Evelyn Brent

# Evelyn Brent

## *The Life and Films of Hollywood's Lady Crook*

LYNN KEAR
*with* JAMES KING

*Foreword by* KEVIN BROWNLOW

McFarland & Company, Inc., Publishers
*Jefferson, North Carolina, and London*

ALSO OF INTEREST

*The Complete Kay Francis Career Record:*
*All Film, Stage, Radio and Television Appearances*
by Lynn Kear and John Rossman (McFarland, 2008)
*Kay Francis: A Passionate Life and Career*
by Lynn Kear and John Rossman (McFarland, 2006)

**Frontispiece: A candid shot of Brent taken by a fan
who later returned to get her autograph.**

LIBRARY OF CONGRESS CATALOGUING-IN-PUBLICATION DATA

Kear, Lynn.
Evelyn Brent : the life and films of Hollywood's lady crook /
Lynn Kear with James King ; foreword by Kevin Brownlow.
p.    cm.
Includes bibliographical references and index.

ISBN 978-0-7864-4363-5
softcover : 50# alkaline paper ∞

1. Brent, Evelyn, 1899–1975.   2. Actors—United States—Biography.
I. King, James.   II. Title.
PN2287.B6853K43   2009        791.4302'8092—dc22 [B]        2009023839

British Library cataloguing data are available

Cover photograph: Evelyn strikes a sensual pose

Manufactured in the United States of America

*McFarland & Company, Inc., Publishers*
*Box 611, Jefferson, North Carolina 28640*
*www.mcfarlandpub.com*

For Kimber Herndon

# Acknowledgments

This book would not have been possible without the help of many people. As always, James Robert Parish was invaluable for his encouragement and advice. Special thanks also go to David Tucker whose friendship and research recommendations were indispensable.

John Oliver went the extra mile for us when he volunteered to sit down and watch *The Eternal Triangle* at the British Film Institute. His information was crucial.

We are especially grateful to those who provided interviews. Kevin Brownlow, Anthony Slide, Hans Wollstein, Grace Siwek, Wesley Musick, Carol Musick, Dick Balduzzi, Lou Valentino, Karl and Mona Malden, Donna Martell, Richard Lamparski, and David Chierichetti were generous with their time and insights.

Others who graciously went out of their way for us included Kimber Herndon, Ben Model, Michelle Vogel, Jon C. Mirsalis, Henry Nicolella, James Gavin, Carol Easton, Keith Lindsay, Andrew Spicer, Jack Tillmany, Eleanor Knowles Dugan, Sybil Jason, John Rossman, GD Hamann, Alex Gildsen, Andre Soares, Michael Pitts, Margie Schultz, Bill Kizer, Howard Mandelbaum, Jeff Cohen, Ron Bowers, E.J. Fleming, Miles Krueger, Stephanie Reeves, Sonya Slutskaya, Susie Hatch, Mike Rinella, Carl Bennett, Richard Schurch, Eileen H. Kramer, Jonathan Prude, Judith Donelan, Harry Waldman, Brian Taves, Elias Savada, Mariana Pinheiro, William J. Mann, Gwinnett County Library System, Lynda Leahy and Laurie Ellis, Schlesinger Library at the Radcliff Institute for Advanced Study, Charles Stumpf, Liane Curtis, Mary Carlisle, Marcy McGuire, John Kerr, Jonas Nordin, Roger Zetterstrom, Laurence Senelick, Susan Drexler, Eastman House, Russ Butner, Margaret Herrick Library, Rosemary Hanes, Library of Congress, Michael Flanagan, Onondaga Historical Society, Albright Memorial Library, Tom Meyers, Fort Lee Film Commission, Richard Koszarski, Charles Silver, Film Study Center at the Museum of Modern Art, Gabby Talmadge, Harry Heuser, Laura Balogh, and Dick Moore.

# Contents

# *Foreword by Kevin Brownlow*

The girl who played the leads in *Underworld* and *The Last Command* brought a level of sophistication to those pictures which helped make them the master-pieces they are. You cannot, for instance, think of *Underworld* without Feathers McCoy—doesn't her name conjure up that magical shot of the feather from her dress floating down the stairs? The fact that half the audience was in love with her made the tragedy of her relationship with "Rolls-Royce" (Clive Brook) and Bull Weed (George Bancroft) all the more convincing and all the more poignant. She had the wit and hard-boiled toughness of those splendid 1920s gals, but she belongs to our age too. Young people seeing her films invariably say "But she's so modern!" (It's meant to be a compliment.) Anyone who can hold their own in the same film as Louise Brooks, as Brent does in *Love 'Em and Leave 'Em*, has to be exceptional.

Opinions of Evelyn Brent varied wildly. Louise Brooks, perhaps motivated by envy, called her "stupid." If that was the case, she would never have become such close friends with Clive and Millie Brook, who told me repeatedly how fond they were of "Betty Brent." (Clive Brook worked with her first in England.) And her director on *Love 'Em and Leave 'Em,* Frank Tuttle, wrote, "The more I knew Betty, the more I admired her. I loved working with her, I loved her—but who didn't?"

It is a pity that biographers of film stars are so dependent on the output of press agents. I remember asking a publicity man of this period how much of what he wrote was true and he replied with a laugh, "None of it!" If a picture was due to play at a specific town, then surprise, surprise!—the star was born in that town. It didn't matter that no one remembered her. All that mattered was that people bought tickets. And no publicity guff could be too ridiculous to appear in print. Fortunately Lynn Kear and James King are well prepared for such stories, and highlight their suspicions whenever necessary.

There is no autobiography, there are no letters; the authors have done an impressive job with so little material. Until I read this book, despite my admiration, I knew little about Evelyn Brent. It made me realise how dependent we are upon dedicated enthusiasts finding out our history for us!

The story is more dramatic and more alarming than I suspected. How sad it is that those who give us most pleasure in life often have so little pleasure in life themselves. However, it is a relief to know that Evelyn Brent seems to have found peace of mind towards the end.

She appeared in an incredible number of pictures, although few of them made much impression, and fewer still survive. But if you only have to make one

*Evelyn Brent*

great picture to be a great director, then just one great performance should be enough to be a great actress. Brent gave three exceptional performances that survive, two for von Sternberg—*Underworld* and *Last Command*—and one for James Cruze called *The Mating Call*, which was rediscovered only recently.

She may not be at the forefront of the roll-call of great stars like Garbo and Dietrich. Nonetheless, as you will discover, Evelyn Brent was one of the glories of the silent era.

*Silent film expert Kevin Brownlow is an award-winning filmmaker, writer, and historian. The author of* The Parade's Gone By *and other books, he has produced several excellent documentaries on Hollywood and the silent era.*

# Preface

*"Do what you please. Have a good time. Don't be burdened with conventions and public opinions and all the meaningless gestures that clutter up life."*[1]

The first time I noticed Evelyn Brent was in *Paramount on Parade*. I was researching the life and career of Kay Francis and came upon Brent's remarkable scene with Maurice Chevalier. I found Brent sophisticated and regal—and wondered what had happened to her and her career. It was years before I had the opportunity to find out, but that mystery led to this book.

Brent began her career in 1914, but it wasn't until 1928 that she reached stardom after appearing in Josef von Sternberg's *Underworld* and *The Last Command*. In that same year she was also chosen by Paramount to appear in their first dialogue film, *Interference*. Although Brent remained in show business for several decades, she would never again reach these heights. In fact, Brent's story, a fascinating one with ups and downs, is a cautionary tale of fame, fortune, choices, and Hollywood.

This book is a biography and filmography. In addition to the first full-length biography on this important silent and dialogue film star, we provide a complete, detailed record of her film career. The filmography includes credits, synopses, behind-the-scenes information, and reviews. Though she made few television appearances, we include a brief section on this part of her career. A chronology is also provided.

# PART ONE

## *Biography*

# 1

# *Playing Hookey*

*She grew up a serious youngster, quite beautiful, but always with*
*a beauty of autumn, of falling leaves and reminiscent rains,*
*of wet violet banks and clouds.*[1]

Evelyn Brent told many fascinating stories about her childhood. Some were almost true. Some were outright fabrications. It was a requirement for movie stars to have an interesting life story for the public. Brent's concoctions, likely produced with the help of studio publicists, had hints of tragedy combined with doses of luck and pluckiness. She wasn't always able to keep the facts straight, but the general themes stayed the same: She was born Mary Elizabeth Riggs to teenage parents who died young, forcing her to struggle to find a career to support herself. Acting became her path out of poverty.

In one interview Brent described her childhood as lonely and sad. "I never had any childhood. I never was a child, or rather, I never was childish—and I knew it. Life had turned a frightful profile to me and I couldn't get away from it. Doubtless it was then that my face settled into the smoldering, secretive lines it is reputed to have today. There wasn't anything to laugh about, you see. I was quiet—and odd, I suppose. I can remember asking a group of girls and boys in to play with me one afternoon. Something I very rarely did. The instant they came romping in I knew that I couldn't stand them. I sent them away, stony faced, insistent. I had to be alone. I still have to be alone, often. I used to make up plays and act in them. I think that was my only diversion and even that could hardly be called diversion since I cried for hours after I had given one of my 'dramatic interpretations.' My mother finally made me stop doing them. They upset me so. Otherwise, I had no play spirit. I didn't skate or roll hoops or play dolls. None of the usual childhood things. I always read everything I could find and took every word to heart."[2]

She lied many times about her birth year. Of course, this is not unusual, and you'd have a difficult time finding a contemporary Hollywood actress who didn't do the same thing. Most commonly, she claimed her birth year was 1899, though she was probably born in 1895.[3] We believe her parents' names were Arthur Riggs and Eleanor Warner Riggs.

She liked to tell the story about how she was born in Tampa, Florida. However, according to State of Florida Vital Statistics, there is no official birth record for Mary Elizabeth Riggs born between the years of 1865 to 1915. Either Brent was not born in Tampa or the birth was not recorded. Still, when Brent was interviewed on the radio in 1969 she continued to tell the tale of her Florida birth. "I was born in Florida," she said, adding, "but by accident. My mother was traveling.... I was really from Syracuse, New York.... She just traveled some place with my father, and she should have been home, and she wasn't."[4] There is also no official birth record for Mary Elizabeth Riggs in New York State born between the years 1894 and 1899.

Brent claimed that her parents were teenagers when she was born. For example, in a 1930 interview Brent explained that her mother was 14 and her father 17. In that same interview she said her earliest memory was when she learned her father had been killed in a horse track accident and that she was orphaned at 14 when her mother died.[5]

In yet another version, Brent told interviewer Gladys Hall in 1929 (while inexplicably sitting in a "green and gold boudoir, filled with flagons of perfume[7] and adorned with a huge toy rabbit") that her parents were mismatched and impossibly young. "I was born when my mother was 14. She was married when she was 13. My father was 17. Of such a violent young love match did I come into existence. My mother was an Italian, born in Italy. She was indescribably beautiful, with long straight black hair, a white, haunting face. Eyes that told strange things. I knew they were strange even when I was a child. My father was—just an American. With a dash of Irish [in official records, she sometimes identifies him as German]. Hybrid. He was extremely fond of horses and of racing. And we lived in Florida so that he might indulge this hobby, which amounted to a passion. One day when I was about three, my mother and grandmother were in the kitchen, baking or something of the sort. I was meddling about, getting in the way. Two men walked in. They carried something between them. It was my father—dead. He had been killed in an accident on the race-course. There was no preliminary softening of the blow. He had simply gone out, alive. They brought him home to us—dead. I suppose that is my earliest, conscious recollection. Time hasn't blurred it much. My mother was expecting another baby at the time. When the two men with their tragic burden walked in, she screamed, fainted, and fell to the floor. She was horribly ill for months and months. There was no other baby. After that we moved to Syracuse, lived there for a brief and uneventful period and then moved to Brooklyn. We lived in the two upper stories of a large brownstone house, owned and also lived in by an Irish family of whom Kathleen Norris might have written. There were 19 children, and the Irish mother had a heart capacious enough to hold them all and, later on, me, too. She was, and is, a grand person. I always see her when I am in the East."[6]

A newspaper account stated that Brent's father died when she was four and living in Syracuse. In another account, Arthur Riggs is described as an "interior decorator ... [who] loved horses and gambling more than his profession. He owned, not a stable, but two or three horses when Evelyn was born. He never made very much money."[7]

Brent's father is a mysterious figure who is either totally absent, around for a short time, or a person who figures in her dating life. "Remembering That First Kiss" was a 1929 article that interviewed Hollywood stars about their first romantic adventures. Smacking of a publicist's touch, Brent's is particularly interesting because she claims her father sabotaged a romance when she was 15. "Evelyn Brent, whose charms over men are well known to screen fans, boasts that she was kissed many times by many different boys when she was a child. But the first occasion that meant anything in her life came when she was 15. She was living in Brooklyn at the time and met a boy with beautiful wavy brown hair and brown eyes. They planned to run away and get married, but Evelyn's father put a stop to that. She doesn't remember his name, but he 'did have beautiful brown hair and eyes.' And his kisses could rival those of any cinema lover, Miss Brent asserts."[8] In any event, no death record has been located for Arthur Riggs. Neither has one been located for her mother.

Brent described a childhood heavily influenced by a mother who eventually was institutionalized. "When I was about ten or so, my mother developed a sort of permanent melancholia. She would have frightful fits of screaming and hysteria, after which she would sit for hours and hours, motionless, wordless. A part of this condition of hers was an irrational fear that I would be killed the instant I was out of her sight. I had to stay within her range of vision or risk the horrible consequences. I can shut my eyes today and see her sitting there, white, immovable, voiceless. I can remember my own cold fear. The result of this was, of course, that I missed more schooling than I got. I didn't dare to leave her when she was in that condition. There was little or no money. I had to make the thin ends meet. They didn't, always. Finally, the kind-hearted Irish woman downstairs took things into her own hands. She told me I simply could not go on in that way. She insisted upon a doctor and the doctor insisted upon putting my mother in a sanatorium or nursing home. I went to see her every week until they asked me not to. The sight of me upset her so dreadfully. She had been there for a year or so. One night she died in her sleep. Mercifully. There was nothing physically or rather, there was nothing organically, wrong with her. Life had been wrong. It had given her a dirty deal and she died under it. And to this very day, whenever I indulge myself in two or three expensive gowns at one and the same time, at a hundred or more apiece, when I bought my first real luxury, my special-bodied Cadillac car, I see my mother's face. I think of how young she was. How beautiful. The ghastly waste of a life that produced nothing but—me. I could think of the things I could do for her now. The ways I could make up. The fun we could have together. And it seems so—so awfully useless. Small wonder I look somber, brooding. For so many years there was no other way to look."[9]

An earlier interview told a different version, but her mother was, again, insane. "I had exactly forty dollars left after grandmother was buried.... And mother—well, mother loved violets. I used to bring her some every time I could afford it. One day I came in to find she had gotten hold of a violet-colored silk cord. She was tying it around her neck. I had to take her to a farm house in Connecticut, where there was a doctor who could look after her every minute." The article continues, "A few months later, the little mother went to join the grandmother and the husband, where Evelyn knew she would be more happy."[10]

It's also been hinted that Brent was the result of an affair between an unwed mother and a wealthy New York man. In this version Brent's mother was abandoned by the father and sent to Tampa to have the baby, though mother and daughter eventually returned to New York to live with relatives.[11]

It's likely that most of Brent's childhood was spent in New York.[12] When Evelyn was signed to play Pearl in the 1928 film version of *Broadway*, a Syracuse newspaper proclaimed her a local girl: "Evelyn Brent, known to Syracusians as Mary Elizabeth Riggs [others say she was known as Mary Louise Riggs[13]] when she attended school in this city, but now widely known to fame as a screen star, has been signed by Universal Pictures to play the role of Pearl in *Broadway*."[14] Other reports stated that she lived on Temple Street and attended Montgomery School.

When Brent reached the age when she could attend normal school, she and her mother moved to New York so she could study to be a school teacher.[15] From Gladys Hall's interview with Brent: "'Because we nearly always were in precarious financial circumstances it was early decided that I should become a school teacher. I was quite in accord with this,' she smiles, with a funny and rather dubious twist of her small, firm, pretty mouth. She quite expected to eventually support her mother and herself by teaching school. At the age of 16 she was in her first year at a normal school in New York City."[16]

As for childhood romances, Brent appeared to have little interest. "I did very little running about anyway, with anyone. Didn't have much time and had less inclination. I'd had one childish love affair. One very young romance with a boy I'd known since I was ten. One of those things where we'd look mooney and say, 'Some day, when we're married.' It petered out. Those things usually do."[17] Brent also told of a romantic adventure that was ended by her mother. "Evelyn Brent and her Herbert could not bear life apart; as Evelyn was about to climb from her bedroom window to her waiting lover, her mother arrived on the scene. Humiliation for both the Juliet and her Romeo followed."[18]

Her early life—or the way press agents envisioned it—sometimes presented problems for Brent. In one case, Syracuse citizens accused her of going high-hat on them and having a poor memory:

> "YOU'RE ANOTHER" That's the answer of Evelyn Brent, screen star, to those Syracusians who, claiming to have been her intimates in childhood here, have accused the actress of having a "short memory." The exchange of compliments between Miss Brent and Syracusians who "knew her when" had their inception when a press agent innocently denied that the actress had ever lived in this city, and built for her instead a picturesque background that ranged from Tampa, Fla. to New York City. The Syracusians averred that in the long ago, Miss Brent was "little Minnie Riggs of Temple Street" and that her education was gained periodically in a local grade school, and not the Normal College of the city of New York, as her authorized press biographies had it. But the chief accusation of "poor memory" hurled at Miss Brent by her Syracuse critics is of a more serious nature. The screen star reports receiving a letter from one caustically inquiring why she did not support her sister. "I never had a sister," indignantly states Miss Brent. "I only had one brother, and he lived but five days." She also emphatically claimed that she had never been called Minnie. Her nickname among friends and relatives was always Betty. [In fact, all of Brent's close friends and professional colleagues called her Betty throughout her career.] As for her educational claims, subjected to questioning here, Miss Brent maintains that she never sought to infer that she was a college girl. Miss Brent explains that she started in school in Syracuse and then removed to Brooklyn where she attended the training department (grade school) of the Normal College. Later, she was enrolled in the high school department in the same institution, but her high school career was short. For economic reasons, Miss Brent was forced to leave school and find employment.[19]

Brent later reflected on her childhood experiences and claimed they "led me to expect nothing of life except the fate of the moment."[20] She'd certainly had her share of black luck, but she finally had something in her favor when she considered a film career. She was attractive. In 1914, when she walked onto the World Film Studios lot in Fort Lee, New Jersey, and was quickly offered a job as an extra, her striking looks gave her one of the first breaks she'd had in life.

Brent's tales of how she entered the movie business also have several variations, but the key points are that she was desperate for money and/or she ended up on a movie lot because of a lark. "Decided to become a screen actress after she had heard that it was the quickest way to make money. Walked miles to the old Fort Lee studios, and managed to secure work as an extra. Smiled for the first time in years."[21]

Sometimes Brent told interviewers that her mother's death led her to a filmmaking career. Other times it was a grandmother's demise. In one interview, it's her father's. "Her father died when she was in high school and she entered pictures because.... 'It seemed to be the only thing a young girl could do without any particular preparation!'" She explained she received small roles at various New York studios until she was discovered at Universal. "[F]inally, one day Matt Moore saw her standing at the entrance to the casting office of the old Universal studio. 'He told me to come in and go to work.... He didn't even give me a test. The picture was a two-reeler and he directed it and acted in it.'"[22]

Years later, Brent explained that when she entered the film industry, she had no one to depend on. Her career came about "quite by accident. I had to earn a living.... My mother and father died. My grandmother died. And I had nobody. And I had no money. So I had to go to work. First, I modeled a little, posed for artists and whatnot, and then quite by accident another girl said that they were looking for people at some studio. So we went over, and in those days there was no protocol about it at all. You could just walk in any studio, you know. So they said, 'Well, there's a pretty little girl. Let's have her in this.' Or something or other. So that was how I first started."[23]

Brent always maintained that she was a teenager, a mere child at that, when she entered show business in 1914 in Fort Lee. However, if she was born in 1895 she was in fact around 19 when she started earning her living as an actress.

Brent also liked to explain that her movie career started when several friends, including Priscilla Dean, convinced her to join them on a jaunt to Fort Lee, New Jersey. "I played hookey ... as did some of the other embryo teachers. It all happened after we had visited, as sight-seers, the World Film Studio at Fort Lee, New Jersey. Some of us went back again, and took occasional 'extra' work at $3 or $5 a day. I finally got into a 'bit' with the late Tom Wise in one scene and was given a contract for $15 a week. Some weeks I made $20 or $25. The contract really was a guarantee of three days work at $5 a day as a minimum weekly income. Of course, I quit the normal school. My mother and I needed the money. After a time I met Mr. and Mrs. Herbert Blaché, who ran the Solax studio, also at Fort Lee. They gave me a job in the cast of *Dangerous Dan McGrew* which starred Edmund Breese. I was the daughter of 'the lady that's known as Lou!'"[24]

The film with Tom Wise was *A Gentleman from Mississippi*. According to DeWitt Bodeen, Brent sometimes referred to it as *A Man from Mars*, either in fun or because she'd forgotten its name. The production was not uneventful. A fire broke out at the two-block long Éclair Moving Picture Company in Fort Lee. Much equipment was destroyed, along with the negative department and storage vaults. All told, the fire caused $300,000 in damage. One reason the damage was so great was because the water pressure was insufficient. In fact, the Fort Lee City Council agreed on a resolution that blamed the Hackensack Water Company. Two people were injured in the fire, including director and cinematographer Francis Doublier who suffered from smoke inhalation and Robert Klein whose hand was crushed. It could have been worse, but a brave employee succeeded in getting dozens of people out of the way. "The heroine of the day was Irene Whipple, a young woman employee of the company, who hurried through the hall to different departments and warned a hundred employees to run for safety."[25]

Cast members from *A Gentleman from Mississippi* were directly involved. "The studio, when the fire started, was filled with actors who were rehearsing The [sic] *Gentleman from Mississippi*, in which Thomas Wise appears. All the actors hurried from the studio, and did what they could to aid in saving property."

Another early Brent film was Maurice Tourneur's *The Pit* in 1914. The French filmmaker had arrived in New York in May 1914 and begun working at Éclair in Fort Lee. The studio's factory had been destroyed in the March 1914 fire, so Éclair opted to build a larger, fireproof studio which was called Peerless Studios. Francis Doublier, who had been injured in the fire, designed the new studio. It was said to be the most modern motion picture studio of its time. "The studio property covered five acres on the crest of a small valley. Costing almost a million dollars to build, the studio was equipped with a two hundred foot stage and a film laboratory capable of developing 2,000,000 feet of film a year."[26]

Éclair made Maurice Tourneur its producer-director while also working closely with World Pictures and Louis J. Selznick and William A. Brady.[27] Tourneur produced four films at Éclair in 1914 (*The Pit, Mother, The Man of the Hour,* and *The Wishing Ring*). *The Pit*, Tourneur's last film for Éclair, was based on Channing Pollock's stage adaptation of a Frank Norris novel. The play had been produced in 1904 by Brady in New York. The film featured the screen debut of Milton Sills and has been described as "hard-edged."[28] Brent had a bit part as a maid. *The Pit* was successful at the box office, grossing more than $70,000 by December 25, 1915.

No doubt working with Tourneur was an education for the young Brent. Her mentor Olga Petrova, an early film vamp, later described the joy of collaborating with this genius director. "For the first time since I had faced a camera lens, I could relax from the tension of worry, fear and distrust, and place myself without question under the guidance of a man who, I knew, *knew*; a man who knew that he knew; a man of culture and imagination…. [I]t was in the treatment of individual human emotions that he excelled. His methods of lighting were a revelation to me. Sets, instead of being uniformly flooded with harsh blinding whiteness, were shadowed or high-lighted in spots, suggesting or emphasizing, as the case might be. This treatment of chiaroscuro created a subtler and more spiritual approach to the observer than could possibly be achieved by the older system of flat or back lighting."[29]

The *Los Angeles Times* claimed that Brent appeared in *The White Feather* in 1914, though she is not listed in the credits. Still, in 1928 the newspaper reported, "Thirteen years ago, Adolphe Menjou was playing a 'bit' in Olga Petrova's starring picture *The White Feather* at the old World Film Studios in New York. He received $75 every seven days. One of the $30-a-week players in the picture was Evelyn Brent, at that time just a youngster with an ambition."[30]

Brent later explained that movie work was sporadic, and she sometimes worked as a model, all the while thinking about the possibility of stardom. "Fortunately for me, it was quite the thing in those days for girls to go over to the Fort Lee Studios and work extra — when they could. I went along two or three times. We all thought it was fun. And after my mother's death I started to do it, not for fun, but for what there was in it. Sometimes I had three days' work in one week. Finally I had a guarantee of three days' work. Fifteen dollars. Now and then, between times, I worked in a wholesale hat warehouse as a model. Things like that. Gradually, oh, very gradually, I got more and more work to do. In the studios. Every day I'd take the long trip from Brooklyn to Fort Lee, riding on trolleys, subways and ferry boats, walking whenever I could in order to save a nickel. I thought, then, that I was very famous. I imagined that everyone on the subways and ferries was staring at me and saying, 'That's Evelyn Brent.'"[31]

Brent became a protégée of Olga Petrova, who was fond of the dark-haired, pretty actress. Cast as Betty (sometimes Bettie) Riggs, Brent first appeared in bit roles with Petrova, "whose plays were always full of dark, sinister vamping, international conspiracies, passions, problems and bloodshed."[32]

Petrova often worked for film pioneer Alice Blaché. A 1915 issue of *Metro Pictures Magazine* referred to her as "the foremost woman producer of motion pictures in the world, and one of the ablest directors of the silent drama."[33] According to Petrova, Blaché was "a charming and cultured French woman."[34] Truly ahead of her time, Blaché saw no reason why women couldn't succeed in the film industry. "It has long been a source of wonder to me … that many women have not seized upon the wonderful opportunities offered to them by the motion picture art to make their way to fame and fortune as directors of photodramas. Of all the arts there is probably none in which they can make such splendid use of talents so much more natural to a woman than to a man and so necessary to its perfection."[35]

Petrova, who had been a stage star, was astonished at the slow pace of motion picture making. "The first thing that struck me, and most forcibly, was the extraordinary amount of time apparently wasted. One arrived at the studio somewhere around half past nine in the morning and reported, dressed and made up, on the set by ten. Then it was quite possible to sit and sit and sit until lunchtime, when one was free for an hour. After lunch a little friendly chat, to allow for a very proper and necessary digestion, might well bring one to three o'clock before making any kind of a start on the business of the day. By this time one's make-up was messy and one's verve well below par."[36]

Petrova described an almost chaotic atmosphere on the set. "Although the scenarios were always read to me for approval, it was quite possible for a director to change them out of all recognition as we went along. Members of the supporting cast rarely knew more of the piece than the episodes in which they appeared. These scenes were outlined by the director, but for the most part he left the dialogue to the imagination of the performer. As it was considered very amusing by some artists to try to break one another up, the dialogue, during the actual photographing of the scene, had very often nothing in common with the action."[37]

Years later, Brent still spoke highly of Petrova, who even then sent her former protégée Christmas cards from Florida. According to Brent, Petrova "was very sweet to me. She found me crying one day on the set about something. I can't remember what, and she took me into her dressing room and gave me a talking-to ... and I'll never forget it. You know, 'You can't let these things upset you this way because they aren't worth it.'"[38]

The first known film that Brent made with Petrova was *The Heart of a Painted Woman*, directed by Alice Blaché and released in 1915. Brent played a small role in this picture, which, like most of Brent's early films, is presumed lost. Too bad because one contemporary reviewer complained about the director's "'strange tendency to ultra-sensationalism of the morbid order,' such as the use of a hypodermic needle as well as gunplay and an execution scene."[39]

*The Lure of Heart's Desire* (1916) marked the first time Mary Elizabeth Riggs was credited as Evelyn Brent. In the Metro picture, Brent played Little Snowbird, and the cast included Edmund Breese.

While shooting *Playing with Fire* (1916) with Petrova, Brent made it into the newspapers because of her antics on a tugboat. It was one of the first publicity pieces designed to promote Brent's career. "Shipping men in the upper bay New York were surprised to see a beautiful young girl at the wheel in the pilot house of a sea-going tug that picked its way to the Battery wall. All along the route they blew their whistles and sirens in salutation and the girl responded with short toots, as she was too busy at the wheel to devote much time in exchanging greetings. The girl was Evelyn Brent, the pretty young ingénue who is appearing in Metro plays and who, with several members of the Popular Plays and Players, had been out to the lighthouse to make the final scenes for *Playing with Fire*.... On the return from Sandy Hook, Miss Brent asked permission to run the boat, assuring the captain that she could, as she knew everything about an automobile and motor boat. He agreed and she had the time of her life."[40]

This article and others like it represented a push for Brent in which her name often appeared in newspapers. For example, in July a newspaper reported that Brent was a member of New York's Polar Bears, the name given to those hardy enough to swim in the ocean by Coney Island during the winter months.[41] In November a Canadian newspaper reported her fondness for skating. "Evelyn Brent is having a new skating costume made, to be all ready for the skating craze that promises to rage harder this year than it did last. After a hard day's work in Metro studios, the little ingénue will find her needed relaxation in skating. Evelyn says her costume is practical—that New York women as a rule think to [sic] much about how they look, and do not wear sensible outing clothes. But, then, Evelyn couldn't look ugly even if she tried."[42]

Another 1916 film appearance was in *The Spell of the Yukon*. Described by publicists as "a vivid drama of Alaskan life in five acts filled with thrills and smashing climaxes,"[43] it opened in May in Los Angeles.

*"A charming young actress has been discovered recently whose name has been added to the Metro ranks."*[44]

Throughout her life Brent often developed intense friendships with women. One of her first was with Imogene, whom she met during her early days in New York filmmaking. "After several months of this [trying to find work on movie sets], I met a girl standing about the studio grounds. She wanted to get in to see the studio manager. She hoped to get extra work, too. I was very grand about it and took her in with me. We became great friends and I moved to New York and we took a furnished room together. By this time I was a member of the stock company, getting twenty-five dollars a week. There came the time, though, when both of us had been out of work for some time. We were down to—nothing. Not so much as a dime. Nothing to eat for three days. I was very ill, too, with pleurisy."[45]

In a later article, the room was described: "The furniture ... was scarred and yellow and dreary. [Brent] and her roommate hoarded nickels and dimes to buy a few homey odds and ends for the poisonous place. Betty haunted auction rooms and, one gala day, picked up a colorful shawl. This relieved one chair of its boarding house bleakness."[46]

Throughout her life Brent attempted suicide several times, usually precipitated by romantic or career woes. During the time she lived with Imogene, Brent made one of her first attempts. "I tried to commit suicide by cutting my wrists. Of course, I couldn't have succeeded. It was a childish gesture of despair. I never would have had the strength to cut deeply enough to reach the main artery. And I never would have had the nerve even if I had had the strength. I fainted at the first sight of blood and staggered in for water and bandages. Those were very grim days. Imogene went back to Omaha where she had come from."[47]

After Imogene there was Fay. In order to support both of them, Brent accepted a role that was not her first choice. "Another girl I had met at the studio came to live with me and share expenses. Fay. One day I had a call from the Metro studio. I borrowed a nickel from the switchboard boy, some flimsy pretext or other. 'No change,' one of those things. They were casting an allegorical story at Metro, it seemed. They wanted a young, unformed adolescent girl to play the symbol role of Sin. She had to be very young, very slender and wear nothing at all but a long black wig. I said that I couldn't possibly do a thing like that. They offered me twenty-five dollars a day to play the part. It would go on for close to two weeks, they said. I couldn't resist that. It was more money than I had ever dreamed of. It was all the money in the world. And—I was again next door to starvation. I did it—and Sin bought Fay and me some much needed square meals and a winter coat apiece. We hadn't had any. I also bought myself a dark blue tailored suit. I always bought a new suit when I was in funds. I knew that if I had a decent suit and a couple of blouses I could always put up an appearance when I was looking for work." [48]

In March 1917 the United States had not yet joined the allies in World War I, but a newspaper reported that Brent was "intensely patriotic" and stated that "if war takes place in the United States she will don male attire and enlist as a soldier." According to Brent, "Most of the girls will be wanting to serve as trained nurses.... What the United States really will need will be people who know how to shoot. And I know how to shoot. I am young. I am strong. Therefore, why should I not be able to fight as well as a man?"[49]

In that same year, Brent earned her first lead. "I played the feminine lead opposite Lionel Barrymore in *The Millionaire's Double*. He was very kind to me. He is eccentric but kind, and not as destructive as his brother, John. Louis Wolheim was in the cast, too having just forsaken a position as a professor of mathematics at some eastern college, Harvard, I think."[50] Brent told another interviewer that her casting "was absolutely the happiest day of my life— and my last job for many months."[51] When the film was released in May 1917, Brent received second billing. Barrymore, of course, was the star and *Variety* gave him all the accolades, ignoring Brent's performance. "Lionel Barrymore has the leading heroic role and plays it exceedingly well. It is one of those parts in which he is so admirably suited ... and his followers ... will rave over him."[52]

In June 1917, *Who's Your Neighbor* held a private showing. *Variety* was on hand to review it and applauded the director, stars, and film, though Brent did not rate a mention.

By the end of 1917, *Raffles, the Amateur Cracksman* had opened to great reviews, especially for the male lead, Lionel's brother John Barrymore. Brent played the role of Ethel, but her screen time was minimal. Barrymore gave her advice about smiling. "John Barrymore once told her that she didn't smile well, that she should learn to smile only with her eyes."[53] She took it to heart. Years later a newspaper writer commented that her rare smiles made her stand out from other actresses. "Evelyn Brent is 'different.' Her unsmiling loveliness is in demand because she does not follow a type."[54]

Brent made only one film in 1918: Released by Metro in January, *Daybreak* starred Emily Stevens and Julian L'Estrange. For the most part, reviewers ignored her.

In the fall of 1918, Brent was up for an important stage role. According to her, it came about through the efforts of John Barrymore. "This was way back when he was quite a young man—and very handsome. He was going to do a series of plays for Arthur Hopkins. One of them was *Redemption*. He wanted me to come and do the one part in it, and I was scared to death. Frightened to death! I'd never been on the stage at that time. Petrified! In New York, no less. And with John Barrymore. So I might have had an entirely different career had I tried to do it, anyway. I don't know how good I would have been at that time because I was a kid. I was about 14 years old."[55] (She was probably closer to 23.)

Brent also described missing out on a role. "I took a test for Selznick for a dramatic part. But they said I hadn't enough experience and hired Martha Mansfield. That seemed my last chance. There seemed nothing whatever left for me."[56]

That fall, Brent almost became a victim of the Spanish flu epidemic of 1918. She became ill, and her career was interrupted while she recovered. During the epidemic, several entertainment celebrities died from their illness, including actors Harold Lockwood, Ronald Byram, and Julian L'Estrange (who had appeared with Brent in *Daybreak*). In addition, John H. Collins, an Edison director who was married to actress Viola Dana, succumbed to the epidemic.

The illness led to a suicide attempt. "Pneumonia and pleurisy followed. I didn't have any money at all. A friend of grandmother's had taken me to her house. But I didn't like that. I was used to earning my own living. All that I asked of life was to be a dramatic actress—and that seemed forbidden. The doctors had given me morphine. I took the whole bottle. A stomach pump was all I got for my trouble!"[57]

Brent eventually recovered and had a productive 1919, appearing in five films. *Fool's Gold* was a comeback of sorts for lead actress Florence Turner who had not made a film since 1916, and had recently returned from Europe where she'd been doing World War I relief work. According to publicists, "Photographed in the beautiful Cascade mountains near Spokane, Washington, the result is a combination of good scenery and excellent photography that really makes the picture of special interest."[58] Though Brent's part was small, *Variety* found her charming.

Brent also appeared in *Help! Help! Police!* It starred athletic actor George Walsh, and *Variety* favorably commented on Brent's acting and physical attributes.

That same year Brent had a small part in *The Other Man's Wife*. It was viewed as a poorly produced piece of hackneyed propaganda for women's rights; *Variety* found it dated and mediocre. "Certainly a more blatantly crude bid for the approval of women who have banded together to assert their superiority to men has rarely been made in these parts in a picture, a piece of writing or a speech."[59]

In November 1919, Brent's film *The Glorious Lady* opened. It starred Olive Thomas and Matt Moore. Brent's role was so small it did not rate a mention with *Variety*.

The reality of working in the film industry was hardly glamorous, and there was no steady paycheck. "A contract for six months here. Bits now and then. Nothing at all for weeks. A chance with Olive Thomas [*The Glorious Lady*], one of the swellest girls I ever knew. One thing and then another."[60]

This was not an easy time for Brent. In what became a pattern for her life, her initial success suddenly ended, leading her to desperation. "[A]fter making one picture in which Olive Thomas was starred ... she encountered a run of downright black luck. 'I just couldn't get a job,' she says, darkly impassive, 'and I seemed to be all wrong. Nobody seemed to like me. I was very unhappy and often hungry.'"[61]

During one particularly trying time, Brent was approached with a different kind of offer. "I had my first whack at what is popularly known as going wrong. An elderly gentleman was my 'tempter.' I refused. Later on I had another opportunity of the same species. I refused that, or him, too. His offer was to take me to California and make a star of me 'overnight.' I didn't want to go to California. And I didn't want to be starred—on those terms. He told me that if I refused him I would never work again. I would be through. I took a chance on that, walked out of his studio, down the block to the next studio and signed up there within ten minutes. I felt pretty cocky. Virtue was being its own reward, right before my very eyes. Though it may not have been so much virtue as it was revulsion. Perhaps if he had been young and handsome and had appealed to me—well, who knows? Who is to say what one will or will not do? But under the circumstances I couldn't see where I'd get any fun out of it."[62]

Brent was still shaken from her near death in the flu epidemic when she decided to move to Augusta, Maine, to make films with the Edgar Jones Production Co. Formed in 1918, the company was named for actor-producer-director Edgar Jones. According to a newspaper report, the film company, the first of its kind in Maine, was based in what had once been a Children's Home at 129 Sewall Street. Other actors in the company included Francis M. Smith, Edward Brennan, Edwin Keough, Carlton Brickert, Walter Arthur, Edna May Sperl, Florence Ashbrooke, and Charles Nikkari. According to a newspaper report, Jones planned "a series of photoplays adapted from stories and novels dealing with raw-boned, passionate men of the frontiers, the lumber camps and the woodlands of the north. He established a studio in Augusta, Maine, and went into the heart of the woods in that state for its exteriors."[63] Jones had an ambitious plan: "The company has come to Maine to stay and plans to put out a picture every ten days or two weeks."[64] The president of the company was Blaine S. Viles, the former mayor of Augusta, and local dignitary William B. Williams provided additional funding.

According to one report, the New York actors who relocated to Augusta lived "in a sort of communal arrangement."[65] It was a difficult situation for many of them. Mary Astor later recalled it as "a miserable, remote place to work," complete with pestering black flies. It would be an understatement to say that these were low-budget films. "At the very beginning, the only set ... consisted of three walls set up outside.... [I]n the winter, the actors had to hold their breath during the scenes so that the camera wouldn't pick up the vapor coming from their mouths. Even the cameramen had to stop breathing for short periods so they would not fog up the cameras."[66]

About a month or so after she arrived in Augusta, Brent suffered an appendicitis attack— or so it was reported. The illness required hospitalization that July in Augusta. Quite often, appendicitis is a euphemism for a more scandalous or embarrassing incident for actresses. Perhaps in Brent's case, it really was appendicitis, but it also could have been another suicide attempt.[67] A July 31, 1919, newspaper article stated that Brent was still in Augusta General Hospital recovering from surgery.[68] The newspaper made it clear that Brent had already wowed Augustans. "Lots and lots of dark hair, wonderful in texture, expressive eyes, charm- ing manners, all are Miss Bent's [sic] acquisitions."[69] A few months later, Brent was described as a six-month resident of Augusta. "As leading woman of the Edgar Jones Production Co., which has been making motion picture plays in and about the city, she has become acquainted with many people in the Capital City and many people have come to know her and to like her."[70] In fact, the newspaper reported there was lots of excitement when an Evelyn Brent film came to town to play at the local theater.

In September, Brent briefly returned home to New York City for a short visit, accom- panied by a female friend. "Miss Evelyn Brent, the leading lady of the Jones Moving Picture Production Co., engaged in making pictures in Maine, has gone to her home in New York City for a few days. She was accompanied by her friend, Miss Bernice Allen, who returned to her home in New York after a short visit in this city."[71] It's likely this was another intense friendship, one that did not end well.

Little is known about the picture (or pictures) Brent made while living in Maine. Titled *Border River*, the cast included Brent, Jones, Ben Hendricks, Jr., and Carlton Brickert. It is reportedly a short Western about moonshiners. It was possibly released as early as January 1920, and Jones may have recut the film many times and released it under different titles. In any event, by the time of its release, Brent had left the country. Brent's career was not pro- gressing as quickly as she'd hoped. "I felt I was a decided failure.... I made a succession of pictures that were anything but inspiring They were turned out by a fly-by-night company and never exhibited in any of the big cities or any place where they were heard of."[72]

Brent was apparently unhappy in Augusta (and perhaps the United States) and eager for a change.[73] Fortunately, she was offered a unique adventure. A combination of personal and career difficulties made it easy for her to accept the offer to be a companion to a wealthy woman on a trip to Europe. The woman who made the generous offer was reportedly the wife of an importer. Brent later identified her only as Lola. Another interviewer identified her as her grandmother's friend, the same woman who nursed her when she was sick with pneumonia. Brent's benefactor was willing to pay for the companionship of a sweet, charm- ing, beautiful young girl. According to Brent, the timing was perfect. "When I thought I had reached the end of everything the unexpected happened. A friend of my mother looked me up. She said she was going to Europe and would enjoy taking me along for company. I could have fallen down and worshipped her, I was so overjoyed."[74] Brent seemed eager to escape the United States, perhaps because of a failed romance or a loss of confidence in her career. Or both. In truth, Brent would later claim that this first trip to Europe in late 1919 was one of her happiest times. She later described it as "the most carefree time of my life!"[75]

Brent summed up the experience to an interviewer in 1929. "Toward the end of the war a friend of mine invited me to go abroad with her. To Paris and to London. I had five hun- dred dollars saved up. My entire capital. She told me that she would pay all expenses and that I could bring my five hundred along and blow it in having a good time in Paris. The words 'good time' rang like bells to me. I'd never had any. I wanted them. I went. And I had them, the good times."[76]

# 2

# *Europe*

*Once she was contemplated for a lead with Eugene O'Brien but she was told that
the part was too difficult for her—rather amusing in the light of her present success.
She gave up pictures here and went to England.*[1]

Arriving in Europe on her Grand Tour, Brent first went to France. "We lived in the French quarters and saw only French people. Oh, the French people, the real middle-class French people, know how to be always happy."[2]

Brent moved on to London where she felt an immediate connection. She told several interviewers that she believed in reincarnation and thought she had once lived in England. "After Paris, which was gorgeous, we went to London. And London is my home. Not by right of birth but by right of—well, who knows? Maybe a birth in some other incarnation. I belong there. And in London I had the happiest time I have ever had in all my life. I shall live there again some day. Buy a house there. It is the only spot on earth where I want to own a home."[3] Brent echoed this sentiment for years afterward.

Brent took an apartment on London's Duchess Street, expecting to stay there only a short time before returning to the United States. However, an opportunity to appear on the British stage fell into her lap, and before she knew it she was working at London's Comedy Theater. Through the dancers Maurice and Lenora Hughes, Brent met John Cromwell who cast her in the stage play *The Ruined Lady*. "I had met ... them in New York, and they were in London. And they invited me to come see them dancing. I think it was at the Savoy, and I met John Cromwell there, who was casting the play, and that's how I got into it. That's when it all started to happen."[4]

The role was perfect for Brent: a scrappy American chorus girl who was vacationing in London. Brent, who was on the verge of turning 25, made quite an impact. A 1920 Atlanta newspaper reported that she played a "slangy" and tough chorus girl, and her performance was so different from what was usually seen on the British stage that producers sent British actresses to study her. Brent's style was described as having a "rattling delivery, slickness and mental agility."[5]

Interestingly, Naomi Jacob, playing an inebriated cook, was also singled out by the Atlanta newspaper for being, like Brent, an American actress. This was the notorious lesbian novelist who was *not* an American but a British writer who enjoyed a brief career on stage before turning her attention to cranking out potboilers. Other cast members were Rosa Lynd, C. Aubrey Smith, and Nigel Bruce.[6] Jacob, known to friends as Micky, remained friendly with Bruce after he went to Hollywood and found success as Dr. Watson in the Sherlock Holmes movies. Bruce later reminisced about *The Ruined Lady* and his work with Jacob: "We were as bad as each other; together we must have contributed very little to the success of the play."[7]

*The Ruined Lady* led to further opportunities for Brent. "The second week of the show— it ran for six months—the leading man [C. Aubrey Smith] asked her to play opposite him in a picture [*The Shuttle of Life*, her first film in England], when he found she had worked in pictures in America. She was billed as 'the American Star' in the production, but when it made a hit she was promptly billed as 'Evelyn Brent, the British Star.'"[8] In fact, there would later be some confusion about Brent's nationality because of this early success in England.

British filmmakers were impressed that Brent had worked on American pictures. "After [*The Shuttle of Life*] there were pictures to do at thirty pounds a week, which was phenomenal to me and which I only got because I had had American experience. You could have got anything there at that time, on that premise."[9] *The Shuttle of Life* (1920) starred Smith and was based on a novel by Isobel Bray. A reviewer remarked on Brent's "charm and extreme beauty."[10]

Partly due to this performance, Brent was scheduled to be cast in the British film *A Romance of Old Bagdad*, starring Matheson Lang. However, her name was not included in the final cast list.

In 1921 Brent appeared in *Sonia* as a young British woman who is changed by World War I. According to the *London Times*, the film was one of the best British films of the year. "Mr. Denison Clift, in the short time that he has been in this country, has given us a series of films of great merit and has been largely responsible for putting the Ideal pictures in the very first rank not only of British, but of world production. But his film version of Mr. Stephen McKenna's novel *Sonia* is easily his best piece of work, and he has been helped by some of the best acting that has been seen on our screens for a long time."[11]

Another 1921 British film, *The Door That Has No Key*, was so bad it's surprising it didn't end Brent's career. Although the *London Times* liked the film, other reviewers found it horribly bad—and in poor taste, too. In fact, a New York reviewer remarked that audiences were laughing in the wrong places.

After making several English pictures, Brent traveled to Holland to make *Laughter and Tears*, an Anglo-Dutch production. In the fall it opened in London and then premiered in the Netherlands in October. Although the film was not released in the United States, it did open in France, Portugal, Hungary, and Austria which indicates it enjoyed a fair amount of success, possibly due to the scenic Venice and Paris locations as well as the international cast.

This set the stage for *Spanish Jade*, a picture that eventually led to her return to America. Signed by Famous Players–Lasky, Brent traveled to Seville, Spain, for three months to film location shots, and then returned to England to film the interior shots. While in Spain Brent and David Powell took an hour each day to learn "the steps of a 'Sevilliano' to their own accompaniment with the castanets. This dance is to be one of the incidents of the big 'fiesta' scene which is being staged in the market-place of Carmona, Spain. In order that every step and movement of the dancers shall be accurate, they are receiving a special course of instruction from Senor Otero, expert on Spain's national dances."[12]

According to Brent, the trip to Europe

**Brent worked in Europe in the mid–1920s.**

had turned into a windfall. "My, but I thought I was wealthy.... I made fourteen pictures in England, saved up quite a lot of money and thought my life was straight sailing—but, I fell in love!"[13]

Brent reminisced about a romantic relationship during her time in England. "I had my second romance. It might almost be called my first. It was a beautiful thing and every memory of it is perfect. It, too, was one of those things where we'd say, 'Some day, when we're married. Some day we will be married, and then—' But in the meantime there was today. And tomorrow. And what todays and tomorrows! He was a young solicitor. He had a charming house, a charming mother who gave charming parties, and everything he did was charming. We went everywhere together, did everything together. He was proud of my work, proud of me, thoughtful, kind—and fun. And all of this against the background of English country life which is the most divine mode of living left anywhere in the world. It was a glorious experience. It lacked only that compelling force which motivate or thrusts people into matrimony.... There seemed to be no immediate reason for changing so idyllic a state. And so, we didn't change it—and I'm glad. For all my life I have that memory, intact, perfect."[14]

In another version, Brent described the man as her first love—and married. "It was hopeless from the very beginning. He had a wife and children. Although he had not been living with them for some time, what could I offer in comparison? I wouldn't give up my career for any man living. Oh, it was just no use. But it was the first time I had been in love. I told him he must go. He went to America to get away from me."[15]

Brent's film career was characterized by its highs and lows. She would find abundant work—and then there'd be nothing. It was literally feast or famine. This was true in England as well. At her height in England, Brent was earning sixty pounds a week. "Then the slump hit British pictures.... They couldn't get an American market."[16]

Once again, Brent turned to the stage, but this time disaster struck. "I accepted a stage engagement, a lead with Cyril Maude. We had to rehearse in a cold damp theater. London was still rationed in coal although the war was past. I caught pneumonia, inflammatory rheumatism, and all the other pleasant complications. For a year I couldn't work—all the while my money growing less and less."[17]

The story was retold by Brent with greater drama in 1929. "I was rehearsing a play with Cyril Maude when I had what came close to being my last illness. Thought I had a bad cold. Got up in the night to get some aspirin, fell to the floor and never knew another thing for weeks and weeks. Pneumonia, muscular rheumatism, complicated by a bad nervous smash-up. When I finally came to again, I had to spend several weeks in a nursing home resting and eating in order to put on some weight. Picture work had fallen off meanwhile."[18]

The best version of this story, though, might be the one she told in 1928. Brent explained that the illness followed the end of her romance. "'Funny how one heartache leads to another, isn't it? He had no more than gone, when there came a slump in the English productions. They couldn't compete with the Americans. I couldn't find a thing to do. Finally, there came a chance on the stage. It was my last hope. On the fourth day—I caught a cold. All I can remember is getting home. They found me on the floor of the bathroom, six hours later, unconscious. Pneumonia, pleurisy and, this time, rheumatism with it.' Easter Sunday was to be Evelyn's last day, according to the physician. But again she defied the fates. Four weeks in the country with a trained nurse, and she returned to London without a penny left of her savings. And the day she returned, a cablegram informed her that the man she had loved had died in New York City."[19]

Once again, Brent's mental state became unstable, and she attempted suicide. "I took iodine this time. I didn't know that a person cannot swallow enough iodine to kill them. Another illness was all I had this time for my trouble!"[20]

Personal and career difficulties led to Brent's return to America. "For six months I could scarcely look at anyone. Many times I wanted to die. I went down to 87 pounds. When I got strong enough to go, I acceded to a girlfriend's wish that I accompany her back to New York."[21]

Brent learned of an unusual opportunity that enabled her to return to the States at no cost to herself. "The Cunard Line was doping out a picture to be made for advertising purposes. They asked me to play in it for transportation, round trip, and several pounds besides. I decided to do it, on the spur of the moment. I did do it. The picture went flooey for lack of funds. And I found myself in America again."[22]

In fact, Brent was in New York when she had another bit of good luck. Douglas Fairbanks, Charles Chaplin, and Mary Pickford had seen Brent in *Spanish Jade*. Brent was staying in New York at the Algonquin Hotel and was invited to lunch with Fairbanks and Pickford. They offered her a contract. In a "better" version of how Fairbanks discovered her, it was said that Fairbanks and Pickford were attending the theater regularly in New York. "They were looking for talent for their pictures. One night Evelyn Brent walked on the stage and Mary said to Doug, 'There she is!' And in the same breath Doug said to Mary, 'There she is!'"[23] Regardless of the real story, it was a huge break for Brent, but it meant she had to move to Hollywood.

# 3

# *Hollywood*

*I do not care for money. I am an artist,*
*and I have a right to appear before the public.*[1]

On November 28, 1922, Brent arrived in Pasadena on the California Limited with Douglas Fairbanks and Mary Pickford—and their twenty-seven suitcases. The next day the *Los Angeles Times* announced that Fairbanks had a new leading lady. "Miss Brent, a striking brunette, 24 years old [she would have just turned 27], first attracted Doug's attention when she starred in *Spanish Jade*, a picture made in Spain with David Powell in the male role. She arrived yesterday on her visit to California and with the declaration that it would be her home 'forever and a day.'"[2]

According to the paper, Brent had been in New York since September, and was now more than happy to be in sunny California. "'I love California,' Miss Brent said yesterday at the Hollywood Hotel, where she is staying, 'and I am anxious to get to work. We had a hard trip especially at Chicago, where the crowds nearly mobbed us. It is a wonderful change from the foggy nights of London and already I feel quite at home with the California people.'"[3]

Brent immediately demonstrated her ability to be discreet when a reporter "asked whether she thought that the irrepressible Doug would prove to be too fast a partner, Miss Brent merely smiled and remarked that the California flowers were wonderful."[4]

Housing was a problem for actors as many landlords refused to rent to them. As a result, producers Jesse Lasky and Samuel Goldwyn built the Hillview Apartments at 6531 Hollywood Boulevard in 1917. "The Hillview Apartments soon became one of the most desirable residences, housing some of the era's biggest film stars including Mae Busch. According to director Douglas Carlton, 'Everybody that was anybody in the silent movie days lived there.' The 54-unit Moorish- or Mediterranean-style apartment complex offered the latest amenities including a large parlor lobby, a writing room, a ladies waiting room, garbage incinerators, automatic elevators, and a rehearsal space in the basement. The ground level of the first multi-story building in Hollywood was home to a Speakeasy."[5] The Hillview Apartments became Brent's home.

Years later Brent reflected back on Hollywood upon her arrival. "It was a small town. Sometimes I drive down to Hollywood and I just cannot believe what has happened to it. There used to be just a few blocks where they had two or three restaurants and one that was open all night where we used to go to eat after we had worked late, at one or two in the morning.... They had one traffic cop, and that was only in rush hours. He stood up on a box on the corner of Vine and Hollywood between five and six in the evening and in the morning rush. At night it was like being in a deserted village."[6]

Being signed by Fairbanks was Brent's biggest career break up to that point. Perhaps not coincidentally, on March 6, 1923, the *Los Angeles Times* reported that Brent had announced plans to marry producer Bernie P. Fineman. Fineman had once been a backer of actress Katherine MacDonald, nicknamed "The American Beauty," and previously worked with film producer-presenter Sam Rork, but was now hoping to produce his own motion pictures. The newspaper further reported that the couple had known each other for a long time—Brent often told people he was the brother of a schoolgirl friend from Syracuse—and were planning a honeymoon. The article described how Brent had worked in films in Spain and England, and was now employed by Pickford and Fairbanks. "She had most interesting experiences and declares she wouldn't take anything for the training she received under foreign directors."[7]

The engagement announcement was disinformation at its best. On March 27, 1923, the *Los Angeles Times* reported that Brent and Fineman had already married—on November 1, 1922, in New York City. In truth, the couple actually married on November 21. Fineman, an assistant to the head of production at Paramount, arranged with his company to relocate to Hollywood just as Brent signed a contract with Fairbanks and Pickford. Although it was never clear why the couple decided to keep their marriage a secret, Evelyn seemed relieved when the news finally broke. "'Happy?' said Miss Brent, as she stood on the steps of Fineman's studio. 'I should say we are. You see, we thought we would keep it all a big secret until this summer when we planned a big reception, but somehow it just could not keep no matter how hard we tried.'"[8]

Brent insisted that Hollywood would be their permanent home. "[Y]ou bet we will stay here. I love California and love my screen work. We will start building our home next month."[9] The newspaper (or some press agent) exaggerated Brent's husband's importance a bit—or confused him with B.P. Schulberg—by claiming "Fineman is well-known in the film circles, having been an executive of production under his own film banner for many years. He is beginning a series of feature pictures, the first of which is now under production at

Principal Pictures Corporation studios, Hollywood."[10] The article also went to great lengths to point out how much time they spent together. "Fineman's studios adjoin those of the Fairbanks-Pickford Corporation. Each noon time Miss Brent dashes across the 'lot' to her hubby's studios and together they stroll across the street for luncheon. 'This is great,' laughed Fineman, as the couple started across the street for lunch. 'While Miss Brent's work is so close to my office, it is easy for us to find time for luncheon together and to learn what happened since leaving each other early in the morning.'"[11]

In truth, Brent and Fineman were not a good match, and the marriage was more of a business relationship than a romantic one. In 1929 Brent presented a different version of their marriage and eventual separation. According to her, after returning to New York from England, "I met Bernie Fineman. Or rather, I met him again. I had known

*Evelyn shortly after moving to Hollywood.*

his sister [Frances[12]] during my school-days. And I'd seen him occasionally. He'd had a sort of boyish crush on me. We met again at the Algonquin and—it was just one of those things—ending in a whirlwind marriage and an immediate trip to Hollywood. I am not in the slightest degree domestic. I know less than nothing about running a house, ordering meals or putting away the laundry. I'm not even sure that there is any laundry. Which is an unsatisfactory way for a wife to be so far as nine out of ten men are concerned.... Bernie and I lived in an apartment hotel. And it lasted about four years, unhappy years for him as well as for me. It just wasn't right. After the four years we separated by mutual agreement and in a friendly spirit which even now still exists between us."[13]

Fineman was born Bernhard Powell Fineman, the son of Sonia Paul Fineman and Dennis Fineman. Both parents were Russian Jews "who had emigrated to America from the Kiev area of the Ukraine in the late nineteenth century. Sonia was a petite, red-haired beauty with ... finely boned, delicate features and strong-willed temperament. 'Sonia spoke Russian and always emphasized that she was high-born,' recalls her granddaughter. 'She was quite a free-thinking lady.'"[14]

Bernie's parents had married in 1896 while Sonia was pregnant with Bernie. The marriage was unhappy, and Sonia began an affair in 1911 with wealthy Texan Morris Brown. Sonia eventually married Brown and changed her name to Sophia Powell Brown. Little is known about what happened to Dennis, but Sonia (or Sophia) remained a forceful woman who exerted control over the lives of both of her children.[15]

There is no evidence that Brent had anti–Semitic feelings. She married two Jewish men, and many of her closest friends, including Dorothy Herzog, were Jewish. In fact, some in Hollywood seemed to think Brent was herself Jewish. In Budd Schulberg's autobiography he referred to her as a Jewish charmer.[16]

Although the Brent-Fineman marriage was unsuccessful, Fineman did an excellent job of promoting Brent in her film career. In April 1923 Brent was announced as a Wampas Baby Star. This publicity coup was probably due to the efforts of Fairbanks or Fineman. Founded in 1920, the Western Associated Motion Picture Advertisers (WAMPAS) nominated young actresses working in the movie industry to be Baby Stars. According to writer Roy Liebman, "From 1922 to 1934 there were almost 150 young actresses who proudly bore the designation—especially in its mid-to-late-1920s heyday—and it was a much sought-after honor to be so designated. In the days before Academy Awards, it was a signal [of] recognition, and many actresses who became major stars were first recognized in this way.... The idea was conceived to select 13 young women with potential star power and to publicize them to a fare-thee-well. The future stars were to be known as the Wampas Baby Stars; the 'Baby' not meaning infants but rather 'junior' stars. At first, the organization's desire to publicize Wampas, rather than the actresses, was undoubtedly at the forefront.... The studios realized the inherent promotional value of this hoopla and gave the idea their enthusiastic blessing."[17]

The first group of actresses honored in 1922 included Lila Lee, Bessie Love, Patsy Ruth Miller, Colleen Moore, Lois Wilson, Marion Aye, Helen Ferguson, Jacqueline Logan, Louise Lorraine, Kathryn McGuire, Mary Philbin, Pauline Starke, and Claire Windsor. Among Evelyn's co-nominees in 1923 were Eleanor Boardman, Dorothy Devore, Virginia Brown Faire, Betty Francisco, Pauline Garon, Kathleen Key, Laura La Plante, Margaret Leahy, Helen Lynch, Derelys Perdue, Jobyna Ralston, and Ethel Shannon. Of all of them, Evelyn was by far the most seasoned actress, having worked in films for almost ten years. In any event, the selection provided huge publicity for the studios, and required the women to appear at events such as a photo shoot with golfer Gene Sarazen. In the coming years, Brent, like many previous honorees, continued to participate in Wampas publicity events.

Brent was signed by Fairbanks for seven months while he tried to decide between *Mon-*

*sieur Beaucaire* (later made by Valentino) or *The Black Pirate* (made with Fairbanks and Billie Dove in 1926). When he finally decided to instead make *The Thief of Bagdad* he chose a princess role for Brent. It was a mistake. "I was too terrible in the tests.... What they wanted was a fairy princess who would seem to be wafted about on air rather than walk. Well, again, I was not the type. I obtained a release from the contract."[18]

It was in May 1923 that Brent made that unusual career move. "[T]his announcement is one of the sensational items of the film world. Hardly a woman in films but would be flattered by an offer to play opposite Doug, yet this American girl, who is a star in her own right in English films, yesterday definitely refused to renew her expired contract with the Fairbanks organization."[19] Brent's contract with Fairbanks had ended on May 18, and she made her announcement the following day.

Brent received advice from husband Fineman about how to get out of the restrictive contract. "I just didn't like the part of the princess in *Thief of Bagdad*. I remember going to Bernie and saying, 'I cannot do that part.' After I had been in the studio and talked and done still pictures with Fairbanks holding me up in one hand and all of that silly stuff. I just didn't like the setup."[20]

At the time Brent was more diplomatic. "When I signed my contract with Mr. Fairbanks, it was understood that he was to commence production on *The Black Pirate* almost immediately. Six months have passed and I have not yet appeared before the camera. Even if work on *The Thief of Bagdad* were commenced at once it would be more than eighteen months from the time I first signed with Mr. Fairbanks before my first work with him would be shown to the public. I do not feel that I am willing to stay off the screen for that length of time, more especially since I have had several very flattering offers since my arrival in Hollywood. I love California and I intend to stay here a long time. But to stay in idleness is beyond me. I must work to be happy."[21]

Fairbanks agreed to end their business relationship with good wishes. "It is essential to a new star that she appear as often as possible in new productions that offer her characterizations that will build up a following for her.... I wish Miss Brent every possible good luck and I am sure that the faith both Miss Pickford and I have in her eventual success will be amply justified."[22]

In June 1923, Julanne Johnston was hired by Fairbanks to play the princess in *The Thief of Bagdad*. "It was dexterity in handling costumes, learned from dancing, together with grace and a distinguished carriage, which impressed Fairbanks while Miss Johnston was being tested.... Miss Johnston, who is also a talented costume designer and writer of verse, was signed up by Fairbanks at the expiration of Evelyn Brent's contract. Miss Brent, it is understood, was not just the type required for Doug's forthcoming novelty spectacle."[23]

By the end of 1923 Brent was no longer Fairbanks' protégée. Much of the negotiations to get her out of the contract were conducted by Fineman. This was a sign of things to come as Fineman successfully guided her career for the next several years. Not only did Fineman direct Brent's career, he might even have been accused of overworking her in the mid–1920s. Over the next few years Brent appeared in many films, and the heavy workload produced physical and mental problems.

*"Evelyn Brent ... has admitted, that, while the sea is beautiful to watch and beach bathing thoroughly enjoyable, she prefers an evening in the library with her books."*[24]

Finally free from the contract with Fairbanks, Brent did not immediately sign with another company. She complained that the roles offered to her "called for little but to look pretty and 'to walk thru the picture.'"[25] Eventually she and Fineman decided it was time to appear in a film. Her first American film in years was *Loving Lies*.

The film's production was not without its own drama. While filming in the Los Angeles Harbor on the *G.C. Lindauer* several miles out to sea, the crew, working under the direction of W.S. Van Dyke, simulated a storm at sea. The lightning machine produced enormous flashes which fire department boats interpreted as desperate calls for assistance. "After profuse explanations by Director W.S. Van Dyke and no little chagrin on the part of the seagoing fire-fighters, they stood by and watched several scenes photographed."[26]

Even worse, Brent came close to suffering a serious injury during production. "In the development of the climax of the story Miss Brent is aboard a ship which is being battered by a storm as it sways helplessly on the rocks. The script demanded that she be tied in a breeches buoy and pulled along the life line from the mast of the sinking ship to the top of a high cliff on shore. Halfway along the life line the rope broke and Miss Brent, who insisted on doing the scene herself, fell into the water. Waves dashed over her head and frantically Monte Blue pulled at her rope to get her ashore. After some work the buoy, with Miss Brent, reached the bottom of the cliff where, fearing that she might have been hurt, Thompson Buchanan ordered the cameras to stop before Miss Brent was to be pulled to the top of the cliff. But Miss Brent would not pause and pulled at the rope for Mr. Blue to finish the scenes without a stop. After three attempts Miss Brent was finally brought to the top of the cliff. 'I'll bet Mr. Blue thought I was an awful coward when I screamed the last time his rope slipped,' was Miss Brent's only comment."[27] Brent's heroics went for naught. When the film was released in 1924, *Variety* found it depressing and slow-moving and did not remark on Brent's performance.

In the summer of 1923, while Brent was finishing up *Loving Lies* with Associated Authors, Metro signed her for *Held to Answer.* "In order to allow Miss Brent to appear in the Metro

*Brent had not yet bobbed her hair in this photograph taken shortly after leaving Douglas Fairbanks' film company.*

film, Associated Authors are rushing the most important scenes for *Harbor Bar* [*Loving Lies* upon its release], in which Miss Brent participates. After working night and day for the past week Miss Brent is now enabled to start immediately on the Metro film and conclude her work at the Ince Studio when not actually appearing before the camera in *Held to Answer.*"[28]

Unfortunately, the hard work took its toll. During production of *Held to Answer,* Brent had a mental collapse and could not return to the set. On August 3, 1923, the *Los Angeles Times* referred to her as the "popular English star," and reported, "A week ago Miss Brent suffered a nervous breakdown following months of continuous work before the cameras of various producers. Her absence from the Metro Studio where *Held to Answer* was under production, has held up the completion of this picture, involving many thousands of dollars. Further delay would not only have brought about cancellations of many bookings already made throughout the country, but also would have upset the general releasing schedule of forthcoming pictures."[29]

Although Brent volunteered to go back to the studio to complete the film, her physician, Dr. Leo Schulman, advised against it. Finally, in desperation, director Harold Shaw and cameraman Milton Brown arrived with a crew at her Hillview apartment and finished filming her scenes in her bedroom. (It's interesting to note that after her marriage to Fineman, Evelyn maintained her residence at the Hillview Apartments. Furthermore, there was no mention of husband Fineman in the *Los Angeles Times* article.) The *New York Times* reported the story with a whimsical spin: "Fancy a girl, very much under the weather, having to smear make-up on her face and try to look well when fired upon by cameras in her own boudoir!"[30]

Another unusual occurrence was reported during the production of *Held to Answer*. According to a newspaper report, Brent was on the verge of adopting a child. The whole thing sounds suspicious. Perhaps it was an attempt to rehabilitate Brent after the news of her breakdown. "Evelyn Brent ... is going to adopt a child. Little Marie Mobray. One day recently Miss Brent was spending a day at the beach. She came upon a little girl who was crying. She was lost. Miss Brent told her stories and comforted her until a frantic aunt turned up. It developed in the conversation that the child was an orphan and Miss Brent successfully opened up negotiations for adoption."[31] Nothing was ever said about little Marie again.

When *Held to Answer* was released that fall, *Variety* found it suspenseful and singled out Brent's performance: "Evelyn Brent plays the lead opposite rather effectively in an ingénue manner."[32]

Brent apparently made a quick recovery from her breakdown because an article on August 19, 1923, mentioned her coming out of the Hillview Apartments: "...trim, small and dark, tripping out in a white silk sweater and sport skirt, a bag of golf clubs slung over her shoulder."[33]

Although being groomed for stardom by Fineman, Brent did not want to be a star. She often went on record that she preferred character roles. In a 1923 interview she talked frankly about her looks and fancied herself a non-conformist. "I have no delusions about my appearance. I couldn't be, if I wanted to be, a pretty-pretty ingénue lead. I want to exploit character roles. So many directors seem intent on making girls conform to a certain type, discarding all their native characteristics. Because curls were once the token of a movie ingénue, all must now friz their hair. Because D.W. Griffith once ordered three dabs of red on a pair of lips, all film ladies must now have cupid-bows. This conformity holds good not alone in the studios but in the streets as well—American women in all walks seeking to look and act exactly like. Depressing monotony. I rebel."[34]

The interviewer went on to describe Brent as no-nonsense. "She doesn't gush. She has no all's-right-with-the-movies smirk. She is deliberate rather than shy. She says she has lived more mentally than physically, although her arms are tanned and hard from beach swimming and riding. She refuses to accept the toothful for photographers merely to 'look cheerful.' She knows what she wants, what she believes herself capable of and she doesn't swerve."[35]

In the fall of 1923, Brent reportedly turned down a lucrative offer to return to the British stage, choosing instead to remain in Hollywood and focus on her motion picture career. "Miss Brent made her decision yesterday [September 4] when she cabled a refusal to an offer of a theatrical contract in England, where she had a particularly large following resulting from her two and a half years on the stage and before the camera. For several days Miss Brent has been trying to make a decision on the theatrical offer which would establish her as a stage star in her own right in England. Several motion-picture contracts which are now under negotiation decided the matter for her."[36] Again, Brent indicated that her greatest ambition was to "portray a heavy emotional character many years older than her own age."[37]

One of the most scandalous events in Brent's life occurred about a month later. In late 1923, *Screenland Magazine* reported that she'd had an affair with former employer Douglas Fairbanks. The magazine published a blurb which claimed Fairbanks and Mary Pickford had argued over his attentions to Brent. Other publications picked up the story, though they avoided naming the principals. The Fairbanks promptly telegraphed their attorneys and indicated they were suing for libel. Bernie Fineman added that Brent was suing as well.[38]

Pickford seemed to take the greatest offense. According to her, "That was a nasty story, an unjust story." Fairbanks, too, blew a gasket. "Mental perverts have been talking about me for years.... As a matter of fact, Mary and I were never so happy in our lives."[39] Fairbanks thought it important to add that his relationship with Brent was strictly business and he "never talked with her more than 20 minutes at a time." Brent insisted she left Fairbanks' employment because no suitable role had been found for her. She added, "The only relations I have with Mr. Fairbanks were business relations. Since leaving his studio I have seen him only twice. I parted the best of friends with Miss Pickford. I think she is a very sweet and charming woman."[40] As for husband Bernie, Brent indicated they had no marital problems and seemed downright defensive about it. "I am married—happily married. I married my husband because I loved him, and I still love him."[41]

Pickford was particularly upset that the story might affect Brent's career. She released a bizarrely worded statement that perhaps did not come out the way she intended. "The malicious stories that Miss Brent caused differences between myself and Mr. Fairbanks are extremely unfair to her. I think she is a beautiful girl, and I love to see beautiful women in Mr. Fairbanks' pictures. They are like flowers and other beautiful things. I helped select Miss Brent for the picture in which she appeared with my husband; I am always looking over chorus girls and women for him."[42]

Pickford concluded that the rumors stating that she and Fairbanks had separated were ridiculous; "Douglas and I have not been separated one night since we have been married, and we don't intend to be." According to her, "We are bringing this suit to protect not only ourselves, but all others who are attacked by such stories."[43] The story, which apparently had no truth to it, eventually died down, but for some time Brent was the subject of much unwanted gossip. Interestingly, there were many cynics in the film community who saw the whole thing as a publicity stunt. Apparently the press conference was a little too carefully staged. Reporters were called to Pickfair where they found Fairbanks getting a massage. He gave them his side of things. A reporter described what happened next. "Then Mary—charming Mary—in quaint costume of an olden day—backed up by the ever present 'Ma' (Pickford) Smith appeared in a becoming doorway and had her little say."[44]

By the end of the year, the publisher of *Screenland*, Myron Zobel, responded to threats of a lawsuit by claiming that the whole thing was a publicity stunt. He wrote, in part: "It is the intention of this magazine to fight with redoubled vigor its battle for freedom of the screen. It is the belief of the supporters and editors of this magazine that the hope of a free screen lies first and foremost in a free screen press. It is the intention of this magazine to mould its editorial policy towards the one sole object to the improvement of screen conditions and a higher quality of screen products. In this struggle individual vanities and personal pride must frequently suffer. The motion picture is no longer a commercialized industry. It has become a public institution and a public trust and as such is subject to public scrutiny and public comment. My magazine declines to become the vehicle for paid propaganda."[45]

Years later Brent claimed that she didn't even like Fairbanks. "I had three personal contacts with them—one at the Algonquin, one when I came out here and they asked me to come to some story conference or something, and Mary was not there but he was ... among the executives and Mary's mother and the whole bit! Then I was told to come and make the still pictures. Those were the only contacts I had with him."[46]

In October 1923, Brent began filming her scenes in George Archainbaud's *The Shadow of the East* for Fox. Other cast members included Frank Mayo, Norman Kerry, and Mildred Harris, ex-wife of Charles Chaplin. Publicists claimed Brent wore her own jewelry in this picture. "Evelyn Brent has had a passion all her life for collecting jewels that border on the barbaric, but never until she played her recent role as a native girl in *The Shadow of the East* did she have a chance to wear her collection. It includes a string of coral beads strung with bits of silver which she bought from a Navajo Indian; jade earrings made in a design taken from Egyptian pottery, and so long that they almost touch her shoulders; amber beads as large as plums, and bracelets of carved jet. All these, and more, came out of a satin-lined morocco box, where they had so long lain, to add greater beauty to the smoothness of her olive skin and the charm of her clear-cut features."[47] *The Shadow of the East* would be released in January 1924, along with nine other films featuring Brent.

While working on *The Arizona Express* in December, Brent restated one of her favorite themes: She preferred playing anything but straight leads. "A straight lead, to me, means the portrayal of a general feminine type. A characterization must be qualified by a given type, a finely drawn individual. Personally, I have never been interested in straight leads. I am extremely interested in any individual who plays a specific role in life. That is why motion pictures intrigue me. The dramatic scope they can and do cover offers beautiful opportunities for character interpretations."[48] In the spring of 1924, *The Arizona Express* opened to a solid review by *Variety*'s critic who suggested that Brent stole the film from Pauline Starke. "[David] Butler and Miss Starke both do well, but they must surrender honors to Harold Goodwin as the brother and Evelyn Brent as the dancer, two remarkably good performances."[49] The picture was action-packed and required lots of stunts. Brent told one interviewer, "I've played in many thrilling scenes but nothing ever required so much action and quick performance."[50]

Brent's first two films of 1924 were directly influenced by Bernie Fineman, who had joined Film Booking Offices of America (F.B.O.) near the end of 1923.[51] It was an important career move for him and, ultimately, Brent when he brought her into the studio. According to a *Los Angeles Times* article written a couple years later, Fineman saved the studio. "When Fineman arrived in December, 1923, F.B.O. was making one- and two-reelers on a sort of a hand-to-mouth policy and losing money every day. During the two previous years, $336,000 had been sunk. He drew the big pruning knife and started in. He reorganized the business. He adopted the policy of using only original stories on the theory that the cost of picture rights to successful novels and plays was out of all proportion to box-office returns. Last year F.B.O. lost only $36,000."[52]

In July 1924, Brent began work on *My Husband's Wives*. Her director was Maurice Elvey, a Britisher who had been signed to a Fox contract. Brent had known Elvey when the two lived in England. Elvey quickly realized Hollywood's advantages over England. "I have never before visited Hollywood and truly this thriving and beautiful community is a revelation to me. What with your picturesque location, attractive homes and constant sunshine and flowers, there is no other place in the world that can take Hollywood's dominating position in filmdom away from her. In England, and especially about London, we must contend with fog, smoke and like unfavorable conditions."[53]

The film, written by doomed actress Barbara LaMarr, cast Brent in the role of vamp. It simply didn't fit her. However, publicity for the film suggested that in the role, "the beautiful Evelyn portrays a girl who is decidedly dangerous to the masculine sex. The technique she uses in this role expresses the epitome of the satirical. She emphasizes the fact that, while feeding her vanity on the admiration of men, deep in her heart she despises them for succumbing to her charms. To her they are mere pawns in a mighty game, and she is oblivious to the feeling of her victims. Miss Brent also wears gowns which are gorgeous creations of art and has developed a totally different personality for the picture."[54]

In the summer of 1924, *The Desert Outlaw* was released. This Buck Jones Western was well-received. *Variety* went ga-ga over Brent's physical appeal. "Evelyn Brent ... is given no opportunity to wear colorful clothes but [she] is startlingly attractive even in shirtwaist and skirt."[55] Publicists insisted that the stunts were truly dangerous, including a scene where Brent was scripted to jump from a carriage into Jones' arms. "At this critical moment, accidental realism was injected into the scene unexpectedly. On the steep downgrade, the right hind wheel of the rickety stagecoach broke and Miss Brent was thrown out. Luckily, Buck Jones was Johnny on the spot, and fair Evelyn actually did drop into his doubly eager arms."[56]

In September 1924, Brent signed a long-term contract with Gothic, whose films were distributed by F.B.O. According to Fineman's new strategy, Brent would only star in novel adaptations. "Gothic Productions, Inc., will star Miss Brent in adaptations of well-known novels only. Each story was selected because of its adaptability to the screen and because its leading feminine character corresponded to the types Miss Brent has been most successful in the past."[57]

Brent's next picture was directed by Tod Browning, who had made several pictures with Brent's childhood friend Priscilla Dean. Fineman was Browning's friend and a fan of his work, so the eccentric director got the job despite his well-known personal issues. Browning made two pictures for F.B.O. Neither was successful, and Browning moved on to MGM. The wife of Lucien Andriot, cinematographer on *Dangerous Flirt* [*Prude*], told Browning's biographers that although the director may not have had his usual problems with alcohol he *was* having woman problems at the time.

> "He was quite a lady's man," she recalled. Browning, she stated, was dating a woman other than his wife and other than Anna May Wong during the F.B.O. period. Mrs. Andriot declined to give the woman's name, but recalled her clearly as a friend of hers given acting bit parts by Browning.[58]

Brent admitted she was worried about working with Browning: "I was scared when I first worked with him, because I'd heard the stories." However, Brent grew to like Browning and his wife Alice. "Brent was relieved by the sobriety, courtesy, and professionalism Browning exhibited at all times. Alice was at her husband's side constantly, a 'very steady' presence, Brent remembered. 'She kept her eye on everything,' and even accepted a role in Browning's ... final F.B.O. film, *Silk Stocking Sal*, a crook drama again starring Brent. Alice played a gun moll named, 'Gina, the wop.' [In the credits, Alice's character is renamed the slightly more politically correct Bargain Basement Annie.] Brent noted that 'Tod Browning was the first director who made you use voice when you worked.' In the silent films Brent had earlier worked in, 'the actors would make up lines, just say anything, throw it away.' But Browning, audaciously, asked actors to speak lines that corresponded with the story. 'He was a good director,' Brent said, 'a damned good director.'"[59]

*Prude*'s title was later changed to *Dangerous Flirt*. *Variety* found it noticeably low-budget, in poor taste, and didn't think much of Brent's ability to draw audiences. "Miss Brent as the girl probably doesn't mean anything as a draw, although starred. The rest of the cast is fair, while the sets, etc., are cheap."[60]

*"I must look crooked, because I always had to play underworld characters."*[61]

In January 1925, F.B.O.'s *Midnight Molly* was released while Brent was working on *Lawless Blood* for director Tom Buckingham. Many scenes were filmed at Balboa, resulting in serious cases of seasickness among the cast and crew; "Although most of the company, including Brent, were ill most of the time, they managed to shoot all scenes according to schedule."[62] The title was changed to *Forbidden Cargo* by the time it was released in February 1925. A letter purportedly written by Brent, but likely from the pen of a publicity writer, stated: "I must go up to the land again, to the lonely land that is nigh, and all I ask is an automobile, and a wheel to steer it by. Paraphrasing the immortal words of John Mansfield,[63] that is the way I feel about this bilious body of fluid they call the sea. Don't say the word sea to me again! Don't ever, Stella [the name of the columnist to whom the letter was supposedly written], let them sell you this 'fair wind and a flowing sea' stuff and all that sort of thing. For me, hereafter, the great open spaces away from the seaboard, where stomachs stay put!"[64]

Buckingham was crucial to the film, at least in the mind of Fineman. "I had to keep Evelyn Brent idle, though under contract and on this payroll for three weeks before starting *Forbidden Cargo* because I couldn't get Tom Buckingham. He was positively the only director in the business whom I would permit to handle the filming of that story."[65]

Boris Karloff was also in *Forbidden Cargo*. Years later Brent explained that Karloff was struggling to find work as an extra. "Boris was just one of a pool of actors who would hear of a film being shot, then go and stand in front of the studio and the director would come out and say, 'Okay, you,' and grab one. I saw Boris picked that way twice. He worked, I think, in three films with me." When asked to identify the films, Brent laughed and said, "Lord— I don't know! I used to make two pictures a day—one in the day and one at night—I couldn't possibly remember the titles of any of them!" She did remember, however, that Boris was a charming, gentle man,[66] nothing at all like the horrible character he played in the film who gets the idea to pour molten lead into the eyes of Robert Ellis.

The F.B.O. films, as Brent intimated, were virtually indistinguishable from each other. According to DeWitt Bodeen, "She was usually a lady crook, or a secret service agent posing as a crook, or a chorus girl in melodramatic post-chorus adventures.... [A]ll involved jewel robberies and impersonations. Elegant on the surface, but cotton-backed silk."[67]

Incompatibility and the relentless pace of moviemaking ruined the marriage between Fineman and Brent. They separated on February 25, 1925, but this detail did not come out until their 1927 divorce proceedings. A few weeks after separating, while working on *Alias Mary Flynn* with director Ralph Ince, Brent tried to commit suicide. Although the newspapers called it an accident, the details suggest otherwise. According to the *Los Angeles Times* (March 15), she "suffered a severed artery in her wrist Friday afternoon, when a faucet on her shower-bath broke in her hand. The quick action of a maid in applying a tourniquet is believed to have saved Miss Brent's life. The actress was reported out of danger yesterday, though she was weak from loss of blood. Three stitches were taken in the wound by Dr. E.B. Wolfan, who was summoned by B.P. Fineman, Miss Brent's husband. Fineman was at the Film Booking Offices studio, of which he is general manager, when he received word of the accident. He rushed home and found his wife in a weakened condition with the makeshift tourniquet, however, preventing her from bleeding to death."[68] Another newspaper report provided a different version. Headlined "ACTRESS SLASHES ARTERY IN WRIST," this article explained that it was not a faucet but a glass door knob that injured Brent. Also, in this version Fineman was summoned home by a hysterical maid who phoned him with the message that Brent was "bleeding to death."[69]

A day later, the *Los Angeles Times* ran an article about Hollywood celebrity superstitions. "Evelyn Brent and B.P. Fineman, happily wedded star and producer, will pass up most superstitions as mere bosh. But they will never permit pillar, post nor person to come between and separate them when they are out walking. For that is supposed to betoken a marital rift."[70]

Studio publicists were employed to keep stars' names in newspapers and magazines. Many times desperate measures were called for, and the resulting blurbs were full of lies and half-truths. Perhaps the most bizarre publicity story for Evelyn Brent appeared on March 22, 1925, in the *San Antonio Express*. The headline only suggested the story: "Snapping, Hissing Reptiles the Crop on This Farm." The subtitle made this preposterous claim: "Evelyn Brent of Los Angeles Only Woman in the World Who Is Raising Alligators for Commerce—Make Good Pets, Also." The article was a long one, several columns, and featured three photographs of Brent with, yes, alligators.[71] It reads like an April Fool's joke. One photo shows Brent straddling an alligator and opening the jaws of what is described as a "200-year-old crocodile." The caption states that Brent's interest was formed when she was a little girl in South Africa.[72] Even more remarkable, the farm, it was said, provided an excellent second income for the movie star: "Altogether, these sales of live reptiles and of hides, combined with money taken in for admission to the farm from curiosity seekers, total up to a tidy income each month." Another newspaper used a similar photograph (Brent straddling an open-mouthed alligator), but this time the alligator was said to be a gift from "an admiring fan."[73] By the way, there were also photographs that same month of Brent riding an ostrich. Apparently some newspapers didn't want to play along. An Ohio paper published the photo but a writer rather snippily commented, "Ostrich-riding is becoming a sport around Los Angeles, due to the efforts of Evelyn Brent and her press agent."[74]

There were also articles concerned with filmmaking. For example, Fineman acknowledged that he and Brent agreed that melodramas offered the best entertainment to American audiences. "The best kind of a picture is a good picture but—we, the average, you and I, prefer melodrama. Logical, apparently real, it appears to be a happening within our own possible experience. But it must be sufficiently exaggerated to be striking," declared Fineman.[75] He also defended Brent against charges of favoritism. "'It is rather a difficult position,' Fineman admits. 'For instance, if another actress is ill, that is all there is to it. But if it is my wife—I can't have people saying she gets out of working just because she is the boss's wife. However, I believe no one can truthfully accuse Evelyn Brent of shirking. She is always the one who insists on finishing the episode before quitting for the day—or night. And she possesses that remarkable faculty of being able to make a melodramatic heroine appear real while you are seeing her on the screen.'"[76]

Fineman and his publicists did an excellent job keeping Brent's name and photograph in the newspapers. In February 1925 one article concerned the fad of bobbing hair. "Screen stars with unbobbed heads are scarce and getting scarcer in Hollywood. Evelyn Brent is one of the few who still retains her long, raven tresses. 'Evelyn Brent without her hair would be like Mary Pickford without her curls,' says B.P. Fineman.... 'Producers seem to want me with long hair, so I'm not going to cut my throat by cutting my hair,' says Miss Brent."[77]

Brent finished filming *Alias Mary Flynn* on Saturday, April 4, 1925. Her physician ordered her to bed for a week so she could continue recovering from the "accident." Perhaps thinking that his wife simply needed lighter film roles to improve her suicidal mood, Fineman next cast Evelyn in a comedic role. "For the first time in her career Evelyn Brent is to play a light comedy part when she starts work on *Flash Annie*, the second production under her new contract with F.B.O."[78] It was based on *The Chatterbox*, a play by Bayard Veiller; the title was later changed to *Smooth as Satin*. According to reports, Fineman decided to cast Brent in a comedy after noticing she'd done some comedy bits quite well in *Alias Mary Flynn*.

During production of *Smooth as Satin*—and despite Fineman's protests to the contrary—Brent's illnesses created delays. The *Los Angeles Times* reported on April 18 that "Miss Brent, who has been confined to her bed for more than a week, is now up and around her home, and it is expected that she will be able to start work within a few days. Her illness has been occasioned by the loss of blood incurred when she severed an artery in her wrist several weeks ago."[79] It is likely that Brent was again suffering from mental issues.

Brent's role in *Smooth as Satin* was less glamorous than usual. "The day when the only role which a motion-picture star would consent to accept was that of a beautiful young society girl who walked through the picture in gorgeous gowns is almost past. Evelyn Brent is the latest of the beautiful young women of Hollywood deliberately to mar her attractiveness with ugly gowns and hats. In *Smooth as Satin* ... she plays the part of a pert and pretty French maid.... But in a long sequence she wears spectacles and a black bombazine skirt, which sweeps the ground."[80]

The budget for *Smooth as Satin* was $28,000 which was almost guaranteed to produce a financial windfall for F.B.O. According to Fineman, "We are making pictures which are of the simply, homely sort, and we find that the American public likes them. No great amount of money, as compared to some productions, goes into them. All of Miss Brent's pictures have been successes. There hasn't been a slump. F.B.O., this year, will make money."[81]

Brent concurred with the sentiments of her husband. "It isn't necessary to spend a pot of money to make an interesting picture play. People like melodrama—always will like melodrama and I believe nothing can supplant it. And it doesn't necessarily involve huge expenditures"[82] Brent made these comments in an interesting interview she gave to the *Los Angeles Times*, again explaining that character roles were her favorite. "I like character parts because they give you an opportunity to develop something through your own initiative. Society drama does not appeal to me at all. You hear a lot of young women say they want to play the role of the good little bad girl or the bad little good girl, and I'm one of them if there's a clean heart-story through it. What success I have achieved has been largely through such roles."[83]

Upon its release, *Smooth as Satin* garnered decent reviews. *Variety* noted its low-budget pedigree, but added, "For a cheap picture this one is at least entertaining." It also gave Brent faint praise, saying her part was "fairly well played."[84] Another critic credited Brent as being "the one bright spot."[85] F.B.O. kept up the publicity machine. When the picture played on Broadway at the Capitol Theater, a report declared that the film was "Miss Brent's sixth starring vehicle for F.B.O. Each has been a financial and artistic success. This is an unusual record, for even the best known stars usually have failures marked against their records between successes."[86]

By May 1925 Brent seemed to have regained her sense of humor. It may have been the result of a small bequest made to her "[f]rom an aged scene-shifter in England, to whom she was kind when on the stage."[87] According to the report, she received one hundred pounds. In that same month, the *Los Angeles Times* reported that she was the leader of a group that was fighting to ban corsets. Apparently some Parisian fashion designers had decided that the corset should return. No way, Brent responded, and formed the No-Corset-Never-Club. She was promptly named chairperson. All club members vowed never to wear a corset and enlisted the support of physician Dr. William E. Balsinger. "'Corsets are a peril to a woman's health and beauty,' says Dr. Balsinger. 'They interfere with digestion and breathing and impede the function of all the vital organs. The movement started by Miss Brent is worthy of support.'"[88] Club members planned to enlist the support of other stars as well as Hollywood costume designers. "'The safeguarding of health is the strongest reason for not wearing corsets,' Miss Brent says. 'But the club's appeal will be made principally to the desire for beauty and style. The modern demand for comfort also will be used in our propaganda.'"[89] Again, it appears the F.B.O. publicity machine was on the job. Furthermore, on May 13 the *Los Angeles Times* published an article with Brent suggesting that women should design men's clothing: "'Clothes make the man' should be changed to 'Women make the clothes that make the man.'"[90]

A major announcement appeared on May 24: Evelyn Brent had gone ahead and bobbed her hair. Yes, she had earlier said it would be like cutting her own throat, but the decision was made after her fans had been polled. Furthermore, her friends had been applying pressure. "It took two years' argument on the part of her friends and the demands of 1240 fans to get Evelyn Brent to bob her hair. And 12,400,000 fans couldn't induce her to let it grow again. Five times postponing the severing of her beautiful black hair for three months in the hope that Dame Fashion would put an end to the bobbed-hair craze, Miss Brent finally decided to do as her fans willed. The decision was announced in fan magazines and newspapers throughout the country. An avalanche of letters left no doubt as to the wishes of the movie-goers. When Miss Brent stopped counting there were 1240 votes for immediate bobbing and 310 against."[91]

Apparently Brent (or her press agent) researched hairstyles and discovered that the bob was not new: "[A] picture in the Metropolitan Museum shows Miss Baring, daughter of Sir Thomas Baring, wearing a center-part bob. There is another eighteenth century picture by Samuel Isham, which shows a girl with a characteristic high-part bob, and the cutest Gainsborough showing a regular eighteenth century flapper with an ultra-boyish shingle."[92]

In June 1925, F.B.O. announced that Brent and director Ralph Ince would re-team for their third production. "It will be based on an original story, *Tizona—the Firebrand*, with a Spanish locale, and the leading role will provide Miss Brent with a sort of female 'Mark of Zorro' character, in which the comedy high lights will be stressed."[93] The title would later be changed to *Lady Robinhood*. *Variety* was unimpressed with the film, but found Brent's performance charming.

Brent finished her scenes on July 4; she'd been working extra hours in a frantic attempt to complete the film earlier than expected. She wanted to attend the opening of *Smooth as Satin* at New York's Capitol Theater because it represented her Broadway debut. Her best efforts failed, however, and Brent missed the opening. She consoled herself with the fact that she'd start her next film the next week and be two weeks ahead of schedule. This was important because after finishing the next film, *Three Wise Crooks*, she planned a trip to Europe.[94] Meanwhile, Ince was outspoken about Brent's talent, predicting that she would become a star: "Mr. Ince acclaims Miss Brent as one of the great stars looming in the film firmament."[95]

An interesting news blurb on June 29, 1925, suggested that Brent did more than act for F.B.O.. "Evelyn Brent has been delegated the task of choosing the final title for the picture she is completing this week at the F.B.O. studios. It will be the third picture which she has both acted in and named. The other two [unnamed] have 'gone over big,' and the F.B.O. management has decided the star has a gift for this difficult factor in production."[96]

In July 1925, Brent celebrated her success by buying a fancy new car, a Pierce Arrow 80 Roadster. Her purchase was made through William E. Bush, Inc., the only Southern California Pierce Arrow dealer. This was a flashy, impressive automobile, one that signaled the driver was important and rich.[97] There is no question that Fineman's management of her career had made Brent a wealthy woman. He also made sure she was one of the most publicized stars of her era.

Believe it or not, Brent made the news in August 1925 for complaining about publicists. In a rather novel way to get publicity, Brent was interviewed about how stupid she found publicity, calling it "moron press-agentry." She further claimed that she only participated when the subject was newsworthy. "Yes I have publicity men.... Just the same as I have doctors and lawyers. But my press agents know better than to ask me to pose with rolled stockings and slave-bracelets around my anklets. I believe in legitimate news."[98] One columnist could not take Brent's hypocrisy and scolded her: "Just after I write a story about Evelyn Brent ... partially praising her for not allowing press agents to take photos of her ankles, knees and thighs, I received word that she is going to have a plaster cast made of ankles for the British Society Anatomists in London."[99] Apparently when Brent was working in England she received an award for "the most perfect ankle" in Great Britain.[100]

That same month, Brent started work on *Three Wise Crooks*, but Fineman was wondering if she shouldn't be in a drawing room drama. Brent was not enthusiastic. "The F.B.O. star is a fervent admirer of the thriller type of picture, believing it is better entertainment and provides superior opportunities for acting. 'These drawing-room pictures, in which you have to play the part of the animated clothes-horse, give me a pain.... They give you no chance whatever to develop individuality or character.'"[101] Fineman, however, insisted that fans were clamoring for an Evelyn Brent society drama. "It is what her public likes—and many of her admirers have expressed a desire to see the beautiful Evelyn in a modern society picture."[102] As for *Three Wise Crooks*, F.B.O. admitted that the role was similar to the ones Brent played in *Silk Stocking Sal*, *Smooth as Satin*, and others, but believed this role offered "more sentiment in the development of character."[103] To Brent, though, it was more of the same. One reviewer concluded, "Pretty bad. Evelyn Brent tries to rescue the picture from mediocrity by some good acting, but to no avail."[104]

Upon finishing the film, Brent took a trip to New York City and stayed at the Commodore Hotel. "Just going to put in a few weeks in the old home town,"[105] she said. Just before leaving, Brent signed a contract with F.B.O. for eight new films. The new pictures, it was promised, would be a departure from the crook melodramas. "Her new schedule, Mr. Fineman said, will contain several pictures which will give Miss Brent new opportunities for the humorous characterization work which has distinguished her recent vehicles, notably *Smooth as Satin* and *Lady Robinhood*."[106] In fact, F.B.O. was now seeking more comedy in all of their films, but especially in Brent's films, mainly due to exhibitors' requests.[107]

In truth the films Brent made at F.B.O. were low-cost productions that were rarely seen at first-run theaters. A Syracuse newspaper accurately—if undiplomatically—described the type of production: "These pictures were cheaply and hastily produced. The stories were hashed together. The directors were hacks or novices. And usually, Miss Brent's supporting players were mediocre performers who threw the entire brunt of the acting on her shoulders. Since speed was the slogan of the producers, there were few opportunities to re-take scenes and Miss Brent soon acquired a remarkable facility for making her characterizations sure the first try. These productions—there were about twenty of them—paid Miss Brent a lot of money, but they were such quality that few of them ever played the big theaters."[108]

Meanwhile, a rumor had started that Fineman was planning to leave F.B.O. for one of the large studios. Fineman denied it. "'I am satisfied with what we are achieving at F.B.O.,' Mr. Fineman said yesterday [August 28, 1925], 'and have no intention of going anywhere else.'"[109] Meanwhile, the *Los Angeles Times* reported that Brent was traveling to New York alone. The newspaper offered a hint of marital trouble, writing that Fineman "did not accompany her, being detained here, it was said, by press of work."[110] The couple still had not announced that they were separated.

While Brent was on her New York vacation, one newspaper thought it important to report that she had forgotten her shoe trunk. "Miss Brent's pet extravagance is shoes and her wardrobe usually contains a half hundred pairs made to order by a Hollywood bootmaker. When she travels they occupy a special trunk. But this time the trunk was left at the Hollywood home."[111]

A month later, Brent was still in New York, unable (because of work obligations) to make that trip to Europe. However, she had procured some French fashions. While in New York, Brent met up with old friend Marie Degenais who sketched the gowns worn by a New York visitor who had just arrived from France—someone Miss Degenais knew would be wearing the latest fashions. "After a little while Miss Brent had a collection of scores of sketches of suits, gowns and dresses from Worth, Poirot, Le Long, Chanel and half a dozen of the great French couturiers. Then Mlle. Degenais took her to a French dressmaker who for years before her arrival in New York a few months ago had made a business of copying the work of the great Parisian masters for American buyers. So Miss Brent is returning to Los Angeles with her French clothes."[112]

A few days later, publicists who were earning their keep while Brent was in New York, got a story published in the *Los Angeles Times* in which they claimed Brent had been suspected of being a society crook by detective James Tait. He apparently recognized Brent from her pictures, but in his confusion thought she was a real-life crook and followed her back to her hotel. Upon realizing his error, he sent her a letter, they got together, and he took her to the New York police department where she viewed a gallery of mug shots. "During the visit to 'mug row,' as it is known to New York detectives, Miss Brent examined several hundred of the thousands of photographs held by the police. She informed the detectives that the visit would be of great value to her in future pictures, should she continue criminal roles. The data on crook characteristics alone, said Miss Brent, are invaluable to an actress playing crook roles. At 'headquarters' Miss Brent was introduced to other detectives who complimented her on her work, but who at the same time joshed Tait for his 'fall.'"[113]

Brent finally returned to Los Angeles in early October, greeted by many friends who awaited the arrival of her train. Brent stayed busy with social occasions. Just after Thanksgiving she attended the premiere of Cecil B. DeMille's[114] *The Road to Yesterday* at the opening of the new Figueroa Theater.[115] "The gorgeous gold and crimson of the theater's decoration was a colorful background for the lovely gowns of the women as they entered the flower-banked lobby.... Evelyn Brent showed her dark beauty in a gown of pink satin with a French blue velvet cloak."[116] Other attendees that night included Mrs. DeMille, Claire Windsor, Priscilla Dean, Blanche Sweet, Joan Crawford, Norman Kerry, Carmel Myers, June Mathis, Jacqueline Logan, and Margaret Livingston.

In November 1925, another scandal touched Evelyn Brent when Bernie and F.B.O. were sued by showgirl Peggy Udell. The news was scarcely covered by most American newspapers, but a short blurb in a Canadian paper suggested the story was unsavory. "Peggy Udell, film 'extra' de luxe and former follies beauty, has filed suit for $501,500 damages against B.P. 'Bernie' Fineman, general manager of the F.B.O. Studios and husband of Evelyn Brent."[117] A more detailed explanation of her accusations was reported in a Fresno newspaper. "Fineman is alleged to have attempted to become familiar with the actress during business interviews in his office, where he is also accused of detaining her with the aid of a detective on the occasion of the second visit."[118] The news, coming on the eve of the couple's third wedding anniversary, could not have made Brent happy, to say the very least, even if they were separated. For his part, Fineman claimed blackmail when Udell specifically complained of "two attempts of criminal attack and false imprisonment."[119] In another report she claimed that "Fineman and detectives held her a prisoner in the film office as part of an alleged scheme of intimidation."[120] Udell may have received some kind of settlement, but the suit never made it to trial.

Peggy Udell (*née* N'ertle[121]) was an interesting woman. On the stage at the age of four, she was often in the news, and it was usually—well, let's be more precise, *often*—for scandalous reasons. The first scandal hit in January 1922 when she married wealthy Philadelphian John Montgomery. Montgomery asked for an annulment ten days later based on the grounds that he was drunk—and she'd seduced him. According to him, he was "vamped and married the Midnight Frolics girl at dawn while he was intoxicated." Udell's age was variously reported as 16 and 17. The court case began in June. At the end of July, the judge more or less said "tough" to Mr. Montgomery. "'The escapade' was fraught with serious results, the judge's opinion said. He gave the girl $50 a month support."[122] Then, the ruling was overturned, the annulment granted, and Udell received nothing.

Udell quickly remarried. Her new husband was football player James Conzelman. However, by June 1924 she was asking for a divorce.[123] In 1928 Udell was in the news because of a brawl with fellow showgirl Peggy Green. They were appearing together in *Show Boat* and had apparently been feuding for some time. "Peggy Udell emerged from the battle with a discolored optic and two missing molars."[124] Udell and Green were fired from the show.

But wait—there's more. In what might be our favorite twist, Udell announced in 1929 that she was giving up the fast life—to join a convent. Yep, at the age of 21 she decided she'd seen and done it all. According to a newspaper report, "she decide[d] that the world, especially men, is just a snare and a delusion and has arranged to enter a convent in Canada, as far away as possible from the sham and tinsel of Broadway and its horrid men."[125] Of course, she never followed through. Still, for you cynics out there, be aware that, according to the article, when Peggy was 14 she chose between becoming a showgirl and her other ambition— entering a convent.

In March 1930, Udell married again. This time it was to vaudevillian Peter Michon.[126] Very soon both were in the news. Around Christmas 1932 the Michons crossed paths with Frederick Hansen. It happened in a minor traffic accident that suddenly escalated to fisticuffs between the two men. Udell contributed to the mayhem by grinding Hansen's eyeglasses into the ground. She paid $15 to replace the spectacles.[127] Udell seems to have disappeared after this, though we can't help wondering what happened to her. Where is Richard Lamparski when we need him? The only information we found was that she apparently lived to a ripe old age—outliving both Brent and Fineman. Peggy Unertel Udell died in December 1984 in Los Angeles.

Though Brent's personal life was nowhere as eventful as Udell's—thank goodness—her personal life by the end of 1925 was in shambles. Still, she was an honest-to-God movie star. The *Chicago Herald* on December 4, 1925, advertised that the Bensonville Center Theatre had twelve current or upcoming movies. Three of them starred Brent—*Lady Robinhood*, *Midnight Molly*, and *Smooth as Satin*.[128]

*Silk Stocking Sal*, released in January 1926, was an important step for Brent, at least according to publicists. "For the first time in her career, Evelyn Brent, brilliant and beautiful young star of the cinema, essays the role of an underworld character and comes off with flying colors. The part of 'Stormy' Martin, a girl of the slums who associated with crooks only to find that love changes her from a lawbreaker into a fine, upstanding young woman, fits the capabilities of the star as snugly as a new glove."[129] Yes, it was another crook drama.

Fineman left F.B.O. in February 1926. It's difficult to determine whether the Udell suit had anything to do with it, but a news report explained that he resigned to become supervisor of a unit at First National Pictures. Eventually Fineman became an assistant to B.P. Schulberg, Paramount's West Coast production supervisor, by the fall. In the two-plus years he was at F.B.O., he had helped make Brent a star and a fortune. As for Brent, she still had four more pictures left on her contract with the studio.[130]

In April 1926, *Queen o' Diamonds* was released, and *Variety* loved Brent in it. "Miss Brent is the perfect crookess. It would take much to resist her stealing ways. She steals hearts." In the film, Brent played a dual role—a good girl *and* a bad girl. "As the nice girl she is lovable, but as the crooked, sophisticated actress, great!"[131]

*The Impostor* was also released around the same time. The critics were becoming restless. One simply wrote, "A carbon copy of the former Evelyn Brent productions."[132] Another echoed that critique: "If it's an Evelyn Brent picture it will eventually turn crooked. Even though we always enjoy her pictures, we are of the opinion that Evelyn should quit harping on this crook idea continually."[133] When *The Jade Cup* was released that same year, the critics complained again. "Evelyn Brent does her best, but it isn't her fault that this is barely palatable. What Evelyn needs is a new type of story."[134]

The Finemans continued the pretense of being married. On May 16, 1926, it was noted in the Glimpses of Hollywood column that the couple was seen at the Cocoanut Grove. That same month the Finemans were invited to a dinner party at the 1775 North Sycamore Avenue of home of stage star Mrs. Leslie Carter. Other guests included Pauline Garon and husband Lowell Sherman, Mrs. Adolphus Busch, Jr., Lou Payne, and John Colton. According to the *Los Angeles Times*, "The event was one of the exclusive affairs of the week."[135]

By June, Brent was still at F.B.O., but publicity was not as carefully honed as it had been under Fineman. For example, one report appeared to have been written by someone who'd never heard of Brent. Or Mabel Normand, for that matter. "Evelyn Brent, a little southern girl, with English training, darkeyed, vibrant, with heaps of personality, was picked up by F.B.O. a bare two years ago—and today she stands at the top of the melodramatic list of actresses. A prominent film man recently called her 'the logical successor to Mabel Normand.' In stirring melodramatic roles she is superb. Her fame, now spreading rapidly, is another result of F.B.O.'s vision."[136] Though both were quite talented, there were few similarities between Brent and Normand.

Brent finally got out of her F.B.O. contract. In July 1926 it was reported that she had left for Arrowhood Lake for treatment of an abscessed ear and to recuperate. She had suffered, it was said, from the condition for ten days. "She was taken ill after she went swimming at the beach when already suffering from a cold. Her condition became so acute that the services of three physicians, Dr. P. Newmark, Dr. M. Lovejoy and Dr. Joseph Goldstein, were required."[137] It was expected her recuperation would take several weeks. This meant that the film she was scheduled to make, *The Adorable Deceiver*, was re-cast with Alberta Vaughn.[138]

Another article made reports of her illness suspicious. On July 15, Brent notified F.B.O. that she was breaking her contract with them in order to pursue other filmmaking opportunities. According to the *Los Angeles Times*, the split with F.B.O. was "arrived at most amicably."[139] Brent made it clear that she no longer wanted to deal with "entangling alliances."[140] A month later, the same newspaper reported that Brent had fulfilled the terms of her contract with F.B.O. and was moving on. "Having recently completed the last of her F.B.O. vehicles, *Flame of the Argentine*, the young star has responded to the demand for her services in several studios by announcing her freedom from contractual obligations and is now considering which role of three offered will give her free-lance career the greatest impetus."[141]

# 4

# *Stardom*

*Miss Brent's personality is peculiarly adaptable to fulfilling roles of crookdom.*
*It suggests mystery, intrigue, lurking danger, every element that popular*
*conception has conceived of the fascinating "lady crook."[1]*

In September 1926, Evelyn started work on Paramount's *Love 'Em and Leave 'Em* in Astoria, New York. Many of Paramount's productions were made in New York, and this change meant Brent had to temporarily move back to the East Coast. Meanwhile, Bernie remained in Hollywood.

Brent and director Frank Tuttle traveled on the same steamy New York–bound train. According to Tuttle, "Miss Brent had a drawing room in the car next to mine.... This was in the days before air conditioning, and Miss Brent was doing her best to fight off the heat with an electric fan. She was a slender, dark-haired young lady, with a fine forehead and wonderful, intelligent eyes. I had admired her sensitive performances with Clive Brook and George Bancroft.[2] We sweltered through the conventional, conversational gambits, then, as we got to know one another, I discovered that she was a warm and wonderful person. When I left, I felt that working with her would be a stimulating experience."[3]

Shortly after production began, however, Brent was taken out of the film—at least for a short time. "On the morning we started shooting," Tuttle explained, "I was astonished to find that Esther Ralston had replaced Evelyn Brent. Let me quickly add that Esther had nothing to do with the switch, which had originated in the front office for some reason I have never been able to fathom. Perhaps the higher ups were trying to capitalize on a recent Ralston hit. In any case, it was a real contretemps. Fond as I was of Esther, I couldn't help feeling that Evelyn Brent's qualities and appearance suited the part perfectly. I did the best I could to readjust myself to the change. Esther was her usual cooperative self and we finished the day's work with only a slight feeling of tension. Next morning, Evelyn Brent walked onto the set. The powers that be had switched the switch. I never found out the 'whys and wherefores' of this one either. My guess was that Betty's husband, Bernie Fineman, had heard the news in Hollywood and raised long-distance hell."[4]

Tuttle was left in the unenviable position of soothing Brent's bruised ego. "What kind of people, I thought, would assign a role to an actress because she is talented and sensitive and then slap her face by yanking her out of the part. Russ Mathews, my assistant, and I did our darnedest to salve our star's *amour propre* and make our sympathy and understanding obvious. Like us, Osgood [Perkins] had fallen for Betty like a ton of brick-a-brac and she reciprocated. After the picture had really begun to swing, Betty told me that if all of us hadn't been so considerate she would have quit the show. Naturally none of this affected her performance, which was exceptionally convincing."[5]

Brent's co-star Louise Brooks was not a fan of Brent's. Brooks had gone to the trouble of having her shopgirl costume customized at Milgram's. Brent was not so picky. According to Brooks, Evelyn arrived from Hollywood and immediately went to the wardrobe department. "For a shocking half hour I sat amazed watching Herman [Smith] and her assemble a complete wardrobe for the film in which she played the lead, and my sister. From a pipe stand of worn size 12s they selected her clothes, and from the shoe shelves they selected my castoff slippers (we wore the same size 4). All this time her manner was warm and friendly, but I found later she was like a Baked Alaska—very cold inside."[6]

Brooks, who apparently drank her milk from a saucer, further hinted that Evelyn's rise had been due to marrying B.P. Schulberg's new assistant Bernie Fineman, and insisted that Brent was demoralized. "After much careful handling and coaxing, Tuttle was finally succeeding at relaxing her performance ... when Schulberg wired from the coast that he had seen the rushes and he wanted Evelyn photographed to look much younger. And more beautiful. As a consequence, all her carefully nurtured ease and confidence withered away during the rest of the filming, while the makeup man and our camera man, George Webber, worked on the lines under her eyes and around her mouth."[7] Brooks concluded that "Evelyn was indeed in a class by herself. After all these years the possibility of stardom put her in an emotional state of anxiety, the result of which being that she acted with an intensity better suited to Mata Hari before the firing squad than a shopgirl in a comedy."[8]

Tuttle held a vastly different opinion: He adored Brent. He and Osgood Perkins, father of Anthony, sought out her company. "At coffee break time, Os Perkins and I talked about everything imaginable with Evelyn Brent. You usually get to know your leading players and what makes them tick before you've finished directing a picture. The more I knew Betty the more I admired her. I loved working with her and I loved her—but who didn't? Less than a year after *Love 'Em and Leave 'Em* was previewed, I returned to Hollywood. I still treasure the photograph Evelyn Brent gave me. On it she had written, 'Love 'em and leave 'em and send 'em a photo—Betty.'"[9]

*Love 'Em and Leave 'Em* was Brent's first Paramount feature upon leaving F.B.O. The *Los Angeles Times* wrote that her newest role "marks another step up the ladder of accomplishment for this young actress who for more than two years was the leading feminine drawing card in theaters that featured the product of F.B.O. and who is now a scintillating figure in her first Paramount feature. It is this picture which is said to mark Miss Brent's entry into the small group of free-lance stars determined to play 'better roles in the best films.'"[10]

The next film on her schedule was *Love's Greatest Mistake*. Based on a magazine serial story, it, too, was filmed in New York. The roles in the two films, however, were quite different. Brent insisted she was eager for variety: "A young actress wins her histrionic spurs only by playing a diversity of roles. Added years may limit her variety but youth permits latitude of work."[11] *Variety*'s critic ignored Brent's performance and thought Josephine Dunn stole the picture: "Miss Dunn looks like a potential Garbo. This one shows that the girl has pretty much everything needed to carry her through, and if she is supplied with the right type of roles, there is no reason why she shouldn't land in the big money."[12] Although Brent received top billing—William Powell second—*Variety* complained that "there isn't a star name anywhere in the cast."

It was announced in December 1926 that Brent would play the lead opposite Thomas Meighan in *Fate*. "The picture holds unusual promise because it is an original by Owen Davis, the playwright who knows his dramatic onions and has successfully squeezed the juice from them these many, many years."[13] The film's title was changed to *Blind Alleys* when it was released in March 1927. Mordaunt Hall, the *New York Times* film critic, found it laughably bad, as did the audience with whom he attended the showing. He described how the final scene, which was supposed to be poignant, "moved the audience to vociferous mirth."[14] *Vari-*

*ety* also reported that audiences laughed at scenes that weren't supposed to be funny, and credited villain Brent with stealing the film from co-star Greta Nissen.

Brent had spent the last three months of 1926 at the Hotel Chatham in New York making films before returning to Hollywood in January. In early 1927, Hollywood was proclaiming Brent the queen of the underworld. Newspaper columnist Whitney Williams wrote, "Evelyn Brent seems to have taken Priscilla Dean's place as 'the lady crook of the screen,' now that Priscilla has forsaken the lowly crook roles for comedy of a far broader nature.... In Miss Brent is glimpsed the exotic, the mysterious, the romantic—everything that goes hand in hand with the appearance of such a character. For the heroine in plays of this nature must have qualities as fascinating as she must be beautiful. And Miss Brent qualifies."[15]

There was talk that Brent would join Harry Cohn and Columbia Pictures to make two movies. Perhaps most enticing to Brent was Cohn's suggestion that she could make the films in Europe. However, nothing came of it.[16]

Brent's favorite hangout around this time was the Montmartre Cafe. Sometimes she was seen with Fineman, other times accompanied by female friends including Lilyan Tashman, Priscilla Dean, and her closest companion Dorothy Herzog. In February 1927, Mrs. Benjamin Glazer (actress Sharon Lynn) hosted a party at the Montmartre for Brent's return. Other guests included Louella Parsons, Dorothy Cumming—and Herzog.[17] Herzog had become a constant companion and eventual roommate after Brent separated from Fineman. Brent later told an interviewer, "After the separation my good friend Dorothy Herzog came to live with me."[18] Born on December 4, 1899, in Memphis, Tennessee, Herzog was the daughter of Henrietta and Adolph Herzog. Raised in New York, she'd worked as a journalist in New York before coming to Hollywood to write for newspapers and magazines. Others noticed that Brent and Herzog were a couple. "Frequently she may be seen lunching at the Montmartre, usually with her chosen crony, one of the newspaper women devoted to the doings and undoings of the Hollywoodians."[19] Once, when talking to Herzog, George Bancroft referred to Brent as "that girl you go with."[20]

For much of 1927 and well into 1928, Herzog and Brent were often mentioned in the same news articles. For example, in May 1927 Brent joined Herzog and Priscilla Dean as judges in a bathing beauty contest held at Ocean Park. The contestants numbered 200, and the annual event was sponsored by the Ocean Park Business Men's Association.[21]

*"Evelyn Brent was a smouldering-eyed brunette whose look was supposed to be sultry but could just as well have been described as sullen."*[22]

If there is only one movie that Evelyn Brent will be remembered for, that film is likely to be *Underworld* (1927). At least one newspaper got it right when it announced that the role would prove to be "one of the greatest opportunities of her screen career."[23] Noted film historian Kevin Brownlow described Evelyn's appearance as "disturbingly attractive."[24] An international writer, based in Berlin for *Vossische Zeltung,* referred to Brent as "probably the most talented of the younger generation ... in the United States."[25] According to James Card, Brent was a force in Josef von Sternberg's *Underworld* and *The Last Command* (1928). "She had been unnoticeable in a lot of things, but when Sternberg got hold of her, he shot all that cigarette smoke around her face. He was a genius at lighting up a person's face and making it sing and shimmer. He made Evelyn Brent look more beautiful than Garbo."[26] According to the *Los Angeles Times,* "As a gang leader's sweetheart in *Underworld,* Evelyn Brent is said to give one of her finest interpretations. The film is a crook drama and serves to bring into the spotlight Miss Brent's unusual type of beauty."[27]

Louise Brooks, who went to a lot of trouble to say some fairly mean things about Brent, grudgingly agreed that von Sternberg got a great performance out of her. "I made a picture

*Dorothy Herzog was included in this promotional photograph for* A Man's Home *(1921). Front row: Grace Valentine, Anna Steese Richardson, Margaret Seddon. Middle row: Mrs. Sime Silverman, Dorothy Moran, Mary Kelly, Miss Fergus, Lillian Gale, Herzog. Back row: Ruth Rosenberg, Wilhelmenia Burch, Mrs. William Johnston, Agnes Johnston, Caroline Harding. At the time, Herzog was working for* Motion Picture News.

with her, and Evelyn's idea of acting was to march into a scene, spread her legs and stand flat-footed and read her lines with masculine defiance. Oh, I thought she was dreadful, and then I saw her in *Underworld*, and Sternberg softened her with all these feathers, and he never let her strike attitudes at all. He made her move. I remember the opening of *Underworld*.... [H]e makes her entrance the loveliest, most feminine thing, like bringing her from standing at the top of these stairs and reaching down, pulling up her dress, fixing her garter, I think. Anyhow, it's lovely, it established her as lovely and feminine."[28]

It wasn't easy to be a von Sternberg actor. According to Budd Schulberg, the director "had a way of talking to his actors as if they were slightly retarded children."[29] Film critic Blake Lucas added that to be a von Sternberg actor called for a different kind of talent. "The attempted suppression of emotion typical of Sternberg characters required an acting language in which physical gestures and mask-like countenance would permit the characters' deepest feelings to emerge seemingly against their will."[30]

Nowhere in his 1965 autobiography does von Sternberg mention Brent by name though he does write several pages each about *Underworld* and *The Last Command*. His most telling reference is when he describes the casting for *Underworld*. "The wife of one of the studio officials was assigned to me as leading lady and several other unimportant players were added, making certain that no valuable personality would be risked in this gamble." It's likely that he was not the only person in Hollywood who thought of Brent only in terms of who she had married. He later acknowledged that the film made her a star. "The studio officials shook hands with each other for having made a film with nothing and for nothing and having emerged with three new star players and one director."[31]

Brent had a different recollection of *Underworld*'s casting. According to her, Paramount insisted on Estelle Taylor, a very good actress who Evelyn liked and stayed friendly with for years, "but Sternberg wanted me. I guess he liked my work and thought I could do it."[32] She told another interviewer that von Sternberg remembered her from Europe. "Von Sternberg had been an assistant something-or-other in England. I didn't remember him, but fortunately, he remembered me. He insisted on having me for the lead in *Underworld* with George Bancroft, which, after twelve years, was my first real break in pictures."[33] Brent also suggested that von Sternberg had seen her in Tod Browning's pictures and decided to use her.

Brent was signed as the female lead in *Underworld* in December 1926 by B.P. Schulberg. The *Los Angeles Times* knew how important the role would be. "When Evelyn Brent returns to Hollywood from New York she will. ... play the leading feminine role in what promises to be one of the foremost pictures of the coming year. ... Miss Brent is to play the role of the sweetheart of the underworld chief, which part, it is declared, gives her the opportunity for a characterization of exceptional power. She won the role as a result of the brilliant work she has done in three successive Paramount pictures made at the Long Island studio."[34] Production on the film was scheduled to begin on February 1, 1927.

Brent later suggested that the set was stormy. "As a director ... he gives much to the players he is directing. I believe it is the fact that he is constantly putting up an argument, getting one into a fury and thereby bringing forth her best talent."[35] Brent explained that she, Fred Kohler, and Clive Brook lost their tempers at one time or another on the set with von Sternberg. "It was [due to] working too many hours, and under difficult conditions, too fast. It's cold working out in the back lot at night, you have no idea what it could be like. They didn't have portable dressing rooms in those days, they had what they called a stove, that if you stood right up against it you could get a little warm. But you couldn't stay there very long. There weren't the comforts that they've got today.... Oh, that back lot at Paramount was miserable, so cold[;] even on a hot day the nights were cold. And the fog machines going, see? It was beautiful on the screen, but difficult to do."[36]

In another interview she praised von Sternberg but also indicated that he was volatile. "She feels that her best work is dragged from her by Josef von Sternberg. They are always scrapping. Liking and admiring each other tremendously, their scrapping is without malice or bitterness. 'But don't make any mistake that it isn't real.... There isn't a foot of the Paramount lot that doesn't remind me of a fight I have had with von Sternberg. We argued for half a day about whether I was to sneer with my top lip or bottom lip. Sometimes we start on the set and wind up in my dressing-room, and sometimes we start in my dressing-room and wind up on the set, and between the two places we cover every inch of space in a battle royal. But we understand each other perfectly and I often think he does it on purpose just to get me into the mood to "show him," and I always rise to do it, in spirit at least.'"[37]

Von Sternberg required that the actors watch the rushes. "Joe was a stickler for making you see rushes every day. It helped you get an understanding what he was taking the time to try to do. He got very angry if anybody missed seeing the rushes. We used to go in every day."[38]

Brent later described *Underworld* as a "sensation" and claimed it established not only her career but Bancroft's and von Sternberg's.[39] Late in life Brent was asked if von Sternberg had been strange. "Always. But a very nice man. I first knew him in England, slightly. He worked at studios there. Not as a director. I think he designed sets or something, as I remember." When asked if he was eccentric, she replied, "Yes. But a good director. He had one thing that I don't think I ever found another director to have and that was a feeling for the sweep of a picture and the movement. The people were incidental. It's true. It was a whoosh ... like that. And the people did their thing, you know, as it went along. And it was a most effective technique, I think. I saw *Underworld* not long ago down at the Academy Theater, and I was impressed by it then.... It was still a good picture!"[40]

A distinctive look for Brent during this time was the wearing of a cloche hat. "Travis Banton ... was the designer at Paramount in those days. We had no union then, you see, and we could work 24 hours straight through. There was no such thing as 8 hours, and then you'd go home.... You'd finish at 3 in the morning, and they'd blithely say, 'On the set at 7!' You know, 3 o'clock in the morning! So I got an idea that if I didn't have to sit and have my hair done every morning and then dried, I could save time. So Travis designed the hats; the feathered ones for *Underworld* were the first. Then in each picture he designed them with either flowers or leaves or something. And it really saved me about two hours every morning."[41] Brent called Banton "a damn good designer."[42] She also said, "I shall never forget that marvelous man.... The gowns he designed for me were always sheer perfection. An actress could move in them, use them as if they were a part of her body."[43]

Brent's feather turban became a hit. A contemporary ad featured "Feather Turbans as worn by Evelyn Brent." Described as "The Latest Sensation on the Pacific Coast," the turbans were being sold at Frost Bros. Department Store, ranging in price from $10 to $22.50.[44]

*Underworld* has proven to be a tremendously influential film. According to James Card, "*Underworld* became the archetypal gangster film, with arresting touches that other directors did not hesitate to copy."[45] Writer-researcher William Everson made the excellent point that the first gangster films were simply a variation on Westerns. "With the 1920s, Prohibition, and the rise to notoriety of men like Al Capone, gangsterism made the headlines, and provided hot, topical fodder for the movies. But as yet, Hollywood really knew nothing about the gangster or the social forces that created and sustained him. As a result, the new gangster films, spearheaded by Josef von Sternberg's *Underworld* (1927) ... merely transplanted William S. Hart's good bad man to a big-city milieu."[46]

*Underworld* still seems so fresh and original, but Everson rightly points out its clichés, "ranging from gang-leader Fred Kohler's humiliation of the hero (Clive Brook) in a saloon ... to the ultimate showdown and street shoot-out between the lone badman and virtually the city's entire and fully mechanized police force.... In keeping with the good-badman image transposed from the West, he was a man of honor whose death was brought about in a self-sacrificing manner, usually to unite the unspoiled young lovers who sought to escape the underworld environment."[47]

There is no doubt that *Underworld* was the most important picture Brent had yet made. According to James Card, von Sternberg "rescued Evelyn Brent from a fading career by transforming an ordinary face into that of an earthy Madonna."[48] When the film opened in L.A. in August 1927, a *Los Angeles Times* critic wrote, "It is bound to be one of the significant pictures of the year, and comes near being the best crook melodrama to hit the screen.... Evelyn Brent hasn't been seen to such advantage for many a month. It will return her to high favor."[49]

Though Paramount had misgivings about whether the film would prove to be successful, they touted it as the "greatest underworld thriller in years."[50] Upon its release, it was a huge hit in Los Angeles. "*Underworld* at the Paramount has made such a hit with the public that midnight showings have been the rule. Doubtless, it should remain for an indefinite engagement but the policy of the theater admits no deviation from a weekly change of program, consequently *Hula* goes in today."

New York critics were a bit tougher on the film but still applauded the effort. "The consensus of opinion is that *Underworld* might have been immeasurably finer, but in its present form it cannot be denied that it will prove a great money-maker, even though its palpable identification with Chicago may raise some protest in that quarter."[51]

*Underworld*'s style was more similar to German Expressionism than what we think of as a typical gangster film. According to Harry Hossent, "It owes more to the Germanic overtones of *Dr. Mabuse* than it does to the *Chicago Tribune*. Furthermore, 'Bull' Weed is not a gangster in the Capone pattern; he robs banks instead of existing on an empire of booze and vice. The characters seem to live in a dream world which had little to do with the streets of the 1920s. They are not documented gangsters lifted from the news-pages and enlarged upon, but more figures in a grand tragedy."[52]

By 1930 the *New York Times* reported that *Underworld* had become a cult favorite in Paris, where its title was *Nuits de Chicago*. According to Paris correspondent Morris Gilbert, "the piece was a furor. In the minds of those enterprisers of the serious film here in Paris — and it must be said that Paris offers much more opportunity for experiment, for artistic effort, for the cultivation of the cinema as an art, than New York does — the picture is a film classic.... The work of Bancroft never loses its power to magnetize this city, and Evelyn Brent is only a little less esteemed."[53]

Some have argued that Brent not only became typecast after vividly playing Feathers but that she played every role afterward as if she were Feathers. Richard Griffith wrote,

> Miss Brent continued to play Feathers with slight variations for the rest of her starring career. The stereotype she established provoked the following immortal exchange from S.J. Perelman:
>
> FEATHERS: Hello, you two-timing bastard.
> TYRONE RUKEYSER: Why, what's the matter, Feathers?
> FEATHERS: Nothing. I always say that when I come into a room.[54]

*Underworld* helped make Brent a star whether or not she wanted to be one. The same month that *Underworld* was released, Brent was quoted in an article discussing the flip side of fame. She explained that several Hollywood actors had taken their names out of the telephone book because obsessed fans, real estate agents, scamsters, and so-called financiers were making stars' lives a living hell. For example, poor Clara Bow, who already had a private number, had to change her number every month or so because of telephone harassment. According to Brent, she too was forced to go with a private telephone number. "She tried hard to be different ... but it did not work out. At all hours of the day and night the telephone rang in her apartment. It disturbed her so much she had to get a private number."[55]

The next film released after *Underworld* was *Women's Wares*, but it did not measure up. According to *Variety*, "Evelyn Brent is photographed disadvantageously at times. She contributes satisfactory acting, not up to her previous work."[56]

Long separated from Fineman, Evelyn finally filed for divorce on June 22, 1927, in Los Angeles, charging her husband with mental cruelty.[57] When reporters caught up with Fineman, he explained that though they were still friendly, divorce was the best solution. They were indeed friendly. Many times the *Los Angeles Times* reported that the couple attended social gatherings together before and after the divorce. Ruth Biery noted in 1928 that Brent "and Mr. Fineman are seen lunching together at least once a week."[58] After Brent married Harry Edwards in 1928, a newspaper writer referred to Brent's "maternal consideration of her ex-spouse."[59] Furthermore, the *Los Angeles Times* reported in March 1930 that Fineman still kept a life-size photograph of Brent in his private office.[60] Though Brent told an interviewer, "We were unhappy together,"[61] Brent and Fineman remained in close contact after the divorce. Brent explained, "He is still my best friend. We just get along better as friends than we do as husband and wife."[62]

Their divorce was granted on August 18, and more details emerged about the marriage. According to Evelyn, her legal name was Mary Elizabeth Riggs Fineman. She complained that her husband became unfriendly when her friends visited and described him as rude. "'Such a rude man,' exclaimed Miss Brent. 'Why, he made it impossible for me to have any of my friends in our home. He told me our home was for his friends, not for mine. Mine he would insult.'"[63] Priscilla Dean testified that Bernie "was the rudest man I ever saw, at times."[64] Dean continued, "Such insults.... They would make Miss Brent quite ill. I have been there many times and heard the insults and seen Miss Brent ill afterward."[65] Keep in mind that in order to get a divorce granted at this time, it was sometimes necessary to exaggerate or even make up marital offenses. Years later Fineman wrote a letter to sister Frances in which he stated his belief that once it was recognized that a marriage was not going to work, it was better for both parties to agree to a divorce—and the sooner the better.[66]

The divorce settlement was generous. Brent was to receive $200 a week in alimony until she was paid $52,000. She also received jewelry and investments including stocks and bonds worth $50,000. In addition, Fineman was required to take out a life insurance policy naming Brent as beneficiary in the amount of $50,000. In 1926 the average American income was $770 a year, so Brent's settlement represented some significant change.

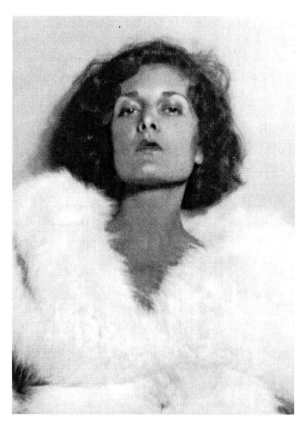

*Evelyn strikes a sultry pose.*

Less than a year after the divorce, Fineman was dating Greta Nissen,[67] but the relationship was short-lived. By September 1929 Fineman had resigned from Paramount Famous–Lasky, eventually moving to MGM in April 1930 where he continued as a producer.[68] Fineman married twice more. In September 1930 Agnes B. de Mille became Fineman's sister-in-law when he married her sister Margaret. "Margaret, now twenty and as beautiful as ever, had accompanied her [Agnes] on an interview at MGM. Bernard P. Fineman, an attractive middle-aged executive they met with, did not think Agnes's dance talent had a future in film, but as they left his office, Margaret turned to her and remarked quietly, 'I think I'll marry that man.' Six weeks later, they were wed in a Tucson courtroom with Agnes and Anna [Margaret and Agnes's mother]."[69] Agnes was opposed to the marriage because she considered

Bernie "an upstart manipulator."[70] Anna feared a negative reaction from marrying a Jew. "Mr. and Mrs. Bernie Fineman may find hotel doors and other gates closed to them. It's isn't just or pretty, but it's true."[71] Still, Margaret was in love and married Fineman; the marriage ended in divorce in 1937. Margaret, an actress who used the name Peggy George,[72] had one daughter with Fineman named Judith.[73] At one point in the marriage, Fineman was his father-in-law's (William de Mille) boss. According to Agnes, "Both men handled this delicate situation with tact."[74] After his second divorce, Fineman married newspaper writer Miriam Miller; that marriage also did not last.[75] They had one daughter. Fineman was out of the movie business by the mid–1940s. According to extensive and heavily redacted FBI files he became involved in obtaining "tanks, guns, and ammunition" for Israel in the late 1940s and was very fortunate to avoid indictment. Fineman was running an executive placement company in the 1950s and died in California on September 28, 1971.

Perhaps Brent's recent divorce led to rumors of an affair with Gary Cooper on the set of her next film *Beau Sabreur*. She played "an English girl, very sweet and innocent."[76] Paramount location scouts found a stand-in for the Sahara's Ibra Pass in Red Rock Canyon in the California desert.[77] Much preparation was needed for the difficult shoot. "More than a thousand various styles of carbines, rifles and pistols, spears and lances will be required to arm the players who will appear as Arabs and Legionnaires in the photoplay.... Some of the finest blooded Arabian horses available in the United States will be ridden by the principals and at least a score of camels will appear in the caravans. Five hundred men and women will occupy the oasis, to be constructed on the desert, and half of these will live in goatskin tents for the purposes of the picture, while a more modern and sanitary camp will house them during their leisure."[78]

The set began to be referred to as Sabreur, California, and bored cast and crew quickly came up with ways to make the time pass quickly. Brent and Joan Standing, who played Brent's maid in the film, were reported to be sleigh-riding on the sands. "Evelyn Brent and Joan Standing, the only women in a cast of 500 motion-picture players ... go sleigh riding daily behind four prancing steeds. From a standing start in their sand sleds, which were specially constructed for transportation over the desert, they can accelerate to a speed of two miles an hour on the level. Nevertheless the actresses prefer the sand sleds to the camels, which are also provided for transportation.... The powder-like sand of the mountainous dunes will not sustain any kind of a wheel, and to pull a 500-pound load with a sled requires four horses, which, sinking almost knee deep with every step, can draw little besides their own weight. Daily the two women make the trip from the town of Sabreur at the edge of the desert, about four miles away, on the sand sleds. The remainder of the company travel back and forth on horseback, while the equipment, reflectors, cameras, film and food for luncheon, also is taken by sand sled." [79]

Despite safety precautions, the *Beau Sabreur* set proved dangerous to Brent. In mid–July, it was reported that she lost "several square inches of skin in a bathing pool plunge,"[80] and later that month she received a spider bite on her foot. "[S]he didn't pay sufficient heed to the seriousness of her wound, but went right on working. Yesterday the wound showed signs of infection and she was ordered to bed by her physician and will not be able to work for a few days at least."[81] Brent was also reported to have suffered from Kleig eyes,[82] which is caused by the bright lights often used in close-ups. Symptoms include eye pain, temporary blindness, and excessive tearing.

Dorothy Herzog and Brent's maid Helen Brown were with Brent while she was on the set of *Beau Sabreur*. Herzog related this in June 1929 while writing about Brent and Helen Brown: According to Herzog, Brown had been employed by Brent for about six years, ever since Brent came to Hollywood. She'd also been fired umpteen times. "Helen has been fired more than any hundreds put together. I was present at one such scene. It transpired about a year ago, whilst Miss Brent was locationing at Guadalupe, making scenes for *Beau Sabruer*. Something went wrong. Helen forgot some trifle or other. Betty hit the ceiling. Yes, she exploded like a keg of T.N.T."[83] Of course, Brown ignored the firing, and Brent apologized.

When *Beau Sabreur* opened in Los Angeles in 1928, the *Times* reviewer thought it above average, but weak compared to *Beau Geste*. Philip K. Scheuer also thought Brent was miscast. "Evelyn Brent—who miraculously succeeds in keeping her extensive wardrobe and her coiffure intact through all the vicissitudes of desert life—hardly suggests the lady novelist ... but she makes a charming heroine."[84]

Brent later characterized her lightweight part as one of her worst; she preferred "heavy" roles. "They give you something to get hold of."[85] *Variety* agreed, writing, "Miss Brent leaves the imprint of having been miscast."[86] Nevertheless, her pairing with Gary Cooper led to rumors that they had an affair. Cooper's mother approved of Brent, perhaps because the alternative was the tempestuous and unsuitable Lupe Velez: According to Cooper's mom, "Evelyn Brent has been good to Gary; she has given him poise, she has taught him to think; her influence has been excellent, and I will always regard her with affection and gratitude."[87] Photographer John Engstead also believed Cooper and Brent shared a romantic affair, and he credited her with being the "sophisticated" girlfriend who "polished up some of the rough edges for a few months."[88] Years later Joel McCrea corroborated the affair. According to McCrea, Brent would have married Cooper, but Cooper was reluctant. Oddly, most contemporary magazines and newspapers largely ignored the romance, if indeed there was one.

Years later Brent told John Kobal that the affair with Cooper was brief. "When I first met him and we made [*Beau Sabreur*], it was quite a thing, but it didn't last very long. I don't know why, but I went to New York. The time I broke with him was the time Valentino died,[89] because I was on the way when the news came in that he'd died. I wanted out of it, [sic] I liked Gary very much, but you know...."[90] Brent later described Cooper as a "very, very nice man. When I met him first he hadn't done much, you know, and he was very shy. But very, very nice. And a lot of fun.... He was very shy and very withdrawn.... I don't think he ever got to be an extrovert. I liked him on the screen. I thought he was wonderful."[91]

By the end of 1927 Brent was making her second great film with director von Sternberg. *The Last Command* was also the first of several films with debonair star William Powell, who at the time was known as one of the screen's best "heavies." They made an odd if satisfying pairing. According to writer Lawrence Quirk, "Evelyn Brent was a dark-haired beauty with a somewhat glum and sinister aura which she employed to good effect in gangster films and other low-life cinematic ambiences. She and Powell were to meet again for more films, in which their respective chemistries matched well, her rueful cynicism dovetailing with his polished malfeasances."[92]

In November while working on *The Last Command*, Brent was often seen on and off the set carrying a German textbook. She explained to an interviewer that she was learning the German language. "I never realized the importance of being able to speak a foreign tongue until I started working with Emil Jannings.... I couldn't see what difference it made how a person talked before the camera and I often used to just pretend I was talking. I figured that the title writers did my speaking for me. Since working with Jannings I have come to regard my talking as important as any other phase of acting. Jannings always speaks German—in fact he knows only a few English words. And when he talks he has more force on the screen [than] any other actor I have seen. The reason is that foreign words as a rule are longer than ours. The additional syllables seem to put life into an otherwise dead speech."[93] According to the interviewer, the rushes indicated that Evelyn's performance was indeed improving, her foreign language study "[adding] a sparkle she lacked before."

Brent later gave an interesting interview to the *Los Angeles Times*. It was supposed to be about her, but she focused on Emil Jannings and seemed reticent to talk about herself. "The Paramount people will tell you about Miss Brent—how skillful is her acting, how full of fervor, intelligence and understanding. So will the critics. Probably, like most clever people, she doesn't half know herself just how she does things. And, like the sensible person she is, she doesn't try to explain herself. But she can, for instance, tell you all about Emil Jannings—or cabbages and kings, in case you happen to be curious concerning anything as commonplace as cabbages or so archaic as kings. Her brown eyes reflect all sorts of intelligence and emotions—when she talks about other people and books and current topics."[94] In the interview, Brent focused on Jannings' technique and personality. "Jannings is lovable and nice to work with—except when he gets sulky. He gets sulky sometimes over trifles. He didn't, for instance, like the fur coat I was wearing in one scene, and when I had taken it off and laid it aside on the set, he used to go over and kick it, for all the world like a petulant kid."[95] She also described the actor as professional, generous, and thorough. He also, she claimed, helped with the script. "He wants every detail right, and to this end he will do anything to help another. He worked an hour and a half with an extra woman at the end of the day when everybody was dog tired, in order that she might do her work well. He was sympathetic with her, too. One could see that. And she was just a poor old soul at that."[96]

Brent and Jannings hit some rough spots before the film even began. Jannings, for some unknown reason, let it be known that Brent wasn't his type. His comments got back to her, and she let him know she felt the same about him. "I heard what you said about me.... I'd just like to say that *you're* not the sort of man I'd fall in love with. You're ten years too old, and forty pounds too fat." Although they came to respect each other, it was a tad icy in the beginning. "Evelyn glowered, and whenever Jannings had a chance he ignored her."[97]

There is no question that Brent found Jannings difficult, but she also knew his talent bordered on genius. "He is such a splendid actor that one is fired on to give her best in a Jannings picture in order to cope with the work of the star."[98]

Brent thought her role in *The Last Command* was one of her most difficult. "The slow speech and thought of the Russians is the reason, she believes, for the difficulty in bringing such a character to the screen."[99] A couple of weeks later, the *Los Angeles Times* ran another publicity-type article on Brent, this time suggesting that she might be the reincarnation of Catherine the Great. A former Russian general who was working on the set of *The Last Command* saw a resemblance—and more. "'Not only in appearance, but I find Miss Brent's ability to learn Russian words is amazing,' says the general. 'I was talking with another Russian on the set the other day in our native language. Miss Brent was sitting nearby and asked me later if the thread of my conversation had been something about the arrival in America of some friend. I was astonished and asked her if she knew Russian, for that had been exactly what I had been talking about. She told me that she had never studied Russian, but that she had a great feeling for the language and that she believed she could learn to speak it easily.'"[100]

*The Last Command* was critically acclaimed upon its release. According to the *London Daily Sketch* reviewer, "It is the greatest film in the world. There is no qualifying sentence to that praise of *The Last Command*."[101] James Card considers it von Sternberg's masterpiece. On January 26, 1928, Brent, William Powell, and Jannings attended the world premiere of *The Last Command* at the Million Dollar Theatre in Los Angeles.[102] A couple of days later, the *Los Angeles Times* reviewed the film and found it commendable but flawed: "It is an accomplishment to be extolled, but with a certain restraint and with reservations." However, the reviewer had no qualms about Brent's performance. "Evelyn Brent as the Russian girl gives a vivid performance and enjoys considerable opportunity. She has a definite screen magnetism, and enacts her role very skillfully."[103] DeWitt Bodeen thought *The Last Command* was Brent's best film. "The variety of changing moods it affords her is fantastic: she was superlative however you fancied her—as the well-gowned lure; the devoted revolutionary; the soft, eager romantic; the hard, fighting woman."[104]

"A vintage year for silent films was 1928," James Card wrote. "Alas, most of the silent movies at the time were completely overlooked in the excitement of beginning dialogue. Ironically, 1928 was the year in which the silent cinema had reached its highest point in perfection. But its masterpieces were ignored by the public, entranced by the aural inanities of Jolson's *The Singing Fool* and the early talkies *Sal of Singapore*, *The Carnation Kid*, *Mother Knows Best*, *State Street Sadie*, *Tenderloin* and *The Terror*."[105] Ivan Butler echoed this sentiment: "For anyone traveling from town to town across Britain, as I was, a part-talkie was still a curiosity, and an all-talkie, let alone an all-talking-all-singing-all-dancing talkie, rarer still. In general we did not feel in any deprived. We had a highly developed art form available to us (even if it did not often achieve sublimity), and though we looked forward to hearing the voices of a favourite player there were plenty of voiceless movies around, either from former years or from the current output. Josef von Sternberg's *The Last Command*, for instance, stands comparison with anything of the period."[106]

In early 1928 it was announced that Brent would support Adolphe Menjou in the film adaptation of the stage play *Captain Ferreol* (later renamed *A Night of Mystery*). The *Los Angeles Times* pointed out that "Miss Brent has been scoring heavily of late in all the pictures in which she has appeared."[107] However, when the newspaper reviewed the film upon its release, it complained that it was confusing. Still, the critic liked Brent: "Evelyn Brent, as the judge's wife, looks beautiful as usual, and is a consummate actress in the few scenes that fall her way, but the part is negligible."[108] *Variety* also complained, "Evelyn Brent does nothing, although featured."[109]

On January 18, 1928, the *Los Angeles Times* reported that Brent had purchased land from actor Noah Beery, her co-star in *Beau Sabreur*, with plans to build a cabin near Victorville.[110] At the time Victorville was a small desert town in Southern California. In 1926, it had become part of the legendary highway system known as Route 66 linking Chicago and the Midwest to California. She wasted little time getting started on her project. By the end of the month it was reported that "Evelyn Brent, who desires the quiet and restful places among the 'whispering' pines at the end of the week's strenuous week has built a charming stone and log cabin high in the San Bernardino Mountains."[111]

In early February, Brent was stricken with tonsillitis but went on a spending spree when she recovered. She purchased a new car and planned a week-long driving trip to San Francisco.[112] Her recent purchases made it clear that Brent was beginning to enjoy her financial success.

Around this time, magazine writer Helen Louise Walker interviewed Brent at the actress' favorite place, the Montmartre. She found Brent relaxed and happy. The interview got off on the right foot when Brent was asked what part she most wanted to play, and she answered with a joke: Juliet. "Wouldn't I be dandy!" she joshed. She insisted that she was perfectly happy playing her underworld characters.[113] "I have already played almost every kind of role you can imagine. I started by doing ingénues, and I went on to do almost everything else, before I finally settled down to the habitual portrayal of lady crooks.... I am always interested in just what sort of person a girl crook is—how she happened to become one.... [F]irst and foremost, she is a human being. She has had her reasons for 'going bad.'" Brent's favorite bad girl crooks were those who did it for the fun of it. "The fascination of crime gets hold of her.... It isn't the money or the jewels she wants so much as the 'thrill of putting over a job.' The admiration of her companions in crime when she displays unusual ingenuity, her reputation for cleverness—these are the things which are meat and drink to her. It must be horrible, really, to live like that. Always in danger. Never a moment of security."[114]

Perhaps the most interesting tidbit in the interview, however, was the information that Brent was furnishing an apartment. She asked the writer to accompany her (in her cream-colored roadster) as she purchased a lamp and some pillows. "I must stop and buy a lamp I saw on my way here.... I'm just furnishing an apartment, and every time I go home I go loaded with bundles. It's such fun!"[115] (Knowing the financial difficulties Brent would later face, one feels tempted to gently but sternly suggest she immediately put that lamp and cushions back.)

Walker concluded by offering a picture of a contented woman. "She has an Oriental sort of beauty. Her voice is husky, and she is direct almost to the point of abruptness. It is difficult to make her be serious about herself. Her eyes twinkle constantly, and her laugh is always threatening to well up and brim over. I fancy she has few illusions about life or people or her job—or her own importance in the scheme of things."[116]

Brent later commented that people seemed surprised when meeting her in person. "I'd meet people ... and they would always be surprised that I was so small. They always figured I was tall because I wore four-and-a-half inch heels all the time. And the clothes had a tendency to have long lines, and that surprised them. A lot of people also have said that they were surprised that I always so quiet. I don't know what they even expected."[117]

On March 21, 1928, the *Los Angeles Times* reported that Evelyn was assigned to play opposite George Bancroft in *Swag*, the $5,000 prize-winning story written by Rena Vale and published by *Photoplay*. According to the report, hosiery salesperson Vale had once been a cowgirl in Montana and Arizona. The story was about the underworld, a gangster, and his moll.[118] The picture was apparently never made.

*His Tiger Lady*, released in the late spring of 1928, did little for Brent's career. It co-starred Adolphe Menjou again, and The *Los Angeles Times* described it as uninspired and found Brent "stiff and unnatural.... Miss Brent does not have an opportunity to reveal her true charm and ability as an actress. She is seen, however, in an array of beautiful gowns that enhance her exotic beauty."[119] *Variety* also found Brent's costuming a highlight: "Miss Brent looks great ... and wears a couple of nifty gowns."[120]

Like many actresses, Brent was often announced for roles and pictures that never materialized. A May 1928 *Los Angeles Times* news blurb announced that Brent and Clive Brook would appear in a film version of *The Letter*.[121] The Somerset Maugham Broadway play had starred Katharine Cornell. Although as late as August, Brent and Brook (and then Paul Lukas) were still listed as cast members, Jeanne Eagels ended up with the film role when it began production in October 1928. Her supporting cast included Herbert Marshall and Reginald Owen.

In the summer of 1928, *The Showdown* was released. Co-starring George Bancroft, this, along with *The Last Command*, was one of Brent's favorite pictures. "She feels that, of the scores of photoplays she has been in, that she did her best work in *The Showdown*, opposite Bancroft in which she played a woman's gradual dissolution in the loneliness and sensuousness of tropical life."[122] Her hometown Syracuse newspaper commented on her able performance as well as her great beauty: "As the white woman who, what with the heat and the rain and the oil wells gets to tearing her hair and losing her morals, she gives an intelligently dramatic performance. Miss Brent is not only an unusually competent actress but a remarkably good looking one as well."[123]

It seemed like a great idea to reteam Brent with George Bancroft and Josef von Sternberg, and Brent and Bancroft were cast in von Sternberg's *The Night Stick*. The picture's title was later changed to *The Dragnet* (it is sometimes written as *The Drag Net*). When the film was released, critics, especially Mordaunt Hall, complained that it was gratuitously violent and excessive. "There could be more drama to a scratch or a slap in the face than there is to all the gun-play and wholesale slaughter in this picture. Mr. von Sternberg is inclined to break the camel's back with the proverbial straw. He shows Mr. Bancroft and Miss Brent reviling each other, both volleying expletives. Once is even too much, but when it comes on two or three times it is a bore."[124] The *Los Angeles Times*, however, liked the film, and found Brent to be perfectly cast: "Miss Brent attains the perfect impression of being sinister. Her repression and pose are notable."[125] Indeed, according to James Robert Parish, "*The Dragnet* had its own group of film champions, who found deep meaning in the emotion-charged encounters between lawless Evelyn Brent and gangster Bancroft."[126] In the book *Hollywood in the Twenties* (1968), David Robinson praised the film: "Sternberg's pictorialism proved an entirely dynamic and in no way static element; the story and its characters are developed through well-observed visual details.'" DeWitt Bodeen lamented its status as a lost film: "I hope it turns up, because it's worthwhile, and Miss Brent, as usual, is brilliant; in fact, some regard it as her most important appearance for von Sternberg, the role that really set her in the moll image."[127]

In the summer of 1928 Brent gave an interesting interview at her Malibu cottage where she again claimed she had no desire to be a star. She had just returned from a month-long vacation in New York ("She saw most of the shows, bought a lot of new clothes, and gave a tony tea at which only one cup of tea was upset—that on her favorite dress"[128]), apparently using the time to reflect on her career. She indicated she was not looking forward to *The Mating Call*. She had first been considered for the role of the immigrant wife but instead ended up as the vampish ex-wife. "'It isn't my sort of role,' she explained. 'I think I know my own capabilities and I dislike playing a part for which I am unsuited. All I ask is to be left alone as I am going now. I don't want to star. Program stars get bad stories and all the blame.'"[129]

When *The Mating Call* was released, the *Los Angeles Times* was unimpressed, though the critic found Brent in fine form. "Evelyn Brent looks ravishingly lovely as the fickle wife, and plays the role with just the right dash of burlesque."[130] The film did well, mainly because it featured nudity and "steamy sexual undercurrents." In fact, some cities banned it which, of course, made it even more popular with audiences. "The public, learning that the film has been banned in some cities, is doubly anxious to see it. Packed theaters are the result."[131] It was one of the first films Howard Hughes produced. According to Geoff Schumacher, because of *The Racket* and *The Mating Call*, "Hughes had become a force in the silent film era."[132]

Writer Marquis Busby profiled Brent and found her much different from the typical Hollywood actress. "This dusky-haired, vital Evelyn is as candid a person as one could meet in Hollywood. What is even more strange is her candor about herself. She is absolutely lacking in conceit. 'I don't dare become conceited,' she explained. 'If I should, sooner or later it would show in my work. It always does. I know of a very popular actress on the stage who always gives me the impression of saying under her breath—"I'm a success, why should I work." It annoys me, and I know it annoys other people.'"[133]

Brent was financially secure. In a 1928 interview she explained that she was saving $4,000 a month. "[O]ne thousand dollars of Evelyn's salary automatically goes into a trust fund each week, where she has no opportunity to spend it."[134]

*Evelyn in 1928.*

Brent also described herself as happy and admitted that she had been foolish to attempt suicide in the past. "[S]uicide doesn't pay. It's foolish. Every time I tried it, the next day something splendid happened. You get so low in life, and then something good is sure to happen. Suicide doesn't help any. If you succeed, you pass out and never know the break that is just around the corner; if you don't, you're downright sick and feel like a dumb-bell for causing so much trouble. It's taken me twenty-six years, but I've gotten there and I'm happy."[135]

Brent's personal life and career were humming along in 1928. She was content and hopeful about the future. Sadly, she was headed for a terrible fall precipitated by an ill-conceived marriage.

# *A Surprise Marriage*

*My knees trembled so much that I could scarcely stand, and I've never*
*been frightened before the footlights. The first time I tried to speak my lips moved,*
*and not a sound came forth.*[1]

Not everyone found Evelyn Brent a delight. At Paramount she developed a reputation for being difficult. One writer was beyond annoyed when she did not show up for an appointment. Albert Richard Wetjen had been assigned to interview various actors. "Evelyn Brent was the one that finally disgusted me with the whole interview series. I had a date to lunch with her and do a story. She didn't show up. I waited an hour and a half and then called her house. Her secretary said, 'Miss Brent had forgotten all about the date.' I was so mad I could have torn up the streets. I was a more or less a prominent writer and I wasn't used to being treated like that."[2]

Portrait photographer John Engstead found Brent unwilling to play the game. "She was a snazzy woman. But she was stupid. In a way. Evelyn Brent was married to B.P. Fineman, who was Schulberg's assistant, and she was a *big* star. I remember her coming in to the publicity department one day. Julie Lang was handling the magazines at the time, and she was handling the sittings. So she came up to Evelyn and said: 'Evelyn, we'd like to make a portrait sitting of you.' And Evelyn said: 'Oh, fine, that's all right. We'll do it Friday at 2:30 ... what'll I wear?' And Julie said: 'Can't you bring something to wear?' And Evelyn said: 'I wouldn't *dream* of wearing my clothes in *front* of the camera. I buy these at I. Magnin's. These are $500, $600, $1000 apiece. If you want to *buy* one, you can buy it and I'll pose in it, but I'm not going to use my own for the thing.' Well, she'd only been doing *The Last Command* and that sort of thing, which didn't have much wardrobe changes, so she didn't have any clothes from the studio. So Julie said: 'Well, I'll see what I can get from the wardrobe,' and Evelyn said: 'Look, I'm not going to wear anything cast off by Louise Brooks or Clara Bow or any of these other women. I can't do it. So you'll have to figure out something I can wear.' Julie said: 'Well, what if I get some furs?' So they just got furs and they did her in furs, and then they sent the furs back. And that's the way they did the sitting. But this was stupid of this woman. Nobody else ever said this. And B.P. Fineman was standing right beside her, and you'd think he'd say: 'Well, why don't you want to do it?' I'll never forget this. And then, of course, she went downhill two or three years after that to *nothing*. Later on she came back to the lot and she did a little tiny bit in a picture, and Travis Banton called me up, because he loved Evelyn, you see.... [S]he was very chic, you know ... and he said: 'Look, Evelyn's in this, and she needs a couple of pictures. Could you have Gene make a couple pictures of Evelyn?' I said: 'Why, sure.' And she came down ... and this time she used her own clothes."[3]

Despite (or maybe because of) shots with the ostrich and alligator, Brent reportedly bristled when asked to pose for silly promotional photographs. "She refuses to do gag publicity pictures because she believes that she isn't the type to wear hand painted socks with rabbits skipping over the cuffs."[4] Brent did, however, occasionally appear in advertising for such products as soap and perfume.

Brent's next Paramount production in 1928 was *Interference*. Based on a successful stage play the material featured an English setting which was perfect for Brent considering her previous experience on English stages. It started out as a silent film, but at some point became Paramount's first talkie. The studio went into the endeavor with reluctance, but finally announced in September that *Interference* would be its first 100 percent talkie.

Jesse Lasky spoke for many when he once pointed at a landscape oil painting by wife Bessie and asked, "Do you have to hear the wind to appreciate the artist's intention?"[5] Many thought sound pictures were a novelty, a fad, something that would make a lot of noise, literally, and then be forgotten. Lasky was finally convinced when he read an article in the *Hollywood Spectator* by Welford Beaton. According to Lasky, Beaton, who had once thought talkies would soon disappear, reversed course. He "called on the producers to wake up to the fact that silent pictures were doomed. It was such a discerning analysis of the new development's indications that it gave me [Lasky] pause."[6]

The man who was in the right place at the right time was special effects man Roy Pomeroy. He had successfully recorded sound segments for *Wings* including gunfire and other effects. "It enhanced the realism of those scenes so much that each of a dozen road-show units of the picture carried turntables and a prop man to watch the picture from the wings of the theatre and turn on the records at appropriate times."[7] Lasky had enormous respect for Pomeroy and his creativity. He, after all, had also been credited with parting the Red Sea in *The Ten Commandments* and other amazing feats. Lasky was only half-kidding when he wrote, "Perhaps it isn't strange under the circumstances that he came to feel he was God."[8] For his part, Lasky came to feel he'd created a monster by making Pomeroy feel indispensable.

Pomeroy was sent for training to Western Electric and RCA and "returned to Hollywood as something of a sacred oracle, the only one in our company who knew anything at all about the new science."[9] Pomeroy was given control, and the once meek man became a tyrant. According to Lasky, "It might have been called '*No Interference*,' for Roy Pomeroy took complete charge, insisted on directing it himself, a function he had never performed, and demanded a salary raise from $250 to $2,500 a week. He knew that he had us where he wanted us. So our first talkie was directed by a special-effects man who became a sound engineer by virtue of a trip through the laboratories of Western Electric and RCA. We couldn't have treated him with more awe and homage if he had been Edison himself."[10]

Only cast and crew were allowed on Stage 5 where Pomeroy operated with supreme secrecy. Lasky assigned William de Mille to be Pomeroy's assistant so they could keep an eye on him. "It flattered the self-elevated director [Pomeroy] to have such an important man [de Mille] working as his underling."[11] The *Los Angeles Times* managed to get a reporter inside one day. The result was an intriguing look at how this new technology worked: "Roy J. Pomeroy, director of the picture, sits in a chair giving last-minute instructions to the players, Evelyn Brent and William Powell, featured with Clive Brook and Doris Kenyon in the film. Giant doors swing shut at Pomeroy's signal. A peculiar silence dominates the stage. Now and then whispered conversation is heard. Voices trail off strangely.... [A]ll resonance and echo has been banished. Incandescent lamps flood the set with light. Strange camera 'tanks' ... soundproof booths ... crouch on the edge of the set. Microphones are suspended over the players' heads. A pair of eyes looks down upon the stage. They belong to an engineer who sits in a tiny room tucked up under the ceiling. It is isolated with plate-glass windows. The man studies the positions of the 'mikes.' He is the 'mixer.' He hears everything through giant horns. His duty is to regulate the volume of the voices that are picked up by the 'mikes.' Downstairs a voice is heard over a telephone. It gives the magic word: 'Interlock!' The familiar cry of 'Camera!' is never heard here. 'Interlock!' has supplanted it. It means that cameras and recording machines are synchronized and ready to go. A bell rings somewhere outside ... a signal for carpenters to cease work. Someone says: 'Ready! Quiet, please!' A green light glows on a switchboard. The buzzing of conversation dies away. The doors of the 'tanks' are closed and locked ... the operators sealed in soundless tombs. The musical notes of a three-toned horn are faintly heard ... the final signal. A red light flashes. The operator signals Miss Brent and Powell. They have been watching him. Now the cameras are turning. The microphones are 'alive' and sensitive to the slightest sound...."[12]

After all that, it's amazing anything ever got filmed. Paramount called Pomeroy's bluff when he asked for an additional $1,000 a week increase, and just like that Pomeroy's directing career was over. When Brent was interviewed in the 1970s by John Kobal, she couldn't even remember his last name.

The talkie experience was traumatic for actors who had no experience with a microphone. Clive Brook explained that the first time he heard his voice played back he didn't recognize it. "It alternately faded into nothingness and then rang out in a thunderous crescendo. Pomeroy smiled at me. 'Was that my voice?' I asked. 'Yes, but you couldn't recognize it, could you? Try it again,' he said, 'and speak just as you would in a small room at home....' Soon I heard the voice in the loudspeakers again. This time it was unmistakably my own.... Although it was not loud, somehow it seemed to fill every corner of the huge room.... I had learnt my first lesson in microphone recording."[13]

The first time Brent heard her voice she thought her career was over. "Scared the daylights out of me ... I thought, 'This is it.' I sounded like this British singer Dame Clara Butt[14] ... with an enormous voice ... I didn't know at the time that they'd stepped the volume up. I found out ... I went to Roy and I said, 'This is terrible.' And he said, 'Wait until we've got it adjusted and you'll hear how it really sounds.' They had boomed it up because of bad facilities in the studio, because it was experimental then."[15]

In a 1969 interview, Brent could still recall the excruciating feeling she had the first time she heard her voice. She thought, "'Oh, I've got to get out of this business.' I sounded like an enormous six foot woman with the biggest voice I'd ever heard in my life. It scared me to death. I said, 'It can't be my voice!' I didn't realize it then that they amplified it. When they played it back for you to listen to, it was amplified I don't know how many times. Everybody sounded BOOM!" Brent also recalled that during that time, other studios sent their contract players over to do sound tests. "I remember Colleen [Moore], particularly because she was about as scared as I was the first day."[16]

Another problem was the sensitivity of the microphones. One time Clive Brook, upset with a ruined take, clapped his hands together. He blew out all the microphones, and the cast waited all night before they could be repaired. Brent also explained that an inadvertent sneeze could "blow out the sound"[17] and leave the cast idled.

*Interference* was a class production. Alexander Walker described it as having "[p]ossibly the most distinguished cast of any talkie to that date.... All the people in it were cultured, educated: they did not shout, run, fight, fire guns or bootleg hooch."[18]

Lasky was excited about the film when it was released in 1928. His hyperbole rang out loud and clear in this announcement: "The bringing of this stage play to the screen as an all-talking picture is one of the most significant things Paramount has ever done.... I regard it as one of the outstanding important films of the year.... For sheer drama, gripping and realistic, it is unmatched by anything that has so far been produced."[19] It was claimed that the film was the first play adaptation that did not change any of the original scripted words.[20]

When the film opened, it was introduced by Daniel Frohman. His statements made clear the idea that the film industry believed *Interference* represented a major innovation. "I speak to you from the screen itself—triumphantly and with utter confidence in the new future that stretches before us. It was only last Winter that this play we are about to see tonight was enacted on the boards of the Lyceum Theatre. It was presented by the company which was founded by my brother, the late Charles Frohman. Tonight, carrying on the Frohman tradition, I once more welcome you on behalf of Mr. Zukor and Mr. Lasky to the inauguration of the greatest era in entertainment—an era made possible through this miraculous invention, the talking picture. No more will our best plays be confined to the few big cities. These plays, with their stirring drama enhanced by the richness of the human voice, will go to the whole world."[21]

Reviewer Mordaunt Hall marveled at everyday sounds reproduced. "The ringing of a telephone bell was natural and so was the knock on a door. One even heard a pen scratching its way over the paper as Evelyn Brent wrote a missive with her left hand.... Mr. Pomeroy even gives the voice of an unseen person over the telephone, and one felt intensely thankful that this excellent piece of work was not marred by a love song as Sir John Marlay told his wife how much he adored her."[22]

The film opened at the Carthay in Los Angeles on November 18, 1928. Brent attended the premiere with future husband Harry Edwards. "Evelyn Brent ... was resplendent in a gown fashioned entirely of gold sequins. It was short in the skirt giving diversity on the stage when she stood next to Doris Kenyon whose skirt touched the floor all around."[23] *Interference* was almost immediately pulled in order to fine-tune it before its re-release on January 5, 1929.

Not every critic was impressed. Dan Thomas (more about him later) complained, "Still we wait for that talking picture which we can call good.... Its salvation was the performances of the four principals in the cast, Evelyn Brent, Clive Brook, William Powell, and Doris Kenyon, with Miss Brent excelling by a wide margin."[24]

Most critics thought the stage version of *Interference* was much better entertainment though the film did have the novelty of spoken dialogue which was certain to appeal to audiences. Norbert Lusk wrote about the reaction from New York critics: "Every player is effective, from the principals down to Donald Stuart, as the page in the London apartment-house, and praise has been given them all, but the sensational high lights vocally are, of course, Evelyn Brent and William Powell. Miss Brent's low-pitched vibrant voice fits perfectly the character she plays and her appearance though unfortunately the photography does not grant her her usual cameo clearness of feature. In achieving success on the screen the process of synchronization has not yet been able to give any of the players, in this or any other picture, his usual photographic value."[25]

Critic Arthur S. Mom wrote for *La Nación* and was an Evelyn Brent fan, but he, like many others, believed silent films far surpassed sound films in terms of expression and drama. "I believe that Evelyn Brent is the artist who has done the best work in talking pictures thus far. But, with all that, what an abysmal difference between the Debora [sic] Kane of *Interference* and the beautiful, untamed, adorable and silent revolutionary of *The Last Command*." Interestingly, in a 1940 interview Brent named *Interference* and *The Last Command* as her two favorite films.

As for Brent's voice, Forney Wyly spoke for all when he noted that Brent "has nothing to fear."[26] Brent believed that her work in motion pictures had been better preparation for dialogue films than her stage work. She provided an interesting comparison between acting in silents and talkies: "Film players will have to learn to think again. In silent pictures it was easy to walk through a part with your brain on a shopping tour for a new hat. In talking pictures you have to think of what you're doing, and remember lines at the same time. The director cannot tell you what to do next."[27]

She also reminisced about her days in London when she supported Cyril Maude. She longed to return there after her Hollywood career ended. "Londoners are different than we Americans. If you once make a success in London, you are remembered, even if it is years later." Brent also remarked that her Paramount contract was coming up for renewal in December, and she wasn't certain it would be extended. "She admits she has the habit of saying what she thinks, and sometimes what she thinks hurts the feelings of the dignitaries, stellar and otherwise. However, if she doesn't get the contract, she's going to treat herself to a three months' vacation in Europe."[28]

Writer Marquis Busby was obviously a fan of Brent's. "There's no one else on the screen quite like Evelyn Brent, which undoubtedly is not an original discovery on my part. She has the courage to say what she thinks, but she isn't petty or she doesn't indulge in gossipy small talk. She is a sophisticate, but she admits she wept at *The Singing Fool*. She has a sense of humor, and perhaps that is why she wishes fervently never to be made a star. She also smiles at a magazine writer who proclaimed her to be the leader of Hollywood's 'fastest set.' If Hollywood has a 'fast set,' Evelyn certainly doesn't lead it. I know that she goes to fewer parties than almost any celebrity in Hollywood, and she does little entertaining. Her social appearances are limited pretty much to daily lunches at the Montmartre, when she isn't working, and she works most of the time."[29]

Busby got Brent to admit that her dream role would be Salome, the part that Alla Nazimova had played a few years before. She also expressed doubts about a second marriage. "Sometimes I think it would be nice to be married to a sensible, well-balanced person. I'd like to lead a sane life again, although in all probability it would be bothersome. I can't think of anything worse than an actress marrying an actor. I'm sure I'll never do that."[30]

On November 3, 1928, the *Los Angeles Times* announced that Brent had signed a new contract with Paramount. Although there had been talk that the studio and star would not reach an agreement, "everything is ironed out ... and she is to stay on and give the company another chance. And, what's more, it is a contract which promises to lead to stardom, we are advised. The new agreement specifies Miss Brent's continued appearances in both sound and silent pictures, stress being placed on dialogue parts by reason of her excellent performance in *Interference*."[31]

It is likely that the contract brought certain pressures on Brent. According to film historian Anthony Slide, "The better-known lesbians in Hollywood during the silent era include Evelyn Brent, Nita Naldi, Alla Nazimova, and Lilyan Tashman."[32] Furthermore, social historian Lilian Faderman concurred: "Throughout the 1920s, the lesbian cavortings of silent film stars such as Evelyn Brent, Nita Naldi, Pola Negri, and Lilyan Tashman were Hollywood's open secret."[33] John Kobal said it without saying it. "More often than not, she came across as a hard woman lacking femininity." Louise Brooks also hinted that Brent had masculine traits.[34] Writer David Chierichetti assisted John Engstead when he wrote his book *Star Shots*. "I got the impression that John Engstead thought that she had become a lesbian, that she was living with some girl in Westwood on very reduced circumstances just a couple years after she left Paramount."[35]

On November 20, 1928 Brent suddenly married Harry D. Edwards. It was just two days after the *Interference* premiere where she was escorted by Edwards. *Photoplay* characterized it as the surprise marriage of the season, and explained that the couple had eloped to Tijuana, Mexico, "thereby cheating their friends out of a big wedding and celebration."[36] Newspaper and magazine accounts described Evelyn's friends as shocked, puzzled, baffled—you name it. No one was expecting Brent to marry Mr. Edwards.[37]

*Atlanta Constitution* columnist Forney Wyly interviewed Clive Brook in late December. "Mr. Brook told me that Evelyn Brent's recent marriage was quite a surprise to Hollywood. The alluring Evelyn seems to have pulled a surprise on everybody when she wed the director, Harry Edwards."[38] (Be aware that this is not the same Harry Edwards who directed the Harry Langdon comedies.) *Photoplay* reminded readers that everyone thought Brent was going to marry Gary Cooper. "The marriage of Evelyn Brent and Harry Edwards has caused a ripple of comment on Hollywood's untroubled seas. It was sudden. It was unexpected. Nobody, except one dear friend [perhaps Dorothy Herzog?], had an inkling that it was to take place. Evelyn tried to keep it quiet.... The fact remains that she looks radiantly happy, and Mr. Edwards isn't pulling a long face."[39]

Despite the intense surprise, Brent had been linked to Edwards in September 1928 when reporters spied a diamond ring on Brent's left hand and wondered if she'd received it from occasional escort Edwards. A suddenly defensive Brent reacted with hostility. "I bought that diamond myself and if you want to see the receipt I'll show it to you; I get out so seldom in Hollywood, on account of my work at the studio, that when I do, somebody always starts talk that I am engaged. I am not engaged to anybody and when I am I'll let you know." Brent further informed reporters that she and Edwards, who worked for the Christie organization, were just friends.[40] It seems odd for a woman to buy herself a diamond ring and wear it on her left hand. Brent could have been covering up the fact that Herzog had purchased the ring for her. Or maybe Brent bought the ring for Edwards to give to her. Or maybe Edwards did buy it for her. The whole Edwards affair is baffling.

Henry Donald Edwards[41] was born on April 11, 1887,[42] in New York City. The Edwards family resided at 648 6th Avenue in Manhattan at the time of Henry's birth.[43] Little is known about his family life other than that father

*A sly-looking Evelyn with Harry Edwards after their marriage announcement in 1928.*

Nathan Edwards was born in New York City[44] and mother Mary (Barry) Edwards was born in East Constable, New York.[45]

When Harry was a young man he was employed as a theatrical manager in New York City. In December 1916, with a personal endorsement from Eliot Norton,[46] Henry departed for France aboard the *Rochambeau* as a volunteer for the American Volunteer Motor Ambulance Corps. He may have sustained an injury while a volunteer overseas because his 1917 World War I draft card listed an unspecified physical disability. By June of 1917 Harry was back in New York City and employed as a car salesman for Alexander G. Harris at 1700 Broadway.[47] Sometime around 1917 or 1918 Edwards left this job to pursue a career in motion pictures where his salesman skills no doubt came in handy. In just three short years he was already a vital part of the rapidly expanding film industry, employed as a motion picture director with the pioneering Christie Film Company. It's likely that Edwards had made the acquaintance of writer Frank Conklin[48] while in New York, or while both were overseas as volunteers in the Ambulance Corps. Possibly through this relationship, he ended up working at the studio. It is also possible that Edwards already knew Al Christie from Christie's days as a fellow theatrical manager[49] in New York. By June 1919 Edwards was using the name Harry almost exclusively. Early in his career at the studio, Edwards may have held other positions, including actor[50] and director.[51] He apparently did well enough to be promoted to department head and was listed as Christie Film Company's production manager in 1921's *Motion Picture Studio Directory and Trade Annual*. In 1922 Harry's new position with the studio required that he be sent on a business trip to Europe[52] where he spent most of the next two years.

A few months after the surprise marriage, Brent romanticized her courtship with Edwards. "I went to New York and while there I met Harry. He was passing through on his way to Europe. I knew, at once. It was one of those instantaneous things. He made the European trip, sent me cables and things and wrote me the letters lovers write and it was settled between us that one day—not the indefinite 'some day' of the other affairs. Very definite this time. Inevitable. I came back to Hollywood. My personal affairs were settled and Harry and I were married—and here we are. I think I know what attracted me to him was his thoughtfulness. To me, that is the prime essential in any man. And he knows me. When I come home from the studio after a difficult day, he knows that I cry the instant anyone speaks to me. And so, he doesn't speak to me. He leaves me alone. He watches what I eat and how I feel. He knows the things I like to do and he likes to do them, too. We like the same people, the same way of running our lives. Putting it all together, it spells love." She hastened to add that they had no plans to start a family. "I don't believe I want children. I'd like to have had them. I doubt that I ever will, now."[53]

Despite her quickie marriage, something extraordinary happened in December 1928. On December 2, Evelyn and girlfriend Dorothy Herzog were essentially "outed" by newspaper columnist Dan Thomas. He described them as "about the most inseparable companions in the cinema colony ... and incidentally two of the Montmartre's best customers."[54] Indeed, when scanning the *Los Angeles Times* society pages, there were numerous mentions of Herzog and Brent attending events together at the Montmartre. Sometimes Herzog was accompanied by her sister and mother.

Thomas had a propensity for making sly comments about certain Hollywood lesbians or bisexuals. For example, in a May 1, 1935, syndicated column he identified several actresses who had "gal pals," including Katharine Hepburn (Laura Harding), Dolores Del Rio (Sandra Shaw), Carole Lombard (Madeline Fields), and Claudette Colbert (Elizabeth Wilson). On September 29, 1935, he also reminded readers that Hepburn, then starring in the crossdressing *Sylvia Scarlett*, "has not been linked with any ... man."[55]

One can only imagine the flurry of nervous excitement this column caused Brent, Herzog, and Paramount. One clear effect was that Brent and Herzog stopped being seen together publicly for months to come.

Brent's world changed almost immediately upon her marriage to Edwards. On February 12, 1929, Brent's chauffeur was arrested for waving a gun at another driver. It's likely the ruffian chauffeur came from the world of Edwards. Eric Bryfogel, 21 years old, "was taken into custody late Monday ... on the complaint of Martin McCurres of 850 South Manhattan Place. McCurres stated that Bryfogel threatened him with a revolver as the climax to an argument over a traffic difficulty.... The chauffeur gave his home address as 227½ South Western Avenue. He denied that he threatened McCurres with a gun."[56]

Brent's surprise marriage to Harry Edwards near the end of 1928 marked the beginning of the end of her film career and personal fortune. Within a few short years, she'd be abandoned by Edwards, and her film credits would dwindle to bit parts. Edwards essentially took over the role that Fineman had played in Brent's career. However, while Fineman's guidance had led to stardom and wealth, Edwards' management was a disaster, eventually leading her into bankruptcy.

# 6

# *Life with Harry Edwards*

*I do not play the social game in Hollywood. I like whom I like*
*no matter what they are or what they have done.[1]*

It's difficult to conjecture exactly why Brent married Edwards. However, there is no denying that Brent and Herzog were close, intimate friends who shared Brent's residence. It is assumed that Herzog moved out after the marriage. It's also possible that Herzog and Brent continued their relationship, and Brent and Edwards were married in name only. Perhaps Edwards may have been friendly toward Brent and Herzog and offered to marry Brent when it seemed a marriage might make for better public relations. The three of them—Brent, Edwards, and Herzog—may have agreed that marriage to a friend was the best path to take.

It's possible, too, that Brent met Edwards, fell in love, and married him, hoping to spend the rest of her life with him. However, the two were not often seen together, and the marriage rapidly fell apart, finally ending years later in a bitter divorce. In addition, Edwards' future behavior lends credence to the idea that something was not right about the marriage or Harry. He associated with underworld figures and eventually ended up marrying the wealthy ex-wife of a gangster.[2]

Dorothy Herzog, who often ended her popular syndicated columns with "And—That's all" or "Well, I'll be seeing you," published her first novel *Some Like It Hot* in 1930. The book, which has nothing to do with the film of the same name, was written in a contemporary, slang-filled style and featured a lead character named Patricia who goes to business school, takes a job in show business, hates her father, loves her mother, gets pregnant, has an affair with a wealthy man, gets an abortion, marries a moody writer, loses her mother, has a breakdown of sorts, and ultimately reconciles with the now *less* moody writer. Unfortunately, it's not well-written, though Herzog was certainly a capable and entertaining newspaper columnist. It should be noted that Herzog's hometown of Memphis considered it steamy enough to ban.[3] The only thing interesting these days about the novel is its dedication to MER which likely stands for Mary Elizabeth Riggs, Evelyn Brent's real name. Brent hosted a book release party for Herzog in March 1930 at the Embassy Club. Guests included Harry Edwards, Margaret Ettinger, Marquis Busby, Mickie (Rita) Flynn, and Elise Bartlett. Brent also plugged it in a 1930 magazine article: "Dorothy Herzog, the writer, is Evelyn's one intimate. Betty feels as happy about Dorothy's first book, *Some Like It Hot*, just off the presses, as though she had written it and says so to anyone who will let her."[4]

The friendship obviously continued in one way or another because Herzog's second novel *Intimate Strangers* was dedicated to "Betty" when it was published in 1933. *The Syracuse Herald* verified that the book was indeed dedicated to "Syracuse's erstwhile Mary Elizabeth Riggs, i.e., Evelyn 'Betty' Brent."[5] The floridly written novel featured a lead character who was an actress and strongly resembled Brent: "Nacia Connors was average height, twenty-six, brunette, slender. Glossy black hair parted in the middle, knotted at the nape of shapely head, clipped to small ears. The upper lip bowed just a little above the full lower lip. A glow of Latin heritage showed in the olive of clear complexion. A challenge of Irish glimmered in the gray eyes." Herzog may have hoped to sell the story to a movie studio—and perhaps provide a movie role for Brent. It featured a ruthless Chicago underworld gangster, but, unfortunately, offered a punchless climax.

It should be noted that immediately after the marriage to Edwards there were few Brent sightings at the Montmartre. There were no sightings of her with Herzog until March 1929 when they again began frequenting the Montmartre together.

Brent and Edwards became regulars at the Embassy Club, a private club which was a bit more upscale than the Montmartre. Designed by architect Carl Weyl at a cost of $300,000, the club opened on December 14, 1929. The style was Spanish and Byzantine. "One of the features of the building will be a roof promenade, glass inclosed [sic] and lounge, with a view of the Hollywood hills. The club will be lighted by a new crystal lighting effect. The portieres will be composed of Russian gold. Mr. and Mrs. D.H. Gardner Soper are providing the interior scenic effects and decorations which will be of the modern period. The construction of the Embassy Club was arranged by the Christie Realty Company."[6]

It was an exclusive club, originally limited to 300 members. "The Embassy Club is bringing together some of Cinemaland's best 'mixers' with others who used to be rather exclusive as to where they took their pleasure. Not, of course, that the Embassy Club isn't about one of the most aristocratic places one could choose."[7] Someone, it seemed, was interested in social climbing. And it wasn't Brent.

The Embassy Club was in a two-story building on Hollywood Boulevard near Highland, adjacent to Brent's favorite restaurant, the Montmartre. In fact, Eddie Brandstatter, owner of the Montmartre, was responsible for the catering and management. Though no one knew—or were willing to say—how one became a member of the Embassy Club, it did appear to be invitation only. Rupert Hughes was the president and Charles Chaplin vice-president. Antonio Moreno was the second vice-president. The directors included Brent, John Gilbert, Harry D'Arrast, Betty Compson, Bebe Daniels, Constance Talmadge, Norma Talmadge, Gloria Swanson, Marion Davies, King Vidor, and Ruth Roland.[8] Members included Tod Browning, Clarence Brown, Paul Bern, Lina Basquette, Joe E. Brown, Reginald Denny, William de Mille, Louise Fazenda, Hoot Gibson, James Gleason, Jean Hersholt, Elsie Janis, Robert Leonard, Carl Laemmle, Jr., Jesse Lasky, Lila Lee, Mervyn LeRoy, Harold Lloyd, Millard Webb, and many others.[9]

Louise Brooks, of all people, visited Brent around this time and got a sense that all was not well. "The next time I saw Evelyn was in Hollywood in 1928 [it's more likely it was in 1929 since Brent did not marry Edwards until November 1928] after she had made a great hit in *Underworld*. She had divorced Bernie Fineman and married Harry Edwards, a low-rate actor, director and con man. When I visited her at her expensive new house in Brentwood [this was probably her house at 8419 DeLongpre Avenue where the neighbors included Kay Francis and Clive Brook] I hoped to find a happy and secure Evelyn—and she did appear to be living in the Hollywood dream world of unending grandeur. But behind it I saw the same old tight little smile and heard the same old dry laughter."[10]

It's fascinating that Brooks pegged Edwards as a con man. It's also interesting that the show of wealth did not seem to make Brent happy. In fact, the couple was living beyond their means in an attempt to establish Edwards as a high-powered Hollywood producer.

Margaret Chute wrote an article that suggested Brent's marriage to Edwards had drastically changed her life—for the better. "[T]he caustic, saddened girl of a year ago has vanished.... And for the first time in her life is happy; really happy.... She smiled, a real smile that lighted her eyes, as she went on—' ... [E]verything seemed to happen at once. Success in my work. Good parts. Advancement. A chance in an important talking film, *Interference*; that was a fine adventure. And then my new marriage."[11]

With Fineman's departure, Brent's roles at Paramount were not as good as they had once been. In June 1929 Brent was working on *Woman Trap*. "It is the first time Evelyn has been a nice, good girl in pictures ... and she rather likes it."[12] Unfortunately, by the time the film was released in the fall of 1929, critics were lukewarm, and most didn't even bother to mention Brent. Still, *Photoplay* noticed, describing her performance as "really splendid."[13]

Later that month, Jesse Lasky made a major announcement concerning Brent's career. While attending a business conference, Lasky "promoted" Brent, Richard Arlen, Nancy Carroll, Ruth Chatterton, Gary Cooper, and William Powell. "It is with the greatest pleasure that I announce the elevation of these players to stardom.... The pleasure is mixed with pride.... All these players have been under contract to Paramount for some time. All have established large popular followings. All have demonstrated unusual and extraordinary ability. All have unusual and extraordinary physical attributes. They have succeeded."[14]

The "promotion" did little to benefit any of these stars, except perhaps Cooper. A cynical William Powell was reported to have "clutched her [Brent] warmly by the hand and said with a choke in his microphone voice, 'Congratulations Betty, Isn't it marvelous to be a star? Think of all the advantages. Now you can ride in Shriners' parades.'"[15]

*"I wonder why I keep on making pictures. Perhaps I think some day I'll make a good one."*[16]

In the summer of 1929, Brent gave a surprisingly honest interview. At the time married less than a year to Edwards, she discussed her state of mind—and it wasn't pretty. "I'm mortally afraid of death. Time and time again I wake from a hideous sensation—not a dream at all—a frightful sensation of something immense and smothering, and I wake in an icy sweat, shaking and unnerved for the rest of the night. I want to live forever. Not that life is so surpassingly sweet but that death is so terrible. I don't care anything about luxury. I do care about comfort. Rococo swimming pools, immense estates, blooded dogs—those things are out for me. My chief objective in life is to have enough money to enable me to live in London and to be on the stage. As to what it's all about, I'll confess that I don't know. There is something. Perhaps it's the reincarnation theory, perhaps not. Who does know?"[17]

Brent craved privacy and a quiet life out of the limelight. "In Hollywood, Evelyn Brent is called smoldering, slumberous, secretive, silent. She evades the probe and lancet of the interviewer, of public curiosity. It is known that she will not reveal herself to casual persons or even to persons not so casual. It is also said of her that while she looks capable of enacting the part of a Medici, a Borgia, a Beatrice, because of her carven face and torrid reticences, she is not like that all. Not really. She is also known as a trouper of detailed experience and extreme efficiency. She debunks producers, roles, rules and the usual hocus-pocus of Hollywood. Now and then, there is a publicity flare, an angle. She has tried to commit suicide. She is engaged to this or that young man. She has suddenly been married. Then there is the lapse into silence again and people continue to go about saying, 'Well, what is Evelyn Brent really like? What does she think of back of that impenetrably beautiful, silent face of hers? Why is she as she is? What has gone before?' ... [S]he lives in a white ... house. A house filled with interesting books: Sudermann, Hugh Walpole, Ernest Hemingway, Robinson Jeffers, Shaw, first editions. It is also filled with an enormous collection of perfumes. Evelyn plays bridge, eats caviar and goes to bed early the nights she works, which are most nights."[18]

What was married life with Harry D. Edwards really like? A truly bizarre *Photoplay* magazine article titled "She Eats and Tells!," written by Katherine Albert and published in January 1931, provided a glimpse. According to the writer, she had phoned to ask Brent to attend a fall fashion show with her. Because she was working, Brent declined—but instead asked

Miss Albert to spend the weekend with her. Even accounting for phony publicity writing, this seems a bit strange. But, nevertheless, Miss Albert reported that she spent the weekend at the home of Brent and Edwards. The producer was away in London on business so they had the house to themselves, except for some servants and Nig, the family dog. Albert provided a thorough description of the house and its contents, reasonably certain that the magazine's readers would find it of interest. She first described it as a "palatial mansion" and then went on to write that it's "an amazing house. From the outside it looks enormous, like some ancient white palace, but, in reality, it is small and intimate inside. The upstairs consists only of a frivolous dressing room, all satin chairs and enormous perfume cabinet loaded with hundreds of bottles, a hall and a big bath room and practical sleeping quarters, almost a sun porch, with twin beds and a long table arrangement where Betty has massages.[19] Downstairs—spacious living room, dining room, breakfast nook, kitchen, bedroom and den."[20]

Despite Brent's display of wealth, Albert found her unpretentious. She arrived on a Saturday night, and sections of the Sunday newspaper were spread on the floor. Brent was without makeup, and it was clear that there was no furniture that was "off limits." According to Brent, "I haven't a piece of furniture here that you can't put your feet on or jump up and down on if you like. You see, before I married Harry I had just furnished an apartment of my own and I was pretty attached to everything so instead of getting rid of that we simply added more things and moved them all here. But I can't bear having anything you've got to be careful about. Furniture is to be used, isn't it? Well, then, use it."[21]

Still, Albert noticed that Brent brought a touch of elegance to the details in her home. "Betty does things well. Her table looked lovely ... and there is a warmth, a friendly sort of glow in the dining room. We had oyster cocktails, fried chicken, whipped potatoes, string beans—and surprise!—turnips. Bet you never thought a lowly turnip was admitted to a star's home. Then there was ice cream, cake, and coffee."[22] Brent, an avid coffee drinker, drank it morning, noon, and night—and even claimed it helped her sleep.

Brent seemed overly concerned about the home's security. The unfortunately named pet was a police dog, and Brent claimed they also had a night watchman. Still, Brent decided to take a gun and investigate the grounds herself. "Of course," Albert wrote, "I know she's played in a lot of gangster pictures, but when I saw her with that revolver she got out of a drawer in the den I wasn't any too comfortable. I was much more afraid of Betty and the pistol than of any burglar in the world."[23]

Finally, Brent put away the gun and bared her soul to the reporter. Perhaps most telling, if true, was the dream she'd recently had. "I thought that there was a great earthquake that shook down all of Hollywood except this house and destroyed everybody but me and I remember that I stood in the midst of the rain and instead of being upset about it I was glorified. Slivers of delight ran up and down my spine. My whole being was enthralled by the tremendous aloneness."[24]

After what was no doubt an awkward moment, the topic turned to her husband. "Harry Edwards is the one ideal man for me. He has a great wealth of sympathy. We like doing the same things. Sometimes I wake up in the middle of the night and want to walk, particularly if it is raining. He doesn't think me mad. He walks with me. Marriage is grand when you've someone who understands you. I've always been so alone and loved it. Even when I was married to Bernard Fineman I was alone. An executive's life takes him away. But with Harry it's different. We have so much fun together.... Harry and I hope to live in Europe one day."[25]

In addition to the rented mansion, Brent and Edwards also rented a Malibu beach house which is where she stayed most weekends. She took Albert to Malibu. Before leaving for the beach, they enjoyed a huge breakfast of pancakes, sausage, grapefruit juice, and, of course, coffee. "When we set off in a long-nosed touring car Betty, in a white dress, socks, flat-heeled shoes, beret and a pair of dark glasses, looked about as much like a picture star as Cal Coolidge."[26]

Another article described more about the house and lifestyle. "Mr. and Mrs. Edwards live in a two-story, six-room, Italian villa style house in a quiet side street of Hollywood, only a few blocks from Hollywood Boulevard and close to the business section. It is white stucco, with a green overlapping tile roof. They rent it unfurnished because to rent is less responsibility than to own and they feel they may pack their bags at any moment and go to Europe for an indefinite period. They chose the furnishings together. They are modernistic without being violently futuristic. The color downstairs is rust and green. The rugs, green; the drapes, rust. There is a piano, a radio, a gramophone and a ukulele. Harry plays them all; Betty listens. They sleep in one huge bedroom but in separate double beds. Each has his own dressing room; there is one bathroom in the upstairs quarters and one downstairs for the servants.... Four servants manage this home for her. A cook and a second girl who live in the house; a personal maid and a chauffeur who go home each evening."[27]

In this 1930 article the most ominous note was the one concerning Brent's finances. "Harry Edwards is his wife's business manager. She is frank to admit she never saved money until this second marriage [there is no mention of the $4,000 a month she once said she was saving]. Now, she does not have to worry over her future. They both admit, with an emphasis which no one would venture to question, that they like this arrangement; that they are happy."[28] A 1931 article also made it clear that Brent's finances were controlled by Edwards. "Mr. Edwards. ... babies the smoldering siren. She is more his wife to him than she is the film star. He gives her playful spankings—imagine Brent being *spanked*—and takes care of her income tax."[29] Unfortunately, you'll soon see that he did not, in fact, take care of her income tax. As for the spankings, well, who knows?

*"I will not do anything which I cannot do well.... If I am not good I feel like an utter fool."*[30]

*Broadway* was Brent's most important film of 1929; she begged for the

*Evelyn at the doorway of her beach cottage.*

role of Pearl. "I wanted to play the part of Pearl on the screen from the moment I first saw the play.... The company could not visualize me as that character until they heard my voice in *Interference*."[31] It was announced in May that she'd won the role, but only after finally convincing Universal's Carl Laemmle, Jr. However, Brent came to regret her efforts, concluding that "it doesn't quite come up to her expectations of it."[32] In fact, Brent was so disappointed in her performance that she claimed she'd never begged for the role and was assigned it over her objections. "She had gone to Universal in the first place against her will. She had taken the role in the picture against her better judgment." As a result, Brent refused to attend the film's opening. "She thought she gave a bad performance and for that reason did not want to take her bow at the opening. 'I didn't do anything to bow for,' she said."[33]

In any event, the role was yet another bad girl character. "It is curious that she should love and shine in these 'bad' girl roles, for Evelyn gives an immediate impression of 'class.' Her small, refined face, her clear, dauntless eyes, her air of restraint, her good mind, ardently self-educated, her taste for sartorial simplicity, all convey anything but an 'underworld' idea ... yet she is forever murdering or being murdered, or at least portraying a most reprehensible character in her pictures."[34]

*Broadway* did quite well in Los Angeles when it opened at the Million Dollar Theater in late October. It was held over for a second week, marking the first time a picture had done this since the theater had re-opened. According to Louella O. Parsons, Brent stole the picture. "Evelyn Brent in *Broadway*, which was by no means one of the good pictures of the year, should go down in history, largely because she made the most of a very small part. She walked away with honors so completely that the principals didn't have a chance."[35]

Following her performances in *Interference* and *Broadway*, Brent told an interviewer that she wanted to focus only on talking pictures—which was a wise idea since that was the future of film. However, she also remarked that working on dialogue pictures was a lot more complicated than silent pictures or even plays. "Working in the talking film means an additional amount of work, of course. Studying lines at night, spending days on rehearsing prior to filming the scenes—all means much more time and work devoted to the production. It is so much more strenuous than learning a part in a stage play, because there, once you have it, once you finish your final rehearsal, you [are] working only during the hours allotted to the running of the play."[36]

"*A kibitzer is the person who wires asking a favor and sends the telegram collect.*"[37] Evelyn Brent, September 1929

By the fall of 1929 Brent no longer had Bernie Fineman to protect her at the studio. Perhaps not coincidentally, Brent's temperamental reputation was peaking. According to Brent, the whole thing stemmed from an incident during production of *Why Bring That Up?* when she refused to stand on a trapeze several feet off the ground because she had a fear of heights and quickly became dizzy at any height.[38] *Photoplay* included a description of the incident and defended Brent: "Word sped around the Paramount lot that Evelyn Brent had 'gone actress' on the Moran and Mack set, when she refused to stand on a trapeze only ten feet high. It is an actual fact (and if you don't believe it, her doctor's name will be furnished upon request) that Betty suffers from vertigo and cannot look out of a second story window without becoming dizzy. She did, at last, because of the keen criticism, stand on the trapeze. She was ill and had to come down."[39]

Moran and Mack, the popular blackface comedians known as the Two Black Crows, were vaudeville performers who had appeared on radio and records. Although critics weren't crazy about the film, audiences were. Los Angeles' Paramount theater held it over for a second week—the first time in its history a picture was held over.[40] According to the *Syracuse Her-*

*ald*'s critic, "Evelyn Brent as the temptress makes a favorable impression."[41] Still, it was not helpful to her career. Columnist Louella Parsons issued a plea that there be no more roles like this one: "Evelyn is too fine an actress to be wasted on unimportant roles." Photographer John Engstead bluntly said: "They killed Evelyn Brent with that one movie.... Schulberg *didn't know* what the *hell* to do with these people."[42]

Brent continued to defend herself against the claims of temperament. In one interview she claimed she actually restrained herself on movie sets. "Although born of an Irish-American father and an Italian-American mother, she might be a turbulent woman out of Dostoevsky. One clue to Evelyn Brent's temperament stood out as we were discussing the temperamental fits of certain actors and actresses, notably the hair-raising tantrums of John Barrymore. She smiled quietly, and in her concise, steady tones said: 'How I wish I could publicly weep and rage and tear my hair. How many times have I been utterly out of patience, exasperated with the way some picture I worked in was being maltreated by a director, a writer, a cutter, or an actor! But I have been unable to say a word. My disappointment or anger worked inward rather than outward. When I got home I inevitably collapsed in a heap. My feelings burn so intensely that they seem to be burn me out at times, to drain me of all vitality, to leave me a shell.'"[43]

Others defended Brent. *Atlanta Constitution* writer Forney Wyly reported to his readers that Brent did not play the grand dame off stage. "The movie world knows no more natural person that [sic] Betty Brent. She hasn't any of the airs and affections which makes [sic] some movie queens so uncomfortable to know. She doesn't start long stories about 'My Career' nor go into minute details about 'some of my performances.'"[44]

Hugely popular British writer Edgar Wallace spent time in Hollywood while working on *King Kong*. He had the opportunity to meet many stars including Brent. Following Wallace's death in 1932, his wife serialized his letters in the *London Daily Mail*. In one Wallace described Brent as "very charming" and a "very real person, terribly sane, and without any hokum at all."[45]

Brent was amused by the behavior of some stars, including Ruth Chatterton "who was a very good actress, but she was rather elegant, you know? She came from the theater and she sort of felt superior, I guess. Everybody used to gather and say, 'She's coming off the set!' and they'd all hide to watch her because she had a retinue following her, which none of us had then. She had a long cigarette-holder, and she'd walk like a queen across the lot, trailing a maid and a secretary and a makeup man, all following her."[46]

In the summer of 1929 Brent was still a star at Paramount and celebrated by building a stone Norman-French–style beach cottage in Malibu. It also included a tennis court.[47] A report also came out that summer that Brent's dressing room at Paramount Famous–Lasky was located between Esther Ralston's and Charles (Buddy) Rogers.'[48] A few months later, in October, the *Los Angeles Times* reported that Brent was one of the stars who had requested a grand piano be placed in her dressing room.[49] A follow-up newspaper article explained the purpose: "Talking pictures are probably the reason for the sudden influx of new pianos in the dressing rooms of the Paramount stars. Charles Rogers, Dennis King, Jeanette MacDonald, Evelyn Brent, Mary Brian, Nancy Carroll and Fay Wray have added uprights and small grands to their dressing-room equipment to enable them to practice during the lunch hour and between scenes."[50]

*Darkened Rooms* with Neil Hamilton was released in 1929. Forney Wyly interviewed Hamilton for his "Broadway Banter" column in November of that year; "I gathered from his conversation that he was quite keen about working with 'Betty' Brent."[51] Around this time, there had been a rumor that Brent and Hamilton, both married, were having an affair. Years later, Brent was appalled at the suggestion. "Not Neil, no. No, I wouldn't do that. I knew Neil's wife too well."[52]

As for the film, *Variety* found it—and Brent—unremarkable. "Evelyn Brent's first starring film for Paramount [is] but a weak sister to the previous films which but featured her.... Miss Brent is still the ultra-sophisticated and hard-boiled miss. A bit too much so for her present interpretation."[53] Another critic bemoaned, "Someone should have done better than this for Evelyn Brent in her starring debut."[54] *Photoplay* complained that Brent's talents were wasted in the film and made a direct plea to Jesse Lasky to get her better parts. "We're starting a committee to find a good picture for Evelyn. It's about time. We're appointing Mr. Lasky chairman."[55]

Other newspapers and magazines also noticed that Brent was being miscast and mistreated by the studio. In a *Fast Company* review, *Variety*'s critic wrote, "Evelyn Brent was a little out of character in a role that called for less ice."[56] The *Los Angeles Times* agreed: "Miss Brent has been poorly cast. Her role is devoid of the verve and glamour associated with her name. Photography, too, in her case, is disappointing."[57] In its review of *Fast Company*, *Photoplay* complained, "They must quit kicking Evelyn Brent around! She has been photographed badly and is miscast."[58]

Jack Oakie in his first starring role for Paramount praised Brent's professionalism on the set of *Fast Company*, calling her "a great actress and trouper [who] could have stolen scene after scene from Skeets Gallagher and myself, but she wouldn't, always letting us have the breaks."[59]

At this point in her career, Brent felt comfortable enough with the dialogue film to give advice to fellow actors. She emphasized that it is always a mistake to try to sound like another actor. "I have been greatly amused since the coming of talking pictures to Hollywood to observe the youthful extras and bit players adopting broad A's and the English accent employed by some of our really great stage stars. They do not seem to realize that these stage people they are mimicking were either born in England or adopted the English manner of speaking because it is a tradition of the stage. The talking screen has no such arbitrary traditions, and it does not demand a rubber-stamp mode of speech from its players. A clear, correct personable mode of expression is the chief requisite to success in the talkers."[60] She also suggested that novice actors learn foreign languages. "A really great actress must be able to speak French and Italian as fluently as English.... All countries will clamor for her and in order for them to understand and appreciate her she must speak their tongue. German is regaining its international importance and Spanish is swiftly becoming prominent."[61] She added that, in her opinion, "embryo Thespians" should also study literature, geography, and history.

In 1929 Edwards was working as a producer for Educational Pictures; he and his bride took a belated honeymoon trip to Europe in the fall. "I like the idea of waiting a year for my honeymoon," she was quoted as saying. "Getting married is in itself sufficient excitement for one time. And when that excitement dies down it's lots of fun to get all pepped up again with a honeymoon. Both Harry and I have been all over Europe so we know just where we want to go and what we want to see. We don't intend to lose a single minute because my time is limited. Harry will have to stay another month or so because of business, though. We expect to spend most of our time in London as both of us know a great many persons there. We hope to have a lot of fun and you can believe me when I say it won't be my fault if we don't. I have been working so hard for the last six months that I haven't been able to do a thing I wanted to. I am going to forget I have ever been in pictures. Venice will get some of our time and we will spend a few days in Paris. I never have liked Paris and don't want to waste much time there."[62]

Upon her return, Brent made a terrible mistake: She took her husband's advice and decided to leave Paramount. Columnist Louella O. Parsons was stunned. "Evelyn Brent and Paramount are bidding each other adieu this month. Miss Brent's contract has expired and for some strange reason it is not being renewed. Whether it is at her own volition or because of some misunderstanding I have no way of knowing."[63] Parsons concluded that Brent was one of Hollywood's finest actresses: "Evelyn is one of the greatest dramatic actresses on the screen.... Give a part suited to her talents there is no one who looks better, has a finer personality or who has more ability."

The decision to leave Paramount was not a wise one, and by the end of 1929 Brent was having second thoughts. "There is every chance in the world, we hear, that Evelyn Brent, who quit Paramount a few weeks ago a bit indignant with billing and roles assigned to her, may return to that organization. Miss Brent has been freelancing since leaving Paramount, but it is said to be inclining a not reluctant ear to the idea of returning to the studio where she has been such a success."[64] In fact, Brent was rumored to have been signed to appear in *The Return of Sherlock Holmes* with Clive Brook. However, Betty Lawson ended up playing Dr. Watson's daughter.[65]

*"Miss Brent's frankness and honesty of expression have made her one of the best-like[d] actresses here."*[66]

Brent gave an interview in December that indicated, yet again, her discomfort with being a star. "She was made a star against her wishes. She argued against stardom because she is afraid of it.... The star system, Miss Brent explains, is disastrous to the ordinary, everyday actress, in which class she puts herself. 'For the flamboyant or "circus" personality like Clara Bow or George Bancroft, stardom is all right,' she says. 'Bow shakes her head and waves her hair, and they like it, but unfortunately my hair doesn't wave when I shake my head. The star of a picture takes all the responsibility for its success or its failure. Pictures are good or bad according to the reaction the

*Evelyn and husband Harry Edwards returning from a European honeymoon on the* Aquitania *in 1929.*

*Brent, "Skeets" Gallagher, Gwen Lee, and Eugenie Besserer in* Fast Company *(1929).*

exhibitor gets in his box office. And if a picture in which Brent is starred doesn't make money, the exhibitor writes that "Brent doesn't make us any money." If I am fortunate in getting good stories and have good supporting casts in all of them, being a star will be fine. But one poor story and one weak supporting cast, and Brent will find herself out in the street.'"[67]

Near the end of 1929 Brent signed a contract. However, it was not with Paramount. Her new studio was the much smaller Columbia Pictures, and the deal was for three pictures. Other stars at the independent studio were Jack Holt, Dorothy Revier, and Ralph Graves.[68] This was a step down and a return to an F.B.O. atmosphere in more ways than one. Columbia made their pictures on the RKO lot, which had once belonged to F.B.O. Some believed it was a good choice for Brent. "Evelyn Brent goes over to a company which until recently has not been making much of a splash in the village. They will give here [sic] good drama. This girl has one of the few fine minds in the colony.... Her fight for good stories will probably be shortly rewarded."[69]

In a 1969 interview, Brent was asked about Columbia producer Harry Cohn who had a reputation for being difficult, to say the least. "Everybody loved Harry Cohn," she said tongue in cheek, adding, "I liked his wife very much. ... she was a very nice woman."[70] When pressed about Cohn, Brent said he was quite a character—and had always been one. "When he was a song plugger, he was a character."[71]

In March 1930 Brent was in Helene Costello's wedding party when she married Lowell Sherman in the Beverly-Wilshire Hotel's private ballroom. John Barrymore, married at the time to Helene's sister Dolores, gave the bride away, and Evelyn was matron of honor. Harry Edwards was the best man.[72] Guests included S.N. Behrman, Darryl Zanuck, Allan Dwan,

Jack Warner, the John Gilberts, Mae Murray and Prince Mdivani, Douglas Fairbanks and Mary Pickford, Lionel Barrymore, Lothar Mendes, Hedda Hopper, Al Jolson, Estelle Taylor, Norman Kerry, Frank Fay, Marshall Neilan, and many others. One newspaper described the wedding as "pretentious,"[73] but perhaps the most interesting observation was made by a reporter who attended the event. "Evelyn Brent was matron of honor and looked handsome, but a trifle bored. 'As though ... this wasn't a real wedding, but just a scene in a picture.'"[74] Brent apparently knew something because the not-so-happy couple divorced in 1932. In 1969, Brent remembered things differently. Though Lowell Sherman was a good friend of hers, Brent recalled that she became matron of honor when Dolores Costello could not because of a pregnancy. "So I was the matron of honor, and Jack was the best man, and we laughed all the way up in the elevator. We screamed, you know, about old times and things. It was fun. And Lowell cried at his own wedding."[75]

Paramount's *Slightly Scarlet* was released in April 1930. Co-written by 21-year-old Joseph L. Mankiewicz, who later won Oscars for his screenplays *A Letter to Three Wives* (1949) and *All About Eve* (1950), it was an early talkie that co-starred Clive Brook. Writers were still struggling with the transition from title cards to spoken dialogue. According to Mankiewicz, "Writing dialogue to be spoken is considerably different from writing words to be read.... Lines that read beautifully often sound unnatural when heard. The film dialogue writer must constantly remember that he is creating lines for players to speak. I try to figure out what I would say in the various situations which confront the characters. That helps to judge the naturalness of the words. I always speak the lines, also, to get the ear's reaction."[76]

Brent played a criminal, though a reluctant one, in *Slightly Scarlet*. Around the time of the film's release, a writer attributed Brent's adeptness at such roles to her reading material. "Possibly because she is serious and has regular features, plus beautiful hands, Miss Brent has played more female crook characters than any other actress in Hollywood. Directors like lady crooks who look like ladies. Miss Brent plays these roles with a zest difficult to imitate, and possibly this is because even before she specialized in such parts the study of crooks occupied much of her leisure. In her library are most of the works of fiction ever published in this country."[77] According to Brent, her main objection with such roles was a tendency to want to make the crook break the law because of fear. "I don't object to reforming, nor even to being killed, but I do most thoroughly object to stealing the pearls because somebody scares me into doing so. This, it seems to me, is a worse example to the young—about whom the censors are always concerned—than crime for crime's sake. It's downright immoral...."[78]

This was exactly what happened in *Slightly Scarlet*, and Brent's lack of diplomacy came back to haunt her. Indeed, by the time *Slightly Scarlet* was released in April 1930 Paramount seemed intent on making audiences forget Evelyn. In a review for the film, *Variety* noted that only Clive Brook's name appeared on the marquee. "Miss Brent has first billing on the main title, but house marquee solely bills Clive Brook. That means possibly a lot, or simply that Brook is still under contract to Paramount and Miss Brent is not."[79] The *Los Angeles Times* also noted that Brent was ill-used. "Evelyn Brent, as the lady crook, evinces ability in a part that is not particularly convincing. One wishes for bigger and better roles for this actress." [80] Still, the *Film Daily* critic enjoyed her performance along with her colleagues. "Standing out in the splendid cast are Clive Brook, Evelyn Brent and Eugene Pallette."[81] Critic Harry Mines liked the Brent-Brooks teaming: "Brook, with his polish and reserve, and Miss Brent with her scowling beauty and arresting personality, are nicely cast and contribute interesting performances."[82]

Jimmy Starr, writing for the *Los Angeles Record*, lamented Paramount's misuse of Brent. "It's too bad Evelyn Brent couldn't have been given more productions of this type [*Slightly*

*Scarlet*] before she departed from the Paramount lot. If there was ever a star who unfortunately suffered inferior roles, it was Miss Brent. She struggled along with miserable parts and finally left the studio having but one or two good films to her credit."[83]

*"Let us see what some of our friends in the movies would like to find in their Christmas stockings. I am sure that Evelyn Brent would like a written assurance that she is to have better stories during the coming year."*[84]

Before making any films for Columbia, Brent was first borrowed by RKO. *Framed* was, yes, another crook drama. Director George Archainbaud, who'd worked with Brent years before on Olga Petrova pictures, specifically requested her for this film. "George Archainbaud, one of the screen's leading directors, was the first person in film circles to recognize the dramatic ability of Evelyn Brent.... When Archainbaud was directing pictures at Fort Lee, N.J., he met Miss Brent and through his efforts she was given an important role in support of Olga Petrova.... When Archainbaud was chosen to selected Radio Pictures' all-talking underworld drama *Framed* ... he stipulated in his contract that Evelyn Brent would play the feminine lead."[85] Released in the spring of 1930, *Framed* garnered excellent notices for Brent, especially from the *Los Angeles Times*. "Miss Brent ... is not only good, she is excellent in the role that is hers and lends such distinction as the picture possesses by a poised and believable characterization."[86] Critic Chester B. Bahn also liked Brent in the role: "To Miss Brent must go the laurels for ability to look hard though beautiful. She handles her part with conviction. Her charm always has the sufficient metallic edge."[87] The *Los Angeles Examiner's* Kenneth R. Porter gave Brent a rave review. "She is always at her best in underworld atmosphere, but as a [tough] moll of the tenderloin who means to 'square' the death of her father, she is splendid. It is doubtful if she has ever been seen to such advantage as in several highly dramatic scenes."[88]

*Evelyn in 1930.*

*Paramount on Parade* (1930) was Brent's last film for Paramount. It was a musical extravaganza that tried—too hard—to be many things. Writer Lawrence J. Quirk accurately described it as "a lulu," and further explained that the studio had "enlisted the services of the three-dozen stars on the roster, a host of lesser players, musicians, choreographers, dancers, singers—you name it—in a 'rise, decline and fall of the Roman Empire'–style jamboree that snapped, crackled and popped its way through two hours of never-ending activity, some of it sparkling, some of it dull."[89]

Evelyn's appearance with Maurice Chevalier is one of *Paramount on Parade*'s film's highlights. Writer Homer Dickens called her scene "the wildest—and funniest—apache dance ever."[90] Richard Barrios described how Brent and Chevalier "demonstrate the origin of the apache dance. They spat *en boudoir*, bickering, shoving, ripping each other's garments to the strains of the familiar apache song. The scoring is alternately sly, boisterous, and conciliatory, pointing Brent's chic wounded dander against Chevalier's duplicitous caginess, trifling and captivating."[91] The *London Times* in its 1930 review got it absolutely right when it declared that the skit "has the keen French flavour of naughtiness permissible to a revue."[92]

Brent found director Ernst Lubitsch to be "a sweet little man with a great sense of humor."[93] She also called working with Chevalier "a dream" and attributed the sequence's success to Lubitsch and Chevalier. "That cute little slapping sequence, about the husband and wife. I don't know how it all came about 'cause all of a sudden I was doing it, and I liked Chevalier so much. I had admired him so, for many years, I thought he was so wonderful. We had fun doing it, and I had never worked music before.... [I]t was timed to the music of 'My Man' like an 'Apache' number.... Between Lubitsch and Chevalier, they made it very easy for me to do. I was scared to death when I started it, because I'd never done that type of thing before, but they made it so easy."[94]

According to Edwin M. Bradley, the film "resembles an informal tour of the studio backlot."[95] While an important picture for Paramount, the set's atmosphere was casual. For example, Clara Bow's scenes were filmed with little rehearsal while she took a break from a different movie set. She even claimed that she was responsible for styling her own hair.

Meanwhile, Harry Edwards had decided that he would not only manage Brent's career but become her producer. He still hoped to become a studio executive, perhaps like Bernie Fineman, and Brent seemed to be the ticket. Somewhere along the way he'd met British entertainer Jack Buchanan, and the two planned a production company. While Buchanan was in America to iron out the business details, they were involved in an automobile accident. On May 12, 1930, old friend Dorothy Herzog reported that Brent had been involved in the accident along with husband Harry, Buchanan, and Buchanan's mother. According to Herzog, the foursome had gone to a movie and upon their return Mr. Buchanan's Cadillac Phaeton skidded on the rain-slickened road into a parked car. Brent, who had been sitting in the back seat with Mother Buchanan, banged her head on the window glass. "Fortunately, it was nonbreakable glass," Herzog cheerfully added, "otherwise her face might have been cut into ribbons."[96] Despite bumps and bruises, there were no serious injuries to the other parties.[97] The accident, however, was an omen of the coming disaster.

# 7

# *Financial Disaster*

*Innocence was not her forte.*[1]

Joel McCrea got a huge career break in 1930: It was announced that he would be Brent's lead in *The Silver Horde*. This was a major opportunity for McCrea who had only had small roles up this point though he'd been under contract to RKO for about a year.[2] Original director Mel Brown was re-assigned to work on the talkie debut of Amos and Andy. He was replaced by Brent's friend George Archainbaud. Cast and crew traveled to Ketchikan, Alaska, in July to film.[3] However, they stayed in Alaska for only a couple weeks for an unusual reason: "[T]hey found it too hot to work there. They will produce the whole picture in sets made at the studio and on nearby locations."[4]

The weather wasn't the only thing that was hot during the making of *The Silver Horde*. McCrea admitted to interviewer John Kobal that he and Brent had an affair. "I went into [producer] Bill Sistrom's office, and while I was there, Evelyn Brent came in. And I took a look at her. I knew Coop [Gary Cooper] had had a crush on her.... [T]hey really had a thing going, but it was over. She would have married him, too. But he hung back. So, anyway, Sistrom looked at me and then looked at her and said, 'It's going to be incest.' I wasn't sure what that meant, but it sounded good! And when we got on the boat to go up to the location in Hotchkotch, Alaska, and I began having dinner with Evelyn, we got to talking about Coop. And we got on pretty good. And when we got back, I would like to have carried it on, but she was married to a guy."[5] McCrea would later blame the "guy" for ruining Brent's career.

RKO liked what they saw in Brent and awarded her a new contract based on her work in *The Silver Horde*. "When William LeBaron and other studio executives saw the rushes ... they went into immediate conference and decided that Miss Brent ought to keep her makeup box parked permanently on their lot. The result: The new contract, calling for two more RKO productions. Her first piece of work under the new agreement will be her third for the studio. There is some talk that it will be *Quest*, an English play."[6] Indeed, the reviews were generally good for the picture and Brent's performance. According to critic Norbert Lusk, "The presence of Evelyn Brent is decidedly an asset and she injects humanness and subtlety into the wholly theatrical character of Cherry Malotte, who must be recognized as the forerunner of all the good bad ladies the screen has given us. Miss Brent makes her curiously lifelike and always sympathetic, achieving one of the best characterizations."[7] Dan Thomas commented, "Evelyn Brent runs off with the acting honors although she is pushed rather closely by Louis Wolheim and Raymond Hatton."[8] He added that it was "an entertaining picture with a couple of good fights."

In June 1930, Columbia announced their slate of films and reported that Brent would be appearing in *Madonna of the Streets* and a reincarnation picture titled *The Woman Who Came Back* to be written by John Howard Lawson (later blacklisted because of his activities with the Communist Party). According to the *Syracuse Herald*, Brent's appearance in *Madonna of the Streets* was to fulfill "an old agreement with [Columbia's] Harry Cohn."[9]

*Madonna of the Streets* almost co-starred Clark Gable. When casting decisions were being made, Brent suggested the relatively unknown Gable for her male lead. she was ignored, though producer Harry Cohn later came to regret it. "In her quiet way La Brent suggested a young fellow named Clarke [sic] Gable whom she had just met with his agent, Ruth Collier. 'Who ever heard of him?' grunted Harry Cohn. 'No. We gotta have a man with a reputation.'" When Cohn was later unable to sign him at a reasonable price, Evelyn reminded him of his mistake. "'I told you so,' said Betty Brent, at risk of losing a producer's good will. And the producer had the good taste to grin and take it on the chin."[10] Robert Ames instead was cast.

When *Madonna of the Streets* was released, critics were disappointed, though Brent received good notices. John Scott of the *Los Angeles Times* wrote that Brent "gives an even performance, hampered only by the multitude of words put into her mouth. The actress is capable of presenting better characterization given the opportunity."[11] The critic for the *Illustrated Daily News* wrote, "Evelyn ... is very good. There are few surer actresses in pictures and in anything she does, Miss Brent always does a complete job of it. What she needs now is an interesting part in a really fine picture."[12] Jerry Hoffman echoed these sentiments in his review in the *Los Angeles Examiner*. "Evelyn Brent, as fine an actress as the screen has ever given us, makes the best of a role which suffers from dull dialogue. With the natural ability that Miss Brent has, and more dramatic moments, it would have been splendid."[13]

In October 1930, Brent signed a contract with RKO to appear in a Rex Beach project, *Recoil*. The name was later changed to *White Shoulders*. In November the *Syracuse Herald* wrote that Brent would appear in *White Shoulders* with Ricardo Cortez after her appearance in *Madame Julie*, based on a French play.[14] She ultimately appeared in neither. In December *White Shoulders* was postponed because of "the dearth of leading men."[15] Brent was eventually replaced in the cast by Mary Astor. *Madame Julie* was retitled *The Woman Between*, and Lili Damita was given the starring role.

That same month, gossip columnist Louella O. Parsons reported that Brent was feuding with Columbia and Harry Cohn. According to Brent, Columbia's inactivity led her to sign to appear in *Women Like Men* (later changed to *The Mad Parade*). However, Columbia said that Brent had promised to be at the studio on January 2 to make a film with them. "Cohn is still hopeful that Betty will have a change of heart and come back to Columbia, but Betty says not a chance."[16]

By the end of 1930 Brent was strongly associated with playing beaten-down, disillusioned women. It shouldn't have been much of a surprise to learn that she received many letters from women in similar straits, including women in prison. "The letters they write me are tragic letters. Groping. Frustrated. Too often disappointed. Defeated. Striving to grasp some hope on the very grave of hope. I seldom get a happy letter.... It may be because of the pictures I have made. The sort of thing I have so often done probably draws letters from an unfortunate group. But there are so *many* of them!" Brent, who was never a frequent letter writer herself, explained that her advice was to persevere. "I tell them that life is a fight. A fight from the time we struggle to get our first breath to the day when we struggle not to lose it. I tell them that we can't sit down and we can't just drift. I tell them that we can't wait for Fortune or Fate to drop plums into our mouths. We have weapons, all of us. We have to keep them sharp—and use them."

Some women thought Brent could save them. "Women behind worse bars than prison bars write to me. One woman here in Los Angeles. I have had dozens of frantic letters from her. I would believe her mad, if the letters were not fairly coherent, and showing glimpses of a muddled intellect. She tells me she is imprisoned in a room in the city and cannot get out.

She writes of horrors that keep her jailed there so that she never sees the sun. She labors under the delusion that there is some kinship between herself and me and that I am somehow obligated to break her bonds. She is probably a drug addict. Apparently, she once saw one of my pictures and some circumstance in the story was similar to some circumstance in her own life. I should say that the great majority of women write, asking me for money to get a new start in life.... These women never seem to feel that they should be cared for. There is nothing ... parasitical in the women of America, judging from the letters they write to me. They do ask for an initial loan with which they hope to become self-supporting."[17]

Women also wrote Brent for advice about relationships. "They know that I have been married twice. They want to know what happened to my first marriage so that they may avoid any mistakes I made. They want to know how I am 'managing' my second marriage. One girl wrote me all through the period of her engagement. She asked the most personal and detailed questions about the relationship between Harry and myself. I could feel that this was no idle curiosity, but a genuine desire to profit by the experience of others. She was so eager to make a go of it!"[18]

Of course, there was the occasional inappropriate letter, too. "Sex seems to be the least of their considerations, the least of their problems. If any such letters do come, they are very obviously from psychopathic cases, too filthy to read. And these few do not come from women, but from men."

Brent also received letters asking for fashion advice—or even the opportunity to buy her personal wardrobe. "Of course, there is a percentage of letters, usually from young girls, on how to make up, what type of clothes men like, how they should do their hair ... things like that. I have had innumerable letters asking to buy the little feathered helmets I have worn in several pictures. Some of them ask me to give them to them. Most of them ask to buy them."[19] Finally, one of the strangest letters she received was from a woman who apparently didn't understand the difference between a character in a picture and an actress. "I saw you cooking in a scene in one of your pictures, and the spaghetti looked so good I wondered if you'd send me the recipe," a housewife asked Brent.[20]

Meanwhile, Brent's career looked hopeful at RKO. When the studio announced that it would build six penthouses at its studios, some conjectured that Brent might be one of the recipients. "Plans are now being drafted for two groups of bungalows to adorn the roofs of the three-story administration buildings of Radio Pictures studios. The penthouse bungalows will be star dressing room suites, and there probably will be six of them all told. What stars are to occupy them is information kept secret at this date. On the Radio personnel list are Bebe Daniels, Richard Dix, Betty Compson, Irene Dunne, Dorothy Lee, Evelyn Brent, Bert Wheeler and Robert Woolsey and several other likely candidates."[21]

In that same year Brent moved out of the rental house and into the Beverly Wilshire. She said it was because a nearby apartment building was undergoing renovation. "She was scheduled to begin a picture within a week. There was no time for house-hunting. She shunted her household goods into storage and took up quarters in the Beverly Wilshire.... The night I [Gladys Hall] dined with her there, I saw the tangible manifestations of the home-making hand. Three hundred books, at the very least, jammed the tables in the living room. Flowers were spilling their fragrance from Betty's own vases. Scarves and tiny objects of all sorts littered mantle and couches. In the bedroom the three-shelved glass perfume table bore its glittering load. The place was a *home*. Betty had her own maid, who served us dinner, including, of course, caviar."[22] There was no mention of Harry Edwards.

*The Mad Parade* was an all-woman feature originally titled *Women Like Men*.[23] "'Although it seems a bit unusual, I don't think we are going to notice the lack of men at all,' said Miss Brent, archly commenting. 'The story is so different and the roles in it are so vital that I think we all will be able to play them without the slightest aid from the other sex—except, of course from the director, cameramen and technicians.'"[24]

The World War I drama was not an easy shoot. The women were asked to do all kinds of physical stunts and often ended up with bumps and bruises. Director William Beaudine recalled one particularly difficult scene: "Evelyn Brent went on her face and stomach for a good hundred yards over the most uneven mud that we could make. It was a day's work to walk across it, and she had to crawl. Did it once and then, gosh, I had to have a retake. I was afraid to tell her, but I did. She never said a word. Just walked out and got herself soaked all over again.'"[25]

*The Mad Parade* was released in the fall of 1931. It is a remarkable film that still packs a punch today. A woman-only picture set among an ambulance corps during World War I, it was considered experimental[26] and did not get good reviews upon its release. Louella O. Parsons was particularly critical. "The idea of *The Mad Parade* is original, but the execution is poor.... A pity to waste an actress of Miss Brent's mentality and ability on a role that at best is a burlesque."[27] Brent was noted by *Variety* who said she gave "a steady, brilliant performance except for the first few hundred feet." Norbert Lusk added that Brent "played with brilliant authority."[28] Eleanor Barnes wrote, "Miss Brent certainly made the character of Monica sizzle."[29] Even though the film was not a critical or popular success, it did do well with certain female crowds who often became rowdy while watching the picture.

Brent worked on the picture over a period of eight months. This caused problems. "During that time she acquired a mahogany coat of tan at Malibu and let her eyebrows grow in. When *The Mad Parade* started at the Liberty studios she wore her eyebrows plucked in the familiar Brent manner. In the interval, when Paramount took over the production, called for retakes, and finished it, she had abandoned the thin, arched circle over each eye for a heavier, lower line which naturally follows the frontal bone and makes a tremendous difference in her expression. It gives her an eagle-like strength missing before. It also raised hob with matching the retakes with close-ups made at the start of the production."[30]

This information came from an interview conducted at the Embassy Club. Brent was described as wearing "a close-fitting sort of helmet, a barbaric green necklace and red fingernails." "I am glad to see the producers going back to action,' she said. 'Sophistication and the stage might go hand in hand, but not necessarily so when it comes to pictures.' She believes the picture public wants action, not words, and she sees the dominance of dialogue which came with the deluge of strictly stage players and producers soon ending. 'I still remember *Alibi* as a great picture,' says she, 'because it was primarily action in pictures. You could have deleted every word from it and it would still have been great entertainment.'" Brent admitted that she was a fan of motion pictures and theater. "I am a good audience. I can never see a good picture or play without getting emotionally all tied up. Some shows I go back to see time after time. During my trip to London last year I went to see *Bitter Sweet* eight times. Other shows I have cried over are *Peter Ibbetson* and *Journey's End*."[31] A few days later, Brent claimed she was through attending plays. "At the opening of *Camille* at the Belasco she cried, and got mascara all over her ermine coat."[32]

*"Evelyn Brent has an unusual superstition. She will not permit anyone at table to pass her the salt-celler. Just what 'bad luck' is associated with a salt-celler, Evelyn doesn't know, but the superstition is a decisive one. Miss Brent's next talkie will be* Pagan Lady, *in which she will enact the name part."*[33]

Apparently someone passed Brent the salt cellar because around the time of *The Pagan Lady*, Brent's bad luck increased. According to reports, *The Pagan Lady* came about due to the hard work of husband Harry Edwards. In 1930 and 1931, Edwards made numerous trips to England to meet with popular British actor Jack Buchanan.

Columnist Elizabeth Yeaman (who sounded like she'd gotten her hands on a press release) explained that Edwards had formed a company with Buchanan. "Harry Edwards has been traveling back and forth to England for well over a year now. Everyone has been wondering what necessitated such frequent trips, and now the secret is out. He has been busy with the formation of a British-American producing company incorporated under the trade name of B & E. Ltd., with offices in Hollywood and London. Jack Buchanan, popular stage and screen star in England and America, is president of the company and Edwards, who is prominent as a Hollywood producer, is vice president in charge of production. Headquarters have been established at Tec Art Studios, and Edwards told me this morning that *Pagan Lady* will be the first picture produced by the new organization. Associated with him in this production is Walter Camp, president of Inspiration Pictures. *Pagan Lady*, the David Belasco production starring Lenore Ulric in New York, was bought some time ago by Columbia Pictures. B & E Ltd. will make the picture for Columbia release, but as all the Columbia product is purchased by RKO, it will, in reality, be released by that distributing organization.... An equal number of pictures will be made in Hollywood and London by B. & E. Ltd., and the best stories and cast will be engaged in these productions according to Edwards."[34]

There was no mention of the partnership in the detailed biography of Buchanan by Michael Marshall. In addition, a chronology in the book's appendix made no reference to *The Pagan Lady*. According to Marshall, Buchanan lived in California in 1929 and 1930 and described it as "the place of lovely blue skies and magnificent green trees and scrub."[35] Marshall reported that Buchanan spent most of his free time not with Brent and Edwards but with the elite of Hollywood—Charles Chaplin, Pauline Frederick, Harold Lloyd, and Mary Pickford and Douglas Fairbanks. He and his mother also enjoyed spending time with Elsie Janis and Marie Dressler.

*The Pagan Lady* was produced by Harry Edwards for Columbia. Initial casting was announced in May 1931. Based on a play by William DuBois starring Lenore Ulric, the production borrowed Charles Bickford and Conrad Nagel from MGM. According to columnist Elizabeth Yeaman, "Edwards, who has long been associated with the moving picture industry and for years was general production executive for the Christie Brothers, is vice president of B. & E. Ltd., a British-American producing firm in which he is to produce in partnership with Jack Buchanan." Edwards relied heavily on advice from writer Benjamin Glazer. "Barney [sic] is a little bit more than writer on this story, for Harry is greatly influenced by his judgment on players, sets, etc."[36] It was also around this time that Harry began insisting that people refer to him as H.D. Edwards because of confusion resulting from another Harry Edwards in Hollywood.[37]

Upon its release in the fall of 1931, the film failed at the box office and with the critics. It's very likely, in fact, that Brent and Buchanan lost a good amount of their personal fortunes. *The Pagan Lady* proved disastrous to Evelyn's career. It would be one of her last big-budget starring vehicles. Edwards never produced a major feature film again. According to *Variety*, the picture "is something of a lightweight through thinness and familiarity of story," and added, "Evelyn Brent as the bad girl never looked it, and photography didn't help that handicap. It seemed miscasting for Miss Brent."[38] Harry Mines, writing for the *Illustrated Daily News*, disagreed. "Evelyn Brent is really the star by rights, bringing her hard-boiled, scowling personality into the character of Dot Hunter, a roughneck bartender down in the tropics.... The dialogue savors of the torrid, and Miss Brent slings it out for all its worth."[39]

In any event, the failure of the film appeared to end the business relationship with Jack Buchanan, who returned to England to focus on British filmmaking.

The marriage between Brent and Edwards was in trouble. A small blurb may or may not have given us some insight into the state of the marriage: "Evelyn Brent confesses her favorite indoor sport is playing solitaire."[40] In fact, around the time that *The Pagan Lady* was released, Brent gave an interview that strongly indicated she was in a mood. The article suggested that Brent had earned a well-deserved reputation for being temperamental. "[D]irectors soon found out that Evelyn's education, knowledge of the world and own personality made her difficult to handle at times." Dubbing her the Pagan Lady of Hollywood, the article quoted Brent as saying she was going to do whatever she wanted—and people could simply deal with it. Or not. "If, by trying to give as nearly an authentic characterization as physically and humanly as possible, and to do so means to oppose ideas which would prevent such a characterization—then I am pagan! I don't choose to attend so-called parties and simply refuse to go Hollywood. I'm dubbed 'high hat.' We all have our own lives to live and I, for one, propose to live mine as I see fit, and to enjoy those things that interest me when and where I want to. All I ask is to be allowed to continue my life in my own way. Whether or not it gives me the title of 'Pagan Lady' by so doing, I care little."[41]

In March 1931, RKO dropped Brent along with Sue Carol.[42] Brent announced to the press that when she completed the 1931 films she planned to take several weeks of vacation at her Malibu cottage house. By 1931, Malibu was no longer a rustic get-away that provided little in creature comforts. Though still a small town by many standards, it boasted paved roads, telephone service, and electricity—and many film stars. "In addition to two divorce lawyers, several real estate men, one doctor, a manager and several civilians—six Chows, seven wire-hair terriers, one Great Dane, eleven Scotch terriers, a flock of Pekingese and several species of cats, Malibu Beach is inhabited by that mysterious clan known to points Middle West as 'movie-people.' Here they frolic on the sands and gambol on the porches, eat hot dogs and rust the nickel plate of their Rolls-Royces."[43] Inhabitants included Warner Baxter, Jack Warner, Anna Q. Nilsson, Dolores Del Rio, Ralph Ince, Herbert Brenon, Constance Bennett, Joan Bennett, Chico Marx, John Gilbert, Barbara Stanwyck, Frank Capra, Bert Wheeler, Clara Bow, Louise Fazenda, Marie Prevost, Tod Browning, Robert Leonard, Wesley Ruggles, Lilyan Tashman, Neil Hamilton and many others. "None of the land is owned by its occupants. It stretches for two miles and includes more than 100 houses, ranging from shingled bungalows to fifteen-room mansions. The lots are, for the most part, thirty feet, and the rental originally very low is now $75 a month. The leases run for six more years and it is said that the lessees have been promised an extension of five more years, making eleven in all that they can count on before they can be tossed off the beach and their homes claimed." [44]

In order to keep their sanctuary private, a gateman was hired to keep out stray cars and tourists. "Seven patrolmen are on duty night and day. Protecting the homes from gate crashers that may have gotten past the gateman, souvenir seekers, over-eager fans and yes, gangsters."[45] During the week, Malibu was relatively quiet, but on Saturdays movie stars gathered for parties, fishing, yachting, tennis, and swimming. Brent was well-known for her love of the water. "Betty Brent is the champion get-wetter."[46]

By the end of 1930, Brent clearly stated her two goals: "(1) to have enough money to live in London; and (2) to return to the legitimate stage."[47] Her hobbies included reading, playing bridge and collecting rare first edition books as well as exotic perfumes.[48] Among her most prized books were first editions of Mark Twain's *Huckleberry Finn*[49], James Barrie's *Sentimental Tommy*, and Sarah Bernhardt's *Memoirs of My Life*. She also owned works by John Galsworthy, James Stephens, and Liam O'Flaherty.[50] It was thought that Brent owned one of Hollywood's finest libraries. Still, Dorothy Herzog once reported in her column that Brent's household employees were unimpressed. "Evelyn Brent has a very large library. She's a little proud of her library. Picture her disconcerted face when she overheard her cook comment to a visiting friend: 'Yes, Miss Brent has a lot of books, but I do wish she'd get books that are interesting to read.'"[51] A newspaper blurb in 1931 also reported that Brent had become interested in art, and was in the market to purchase Rodin sculptures.[52]

Brent was on the verge of losing her fortune and going into debt but continued to spend money on clothing. "Betty Brent has chosen two prints for spring right atop the fatal announcement of Chanel's 'prints are out.' One afternoon gown is a printed frock in beige, brown and white with a light-weight woolen coat of brown lined with the print. And of evenings she is going to wear a white and green print, cool as a crème de menthe frappe. The skirt had three shirred flounces of the print. Evelyn Brent has a liking for London: her husband is tied up in an American-English motion picture producing concern. So when a wag looked her printed gown up and said: 'You didn't get that one from Mme. Chanel...' Betty Brent replied airily, 'This is from the English Chanel.'"[53]

An interesting article about Hollywood stars' personal wardrobe provided a peek into Brent's closet. "Evelyn Brent's 15 evening gowns are mostly in black and white, with an occasional green. They are guarded by seven wraps of velvet and brocade, and are flanked by twelve street suits and or frocks."[54] It was estimated that well-known actresses spent anywhere from $10,000 to $15,000 a year on their personal wardrobes.

Brent and Edwards continued living it up, moving into a house on Vine Street in April 1931. According to Louella O. Parsons, the couple gave "an impromptu house warming at their new home."[55]

Around this same time, Brent told the *Los Angeles Times* that she might leave for London to appear on stage. "She had two offers when she was there last year, and we are told that these offers will be renewed if she cares to take advantage of them."[56] She would have been wise to leave.

Ironically, in the spring of 1931 Brent was one of the main organizers for a tea benefit held at the Montmartre to help one of Hollywood's own. It was sponsored by the Hollywood Women's Press Club; other hostesses besides Brent included Mrs. James (Lucille) Gleason and

*Evelyn in 1931.*

June Collyer. The bridge-tea was being held "in honor of a beloved and once famous movie star, who now is in dire straits."[57] For privacy reasons the name of the person was never released. Gloria Swanson donated a $100 money order to be used at Robinson's department store. Other prizes were awarded, and tickets were $10 for a table or $2.50 for a single ticket. Guests included Marie Dressler, Joan Crawford, Edward G. Robinson, Barbara Stanwyck, Bessie Love, Esther Ralston, Louise Dresser, Robert Z. Leonard, and others. The event was a success. Columnist Grace Kingsley wrote, "Betty Brent was there ... working like a major to see that all the guests were made comfortable and all were served their sandwiches and tea."[58] Brent was fashionable, too. "Miss Brent appeared in a brown and white print dress fashioned with short, cap sleeves, with brown felt hat; and brown and white slippers."[59]

*"Evelyn Brent discovered that under-sea swimming is the greatest eye-beautifier in the world today. Seems it improves the clarity and luster of the eye and makes the white as hard and clean as Carrara marble."*[60]

Brent and Edwards were still pretending to be wealthy film people, but something was beginning to go seriously wrong with Brent's career. An interesting observation was made by Roger Bryant, who has written a book examining William Powell's films: "The contrast between the mysterious beauty of *The Last Command* and the sullen woman in *High Pressure* is remarkable. When sound came her voice was revealed to be perfectly acceptable; but sound destroyed the illusion of the figure created by Josef von Sternberg."[61]

It was more than sound that ruined Brent's career. Mismanagement and the lack of a Bernie Fineman to give astute advice and protection also figured in. In the summer of 1931, columnist Grace Kingsley made a pointed comment about why Brent's RKO contract had not been renewed: "It was known that Miss Brent was a drawing card, and all the critics agreed that she was one of the finest actresses on the screen. It has been learned that the facts behind Miss Brent's withdrawal from Radio had to do with one postponement after another of her starring vehicles, a substitution of Lili Damita in one of them."[62] Apparently Brent was intent on sabotaging her career—or she was receiving bad advice.

Evelyn was still frequenting the Embassy Club. By the way, Brent's favorite meal, whether at the Montmartre or Embassy Club, was bacon and eggs. In July the *Los Angeles Times* columnist Margaret Nye wrote, "Everyone turned to look at Evelyn Brent as she passed, because of her newly acquired coat of tan, which blended beautifully with her smart sport dress of yellow, orange and brown."[63] Later that month, the Embassy Club roof was opened. "With a staff of decorators and builders working night and day the past week under the personal supervision of Harry Grieves and Jetta Goudal, the new Embassy Club roof at Hollywood Boulevard and Highland is in readiness for its gala premiere tonight [July 29, 1931], according to the announcement of Eddie Brandstatter and Jacques De Bujac, who will operate it."[64]

It's important to note that neither column mentions included the name Harry Edwards. A few days before the Embassy Club roof premiere, on July 26, 1931, something unusual happened at Malibu Beach. According to the *Los Angeles Times*, Brent, who was known to be an excellent swimmer, almost drowned—only to be saved by husband Harry. "Miss Brent was swimming before her home in Malibu, and went far out. Heading back, she sensed an undertow, and decided to take the waves by diving. The surf was high, and she took one wave, but it broke just as she dived into it, knocking her under. Coming up well nigh exhausted, another wave caught her before she could regain her breath. She attempted to dive, struck bottom, and says she remembers nothing more until she found herself on the beach. Miss Brent's husband, Harry Edwards, is the hero of this tale, as he swam out, dressed in his flannels as he was, and dragged his wife to safety."[65] Sounding somewhat reminiscent of the faucet incident that occurred when Brent was married to Fineman, the story had a sinister tone as well. Louella O. Parsons reported it with this detail: "[Harry] caught hold of her arm so tightly that she has black and blue marks."[66] In Parsons' version, Mrs. Sam Jaffe was also part of the incident. "Mrs. Jaffe ... was so hysterical from fright that she had all her neighbors calming her."

A day before the newspaper report about her near-drowning, a column written by Dan Thomas described Brent's life in Malibu—and her desire to live on the beach. According to Thomas, he received a phone call from Brent inviting him to swim with her. The only mention of Edwards was that Brent is also known as Mrs. Harry Edwards. According to Thomas, Brent's beach house was simple. "Her house has three bedrooms, a kitchen and a living room which also serves as the dining room. It is a very serviceable beach house, too. Wicker furniture predominates and the linoleum covered floors can't be harmed by the wet bathers."[67] Although Edwards did not seem to be at home, Thomas explained that Brent did not live alone. "Wherever you find Miss Brent, you always find Elsie. For one thing the star has a great weakness for Elsie's cooking. Also, Elsie is more than a cook. She is sort of a general manager of the Edwards household, at Hollywood and at the beach. She looks after everything from buying provisions to paying bills. She even spends her day off pasting clippings in Betty's scrapbook."[68]

Brent described her idyllic life away from the stresses of Hollywood by recounting her daily activities. "I spend practically all of my time on the beach.... Ordinarily I get up about nine o'clock, take a quick dip in the ocean and then have a very light breakfast. After that I go out on the beach again, dividing my time between the water and the sand until about one-thirty when I come in for lunch. Then I go back to the beach again. Of course, I don't spend all of my time in the water. That would be too tiring. Part of the time I sleep and part of the time I go visiting—the gang at Malibu are like a big family.... I'm also out in the sun. If sunshine makes one healthy, I certainly should have enough health to last a while."[69] Like many, Thomas was surprised to see how tan Brent was. "Having lived at Malibu for the past several weeks, she resembles a native Hawaiian girl more than a motion picture actress. Boy, she's brown!"[70]

Brent preferred life on the beach to working on a set. "I haven't the slightest idea when I start my next picture or what it will be. But I had better start pretty soon or I'll be out of the notion of working. This beach life gets into my blood."[71]

In the fall of 1931, Brent and Edwards left Malibu. Brent blamed the weather. "It was too cold for words down there the other day, and all of a sudden everybody down there decided to come home."[72] In truth the reasons may have been financial. A terse report in the *Los Angeles Times* stated: "Evelyn Brent has given up her cottage at Malibu Beach and moved back to her Hollywood home."[73]

Around this time, Brent made comments about poor reviews. "If the criticism is justified I don't mind it, but many times players are roasted for performances that are not entirely their fault. If they say I am bad in a picture, I don't resent it.... [But] [v]ery often the things to which they object are due to the mechanics of direction, or because the film has been badly cut or poorly edited." She was also asked her reaction to comments suggesting she had been miscast. "I get sore at the casting office,"[74] she said in no uncertain terms.

Christmas Eve 1931 was eventful for Brent and her friends. Estelle Taylor was involved in a serious automobile accident, and Evelyn and Harry showed up at the hospital to take her home. Taylor, in the middle of a divorce from boxer Jack Dempsey, was a passenger in a Rolls Royce driven by Frank Joyce's chauffeur Noel Scott. "Estelle Taylor ... was injured painfully early today when her expensive automobile leaped a curb in front of 121 South Normandie Avenue and crashed into a palm tree. The injuries to the screen actress climaxed a Christmas Eve of wild driving and collisions seldom equaled in receiving hospital records. Twenty-six accident victims were treated at the Hollywood Receiving Hospital. Miss Taylor's injuries were diagnosed by police surgeon H.W. Deane of the Hollywood Receiving Hospital as a two-inch cut on the upper left side of the head, bumps on the right side of the head and left cheek and bruises on the left knee and hip. She was thrown against the top of the car. Accompanying the actress were Frank Joyce, film producer, and her chauffeur, Noel Scott, who was not injured.... The chauffeur said at first that he believed another machine had sideswiped Miss Taylor's car, forcing it from the road. Later, however, he admitted that he might have fallen asleep momentarily, according to policemen Dillard and Hansen of the Wilshire police division. He said he had 'not had much sleep recently.' Because of the absence of marks of a collision, no official report of the accident had been made up to this morning. The Taylor car was a Rolls Royce, believed to be the machine involved in the legal warfare of the Dempsey divorce. The accident occurred at 3:15 am. Miss Taylor and Mr. Joyce were returning from a hotel dance when the crash occurred. The actress gave her age as 31 and her address as 5352 Los Feliz Boulevard. She remained at the Hollywood Receiving Hospital for an hour and then was called for by Evelyn Brent, film actress and her husband, Harry D. Edwards, who took her home. She is under the care of Dr. Maurice Kahn. Her injuries may well keep her from the vaudeville stage and screen for a short time, it was said."[75] Taylor later sued Scott and Joyce for $150,000, claiming Scott was intoxicated.[76]

This event was much more exciting than anything happening with Brent's career. By the end of 1931 she was included in an article about stars who had been lost in the shuffle. Alma Whitaker also detailed the career woes of Colleen Moore, ZaSu Pitts, May McAvoy, Aileen Pringle, and others. She blamed Evelyn's career decline on one bad picture. "It took Evelyn ever so long to get her chance in *The Mad Parade*, that all-woman picture which might have been so great, but it turned out a failure and down went Evelyn's screen opportunities with it."[77]

In the winter of 1932 it was incorrectly announced that Brent would soon be appearing in British talkies.[78] In addition, it was reported that Brent would play opposite Marlene Dietrich in Josef von Sternberg's 1932 film *Blonde Venus*. The role of Taxi Belle eventually went to Rita La Roy who was rumored to be Dietrich's lover at the time. Losing that role might have been a blessing in disguise because Taxi Belle's role was severely cut. According to Hans J. Wollstein, "the role of 'Taxi Belle' had been written for an earlier Sternberg favorite, Evelyn Brent, but Paramount executive B.P. Schulberg, his gaze firmly on the Production Code, demanded a rewrite of the censurable script. Sternberg was forced to cut the role to the bare minimum (and, even more fatal to the end result, add a ludicrous happy ending!), with the result that Evelyn Brent, too big a star to waste in a bit role, was out."[79]

Brent's first picture released in 1932 was *High Pressure*. According to gossip columnist Louella O. Parsons, "I hear all the way from Hollywood that William Powell asked for Evelyn Brent for his next picture, *High Pressure*. Betty used to play in Bill's underworld stories at Paramount and she always did a good job. She has been more or less free-lancing since she left Paramount and this is the first time she has been on the Warner lot."[80]

Powell reflected back on the experience he and Brent shared when they worked on *Interference* and found it truly remarkable how advanced sound picture had become in just a few short years. "*Interference* was a wonderful picture, but to compare it with *High Pressure* is like lining a 1915 Haynes alongside a 1932 model car."[81]

*High Pressure* was generally popular with audiences and critics. Critic Norbert Lusk raved about Powell: "In this he shines brilliantly, engagingly, the suavity that served for many of his recent performances giving way to a vital expressiveness that makes his present characterization the most lifelike and arresting that he has played in several years.... Then, too, the cast is extraordinarily fine, as must be the case when Alison Skipworth, Lucien Littlefield and John Wray play bits in support of Evelyn Brent, Evalyn Knapp, George Sidney and Frank McHugh, all of whom couldn't be bettered. In short, this is a picture that is first of all entertaining and irresistibly amusing."[82] This was one of the first roles in some time where Brent was given a glamorous wardrobe. "Miss Brent's role calls for several smart evening gowns and street frocks. The clothes are being especially designed for her by the First National fashion department."[83] James Robert Parish described it as a "fast-talking melodrama that zipped through its seventy-four minutes so quickly that viewers scarcely had the opportunity to analyze, let alone comprehend, its confused plot."[84]

In the spring of 1932 Brent was on the verge of signing another contract with Columbia.[85] According to her hometown newspaper, she had been summoned to a contract conference. In truth, Brent was eager to sign because she needed the money.

The first sign of financial difficulties appeared in the *Los Angeles Times* on March 31, 1931. Brent owed Chanel, Inc., $400.30 for gowns she had purchased and not paid for. A complaint had been filed in court the previous day.[86] Ironically, on the same day Harrison Carroll reported that Brent had purchased a swimming pool. "Evelyn Brent now has joined the Hollywood order of swimming pool owners. It goes with her new house overlooking the film capital."[87] Perhaps more ominously, it had been reported a day earlier that Brent had met with attorney Ralph Blum, husband of Carmel Myers.[88]

Later that year, Brent attempted to explain away the lawsuit when Dan Thomas wrote a newspaper report titled "Shop Owners Cheat Stars." "One of the greatest annoyances so far as film folk are concerned is fly-by-night shop owners who often sue for bills not due them—and very often collect as many of our stars would rather pay than suffer the adverse publicity brought about by court proceedings." Brent described to Thomas an incident where a man jumped on her car's running board in order to thrust a summons at her. "The fact that she had a receipt to show that she had paid meant nothing to him. He figured she would pay again rather than go into court. But for once he figured wrong."[89]

In the summer of 1931 when *Traveling Husbands* was released, critics were generally kind to Brent. According to *Variety*, "Miss Brent plays the 10-minute egg quite nicely. She puts plenty of scorn into her glances and as much snap in the dialog."[90] The *Los Angeles Times* added, "Miss Brent, a pivotal member of the cast, contributes one of her usual taciturn demimondaines to the proceedings."[91] *Film Daily* raved about this pre–Code gem: "Thoroughly worth-

*Evelyn in 1932.*

while entertainment from every angle. The pace is fast, the comedy smooth and spontaneous, and the cast is capable and convincing.... Any audience, anywhere will like this offering."[92] Marquis Busby, writing for the *Los Angeles Examiner*, concurred: "[I]t is a good many notches above the average motion picture."[93] He added, "Evelyn Brent has never given a finer performance."

The good reviews didn't matter. Brent released three good films in 1931, but 1932 was marked by financial setbacks. On January 8 a newspaper reported that Brent and Edwards were being sued by the Robertson Company for their failure to pay for $366.88 worth of furniture and drapes.[94] In April they were sued by a collection agency for clothing they had purchased. According to the *Los Angeles Times*, they owed $409 to the Machin Shirt Company and $76.85 to the Ambassador Importation Company.[95] The *Los Angeles Times* also reported that same month that a judge awarded Stanley Rose Ltd. a $724 judgment for books sold to Brent and not paid for. The transaction had occurred months before, and Brent had not answered the complaint.[96]

On April 30 it was a furrier who was suing Brent. "During the past two years Evelyn Brent, film actress, has purchased fur coats and neckpieces from Louis B. Spiegel, operator of a fur store at 329 North Beverly Drive, Beverly Hills, valued at $1881 for which she has neglected to pay."[97] Harry Edwards was also named as a defendant in the case.

On August 6 a veterinarian sued the couple for $537.50. Dr. J.E. Hapenney claimed that the hospitalization charges accumulated over several months.[98] At the time, Brent owned a Pekingese and a wire-haired terrier.[99] A 1930 article described the pets in greater detail. "In the rear of their home is a large, fenced lawn-space for 'Tricksick,' a wire-haired terrier, and 'Kim,' the Pekingese. Both young thoroughbreds are very much a part of the family and up through the house at night; they are never admitted during the day unless it is raining."[100]

In September, I. Miller, a shoe company, took Brent to court for bills totaling $1,218.85. "The shoes, the company asserts, were sold to Miss Brent at her 'special instance and request,' the bill for them becoming due on January 7, last. She has failed to pay the bill ... although she 'promised to pay.'"[101] The charges were filed against Mary Elizabeth Edwards.

On November 25, 1932, the *Los Angeles Times* reported that Brent and Edwards were being sued for clothing they had purchased in 1931. Hawes and Curtis, Ltd., an English company, claimed the couple owed $585 on a bill that had come due January 23, 1931. A second company, C. Ebeglou (doing business as Maison "Saint Maur")[102], also made a claim for monies owed them since June 30, 1931.

Little wonder when a newspaper blurb reported that Brent was having trouble sleeping at night.[103] Ironically, a newspaper reported around this same time Brent was able to ask for—and receive—$1,000 a week for her acting services.[104] Regardless, Evelyn and Harry Edwards were living far beyond their means. Brent wasn't helping herself. In July 1932 she turned down a role in Robert Florey's *Those We Love* (1932) and was replaced by Lilyan Tashman. According to columnist Harrison Carroll, Brent "withdrew from the cast at the last minute after an argument over billing."[105]

Meanwhile, Brent's films were not doing well. In the fall of 1932 *Attorney for the Defense* came out. The Columbia release was low-budget and looked it. *Variety* unkindly reminded readers that Brent used to be a star. "Brent as the usual tough trollop was of secondary importance, although it as fair a role as they get handed out these days. She worked for Columbia previously as a full-fledged star."[106]

Louella O. Parsons, however, pointed out that Brent still had it. "Evelyn Brent ... has all the allure that made her so much talked about in *Underworld*. She can play a tough girl in the most ladylike fashion of any actress I know."[107] Parsons was such an adamant supporter of Brent that someone accused her of being her press agent. She responded in a huff: "I deny that I am anyone's press agent, but I do like to see the Hollywood girls get a break before the newcomers."[108]

Eleanor Barnes, writing for the *Illustrated Daily News*, also made a case that Brent deserved more attention. "Evelyn Brent, as the bad brittle woman who two-times the prosecutor, once again turns out a neat performance. Why can't some director make an honest woman out of Evelyn? For class, smoothness of acting, for beauty and intelligence, Miss Brent has a lot of dolls backed off the map, but film companies go on forever, miscasting her as a street-walker."[109]

In October *The Crusader* was released. The Majestic release was considered trite, and Brent's performance was largely ignored. Not surprisingly, a newspaper blurb hinted that Brent and Edwards were having marital troubles: Hollywood gossip columnist Dan Thomas (him again) reported that Hollywood's only real night club, the Club New Yorker, had just opened and drawn a lot of celebrities. Thomas observed, "Wallace Beery and his wife only attempted one dance.... Evelyn Brent and Harry Edwards didn't even do that."[110]

In October, Brent was up for a role in *Air Hostess* at Columbia, and then in November she was rumored to be in contention for a Houdini film at RKO with Adolphe Menjou. Neither came to pass. Around the first of the new year (1933) Edwin Martin noted in the *Hollywood Citizen News* that Brent was sighted attending a Ruth Chatterton play. Calling her "ever-glamorous," he lamented, "why, oh, why don't we see more of her on the screen!"[111]

By 1933 Evelyn's career was skidding to a halt. Her personal life wasn't going so well, either. She continued to be served with lawsuits. In April she was sued in small claims court by Bruce Wyndham, who claimed he was owed $10.50 for German books and lessons. Brent's address at the time was 316 North Rossmore.[112]

Columnist Dan Thomas chided Brent for not paying her bills. "While she never has been one of the top-notch stars, Evelyn Brent's salary for years has been in four figures weekly. She hasn't been working regularly of late, but even at that she has earned enough to carry her through life." Thomas then added the most telling information which partially explained the Brents' dramatic reversal of fortune: "It's rumored [that Brent] dropped quite a chunk of money in an independent producing venture with her husband, Harry Edwards. However, she declines to discuss this or any other subject pertaining to the alleged loss of her wealth."[113] Louella O. Parsons spoke up for Brent around the same time. "High time that some of these producers signed Evelyn Brent. For no good reason she has been idle for months and months."[114]

It was soon announced that Brent would appear with Pat O'Brien in *The Public Be Damned* (the picture would later be renamed *The World Gone Mad*). Then in March, Parsons reported that Brent was excited because she was joining Harry Fox in a vaudeville act that would open in March in Omaha. Parsons later reported that she had heard the show was a success. "Evelyn Brent was able to win over the Omaha theatergoers and to get a reception such as few people have ever received in this town which doesn't have particularly enthusiastic audiences."[115]

*The World Gone Mad*, an appropriate title for Brent's life at this point, was released in the spring of 1933. An enjoyable picture, this one gave Brent an opportunity to play a tough cookie yet again. According to *Variety*, "There are first-rate comedy values in sequences dealing with [Pat O'Brien's] campaign to 'make' a gang moll, the latter role smoothly handled by Evelyn Brent."[116] The *Los Angeles Times* noted Brent's return to film, applauding "the welcome reappearance of Evelyn Brent in a smoothly convincing underworld characterization."[117] Still, in an interview publicizing the film, Brent complained about being typecast. "[A]lthough she is rather reconciled to her lot in picture life ... she confesses that she is rather tired of it."[118]

The news got worse. In May it was reported that Brent was being sued by the Internal Revenue Service for money owed on her 1930 income tax return. The IRS placed a lien on her income to the tune of $301.44. Harry got hit with one for $302.[119]

Years later Brent was asked why her career declined. "I think it was my personal life ... I sort of made everything else secondary.... I think I let everything slide. And it was probably due to the one bad husband.... [T]hat whole episode threw me off very much.... I was badly advised."[120]

In fact, Brent was tired of lots of things including Hollywood. Seemingly unable to make a living in films, she made the decision to take her act on the road.

# Vaudeville

*California climate is gorgeous for a time ... but after years of its sameness*
*one longs to be somewhere else. And then I was cast in several films for which*
*I believe I was not suited and so I decided to take the vaudeville engagement.*[1]

By May 1933, Brent realized she needed to make money—and quickly. She hit the vaudeville circuit, teaming up with veteran performer Harry Fox. Born in San Francisco, California, on May 25, 1882,[2] Fox claimed his grandfather was legendary circus clown George L. Fox, but this was not true.[3] In fact, a lot of things Harry Fox said about his early life were not true.

We do know that his real last name was Messman. He had early success with the Millership Sisters, and by 1914 he was a seasoned vaudeville performer, a song-and-dance man who dabbled in comedy, and married to a woman named Lydia. It was around this time that Fox became acquainted with Jenny (sometimes spelled Jennie and sometimes referred to as Yansci), one of the legendary Dolly Sisters twins. "In a carefully calculated move to enhance their careers ... the Dolly Sisters each paired themselves with male partners: Roszika (or Rosy) with specialty dancer Martin Brown, who had recently appeared with them in the 1913 musical *The Merry Countess*, and Yansci (or Jenny) with comic-eccentric dancer Harry Fox. Although critics bemoaned the apparent loss of the popular female team, each of their respective partnerships won critical praise on the vaudeville circuit." Rosy and Martin often relied on erotically charged Spanish dancing while Jenny and Fox "worked more in a light-hearted romantic flirtation vein, combining song and banter. The two teams, who often appeared on the same vaudeville bill, were set up as rivals to create audience interest."[4]

There was a surge of interest in ballroom dancing, and Fox hit the big-time when he got a job at the New York Theatre. "The fox-trot originated in the Jardin de Danse on the roof of the New York Theatre. As part of his act downstairs, Harry Fox was doing trotting steps to ragtime music, and people referred to his dance as 'Fox's Trot.' Wishing to capitalize on this, the management introduced the dance at the roof garden. Harry Fox was undoubtedly spending considerable time in the Jardin de Danse, since he and Yansci Dolly were 'making plans'; in fact, they were married at Long Beach, Long Island, in August of that year [1914]."[5]

Part of that quote is true: Fox did indeed marry Jenny. However, there is much controversy about whether Fox invented the fox-trot. In the book *The Complete Book of Ballroom Dancing* the authors are unequivocal. "There is no question but that the fox-trot was originated in the summer of 1914 by the vaudeville actor Harry Fox."[6] Others say hogwash.

Nevertheless, Jenny became romantically involved with Fox while sister Rosy was linked to songwriter Jean Schwartz, Fox's friend. "The men had been friends since Jean Schwartz had written songs for Harry Fox, and so a double love affair had begun. Within less than two years the two couples would be married."[7]

When Rosy Dolly married Jean Schwartz on April 10, 1913, in Greenwich, Connecticut, the witnesses were Fox and Jenny. Meanwhile, Fox and Jenny continued their act, and it was well received. *Variety* declared, "If there is a better two-act in vaudeville it hasn't made its appearance hereabouts up to date."[8]

While Fox and Jenny were performing at the Hammerstein's Victoria, Harry divorced Lydia. She charged him, not surprisingly, with adultery. He had a cavalier attitude toward

*Harry Fox sheet music (circa 1917).*

marriage vows as evidenced by an exchange with the judge and reporters. "When he was asked by the Divorce Court judge if he would pay his ex-wife $25 per week maintenance, he replied: 'With much pleasure.' On leaving the court, he told reporters: 'I like the way they do business here. I'm always coming here for my divorces in the future.'"[9]

Fox married Jenny on August 28, 1914, and it was a big to-do. "The marriage took place in Greenwich, Connecticut, starting with a wedding breakfast at the Hotel Claridge. Afterwards a big limousine loaned by Diamond Jim Brady[10] took the party for the ceremony shortly before noon. It was a small family affair, with Yansci's parents, Jean Schwartz, Rosy and their brother Eddie. Margarethe, Yansci's mother, was apparently heartbroken by the marriage. First Rosy and now Jenny. She thought they were both too young to marry and that their marriages would mean the end of their careers."[11]

These were first marriages for the Dolly Sisters, who became better known later for collecting millionaire husbands. Both couples resided in nearby apartments in the exclusive section of Riverside Drive, near Central Park. Of course, the compelling question in most people's minds was how the husbands who lived next door to each other could tell their brides apart. "Apparently every precaution was taken against any mix-up—Jenny's room was pink and Rosy's blue (back to the ribbons tied on their legs when they were little girls), and they made a point of dressing differently so that Harry would never mistake Rosy for Jenny and Jean would always be able to identify Rosy, no matter how early in the morning he returned home. Jean Schwartz said that, in order to identify his wife, he made Rosy eat an onion every morning, and Jenny wore an antique ring given to her by Harry. Jean was also believed to possess a sixth sense by which he could always tell the sisters apart."[12]

Harry and Jenny returned to the vaudeville circuit in the fall of 1914. They later appeared in *Maid in America* in 1915 but left after a disagreement with cast member Ina Gould. Jenny starred in the movie *The Call of the Dance*, which is, unfortunately, a lost film. Fox was briefly featured in Charles Dillingham's production of *Stop! Look! Listen!* in December 1915, but it closed three months later. A critic described him as "that good looking and exceedingly unctuous comedian."[13]

In 1916 Fox filmed the serial *Beatrice Fairfax* with co-star Grace Darling in Ithaca, New York. In that same year he summarized his career. "I have done about everything that can be done on the stage. I went in the circus as a clown when I was 10 years old. I have been in vaudeville and in stock companies. I learned to sing and to dance and learned tricks of phrase that will make them laugh."[14]

The following June, Dolly sued Fox for divorce, claiming he had several affairs.[15] Within weeks, the couple had reconciled, and the divorce was called off. The couple requested that the embarrassing divorce papers be destroyed, but the court refused. "Yansci Dolly Fox ... and her husband, Harry Fox, have merely added to the papers in the case by asking that the records of her divorce suit be destroyed. The court has denied the request, and its decision also is filed."[16]

A couple years later, the Dolly Sisters opened with Fox in *Oh Look!* at the Belasco Theatre. The musical production was a success; Harry sang the hit song "I'm Always Chasing Rainbows," which became his theme. Although some critics pointed out that neither the Dolly Sisters nor Fox were great singers, their shows often sold out. In August 1918 in Chicago at the LaSalle Theatre, their act set a record for gross receipts. The show continued to tour well into 1920.

In the fall of 1920, the Dolly Sisters traveled to London for a performance that signaled the end of their marriages. "Rosy said that, when they decided to go to London, both husbands were furious. 'We went anyway and that was how our marriages went on the rocks.

We never went back to our husbands.'"[17] Another problem, according to the Dolly Sisters' biographer Gary Chapman, was the death of Diamond Jim Brady. "Despite the fact that the Dollies were allegedly blissfully married, they had been continually pampered by Diamond Jim Brady, who had provided them with every indulgence. They had been in a unique situation, able to enjoy the best of both worlds. With Diamond Jim's death in April 1917, the sparkle of his generosity evaporated. His absence would have been nothing short of a devastating blow—they had lost their main benefactor and the source of their extravagance and luxury. This gaping void in their lives would have put their marriages into a new perspective."[18]

Jenny later blamed the divorce on hardships and jealousy inherent in an entertainment career. "I realized it was a mistake for an actress to marry an actor. We are still congenial.... He's a dear, sweet boy, but I just knew it was a mistake to have a husband in the profession. Road trips force husband and wife apart, temptations follow and lonesomeness is bound to bring new friendships ... I would never advise an actress to marry an actor."[19] In October 1920 Jenny filed for divorce from Fox.[20]

In truth, Harry Fox was a womanizer. One newspaper hinted that his indiscretions caused the divorce. "Smiling Harry Fox ... who might have lived happily with Yansci Dolly forever after if he had reserved his smile exclusively for her and not, as she alleges in her suit, insisted on sharing it with other ladies."[21] His new girlfriend (and vaudeville partner) was a teenager. Beatrice Antoinette Curtis was the daughter of actress Anna Chandler and booking agent Jack Curtis. Born on September 20, 1901,[22] she told a reporter that Fox was her hero, "especially since he volunteered and went into the naval aviation service during the war." Curtis also said that "she had known Harry Fox nearly all her life....' Why, he carried me around in his arms when I was three years old!' declared Miss Curtis. Maybe [the reporter mused] that wasn't beginning any too soon, when you come to think of it! Ah, certainly Mr. Fox hasn't a wrong moniker!"[23] Curtis was a beauty. "She has a wholesomely rosy skin, perfect features, a red mouth, and big brilliant eyes...." She was painted by artist Harrison Fisher who proclaimed her one of the prettiest girls in America.

Fox's marital mishaps obviously caused financial difficulties because the *New York Times* reported on October 26, 1921, that "Harry Fox, actor of 110 West 48th Street, filed a petition in bankruptcy yesterday, listing liabilities of $17,777 and no assets."[24] Within days of his divorce from Dolly, Fox and Curtis married on February 5, 1922.[25] They later had a son who was named after Harry. Curtis and Fox appeared in the Vitaphone short films *The Fox and the Bee* (1929)[26] and the aptly named *The Play Boy* (1930), but the marriage failed.[27] Fox ended up in Hollywood where he worked with Cosmopolitan Pictures which was owned by his friend William Randolph Hearst. He later appeared in bit roles in Warner Brothers and Twentieth Century–Fox films.

A newspaper reported on August 31, 1948, that Fox and Brent were married. However, no marriage record has been located, and it does not appear that Brent collected from Fox's Social Security after his death. Nevertheless Brent and Fox claimed to be married and lived together as husband and wife. Furthermore, Brent used Fox's name on her tombstone.

In May 1933, Brent ended up in her old hometown of Syracuse with Fox, where they played a week, ironically, at the Paramount. Brent was described as "vibrantly enthusiastic over her venture into vaudeville"; the article further explained that Brent "admitted she is finding a new thrill and is not at all anxious to get back to Hollywood."[28]

Her sunny, optimistic disposition did not appear to be an act. "The wonderful climate we have enjoyed and the beauty of the New York State cities is making my tour an event I never will forget.... We were in Rochester when the lilacs were in full bloom and I believe it was the most beautiful sight I ever saw. I'm anxious to drive through Syracuse and see whether I can remember any of the old landmarks."[29]

In her hometown she was pressed to talk about her past. However, she claimed that because she was so young when she moved from Syracuse (according to her, she was three or four), she could only remember Salina Street. Others, however, claimed to remember her. "I have received literally hundreds of letters from people who say they held me on their knee when I was a child and who probably feel hurt when I write them and tell them I cannot remember them."[30]

Brent blamed a "run of unsuitable pictures" and restlessness as reasons for hitting the road. "I'm really glad I did.... [I]t's proving to be an unforgettable experience."[31] Per usual, Brent claimed that after the vaudeville tour ended she'd go to England, and hinted, yet again, that she was considering a permanent move there that might include a film career. "I have always loved England and would like nothing better than to live there. Possibly I might make a few pictures in that country, that is something that will be decided later. I do not know whether I shall make any more in Hollywood when I return."[32]

Brent, who had probably been asked her favorite type of role at least a hundred times, apparently did not roll her eyes when she was asked this time. But she did sound a bit robotic when she said it was underworld women, "probably because there is so much action in playing these parts."[33]

*Syracuse Herald* critic Chester Bahn urged audiences to see the vaudeville show "to become personally appreciative of the sultry beauty of Evelyn Brent, never fully captured by the camera."[34] The show, *Manhattan Merry-Go-Round*, was a showcase for Brent. "Miss Brent's appearance with Harry Fox, Broadway comedian, is responsible for whatever appeal the stage show holds. Best bet: a jig-saw blackout in which Miss Brent satirizes her cinematic moll. Others seen: Fortunello and Circillino, clowns; George Patten, songster, and the somewhat overstuffed 10 Paramount dancers who will remind dad of the gay choruses in the gay 00's."[35] While in Syracuse on this tour, Brent also played host to the Herald Cinema Critics club at the theater.[36]

In September, Brent faced more financial bad news. She once again fell victim to the Internal Revenue Service's tax lien. This time it was for income she received in 1931. She owed an additional $136.[37]

It was announced in October that Brent would appear with Lew Ayres in *Cross Country Cruise*, a Universal picture that eventually came out in the early part of 1934. However, upon its release Brent was not in the cast list which included June Knight, Alice White, and Minna Gombell.

Apparently the lawsuits, marital estrangement, and career woes caught up with Brent. She gave a fall interview where she sounded burned out, disillusioned, and fed up. "Hollywood is a sort of disease which eats into one's blood, like the tropics, only while tropical sickness is founded on laziness and romance, the Hollywood affliction is nurtured by just one thing—vanity. And do you know what vanity does to a person after a time? It makes him something that's very disagreeable, something which is self-centered, selfish, absolutely impossible to live with in a home. He has developed in an artificial community and his ideas of life are just as artificial. If anything happened to him as a screen star, she could never get him to leave Hollywood because he would be a total washout anywhere else—and he knows it. He just basks in the spotlight of Hollywood and lets it dazzle him."[38] It's likely Brent's criticism were at least partly directed at estranged husband Edwards.

A writer back in her hometown of Syracuse suggested that Evelyn, if properly quoted, had burned her bridges; "No more outspoken indictment of Hollywood and its folks has been printed anywhere in many a day."[39] Brent went so far as to call out some major Hollywood names and suggest their pettiness has contributed to Hollywood's decline. "There's the Mary Pickford crowd, and the Lilyan Tashman crowd, then there's another headed by Marion Davies, and the one ruled by Florence Eldridge, Freddie March's wife. Now each of the girls considers herself the queen of Hollywood society. The women really rule Hollywood."[40]

Perhaps most damaging, Brent lamented the lack of eligible bachelors in Hollywood and commented on three men who had reputations for being homosexual or bisexual. "'Why is it necessary for the girls to seek married men in Hollywood!' Miss Brent declared, 'Don't you know that there are no eligible men in Hollywood!' Pressed more closely with the names of Bill Haines, Buddy Rogers, and Gary Cooper—all bachelors—, cited, in refutation, she added: 'I like all the boys you mention, as friends. So I'll say nothing against them. But when it comes to marriage for myself, let me put it this way—if I married again, I think it would be to a furniture manufacturer. Anyhow, something substantial.'"[41]

On the one hand, Brent seemed to be doing everything she could to make herself unwelcome back in Hollywood. On the other hand, Richard Griffith explained that Brent used a savvy marketing strategy while on tour. "Miss Brent resorted to personal appearances, but she determined to make them mean something. She did not arrive for an engagement in the late afternoon, do her stint, and then catch the midnight choo-choo for her next booking. She came to town with plenty of notice and stayed a week. She made herself available to photographers and press at their convenience, right down to the lowliest high school reporters. She was happy to attend any church social, cornerstone-laying, or ribbon-cutting that might be going locally. If there was already an Evelyn Brent fan club in the community she was visiting, she invited all its members to tea at her hotel; if there was none, she saw to it that one was organized forthwith. She also saw to it, like Miss [Leatrice] Joy, that her act was enjoyable in itself and was not a mere bobbing from the stage. When Miss Brent returned to Hollywood after her tour—she devoted a year to it—she left behind her large audiences who thought of her as a friend."[42]

In other words, she created her own buzz. Exceedingly devoted fans started a letter-writing campaign to Hollywood studios, begging them to cast Brent. The idea was ingenious. However, it was also unsuccessful. Brent continued to be cast in weak roles and productions.

Griffith suggests that there was something more to the Brent story. "Whatever it was that had landed this lovely lady in the bad books of the studio moguls she stayed there. She had got herself on some sort of blacklist, and not even positive, vocal, tangibly demonstrated popular support for her, supposedly the key to success, could get her off it. My friend Arthur Mayer says: 'Nonsense. Her pictures no longer did business.' So, perhaps, she was twice blacklisted—first by a decline in public interest, and then by the trade, despite a revival of public interest. There were mysteries aplenty in the old star system."[43]

*"She has one grave complex. 'I can't borrow money. I can't ask it. I couldn't if I was starving. I always give money to those who ask it from me because I feel so sorry for them. I get more confused and embarrassed than they do. I want to get it over with and change the subject.'"*[44]

Evelyn Brent filed for bankruptcy on September 1, 1933. Filing under the name of Evelyn B. Edwards, she listed her liabilities at $33,955 and claimed she had no assets.[45] The *Los Angeles Times* described how far she had fallen: "Evelyn Brent, who earned a fortune in motion pictures, and collected $100,000 in addition when she divorced her first husband, Bernard Fineman, a few years ago, formally declared herself 'broke.'" The *New York Times* referred to her as an "unemployed actress"[46] and reported on May 24, 1934, that the bankruptcy had been discharged. It listed her address as 334 W. 72nd Street.[47]

According to an April 1, 1934, article, Brent had been away for fifteen months and had returned to Hollywood before going back out on the tour again. "Her partner has been Harry Fox, cheerful vaudevillian; the pair engaged in comedy give-and-take, with a 'serious' finish. Miss Brent lost her well-known tan on tour; with four and five shows a day, you have to make your own sunshine. The big cities, she said, remember their Hollywood favorites; in the sticks, you're just another act. Business was terrible last summer and fall, but has picked up considerably—except in Canada, which apparently has been hit by repeal and a consequent falling-off in the number of American visitors."[48]

Jimmy Starr, columnist for the *Los Angeles Evening Herald Express*, wrote a short blurb in late April that Brent and Fox were doing quite well on their tour. "Evelyn Brent and Harry Fox CLICKED in grand style with their personal appearances in San Francisco."[49] A review in the *Wisconsin State Journal* claimed that the show was mostly Harry. "Evelyn Brent, the movie actress, lets Harry Fox, Broadway comedian, shoulder the load in their act, but the audience seemed satisfied with its glimpse of the comely star."[50]

It's not known what Harry Edwards was doing this time though he was occasionally mentioned in the gossip columns for attending various parties. There were no film credits for him after 1931 until 1942. A mention in a March 1934 Louella O. Parsons column indicated that the rumors about the Brent-Edwards split were just that: "Evelyn Brent proved just how false are that she and Harry Edwards have separated by spending every minute with him on her brief visit to Hollywood."[51] At the end of May, however, Brent announced that they had separated for good. Columnist Jerry Hoffman reported the inevitable news. "Evelyn Brent has returned to Hollywood, but not to her husband, Harry Edwards. Very quietly she slipped into town a few days ago and took an apartment for herself. Harry has moved into bachelor quarters with Jameson Thomas. The news will come as a surprise to the film colony, who knew how Betty worshiped her husband. Although Betty was reluctant to discuss it, she admitted over the telephone today that the separation had taken place and might be permanent. Several picture offers have been made since the success of her personal appearance tour and she may remain in Hollywood."[52]

That same month, Brent was back on the road in the Midwest with Harry Fox. Brent and Fox were invited to meet the governor of Wisconsin, and Brent gave an interesting interview to the *Wisconsin State Journal* where she burned a few more bridges. She first identified her favorite actors—Spencer Tracy, Paul Muni, and Helen Hayes—and then bashed Katharine Hepburn, referring to her as "all pyrotechnics, and a flash in the pan." She also restated her belief that success in acting was mostly luck "Why, I know many girls working as extras who are better actresses than some of our stars." She added that she was sick of appearing in "trashy" movies and was looking forward to any "decent" role upon her return to Hollywood.[53]

*"I've learned to like beer and skittles instead of caviar."*[54]

Early in her vaudeville career, Brent made the same mistake of trusting others to take care of her money. Eventually, she and Harry Fox took over the finances. "[W]hen Harry and I were alone and booked our act and managed our money ourselves, we'd often have $500 weeks. After all railroad fares, hotel bills, food, dry-cleaning and so on had to be paid there'd still be plenty left. I began to learn the value of money then. I began to learn what it means to shop for a dress costing $16.75 and not another cent because there isn't another cent for it. I had already learned, you see, what it feels like to wonder when there will be another meal, or how to finagle a jump from one town to another. And I swear I didn't mind it. It was fun!"[55]

Increasingly desperate for work, Brent turned to radio. On July 23, 1934, she appeared with Henry B. Walthall on KFI's *The Show*. They performed together in a scene from *Leah Kleschna*, which had been a stage play starring George Arliss.[56]

Louella O. Parsons again went to bat for Brent in July. "Evelyn Brent had a good right to be discouraged. Yet she has never let the movies get her down. At one time a topnotcher, she has had difficulty convincing these producers that she is still a good actress and still knows her stuff."[57] Parsons announced that Brent would appear in *Without Children*. Dan Thomas summed up Brent's career: "Evelyn Brent certainly wasn't born under a lucky star.... [H]er first marriage went to smash several years ago and now her second one is on the rocks ... and she hasn't been able to get a break in pictures of late ... but prospects are brighter now."[58]

Finally, in September 1934, Brent got a movie job. This time she was on the set of *Code of the West*, a Zane Grey Western, replacing Grace Bradley.[59] Upon release, the title was changed to *Home on the Range*. Muriel Babcock wrote, "I found Evelyn Brent's work most interesting. Why she doesn't make a good comeback in films is beyond me, for she has a fine presence, a good voice and looks well."[60] Dan Thomas also put in a good word for Brent. "Evelyn Brent is hard at work again and all Hollywood is pulling for her to climb right up to the top."[61]

Some time in 1934 Brent's dear friend Dorothy Herzog wrote a magazine article titled "The Strange Case of Miss Brent," beginning it with, "'Fickle' is not a complimentary word. The picture public is said to be fickle. Producers say so. Producers also say the public is quick to turn from the favorites of yesterday and seek new ones for tomorrow. I have always been of the opinion that it isn't the public who is fickle, but the producers. For several years now, Evelyn Brent has been absent from the screen."[62]

Herzog included an interesting interview with Brent in which she, among other things, talked about stars who were popular with small-town America, including Bessie Love, Kay Francis, Wallace Beery, Marie Dressler, Helen Hayes, and Tom Mix. Not once in the piece was Brent's marriage to Harry Edward's mentioned. Herzog concluded her article by virtually demanding that Brent be hired again in Hollywood. "Perhaps when Evelyn Brent returns to the Coast, some shrewd director will forget that producer opinion, not public opinion, decided she was no longer box-office. It seems to be the hope of the thousands Betty has met on her tour. I'm among those who hope this vital actress will get her chance again. Aren't you?"[63]

The first hint of a personal relationship between Fox and Brent came from a Louella O. Parsons blurb. "I keep hearing of a romance between Evelyn Brent and Harry Fox. Interesting, if true, since they were vaudeville partners and appeared in an act for over a year. Miss Brent was formerly married to Harry Edwards and only recently filed suit of divorce against him.... [Fox] now has a position with the Fox Company and, according to his friends, is working hard to establish himself in the movies."[64] Actually there is no record that Brent filed for divorce in the 1930s.

Brent's legal troubles did not end with her bankruptcy. She was sued by former secretary Sunshine Duncan in 1935 for back wages totaling $3,000. According to Duncan, Brent employed her from March to October 1933 for $100 a week. "Miss Brent and her counsel, Vernon L. Gray, denied having employed Miss Duncan. In this connection the actress said she [Brent] signed a contract with Harry Edwards, her husband and agent, for a theatrical tour and that it was Edwards who had employed Miss Duncan. Edwards, Miss Brent added, recently went through bankruptcy."[65] The case was dismissed on a technicality on May 7, 1935, because "it was brought out that Miss Duncan had been married in Tijuana before she filed her suit for salary and that her husband had failed to join in the assignment.... Although

Miss Duncan said that she only lived with her husband for one day, the case was dismissed on technical grounds without prejudice."[66]

Not surprisingly, Brent struck a sour note when discussing servants later that month. "Evelyn Brent will hire no servants who have worked for other motion picture people. The star used to favor credentials of this sort, but has changed her policy because of her dislike for gossip. 'I'm tired of having my friends talked about [and no doubt herself] by their ex-servants,' declares the actress. 'Hereafter, I'll stick to the help who know nothing of motion pictures or their people.'"[67]

The mid–1930s were tough years for Brent as they were for many Americans. She went bankrupt, and her film career stalled. Her career woes got worse as the decade went on. Surprisingly, Brent claimed she was the happiest she'd ever been.

# Finished

*I really blame no one but myself.*[1]

In the winter of 1935, a columnist labeled Brent as finished. "Evelyn Brent, who was once director Josef von Sternberg's Dietrich, is still alluring, still knows as much about acting as she ever did; yet someone tapped her on the shoulder and said, 'You're all washed up.'"[2]

Brent, who had lost her fortune by this time, gave an interesting interview in March 1935 which suggested misfortune had given her a different perspective on materialism. "Lavish, expensive Hollywood parties came in for a panning from Evelyn Brent yesterday at the Radio Studio where she is working in the new Wheeler and Woolsey opus. Miss Brent pointed out that she has been up and down the ladder and that when she was up she gave many big blowouts. They never brought her anything but headaches, she opines. Since she has worked as a free-lance actress she has come in contact with a great many down-and-outers. If she had her way she would take all this party money and put it into a fund to give three square meals a day to those less fortunate."[3]

A few weeks later, the Internal Revenue Service again placed a lien on Brent and estranged husband Harry Edwards in the amount of $92. It could have been worse. Ruth Chatterton owed $11,064, and husband George Brent owed the IRS $11,613. Still, it was yet another public embarrassment.[4]

In a 1935 interview, Brent detailed the possessions she had lost. "Three years ago, I had a wardrobe containing, among other things, twenty evening gowns which I had never worn. Each one of them cost a minimum of $350. In the past two years, by actual memoranda, I have spent exactly $125 on my clothes, including everything. I used to travel, when I was a star, with five trunks and as many as hat and shoe trunks. On the road I used one suitcase and my things rattled around in that. I kept my jewels in a vault at the bank. Among other things was a diamond necklace I bought myself as a pat on the back gift for the opening of *Interference*, my first talkie. And now ... here on my person, you behold every piece of jewelry I possess—signet ring, wrist watch, bracelet with good luck charms." Surprisingly, she seemed to have no bitterness and even seemed grateful. "I wasn't happy then. I am happy now.... I get far more kick now out of affording one new pair of slacks than I ever got out of all the furs and gowns and lingerie I didn't need and didn't even know I had."[5]

Brent held her tongue when asked about blame. "Bad management killed me. Bad management of all of my affairs, both personal and professional. My own naiveté completed the slaughter. I will name no names. I have no desire to hurt anyone. It's no fun, being hurt."[6]

However, when you know the real story you quickly realize that Harry Edwards' mismanagement completely blindsided her. "I never handled my own money. I never checked my own accounts. At the first of each month I was told that fifteen or twenty checks were necessary. I scrawled my name on the checks and let it go at that, never asking what they were for; believing, of course, that they were being used to pay household bills, dressmakers, dentists, insurance premiums, and so on. I'd lost all contact with reality. Most of us do, until reality up and smacks us in the face. Which is just what happened to me. One night, as I was leaving my hotel, I was served with a summons. I called my lawyer, who explained that I was being served for non-payment of a bill. It never occurred to me that non-payment of a bill was possible. Hadn't I paid bills, thousands of dollars worth of them, with weekly checks of three and four thousand dollars for years? That opened my eyes. I began to dig into things. I found that I was thousands of dollars in debt. I found that scarcely any of my bills had been paid for months. I owed everyone—and never dreamed that I owed a cent.... It took about a year to make me realize that I was a fallen star."[7] According to Brent, she met with her creditors and told them she planned to go on a vaudeville tour in order to pay them back. She warned them, however, that if any of them sued her she'd immediately file for bankruptcy. Someone did—and she did.

When Brent and Fox returned to Los Angeles in 1935, Brent took an apartment at the Chateau Marmont. She knew, however, that she'd have to live frugally. "When I arrived ... I found that a huge apartment had been taken for me.... I took one look, went to the management and said, 'Look here, I don't want the royal suite. I want a place so big, just big enough for me and my bag!' I got it.'" Brent awkwardly added, "I definitely separated from my husband."[8]

As for her career, Brent hired a female agent to find employment in films. She also had dreams for the future. "If ever I do really come back, I'll buy, first of all, a home of my own. And pay for it. A small place, a cottage. I'll have my own things and my books, and I'll have my friends around me who were my real friends before I was a star, while I was a star, and now that I am an ex-star. I'm happy. I know where I am. I was living in a fever then. I am normal again. I lived in the ether and fell out of it. Now I live on earth and I find it very good."[9]

Brent's role in *Home on the Range* (1935) was small and attracted little attention. In fact, by 1935 Evelyn was relegated to minuscule roles. Bill Daniels wrote about her in his syndicated column: "No. Evelyn Brent has not retired from pictures. To the contrary, she's busily staging a comeback. Right now, she and Ralph Graves are making a series of railroad films for one of the smaller companies. And Evelyn did a part with Wheeler and Woolsey in [*The*] *Nitwits*. She looks swell, too, having put on some needed pounds."[10] By the time the film opened, her part had become negligible. According to *Variety*, "Evelyn Brent is almost lost in a brief bit."[11]

*"I'm not afraid of anything anymore."*[12]

Brent reflected on her life in an April 1935 interview. Living in a

*Evelyn upon her return to Hollywood following her vaudeville tour.*

three-room apartment, she gave a candid interview to the man who may have sent her career into a free-fall, columnist Dan Thomas. It was a little more than six years since he'd printed the little blurb about Brent and Herzog being "inseparable." Brent's life had changed immeasurably in that time. As they chain-smoked[13] that day, Thomas recalled that Brent had lived in a 16-room mansion just a few years before. According to Evelyn, adjusting to apartment living was easy. "I wouldn't have another big house if you gave it to me.... I never did like them, was scared to death that someone would break in. But I was told that was the thing to do."

Although she didn't say it, it seemed clear that Harry Edwards was the one who'd wanted the mansion. "I'm through. I like apartments, always have, and am going to live like this from now in [sic]." Although she didn't seem terribly concerned about making a comeback, she did remind Thomas that she'd been written off before. "I'll come back some day if I'm lucky enough to get in the right picture.... I was as dead as they come once before. Then I made *Underworld* and for two years I was kept jumping around like a frog. Maybe I won't get another break like that. If not, I always can go back on the road. I did pretty well there last year."[14]

In the summer of 1935, *Symphony of Living* was released. *Variety* liked the movie but not Brent. "Evelyn Brent is badly miscast as the ungracious mother."[15] While doing publicity for *Symphony of Living*, an optimistic Brent talked about how her vaudeville tour helped her acting. "It seems to me ... that remaining continuously in Los Angeles will tend to give one a provincial attitude that is likely to be reflected in one's work. Getting about gives me an opportunity to learn what other people in the world are doing and thinking, and I am sure it helps me in my screen work."[16]

Brent told a reporter that summer that she was as happy as she had ever been despite losing just about everything. "Evelyn Brent is no longer a film star in Hollywood. She is no longer rich. Instead of two elaborate homes, one at the beach and one in town, she has now only an apartment in one of the better apartment hotels. Instead of having her name at the top of movie casts, she is content to see it somewhere in the list. She no longer spends days and weeks of leisure basking in the sun on the beach and worrying over the thousand and one details of a movie star's life—including the money that movie starring brings."

According to Brent, the money and trappings were burdens. "Having a lot of money was really grief—I've never given that *a snap of the fingers* for money itself, even when I had it. This may sound sappy, I know, but the only reason I miss having more money now is that I know people who could use some. Before I could always help them out."[17]

Brent's financial woes continued. On November 12, 1935, she was ordered to pay two former household employees. The amount she owed was $724.39, plus $134.86 interest. The newspaper account pointed out that husband Harry "was eliminated from the suit as co-defendant when it was shown that he had gone through bankruptcy since the alleged obligations were incurred."[18] Maid Georgiaetta Johnson claimed she worked for Brent from July 1, 1932, to February 9, 1933, and received only $22. Laundress Edna Winder received $100 back pay for her claim.[19]

Around this time, one of Brent's worst films, *Speed Limited*, was released. This one, which starred silent star Ralph Graves, was so bad it fortunately had little distribution. Surprisingly, the plan had been for this to be the first of a series of train movies with Brent and Graves.

By January 1936 Brent was expressing regrets about career decisions. "Four years ago Evelyn Brent belonged to the first flight of stars.... Her salary was $4,250 a week. Her luxury home in Beverly Hills was the nightly rendezvous of ... 'famous friends.' Steely-eyed studio executives trembled at the sound of her voice lest she expressed displeasure over a story or a director. Today Evelyn Brent is grateful for the opportunity of a part in a 'quickie' which lasts for a quarter of an hour on the screen, and is merely included to pad out the programs at second and third run theaters. Her money has gone. Debts have almost overwhelmed her. The 'famous friends' still mill around the house—but someone else occupies it now."[20] What happened? According to Brent, it was her fault. "Evelyn Brent blames her eclipse on the mistake of severing her connection with Paramount when they wanted her to accept a salary 'cut.' She was getting $2,500 a week from them. The wave of economy that swept the studios following the Wall Street crash gave certain smaller concerns the chance of grabbing disgruntled stars. Evelyn Brent was advised to fall for the bait rather than endure the salary 'cut' which Paramount suggested. She went to another company at $3,000 a week, and subsequently succumbed to yet a third offer, which carried $4,250. Alas, the time when the studio paying her the $4,250 found drastic economies necessary, Evelyn Brent, acting on the instructions of her paid advisors, refused to accept the cut. But the studio was adamant, and she found herself jobless. Since then nothing has gone right."

Writers seemed to enjoy reminding readers how far Brent had fallen. "'In the old days of stardom I lived a life of mad excitement. I worked like a dog. I paid no attention to anything else. And thereby I signed my own death warrant,' Miss Brent declared. Thus, did Evelyn Brent confess what it felt like to crash from the peaks of stardom to the abyss of obscurity."

Brent continued to work when she could find roles. In September 1936 she appeared in the strangely titled *It Couldn't Have Happened—But It Did*. The *Variety* critic wrote, "Many customers may add the interrogation, 'Why?' unless they copped a bank night prize.... The biggest mystery about this film is how it could have been done so poorly." In a refrain that was becoming commonplace, the reviewer also wondered why Brent bothered: "Evelyn Brent does as well as could be expected a colorless character."[21]

In the fall of 1936, Brent made a brief appearance in Republic's mediocre film *The President's Mystery*. *Variety* gave her effort faint praise. "Evelyn Brent, as the attorney's wife, does well enough with a disagreeable role that's hardly more than a bit."[22] Norbert Lusk also commented on Brent's appearance: "It is pleasant to record the excellent impression achieved by Evelyn Brent in one of her all too infrequent appearances."[23] The film was based on a series of stories published in *Liberty Magazine* "presumably 'inspired' by President Franklin D. Roosevelt. The stories were actually a sales gimmick to push the faltering weekly."[24] Believe it or not, novelist Nathanael West of *The Day of the Locust* fame was one of the co-writers. Tom Dardis described the movie as "woodenly earnest from beginning to end; there is simply no life in it, and it failed for the same reasons that so much of the 'socially conscious' fiction of the thirties failed just as badly; there is a complete lack of entertainment value."[25]

Brent's last film of 1936 was another Western, *Song of the Trail*. According to *Variety*, "Evelyn Brent and Kermit Maynard share the billing in this formula Western but that's about all they share, for there's no glory to split. ... Miss Brent ... tries hard in a bad spot."[26] Publicists tried to drum up interest by printing a story that claimed Maynard saved Brent's life. According to the report, a runaway steer threatened to trample Brent. "Maynard, who was nearby on his horse, raced to its side, caught the animal by its horns and brought the beast to the ground, saving the heroine."[27]

Old boyfriend Joel McCrea's career was taking off. He'd also married the beautiful Frances Dee in October 1933. Still, he'd never forgotten Betty. "I went out to visit ... the Country Home, and I asked the guy who was running it, 'Where is Evelyn Brent?' And he said that she was on relief, but she and another actress would rather not come into the home, but they had a little apartment in Westwood. That was around 1936. I was at Goldwyn at that time, doing pictures with Wyler, and so I called her. And she said, 'Joey, it's good to hear from you.' I said, 'When can I see you?' She said, 'You can't see me anymore. I don't look like I did when you were crazy about me, Joey.' I said, 'Well, maybe I don't either.' She said, 'Oh, yes. I saw you the other night and you were excellent.' I said, 'Well, it's never changed, I think the world of you. I think both Coop and I blew it when we didn't do better. But have you got everything you need?' And she said, 'Well, not quite. The girl I'm with and I would like to get a little puppy dog.' And so I sent her some money, and then I sent her some again. So that was the end. Then she started going with a fellow named Harry Fox or something, somebody who'd been an ex-vaudevillian. And she said, 'We know that's show business and we've done the tough part and, Joey, I'd rather you remembered me the way we were.'"[28] McCrea concluded that Harry Edwards had ruined Brent after she'd financially supported him.

The actress with whom Brent was living is unknown. Meanwhile, Dorothy Herzog's third—and last—novel, *Undercover Woman*, was published in 1937. The best-written of the three, it featured a tough female heroine named Merle who worked undercover for a New York district attorney. This novel, unlike the previous two, did not have a dedication.[29]

*"Gloria Stuart is now living in an Italian-type house formerly occupied by Anita Louise, Evelyn Brent and Virginia Wertheimer."*[30]

By 1937, Brent and Louise Brooks had something in common. They were both former stars who were frantic for a paycheck. Both ended up being cast in *King of Gamblers*. According to Brooks, director Robert Florey "specialized in giving jobs to destitute and sufficiently grateful actresses."[31] Indeed, columnist Lloyd Pantages of the *Los Angeles Examiner* announced, "Today's boy scout award goes to Robert Florey [for casting] all the ex-movie stars he could get his hands on."[32] The cast included Lloyd Nolan, Claire Trevor, and Buster Crabbe. More than ten years had passed since Brent and Brooks appeared in *Love 'Em and Leave 'Em*. "After saying hello, no further words were spoken between us," Louise recalled. "There was nothing to say.... When Evelyn's scene was finished we went to the still picture gallery where we were photographed [with] Bob Florey. It took no imagination to guess the caption that would appear under the photograph.'"[33] Indeed, newspapers ran stories discussing the comebacks of the two former stars. One newspaper put the roles in perspective: "[T]he two stars ... were handed, not an entire script to learn, but just a few lines of dialogue apiece."[34] Evelyn pleaded her case. "I'm not making what is termed a comeback. I dislike the word. I haven't been away. I've been here all the time just fooling around and not making any particular attempt to get work. My mind is made up now and I'm going to carve a new niche for myself in films. I'll play any kind of a role offered, bad woman, good woman, young woman, old woman. I'm a bad girl in *King of Gamblers*, and I enjoyed playing the character."[35]

Brooks played the role of Lloyd Nolan's fiancée, but her part was completely cut from the finished product. *Variety* seemed surprised to see Brent in the film. "Other roles are minor, even Evelyn Brent having only a bit part."[36] The *Los Angeles Times* ignored Brent's part but found Lloyd Nolan "very sincere" and Akim Tamiroff "stealthily fascinating."[37] Norbert Lusk reported that New York critics were enthusiastic about Brent. "[I]t is gratifying to report that Evelyn Brent, in a deplorably brief role, is singled out by some of the critics for her eloquent portrait of a woman of the underworld who has seen better days."[38] Ever-loyal Louella O. Parsons pointed out that Brent "is still beautiful, vivacious, a fine actress."[39]

In January 1937, *Hopalong Cassidy Returns* was released. Critics were unimpressed, though Brent stood out. *Film Daily* pointed out, "Evelyn Brent is the villainess, who loves Hopalong. Her role is a large one and she acquits herself in fine style."[40] According to *Vari-*

ety, "Evelyn Brent, as the dance hall operator and boss of the lawless element, gives a stand-out performance although handed an unsympathetic role. Chance to make her part more appealing and a substantial feature of the plot is blithely overlooked."[41] It's the only Hopalong Cassidy film where Hoppy kissed the woman (Brent). First and last. It created such an uproar among the twelve-year-old boys in the crowd that it never happened again in a Hopalong Cassidy picture.

By this time, Brent was being talked about as a has-been. One writer suggested that Brent was no longer successful because "she couldn't change her type.... She had several chances at comebacks in lesser roles in pictures but refused most of them, holding out for the starring parts which she thought were due her. Today she lives quietly in a Hollywood apartment house and when she appears in public is seldom recognized by the fans who besieged her in her heyday."[42]

In February 1937, Brent became a regular in a 12-episode serial, *Jungle Jim*. She'd signed to play Shanghai Lil in the fall of 1936. According to *Variety*, it did little to help her career. "Efforts to shape a comeback for Evelyn Brent are still just as stymied by this bit as before."[43] Although it no doubt provided much-needed funds, Brent was horribly miscast. She played the one-dimensional villain as though she were an underworld gun moll, but it didn't work in a jungle setting.

*The Last Train from Madrid* was released in the summer of 1937. It's a mystery as to why Brent was cast. The part was only slightly bigger than an extra's and brought no mention from critics. It was probably just as well she had only a minuscule part. Graham Greene dubbed it "the worst movie I ever saw."[44]

In the summer it was announced that Evelyn would appear in Universal's *Merry-Go-Round of 1938*. The film was made without Brent and released in late 1937. Still, columnist Read Kendall offered encouraging words for Brent and her career: "Evelyn Brent will be right back on the top rung of the film ladder if good breaks keep coming her way."[45] At the same time, Jimmy Fidler recounted how far she had fallen: "...Evelyn Brent was once a famous star, earning several thousand dollars a week. Suddenly, why no one seems to know, she went down the skids. Today, doing extra work and bits at a few dollars a day, she is having a bitter struggle for existence."[46]

Brent earned a role in *Sudden Bill Dorn*, a Buck Jones Western. According to columnist Harriet Parsons (Louella's daughter), Brent welcomed the job. "Evelyn Brent [is] telling friends she likes her part in *Sudden Bill Dorn* and is getting a kick out of starting all over again in pictures."[47]

"*Evelyn Brent, the Bette Davis of silent pictures, has signed for the Mr. Wong, Detective series at Monogram,*" which stars Boris Karloff."[48]

Brent appeared as a villain in *Mr. Wong, Detective* in 1938. This was part of a series of films based on stories written by Hugh Wiley which appeared in *Collier's Magazine*. It was directed by William Nigh who helmed many Monogram pictures. Years later Brent explained that she watched it on late night television and found it "very funny. Not bad."[49]

Brent was warmly greeted when she worked on the set of *Night Club Scandal*. "It was a touching scene at Paramount the other day when Director Ralph Murphy gave Evelyn Brent that long deserved break—a good part in *City Hall Scandal* [it would be renamed upon its release]. The former star's first scene in the picture was to sing a song called 'No More Tears.' When she finished, the extras applauded loudly—and Betty, belying the lyrics she had just sung, broke into tears."[50] The role called for Brent to drive a car. Since she no longer owned one, she had to relearn how to drive.[51] Unfortunately, when the film came out in late 1937, she was largely ignored by critics, as was the film.

Near the end of 1937, Brent's old friend Robert Florey gave her a role in *Daughter of Shanghai*. It wasn't a big role, and it wasn't an important film by any means, but it was a job. "It was both interesting and sad to see such former bright lights of the silent screen as Evelyn Brent and Mae Busch as two of 'the girls' in the waterfront dive. Though both had dialogue, their roles are of little import."[52] Florey himself ended up in the director's chair by default. According to Florey, "'George Archainbaud was supposed to direct it, but it was switched to me by ["B" unit production chief Harold] Hurley over a weekend and I had but a couple of days to get it ready.' Although the story 'was not one of the best,' the film was completed in about twenty days in October 1937."[53] It was fortunate for Brent that Florey was given the job because he tried to help her when he could, and, in this case, he cast her as the jealous girlfriend of tough guy Charles Bickford. It was a comeback of sorts for silent screen star Anna May Wong, daughter of a Chinatown laundryman. According to Wong, "I like my part in this picture better than any I've had before.... This picture gives Chinese a break—we have sympathetic parts for a change."[54]

On November 23, 1937, Brent appeared on the *Big Town* radio show on KNX with Edward G. Robinson and Claire Trevor.[55] The story concerned fraudulently staged accidents for insurance money.

*"In the exact spot on the RKO Radio lot where her star dressing room stood eleven years ago, Evelyn Brent, a top ranking favorite of silent films, is occupying a new room in a new building and starting a new career as a character actress."*[56]

In 1938, syndicated columnist Harrison Carroll wrote that Brent would play a character role at RKO, her old studio, in *The Law West of Tombstone*. He also noted, "This will be good news to Betty's faithful fans who still write to me asking what has become of her."[57]

Writer Jimmy Fidler ran into Brent on the set. He described her as "a few years ago one of my favorite stars and still one of my favorite people. Directors haven't been calling her very frequently of late but she refuses to be discouraged. I asked her what she is doing in this picture and she shrugged. 'Just a bit—a French music hall singer, but I'm mighty glad to play it—it's a chance to prove that I can still act.' I like the courage with which she has turned her back on all the glamour that surrounded her stardom. And if there is an ounce of fairness in Hollywood, it should have a spot."[58]

Anne Shirley refused a role in the film and was suspended by RKO. Her replacement was Jean Rouverol. "Miss Shirley was quoted to the effect that she did not believe the role suited ... her personality and ability."[59] Shirley probably thought the picture would stink, and she was right. A Los Angeles critic was unimpressed: "The film is ... just one of those run-of-the-mill 'mellers' that are so popular in the South and Middle Western small towns. The preview audience last night got a lot of laughs out of it, mostly in the serious parts."[60]

*Tip-off Girls* was released in 1938, and Brent, per usual, played a villain. It was a small role, but the *Los Angeles Times* noted that it was "nice to see her again."[61] Years later Brent saw it on television and pointed out that *Tip-Off Girls* "was a quickie—cost practically nothing to make.... *Tip-Off Girls* was a silly cops and robbers bit. Everybody chased everybody else.... I made a lot of those."[62]

*Tip-Off Girls*, like her early movies, was about gangsters. In an interview with Frederick C. Othman, she explained that earlier typecasting had not helped her career—nor had her vaudeville tour. "I was typed for criminal parts.... The producers never gave me anything to do, except roles in which I helped glorify the criminal. They were the heroes, instead of the G-men, in those days. About four years ago I left Hollywood for a personal appearance tour, which took me all over the United States in vaudeville. When I returned, I wasn't a star anymore. I stayed away too long. Hollywood was full of new faces, new studios, and new production methods. Furthermore, nobody was making gangster pictures. So I had to take small parts in many pictures. It was a sort of comedown, but I didn't particularly mind. That lasted for a couple of years, and first thing I knew, here was Hollywood making gangster pictures again! The only difference now is that the G-men are the heroes, and the gangsters are the villains. So I seem to be flying high again."[63]

Meanwhile, Harry Edwards completed his Social Security application in February 1938. He listed his address as 2323 St. George in Los Angeles. For his employer, he wrote "Unemployed."

A tantalizing tidbit concerning casting for *Gone with the Wind* appeared in the *Hollywood Citizen News* in January 1939: "Evelyn Brent ... is being tested for the Belle Watling role."[64] Of course, the part went to Ona Munson, and Brent missed out on appearing in one of Hollywood's most famous movies.

On March 1, 1939, the *New York Times* reported that Brent had been cast in a picture titled *The Second Shot*. Other cast members were said to include Abner Biberman and Steffi Duna. Around this time, an article came out explaining that some directors liked to help struggling oldtimers by giving them small roles. "Directors are a sentimental lot, the proof being that few of them will cast a picture without casting a sympathetic eye toward the old-time stars now in the twilight of their careers." This description, unfortunately, fit Brent. "Leo McCarey at RKO always tries to use Evelyn Brent and Herbert Rawlinson."[65] *The Second Shot* was later retitled *Panama Lady*.

Brent offered a unique perspective on the longevity of a star's career when she noticed something interesting on the RKO lot in 1939. "Do you ever think that the men behind the camera are luckier than those in front? Well, Evelyn Brent thinks so. She's working at RKO with four technicians who have kept the same jobs for 10 years. Then, she was a star."[66]

Columnist Robbin Coons tried to boost Brent's popularity: "Today's song of unstinted admiration is dedicated to a little woman who isn't 'important' any more. Unless you were a movie fan eight or nine years ago you won't even recognize her name. It's Evelyn Brent. Remember?" Coons explained that Brent had lost everything but her good humor. "'Bitter?' she laughs. 'Why should I be? I'm happier now than I ever was. I'm not sorry for anything that happened. Once I had things, now I haven't.... Funny ... how little it hurt when the crowds dropped away. It happened as soon as I gave up my house and took a little apartment. I was stunned at first, and then I laughed.... When you have things, you bother about them. Now I don't worry. I have my friends—mostly outside pictures—and I read and practice my wood-carving, and I knit. It's very peaceful, and fun. I'm enjoying life again.'"

Brent told Coons that there was only one experience that hurt her. "There was a little girl—a star now—who always seemed to be my friend. Always came around with the others. One evening in a [Brown] Derby booth next to hers, I overheard someone ask her why she hadn't been around to see me. She said, 'They tell me never to associate with failures—only with successes' ... And that really hurt!'"[67]

While working on *Panama Lady* with Lucille Ball, Brent rehearsed a new vaudeville act with partner Harry Fox. "The entire cast was assembled in the East and rushed to Hollywood, where, in between 'takes,' Miss Brent rehearsed with them."[68] In the fall of 1939, Brent headed back on the road with Fox in a show called *Streets de Paree*. When she appeared in Zanesville, Ohio, at the Liberty Theatre, along with Jack Greenman and Johnny D'Arco, Brent was advertised as "the glamorous gorgeous screen star," and the show was billed as offering "popular prices!"[69] Interestingly, Brent's act was said to include a spoof on her famous roles as an underworld moll. In addition, the bill featured a dance act called The Fredericks, Victor Charles and the International Puppeteers, chorus girls called the Hollywood Models, and music by the Latin Quarter Artists Band. When Brent was asked to described it, she said it was a "kind of miniature musical comedy."[70] Brent was particularly a fan of Greenman and D'Arco, and claimed she still "laughed in the wings" at their on-stage antics."[71]

Believe it or not, one of the promotions for this particular show was a prize awarded for the first person who could *recognize* Evelyn Brent. "Evelyn Brent, glamorous movie star, will appear in person at Roberts [Diamond Store] between the hours of 11 A.M. and 1 P.M. Saturday. The first person who identifies Miss Brent by saying: 'ARE YOU MISS EVELYN BRENT APPEARING ON THE STAGE OF THE LIBERTY THEATRE TODAY?' will be awarded a merchandise prize and two guest tickets by Roberts and Company."[72]

While in Uniontown, Pennsylvania, Brent offered an interesting interview about character actors. "You have to be bad to be good.... This may seem odd to theatergoers, but if you will watch your next picture carefully you will see what I mean. Acting honors on the woman's side will invariably fall to the character actress.... You may hiss the lass who lures Handsome Harold away from the stern path of duty ... but you won't be likely to forget her, and that ... is the secret of a successful career in pictures."[73]

In November, Brent and company were in Burlington, North Carolina, at the Carolina Theater. Amazingly, there were four performances a day—at 1:15 P.M., 3:45 P.M., 7:00 P.M., and 9:30 P.M. Other acts on this bill included Chisholm and Lamps, Gene Fields, and Can-Can dancer Mlle. Cherie. A local reporter interviewed Brent and found her "unexpectedly lovely and youthful as she donned makeup in the small dressing room.... After years as an actress, both on the stage and screen, Brent had all of the poise and self-assurance of a veteran. With only five minutes before curtain-call, she calmly answered questions.... She admits that she fosters nostalgia for the old 'silents,' because making them is more fun and exciting."[74] Still, she chose as her favorite film a sound picture, *The Silver Horde*, "in spite of the fact that the entire cast had to suffer four weeks of frost-bitten fingers and noses in Alaska.... It was during the making of this picture that Miss Brent was closely associated with the late Louis Wolheim, whom she considers not only one of the greatest actors early Hollywood can claim, but also one of her dearest friends."[75]

Brent admitted that the experience of the vaudeville act was a new one for her. "Though this is not Miss Brent's first personal appearance tour, it is the first time she has ever been connected with an 'act.' She says that she thinks the stage has a slight edge over the screen, as there is a much more intimate feeling between actor and audience and that once a picture is completed, it is forgotten while a player never forgets the excitement of the stage, or the parts played on it. The actress has a trouper's genuine love for traveling, and admits that, forgetting the inconveniences of poor dressing accommodations and poorly equipped theaters, she enjoys 'living in a trunk.' The South, she finds, is an ideal place to travel, not only because of its beautiful country, but because of the friendly and gracious people. Though she would not like for the Los Angeles Chamber of Commerce to hear her say it, she says that to her the South has much more beauty to brag of than California, and she would not give anything for having had the opportunity to see North Carolina in autumn."[76] Tellingly, Brent incorrectly informed the reporter that she had been married twice—and divorced twice. Although long separated from Edwards, she would not divorce him for another eight years.

In January 1940—the dead of winter—Brent was still on the road. A Waterloo, Iowa, reporter caught up with her at the Hotel Russell-Lamson beauty parlor. Brent was in Waterloo for a three-night engagement (Friday through Sunday) at the Orpheum Theatre, and the reporter expected Brent's on-screen persona to arrive. "Reporters asked questions intended to bring flashes of the Brent screen temper, a sneer thru an angry haze of cigarette smoke."[77]

However, Brent proved to be a delight, even when a photographer took a less-than-flattering shot of her in the salon's chair. "[T]he real-life Evelyn, a gracious, friendly, good-humor girl, was unperturbed."[78] She good-naturedly answered all the questions, proclaiming she was thrilled to be doing vaudeville, enjoyed Disney cartoons, respected Orson Welles, and had no problem with radio stars going into motion pictures. "I'd rather see people with entertainment backgrounds, stage, radio, or anything, come into the pictures than those with no professional background."[79] The only notes of complaint concerned Florida audiences and the winter weather. "I think it must be that people only go to Florida when they're too old and sour to laugh." Having lived much of her life in California, she was not used to the snow and single digit temperatures in the wintry Midwest. "We got stuck in Illinois snow banks. Had to give up cars and take trains. Not long ago, in one-night stands, I didn't sleep in a bed for four nights. I got very bad-tempered."[80] Brent also revealed that she liked Spencer Tracy, Paul Muni, and Robert Taylor, but criticized Taylor's publicity efforts, saying it "has been so stupid." As for her own career, Brent concluded that she preferred vaudeville over motion picture acting though movies paid much better. "If profits were the same, she would take 'vaudeville any time—all the time.'"[81]

Joining Brent in Iowa was 14-year-old Donald "Small Fry" O'Connor and sister Patsy. Already a veteran vaudeville performer, the dancer-singer had first appeared in a family act.

On March 10, 1940, a listing for a radio show appeared in the *New York Times*. She performed with Francis X. Bushman in the half hour show *Fifth Row Center* on WOR in a play titled "Make Believe."

Near the end of the year, Jimmy Fidler published a strange blurb, claiming that Brent owned a dress shop. "Who said ex-star Evelyn Brent is broke—she's the owner of an exclusive Beverly Hills dress shop."[82] It's difficult to determine if this was a joke or mistake, but it was highly improbable that Brent owned anything, least of all a retail store.

*"Miss Brent has been playing in vaudeville and has been visiting some very obscure towns. One of her shorter tours included a trip through New England in which she made the front pages as being the first film star ever to visit several of the towns."*[83]

Brent returned to Hollywood to make *Forced Landing*, a low-budget quickie released in 1941. The budget was $80,000, and the shoot took 12 days. It was shot on the Fine Arts studio lot and released by Paramount. Producers William H. Pine and William C. Thomas often hired oldtimers such as Brent in order to save money. "Thomas explained that economy is achieved by paying $100 to a good actor who can go straight through a scene instead of hiring some $25 punk who may waste $500 worth of production time."[84]

Director Gordon Wiles trained as an artist and received an Oscar for his sets on *Transatlantic* (1931). He took ten weeks to prepare *Forced Landing* for shooting. A fan of silent filmmaker F. W. Murnau, Wiles had an unusual approach to filming, focusing more on the illusion. "Wiles believes in 'composing' a shot for maximum story value. When sound came in, the illusion artists were kicked out and replaced by architectural designers, he says—men who could construct a room with four walls or three, but who had no eye for cinema dramatics. Four walls were considered better for the mike than one or two; the sound was 'fuller, more solid.' 'Bunk,' says Wiles—and he's out to prove it."[85] Considering it was a definite "B" film, it garnered decent reviews, though Brent was rarely mentioned. The *Los Angeles Times* called it "an effective melodrama of aviation."[86]

In the summer of 1941 *Wide Open Town* was released. Brent had a sizable role in this low-budget Hopalong Cassidy Western and received good notices. According to *Film Daily*, "Evelyn Brent ... doesn't show a single reason why she has been kept from the screen so long."[87] Louella O. Parsons also chimed in: "Betty (Evelyn) Brent, who in her heyday was an important star, is still beautiful. She is now in a Harry Sherman picture. Hollywood should never forget Betty, whose generosity to less fortunate people when she had it, is still remembered."[88]

In 1941 Brent also appeared in *Emergency Landing, Dangerous Lady,* and *Ellery Queen and the Murder Ring.* She also got the very-welcome gig of working in a serial starring Jack Holt, *Holt of the Secret Service.* "[F]or the first time in movie history the star's name is to be used in picture titles." Producer Larry Darmour created the serial for grown-ups rather than kids. "That is why he got Holt and Evelyn Brent to appear in this serial for adults. Holt has an excellent record for not overacting. Darmour argued that if he could get a serial which was both thrilling and logical and never impossible it would be just as entertaining for the grown-up audience as a magazine serial would, and would still delight the youngsters."[89] Holt, who'd previously appeared in the serials *The Broken Coin* and *Liberty,* was paid $5,000 a week. It was a fast-paced production, producing 15 chapters in one month. "Behind this were six months of preparation and a complete script. Darmour demanded that the thrills be 'believable'; he threw out 'tintype characters' and employed Evelyn Brent as the girl, besides other names not identifiable with the usual serials.... James Horne, an old hand at dangling the Sword of Damocles, directed, using 200-odd sets at three studios and Columbia Ranch."[90] Brent was not miscast in this thrilling serial and got to play a hard-boiled character to perfection. Columnist Robbin Coons once again put in a good word for her: "Miss Brent ... isn't bitter about lost stardom or lost fortune.... She's as good now as she ever was, and that was plenty good. Is there a Broadway producer in the house?"[91]

In 1941, Brent appeared with Neil Hamilton in *Dangerous Lady.* The following year saw her in *Westward Ho,* yet another Western. *Film Daily* found her to be a great villain. "The male baddies have nothing on her when it comes to playing mean."[92]

Newspapers were reporting in 1942 that Evelyn had returned to Paramount, the scene of some of her greatest successes. The occasion was to work on *Wrecking Crew.* Louella Parsons wished her well. "Ran into Evelyn Brent on the Para [sic] lot—and she looks wonderful. It was here she made her biggest hit in *Underworld,* and she feels this studio is lucky for her. I hope so for there are few better actresses than Evelyn."[93] According to a newspaper report, Brent received other moral support. "The first day at work her old friends crowded the stage to wish her success."[94]

Brent also made *The Pay Off* in 1942. The most remarkable aspect of that film was that the associate producer was none other than Brent's estranged husband, Harry D. Edwards. By the early 1940s Edwards had gotten back on his feet and was working with Jack Schwarz at Monogram Pictures. In late 1942, Schwarz produced and Edwards associate-produced *The Pay Off,* with Brent appearing in a featured role. This was the last time Brent and Edwards worked together.

In May 1943, syndicated columnist Sheilah Graham reported that Brent was returning to films via Val Lewton's creepy *The Seventh Victim.* According to Graham, Brent had been absent from films for a year due to illness. Graham added that Brent was "one of my favorite actresses in the early gangster flickers."[95] Screenwriter DeWitt Bodeen was eager to meet Brent. "She was most charming, and looked very svelte."[96] *The Seventh Victim* was an atmospheric, disturbing film about devil worship. Doug McClelland wrote that it "remains one of the most absorbing, creative chillers of any day. As an adventure in stylish diabolism, real or unreal, it makes *Rosemary's Baby* look like *Blondie's Blessed Event.*"[97]

In 1944, Brent appeared in a movie with the East Side Kids, *Bowery Champs.* Along with her were Bobby Jordan, Ann Sterling, Ian Keith, and Thelma White. In this one, Brent did some cross-dressing; the film is quite good despite its low-budget pedigree. According to

David Hayes and Brent Walker, "An East Side Kids film that whizzes by, *Bowery Champs* is one of the best of the series."[98]

"At one time Miss Brent had all but decided to quit the cinema game, but the old lure worked,"[99] proclaimed a *Los Angeles Times* article on August 16, 1946, heralding Brent's return to Monogram. A few days later, on August 19, the *New York Times* reported that Brent was returning to films after a three-year "retirement."[100] According to the reports, Brent was to appear in Monogram's *Draw When You're Ready* with Johnny Mack Brown. The title was changed to *Raiders of the South* when it was released. "They were pretty tight schedules, and they didn't waste any money," Brent later said about the Poverty Row studios.

The following month, Harry Fox sued 20th Century–Fox, along with Jean Schwartz, for the way they were depicted in the film *The Dolly Sisters*. Newspapers failed to report the disposition of the case, but it's unlikely Fox was successful. Perhaps the cruelest blow was the quote from Rosy Dolly who laughed about the lawsuit and quipped, "Harry Fox doesn't remember whether he was married to me or Jennie [sic]."[101]

In April 1947, after almost 20 years of marriage, most of them lived apart, Harry Edwards finally filed for divorce from Evelyn Brent. He wanted to marry heiress Jackie Freeman Wertheimer. Previously married to Palm Springs night club owner (and reputed Purple Gang mobster) Al Wertheimer,[102] Jackie was the daughter of Sidney Freeman who owned Duggan Stuart, once the largest legal gambling and book-making company in the world. His brother Spencer, born in Wales and educated in South Africa, was an engineer who made a fortune as one of the promoters of the Irish Sweepstakes, officially known as the Irish Free State Hospital Sweepstakes. Sidney Freeman was described as "the picture book figure of the professionally gambling man—gaudy, adventurous and tough."[103] Jackie, 24, was reportedly worth millions. Harry Edwards wasn't letting this one get away.

Jackie had already had one annulment and one divorce. Brent answered Edwards' complaint with her own. She named Mrs. Wertheimer as co-respondent and asked for $500 a month, along with $1,000 in attorney's fees, claiming that Edwards was living in Los Angeles and Las Vegas with Jackie.[104] In fact, Harry and Jackie had been living together at least since January 1947. A January 16, 1947, Pan Am passenger list showed that the two traveled together from London to New York. On the manifest both listed their address as 8221 Sunset Boulevard in Los Angeles. The address is the site of the legendary Chateau Marmont Hotel and Bungalows in West Hollywood where Brent had also taken an apartment at one time. Harry listed his age as 59 and his occupation as producer. Jackie stated she was 25 and a restaurateur. At the time Jackie was still married to Wertheimer. Her divorce did not become final until March 6, 1947.

The Las Vegas court temporarily gave Brent a stunningly low stipend, nowhere near the $500 a month she'd requested. She was given $8 a day (some reports say $10), and $200 for attorney fees.[105] At the time, the average median family income in 1947 was around $3,000.

By May the divorce was getting nasty. In response to Brent's charges of adultery with Jackie, Edwards accused his wife of living with Harry Fox in Hollywood for the previous three years.[106]

In June 1947 a settlement was reached. Edwards hustled back to Los Angeles to marry Jackie within a day of divorcing Brent. To Brent's no-doubt-considerable relief, Edwards decided he and his new wife would leave the country following the marriage on June 11. "After their wedding today Edwards and his bride plan to live in Cannes, France, where her parents have bought them a fully staffed villa. Edwards also plans to produce films in France."[107] The wedding was held in the Sunset Boulevard apartment of Rena Borzage, exwife of director Frank, with Superior Court Judge Stanley Mosk officiating. Rena also served as matron of honor, and producer Al Christie was Edwards' best man. Jeffrie Gill gave the bride away and also sang "Peg o' My Heart." In addition to the villa on the French Riviera, kindly paid for by the bride's father, the couple also kept an address in New York City, often traveling between the city and their residence in France during the late 1940s and early 1950s.

There are many puzzling aspects to the Brent-Edwards marriage and one of the most baffling is why the divorce did not happen sooner. The marriage was for all intents and purposes over in the early 1930s. Certainly Edwards was not a member of Brent's household for many years. Why didn't Brent divorce him? Although married, he apparently didn't contribute to her financially. Why didn't she ask for alimony? One has to wonder if Edwards had something on her that made Brent reluctant to divorce or sue him for abandonment.

Brent later described Edwards as "a bad one. He was an attractive man and he had good manners. It was a mistake, unfortunately."[108] Harry D. Edwards, actor, director, producer and con man, husband of wealthy women, and spender of fortunes, who once described President Herbert Hoover as "one of America's all-time greats,"[109] died in France in 1969 and is buried in California. When he died, he was still married to Jackie.

In 1947, the same year that she was finally divorced from Edwards, Brent had two films released. *Robin Hood of Monterey* with Gilbert Roland was a real cheapie, with Brent playing the villain. Donna Martell was in the cast, and in 1997 told *Classic Images* about her experience. "We shot it on location ... not too far away in Newhall [California]; and in those days, that was a location!.... It was blistering hot and raining buckets, but it turned out to be loads of fun. Evelyn Brent was a silent screen actress, and she helped me out in some key areas on this picture, offering good advice and other things helpful to my work."[110]

Ten years after this interview, Martell explained that Brent mostly kept to herself. She also related an unusual anecdote. "At one point, I was working and she wasn't, and somehow she got into my room. I'll never forget this as long as I live. I had a brand new bathing suit that I had never even worn. She got into my bathing suit, and she went swimming. I'm not kidding. I thought that was a little much. It wasn't funny. That's something that molds to your own body, I never even had it on. I came in after working all day and saw it hanging on the bathroom door. No explanation. True story. I've never forgotten it, because, you know, I wasn't raised that way."[111]

In August 1948, Louella O. Parsons reported that Harry Fox was writing his life story, calling it *Chasing Rainbows*. Fox planned on pitching the idea to a movie studio. Parsons added that Harry Edwards was still thriving. "I met Evelyn's ex, Harry Edwards, who lives in Cannes in a gorgeous villa. His wife's father is the man who controls the Irish Sweepstakes and is reported to be very rich."[112]

The following month Brent could be seen in a new Charlie Chan film, *The Golden Eye*. It starred Roland Winters and did nothing to help her comeback attempt.

Brent did not work again until 1950. In March of that year, Louella O. Parsons, who seemed to always have a kind word for Brent, reminded readers that Brent was "at one time one of the biggest stars in motion pictures."[113] Parsons reported that Brent was on the comeback trail. "She will have an important role in a religious film based on the life of St. Paul, for Cathedral Films. It is part of a series on the apostles, and is titled *The Second Journey in the Life of St. Paul*." Parsons quoted Brent as saying, "I am just like an old fire horse—I never really got motion pictures out of my blood." Parsons tersely added, "She is married to Harry Fox and is happy with him."

Although that role never came to fruition, in May 1950 Brent was added to the cast of

*Again ... Pioneers*, a Protestant Film Commission production focusing on migrant workers. The film was released on November 6 with special showings in approximately 100 cities in the United States and Canada. The media largely ignored the film and Brent.

Brent summed up her film career in her later years: "I think I really enjoyed being a movie star. Not always in reality, but now in memory, yes, because I only remember the good times. That's why I stuck at it so long. I did so many that I can't remember them all. I made far too many, really. But I do wish I'd had the luck to do more like the three I made for von Sternberg. If I'm remembered for any movie, it'll be for the ones I did for him."[114]

# A Cult Figure

*I only remember the good times.[1]*

Not much was heard from Brent in the 1950s. A newspaper blurb reported that she was living in Westwood Village in 1953.[2] Presumably she was living with Harry Fox at this time, though the newspaper did not mention him. Fox finally gave up show business for a steady job as a photo lab technician at Douglas Aircraft and retired in 1956 due to illness.

In 1957 the syndicated Hollywood column "Chatterbox" reported in the *Dallas Morning News* that Evelyn was considering film roles again—but this time not as a leading lady. "Oldtime screen heartthrob Evelyn Brent plans a comeback in character roles."[3]

It simply never happened. Fox died on July 20, 1959, at the age of 76. He had been living in the Motion Picture Country Home for some time. According to a July 25, 1959, newspaper columnist, Brent was a constant visitor. "Every day during the two years he was there, she showed up around 1:30 P.M. and stayed until he went to sleep at night. I always liked that gal and what a fine actress."[4] Brent later said the marriage had been good. "When he died, I said, 'I had a good one, now let it go.' Ways of life change. But Harry was the best one."[5] According to friend Dick Balduzzi, who knew Brent in the last years of her life, "Harry Fox, she really loved. That was a pretty good romance."[6]

Following Fox's death, Brent appeared in a 1960 *Wagon Train* episode as well as in a *Walt Disney Presents* TV movie in that same year (*Elfego Baca*). Later that year she showed up on the set of *Harrigan and Son* to wish Pat O'Brien a happy 60th birthday. It also marked the 40th anniversary of his start in show business. Brent was referred to as a "former film star."[7]

Following her retirement, Brent complained about the lack of good will on the sets, especially compared to what she remembered from the old days. "I've been on sets of some of those TV things, and the principals, the regulars, seem not to want to be bothered ... they're like in a class by themselves. Almost to the point of rudeness.... During the last few things I did, there was a lack of warmth, a lack of working together.... Now, in those days, when they'd have a scene that called for a lot of people, they would get together all the old-timers who weren't doing so well and get 'em in to work. And you'd knock yourself out being nice to them. I don't think that exists any more."[8] According to John Kobal, Brent was still listed as being available for small acting roles up till the day she died.

In late 1960, Brent took a position at Thelma White's agency. Columnist Mike Connolly reported that Brent was employed as a "television assistant."[9] According to actor Dick Balduzzi, who later became a client of the agency, White hired Brent to help her out financially. Brent's money was long gone, much of it spent on Harry Fox's medical care over the years, and White was known to be soft-hearted and generous.

Brent phoned old pal Louella O. Parsons in March 1961 to say that she was no longer an agent and was returning to acting.[10] However, there was no news to report on Brent's acting career until July 1963 when it was announced that she would appear in an episode of *Day in Court.* According to Fred H. Russell's blurb, other stars slated for the show included Patsy Kelly, Johnny Mack Brown, Gertrude Michael, Iris Adrian, Viola Dana, and Isabel Jewell.[11] Brent appeared as a cleaning woman who makes a claim for reward money. The premise of the ABC daytime show was ahead of its time. Real attorneys argued their cases in front of a real judge while witnesses and defendants were portrayed by actors. *Day in Court* was Brent's final television appearance.

Poor health plagued Brent in her final years. She was hospitalized at the Motion Picture Country Hospital in January 1965. Columnist Mike Connolly referred to her as "one of Hollywood's greats and also one of the founders of the Motion Picture Country Hospital."[12] Many stars ended up living their final years in the neighboring Motion Picture Country Home, a kind of retirement center. John Barbour described it in the late 1970s: "The freeway flashes by only a hundred yards away, but it is unnoticed in the tranquil cloisters of this precious 41 acres with their red geraniums, purple jacaranda, gracious trees and flowing gardens.... This is the Motion Picture Country Home, for the retired of the industry, from cartoonists to hair dressers, from accountants to stagehands, from wranglers to writers, and an occasional star."[13] In February, Louella O. Parsons wrote that Brent was still hospitalized, and "it will make her very happy to hear from her old friends."[14]

In January 1969, Brent, out of the public eye for many years, appeared on Richard Lamparski's radio program sounding down-to-earth, happy, and remarkably at peace. Though she sometimes confused her movie roles and titles, she spoke clearly with strong diction and was upbeat and positive about her career and the people with whom she'd worked.

"I had a wonderful time!" she insisted. "I loved every minute of it." Lamparski asked why she no longer socialized much. "I would much rather do something a little more useful than go to parties. I'd rather go out to the hospitals and visit people which I do quite a lot." She mentioned that she visited the Motion Picture Home. "A lot of old-timers out there. Some of them have cottages, and they can get around. And some of them can't. And I go out there quite often."[15]

Brent was also asked if she had lived extravagantly. "Sure," she replied. "Much to my chagrin now.... I had a nice house, you know. Not a showplace by any matter or means, but it was comfortable. It had a swimming pool, and it was fun. I liked Cadillacs so I always had a Cadillac.... Once I had two. I had a chauffeur, see, because when you worked then you worked very late at night.[16] You'd come home at four and five in the morning, and you were tired. And I just didn't believe in driving when I was that tired.... And then I had an open car that I used to go to the beach because I had a little house at Malibu, too. And I used to go down there and stay a lot ... I had fun."[17]

When asked if she missed the glamorous life, Brent found the question ridiculous. "Look, I'm older now, you know, and I think the same sort of thing probably wouldn't appeal to me so much now." Still, she had no regrets. "There wasn't one bit of it that I didn't love."[18] Brent further explained there were few feuds. "There was no envy. There was no 'Oh, I should have had that part.' ... Everybody liked everybody else.... Nobody hated somebody because they got a good part."

After talking to Brent for a little more than twenty minutes, Lamparski commented on the fact that she was "one of the least theatrical actresses I've ever met. And your image was anything but that." He concluded by commenting that she "looked great. That bone structure they gave you really held on."[19]

Lamparski included Brent's story in the 1970 edition of his *Whatever Became Of...?* book series. A renewed interest in old Hollywood had made her popular again. "Lately, a cult of film buffs has enshrined her in a niche rivaling some of the superstars of her era. Widowed since 1959, Evelyn shares a small apartment in Westwood Village, California, with her friend of forty years, Dorothy Herzog. Here she receives loyal fans from everywhere, many born well after her best films were made. Philosophical over the fact that her fortune is gone (she lives on a very small income) and that her canonization by fans has come too late, she replied recently to one fan, thanking him for his compliment and interest: '...but where were all you people when I needed you?'"[20]

It appears that at some time Dorothy Herzog reconnected with Brent. If she did, then Herzog was out of the picture by the late 1960s.[21] A new friend, another Dorothy, became Brent's roommate until the end of her life. Dorothy Konrad, born Dorothy Rita Konkowski in Chicago in 1912, was a character actress and acting teacher who encouraged Brent to move into her West Hollywood apartment around 1969 or 1970 and took care of her for the rest of Brent's life.

They met when Brent was at Thelma White's talent agency. Konrad was one of White's clients. Like Herzog, Konrad never married. She had previously taken care of her invalid mother for years in Illinois. A graduate of Rosary College, she had taught at Chicago's Tuley High School and DePaul University. Although she was never officially adopted by Konrad, Grace Siwek[22] went to live with her in her Chicago home when she was nine and considered Konrad her mother. In fact, when Konrad moved to California following the death of her mother in the late 1950s, she requested that Grace accompany her. However, by this time Grace was engaged and chose to stay in Illinois.

According to Siwek, her mother befriended Brent. "Evelyn had no money. She was completely broke. So my mother more or less supported her because she did like her a lot." Dick Balduzzi concurred: "[Dorothy] told me that she rescued a famous person who was down and out. Evelyn was completely broke and really looked terrible. She hadn't been eating or anything. Dorothy. ... brought her back to health."[23] According to Balduzzi, "They did a lot of things together. They went to the theater. They went to films. They went to different functions. Dorothy was very instrumental in getting her back to her life."

Konrad moved Brent into her own apartment in a building just off Santa Monica Boulevard. The front yard had a wrought iron fence. "You had to go up the stairs to go into their apartment," Siwek explained, "and it was a really nice apartment. You felt when you walked in that you were welcomed. Just about everything in there was my mother's, of course, because [Brent] had nothing. The only thing she had was her clothes and a few odds and ends." Siwek did recall one piece of furniture that Brent still owned. "Evelyn did have a dresser. I thought it was not that nice, but everybody else seemed to think it was beautiful. Hand-made, you know, and she had it all fixed up with carvings on—paintings on it. You know, like flowers on it and things like that."

Dorothy Konrad had traveled the world, and her interior included many of her finds, including a round metal table from Egypt that sat in the front room. The walls were covered with photographs and art, and they also had a bookcase that covered one wall and displayed many of their mementos (including signed photographs of stars such as Lucille Ball and Spencer Tracy). Siwek also remembered seeing a photograph of Brent from one of her films. In addition, the couple had numerous photo scrapbooks that held additional photos of fellow stars as well as themselves.

Siwek remembered her mother saying, "It's such a shame that she would end up like this." At the time, Brent was unable to work. "I think that she couldn't work, to tell you the truth. Because when I met her, she was an elderly, feeble woman. You know, she was quite a small woman, and so she really didn't have all that kind of strength."

An intimate picture of Brent's final years is provided by Siwek. According to her, Brent

*Evelyn surrounded by Dorothy Konrad's relatives (circa early 1970s) (courtesy Grace Siwek).*

and Konrad had a good life together. "When I talked to her, she was just an ordinary lady who was very nice and very sweet. My mother always got along with her. They had good times, and as far as I know, they never argued about anything. They had a comfortable life. She was very pleased about it. And when my mother would go some place she would take Evelyn with her." The two often attended services at the Catholic Church near them. "I know she went to church with my mother, and I know that they were both very religious people." Interestingly, in 1930 Brent discussed her religious beliefs. "When I was a kid I was a Catholic, and I believed everything I was taught, even that a girl might go to Hell if she isn't careful. Now I just don't know what I believe. I don't know what it's all about, but—you know—a person never gets over childhood training. And that's why, whenever I die, I'm going to call for a priest."[24]

Brent's life with Konrad was simple but satisfying. The apartment was a two-bedroom, two-bath residence, and a cleaning lady came in occasionally. They did their own cooking. According to Siwek, "She was happy. She lived a good life. They got up in the morning. They had their robes on, and they sat around, talked, and ate their little breakfast, and then they would get dressed up in lounging clothes. Like a house dress or something like that. They didn't wear makeup until they went out. If they went out, they would fix themselves up."

One of the highlights for Evelyn and Dorothy was when Dorothy's brother Richard visited California once a year or so. "He'd take the ladies out and treat them like they were royalty. He would give them money, and he would take them to nice places. And he would make them feel very special. He did a lot for them. He paid some of their bills off—my mother was making money, but it was always nice when her brother came out there because he would add a little more money to their little pot."

In 1972 Grace and her children vacationed in California and met Brent. "She was a very, very nice woman. She was very down to earth, and she was really good with my kids which surprised me because my kids were a little rowdy. We were at the beach [Redondo Beach] and then, of course, Disneyland. Well, they were running their legs off, and those two old ladies [Brent and Konrad] were kind of following along. She was very patient with kids. I don't remember how old she was at the time, but she was very patient, never got cross. She was very good with them." A couple of times one of Siwek's children called Brent "Grandma." Thinking of Brent's many roles as tough ladies, we immediately imagined her putting her hand on her hip, leaning forward, narrowing her eyes, and sneering at the little guy. "Listen, kid, I'm no grandma. *See?*" But that's not what happened. "She was pleasant. She didn't make any kind of remark. It was just A-OK with her."

Siwek also recalled her mother telling her about how Brent drank a little. "When she got older she liked to have a drink or two. So one time she was talking to her doctor, and she said something about her drinking. And he said, 'A shot a night will help you.' So every night she took a shot whether she needed it or not. And that was her excuse."[25]

Although Brent didn't talk much about her past career, she sometimes reminisced about her leading men and spoke in general terms about many affairs. "She said that she loved every one of her leading men. She said she fell in love with each and every one of them. She loved them all. She loved her men. That much I do know because she would always brag about them." Siwek recalled words of wisdom Brent told her mother about her love life: "Dorothy, every time you see a big man, you know he's going to have a little penis. And I know. I've seen them all. Believe me, I know."

Interestingly, Siwek was not aware of anyone calling Brent by her nickname of Betty. According to her, she and her mother called her Evelyn or Ev. Dick Balduzzi said the same thing.

John Kobal, in contrast to Siwek's observations, depicted Brent as a sad, disillusioned woman in her last years. He seemed surprised to find that the once beautiful actress had aged. "This woman, strangely awkward in her stance, like someone who had never been comfortable with her body, as if she were afraid it might give her away, neat but prim in her plain red-checkered dress, would have looked more natural standing in a farmhouse doorway out of Depression photos.... I might have thought this was the wrong door, and she the wrong person, a next-door neighbor, a friend looking after the house, anyone but the woman I'd sought out, the Garboesque silent film beauty Evelyn Brent."[26] Kobal described the house she shared with Dorothy and their cats[27] as spotless but bare and small. "All these decades later," Kobal claimed, "she had not one picture of herself from any of the films or any of the portrait sittings with the masters. Not one. And she didn't want any."[28]

Wesley Musick's memories coincided more with Siwek's than Kobal's. He and his family visited Dorothy Konrad in the late 1960s and were introduced to Brent. At some point Musick learned that Brent had been a silent film star. "I think it was Dorothy that mentioned the fact that Evelyn was a movie star in her own right in her day. And I said, 'Oh really?' And she said, 'Yeah, in the silent movies.' And I thought, wow, that's really something because she was such a little bitty thing. She was still a pretty little thing, if you ask me. Even for her age."[29]

Musick described their apartment as small but very neat. He was shown a scrapbook filled with photos of Brent during her acting career. "I was just totally swept away on how beautiful she was as a young actress." Someone mentioned that Brent also had a star on Hollywood Boulevard. Musick was keen to see it. "When we went to Hollywood Boulevard, she [Evelyn] didn't rave about it. I got the impression that she was sort of embarrassed that I was making a big deal out of it. She didn't say much, [though] she smiled and seemed to be happy about it. I remember some guy trying to pick up on me or something. They [Evelyn and Dorothy] were laughing at me. 'Well, *that's* Hollywood.'"[30]

Musick also recalled seeing a signed photo of Karl Malden in the apartment. Musick asked Dorothy about it. "She said, 'Oh yeah, he's a real good friend of ours.'" Malden wasn't the only star the two knew. "When we were driving around I remember Dorothy honked the horn, and there was Richard Widmark. I was just blown away. 'Wow—you know him?' 'Yeah, we know him, too.'"

Indeed, Mona and Karl Malden were close friends. According to Mrs. Malden,

*Evelyn Brent's Hollywood star is located at 6548 Hollywood Boulevard.*

Brent "was a sweet, kind, unassuming person. You would never guess she was a well known actress. We had many dinners together. Evelyn gave me an exquisite beaded purse that I think Gary Cooper had given her."[31]

Brent, according to Musick, was modest about her career. Like Siwek, Konrad, and Balduzzi, he also called her Evelyn. "I never called her anything but Evelyn. She never impressed upon us—Dorothy never did, either—that she should be called anything else. It wasn't like 'She's a movie star. She should be treated like royalty.' Never, never got that impression."

Brent harbored no sour feelings about what had happened to her. "Not at all. She was a sweet lady. I never caught any bitterness at all. I didn't see any sadness, any bitterness. She was very pleasant to us. I got no impression at all that she was a sad person."

Musick was so struck by meeting Brent that upon arrival back home he sought out a copy of *The Last Command* after Dorothy or Evelyn mentioned he might like it. "I remember coming home after that and renting one of the silent movies that she was in just to see her. She was just an angel to me. And in the movie, she didn't disappoint me. I would have fell in love with her in a minute. I thought, you know what, this is fun. It was actually a good movie. I was thrilled. I never thought I'd enjoy a silent movie. I'd never seen one before that."

Far from being a recluse after meeting Konrad, Brent became more social and outgoing. She saw friends from Hollywood such as Thelma White and Viola Dana, a childhood friend. She also became reacquainted with Lucille Ball, who was a friend of Dorothy Konrad's. According to Balduzzi, Brent and Konrad often ate dinner at his house and also went to his annual Christmas party. "She was very good friends with us. She'd come to our house for dinner. Evelyn was very happy in those days. She'd visit us a lot. She enjoyed my cooking because I'm an Italian chef. I'm a good cook, and she loved coming over and having Italian food." He also insisted that she harbored no bitterness. "She was a lovely, lovely lady and had class. Even though she was down in the doldrums she still had class." Balduzzi also said that Brent told him her favorite movie was *Underworld*. As for von Sternberg, "She said he was a strict, disciplined guy, but she enjoyed working for him."

Several fans have reported that they simply showed up at her door and knocked—both at her apartment and when she lived at the Motion Picture Home—and she graciously greeted them. She was also, as Lamparski described, popular with film buffs who held parties and film showings in her honor. Writer Clive Hirschhorn described one event: "I met Evelyn Brent once—in 1974. It was at an afternoon party being given in her honor in a home in Hollywood. It was a strange occasion. People were literally sitting at her feet while she held court—with both wrists bandaged [no explanation was given]. The food on display was more appropriate to a kiddie's party (Jell-O, soft drinks, assorted candy, cupcakes, etc). The guests included Tony Dexter (who I think once played Valentino),[32] and a Miss Lux Girl of 1943. I also met an avid Valentino collector, whose latest proud purchase was the set of gates at Valentino's ranch. And I remember a Garland collector who offered to make copies for me of most of her TV shows. What I actually said to Miss Brent when introduced, or what she said to me, remains lost in the mists of time."[33]

Writer David Chierichetti met Brent at one of Marvin Braum's monthly parties. According to Chierichetti, Brent served as an unofficial hostess, helping to pass out refreshments. She was not overly friendly or talkative. "She was just an old woman at that time. Not too friendly or anything, so people didn't pay much attention to her. I don't think people knew that much about her. She was there, and she was pouring the coffee or whatever they were serving, but she wasn't talking much about herself."

Chierichetti worked up his nerve to ask her about Gary Cooper. "I asked her what she remembered about Gary Cooper, and she said, "Mmmm ... A great many things."[34] Chierichetti, who was working on an Edith Head biography at the time, also inquired about Travis Banton. "She said that she didn't remember him very well, but she remembered Edith Head who was Banton's unknown assistant at the time.... She told me she would leave at the end of a long day, and she'd pass by the wardrobe department. She said, 'Poor Edith would still be working.'"

Lou Valentino remembered meeting Brent at a film showing in a private home. "She was simply dressed, little makeup and surprisingly petite.[35] Surprising since she was such a force of nature in her films. She was also soft-spoken and very modest about all the adulation the group (about a dozen local and visiting film buffs) afforded her. She appreciated but didn't understand all the fuss. I can't remember what 16mm film Marvin [Braum] showed but I do remember it was a sunny (what else?) Sunday afternoon in Hollywood. I also remember walking back to my car on a cloud. I loved her."[36]

Writer Anthony Slide also met her at a private screening. He noted that "she seemed very pleasant and jovial, and I was certainly unaware of any bitterness toward Hollywood."[37]

DeWitt Bodeen attended a showing of *The Last Command* at a private home. "Afterwards, she spoke of her acting days, especially as a Paramount player. Her memory was keen, and her views as perceptive as ever."[38]

In 1975 Brent was interviewed by writer Cynthia Lindsay who was researching a book on Boris Karloff. "I had the great pleasure of meeting Miss Brent shortly before she died. She was still an enchanting, humorous, and very beautiful woman."[39] Lindsay also wrote that Brent supplied several stills that were used in the published book *Dear Boris: The Life of William Henry Pratt a.k.a. Boris Karloff.*

Unless she pulled off the best acting job of her career, Brent was a content, down-to-earth, humble woman. Despite losing fame and fortune, she appeared to realize the importance of simple things. Some actresses of her era ended up penniless and bitter, raging at the injustices done to them. Others wound up wealthy but lonely, sad that they'd been forgotten and their beauty gone. Brent, on the other hand, and for whatever reason, found peace and wisdom about what was truly important in life.

After being in and out of the Motion Picture Home, Evelyn Brent finally died at home of heart disease and emphysema shortly before noon on June 4, 1975. According to Dick Balduzzi, Dorothy heard a noise from the bathroom and checked on her. "She heard a thump, like a fall, and she went in there. She was gone." The *Pasadena Star-News* reported that Brent died "in the apartment she shared with her longtime friend, Dorothy Conrad [sic], a character actress."[40] Siwek recalled getting the phone call from her mother. "She was really upset about it."

Siwek suspects Brent's funeral was paid for by Konrad and her brother Richard. Rosary was read for Brent on Friday, June 6, at St. Paul's Catholic Church (10750 Ohio Avenue) in West Los Angeles. The Requiem Mass was celebrated the following morning; this was followed by her burial in San Fernando Mission Cemetery. [41]

Brent's tombstone reads EVELYN BRENT FOX. Inscribed are the years 1901–1975 along with a cross. Harry Fox is buried next to her.[42] According to Grace Siwek, Brent had no will. "She had nothing so there was no need to have a will."

Brent made her last film in the 1950s. She is still a favorite among many fans. What is her reputation among researchers and film buffs? James Card considered Brent, along with Lil Dagover and Louise Brooks, to be "among the greatest actresses during the era of the silent film."[43] Historian and writer Anthony Slide claimed, "She is really a very, very good actress, both in silent and sound films. She is excellent in Paramount's first talkie, *Interference*."[44]

Western movie fans were particular fans of hers. According to Buck Rainey, "Though she made only two serials and a handful of Westerns, her unique personality and style made them memorable."[45]

Part of Evelyn's appeal is that she is unmistakably a woman. Brent played women who were knowing, mature, experienced, and sophisticated. "[T]his world-weary woman was absolutely sexier and more wonderful than any of the others," James Card said. "There is something about a woman like her that is challenging to a man in a way that's quite different from the bouncy sexuality of a Clara Bow. That was high school prom stuff compared to a real woman like Evelyn Brent or Jeanne Eagels."[46]

Writer and research Roy Liebman summed up Evelyn's appeal: "Of dark and exotic mien, Evelyn Brent did not look like the average leading lady of the '20s and '30s. She had a certain toughness ... that consigned her to 'bad girl' parts, but it was typecasting that cut two ways. It gave her the niche which led to stardom; on the other hand, it was a box that eventually ended her starring career.... She was a watchable actress who probably deserved better."[47]

DeWitt Bodeen worked with Brent and was also her friend. "The dark, cynical eyes: the sardonic mouth—these were what made the Brent mystique, and she remained a vitally interesting film personality for more than three decades in the New York, London, and Hollywood film worlds."[48]

John Kobal conducted a fascinating, wide-ranging interview with Brent in 1972. He concluded the piece with these words: "There was no failure in Evelyn's life—the failure lay in others, those who tried to make her a star. Evelyn didn't want to be a star, she just wanted to work. And at that she was a success, right to the end."[49]

# PART TWO

*Filmography*

# The Films, 1914–1950

## A Gentleman from Mississippi

(William A. Brady Picture Plays, Inc.) 5 reels. Released on September 25, 1914.

*Survival Status:* Presumed lost.

*Credits:* Producer, William A. Brady; director, George L. Sargent; assistant director, Harry Weir; based on the play by Thomas A. Wise and Harrison Garfield Rhodes; photography, Arthur Edeson.

*Cast:* Thomas A. Wise (Senator William H. Langdon); Betty Riggs [Evelyn Brent], Chester Barnett (undetermined roles).

Newly elected Senator William H. Langdon moves from Mississippi to Washington, D.C., with children Caroline, Hope, and Randolph. Caroline's husband-to-be is a corrupt Congressman who uses money provided by Caroline and Randolph for an unscrupulous land deal. Langdon finds out about it and delivers a heartfelt speech decrying corruption.

Thomas A. Wise created the role of Senator Langdon on Broadway. The popular play, also produced by William A. Brady, opened on September 29, 1908, and closed in September 1909 after 407 performances. Cast members included Douglas Fairbanks.

Some scenes were filmed in Natchez, Mississippi. Rehearsals were disrupted by a fire on March 19, 1914, at the Éclair Moving Picture Company's factory. The film did good—not great—business for World Film Corporation. By its 64th week in release it had grossed $56,832.55. In comparison, *Dollar Mark* had been in release for 66 weeks and had grossed $85,643.83; *Mother* for 65 weeks, $55,985.20; *The Man of the Hour*, 63 weeks, $73,781.22; *Mystery of Edwin Drood*, 62 weeks, $28,507.90. One of World's most successful films was *Alias Jimmy Valentine* which grossed $72,674.61 in only 44 weeks.

Advertising proclaimed, "The trials and pleasures of a new senator. A comedy drama that Teddy Roosevelt said was 'Bully.'"

Thomas A. Wise was born in England in 1865. The stage actor made only a handful of movies. This was his first. He died in New York in 1928.

Producer William A. Brady was born in San Francisco in 1863 and died in 1950. He was married to Rose Marie René, and their daughter was actress Alice Brady. After Rose Marie's death in 1896 he married Grace George in 1897. They had one son, Bill Brady, Jr.

Cameraman Arthur Edeson was born in New York in 1891. He received Oscar nominations for *In Old Arizona* (1928), *All Quiet on the Western Front* (1930), and *Casablanca* (1942). He died in 1970.

*Reviews:* "All of the characters are naturally presented, whereas settings and photography may be numbered among the good points of a satisfactory production" (*New York Dramatic Mirror*, September 30, 1914).

"A fair picture, not strong on action" (*Variety*, September 26, 1914).

## The Pit

(William A. Brady Picture Plays, Inc.) 5 reels. Released on December 28, 1914.

*Survival Status:* Presumed lost.

*Credits:* Producer, William A. Brady; director, Maurice Tourneur; writer, Channing Pollock; based on the novel *The Pit* by Frank Norris; photography, John van den Brock.

*Cast:* Milton Sills (Sheldon Corthell); Hattie Delaro (Mrs. Cressler); Alec B. Francis (Charles Cressler); Gail Kane (Laura Dearborn); Wilton Lackaye (Curtis Jadwin); Chester Barnett (Landry); E. F. Roseman (Crookes); Bert Starkey (Scannell); Sim Wiltsie (Hargus); W. A. Orlemond, Gunnis Davis (Crookes's clerks); George Ingleton (Jadwin's butler); Jessie Lewis (Page); Julia Stuart (Aunt Wess); Betty Riggs [Evelyn Brent] (Maid).

Curtis Jadwin is a commodities trader for the Chicago Board of Trade. He meets future wife Laura at the opera when she arrives with paramour Sheldon Corthell. After their marriage, Jadwin becomes obsessed with getting rich from trading steel and cotton. He neglects Laura, who resumes her affair with Sheldon. Jadwin loses everything through speculation, but Laura returns to her husband.

According to Harry Waldman, Tourneur was a very involved director. It wasn't unusual for him to take on additional duties while on the set: "Tourneur selected costumes and setting, and was not above suggesting how actors were to wear their hair. 'It is true,' he said, 'that I dictate the smallest detail of the action of the players, but it is not because that is my ideal of working. I have to use these methods because there are very few cinema actors who have a sufficient grasp and understanding of their work.... This, no doubt, is due to the relative newness of the art of the screen."[1]

D.W. Griffith directed an earlier adaptation of Norris' novel in 1909. Titled *A Corner in Wheat*, the film featured Griffith's wife Linda Arvidson, along with Frank Powell, Grace Henderson, James Kirkwood, and Henry B. Walthall.

Film director and writer Maurice Tourneur was born in Paris in 1873. A visual artist who later became a stage actor, he eventually turned his attention to silent film directing. The Directors Guild of America awarded him an Honorary Life Member Award in 1945. The father of director Jacques Tourneur, he died in France in 1961 from injuries received in an automobile accident.

Novelist Frank Norris was born in Chicago in 1870. His novel *McTeague* was made into several films, including *Greed* (1924). He died of appendicitis in 1902.

Born in Philadelphia in 1887, Gail Kane made her film debut in *Arizona* (1913). A popular actress between the years 1914 and 1921, she appeared in her last film in 1927. Kane died in 1966.

Wilton Lackaye played the same role in the stage production. One of the founders of Actors' Equity, his most famous film role was Svengali in *Trilby* (1915). Born in Virginia in 1862, he died in 1932.

Milton Sills was born to wealthy parents in Chicago in 1882. Sills was a university professor who later became a Broadway star. A founder of the Academy of Motion Picture Arts, he was married to Doris Kenyon from 1926 until his death in 1930.

*Reviews:* "...*The Pit* is one of the very best releases turned out by the World Film Corporation.... By simply devoting a reasonable amount of attention to detail ... Mr. Tourneur has gained some excellent effects, both by the good acting of almost everyone in the cast and the realistic and faultlessly constructed settings" (*Motion Picture News*, January 2, 1915).

## The Heart of a Painted Woman

(Popular Plays and Players, Inc.) 5 reels. Released on April 19, 1915.

*Survival Status:* Presumed lost.

*Credits:* Producers, Alice Guy Blaché, Herbert Blaché; director, Alice Guy; writer, Aaron Hoffman; photography, Alfred Ortleib.

*Cast:* Olga Petrova (Martha Redmond); Fraunie Fraunholz (undetermined role); Mahlon Hamilton, James O'Neill, Betty Riggs [Evelyn Brent] (undetermined roles).

Artists' model Martha Redmond becomes a prostitute when her artist-lover leaves her. A wealthy man gives her $100,000 to spend as she wishes. She uses the money to open an orphanage. When her former lover is murdered, the wealthy man becomes a suspect. The true murderer is revealed to be the artist's father-in-law. Martha has now fallen in love with her wealthy benefactor.

Born in Paris in 1873, Alice Guy made her first film before the turn of the century. After marrying Herbert Blaché in 1907, they came to the United States and started Solax in 1910. The Blachés divorced in 1922, the same year Solax went into bankruptcy. Alice Blaché died in 1968 in New Jersey. She also co-produced Brent's Popular Plays and Players films with husband Herbert.

Herbert Blaché was born in England in 1882 and died in 1953. He also directed *The Shooting of Dan McGrew* (1915) and co-produced Popular Plays and Players productions with wife Alice.

Olga Petrova was born Muriel Harding in England in 1884. She was married to Louis Willoughby and died in 1977. In her memoirs, Blaché wrote, "Olga Petrova was already known and loved by the public, but she was difficult to direct. One day I wanted her to play a scene of jealousy. 'No,' she told me, 'when the hyacinth is faded it is I who will throw it away....'"[2] Petrova was well paid for the films she made with the Blachés—$1,500 a week.

Mahlon Hamilton, born in Virginia in 1880, also appeared with Brent in *To the Death* (1917). He died in 1960.

*Reviews:* "Though *The Painted Woman* (about five reels) has a couple of spots that are not convincing, partially because of the situations and the direction, the remainder is quite a strong dramatic" (*Variety*, April 23, 1915).

## The Shooting of Dan McGrew

(Popular Plays and Players, Inc.) 5 reels. Released on May 2, 1915.

*Survival Status:* Presumed lost.

*Credits:* Producers, Alice Guy Blaché, Herbert Blaché; director, Alice Guy; writer, James J. Tynan; inspired by the Robert W. Service poem "The Shooting of Dan McGrew" in his *The Spell of the Yukon*; photography, Alfred Ortleib.

*Cast:* William A. Morse (Dan McGrew); Kathryn Adams (Lou Maxwell); Edmund Breese (Jim Maxwell); Audrine Stark (Nell Maxwell as a child); Betty Riggs [Evelyn Brent] (Nell as an adult); Wallace Stopp (Nell's husband).

Alaskan prospector Dan McGrew runs away with Jim's wife, leaving Jim to raise daughter Nell. Nell grows up and marries. When McGrew commits a murder that gets blamed on Nell's husband, Jim, who certainly has had more than enough, shoots him.

Scenes were shot in Canada, Georgia, New York, and Texas. The film was based on a poem by poet Robert W. Service, known as the Canadian Kipling. Born in England in 1874, he died in France in 1958.

During the making of this film, Brent toyed with using the name Dorothy Riggs, but when the film was released she was credited as Betty Riggs.

The film was remade in 1924 with Clarence Badger directing. Barbara La Marr and Lew Cody were the leads, and Mae Busch and Percy Marmont supported. Tex Avery directed an animated spoof adaptation in 1945. Titled *The Shooting of Dan McGoo*, it featured the vocal talents of Paul Frees.

Kathryn Adams was born Ethalinda Colson in St. Louis in 1893. This was her film debut. She died in 1959.

Edmund Breese was born in Brooklyn, New York, in 1871. He began his film career in 1914 and appeared in films through the mid–1930s. Breese died in 1936. He also appeared with Brent in 1916's *The Lure of Heart's Desire*, *The Weakness of Strength*, and *The Spell of the Yukon*.

William Morse was born in 1897 and died of pneumonia in 1918. He appeared in less than a dozen films from 1912 until 1917.

*Reviews:* "As a feature *The Shooting of Dan McGrew* will get double prestige from the reputation of Breese and the popularity of the poem. Too much attention to the snow scenes forced the director to work under a handicap, although he had a chance to make good with the struggle between the male leads and the duel in the dark in the Malamute saloon" (*Variety*, May 14, 1915).

## When Love Laughs

(Independent Moving Pictures Co. of America) 2 reels. Released on December 21, 1915.
 *Survival Status:* Presumed lost.
 *Cast:* Matt Moore, Jane Gail, Betty Riggs [Evelyn Brent], William O'Neill (undetermined roles).

Matt Moore was born in Ireland in 1888. He made his film debut in 1912 and ended his career in 1958. Moore was also a director. Moore never married; he was brother-in-law to Mary Pickford when his brother Owen was married to the silent film star. Moore died in 1960. He also appeared with Brent in *The Glorious Lady* (1919).

Jane Gail was born in New York in 1890. She made her film debut in 1912 and ended her career in 1920. She and Matt Moore appeared in numerous films together. Some of Gail's other films include *Traffic in Souls* (1913), *The Prisoner of Zenda* (1915), and *20,000 Leagues Under the Sea* (1916). Gail died in 1963.

## The Lure of Heart's Desire

(Popular Plays and Players, Inc.) 4775 ft. 5 reels. Released on January 17, 1916.
 *Survival Status:* Presumed lost.
 *Credits:* Producers, Alice Guy Blaché, Herbert Blaché; director, Francis J. Grandon; scenario, Aaron Hoffman; story, Francis J. Grandon; inspired by the Robert W. Service poem "The Spell of the Yukon" in his *The Spell of the Yukon and Other Verses.*
 *Cast:* Edmund Breese (Jim Carew); Arthur Hoops (Thomas Martin); John Mahon (Crazy Jake); Jeannette Horton (Ethel Wyndham); Evelyn Brent (Little Snowbird); Adolphe Menjou (undetermined role).

After being rejected by wealthy girlfriend Ethel, Jim Carew becomes a Yukon prospector. He begins a romance with Little Snowbird but again proposes to Ethel. This time Ethel declines because Thomas Martin threatens her with blackmail. Little Snowbird commits suicide, though not before having Jim's child.

The production's snow scenes were filmed in New York's Adirondack Mountains. The New Year's Eve scene was filmed in New York City at Murray's restaurant.

Arthur Hoops was born in Connecticut in 1870. He made his film debut in 1914 and also appeared with Brent in 1916's *The Soul Market, Playing with Fire,* and *The Spell of the Yukon.* He died in 1916.

Writer Aaron Hoffman (1880–1924) also contributed to scripts for *The Soul Market, Playing with Fire,* and *The Spell of the Yukon* (all 1916).

*Reviews:* "This photoplay abounds with novel and interesting scenes" (*Eureka Reporter*, October 13, 1916).

## The Iron Will

(Biograph Company) 3 reels. Released on February 9, 1916.
 *Survival Status:* Presumed lost.
 *Credits:* Director, J. Farrell MacDonald; based on the novel *Poor Plutocrats* by Maurus Jokai.
 *Cast:* Vera Sisson, G. Raymond Nye, José Ruben (as Jose Ruben), Gretchen Hartman, Jack Drumier, Jack Mulhall, Charles Hill Mailes, Ivan Christy, Evelyn Brent (undetermined roles).

An adventure story about a Hungarian man who leads a double life in the nineteenth century.

*Poor Plutocrats* was published in 1899. Novelist Jokai was born in Hungary in 1825. Many of his works have been adapted for film and television, especially in European countries. He died in 1904.

Vera Sisson was born in Salt Lake City, Utah, in 1891 and died in 1954. She also appeared with Brent in *The Iron Woman* (1916) and *Love 'Em and Leave 'Em* (1926).

Gretchen Hartman was born Grace Barrett in Chicago in 1897 and died in 1979. Married to actor Alan Hale, her son was Alan Hale, Jr., of *Gilligan's Island* fame. Her mother was stage and film actress Agnes A. Hartman.

Director J. Farrell MacDonald (sometimes spelled McDonald) became a character actor after his directing career ended, often appearing in John Ford Westerns. Born in Connecticut in 1875, he died in Hollywood in 1952.

## The Soul Market

(Popular Plays and Players) 5 reels. Released on March 5, 1916.
 *Survival Status:* Presumed lost.
 *Credits:* Producers, Alice Guy Blaché, Herbert Blaché; director, Francis J. Grandon; writer, Aaron Hoffman; photography, George W. Peters.
 *Cast:* Olga Petrova (Elaine Elton); Arthur Hoops (Oscar Billings); Wilmuth Merkyl (Jack Dexter); Fritz De Lint (Dick Gordon); Fraunie Fraunholz (Griggs); Charles Brandt (Sam Franklin); Charles W. Mack (Harvey Theugh); Bert Tuey (Joe Burrows); Grace Florence (Mrs. Wilson); Cora Milholland (Susan); Evelyn Brent (Vivian Austin); Al Thomas (James Austin); Gypsy O'Brien (Billie Simpson); Claire Lillian Barry (undetermined role).

Actress Elaine Elton is desired by two wealthy men. Jack pretends to be a chauffeur to get closer to Elaine. However, Oscar forces Elaine to marry him by telling her she will lose her career if she doesn't. The marriage is unhappy, and Elaine murders Oscar because he cheats on her. While fleeing from the police, Elaine, too, is killed. It all turns out to have been a terrible dream of Elaine's. Still, she sees it as an omen and chooses Jack.

*Reviews:* "[It] rushes off with much promise though encased at the opening with the glamour of back stage, but it soon subsides into a settled, almost staid story" (*Variety*, March 10, 1916).

"Mme. Petrova easily dominates the picture, and gives an impersonation which holds attention throughout. In fact, the picture is very largely Mme. Petrova. Her per-

*A photograph by the renowned portraitist Albert Cheney Johnston.*

sonality and finished acting readily offset a theme which, otherwise, could hardly have been spread over five reels successfully.... [T]he rest of the cast is entirely acceptable.... Views of a theatre, both back stage and out front, are particularly interesting. Direction by Francis J. Grandon plays its part in making the whole a good hour and a quarter of entertainment" (*Motion Picture News*, May 18, 1916).

## Playing with Fire

(Popular Plays and Players) 5 reels. Released on April 17, 1916.
   *Survival Status:* Presumed lost.
   *Credits*: Producers, Alice Guy Blaché, Herbert Blaché; director, Francis J. Grandon; writer, Aaron Hoffman; photography, Robert Smith.
   *Cast:* Olga Petrova (Jean Servian); Arthur Hoops (Geoffrey Vane); Evelyn Brent (Lucille Vane); Pierre LeMay (Philip Derblay); Catherine Calhoun (Rosa Derblay); Philip Hahn (Jacques Gobert); Claire Lillian Barry (undetermined role).

Jean Servian is a married woman willing to expose her infidelity with a former lover in order to prevent her stepdaughter from marrying him.

   *Reviews:* "Pictorially *Playing with Fire* is a corking feature. It is acted by a capable cast who seem to possess a fine sense of dramatic values, and were it not for the fact that the entire story is rather draggy, the feature would rank with the best of the season's output" (*Variety*, April 28, 1916).
   "Evelyn Brent, as the young girl, gives an unusually expressive performance, one which indicates that Miss Brent has genuine screen ability" (*Motion Picture News*, May 13, 1916).

## The Spell of the Yukon

(Popular Plays and Players, Inc.) 5 reels. Released on May 12, 1916.
   *Survival Status:* Presumed lost.
   *Credits*: Producers, Alice Guy Blaché, Herbert Blaché; director, Burton L. King; assistant director, Dale Hanshaw; scenario, Wallace C. Clifton; story, Aaron Hoffman; inspired by the Robert W. Service poem "The Spell of the Yukon" in *Songs of a Sourdough*; photography, Leo Berman.
   *Cast*: Edmund Breese (Jim Carson); Arthur Hoops (Albert Temple); Christine Mayo (Helen Temple); Billy Sherwood (Bob Adams); Evelyn Brent (Dorothy Temple); Frank McArthur (Megar); Joseph S. Chailee (Rusty); Jacques Suzanne (Billy Denny); Mary Reed (Yukon Kate); Harry Moreville (Ike Boring); Baby Volare (Bob Adams as a baby); Claire Lillian Barry (undetermined role).

Believing his sweetheart is having an affair with his boss, Jim Carson leaves the city for the Yukon wilderness. While there he adopts a boy, strikes it rich, and is consumed by his thirst for revenge on his former employer.

Like *The Shooting of Dan McGrew*, this film was based on a poem by Robert W. Service.

Director Burton L. King, born in Cincinnati, Ohio, in 1877, also directed Brent in *To the Death* (1917). He died in 1944. King was also a producer, writer, and actor.

   *Reviews:* "[A] strong, but conventional, melodrama.... The location, detail of direction, acting, etc., all contribute to the general good effect" (*Variety*, May 12, 1916).
   "From start to finish *The Spell of the Yukon* grips one, and it is so realistic that one old timer in New York, who reviewed the picture for one of the big newspapers, declared that it made him 'homesick'" (*Fitchburg Daily Sentinel*, July 26, 1916).

## The Weakness of Strength

[Alternate Title: *The Evil Men Do*] (Popular Plays and Players, Inc.) 5 reels. Released on August 14, 1916.
   *Survival Status:* Presumed lost.
   *Credits*: Producers, Alice Guy Blaché, Herbert Blaché; director, Harry Revier; scenario, Wallace C. Clifton, story, Aaron Hoffman; photography, Joe Seiden.
   *Cast:* Edmund Breese (Daniel Gaynor); Clifford Bruce (Bill Jackson); Ormi Hawley (Mary Alden); Evelyn Brent (Bessie Alden); Florence Moore (Little Bessie); Clifford B. Gray (Richard Grant).

Edmund Breese played a Maine lumberjack in this drama. He learns an important lesson about what's important when his lifetime of ruthlessness comes back to haunt him. Brent played the ingénue role, and Ormi Hawley was the female lead. Clifford Bruce was Breese's rival and enemy.

Breese was a big-time stage actor who did not do quite as well on film. One newspaper suggested that heavy dramatic parts did not play as well on film as they did on stage—and that Breese was no matinee idol. "Mr. Breese is noted for the roles of strength which he has created on the stage. His picture career has not been so eminently satisfactory, however, because in the movies we don't like things too heavy. We are strong on the 'grab and kiss' finish and we like our heroes young and good looking. Not even his mother could say that of Mr. Breese."[3] Ouch.

Director Harry Revier was born in Pennsylvania in 1889 and died in 1957. Married at one time to actress Dorothy Revier, he was also a writer and producer.

Clifford Gray was born Percival Davis in England in 1887. Although he was an actor early in his career, he is much better known for his musical compositions including "If You Were the Only Girl in the World." He died in 1941.

*Reviews:* "*The Weakness of Strength* is admirably done. It commands our sincerest tribute" (*Syracuse Herald*, September 2, 1916).

"[A] story of unusual strength and artistic appeal.... [It] affords Mr. Breese a vehicle which gives the widest range to his notable dramatic powers" (*Logansport Pharos-Reporter* [Indiana], December 5, 1916).

## The Iron Woman

(Popular Plays and Players, Inc.) 6 reels. Released on October 2, 1916.

*Survival Status:* Presumed lost.

*Director:* Producers, Alice Guy Blaché, Herbert Blaché; director, Carl Harbaugh; writer, Wallace C. Clifton; based on the novel *The Iron Woman* by Margaret Deland; photography, Robert Smith.

*Cast:* Nance O'Neil (Sarah Maitland); Einar Linden (David Ritchie); Alfred Hickman (Blair Maitland); Evelyn Brent (Nannie Maitland); Vera Sisson (Elizabeth Ferguson); William Postance (Robert Ferguson); Christine Mayo (Helena Ritchie).

Steel mill owner Sarah Maitland is upset when son Blair marries David's girlfriend Elizabeth. Elizabeth regrets the marriage, but David's mother tells her it's too late. When Sarah is hurt at the mill, David saves her life. A grateful Blair agrees to divorce Elizabeth so she can marry David.

Some scenes in this drama were filmed at a Bethlehem, Pennsylvania, steel plant.

Nance O'Neil had been a renowned stage actress early in her career. One article referred to her as "one of the foremost dramatic actresses in the country."[4] She was also reputed to have been Lizzie Borden's lover. Born Gertrude Lamson in Oakland, California, in 1874, she died in 1965.

O'Neil was married to Alfred Hickman from 1916 until his death in 1931. Hickman, born in London in 1873, had been married at one time to actress Blanche Walsh.

Christine Mayo, who often played vamps, also appeared with Brent in *The Spell of the Yukon* (1916), *Who's Your Neighbor* (1917), and *Raffles* (1917). Mayo was engaged to marry director Marshall Neilan in 1920 when Neilan was married to Gertrude Bambrick. Mayo and Neilan never married, though Neilan did marry Blanche Sweet in 1922. Mayo retired from films in 1924.

Director Carl Harbaugh was also a writer and actor. Born in 1886 in Washington, D.C., he died in 1960. He directed Brent in *The Other Man's Wife* (1919) and was in the cast of *The Last Train from Madrid* (1937).

*Reviews:* "[This is] very much of a jumbled up affair and it is doubtful if there is a possibility of ever getting the story sufficiently straightened out to make it worthwhile.... Pictorially the feature is O.K., but from the standpoint of story and direction it is all wrong. It cannot be rated a feature of the first class" (*Variety*, October 13, 1916).

## The Millionaire's Double

(Rolfe Photoplays, Inc.) 5 reels. Released on April 30, 1917.

*Credits:* Producer, B. A. Rolfe; director, Harry Davenport; writer, June Mathis; photography, John M. Bauman.

*Survival Status:* Presumed lost.

*Cast:* Lionel Barrymore (Bide Bennington); Evelyn Brent (Constance Brent); Harry S. Northrup (Richard Glendon); H. H. Pattee (James Brent); John Smiley (Stevens); Jack Raymond ("Kid" Burns); Louis Wolheim (Bob Holloway).

Brent was second-billed in this film — her highest billing since *A Gentleman from Mississippi.* The film was a melodramatic mystery concerning a Paris millionaire who learns of his estranged wife's death. He returns to New York where a series of events lead many to mistakenly believe he has committed suicide. When a criminal forces a young woman to pretend to be his widow, the millionaire foils the crime — and falls in love with the woman.

Born in Philadelphia in 1878, Barrymore won an Oscar for *A Free Soul* (1931) and received a nomination for *Madame X* (1929). The great-uncle of Drew Barrymore, his siblings included Ethel and John. Ill health forced him to begin using a wheelchair in 1938, and he died in 1954.

Louis Wolheim was born in 1880 in New York. Mentored by Lionel Barrymore, Wolheim first appeared on stage before trying his luck in movies. His disfigured nose was the result of an injury received while playing football at Cornell University. He died in 1931 of stomach cancer while preparing to star in *The Front Page.* His replacement was Adolphe Menjou, who received an Oscar nomination for his performance.

Harry Davenport, born in New York in 1866, cofounded Actors Equity with Eddie Foy. His daughter was actress Dorothy Davenport, who married Wallace Reid. Davenport died in 1949.

Screenwriter June Mathis is credited by some with discovering Rudolph Valentino. She died on July 26, 1927, in New York City while attending a production of *The Squall* at the 48th Street Theater. She screamed out that she was dying. She wasn't kidding. She was taken out to the alley next to the theater where she was pronounced dead. Mathis, a Spiritualist, often included mystical themes in her works. One of Metro's most highly paid employees, Mathis also worked on *The Four Horsemen of the Apocalypse* (1921), *Camille* (1921), *Blood and Sand* (1922), and *Greed* (1924). Her credits with Brent also included *Daybreak* (1918).

*Reviews:* "Here is a corking melodrama, full of thrills and with a corking love interest running through it, that will hold almost any audience and please the majority of those who see pictures as a regular thing" (*Variety*, May 11, 1917).

"A mystery story which affords good acting opportunities for all the principals, is found in *The Millionaire's Double*, which features John [sic] Barrymore, supported by Evelyn Brent, a very charming and talented young woman" (*The Dramatic Mirror*, May 12, 1917).

## To the Death

(Metro Pictures Corp.) 5 reels. Released on August 27, 1917.

*Survival Status:* Presumed lost.

*Credits*: Director, Burton L. King; scenario, Mme. Olga Petrova, L. Case Russell; photography, Harry B. Harris.

*Cast*: Mme. Olga Petrova (Bianca Sylva); Mahlon Hamilton (Etienne Du Inette); Wyndham Standing (Jules Lavinne); Henry Leone (Antonio Manatelli); Evelyn Brent (Rosa); Violet Reed (The woman of mystery); Marion Singer (Maria); Boris Korlin (Valet).

In Paris, lacemaker Bianca falls in love with Etienne, the leader of a secret organization who is on the trail of traitor Jules. When her sister attempts suicide, Bianca returns to her home in Corsica. She learns that "Pierre" is the man behind her sister's suicide attempt. Jules tells Bianca that Etienne is "Pierre." Bianca stabs Etienne but then learns that Lavinne is actually "Pierre." Etienne recovers, and he and Bianca reconcile.

Olga Petrova's co-writer on this scenario was Lillian Case Russell. Born Lulu Case in South Dakota in 1876, Russell wrote some of the first books on screenwriting. She died June 2, 1947, when she accidentally drowned in her son's swimming pool.

Wyndham Standing, born in England in 1880, was the uncle of Joan Standing, who appeared with Brent in *Beau Sabreur* (1928). He died in 1963.

*Reviews:* "The work of Mme. Petrova. ... is excellent, while Evelyn Brent is attractive as Rosa, the younger sister" (*The Daily* [Connellsville, Pennsylvania] *Courier*, October 16, 1917).

## Who's Your Neighbor?

(Master Drama Features, Inc.) 5 reels. Released in October 1917.

*Credits*: Director and scenario, S. Rankin Drew; story, Willard Mack; editor, Frank Lawrence.

*Survival Status:* Presumed lost.

*Cast*: Christine Mayo (Hattie Fenshaw); Anders Randolf (Bryant M. Harding); Evelyn Brent (Betty Hamlin); Frank Morgan (Dudley Carlton); William Sherwood (Hal Harding); Gladys Fairbanks (Mrs. Bowers); Franklyn Hanna (District Attorney Osborne); Mabel Wright (Betty's mother); George Majeroni, Dean Raymond (undetermined roles).

Prostitute Hattie Fenshaw is forced out of the "red light district" because of a new law. She moves into a residential neighborhood and begins plying her trade. The reformers soon learn it's better to keep prostitutes out.

The film's release was delayed, ostensibly because of fears that World War I would hurt movie atten-

dance. However, the real reason may have been the film's content. Because of a condemnation from the National Board of Review, the film was reduced from seven to five reels.

Advertising focused on Evelyn Brent. An ad that appeared in the *Los Angeles Times* on December 4, 1917, proclaimed "Evelyn Brent in a Powerful Drama" and included a large illustration of Brent. At the bottom of the ad was written, "Willard Mack's stirring protest against social conditions is attracting large crowds daily."[5] Another ad described the picture as "A SOCIOLOGICAL CINEMA SPECTACLE OFFERING, THE MOST POWERFUL ARGUMENT EVER PRESENTED ON ANY SCREEN...."

S. (Sidney) was born Rankin Drew in 1892 and died in France on May 19, 1918, when his plane was shot down. The son of actor Sidney Drew, he was a cousin of Ethel, John, and Lionel Barrymore. Drew was also a silent film actor.

Broadway playwright Willard Mack, born Charles Willard McLaughlin in Canada in 1873, is credited by some with convincing Ruby Stevens to change her name to Barbara Stanwyck. Married and divorced from actresses Marjorie Rambeau and Pauline Frederick, he died in 1934.

*Reviews:* "The film does not only tell a graphic story of everyday life in a big city but is splendidly staged and played by a very capable cast" (*Variety*, June 22, 1917).

"The play on the whole is so perfectly balanced that it leaves nothing to be desired except a less unsavory theme.... It is the sort of thing that will set impressionable people speculating on the morals of the two sedate maiden ladies in the house next door" (*New York Dramatic Mirror*, June 23, 1917).

## Raffles, the Amateur Cracksman

(L. Lawrence Weber Photo Dramas, Inc.) 7 reels. Released in December 1917.

*Survival Status:* Museum of Modern Art (New York City); UCLA Film and Television Archive (Los Angeles). Released on video (Grapevine, 52 min.).

*Credits:* Director, George Irving; writer, Anthony P. Kelly; based on the novel *The Amateur Cracksman* by E. W. Hornung and the play *Raffles, the Amateur Cracksman* by E. W. Hornung and Eugene Presbrey; photography, Harry B. Harris.

*Cast:* John Barrymore (Raffles); Frederick Perry (Captain Bedford); H. Cooper Cliffe (Lord Amersteth); Frank Morgan (Bunny Manders); Christine Mayo (Mrs. Vidal); Evelyn Brent (Ethel); Mike Donlin (Crawshay); Mathilde Brundage (Lady Melrose); Nita Allen (Marie); Kathryn Adams (Gwendolyn); Dudley S. Hill (Crowley).

Pretending to be Count de Bauderay, Raffles steals a rare Indian rose pearl and then makes a daring escape from a Mediterranean steamer. Back in England, the champion cricketer is invited to a weekend at a country house with friend Bunny. Raffles is particularly eager because Lady Melrose owns a magnificent necklace. However, upon arriving, Raffles is not pleased to learn that retired detective Bedford is in attendance. To further complicate matters, Raffles is recognized by Mrs. Vidal, who was sailing on the steamer. One of those smart women who makes foolish choices, she has fallen in love with him. "You know a steamship flirtation is never serious," he cautions her. (Barrymore was notorious for disregarding silent film scripts and using foul language instead, so you lip readers out there might want to pay particular attention.) As for Raffles, he has fallen in love with Gwendolyn, Bunny's girlfriend. Mrs. Vidal flies off the handle and threatens him. "I'll see you in prison before I'll let you win Gwendolyn."

Meanwhile, Bunny is on the verge of suicide because he is in debt and has lost his girlfriend. A true friend and gentleman, Raffles promises to help Bunny make good on a bad check and get his girl back.

While everyone prepares to retire for the night, the maid and burglar Crawshay proceed with plans to steal the necklace. Raffles foils the burglary and steals the necklace. Mrs. Vidal insists she will tell the detective about Raffles' true identity. Before he can return to London, the household discovers the necklace is missing.

Bedford, who seems to be on to Raffles, announces that the necklace will be found before midnight. Raffles bets him £150 that it won't be. Raffles returns to his London apartment at the Albany. He is soon joined, separately, by Crawshay and Bedford, who are both in search of the necklace.

Raffles admits to Bunny that he is the amateur cracksman. Bunny reaffirms his loyalty to his old friend. When Crawshay demands the necklace at gunpoint, Bunny leaves with the jewelry hidden in a tobacco pouch.

Raffles convinces Crawshay that he is on the verge of being arrested. He helps him escape, and Crawshay is so grateful he lets Raffles keep the necklace. Once the police break in, Raffles makes it look as though Crawshay attacked him and escaped with the necklace.

While Raffles and Bunny celebrate at the club, Mrs. Vidal shows up at the apartment to seduce Raffles. She finds a letter written by Gwendolyn, who has fallen in love with Raffles though she suspects his true identity. The letter warns him about Mrs. Vidal.

Mrs. Vidal tells Bedford she suspects Raffles is the cracksman. When Raffles returns to his apartment, Mrs. Vidal is waiting for him. "By tomorrow morning, all London will know who you are. You must leave London and you must take me with you." (She just won't give up.) He won't agree to her terms. As she leaves, she tells Bedford that Raffles has returned to his apartment.

"Mr. Raffles, I have a warrant for your arrest," says Bedford. When Gwendolyn arrives, Raffles asks for a moment alone. "I am worse than a thief—I have stolen your love," he admits. With Bedford on the verge of arresting Raffles, it turns midnight. "Midnight, Bedford!" Raffles exclaims. "You haven't recovered the necklace and you owe me one hundred and fifty pounds." Bedford pays Raffles who then gives the money to Bunny to cover his debt.

"I've lost the bet but I've caught the Amateur Cracksman," Bedford cheerfully says. However, Raffles escapes, leaving behind the necklace. "Well, I'm deucedly glad he escaped. He's splendid!" Bedford concludes.

Some of the best scenes in this fast-moving, cleverly written drama are the first ones at sea, featuring shots of the rapidly moving ocean water and a nice shot of Raffles using a mirror to peer into a ship's cabin to watch where the valuable pearl is hidden. Also, watch for the action scene when Barrymore dives into the sea with the stolen jewel. It's also fun to watch the cat-and-mouse game played by Raffles and Bedford.

This is a John Barrymore picture, and he appears in every scene. The film provides an opportunity to see Barrymore as a young matinee idol. He is dynamic and beautiful—this is before he ruined his looks with alcohol. Many shots of him, including the first one, feature his legendary profile. Barrymore and Frederick Perry provide the best acting.

Brent is barely seen in this movie. In fact, the camera seems almost allergic to her. Unfortunately, there are also some unflattering shots of her profile. If not photographed just right, you'll swear you're looking at a Beistle Halloween witch decoration. Barrymore discouraged Brent from smiling on screen. He was right. For some reason, early in her career her smile does not seem warm and welcoming. In fact, it's a downright harsh look.

Stage and screen star Barrymore was born John Sidney Blyth in Philadelphia in 1882. His parents were actors Maurice Barrymore and Georgiana Drew, and his famous siblings were Ethel and Lionel. Barrymore's wives included Katherine Corri Harris, Blanche Oelrichs, Dolores Costello, and Elaine Barrie. Barrymore's two children were John Drew and Diana. John Drew Barrymore was the father of Drew Barrymore, making John her grandfather. John Barrymore died in 1942 of complications related to alcoholism. He also appeared with Brent in *Night Club Scandal* (1937).

Frederick Perry was a well-known Broadway actor and director. He appeared in many stage productions but only a few films.

The ubiquitous Frank Morgan (the wizard in *The Wizard of Oz*) is almost unrecognizable as Bunny, Raffles' loser friend whose debt prompts Raffles to steal the necklace. Morgan, born Francis Wuppermann in New York in 1890, died in 1949. His brother was actor Ralph Morgan. Frank also appeared with Brent in *Who's Your Neighbor* (1917) and *Love's Greatest Mistake* (1927).

Mike Donlin was nicknamed Turkey Mike for his unique walking style. He was a successful baseball player who'd played with the 1905 world champion New York Giants. He retired from baseball in 1912 to become a film actor.

H. Cooper Cliffe, born in Oxford, England in 1862, died in New York in 1939.

Kathryn Adams' real name was Ethalinda Colson.

She also appeared with Brent in *The Shooting of Dan McGrew* (1915). Adams was born in St. Louis in 1893 and died in 1959.

Mathilde (sometimes spelled Mathilda) Brundage was born in Louisville, Kentucky, in 1859. She appeared in dozens of silent films from 1914 to 1928. Brundage died in 1939.

Director George Irving gave up directing in the 1920s and became a character actor. Born in New York in 1874, he appeared as an actor with Brent in *The Law West of Tombstone* (1938). He also directed Brent in *The Glorious Lady* (1919). Irving died in 1961.

Scenario writer Anthony Paul Kelly committed suicide in 1932 in New York at the age of 35. His credits include D.W. Griffith's *Way Down East* (1920) and the play *Three Faces East*.

Versions of this story were also produced in 1905, 1910, 1914, 1920, 1930, 1932 and 1960. Others who played Lady Gwen include Gwendolyn Amersteth, Kay Francis, and Olivia de Havilland. Actors who have played Raffles include J. Barney Sherry, Gerald du Maurier, Kyrle Bellew, House Peters, Ronald Colman, and David Niven.

Ernest William Hornung was Arthur Conan Doyle's brother-in-law; the character of Raffles was created in 1899 to compete with Doyle's Sherlock Holmes. The character first appeared in Hornung's short stories, and then graduated to full-length novels.

*Reviews:* "Anthony Kelly has ... scenarioed flawlessly and George Irving has directed with a delicacy, scenic beauty, and sustained thrill that command for him a place in the ranks of the country's artistic producers. Young Barrymore demonstrates in this play his claim to the dramatic genius of his illustrious father" (*Variety*, December 7, 1917). This *Variety* review credited Brent as Gwendolyn. The role was, in fact, played by Kathryn Adams.

"Mr. Barrymore has a role that suits his peculiar style of acting better than any in which he has hitherto been seen on the screen. As the gentleman thief he has exceptional opportunities to do both serious and comic work. The star is supported by an excellent cast..." (*The Dramatic Mirror*, February 23, 1918).

"Not surprisingly, John Barrymore proves to be the most gentlemanly of all gentlemen thieves in this [film]. Surrounded by an august Broadway cast, Barrymore struts his stuff in the expected way, not forgetting to offer his audience a good long view of that legendary profile.... Kathryn Adams is Gwendolyn, the lovesick leading lady, and appears pleasingly plump in the accepted style of the day, but a very young Evelyn Brent disappears into the background as a society debutante" (Hans J. Wollstein, *All Movie Guide*).

## Daybreak

(Metro Pictures Corp.) 5 reels. Released on January 7, 1918.

*Survival Status:* Presumed lost.

*Credits:* Producer, Maxwell Karger; director, Albert Capellani; adaptation, June Mathis, Albert Capellani; based on the play *Daybreak* by Jane Cowl, Jane Murfin; photography, David Calcagni.

*Cast:* Emily Stevens (Edith Frome); Julian L'Estrange (Arthur Frome); Herman Lieb (Herbert Rankin); Augustus Phillips (Dr. David Brett); Frank Joyner (Carl Peterson, the embezzler); Evelyn Brent (Alma Peterson, the girl detective); Joe Daly (Otway); Mrs. Evelyn Axzell (Meta Thompson).

Edith Frome leaves her successful but heavy-drinking husband Arthur. After a few years she returns but behaves suspiciously. Arthur discovers that Edith has been visiting their ill son. She had given him up because she did not want him raised around alcohol abuse. Arthur resolves to change.

Set in a Long Island home, this society picture was based on a play co-written by Jane Murfin and actress Jane Cowl.

Julian L'Estrange, born in England in 1878, died from the Spanish Flu on October 22, 1918, in New York. His widow was Constance Collier.

Emily Stevens, born in New York in 1882, was the daughter of Robert E. Stevens, a stage and film director. She started her career on stage and did not make her film debut until 1915 when she was well into her thirties. Her short film career ended in 1920. Stevens died in 1928 at the age of 45. Some reports attribute the cause of death to a heart attack while others point to a drug overdose. Her brother was actor Robert Kellard, and her aunt was stage actress Minnie Maddern Fiske.

Actress, director, and playwright Jane Cowl (1884–1950) was born in Boston. She and co-writer Murfin used the name Alan Langdon Martin as a pseudonym on their collaborations. Murfin, born in Michigan in 1892, died in 1955. Cowl and Murfin also wrote the play *Smilin' Through*, which was adapted for the screen in 1932 and 1941. Murfin was at one time married to Donald Crisp.

*Daybreak* was Albert Capellani's directing debut for Metro. Capellani, born in France in 1874, directed many films there before coming to the United States. He also directed the 1915 version of *Camille* with Clara Kimball Young and *The Red Lantern* (1919) with Alla Nazimova. Capellani often collaborated with writer June Mathis. His brother was actor Paul Capellani. He died in 1931.

*Reviews:* "*Daybreak* [is] a much better picture than it was a play.... The feature is very well handled in production. The studio sets showing the home of the Fromes are wonderfully well done, so well they were mistaken by a great many for the genuine..." (*Variety*, January 11, 1918).

## Help! Help! Police!

(Fox Film Corp.) 5 reels. Released on April 14, 1919.

*Survival Status:* Presumed lost.

*Credits:* Director, Edward Dillon; scenario, Raymond Schrock; story, Irving McDonald.

*Cast:* George Walsh (George Welston); Eric Mayne (Edward P. Welston); Henry Hallam (Judson Pendleton); Marie Burke (Mrs. Pendleton); Alice Mann (Eve Pendleton); Alan Edwards (Arthur Trask); Evelyn Brent (Marian Trevor); Joseph Burke (The judge).

In this comedy, George Welston meets Eve at a Palm Beach hotel. She is the daughter of Justin

Pendleton, a business rival of George's father, Edward. George attempts to woo Eve, but his attempts are stymied by a crook named Arthur Trask who has ingratiated himself with Justin. Ultimately George's goodness and Arthur's treachery are revealed. Edward and Justin join forces, and George and Eve marry. Brent played a rich woman who is robbed by Arthur and mistakenly blames George.

Walsh was the brother of director Raoul Walsh. He was married at one time to actress Seena Owen. Born in New York in 1889, he was best known for the athleticism he often showed off in his films. Walsh died in 1981.

Edward Dillon was a silent film actor, writer, and producer. Born in New York in 1879, he is best known today for being Mary Pickford's first leading man. He became a character actor and extra during the sound era and died in 1933. Dillon also directed Brent in *Flame of the Argentine* (1926). His brother was actor John Dillon.

*Reviews:* "A corking picture with a good story.... Evelyn Brent as the daughter of a Pittsburgh millionaire looked well and rested the eyes in a bathing suit, in the beach scenes.... It's the best Walsh picture seen in a long time" (*Variety*, May 2, 1919).

"The action crackles from the introductory flash and the story has enough sustaining value to keep it from resembling a series of stunts" (*Motion Picture News*, May 10, 1919).

## Fool's Gold

[Alternate Title: *Undermined*] (Washington Motion Picture Corp.) 5500 ft. 6 reels. Released in early May 1919.

*Survival Status:* British Film Institute/National Film and Television Archive (London).

*Credits:* Director, Laurence Trimble; assistant director, Philip E. Rosen; writer, M. A. Miller; photography, H. A. Horn.

*Cast:* Mitchell Lewis (Marshall Strong); Wellington Playter (John Moore); Florence Turner (Constance Harvey); Sarah Truex (Lilas Niles); Francis Joyner (Old Niles); Kempton Greene (David Moore); Evelyn Brent (Nancy Smith); Mlle. Marguerite Serruys (Miss Hatch); Harry Hyde (Sir Horace Seaton, Bart); Lone Star Dietz (Chris Kuhn); Elizabeth Du Barry Gill ("Mother").

Marshall and John, partners in a gold mining operation, fall in love with Constance. John ends up marrying her when he lies about Marshall's involvement with someone else. The partners strike it rich, but when Marshall is murdered, John is mistakenly accused. Marshall escapes and changes his name to Mark Smith. He marries Lilas, and they have a daughter, Nancy. Marshall/Mark is again a mine owner, but one who resists safety measures. Nancy falls in love with Constance's son David who works in Marshall's mine. Marshall rescues David after a mine explosion and agrees to safer working conditions. Meanwhile, Nancy and David marry.

This was the first and only film produced by the Washington Motion Picture Company. True to its name, the mission of the company was to produce films in Washington State. In August 1918 the company went bankrupt. The film was sold to investors, and actor Wellington Player bought the studio which he used as a drama school. The film was released by Arrow Film Corporation.

Some scenes were filmed in the Cascade Mountains. One of its backers was Tyrone Power, Sr., and he made quite an impression on the locals. "[He] blew into Spokane in August of 1917 with great fanfare. He had a vision of Spokane's Minnehaha Park becoming the next major movie studio. The park's basalt hills, springs and numerous pine trees were ideal as a background for a variety of settings depicted in Westerns. The park had previously been part of Edgar J. Webster's 'Minnehaha Springs and Health Resort,' after the Lakota word for waterfall. The business failed, leaving the property to fall into other uses that included a brewery, dance hall, brothel and bowling alley. Power advertised his dream in the local newspapers and held a meeting in the grand Marie Antoinette Room of the Davenport Hotel for prospective investors. He promised returns of millions on investments of thousands, and hundreds leapt at the opportunity. They thought the Washington Motion Picture Company couldn't miss, not with Power's box office draw. As promised, a state-of-the-art studio soon was constructed around the old dance hall."[6]

One of the investors was football star Lone Star Dietz, who had recently signed a contract with the new company to act and direct. He especially entered into the agreement with the hope to improve the depiction of Native Americans in films.

*Fool's Gold* was the first project chosen by the company. Power was selected to be the lead (Marshall Strong), and Laurence Trimble would direct. Trimble was best known for his work with Strongheart, the first dog star. After shooting started, Power suffered a nervous collapse and was replaced by Mitchell Lewis. Lewis had been a sensation on the Broadway stage in Rex Beach's *The Barrier*, but he was no match for the box office draw of Tyrone Power, Sr.

The film's box office returns totaled only approximately $43,000, a terrible return on the $39,000 investment. "Without Power and only a marginally profitable film to show for all their money, investors had little taste for throwing in more money to produce another film. Creditors, including the City of Spokane and Lone Star Dietz, were left holding the financial bag."[7]

In November 2006 the former studio's building was destroyed in a fire. "In the building's heyday ... Hollywood actors and actresses, producers, directors and cameramen and locals who wanted to brush elbows with moviemakers danced the nights away on the second floor. By day it was the Washington Motion Picture Company movie studio, where silent films were taped. Stars such as Power, Evelyn Brent and Nell Shipman were filmed at the location, either on the dance floor or outside on an open-air set, or up in the rocks for mountainous scenes."[8]

Laurence Trimble, born in Maine in 1885, was

hired by Vitagraph when he showed up on the set of a Florence Turner movie to write a story for a magazine. His dog Jean was also hired. Married and divorced from writer Jane Murfin, Trimble later married writer-actor Marian Constance Blackton, daughter of director-producer J. Stuart Blackton. He died in 1954.

Tiny Florence Turner (only 4'10") had not made a film since 1916. She was known as "Baby Twinkles" and then "The Vitagraph Girl." She was an expert impersonator (including Marie Dressler, Alla Nazimova, and Charles Chaplin); the *New York Dramatic Mirror* titled a June 1910 story about her "A Motion Picture Star." She was awarded a diamond ring by the *New York Morning Telegraph* for being the world's most beautiful actress. At one time Norma Talmadge said, "I would rather have touched the hem of her skirt than to have shaken hands with St. Peter."[9] Though kept on the MGM payroll in extra parts, Turner faded out of the public view until her death in 1946 in the Motion Picture Country Home. Turner also appeared with Brent in *Flame of the Argentine* (1926).

Mitchell Lewis will forever be remembered for his performance as captain of the Winkie Guards in *The Wizard of Oz* (1939). His long acting career began in 1914 and ended with his death in 1956. He also appeared with Brent in *Beau Sabreur* (1927).

*Reviews:* "[T]his is a disconnected piece of work.... The locations and camera work of the production can be highly praised, but in this instance the good qualities only go to dwarf the story still further. In its present state the picture bears subtitles that are exceedingly poor" (*Motion Picture News*, May 17, 1919).

## The Other Man's Wife

(A Carl Harbaugh Production) 6 reels. Released on June 29, 1919.
*Survival Status:* Presumed lost.
*Credits:* Producer, Frank G. Hall; director, Carl Harbaugh; writer, Mary Murillo; photography, William Crolley.
*Cast:* Ellen Cassidy (Mrs. Fred Hartley); Stuart Holmes (J. Douglas Kerr); Ned Hay (Fred Hartley); Olive Trevor (Elsie Drummond); Halbert Brown (Bruce Drummond); Mrs. Garrison (Mrs. Bruce Drummond); Lesley Casey (Wilbur Drummond); Danny Sullivan (Jimmy Moore); Regina Quinn (Betty Moore); Laura Newman (Mrs. Moore); Georgie Jessel (Davy Simon); Evelyn Brent (Becky Simon).

Devoted family man Fred Hartley enlists during World War I. While he's away, villain Kerr tries to seduce Mrs. Hartley. He even sends her a telegram informing her of her husband's death. However, order is restored when Hartley returns and forgives Mrs. Hartley for her transgressions.

The film was dedicated to women who proved during World War I that they were equal to men.

Stuart Holmes was born Joseph Liebchen in Chicago in 1884. He began his career in 1909 and appeared in more than four hundred films. Holmes died in 1971.

Vaudeville star Georgie Jessel, known as Toastmaster General of the United States, was born in New York City in 1898. The songwriter, actor, producer, writer, and all-around entertainer died in 1981. *The Other Man's Wife* was his first film.

*Reviews:* "It is rather confusing. There is so much in it so scattered about. Among its contents are some well-done scenes, especially those played by George Jessel, Evelyn Brent, and several others ... who enact the members of a Jewish household" (*New York Times*, June 9, 1919).

## The Glorious Lady

(Selznick Pictures Corp.) 4775 ft. 5 reels. Released on October 19, 1919.
*Survival Status:* Nederlands Filmmuseum (Amsterdam)
*Credits:* Director, George Irving; scenario, George M. Arthur; story, Edmund Goulding; photography, Lewis Physioc.
*Cast:* Olive Thomas (Ivis Benson); Matt Moore (The Duke of Loame); Evelyn Brent (Lady Eileen); Robert Taber (Dr. Neuman); Huntley Gordon (Lord Chettington); Marie Burke (Dowager Duchess); Mrs. Henry Clive (Hilda Neuman); Mona Kingsley (Babette).

Ivis meets the Duke of Loame at a horse race. They fall in love and marry, which upsets some because Ivis is a commoner. Family members try to convince the Duke to divorce Ivis by claiming that injuries from the race will prevent her from bearing a child. Ivis, who overhears the divorce plans, pretends to be drunk so the Duke will be embarrassed and leave her. It doesn't work, so Ivis leaves her husband. When the Duke learns from a maid about why she really left, they are reunited, and Ivis bears him a son.

George M. Arthur also co-produced *The Last Train from Madrid* (1937). Born in Brooklyn in 1898, Arthur died in 1949.

Edmund Goulding was born in England in 1891. A brilliant man, he was a writer (novelist, playwright, and screenwriter), director, songwriter, and producer. He also worked with Brent on *Paramount on Parade* (1930). Goulding's personal life was scandalous, and he committed suicide in 1959.

Olive Thomas died in France on September 10, 1920. Her death has been variously reported as an accident, suicide, and even murder. Born Oliveretta Elaine Duffy in Pennsylvania in 1894, Thomas was married to Jack Pickford, Mary's brother, at the time of her death. A former Ziegfeld girl, her ghost is said to haunt the New Amsterdam Theatre.

*Reviews:* "This will assuredly register as an average society melodrama and several attempts at thrills and intense situations have been very well handled.... [A]lthough this is lightweight it should generally satisfy" (*Motion Picture News*, November, 15, 1919).

## Border River

(Arrow Film Corporation.) 2 reels. 23 min. Released January 18, 1920.
*Survival Status:* Library of Congress (Washington, D.C.).
*Credits:* Producer-director; Edgar Jones; writer, Chan-Mac-Laub; photography, Jack Young.

*Cast*: Evelyn Brent (Marie Dubuque); Ben Hendricks, Jr. (Jean Lamont), Carlton Brickert (Buck Dubuque); Edgar Jones (Lt. Dave Blunt).

Steadfast Mountie Dave Blunt is assigned the thorny task of capturing a gang of moonshiners smuggling whiskey across the Border River into the United States. Complications ensue when Blunt falls in love with pretty Marie Dubuque, the sister of one of the moonshiners.

*Border River* was one of a series of shorts produced by Jones and starring him and Brent. A January 8, 1920 article-advert in the *Columbus Ledger-Inquirer* (Georgia) described the films as "*The Northwoods Dramas*.... They are two-reel features, starring Edgar Jones and Evelyn Brent, and a big cast. The first six of these features are ready and include *Strangers*, *Breed of the North* [shown on January 19, 1920], *A Fight for a Soul* [February 9, 1920], *Quicksands* (sic) [February 29, 1920], *Border River*, and *Beloved Brute* [February 15, 1920].... Most of the films deal with logging camp life, and some with the Northwest Mounted Police." Other titles included *Three and a Girl* (April 11, 1920), *In the River* (April 18, 1920), *The Rider of the King Log* (Jones and Brent are not in the cast), and possibly others. Except for *Border River*, it is uncertain which titles included Jones and Brent in the cast. It is possible that footage from *Border River* was re-cut and re-titled for other markets.

Hendricks was born in New York in 1893 and died in 1938. His father was actor Ben Hendricks, Sr. According to a local newspaper, Hendricks' "forte is hero stuff.... In the course of his work he ably acquits himself as a scrapper and in a rough and tumble scene thinks nothing of throwing a man over his head.... Mr. Hendricks is also a good boxer, basketball player, can ride a horse to perfection and swim like a duck."[10] Hendricks portrays a villain in *Border River*. He also appeared with Brent in *The Cyclone Rider* (1924).

In the same local article, Edgar Jones was referred to as "the big boss" since he acted, produced and directed. In fact, the newspaper writer appeared to be crazy about Jones, writing that he "not only is an efficient and dynamic director but possesses exceptional ability as a 'lead.' His grasp of all things pertaining to the work in hand is a source of constant admiration and wonder to his fellow workers." Following the release of the last film he directed, produced, and starred in, *Lonesome Corners* (1922), he seems to have disappeared from public view.

Carlton Brickert was born in Indiana in 1890. He began his film career in 1916 and worked infrequently until his last film appearance in 1923. From 1920 to 1927 he appeared on stage in several plays with Olga Petrova, Josephine Hull, Alma Kruger and Madge Evans. Brickert then went on to become a much-in-demand radio actor until his death in 1943.

## The Shuttle of Life

(Phillips) 4256 ft. Released November 1920.
*Survival Status:* Presumed lost.

*Credits*: Director, D.J. Williams, writer, S.H. Herkomer, based on the novel *The Shuttle of Life* by Isobel Bray.

*Cast*: C. Aubrey Smith (Reverend John Stone); Evelyn Brent (Miriam Grey); Jack Hobbs (Ray Sinclair); Gladys Jennings (Audrey Bland); Bert Darley (Tom); Cecil Ward (Meeson); Rachel de Solla (Mrs. Bland).

D.J. Williams (1869–1949) directed only this one film. He was an actor who began his career in 1920 and made his last film in 1943.

C. (Charles) Aubrey Smith was born in London in 1863, and eventually moved to Hollywood and helped form one of the city's cricket clubs. Smith, who was made a knight in 1944, died in 1948.

*Reviews:* "Miss Evelyn Brent, a newcomer to British films, plays the part with quiet restraint which emphasizes the pitiful struggle to retain her self respect, and gains complete sympathy. Miss Brent has charm and extreme beauty, and we shall look forward with great interest to her future career" (*Bioscope*).

## The Law Divine

(Master Films) 4700 ft. Released in November 1920.
*Survival Status:* Presumed lost.
*Credits*: Producer: H.V. Esmond; directors, H.B. Parkinson, Challis Sanderson; writer, Frank Miller, based on the novel *The Law Divine* by H.V. Esmond and the play *The Law Divine* by H.V. Esmond.
*Cast*: H.V. Esmond (Captain Jack le Bras); Eva Moore (Edie le Bas); Evelyn Brent (Daphne Grey); Mary Brough (Cook); Leonard Upton (Ted le Bas); John Reid (Bill le Bas); Dorothy Wordsworth (Claudia Merton); Florence Wood (Mrs. Gaythorne); Margaret Watson (Kate).

Director H. (Harry) B. Parkinson (1884–1970) was born in England. He was also a writer and producer and is perhaps best known for *The Life of Charlie Chaplin* (1926), which he wrote, produced, and directed. He also directed Brent in *Married to a Mormon* (1922).

London-born Frank Miller (1891–1950) was a prolific British writer and director. He also wrote the screenplay for *Married to a Mormon* (1922).

H.V. Esmond was the father of British actress Jill Esmond. Born in 1869, Henry Esmond was an actor and writer. Married to Eva Moore, he died in 1922.

Eva Moore was born in England in 1870. Her daughter was Jill Esmond, which made her Laurence Olivier's mother-in-law. Moore died in 1955.

Mary Brough, born in London in 1863, also appeared with Brent in *Demos* (1921). She died in 1934.

## Demos

[Alternate Title: *Why Men Forget*] (Ideal) 5700 ft. Released on January 29, 1921.
*Survival Status:* Presumed lost.
*Credits*: Director: Denison Clift; based on the novel *Demos* by George Robert Gissing.
*Cast*: Milton Rosmer (Richard Mortimer); Evelyn Brent (Emma Vine); Warwick Ward (Willis Rodman); Bettina Campbell (Adela Waltham); Olaf Hytten (Daniel Dabbs); Gerald McCarthy (Herbert Eldon); Mary Brough (Mrs. Mortimer); Haidee Wright (Mrs. Eldon); Vivian Gibson (Alice Mortimer); Daisy Campbell (Mrs. Waltham);

James G. Butt (Jim Cullen); Leonard Robson (Long-wood).

Writer-director Denison Clift was born in San Francisco, California, in 1885. The playwright-novelist eventually moved back to California and died in Hollywood in 1961.

Milton Rosmer was born Arthur Milton Lunt in England in 1881. Also a director and writer, he made his film acting debut in 1915. Rosmer died in 1971.

Warwick Ward was born in England in 1891. He also received credits for writing and producing and died in 1967.

If Olaf Hytten (1888–1955) looks familiar, it might be because the Scottish-born actor accrued almost 300 film credits from 1921 until his death. He also appeared with Brent in *Sonia* (1921), *Trapped by the Mormons* (1922), and *Silent Witness* (1943).

## The Door That Has No Key

(Alliance Film Corporation) 5400 ft. Released February 22, 1921.

*Survival Status:* Presumed lost.

Credits: Director, Frank Hall Crane; writer, Adrian Johnstone; based on the novel *The Door That Has No Key* by Cosmo Hamilton.

*Cast:* George Relph (Jack Scorrier); Betty Faire (Margaret Hubbard); Evelyn Brent (Violet Melton); Wilfred Seagram (Pat Mulley); Olive Sloane (Blossy Waveney); W. Cronin Wilson (Yearsley Marrow); Alice De Winton (Lady Emily Scorrier); A. Harding Steerman (Honorable Claude Scorrier); Gordon Craig (Clive).

Director Frank Hall Crane was also an actor. Born in San Francisco in 1873, he made his film acting debut in 1909. Crane died in Los Angeles in 1948. He also directed Brent in *The Jade Cup* (1926).

Novelist and playwright Cosmo Hamilton was married to C. Aubrey Smith's sister, Beryl. Born in England in 1870, Hamilton died in 1942.

George Relph was born in England in 1888. He received a Tony Award nomination in 1958 for *The Entertainer*. Relph died in 1960.

*Reviews:* "...an outstanding film" (*London Times*, March 1, 1922).

The London *Variety* reviewer found the film in poor taste: "Frankly, this production, the second of the many promised by the 'million pound' company, is about as grossly indecent as any ever seen. It has not even the virtue of covering its salaciousness with a strong story" (*Variety*, April 22, 1921).

The New York *Variety* reviewer agreed with his London counterpart. "The picture is as bad as any of the British films.... Properly speaking, it isn't a picture at all, but a novel transcribed to the screen by way of long, verbose titles.... The only merit the picture has is the lovely backgrounds of rural England.... One suspects that [Cosmo] Hamilton's fate has been maltreated in the screen translation. He couldn't have perpetrated anything so awful."

## Laughter and Tears

(Granger-Binger Film [Filmfabriek-Hollandia]) 5947 ft. 59 min. Released on September 27, 1921.

*Survival Status:* British Film Institute/National Film and Television Archive (London) (incomplete); Filmmuseum (Amsterdam) (incomplete).

*Credits:* Producers: A.G. Granger, Maurits H. Binger; director, B.E. Doxat-Pratt; assistant director, Reginald Lawson; based on *Carnaval Tragique*, a one-act play by Adelqui Migliar; screenplay, Adelqui Migliar; camera, Feiko Boersma, Jan Smit; English intertitles, Reginald Lawson.

*Cast:* Adelqui Migliar (Mario Mart); Evelyn Brent (Pierrette); B.E. Doxat-Pratt (Captain Lombardie); E. Story-Gofton (Adolpho); Reginald Garton (Georgio Lario, futurist painter); Bert Darley (Romolo Ferrando); Maudie Dunham (Signorina Zizi); Dorothy Fane (Sonia, Countess Maltakoff); Nico de Jong (Police Commissioner); Norman Doxat-Pratt (bit).

The film begins in Venice during the carnival. Pierrette becomes artist Mario's model and moves into his attic. The lovers agree that if they ever separate, it will be without rancor. When Mario enters an art competition, his piece "Laughter and Tears" wins first place. Mario leaves Venice for Paris to paint Countess Sonia. Pierrette follows him, but he orders her to leave. She lies to him and explains that she is now the mistress of Captain Lombardie, an old flame. Enraged, Mario stabs her and turns himself in to the police. However, Pierrette's wounds are minor. She tells Mario that she lied about her affair, and they return happily together to Venice.

The English translation of this Dutch-English film is *A Laugh and a Tear*. The original working title was *Love in Tears*. It was also released as *Een Lach En Een Traan Een Schilder En Zijn Pierrette* in the Netherlands.

The film was shot on location in Venice and Paris. The Roman Catholic Church advised viewers not to attend the movie because it featured a couple living in sin as well as risqué clothing.

This was one of several Anglo-Dutch productions made in the early 1920s. Writer-director B.E. Doxat-Pratt, born in London in 1896, wrote and directed several of the efforts. He also directed *Circus Jim* (1922).

Reginald Gordon was the pseudonym of writer Reginald Lawson. He also appeared in the credits for *Circus Jim* (1922).

Adelqui Migliar's name was sometimes spelled as Adelqui Millar in English publicity; he changed his name when he moved to England. Migliar was born in Chile in 1891 and became a matinee idol in the Netherlands, often co-starring in productions with Annie Bos. He later worked in the Argentine film industry and died in Chile in 1956. Migliar wrote the screenplay and appeared in the cast of *Circus Jim* (1922) and wrote and directed *Pages of Life* (1922).

Dorothy Fane, sometimes billed as Fayne, was born in England in 1871 and died in 1947.

Maudie Dunham, born in England in 1902, died in 1982.

Norman Doxat-Pratt, the son of the director, was born in 1916 and died in 1982. He also appeared with Brent in *Circus Jim* (1922).

## Sybil

(Ideal) 5300 ft. Released in 1921.

*Survival Status:* Presumed lost.

*Credits:* Director, Jack Denton; writer, Colden Lore; based on the novel *Sybil, or the Two Nations* by Benjamin Disraeli.

*Cast:* Evelyn Brent (Sybil Gerard); Cowley Wright (Honorable Charles Egremont); Gordon Hopkirk (Stephen Hatton); Harry Gilbey (James Hatton); Philip D. Williams (James Marney); William Burchill (Father).

Benjamin Disraeli first became prime minister in 1868 and then served another term beginning in 1874. He has been portrayed many times in films, most notably by George Arliss in *Disraeli* (1929). Born in London in 1804, he died in 1881.

This was Cowley Wright's last film credit. Born in England in 1889, he died in 1923 after appearing in only four films.

## Sonia

(Ideal) 6060 ft. Released 1921.

*Survival Status:* Presumed lost.

*Credits:* Director-writer, Denison Clift; based on the novel *Sonia* by Stephen McKenna.

*Cast:* Evelyn Brent (Sonia Dainton); Clive Brook (David O'Raine); Cyril Raymond (Tom Dainton); Olaf Hytten (Fatty Webster); Henry Vibart (Reverend Burgess); M. Gray Murray (Sir Roger Dainton); Hedda Bartlett (Lady Dainton); Leo Stormont (Sir Adolph Erckmann); Gladys Hamilton (Lady Erckmann); George Travers (Lord Loring); Julie Hartley-Milburn (Lady Loring).

This drama features Brent as a pampered socialite who matures and becomes less self-centered. It was released in the United States as *The Woman Who Came Back.*

Clive Brook would become familiar to Brent. He appeared in several more of her films as studios realized they had a unique chemistry. Born Clifford Hardman Brook in London to opera singer Charlotte Mary and George Alfred Brook, he was married to Mildred Evelyn for more than fifty years. He died in 1974. Brook also appeared with Brent in *The Experiment* (1922), *Married to a Mormon* (1922), *Underworld* (1927), *Interference* (1928), *Slightly Scarlet* (1930), and *Paramount on Parade* (1930).

*Reviews:* "Miss Evelyn Brent manages to convey more successfully than we had dared to hope the wayward moods of Sonia, the spoilt child of fortune, and when towards the end she gets opportunities for real emotional acting she seizes them eagerly. But we would suggest that the scene in which she struggles against the unwelcome attentions of 'Fatty' Webster should be modified and certainly not re-enacted at a later stage of the film. In the novel the incident was bound to be objectionable; on the screen it is acted with so much vigour and frenzy that it becomes very nearly revolting" (*London Times,* September 26, 1921).

"[A]nother weak attempt at something serious. It has all the makings of a tensly dramatic photoplay, so far as the plot itself is concerned, but the action lacks smoothness and the individual acting is none too good.... In the role of Sonia, Evelyn Brent tries awfully hard to act and her

sincere efforts perhaps are worthy of commendation. Her one other noticeable attribute is a head of curly black hair." (*The News-Sentinel* [Fort Wayne, Indiana], September 29, 1922).

## Circus Jim

(Granger-Binger Film [Filmfabriek-Hollandia]) 5000 ft. 70 min. Released on January 9, 1922.

*Survival Status:* British Film Institute/National Film and Television Archive (London); Filmmuseum (Amsterdam) (incomplete); Gosfilmofond of Russia (Moscow).

*Credits:* Producers, A.G. Granger, Maurits H. Binger; directors, B.E. Doxat-Pratt, Adelqui Migliar; screenplay, Adelqui Migliar; camera, Feiko Boersma, Jan Smit.

*Cast:* Adelqui Migliar (Circus Jim); Fred Penley (Anthony Belmore); Evelyn Brent (Iris); Norman Doxat-Pratt (Little Billy); Willem van der Veer (George Munro); Nico de Jong (Sir Henry Rosemount); Jack Doxat-Pratt (his son); Fred Homann (a clown); Filippo (a dwarf); Henri Schmitz and members of Circus Hagenbeck.

Dying, Anthony Belmore tells young daughter Iris about his friend Jim who once saved her life. Iris later gets a job in the same circus where Jim is employed. A jealous Munro tries to thwart a romance between Iris and Jim. Eventually he causes an accident where Jim wounds Iris during their sharpshooting act. Devastated, Jim wants to leave, but Iris finally confesses that she knows all about him through her father. They travel together and meet up with the husband of a woman Jim once saved in a sea storm. The grateful husband appoints Jim the head of a circus that has been purchased from Munro—if Jim and Iris agree to marry. They do.

Produced in 1921, the film was originally titled *The Silver Lining.* It was released in France as *La Cible Vivante.* It was cut by censors before its release in Germany.

Evelyn told an interviewer that she was paid £30 a week due to her success in American pictures.

*Reviews:* "Fine photography and lighting, and an excellent fight at the finish" (unidentified clipping).

"Evelyn Brent gives a beautifully restrained rendering of the part of 'Iris,' a girl of the people, while Adelqui Migliar ... makes a handsome and attractive lover. Norman Doxatt Pratt has the biggest role of his young life (he is only six) in this splendid film" (unidentified clipping).

"Produced by an Anglo-Dutch firm, this silent melodrama was the second and last teaming of Chilean-born actor-producer-writer-director Adelqui Millar and American Evelyn Brent. Badly made with Dutch exteriors that bore no resemblance whatsoever to the London apparently depicted in Migliar's screenplay, *Circus Jim* was typical of the poor domestic fare presented to British audiences in the immediate post–World War I era" (Hans J. Wollstein, *All Movie Guide*).

## The Spanish Jade

(Famous Players–Lasky) 6700 ft. 5 reels. Released on April 30, 1922.

*Survival Status:* Presumed lost.

*Credits:* Producers, Adolph Zukor, Tom J. Geraghty; director, John S. Robertson; writer, Josephine Lovett; based on the play *The Spanish Jade* by Maurice Henry

Hewlett, Louis Joseph Vance; photography, Roy Overbaugh.

*Cast*: David Powell (Gil Pérez); Marc MacDermott (Don Luis Ramónez de Alavia); Charles de Rochefort (Esteban); Evelyn Brent (Mañuela); Lionel D'Aragon (Mañuela's stepfather); Frank Stanmore (Tormillo, Don Luis' servant); Roy Byford (Esteban's spy and confidant); Harry Ham (Oswald Manvers).

Manuela runs away from home when her stepfather wants to use her to pay his gambling debts to evil Esteban. The villain follows her and is killed, resulting in a trial.

Many exterior shots were filmed on location in Carmona, Spain.

David Powell was born in Scotland in 1883. He began his film acting career in 1912 and worked steadily until his death from pneumonia in New York in 1925.

Marc MacDermott (sometimes spelled McDermott) was born in Australia in 1881. He made his film debut in 1909 and enjoyed a prolific career until heavy drinking led to his death in 1929.

Charles de Rochefort, born in France in 1889, was primarily a French stage actor and producer. He died in 1952.

John S. Robertson also directed Brent in *Madonna of the Streets* (1930). Born in Canada in 1930, he's best known for directing John Barrymore in *Dr. Jekyll and Mr. Hyde* (1920). The Byrds recorded a song about him, "Old John Robertson," in the late 1960s. Married to writer Josephine Lovett, he died in 1964.

Josephine Lovett (1877–1958) was born in San Francisco and received an Oscar nomination for *Our Dancing Daughters* (1928).

An earlier version based on the same novel—and with the same title—was produced in 1915. Directed by Wilfred Lucas, it starred Betty Bellairs and Lucas.

*Reviews*: "Mr. Robertson has not done for *The Spanish Jade* what he did for *Dr. Jekyll and Mr. Hyde* and *Sentimental Tommy*. Nor does the original background give birth and color which might be expected.... Manuela ... is played by a Spanish girl, and while she gives evidence of no particular ability, she is pleasant to look at in her role" (unidentified clipping). (Brent must have had some ability if the reviewer believed the part of Manuela was played by a Spanish girl.)

"Included in the cast are such popular players as David Powell and Marc MacDermott. A new and well-received member of the cast was Evelyn Brent" (*La Crosse* [Wisconsin] *Tribune and Leader-Press*, July 13, 1922).

## *Trapped by the Mormons*

(Master Films) 6178 feet. Released in 1922.

*Survival Status*: Academy Film Archive (Beverly Hills); British Film Institute/National Film and Television Archive (London); Cineteca del Friuli (Gemona); George Eastman House (Rochester); UCLA Film and Television Archive (Los Angeles). Released on video (Grapevine, 71 min.).

*Credits*: Producer-director, H.B. Parkinson; writer, Frank Miller; based on the novel *The Love Story of a Mormon* by Winifred Graham; photography, T.R. Thumwood.

*Cast*: Evelyn Brent (Nora Prescott); Lewis Willoughby (Isoldi Keene); Ward McAllister (Elder Kuyler); Olaf Hytten (Elder Marz); Olive Sloan (Sadie Keane); George Wyn [Wynn] (Jim Foster); Cecil Morton York (Mr. Prescott).

Just outside Manchester, Mormon recruiter Isoldi Keene sets his sights on Nora Prescott, "a flower deemed worthy of the plucking." Spooky-eyed Isoldi successfully recruits Nora. "The little world around Nora had suddenly ceased to matter.... The stranger filled her thoughts." Nora's elderly parents (they seem more like grandparents) and boyfriend Jim are vehement Mormon haters, but they cannot change Nora's mind. "Isoldi has caught his bird ... like thousands of other dupes ... lured from home and into the Mormon net."

Nora, in turn, recruits several girlfriends. Isoldi convinces them through trickery that he can raise the dead. Isoldi realizes this seals the deal with Nora, and he thinks about what this will mean. "She shall be for myself alone! Jehovah! What a flower to crush!" Despite a beating from Nora's boyfriend Jim, Isoldi refuses to relinquish control of Nora. He calls Nora out of her bed (a great opportunity to see Brent with long hair), telling her they'll soon be married in London. Nora lies to her parents, explaining that she is leaving for Holland to work as a secretary for writer Sadie. The "writer" is actually one of Isoldi's wives, though she's told she's his sister.

Meanwhile, Jim stays in dogged pursuit. He and his detective friend camp out next to the house where Nora has been taken. The "baptism" scene is worth the price of admission. Several males, led by Isoldi, lead scantily clad females into an area with a walk-in pool. When the first woman walks in and out of the water, there is little left to the imagination.

Later that night, Isoldi takes Nora to a wild jazz club, complete with black musicians, drinking, and women dancing with women. Nora is warned by a waiter (actually Jim's detective) that Isoldi smuggles young girls to Utah. He gives her a piece of cloth to wave outside her window if she is in danger.

Upon returning to the house, Nora is told by a guilt-ridden Sadie that she is Isoldi's wife. Nora confronts Isoldi and unsuccessfully tries to escape.

The next morning Nora overhears the plan to murder Sadie. One of the men suggests they also murder Nora, but Isoldi says, no, she is for him. Isoldi leaves the room for a moment, and Nora overhears the other men insisting that she, too, must die. Unfortunately, Nora is in a windowless room and cannot use the piece of cloth.

Back at Nora's parents' house, a blind Mormon shows up at their door to distribute literature. Nora's father, who has been unable to walk for years, rises in rage and chases him away. He can walk again. "Oh my dear," his wife says, "to think that out of all this evil comes a little bit of good.... You can move! .... you can move!!...." Smiles and nods all around. We are not making this up. We're not sure why this awkward scene is in the movie (or a later one when Nora's mother prays right before her rescue) unless it's to show that the "real" God is on their side, not the Mormons: By the way, Cecil Morton York is particularly hammy in this picture.

Back where Nora is being held captive, Jim and the detective lament that a fog is making it difficult to see the house. Just about that time, Nora is transferred to a different room and places the cloth outside the window. Poisonous gas is released to kill Sadie, and the two men lock Nora in the room with Sadie. The fog lifts, and Jim and the detective contact the police and hurry next door.

The frenzied finale is on. Sex fiend Isoldi arrives in Nora's room. He begins pawing her while Jim is briefly stymied by the other Mormons. Jim successfully rescues Nora, the bad guys are taken away by the police, and the film ends with a passionate kiss by Jim and Nora.

Brent is photographed attractively, though she appears exceedingly thin. She is very good in this rather substantial part.

This British movie, also known as *The Mormon Peril*, is made to look and feel like a horror film. Mormon men are depicted as immoral ghouls, even vampirish. It's difficult to believe there was ever this much hatred and fear of Mormons, but after watching this film you will have viewed one of the most one-sided propaganda pieces ever made in commercial filmmaking. It wasn't alone. There were dozens of anti–Mormon films released in the early part of the 20th century.

Lewis (sometimes spelled Louis) Willoughby plays the Svengali-like Mormon who stalks and then mesmerizes Evelyn's dainty little Nora. Willoughby was married to silent film actress Olga Petrova, with whom Evelyn appeared in several of her earliest films.

Ward McAllister, born in Pennsylvania in 1891, was also a stage actor of note. He died in 1981.

Olive Sloan (sometimes spelled Sloane) was born in London in 1896. She died there in 1963, after amassing many BBC television credits in addition to her film work. She also appeared with Brent in *The Door That Has No Key* (1921).

George Wynn, in addition to acting, directed several British short films in 1922.

Winifred Graham, also known as Mrs. Theodore Cory, was a popular British novelist who often wrote about the dangers of Mormon missionaries. She was considered an expert on Mormons, even writing a history of the faith, though her work is now seen as highly biased and inaccurate.

The movie was based on Graham's *The Love Story of a Mormon*. There was a campy 2005 silent remake of *Trapped by the Mormons* with Emily Riehl-Bedford playing Nora Prescott. Drag king Johnny Kat played Isoldi. Many of the same title cards were used in the remake, though the ending is darker and more horror-oriented.

## The Experiment

(Stoll Picture Productions) 4900 ft. 5 reels. Released 1922.
*Survival Status:* Presumed lost.

*Credits*: Director, Sinclair Hill; writer, William J. Elliot; based on the novel *The Experiment* by Ethel M. Dell.

*Cast*: Evelyn Brent (Doris Fielding); Clive Brook (Vivian Caryll); Templar Powell (Maj. Maurice Brandon); Norma Whalley (Mrs. Lockyard); Charles Croker-King (Philip Abingdon); Cecil Kerr (Fricker); Laura Walker (The Nurse); Hilda Sims (Vera Abingdon).

Novelist Ethel Dell was born in London in 1881. Many of her novels were made into films in the silent era. She died in 1939.

## Married to a Mormon

(Master Films) 5800 ft. Released in April 1922.
*Survival Status:* Presumed lost.
*Credits*: Producer-director, H.B. Parkinson; writer, Frank Miller.
*Cast*: Evelyn Brent (Beryl Fane); Clive Brook (Lionel Daventry); George Wynn (Philip Lorimer); Booth Conway (Bigelow); Molly Adair (undetermined role).
*Reviews:* "[It] gains a little spurious interest owing to the fact that it is more or less topical, and Miss Evelyn Brent and Mr. Clive Brook act well in it" (*London Times*, May 31, 1922).

## Pages of Life

(Adelqui Migliar Productions) 5300 ft. Released in November 1922.
*Survival Status:* Presumed lost.
*Credits*: Director-writer, Adelqui Migliar; photography, Bert Ford.
*Cast*: Evelyn Brent (Mitzi / Dolores); Richard Turner (Valerius); Jack Trevor (Lord Mainwaring); Sunday Wilshin (Phyllis Mainwaring); Luis Hildago, Bardo de Mart (undetermined roles).

Sunday Wilshin, born Sundae Mary Aline Horne-Wilshin in London in 1905, made her film debut in *Pages of Life* and appeared in her last film in 1938. She eventually became a radio actor and producer and also wrote poetry books. She died in 1991.

## Held to Answer

(Metro Pictures Corp.) 6500 feet. Released on October 10, 1923.
*Survival Status:* Presumed lost.
*Credits*: Director, Harold Shaw; writer, Winifred Dunn; based on the novel *Held to Answer* by Peter Clark MacFarlane; photography, George Rizard.
*Cast*: House Peters (John Hampstead); Grace Carlyle (Marian Dounay); John St. Polis (Hiram Burbeck); Evelyn Brent (Bessie Burbeck); James Morrison (Rollie Burbeck); Lydia Knott (Mrs. Burbeck); Bull Montana ("Red" Lizard); Gale Henry (The maid); Thomas Guise (The judge); Robert Daly (The organist); Charles West ("Spider" Welch); Charles Mailes (District Attorney Searle).

John Hampstead leaves his acting career and girlfriend Marian to become a minister. He also finds a new girlfriend, Bessie. A resentful Marian tries to ruin Hampstead's reputation when she blames him for a theft actually committed by Bessie's brother Rollie. Rollie finally confesses, and Hampstead does not lose his congregation.

Brent became so ill during the production that her final scenes had to be filmed at her apartment. The film was described as "a mighty story of spiritual drama and intense passion."[11]

Director Harold Shaw died at the age of 38 in a 1926 automobile accident. He was at one time married to Edna Flugrath, sister of Viola Dana and Shirley Mason. Early in his career, Shaw acted and wrote scenarios.

House Peters was born Robert House Peters in England in 1880. Nicknamed "The Star of a Thousand Emotions," he was a matinee idol during the silent era. Peters made his film debut in 1913 and died in 1967.

James Morrison was born in Mattoon, Illinois, in 1888. He also appeared with Brent in *The Impostor* (1926). Morrison's last picture was released in 1927, and he eventually became a college speech and drama instructor. Morrison died in 1974.

Lydia Knott was born in Tyner, Indiana, in 1866. She appeared in her first film in 1914. Some sources credit her with an appearance with Brent in *The President's Mystery* (1936). Her son was Lambert Hillyer, who directed Brent in *Raiders of the South* (1947). Knott died in 1955.

Bull Montana, born Luigi Montagna in Italy in 1887, was a professional wrestler. He made his film debut in 1917 and died in 1950.

Gale Henry was born in Bear Valley, California, in 1893. Her first film appearance was in 1912, and she enjoyed a long silent screen career. The tall actress

*This publicity photograph was taken just after Evelyn had signed with Douglas Fairbanks.*

(5'9") appeared as Lady Baffles in a detective film series in 1915. Her last film was made in 1933. She died in 1972. Henry also appeared with Brent in *Darkened Rooms* (1929).

*Reviews:* "The action is rather deftly handled at times and there is considerable suspense created" (*Variety*, November 15, 1923).

## *Loving Lies*

(Associated Authors) 6526 ft. 69 min. Released on January 13, 1924.

*Survival Status:* Presumed lost.

*Credits:* Producers, Thompson Buchanan, Elmer Harris, Clark W. Thomas, Frank Woods; director, W. S. Van Dyke; writer, Thompson Buchanan; based on the short story "The Harbor Bar" by Peter Bernard Kyne; music, James C. Bradford.

*Cast:* Evelyn Brent (Ellen Craig); Monte Blue (Capt. Dan Stover); Joan Lowell (Madge Barlow); Charles Gerrard (Tom Hayden); Ralph Faulkner (Jack Ellis); Ethel Wales (Penny Wise); Andrew Waldron (Bill Keenan); Tom Kennedy (Captain Lindstrom).

Tugboat captain Dan Stover has lied about his dangerous career in order to protect wife Ellen. Dan attempts to rescue a ship on the night Ellen goes into labor. The baby dies, and Ellen is led to believe that Dan has been unfaithful to her. Ellen leaves him, but Dan rescues her when her ship begins to sink. They adopt a motherless child and reconcile.

The production was filmed at Laguna Beach and off its coast. Many cast members suffered from seasickness. Awkwardly worded advertising copy stated: "The story of a man who lied to his wife to quell the Fears ever in her heart. Then came the fall of Love and Home founded on Lies of Love—told to save hurt, but that brought only pain." Another took this approach: "What is a lie? Dictionaries say a lie is an intention to deceive. But there are lies, white lies, and loving lies. See this picture story and then Write Your Own Definition."

Director W.S. (Woody) Van Dyke was known as One-Take Woody for his speedy productions. He is best known for directing *The Thin Man* (1934) with William Powell and Myrna Loy. He received an Oscar nomination for that film as well as for *San Francisco* (1936). Born Woodbridge Strong Van Dyke II in San Diego in 1889, he committed suicide in 1943.

Thompson Buchanan, born in New York in 1877, was married to actress Joan Lowell from 1927 to 1929. He died in 1937.

Monte Blue was born in Indianapolis in 1887. At the age of eight, his mother placed him in an orphanage after the death of his father. Blue was a stuntman and assistant for D.W. Griffith early in his career. A popular silent star, he died in 1963.

Joan Lowell, born Helen Wagner in Berkeley, California, in 1902, appeared in only six films in her career. Lowell's book *The Cradle of the Deep* was made into what is supposedly one of the worst movies ever made, *Adventure Girl* (1934). It features Lowell's narration, and though some claim her book was fiction,

Lowell maintains it was non-fiction. Briefly married to Thompson Buchanan in the 1920s, she died in Brazil in 1967.

Ralph Faulkner was born in 1891 in San Antonio, Texas. An Olympic fencer, he was one of Hollywood's best swordfight coordinators in addition to his acting duties. He died in 1987.

Tom Kennedy also appeared with Brent in *Hollywood Boulevard* (1936). Born in New York City in 1885, the onetime boxer died in 1965. His film debut was in 1915, and he was still appearing in television episodes, including *Gunsmoke*, the year he died.

*Reviews:* "It is a depressing sort of a story, with the thrills provided by a series of shipwrecks and deaths. Pictorially it is rather well done, but the direction is decidedly draggy at times" (*Variety*, January 31, 1924).

"This picture is not likely to add to the toil of that municipal department whose duty it is to see that overflow audiences do not stand in the aisles" (*Photoplay*, April 1925).

## *The Shadow of the East*

[Alternate Title: *Shadow of the Desert*] (Fox Film Corp.) 5874 ft. 6 reels. Released on January 27, 1924.

*Survival Status:* Presumed lost.

*Credits:* Producer, William Fox; director, George Archainbaud; scenario, Fanny Hatton, Frederic Hatton; based on the novel *The Shadow of the East* by Edith Maude Hull; photography, Jules Cronjager.

*Cast:* Frank Mayo (Barry Craven); Mildred Harris (Gillian Locke); Norman Kerry (Said); Bertram Grassby (Kunwar Singh); Evelyn Brent (Lolaire); Edythe Chapman (Aunt Caroline); Joseph Swickard (John Locke); Lorimer Johnson (Peter Peters).

Barry Craven is living in India and married to Lolaire. When ex-girlfriend Gillian visits, Lolaire is driven mad with jealousy and kills herself. Barry returns with Gillian to England, but former servant Kunwar casts a spell that threatens the couple's happiness. When Kunwar is killed, the spell disappears.

The film is known as *The Shadow of the Desert* in the United Kingdom. Author Edith Maude Hull wrote the novel that was adapted to make *The Sheik*.

Brent was said to have borrowed a $1,000 sari from J.G. McGee, an assistant to director Archainbaud. "The garment is made of seven yards of silk trimmed with bullion gold and silver brocade and is one of the most fascinating costumes worn by East Indian belles."[12]

George Archainbaud, born in Paris in 1890, enjoyed a long film and television career. He started his film career in 1916. Archainbaud also directed Brent in *Framed* (1930) and *The Silver Horde* (1930). In the 1950s, Archainbaud directed many television shows, including *The Lone Ranger*, *Annie Oakley*, and *Lassie*. He died in 1959.

Writers Fanny (1870–1939) and Frederic Hatton (1879–1946) were married and collaborated on several movies.

Frank Mayo, born in New York in 1886, was married at one time to Dagmar Godowsky. Mayo appeared in many silent films and worked steadily until the late 1940s. He died in 1963. Mayo also appeared

with Brent in *The Plunderer* (1924), *Hollywood Boulevard* (1936), *Jungle Jim* (1937), and *Tip-Off Girls* (1938).

Mildred Harris, born in Cheyenne, Wyoming, in 1901, married Charles Chaplin in 1918. They divorced in 1920. She made her film debut in 1912 and appeared in more than one hundred films before her death in 1944.

Norman Kerry was born Arnold Kaiser in Rochester, New York, in 1894. He made his film debut in 1916 in a small role but eventually became a hugely successful silent film star. He died in 1956.

Edythe Chapman, born in Rochester, New York, in 1863, was nicknamed "Hollywood's Mother." The stage actress made her film debut in 1914 when she was 51 and quickly became a popular actress. She died in 1948.

*Reviews:* "Romance lovers will revel in it" (unidentified clipping).

"Evelyn Brent plays the lovely 'lotus flower' of India, Lolaire, with appailing (sic) charm" (*The Hamilton* [Ohio] *Daily News*, June 21, 1924).

## *The Arizona Express*

(Fox Film Corp.) 6316 ft. 76 min. Released on March 13, 1924.

*Survival Status:* Museum of Modern Art (New York). Released on video (Grapevine, 81 min.).

*Credits:* Producer, William Fox; director, Thomas Buckingham; scenario, Fred Jackson, Robert N. Lee; story, Lincoln J. Carter; photography, Sidney C. Wagner.

*Cast:* Pauline Starke (Katherine Keith); Evelyn Brent (Madeline Nichols); Ann Cornwall (Florence Brown); Harold Goodwin (David Keith); David Butler (Steve Butler); Francis McDonald (Victor Johnson); Frank Beal (Judge Ashton); William Humphrey (Henry MacFarlane).

"Waking peaceful valleys and thundering through granite heights, the Arizona Express speeds westward." This is the first title card for this fast-moving, action-packed silent melodrama. The Los Toros Café is in a New Mexico town that the Arizona Express passes through. "In less than a week Madeline Morgan, the new dancer, has half the masculine hearts of the town at her feet."

Meanwhile, Katherine is being hosted at a farewell dinner before her departure to do relief work in the Far East. To honor Katherine's magnanimous act, old windbag Judge Ashton begins his farewell dinner speech by pontificating, "And so with pride we send this lovely and gracious lady to aid and cheer the stricken people of a foreign—" His ostentatious speechifying is soon interrupted by the family's Asian house servant who announces that Katherine's brother David has a telephone call. It is Madeline, with whom he has been enjoying a dalliance. She convinces him to let her accompany him to the bank later that night (notice how tiny Brent appears next to 6'2" Goodwin). "I'm so lonesome for you tonight, Davie boy—won't you let me go with you to the bank?"

Although David's uncle tells him to stop seeing

Madeline, he's in love and asks her to marry him. This is bad news because she's in cahoots with criminal Victor who is back in town and waiting for her at her apartment. "Well, girlie, how goes it with the simp at the bank?" he asks. She proceeds to draw a map of the bank.

David's uncle visits Madeline in an attempt to end the affair and happens to see the map. Victor kills him. (You know Victor is a terrible man because he not only kills David's uncle, but he's abusive to Madeline's little dog, too.) David has followed his uncle to Lola's apartment. Just at the moment when he's about to enter her apartment, a rainstorm knocks the power out. David and Victor fight in the darkness (except for flashes of light from the lightning).

After Victor escapes out the window, Madeline convinces David he has accidentally killed his uncle. David is tried and found guilty. The newspaper headline says it all: "MUST PAY THE EXTREME PENALTY: Dancer in whose room the fatal blow was struck declares that her love for young bank clerk caused jealous scene which led to crime. Doomed man to go to gallows at eight o'clock Friday morning of next week."

A fairly incredible (in every sense of the word) jailbreak results in David's freedom. He learns from another inmate that Madeline was part of Victor's gang and framed him. Before being killed by a prison guard, the inmate tells David where she can be found. David hops on the Arizona Express where amiable, hunky mail sorter Steve recognizes him as Katherine's brother. After David tells him his story, he promises to help. David is let off the train and goes to the house of the woman who loves him, Florence. She tends to David, who was seriously injured in the jailbreak.

Katherine decides to find Madeline. After reading Madeline's name scrawled across the back of her photograph, Katherine has an epiphany: "That woman is our only means of getting at the truth— I'm sure she knows a lot more than she has told" (the understatement of the year). She infiltrates the Kip Street Gang. However, her ruse is discovered. She pulls a gun on Madeline, escapes, and phones the governor's office claiming to have evidence that will prove her brother's innocence (a letter written by Victor to Madeline). She is told that her brother has been apprehended and will be executed the following morning unless she brings the evidence directly to the governor.

She takes the Arizona Express with the gang hot on her heels. Steve assures her they can make it to the governor's before eight the next morning. One of the gang members, however, jumps on the train to steal the evidence. The gang eventually succeeds in capturing Katherine when, in a remarkable scene, one of the gang members hands Katherine out of the moving train and into a moving automobile. In a sensational, heart-pounding finale, Steve successfully fights off the gang, jumps off the train onto the

ground, rolls down a hill to the edge of a ledge, and then jumps from the ledge into the automobile. He hands off the letter to Katherine, who then jumps out of the automobile. Steve and Victor fall out of the automobile and it careens off a cliff, smashing into bits, killing the other gang members. Katherine finds a horse and heads towards the governor's. Victor, too, is soon on horseback. However, before he can overtake her, the horse falls, and Victor suffers a fatal injury. David is freed from prison.

The last scene is an unfunny bit involving David, Florence, Steve, and Katherine at the dinner table being subjected to the pompous, boring speaker who accidentally keeps calling the butler with a floor buzzer.

Brent appears to have gained some much-needed weight since returning from England. She is photographed quite well and is superb as the vamp. Her character is a glamorous, sophisticated, and knowing woman, though totally amoral. Brent's smile has also significantly improved.

One of the best things about this film are the stunts. There are many of them, and they are really quite gripping and exciting.

Years later David Butler reminisced about the production, explaining that it "was filmed between San Diego and the Mexican border.... I remember that because I played an honest postman in it, and I had to run along the top of a train. I was inside the car with all the mail, and it was robbed. I was going to run up to get the engineer. The director said, 'You just start here and run.' When I got to the middle of the car, five guys dropped on me. That's the way they fought in those days, and you fought your way out of it. There were no doubles or anything else. Then we went over to some place in Mexico to get tequila."[13]

Pauline Starke was a WAMPAS Baby Star of 1922. Born in Missouri in 1901, she was a silent film star but made only a few films after that era ended. She sued director James Cruze because she claimed he hurt her employment opportunities by telling people she had difficulty remembering lines. Starke died in 1977.

Anne (credits listed her as Ann on this film) Cornwall was a WAMPAS Baby Star of 1925. Born in Brooklyn in 1897, she was only 4'10" tall. Cornwall died in 1980.

Harold Goodwin was born in Peoria, Illinois, in 1902. His long career began in 1915 and ended in 1973. He died in 1987. He also appeared with Brent in *Secret Orders* (1926) and *Forced Landing* (1941).

David Butler became a director in 1927. He eventually worked in television, directing such shows as *The Twilight Zone*, *Leave It to Beaver*, and *The Patty Duke Show*. Born in San Francisco in 1894, he survived the 1906 earthquake. Butler died in 1979.

Francis McDonald was a character actor who was married for a time to Mae Busch. Born in 1891, he died in 1968 after appearing in hundreds of movies and dozens of television shows. He also appeared with Brent in *The Dragnet* (1928) and *The Last Train from Madrid* (1937).

Frank Beal was also a writer and director. Born in Cleveland in 1862, his wife was actress Louise Lester, and their son was assistant director Scott R. Beal. Frank Beal died in 1934.

Born in 1875 in Massachusetts, William Humphrey enjoyed a long career as an actor and director. He died in 1942. Humphrey also appeared with Brent in *Lady Robinhood* and *Three Wise Crooks* (both 1925).

Writer Robert N. Lee received an Oscar nomination for *Little Caesar* (1931). Born in Montana in 1890, he died in 1964. His brother was writer-director Rowland V. Lee.

Writer Fred Jackson was born in Pittsburgh in 1886. Jackson, also known professionally as Frederick Jackson, was a playwright and screenwriter. He died in 1953. Jackson is also listed in the credits with Brent in *The Lone Chance* (1924).

Lincoln J. Carter was born in Rochester, New York, in 1865. A playwright who specialized in melodramas, he died in 1926. His name also appears in the credits of Brent's *The Cyclone Rider* (1924).

Director Thomas Buckingham died in 1934 at the age of 39. Born in Chicago in 1895, he also directed Brent in *The Cyclone Rider* (1924) and *Forbidden Cargo* (1925).

*Reviews:* "[I]t is a neat job throughout, and ... never drags" (*Variety*, April 23, 1924).

## The Plunderer

(Fox Film Corp.) 5812 ft. 6 reels. Released on March 30, 1924.

*Survival Status:* Presumed lost.

*Credits*: Producer, William Fox; director, George Archainbaud; scenario, Doty Hobart; story, Roy Norton; photography, Jules Cronjager.

*Cast*: Frank Mayo (Bill Matthews); Evelyn Brent (The Lily); Tom Santschi (Bill Presbey); James Mason (The Wolf); Peggy Shaw (Joan Presbey); Edward Phillips (Richard Townsend); Dan Mason (Bells Parks).

Bill Matthews goes west with friend Richard Townsend to mine for gold. Bill falls in love with saloon owner The Lily who tells him that Richard's girlfriend's father is stealing from their mine. After a confrontation, the father agrees to return the gold.

The film was described as a romantic western set in Gold Pan City. Supposedly there's a sign in Brent's dance hall that cleverly says: "If you want to know who's boss—Start something."

During filming, Frank Mayo became ill with pneumonia and missed several days of work.

Tom Santschi was born in Switzerland in 1878. A writer and director as well, he made his film acting debut in 1908. A leading man for a time, he appeared in more than three hundred films before his death in 1931.

Jim Mason, also known as James Mason, was born in France in 1889. He made his film debut in 1914 and appeared in many westerns. Mason died in 1959.

*Reviews:* "From start to finish the film is almost a continual thrill.... Evelyn Brent of the raven hair and the lovely dusky eyes ... can hardly hope to be cast for any other than

a wicked vampire part while she continues to play such a part so effectively" (*Park* [Utah] *Record*, September 12, 1924).

"An average mining melodrama with a good cast..." (unidentified clipping).

## The Lone Chance

(Fox Film Corp.) 4385 ft. 5 reels. Released on May 18, 1924.

*Survival Status:* Presumed lost.

*Credits*: Producer, William Fox; director, Howard Mitchell; scenario, Charles Kenyon; story, Frederick J. Jackson; photography, Bert Baldridge.

*Cast*: John Gilbert (Jack Saunders); Evelyn Brent (Margaret West); John Miljan (Lew Brody); Edwin Booth Tilton (Governor); Harry Todd (Burke); Frank Beal (Warden).

Inventor Jack Saunders agrees to plead guilty to a murder he did not commit in exchange for $20,000 and an early pardon. However, the deal is broken, and Saunders escapes from jail. It turns out his former girlfriend Margaret committed the murder in self-defense. They are reunited, and the truth comes out.

The working title was *The Mark of Cain*. A contemporary newspaper report described how director Mitchell filmed a wedding scene outdoors: "[H]e decided to use the inhabitants of the fashionable section for atmosphere. Hiding his camera in two leafy trees he started the action. Attracted by a smartly dressed group surrounding John Gilbert and Evelyn Brent, the neighbors gathered on the lawn to view the bride and groom. The scene was taken before the crowd laughingly realized it was being used as a background."[14]

John Gilbert, born John Cecil Pringle in Logan, Utah, in 1897, made his film acting debut in 1915 and became a major Hollywood star in the 1920s. He had celebrated romances with Greta Garbo, Marlene Dietrich, and Laurette Taylor and married and divorced Leatrice Joy, Ina Claire, and Virginia Bruce. Gilbert died in 1936.

Howard Mitchell, born in Pittsburgh, Pennsylvania, in 1883, was also an actor. He directed his last film in 1927 and went on to have a long acting career well into the 1950s. He died in 1958.

This was one of John Miljan's first film appearances. Born in South Dakota in 1892, he also appeared with Brent in *Forced Landing* (1941). Miljan died in 1960.

Writer Charles Kenyon also co-wrote *The Desert Outlaw* (1924). Born in San Francisco in 1880, he died in 1961.

## The Desert Outlaw

(Fox Film Corp.) 5576 ft. 6 reels. 65 min. Released on August 24, 1924.

*Survival Status:* Czech Film Archive.

*Credits*: Producer, William Fox; director, Edmund Mortimer; writer, Charles Kenyon; photography, Joseph Brotherton.

*Cast*: Buck Jones (Sam Langdon); Evelyn Brent (May

Halloway); De Witt Jennings (Doc McChesney); William Haynes (Tom Halloway); Claude Payton (Black Loomis); William Gould (The sheriff); Bob Klein (Mad McTavish).

Prospector Sam Langdon teams up with outlaw Tom Halloway. Both are foes of religious nut Mad McTavish. Eventually they triumph, and a romance develops between Sam and Tom's sister May.

During production, a surprise birthday party was held for villain De Witt Jennings. Refreshments included two cakes and fruit punch, along with Brent's homemade candy. After the festivities the crew visited William Haynes, who was in the hospital recovering from an on-set injury.[15]

Tag lines included "A Picture with a Thousand Throbs and Thrills" and "A blazing story of the cowboy trails."

The picture, like just about every movie Buck Jones starred in, was a western. Jones was born Charles Gebhart in Indiana in 1889. One of the most renowned cowboy film stars, he died in 1942 in a horrific Boston fire. Almost five hundred people died in the blaze at the Cocoanut Grove nightclub where Jones was being honored and doing publicity work for Monogram's Rough Rider movie series. Jones appeared again with Brent in *Sudden Bill Dorn* (1937), which he also produced.

Director Edmund Mortimer, like many other silent film directors, eventually became a character actor when the talkies arrived. Born in New York City in 1874, Mortimer died in 1944.

*Reviews:* "While it has become bromidic to praise the photography in western films, this must be mentioned as the height of artistic and creative camera work from the opening caption to the final fade-out. The riding scenes are well directed, and there is a stirring underwater fight near the end that gets away from the usual cliff-edge stuff" (*Variety*, November 12, 1924).

## The Cyclone Rider

(Fox Film Corp.) 6472 ft. 7 reels. Released on September 1, 1924.

*Survival Status:* Exists in Czech Film Archive.

*Credits:* Director-writer, Tom Buckingham; story, Lincoln J. Carter; photography, Sidney Wagner.

*Cast:* Reed Howes (Richard Armstrong); Alma Bennett (Doris Steele); William Bailey (Reynard Trask); Margaret McWade (Mrs. Armstrong); Frank Beal (Robert Steele); Evelyn Brent ("Weeping Wanda"); Eugene Pallette (Eddie); Ben Deeley ("Silent Dan"); Charles Conklin (Remus); Bud Jamison (Romulus); Ben Hendricks Jr. (Taxi driver).

Inventor Richard Armstrong has fallen in love with Robert Steele's daughter Doris. Steele agrees that Richard can wed his daughter if he wins an automobile race. Armstrong defeats bad guy Trask and gets the girl.

Brent again played a gangster queen in this picture. The "High-Speed Melodrama" was said to contain "Every thrill known on land, on sea, and in the air in one grand panorama of whirling action—Speed and death defying stunts galore." Advertisements proclaimed the picture was "A Roaring Race for Gold and Girl." Publicists also modestly suggested that it was "THE GREATEST THRILL PICTURE THIS YEAR."

Reed Howes was born Herman Reed Howes in Washington, D.C., in 1900. He made his film debut in 1923 and worked steadily until his death in 1964, usually appearing in westerns. A former model for Arrow Collar ads, he was a leading man during the silent film era and then was often seen in villain roles.

Character actor William Bailey, born Gordon Reineck in 1886, made his film debut in 1911. Also a stage actor, Bailey was still acting into the late 1950s. He died in 1962.

Margaret McWade was a former vaudevillian who appeared in an act with Margaret Seddon called the Pixilated Sisters. Born in Illinois in 1872, she died in 1956.

Charles Conklin, also known as Chester and Heinie, was born in San Francisco in 1886. Best known for appearing in Mack Sennett comedies, he died in 1959. He also appeared with Brent in *Traveling Husbands* (1931).

*Reviews:* "There are all sorts of thrills here, from a near-tragedy atop a skeleton of a skyscraper to a smash in an auto race, and, too, there are several wistful love scenes to relieve the tension" (*Syracuse Herald*, January 5, 1925).

"[A] stunt melodrama that does not take itself very seriously. Plenty of thrills, quite a little of humour.... Good entertainment" (unidentified clipping).

## The Dangerous Flirt

(Gothic Pictures Distribution Company) 5297 ft. 6 reels. Released on October 19, 1924.

*Survival Status:* Presumed lost.

*Credits:* Director, Tod Browning; assistant director, Fred Tyler; scenario, E. Richard Schayer; based on the short story "The Prude" by Julie Herne; photography, Lucien Andriot, Maynard Rugg.

*Cast:* Evelyn Brent (Sheila Fairfax); Edward Earle (Dick Morris); Sheldon Lewis (Don Alfonso); Clarissa Selwynne (Aunt Prissy [Priscilla Fairfax]); Pierre Gendron (Captain José Gonzales).

The film is also known as *The Dangerous Flirtation.* The story is an attempt to show how the lack of sex education can damage relationships. Well, sort of. Sheila is raised by an uptight unmarried aunt who frowns on all things sexual. When Sheila marries Dick, he assumes her aloofness means she does not love him. He leaves her and travels to South America. Realizing she *does* love him, Sheila follows him there and they reunite, ostensibly to live happily ever after.

Brent later described Browning as "a very good director. Remember *Freaks* [1932]? That was Tod. Anything weird, away from the ordinary, he loved. Regardless. A script was a very loose thing in those days.... Tod would read us a sequence that was going to be done, and he'd change the whole thing. There was no dialogue, so it was much easier. He had great flair."[16]

Browning, born Charles Albert Browning in

Louisville, Kentucky, in 1880, was also a writer, actor, and producer. He also directed Brent in *Silk Stocking Sal* (1924). Browning died in 1962.

Writer Richard Schayer, born in Washington, D.C., in 1880, also wrote *Silk Stocking Sal* (1924). He died in 1956.

Edward (Eddie) Earle was born in Canada in 1882. He made his film debut in 1914 and became a silent film star. Earle appeared in more than four hundred films and television shows before his death in 1972.

Clarissa Selwynne, born in England in 1886, made her film debut in 1914. She died in 1948. Selwynne also appeared with Brent in *Broadway Lady* (1925).

Publicists had a field day with this one: "WIVES WATCH YOUR HUSBANDS! Come-hither eyes— Long lips—Flashing smile—Pop—Jazz—Speed— Zip—OH HOW SHE CAN FLIRT!" A variation was offered for unmarried women: "GIRLS WATCH YOUR SWEETHEARTS! If you once let her get started—She steals their hearts and makes them like it!"

In some ads, Brent was promoted: "A brilliant and beautiful new star in a stirringly dramatic photoplay about a simple little jenny wren who became a dazzling Bird of Paradise—for whose hand all men clamored."

*Reviews:* "This drama is well-acted, with Evelyn Brent as the girl scoring repeatedly.... [H]er scenes where the husband, played by Edward Earle, misunderstands her timidity are marvels of realism and dramatic force, and the point the story sets out to make is unmistakably accomplished" (*Moving Picture World*, November 29, 1924).

"An intentionally dirty picture with its basis placed upon the fear a young girl holds of her husband on their wedding night. Such stuff is for defter hands than Julie Herne and Tod Browning. From the story the director has fashioned a set of sequences that are as crude as they are distasteful. They leave the picture unsuited to family houses and the better theatres" (*Variety*, December 17, 1924).

"...an intriguing little drama spiced with a dash of the *risqué*" (*Photoplay*).

## My Husband's Wives

(Fox Film Corp.) 4609 ft. 5 reels. Released on November 16, 1924.

*Survival Status:* Presumed lost.

*Credits:* Producer, William Fox; director, Maurice Elvey; scenario, Dorothy Yost; story, Barbara La Marr; photography, Joseph Valentine.

*Cast:* Shirley Mason (Vale Harvey); Bryant Washburn (William Harvey); Evelyn Brent (Marie Wynn); Paulette Duval (Madame Corregio).

The picture was about a newlywed couple who faced complications because of the husband's previous marriage. Bryant Washburn played the husband, Mason was the new wife, and Brent played the ex-wife. Paulette Duval was a busybody who added fuel to the fire as far as the jealous new wife was concerned.

Some scenes were filmed in San Diego. The working title was *Her Husband's Wives*. It was based on

the story penned by tragic actress Barbara La Marr. It had been written years earlier when La Marr was employed as a scenario writer for Fox—before she started her career as one of Hollywood's most memorable vamps. She died on January 30, 1926. The official cause was tuberculosis, but her drinking and drugging lifestyle contributed to her death at the age of 29. According to publicity, the story deals "with the eternal triangle, but with an entirely new and decidedly different twist, which is worked out with a technique different from that usually employed in screen stories."[17]

Maurice Elvey was the first British director signed to a longterm contract by an American company. He was married to actress Isobel Elsom at the time the film was made. Born William Seward Folkard in England in 1887, he died in 1967.

Writer Dorothy Yost was the sister of screenwriter Robert Yost. Born in St. Louis, Missouri, in 1899, she died in 1967.

Shirley Mason was born Leonie Flugrath in Brooklyn in 1900. The sister of Viola Dana and Edna Flugath, she was a child actress who made her film debut in 1911. Mason retired in 1929 and died in 1979.

*Reviews:* "....very lavishly produced, and fairly well played by Shirley Mason, Bryant Washburn, Evelyn Brent, and Paulette Duvall. Feminine fans will like it" (unidentified clipping).

## Silk Stocking Sal

(Gothic Pictures) 5367 ft. 5 reels. Released on November 30, 1924.

*Survival Status:* Presumed lost.

*Credits:* Director, Tod Browning; assistant director, Fred Tyler; writer, E. Richard Schayer; photography, Silvano Balboni.

*Cast:* Evelyn Brent ("Stormy" Sal Martin); Robert Ellis (Bob Cooper); Earl Metcalfe (Bull Reagan); Alice Browning (Bargain Basement Annie); Virginia Madison (Mrs. Cooper); Marylynn Warner (Miss Cooper); John Gough (The "Gopher"); Louis Fitzroy (Abner Bingham).

Brent played a crook who is reformed by a gentleman whose safe she was caught robbing. She later helps him beat a murder rap.

Brent gave Tod Browning credit for starting "the Queen of the Underworld thing." She also thought him a fine director. "I had great respect for him as a director. I think he taught me a lot; he taught me to know what I was doing when I was doing a part, and it was the first time it consciously came to me."[18]

At least one theatre offered an unusual promotion: The Rialto in Waterloo, Iowa, distributed a free pair of "real" silk hose (a $1.50 value) to, one supposes, women attendees.

Earl Metcalfe was born in Kentucky in 1889. Also a silent film director, he made his acting debut in 1912. Metcalfe died under mysterious conditions at the age of 39 in 1928 when he fell out of an airplane in California.

Alice Browning, born in Missouri in 1887, died in

1944. Browning was married to director Tod Browning.

John Gough, born in Boston in 1894, made his film debut in 1915. He appeared in several films with Brent, including *Three Wise Crooks*, *Smooth as Satin*, *Midnight Molly*, *Broadway Lady*, *Alias Mary Flynn* (all 1925), and *Secret Orders* (1926).

*Reviews:* "[T]here is not only considerable action, but real hair-trigger suspense developed because of the good work of the players, excellent direction, and the clever manner in which the heroine uses all of her feminine wiles to taunt the crook into making the desired confession ... *Silk Stocking Sal* should provide good entertainment for patrons who like plenty of punch and suspense" (*Moving Picture World*, January 3, 1925).

## Midnight Molly

(Gothic Pictures) 5400 ft. 6 reels. Released on January 11, 1925.
*Survival Status:* British Film Institute/National Film and Television Archive (London).
*Credits:* Director, Lloyd Ingraham; assistant director, Pan Berman; scenario and story, Fred Kennedy Myton; photography, Silvano Balboni.
*Cast:* Evelyn Brent (Margaret Warren/Midnight Molly); John Dillon (Daley); Bruce Gordon (John Warren); Leon Bary (George Calvin); John Gough (Fogarty).

Brent played a dual role in this melodrama—the wife of an ambitious mayor and a female crook. Publicity writers described it as "A gripping melodrama—so tense it will keep you gasping."

Pan Berman, also known as Pandro S. Berman, was born in Pittsburgh in 1905 and died in 1996. He received an Oscar nomination for *Ivanhoe* (1952) and was awarded the Irving G. Thalberg Memorial Award in 1977. He also worked with Brent on *Smooth as Satin*, *Lady Robinhood*, and *Alias Mary Flynn* (all 1925).

Fred Myton was born in Kansas in 1885 and died in 1955. He began his film writing career in 1916. His name appears in the credits for eight films, all of which were produced between 1925 and 1926.

Born in New Jersey in 1876, John Dillon made his film debut in 1908. He died of pneumonia in 1937. His brother was Edward Dillon.

South African–born Bruce Gordon also appeared with Brent in *Smooth as Satin* (1925) and *Three Wise Crooks* (1925).

*Reviews:* "Dual roles are always fascinating and when coupled with a pretty young lady like Evelyn Brent why it's bound to be enjoyable" (*Photoplay*, April 1925).

"The author stretches our credulity nearly as far as he does our sympathy, and concentrates on his incidents to the great detriment of his artists. Most of these incidents are interesting enough in themselves to grip the onlooker, but at times the almost complete lack of character in his puppets becomes irritating. In spite of everything, Miss Evelyn Brent acts cleverly" (*London Times*, June 23, 1925).

"Evelyn Brent [plays] dual role of the erring wife of a politician and a girl crook who, on the wife's death in an accident, marries the politican and goes straight. The usual far-fetched situations of this type of thing" (unidentified clipping).

## Forbidden Cargo

(Gothic Productions) 4850 ft. 5 reels. Released on Feb 22, 1925.
*Survival Status:* Presumed lost.
*Credits:* Director, Thomas Buckingham; scenario and story, Frederick Kennedy Myton; photography, Silvano Balboni.
*Cast:* Evelyn Brent (Captain Joe/Josephine Drake); Robert Ellis (Jerry Burke); Boris Karloff (Pietro Castillano).

Brent is the daughter of a naval officer who goes by the name of Captain Joe and uses her father's ship to smuggle liquor. A hulking Boris Karloff is first mate Pietro. Robert Ellis plays Secret Service agent Jerry Burke, who comes aboard to secretly investigate the outfit. Forced into labor as a deck hand, Jerry is freed when pirates invade the ship. Jerry rescues Joe, and they end up shipwrecked on an island. As so often happens, Joe's intense dislike for Jerry turns to intense like. Pietro, however, recovers Joe's ship and attempts to rescue Joe and kill Jerry. However, Joe realizes that Pietro's interest in her is ... well, let's just say she doesn't return his feelings. She notifies a Government boat. Pietro starts the ship on fire and escapes with his followers. Meanwhile, Joe releases Jerry before the ship explodes, and the two escape together.

This was the first of two Brent films that Karloff appeared in. The future film star was working part-time as a truck driver for a Los Angeles cement company since film work did not pay enough.

Karloff, born William Henry Pratt in London in 1887, is best known for his horror film roles in such classics as *Frankenstein* (1931), *The Old Dark House* (1932), *The Mummy* (1932), and others. He narrated the television show *How the Grinch Stole Christmas!* in the 1960s. Karloff died in 1969. Karloff also appeared with Brent in *Lady Robinhood* (1925) and *Mr. Wong, Detective* (1938).

Silvano Balboni was born in Italy in 1894. He also worked with Brent on *Alias Mary Flynn*, *Smooth as Satin*, and *Lady Robinhood* (all 1925).

The title was changed to *Dangerous Cargo* in Great Britain because of a Peggy Hyland film already titled *Forbidden Cargoes*.

*Reviews:* "Splendidly directed and intensely interesting" (*Variety*, May 13, 1925).

"Robert Ellis, whose hair on a desert isle suggests he is a bay-rum runner, is a sound hero, and Boris Karloff a typical teeth-gritting villain" (*Kinematograph Weekly*, November 26, 1925).

"Bootlegging on the high seas, plenty of rough stuff, and some good work from Evelyn Brent..." (unidentified clipping).

## Alias Mary Flynn

(Film Booking Offices of America) 5559 ft. 6 reels. Released on May 3, 1925.
*Survival Status:* Presumed lost.
*Credits:* Director, Ralph Ince; assistant director, Pan Berman; scenario, Luella Bender, Frederick Myton; story, Frederick Myton, Edward J. Montagne; photography, Silvano Balboni.

*Cast*: Evelyn Brent (Mary Flynn); Malcolm McGregor (Tim Reagan); William V. Mong (John Reagan); Gladden James (Picadilly Charlie); Lou Payne (Jason Forbes); Wilson Benge (Maurice Deperre); John Gough (Mickey); Jacques D'Auray (Chief of crooks).

Gangster Mary Flynn wants to go straight. John Reagan helps her, but when he gets blackmailed and is forced to steal a valuable gem, Mary becomes involved. Things look dark for both of them, but when the dust settles, Mary emerges as a hero, and she and John's son Tim marry.

During the film's production, Brent attempted suicide. The set was probably not the jolliest in the world A few weeks later, on April 9, 1925, in an apparently unrelated matter, director Ralph Ince announced to the press that he was divorcing his third wife Lucille, an actress and sister of Anita and George Stewart. In the announcement, Ince charged his wife with mental cruelty, accusing her of mistreatment and wrongful accusations. The couple had separated in April 1923 around the time George Stewart was involved in a violent fight with Ince; the injuries effectively ended Stewart's film career, and he died on Christmas Day, 1945.

The original title was *Alias Nora Flynn*. It is yet another underworld drama. Publicity proclaimed that Brent was the equal of stage legend Jane Cowl. "Since the days when Jane Cowl first made a great reputation in *Within the Law* there has been no better exponent of this dramatic school than Miss Brent. In *Midnight Molly* and *Silk Stocking Sal* she registered her worth. In *Forbidden Cargo* she enhanced her reputation. Now comes *Alias Mary Flynn*, a rattling crook drama of the same type yet vastly different from any; and better than her previous productions...."[19] Another ad shouted: "Evelyn Brent, star of *Silk Stocking Sal*, in a new Underworld Drama, better than ever. Hide Your Jewels! Bank Your Money! Hock Your Watch!"

Malcolm McGregor was born in New Jersey in 1892. In 1945 he burned to death in his Hollywood home when his clothing caught fire while he was smoking in bed.

Born in Pennsylvania in 1875, William V. Mong was also a writer and director. He died in 1940.

Wilson Benge often played butlers. Born in England in 1875, he died in 1955. He also acted on stage and occasionally produced stage plays.

This was Brent's first film with Ralph Ince. Born in Boston in 1887, Ince was also an actor, writer, and producer. His brother John was a director and actor, and another brother, Thomas, was the legendary producer, actor, and writer. Ralph Ince died April 10, 1937 in a London car accident. He also directed Brent in *Lady Robinhood* and *Smooth as Satin* (both 1925).

## Smooth as Satin

(R-C Pictures) 6003 ft. 6 reels. Released on June 14, 1925.
*Survival Status*: Presumed lost.
*Credits*: Director, Ralph Ince; assistant director, Pan Berman; based on the play "The Chatterbox" by Bayard

Veiller; adaptation and continuity, Fred Kennedy Myton; photography, Silvano Balboni.
*Cast*: Evelyn Brent (Gertie Jones); Bruce Gordon (Jimmy Hartigan); Fred Kelsey (Kersey); Fred Esmelton (Bill Munson); Mabel Van Buren (Mrs. Manson); John Gough (Henderson).

Brent was announced for the role on April 12, 1925. The film, based on the play *Chatterbox* by Bayard Veiller, was billed as "An Underworld Melodrama, with one of the most beautiful love stories ever projected on the screen." Other newspaper advertising proclaimed it "A roaring crook melodrama born in the fertile imagination of Bayard Veiller, author of *Within the Law* and *The Thirteenth Chair*." A press agent described the film in dramatic terms: "The story is a drama stretched so taut that it quivers like a steel cable under a terrific strain."[20]

Fred Kelsey, who at one time was a silent film director, specialized in portraying detectives. In 1931 it was estimated that he had been killed on-screen 400 times. "Eclipsing his own record as a target for blank cartridges, Kelsey also claims to have made about 700 arrests in his long career as a screen cop. This is probably a conservative estimate, since the actor's grizzled mustache, derby and cigar have been well known to picture fans since 1909."[21] Kelsey also appeared with Brent in *Bowery Champs* (1944). Born in Sandusky, Ohio, in 1884, he died in 1961.

*Reviews*: "Miss Brent is slender and attractive, and she gives a good account of herself as Gertie" (*New York Times*, June 23, 1925).

"The story isn't a strong one and has a theme that has been done before, but it is very well directed and the interest is sustained" (*Variety*, June 24, 1925).

"Evelyn Brent makes one of the best crooks in the business.... This is one of the dandiest crook pictures going, due to the fine suspense interest, and the continuity and direction as they should be" (*Photoplay*, September 1925).

## Lady Robinhood

(R-C Pictures) 5580 ft. 6 reels. 65 min. Released on July 26, 1925.
*Survival Status*: [Trailer only] Library of Congress (Washington, D.C.).
*Credits*: Director, Ralph Ince; assistant director, Pandro S. Berman; story, Burke Jenkins, Clifford Howard; continuity, Frederick Myton; photography, Silvano Balboni; props, Gene Rossi.
*Cast*: Evelyn Brent (Señorita Catalina/La Ortiga); Robert Ellis (Hugh Winthrop); Boris Karloff (Cabraza); William Humphrey (Governor); D'Arcy Corrigan (Padre); Robert Cauterio (Raimundo).

Brent played a double role in this action picture. She was the ward of a Spanish governor and a masked bandit who helped lead the peasants in a revolt against the governor. The governor and his evil assistant Cabraza steal from the peasants, and when Hugh Winthrop realizes their deceit he is arrested. Señorita Catalina, also known as La Ortiga, rescues Winthrop, and the peasants overthrow the governor and Cabraza.

Brent found it difficult to concentrate during her

scenes with the parrots. "[S]he has to sit between two parrots with one about four inches from her right ear and the other equally close. Instead of taking one afternoon, it took two days because Evelyn just couldn't remain still. She positively despises parrots now."[22]

Clifford Howard, born in Bethlehem, Pennsylvania, in 1868, also provided the story for *The Impostor* (1926). He died in 1942.

Writer Burke Jenkins, born in North Carolina in 1879, died in 1948. He is also in the credits of Brent's *Flame of the Argentine* (1926).

*Reviews:* "It would seem F.B.O. expended neither as much money nor as much care on *Lady Robinhood*.... A good many of the Spanish exteriors are obviously faked and most of the action takes place in a none too pretentious Castillian castle. Miss Brent's performance is again a high-light. Her type of beauty suggests particularly a Spanish charmer and she is very much at home in the fiery role of the lady insurgent" (*Variety*, August 26, 1925).

"Evelyn Brent, fiery and languid by turns, does well as the Spanish girl who is a bandit leader" (*Kinematograph Weekly*, October 22, 1925).

## Three Wise Crooks

(Gothic Productions) 6074 ft. 6 reels. Released on September 20, 1925.

*Survival Status:* Presumed lost.

*Credits:* Director, F. Harmon Weight; assistant director, Charles Kerr; scenario, John C. Brownell, Fred Kennedy Myton; story, John C. Brownell, Fred Kennedy Myton; photography, Roy Klaffki; props, Gene Rossi.

*Cast:* Evelyn Brent (Dolly); Fannie Midgley (Ma Dickenson); John Gough (Spug Casey); Bruce Gordon (Dan Pelton); William Humphrey (Grogan); Carroll Nye (Don Gray); Dodo Newton (Betsy).

Jewel robber Dolly hides out at Ma Dickenson's home. Dolly discovers that criminals are planning to steal from Ma and others. She enlists the aid of two cohorts, Spug and Dan, and they foil the attempt.

The British title was *Three of a Kind*. In July 1925, director Weight filmed a scene at the outdoor dining room at Westlake Park as he needed a background with a park and a lake. Weight was assigned the job based on his success with *Drusilla with a Million* (1925) with Mary Carr and Priscilla Bonner. Born in Salt Lake City, Utah, in 1887, he died in 1978.

This was Carroll Nye's film debut. He got his start in film following success on the stage. Mother Myra wrote for the *Los Angeles Times*, as did his sister Peggy, and Carroll himself later became a reporter for the *Times*. He played Scarlett O'Hara's short-lived second husband in *Gone with the Wind* (1939) and was married at one time to actress Helen Lynch. Born in Akron, Ohio, in 1901, he died in 1974. Nye also appeared with Brent in *The Impostor* (1926).

*Reviews:* "Pretty bad. Evelyn Brent tries to rescue the picture from mediocrity by some good acting, but to no avail" (*Photoplay*, February, 1926).

## Broadway Lady

(R-C Pictures) 5500 ft. 6 reels. 60 min. Released on November 15, 1925.

*Survival Status:* Library of Congress (Washington, D.C.).

*Credits:* Director, Wesley Ruggles; assistant director, Frank Geraghty; story and continuity, Fred Myton.

*Cast:* Evelyn Brent (Rosalie Ryan); Marjorie Bonner (Mary Andrews); Theodore von Eltz (Bob Westbrook); Joyce Compton (Phyllis Westbrook); Clarissa Selwyn (Mrs. Westbrook); Ernest Hilliard (Martyn Edwards); Johnny Gough (Johnny).

Brent played a sweet chorus girl who marries into society and becomes involved in a murder.

Director Wesley Ruggles, born in Los Angeles in 1889, received an Oscar nomination for *Cimarron* (1931). His brother was actor Charles Ruggles. Wesley died in 1972.

Marjorie Bonner was born in Washington, D.C., in 1905. The sister of actress Priscilla Bonner, Marjorie was married to English novelist Malcolm Lowery from 1940 until his death in 1957. Bonner died in 1988. She also appeared with Brent in *Secret Orders* (1926).

Theodore von Eltz, born Julius Theodore Von Eltz in New Haven, Connecticut, in 1893, made his film debut in 1915. He was a leading man in the silent film era before becoming a character actor, often cast as a villain. Von Eltz died in 1964. He also appeared with Brent in *Queen o' Diamonds* (1926).

Joyce Compton was born Eleanor Hunt in Lexington, Kentucky, in 1907. This was one of her first films; she went on to enjoy a long career in movies and television. She played dumb blondes to perfection, especially in movies like *The Awful Truth* (1937). Compton died in 1997.

*Reviews:* "Pretty good story with Evelyn Brent as a chorus girl with a heart of gold who marries into society and is innocently involved in a murder." (*Photoplay*, August 1926)

## Twisted Tales: The Eternal Triangle

(Reciprocity) 1186 ft. Released in 1925.

*Survival Status:* Survives at British Film Institute (London)

*Credits:* Producer, G.B. Samuelson; director, Alexander Butler.

*Cast:* Gerald Lawrence (Richard Wayne); Evelyn Brent (Anna).

*The Eternal Triangle* was part of the *Twisted Tales* series. "Produced by G.B. Samuelson and directed by Alexander Butler, ... *Twisted Tales* comprised 12 one-reelers featuring stories with surprise endings."[23] Additional films in the series included *How It Happened*, *The Skeleton Keys*, *The Death of Agnes*, and *Her Great Mistake*.

Unless footage was used from an earlier film Brent made in England circa 1920–1922, it is difficult to explain her appearance in a British film released in 1925, as she was in all probability still under contract to F.B.O. There was a six-week period from September to October 1925 when Brent was between films (and perhaps between contracts) and vacationing in New York City, but there is no evidence to suggest she went to England to make this film. But, as John Oliver, curator at BFI National Archive stated after viewing the film, "[C]haracter names ... in *The Eternal Triangle* are Richard Wayne (the husband), Anna (the wife), Felix Trevor (the lover) and Yoki (the servant). Only Brent and Lawrence are cited by name in the opening credits, but no behind-the-camera credits are listed.... [T]he story concerns an unfaithful wife (Brent) who ... hides her lover up the chimney when her suspicious husband (Gerald Lawrence) unexpectedly arrives home in the hope of catching them together. Realizing that the man is up the chimney the husband starts a fire saying he is ill and cold and needs warming up. The wife believes that her lover is being burnt to death, but it turns out that the lover has been pulled onto the roof from the chimney by the husband's Oriental servant, who then proceeds to drop burnt pieces of meat down the chimney to shock the wife.... The original nitrate print ... has edge codes that date it to 1926."

George Berthold Samuelson was born in Southport, England, in 1888. A pioneer of British cinema, he produced Arthur Conan Doyle's *A Study in Scarlet* in 1914 and later, according to Rachel Low, embarked on an "enterprising jaunt to Hollywood in early 1920 with partner H.H. Laurie, [Alexander] Butler and some of his staff to produce films at Universal City."[24] After Samuelson returned to England, "Reciprocity [Films] ... was formed in December 1924.... Much of Samuelson's production took the form of shorts series such as *Twisted Tales*, *Milestone Melodies* and *Proverbs*. His last handful of films appear to have been produced between 1925 and 1928, under the Reciprocity banner."[25] In 1925 Samuelson produced H. Rider Haggard's *She* starring Betty Blythe. He continued to write and direct films until 1934; and died in 1947. He is the subject of the book *Bertie: The Life and Times of G.B. Samuelson*. Samuelson was the father of cinemaphotographers David and Sydney Samuelson.

Alexander Butler began his directing career in 1913, directing scores of films for producer G.B. Samuelson between 1916 and 1925. Butler, an occasional actor, appeared as Mahomet in *She* (1925).

Gerald Lawrence was born in London in 1873. A successful stage actor, he made his film debut with Herbert Beerbohm Tree in *King John* (1899). Lawrence's next film appearance was twelve years later in *Henry VIII*, also with Tree. Thereafter, he appeared in less than a dozen films. His last appearance was in *The Iron Duke* (1934). Lawrence's marriage to Lillian Braithwaite produced a daughter, actress Joyce Carey. He died in 1957.

## Queen o' Diamonds

(R-C Pictures) 5129 ft. 6 reels. 55 min. Released on January 24, 1926.
*Survival Status*: Presumed lost.

*Credits*: Director, Chet (Chester) Withey; story and continuity, Fred Myton; photography, Roy Klaffki.
*Cast*: Evelyn Brent (Jeanette Durant/Jerry Lyon); Elsa Lorimer (Mrs. Ramsey); Phillips Smalley (Mr. Ramsey); William N. Bailey (LeRoy Phillips); Theodore von Eltz (Daniel Hammon).

Jerry Lyon's resemblance to Broadway actress Jeanette Durant leads to confusion. Jerry becomes involved in thievery and murder, but she ultimately clears herself.

Former silent film actor Chet Withey was also a writer, later providing the story for Brent's *The Jade Cup* (1926). Withey also directed Brent in *Secret Orders* and *The Impostor* (both 1926). Born in Park City, Utah, in 1887, he died in 1939.

Phillips Smalley was also a silent film director, writer, and producer. He was married to Lois Weber, a silent film writer, director, producer, and actress from 1906 to 1922. Born in Brooklyn in 1875, he died in 1939.

*Reviews*: "[Brent] is the perfect crookess. One who could cop the gold out of your teeth while looking into your eyes. That's Evelyn.... In *Queen o' Diamonds* she is the innocently accused chorus girl and also a prominent dramatic actress with thieving aspirations. And superb as both" (*Variety*, April 28, 1926).

"There's not much to recommend in this picture, but we think you'll live through it" (*Photoplay*, August 1926).

## Secret Orders

(R-C Pictures) 5486 ft. 6 reels. Released on March 7, 1926.
*Survival Status*: Presumed lost.
*Credits*: Director, Chet Withey; assistant director, Doran Cox; scenario, J. Grubb Alexander; story, Martin Justice; photography, Roy Klaffki.
*Cast*: Harold Goodwin (Eddie Delano); Robert Frazer (Bruce Corbin); Evelyn Brent (Janet Graham); John Gough (Spike Slavin); Marjorie Bonner (Mary, Janet's friend); Brandon Hurst (Butler); Frank Leigh (Cook).

Brent played a spy in this melodrama.

Frank Leigh, born in London in 1876, died in Hollywood in 1948. He made his film debut in 1917 and also appeared with Brent in *Flame of the Argentine* (1926), *The Impostor* (1926), and *A Night of Mystery* (1928).

*Reviews*: "Good entertainment.... Evelyn Brent is the woman spy and we're here to say the girl's good. Evelyn makes the most of every opportunity afforded her" (*Photoplay*, June 1926).

"The war spy system is again served for your entertainment. You won't object because Evelyn Brent is a treat for the optics" (*Photoplay*, August 1926).

## The Impostor

(Gothic Productions) 5457 ft. 6 reels. Released on April 18, 1926.
*Survival Status*: Presumed lost.
*Credits*: Director; Chet Withey; assistant director, Doran Cox; scenario, Ewart Adamson; story, Clifford Howard; photography, Roy Klaffki.
*Cast*: Evelyn Brent (Judith Gilbert [Canada Nell]); Carroll Nye (Dick Gilbert); James Morrison (Gordon); Frank

Leigh (De Mornoff); Jimmy Quinn (Lefty); Carlton Griffin (Morris); Edna Griffin (Ann Penn).

Brent played a wealthy society girl who helps her wayward brother when he becomes involved with crooks.

Born in Scotland in 1882, writer Ewart Adamson (he also used the name Dayle Douglas) died in 1945. He also appeared in the credits of Brent's *The Jade Cup* and *Flame of the Argentine* (both 1926).

*Reviews:* "If it's an Evelyn Brent picture it will eventually turn crooked. Even though we always enjoy her pictures, we are of the opinion that Evelyn should quit harping on this crook idea continually.... Fair" (*Photoplay*, July 1926).

## The Jade Cup

(Gothic Productions) 4656 ft. 5 reels. Released on May 30, 1926.

*Survival Status:* Presumed lost.

*Credits:* Director, Frank Hall Crane; assistant director, Gene Lowery; story, Chet Withey; continuity, Ewart Adamson; photography, Roy Klaffki.

*Cast:* Evelyn Brent (Peggy Allen); Jack Luden (Billy Crossan); Eugene Borden (Milano the Wop); George Cowl (Antoine Gerhardt); Charles Delaney ("Dice" Morey); Violet Palmer (Poppy).

Brent again played a woman who gets involved with a bunch of crooks—and helps someone who is unjustly accused of murder.

Jack Luden was one of the first graduates of the Paramount Pictures School, a training school for young potential stars. Classmates included Thelma Todd and Charles (Buddy) Rogers. Born Jacob Benson Luden in Reading, Pennsylvania, in 1901, Luden was at one time a pre-med student at Johns Hopkins University. He was also the nephew of the founder of Luden's Cough Drops. Educated in private schools, Luden was a troubled man whose favorite saying was "a crooked buck is sweeter than an honest dollar." Eventually, he was arrested for check fraud and heroin possession and ultimately died in 1951 in San Quentin Prison at the age of 49. He also appeared in *Why Bring That Up?* (1929).

Eugene Borden made his film debut in 1917 and was still acting well into the 1960s on television shows including *Combat!* and *The Donna Reed Show*. Often cast as a waiter, he died in 1971.

*Reviews:* "Evelyn Brent does her best, but it isn't her fault that this is barely palatable. What Evelyn needs is a new type of story" (*Photoplay*, September 1926).

## Flame of the Argentine

(R-C Pictures) 5004 ft. 5 reels. Released July 11, 1926.

*Survival Status:* Presumed lost.

*Credits:* Presenter, Joseph P. Kennedy; director, Edward Dillon; assistant director, Doran Cox; story, Burke Jenkins, Krag Johnson; continuity, Ewart Adamson; photography: Roy Klaffki.

*Cast:* Evelyn Brent (Inez Remírez); Orville Caldwell (Dan Prescott); Frank Leigh (Emilio Tovar); Dan Makarenko (Marsini); Rosita Marstini (Madame Marsini); Evelyn Selbie (Nana); Florence Turner (Doña Aguila).

This is another crook melodrama, but this time set in Argentina. Brent again played a woman who is bad and becomes good.

Yep, the presenter is the same Joseph P. Kennedy who was the father of President John F. Kennedy. Born in Boston in 1888, he died in 1969.

Evelyn Selbie made her film debut in 1911. Nicknamed Jet, she was also known as "The Broncho Billy Girl" because she made many Broncho Billy (Gilbert M. Anderson) films. Born in Ohio in 1871, she died in 1950.

Orville Caldwell was born in 1896 in Oakland, California. He made his film debut in 1923 and retired from films in 1938. In 1940 he was elected deputy manager in Los Angeles. Caldwell died in 1968.

*Reviews:* "A change of scenery is about the only thing new thing in Evelyn Brent's latest" (*Photoplay*, December 1926).

## Love 'Em and Leave 'Em

(Famous Players–Lasky) 62 min. Released on December 6, 1926.

*Survival Status:* British Film Institute/National Film and Television Archive (London); Cineteca del Friuli (Gemona); Cinémathèque Royale (Brussels); George Eastman House (Rochester); Library of Congress (Washington, D.C.). Released on video (Grapevine, 65 min.).

*Credits:* Producer, Jesse Lasky, Adolph Zukor; associate producer, William LeBaron; director, Frank Tuttle; screenplay and adaptation, Townsend Martin; based on the play *Love 'Em and Leave 'Em, a Comedy in Three Acts* by John V. A. Weaver, George Abbott; photography, George Webber; production editor, Ralph Block; editor, Julian Johnson.

*Cast:* Evelyn Brent (Mame Walsh); Lawrence Gray (Bill Billingsley); Louise Brooks (Janie Walsh); Osgood Perkins (Lem Woodruff); Jack Egan (Cartwright); Marcia Harris (Miss Streeter); Edward Garvey (Mr. Whinfer); Vera Sisson (Mrs. Whinfer); Joseph McClunn (August Whinfer); Arthur Donaldson (Mr. Schwartz); Elise Cabanna (Miss Gimple); Dorothy Mathews (Minnie); Anita Page.

"Hark! Hark! The lark at heaven's gate sings!" This first title card is followed by a shot of Mame waking up. "But after waiting up most of the night for her younger sister to get in, Mame Walsh isn't particularly interested in early birds." Right away, we learn that sister Janie is a handful. "When her mother died, Mame promised to take care of Janie—and she has been thankful ever since that Janie isn't twins." Mame also has to care for her no-good boyfriend Bill. "William Billinglsey—a ninety million to one shot for President of the United States." He's lazy, dumb, and conceited. Other than that, he's a great catch.

All three live at the same boardinghouse and work at Ginsburg's. "Ginsburg's Department Store was 'just a happy family of satisfied customer and contented clerks—' according to Mr. Ginsburg's annual speech at the employees' banquet." When Mame comes up with a creative way to enliven the window display (she uses a fan to create the effect of a breeze), Bill takes credit. "You man, I can see you have the artistic touch," he is told. Given the task of decorating the window by himself, Bill hands the assignment to Mame. She includes a live kitten in the display, much to Bill's chagrin. However, the display is a hit, and Bill, again, gets all the credit.

Mame goes on vacation and suggests Bill get Janie to help him. As you might expect, these two immature losers hit it off a little too well. (Besides being lazy, dumb, and conceited, Bill is also a two-timing heel—with the *sister*, yet. What exactly are his redeeming qualities? A nice smile and dimples don't count.) Mame, however, decides to return early because she realizes she's in love with Bill and wants to marry him. She returns home and tells everyone. At that exact moment, Bill and Janie are at a movie theatre. Janie spies a revealing costume on a poster and tells Bill she plans on wearing something like that to the upcoming Welfare League dance. "Well," the not-so-charming Bill says, "you've got two good reasons for wearing it, I'll say."

Mame and her friends hide in Bill's room, hoping to surprise him with a celebration. However, Bill returns with Janie. Hiding behind a door, Mame sees Bill and Janie kiss. Hurt and humiliated, she pretends it doesn't bother her. "Love 'em and leave 'em—that's me."

"I can't help it, can I, if he likes me best?" is the best that Janie can come up with when she speaks to Mame. (Add this to the list of things never to say to your sister if you've stolen her boyfriend.) Meanwhile, Janie is in even more trouble. She's treasurer of the store's Welfare League, but she's embezzled the donations to gamble on the horses. Although she wins her latest bet, Lem cheats her. When Miss Streeter arrives to pick up the donations, Janie claims the money has disappeared. Miss Streeter mistakenly assumes Mame has stolen it. Miss Streeter tells Mame that if she doesn't have the money by eleven o'clock that night, she'll notify the police.

Mame sends Janie to the dance and decides to trick Lem into returning the money. "So, instead of going to the dance, Mame gave Lem a thrill by suggesting a little party in his room." Janie entertains the crowd by dancing the Charleston at the dance, while Mame slow dances with Lem. Also at the dance, Miss Streeter tells Bill about Mame stealing the money. He defends her, and Miss Streeter fires him. Mame manages to steal back the money from Lem. However, while she is trying to call Miss Streeter, Lem violently tries to take it back. Bill, who had taken the phone call, realizes something is wrong and goes to the rooming house. By the time he arrives, Mame has defeated Lem. "Thank God, you're safe!" he says. Mame gives Bill a look. He's in a ridiculous costume, complete with tights. "Put on your pants and don't worry about me," she suggests. Mame arrives at the dance and gives the money to Miss Streeter, who promptly fires her. The store lech promises Janie that he'll give Mame a job. Janie wins a prize and is escorted away by Mr. Ginsburg in his Rolls Royce. We get the feeling they're not on their way to get a cou-ple of ice cream sundaes. Bill and Mame reconcile. They kiss in the display window. "Those dummies look almost human," one drunk says to another.

Overall, the film has a snappy pace and some truly clever lines. It's also an opportunity to see the interior of a 1920s-era department store.

There are two types of people in this world. One group believes that Evelyn Brent ran circles around Louise Brooks, and the other proclaims that Louise Brooks stole the film from Brent. We think this is one of Brent's best performances. She's always believable and shows great range. Also, she is photographed well and is beautiful throughout. Brent is particularly good in the scene where she seduces Lem. It shows she can play coy and flirtatious, but she also had to display a wide range of feelings and emotions and gives a complete characterization to a difficult role.

Brooks, on the other hand, played coy for the whole film. She gives a good performance, but the role is less demanding and includes lots of posing. There's no denying the camera loves Brooks, but we're convinced that Brent gives a superior performance. She is the most intelligent character in the film, a kind, decent, independent, strong, resourceful woman who makes the all-too-common mistake of falling in love with a putz.

Another problem with Brooks' performance is that her character is unlikable. Janie is spoiled, selfish, and shallow, and does not learn from her mistakes. Despite all the mayhem she has wreaked throughout the film, most notably in her sister's life, she indicates she will continue to be a terrible person. In fact, although the film ends happily with Mame reunited with boyfriend Bill, we strongly suspect that Janie will once again try to woo Bill, perhaps while Mame is busy with any future kids.

Brent's face shows lots of emotion, often in the same scene. One of her strongest scenes is when she watches her boyfriend and sister kiss. This was a challenging scene for director Tuttle. "I had already decided to shoot Evelyn's reaction through the narrow opening of the hinged side of a bedroom door, but I hadn't figured the right piece of business for Betty. I told her what was troubling me and we both began to puzzle over the right move. Betty's concentration caused her to press her cheeks with both hands. 'That's it,' I said. So when we took the shot, that's what she did and it worked perfectly."[26] Tuttle later directed Brent again in *Blind Alleys*.

The film was based on a successful stage play by Weaver and Abbott. Tuttle, a Yale graduate who also wrote and produced, admitted his task was difficult. "A story that has been tried and proven a success in another medium is a direct challenge to the director who converts it to the screen."[27]

Filming started on September 3, 1926, at the Paramount studios in Astoria, New York, and was completed on September 29. This was Brent's first film with Paramount since she had signed a long-term contract with them. She received top billing. The movie was awkwardly billed as "A story of modern youths' system of loving."

The film was remade as a dialogue film in 1929 and retitled *The Saturday Night Kid*. (Coincidentally, the director was the recently divorced husband of Louise Brooks, Eddie Sutherland.) Clara Bow played Brent's part, and Jean Arthur played Brooks'.

Louise Brooks was born in Cherryvale, Kansas, in 1906. Known as Brooksie, she was a ballet dancer and showgirl before becoming a popular film star. Bad luck and poor decisions led to a decline in fortunes. In her later life she became a successful writer. Brooks, who was briefly married to director Eddie Sutherland, died in Rochester, New York, in 1985.

George Abbott, also known as "Mr. Broadway," won eleven Tony awards for *The Pajama Game*, *Damn Yankees!*, and others. He also received an Oscar nomination for co-writing *All Quiet on the Western Front* (1930). Born in 1887, he died in 1995 at the age of 107(!).

John V.A. Weaver was also a screenwriter for *The Crowd* (1928), *The Adventures of Tom Sawyer* (1938), and others. Married to actress Peggy Wood, he died of tuberculosis at the age of 44 in 1938.

Editor Julian Johnson was married to Texas Guinan from 1910 to 1920. She was an actress who later became a Prohibition-era night club hostess known for greeting customers with "Hello, suckers!" Born in Chicago in 1885, Johnson died in 1965.

Osgood Perkins was a Broadway star and the father of actor Anthony Perkins. Born in Massachusetts in 1892, he was also a good friend of director Frank Tuttle, having worked with him on *The Cradle Buster* (1922). Osgood died of a heart attack at the age of 45 in 1937.

Jack Egan later appeared in the *Newlyweds and the Baby* comedy shorts (1928–1929) with Derelys Perdue (WAMPAS baby star of 1923) and Sunny Jim McKeen.

This was Vera Sisson's last film. Born in Salt Lake City, Utah, in 1891, she was married to actor-director Richard Rosson, who committed suicide (carbon monoxide poisoning) on May 31, 1953; Sisson killed herself with an overdose of pills on August 6, 1954.

This was Dorothy Mathews' first film role. She left film acting in the late 1940s and became the producer of television's *The Revlon Mirror Theatre* with husband Donald Davis. Born in New York City in 1912, she died in 1977.

Lawrence Gray was born in San Francisco in 1898. He made his last film in 1936 and died in Mexico in 1970.

Ed Garvey had once played football for Notre Dame, and was playing for the Hartford Blues, a professional team, when the film was made.[28] Born in Connecticut in 1865, he died in 1939.

Anita Page was an extra in this film. Born Anita Pomares in Flushing, New York, in 1910, the former leading lady was still appearing in films in 2004. Page died on September 6, 2008.

*Reviews:* "Acting honors go to Evelyn Brent. There is little left over for Louise Brooks and Arthur Donaldson" (*New York Morning Telegraph*, December 6, 1926).

"The film is amusing, with both Evelyn Brent and Louise Brooks doing good work" (*New York Evening Journal*, December 6, 1926).

"Miss Brent helps out quite a bit with the acting" (*New York Telegraph*, December 6, 1926).

"A featherweight comedy drama that should register with the public because of the fine work done by the principals and its amusing gags" (*New York Daily Mirror*, December 6, 1926).

"It deals with shop girls, window-dressers, and a race track tout, and except for a few sequences, it cannot be accused of possessing any vast degree of imagination.... Evelyn Brent is the shining light of the cast. She does as well as she has been permitted to do. Louise Brooks is an interesting type, but her acting in this film is not exactly studious nor can she be for an instant accused of submerging her personality in that of the character" (*New York Times*, December 8, 1926).

"The picture is capably directed with an eye to its comedy values as well as the love story.... Louise Brooks, playing an entirely unsympathetic role ... runs away with the picture.... It's Frank Tuttle's direction as much as anything that puts the picture over" (*Variety*, December 8, 1926).

"[I]nteresting, but not stimulating.... Evelyn Brent is excellent.... This young trouper has personality to burn. Louise Brooks pouts quite distractingly as the spoiled, younger sister. She has a good reason for being in the picture—in fact two of 'em, as one of the characters mentioned.... Lawrence Gray is handsome and agreeable ... and better still is learning how to act" (*Los Angeles Times*, December 11, 1926).

"Amusing true-to-life stuff with Louise Brooks as a cute little vamp" (*Photoplay*, April 1927).

"[T]he film was directed with both zest and sensitivity by Frank Tuttle.... The star is Evelyn Brent, but the picture is stolen by Brooks as Brent's amoral and selfish younger sister..." (Kevin Thomas, *Los Angeles Times*, July 3, 1991).

"The most exciting thing about *Love 'Em and Leave 'Em* was Louise Brooks as the gold-digging sister of Evelyn Brent" (John Douglas Eames, *The Paramount Story*, p. 40).

## Love's Greatest Mistake

(Famous Players–Lasky) 6007 ft. 6 reels. 72 min. Released on February 12, 1927.

*Survival Status:* Presumed lost.

*Credits*: Producers, Jesse L. Lasky, Adolph Zukor; associate producer, William LeBaron; director, Edward Sutherland; scenario, Becky Garner; based on the novel *Love's Greatest Mistake* by Frederic Arnold Kummer; photography, Leo Tover.

*Cast*: Evelyn Brent (Jane); William Powell (Don Kendall); James Hall (Harvey Gibbs); Josephine Dunn (Honey McNeil); Frank Morgan (William Ogden); Iris Gray (Sara Foote); Betty Byrne (Lovey Gibbs).

Brent played an adulterous wife who disappoints younger sister Honey when she has an affair. By the conclusion, Jane comes to her senses and realizes a long-term marriage is more important than a short-lived fling.

The story was serialized in *Liberty* magazine. Some scenes were filmed on New York City's elevated train tracks.

Newspaper advertisements paid particular attention to Brent: "Thrills and Humor reign Supreme in *Love's Greatest Mistake* ... Portrayed by the Brilliant Paramount Star Evelyn Brent.... An absorbing Story of the gay White Way. The intrigues and shadowy night life of the great metropolis. A marvel of dramatic situation, abounding in suspense, excitement and sensational events. An innocent small-town beauty in the toils of a blackmailer."

Josephine Dunn graduated from the Paramount School of Acting, which groomed junior actors. She played Honey, a beautiful but naïve young woman who comes to New York and becomes involved in a scandal. Dunn was born in New York City in 1906. She retired from films shortly after her marriage to Frank Case, owner of New York's Algonquin Hotel. Dunn died in 1983.

William Powell played an evil, self-interested cad, a typical role for him at this point in his career. Born in Pittsburgh, Pennsylvania, in 1892, he received Oscar nominations for *The Thin Man* (1934), *My Man Godfrey* (1936), and *Life with Father* (1947). Powell, who was married to Carole Lombard from 1931 to 1933, died in 1984. This was the first time Powell and Brent were paired together. They ended up appearing in seven films together; the others are *The Last Command* (1928), *Interference* (1928), *The Dragnet* (1928), *Beau Sabreur* (1928), *Paramount on Parade* (1930), and *High Pressure* (1932).

James Hall was a relative newcomer at this point. His big break had been in Pola Negri's *Hotel Imperial* (1927). Born in Dallas, Texas, in 1900, he died in 1940 at the age of 39 of cirrhosis.

Director Sutherland was born Albert Edward Sutherland in London in 1895. His parents were in show business, and his aunt was actress Charlotte Greenwood. He was married to Louise Brooks from 1926 to 1928. Probably best known for directing W.C. Fields and for his work on comedies, Sutherland was also a silent film actor (a Keystone Cop). He died in 1973. Sutherland shares credits with Brent in *Fast Company* (1929) and *Paramount on Parade* (1930).

*Reviews:* "A surprisingly interesting picture.... Surefire..." (*Variety*, February 16, 1927).

"[This] seems to be a maze of unrelated incidents which never quite get together enough to be called a plot. Furthermore, the title is practically all that is left of the original story.... Although Evelyn Brent is extravagantly featured in all advertising, she has but a minor role with no chance to be her usual vivid interesting herself. I entered the Metropolitan when the picture was a third way through, and it wasn't until the final reel that Miss Brent even appeared" (*Los Angeles Times*, February 19, 1927).

"This film ... moves along with all the grace and speed of a snail.... Evelyn Brent, competent though she is as a screen actress, is hardly suited to the role of a flighty, gullible wife" (*New York Times*, February 21, 1927).

"[It] possesses too much story.... [G]ood performances are contributed by William Powell and Evelyn Brent" (*Photoplay*, April 1927).

"There are too many familiar threads woven into the story and it also moves along too slowly" (*Syracuse Herald*, June 19, 1927).

## Blind Alleys

(Famous Players–Lasky) 5597 ft. 6 reels. 68 min. Released on February 26, 1927.

*Survival Status:* Presumed lost.

*Credits:* Producers, Jesse L. Lasky, Adolph Zukor; associate producer, William LeBaron; director, Frank Tuttle; screenplay, Emmet Crozier; story; Owen Davis; photography, Alvin Wyckoff.

*Cast:* Thomas Meighan (Capt. Dan Kirby); Evelyn Brent (Sally Ray); Greta Nissen (María d'Álvarez Kirby); Hugh Miller (Julio Lachados); Thomas Chalmers (Dr. Webster); Tammany Young (Gang leader).

This melodrama featured Meighan as a sea captain and Nissen as his Cuban wife. The couple arrive in New York, only to face all kinds of calamities. Brent played a woman who cares for Meighan when he is injured and falls in love with him.

Frank Tuttle also directed Brent in *Love 'Em and Leave 'Em* (1926). Born in New York City in 1892, the writer-director was a magazine journalist before entering the film industry. He died in 1963.

Born in Pennsylvania in 1879, Thomas Meighan was a silent film star, earning as much as $10,000 a week. His career declined after the coming of sound. His nephew was film director A. Edward Sutherland. Meighan died in 1936. He also appeared in *The Mating Call* (1928) with Brent.

Greta Nissen, born Grethe Ruzt-Nissen in Norway in 1906, suffered a career decline with the advent of sound. Her strong accent resulted in her being replaced by Jean Harlow in *Hell's Angels* (1930). She died in 1988.

*Reviews:* "Although the footage allotted to Evelyn Brent, as an amorous lady with designs on the young captain, was limited, she made the most of it and gave a commendable performance" (*Los Angeles Times*, April 25, 1927).

"[*Blind Alleys*] is a lazy, strained narrative to which Frank Tuttle, the director, has not imparted any great degree of imagination. It might justly be alluded to as a plain case of undershooting the intelligence mark of movie audiences, for spectators in the Paramount Theatre yesterday afternoon willfully laughed when it was intended that they should weep, or, at least, have a lump in their throats" (*New York Times*, March 1, 1927).

"*Blind Alleys* might have better been called *Coincidences*, for that's all it is.... Evelyn Brent, as the heavy, an unthankful role at its best, runs away with the honors" (*Variety*, March 2, 1927).

"The first story written by Owen Davis, the noted playwright, expressly for the screen indicates either his low opinion of that medium or his ignorance of what is required by it.... Greta Nissen, in a dark wig, is easily confused with Evelyn Brent, who, as usual, has too little to do, and the picture is notable for its complete lack of a gleam of humor" (*Los Angeles Times*, March 6, 1927).

"Lots of laughs in this one, but they all come at the serious moments" (*Photoplay*, October 1927).

## Underworld

(Paramount Famous Lasky Corp.) 7643 ft. 8 reels. 75 min. Released on August 20, 1927.

*Survival Status:* Arhiva Nationala de Filme (Bucharest); British Film Institute/National Film and Television Archive (London); Cinémathèque Française (Paris); Cinémathèque Québécoise (Montréal); Cinémathèque Royale (Brussels); Cineteca del Friuli (Gemona); Danish Film Institute (Copenhagen); Filmmuseum/Münchner Stadtmuseum (Munich); Jugoslovenska Kinoteka (Belgrade); George Eastman House (Rochester); Museum of Modern Art (New York); UCLA Film and Television Archive (Los Angeles).

*Credits*: Producers, Jesse Lasky, Adolph Zukor; associate producer, B.P. Schulberg; director, Josef von Sternberg; screenplay, Robert N. Lee; adaptation, Charles Furthman; story, Ben Hecht; titles, George Marion, Jr.; photography, Bert Glennon, Jr.; film editing, E. Lloyd Sheldon; set decoration; Hans Dreier.

*Cast*: George Bancroft (Bull Weed); Clive Brook (Rolls Royce); Evelyn Brent (Feathers); Larry Semon (Slippy Lewis); Fred Kohler (Buck Mulligan); Helen Lynch (His girl); Jerry Mandy (Paloma); Karl Morse (High Collar Sam).

"A great city in the dead of night. ... streets lonely, moon-flooded. ... buildings empty as the cliff-dwellings of a forgotten age." The first shot is a clock superimposed with a skyscraper. It's 2 o'clock. On a dark city street we see a drunk stumbling down the sidewalk. An explosion in a building startles him. "The great Bull Weed—closing another bank account." Bull grabs up the drunk and puts him in his getaway car. The drunk, Rolls Royce, assures Bull he is no squealer.

At the Dreamland Café, we meet Bull's girlfriend, Feathers. Gangster Buck Mulligan gets the not-so-bright idea to flirt with Feathers. He asks Rolls Royce, who's sweeping up, "How'd you like to pick up ten bucks?" Like most of us, Rolls Royce would like it very much. Buck wads up the money and throws it in a spittoon. Rolls Royce decides he doesn't want it that much and goes back to sweeping the floor. "Pick it up or I'll send you to the morgue!" Buck barks. Bull intervenes, which steams Buck.

Bull takes Rolls Royce back to his table and introduces him to Feathers, "my girl." Feathers' expression is priceless; she can't stand Bull. However, there is instant chemistry between Feathers and Rolls Royce. "How long since you had the body washed and polished, Rolls Royce?" she asks the unkempt Rolls. Before they leave the speakeasy, Bull performs a nifty trick where he *bends* a coin with his bare hands.

Outside, a neon sign is flashing **The City Is Yours**. (Five years later, in *Scarface*, obviously borrowing from *Underworld*, a neon sign will read **The World Is Yours**.) Later, Rolls compares Bull to Attila the Hun. "You were born two thousand years too late. You can't get away with your stuff—nowadays." Bull laughs it off and decides to help Rolls get back on his feet.

Bull takes Feathers to their old hideout. There's a heartwarming scene where Bull scolds a young boy for stealing an apple from a fruit cart. He then gives the kid some money and a boot in the pants—just before he eats the stolen apple.

Rolls is already at the hideout. A surprised Feathers sees Rolls cleaned up and looking just like sophis-

ticated, debonair Clive Brook. Bull has taken to calling him Professor. "Look at him," Bull chortles. "Cost me a thousand—looks like a million." Bull shows Feather how the hideout has been made into a fortress with a secret getaway.

Bull steals a piece of jewelry for Feathers (he frames Buck for the heist, thanks to a suggestion from Rolls). This sequence is a brilliant montage of a daring daylight jewel robbery and its immediate aftermath, using 11 cuts in 50 seconds. During the heist, he leaves Feathers and Rolls alone at the hideout. Watch for one of the film's sexiest scenes when Buck lights Feathers' cigarette. In a scene crackling with sexual tension, Feathers learns that Rolls was once a lawyer—and he claims he no longer has interest in women. (Von Sternberg uses close-ups to full effect here. There's not a wasted frame.) She doesn't believe him. The ice is finally broken when Feathers coquettishly tells Rolls, "I wear feathers all over." You can guess what he's thinking. Before you know it, they're fighting to control their urges. Rolls reminds her that Bull is their best friend. "This is the first time in a long while that I've felt ashamed," Feathers admits.

All three attend the gangsters' ball. "The underworld's annual armistice when—until dawn, rival gangsters bury the hatchet and park the machine-gun." Bull becomes jealous when he sees Rolls dancing with Feathers. He humiliates Rolls and drives him to drink again. Feathers cannot convince Rolls not to drink—and she tries very hard.

Later that night Feathers is elected queen of the ball. "[T]he brutal din of cheap music—booze—hate—lust—made a devil's carnival." There's a nice montage sequence showing the faces of the debauched. A distorted mirror shot is used to set the tone. By the way, Feathers' competitors are named Blossom Savoy, Dixie Allen, Trixie McCann, Bella Schmitz, Hazel Maginnis, Kitty Cuneo, Red Nichols (also the name of a famous musician of the period), and Magpie. (In Brent's next film with von Sternberg, *The Dragnet*, she would play a character called The Magpie.)

Bull has passed out, and Buck attempts to rape Feathers. Buck's girl awakens Bull, and Bull confronts Buck, who escapes out a window. Bull follows him back to his flower shop where he shoots him. While Bull is busy with Buck, Rolls and Feathers share a tender moment.

Bull, found guilty of murdering Buck, is sentenced to hang. Rolls hatches a plan to help Bull escape. Rolls plans to leave after the prison break, but Feathers has fallen in love with him. "If I lose you, it's my finish," she pleads. "I love you so—" Feathers convinces Rolls to go away with her, but they change their minds and agree to help Bull because of loyalty. "You see," she tells Rolls, "you taught me how to be decent." Paloma delivers Bull's last wish—a juicy steak—and tells him about the plan. After he leaves, a guard tells Bull that Rolls and Feather have been "carrying on." The plan is foiled, but Bull escapes on his own by overpowering his guard. He returns to the hideout, intending to kill Rolls. In a particularly chilling scene, Bull hears someone outside the door. He opens it to find a kitten and milk bottle. He brings both inside. Just when you think he's going to do something terrible to the kitten, Bull dips his finger inside the bottle and lets the kitten lick the milk off his finger.

A newsboy shouts out the news that Bull has escaped. Bull buys a newspaper and also sees another headline: "FEATHERS MCCOY PROVES FICKLE: Killer's Girl Takes New Sweetheart." Feathers arrives back at the hideout, thinking Bull has been executed. She's thrilled to see him alive, but he's enraged, especially when he learns the police have followed her. "So you've brought the police, too. You little rat!" It seems that about thirty million cops have arrived, though Feathers had nothing to do with it.

Bull plans to escape through a special door behind bookcases. "Now you can wait and take what you framed up for me!" he shouts. Feathers assures him they did try to get him out of prison. Bull can't go through the escape door because Rolls has the keys, and the door is locked. As Bull and the police exchange machine gun fire (totally destroying the apartment building), Rolls arrives. Bull wounds him.

"I'm sorry things went wrong," he apologizes to Bull, "but there's still time—for you—to get away!" Realizing he was wrong about his girlfriend and best pal, Bull sends Rolls and Feathers out the back way. "I've been all wrong, Feathers—I know it now—I've been wrong all the way—"

Bull surrenders with a smile on his face. The policeman scolds him, "And all this got you was another hour!" Bull explains, "There was something I had to find out—and that hour was worth more to me than my whole life!"

If you like gangster films, make sure you see *Underworld*. This is one of the first—and best—in that genre. As for Brent, *Underworld* helped make her a star. Her face is often a mask in this film, and, paradoxically, her lack of expression creates tons of emotion. Still, you can see her abject disgust for Bull early in the film. His charm has obviously worn thin over the years. According to James Card, "*Underworld* gave Sternberg the opportunity to begin his special technique of glamorizing a rather ordinary female face. With magical lighting and a sense of camera angle, which he possessed to a greater degree than any other American director, Sternberg caressed the face of Evelyn Brent, playing the gangster's girl, Feathers. He made her features glow with a luminous translucence that went far deeper than ordinary makeup."[29]

The film still packs a punch—as does Brent's performance. "Once when Sternberg's *Underworld* was being screened and the shimmering close-ups of Evelyn Brent as Feathers, the gangster's moll, were on the screen, one young man fell off his seat, writhing ecstatically in the aisle, happily moaning, 'O Feathers! Feathers!'"[30]

Clive Brook is wonderful in this film. He can sometimes be a bit too stiff in other roles, but in this one he shows vulnerability and intelligence as the reformed drunk who falls in love with Feathers.

Frank Lloyd was originally slated to direct the film. Art Rosson was then hired and fired in favor of Josef von Sternberg. Von Sternberg, who took over in March 1927, had been hired to be "in charge of photographic innovations."[31] Paramount diplomatically announced that Rosson was needed to direct Betty Bronson's *Grounds for Marriage* (later renamed *Ritzy*).

Writer Ben Hecht did not get along with director von Sternberg. However, there were certain things von Sternberg liked about the script, even if he didn't like Hecht's attitude towards him: "It had a good title and dealt with the escapades of a gangster. It was untried material, as no films had as yet been made of this deplorable phase of our culture. Though I considered Hecht an able writer ... he did not consider me an able director, dismissing me, when he heard that I had been assigned to his notes, with 'There are thousands like that guy playing chess on Avenue A.'"[32] Hecht criticized the film before its release and asked that his name be removed from the credits. It wasn't, and he ended up winning an Oscar for his work. When the movie proved to be remarkably successful, often selling out movie houses and setting box office records, Hecht took credit. "I wrote *Underworld* from the newspaper point of view. Fifteen years of reporting in Chicago gave me an unfictional attitude toward criminals, with the result that I feel *Underworld* to be a front-page story rather than a tale cut of the magazine sections."[33]

A stunned von Sternberg marveled at Hecht's behavior. "He failed to show embarrassment of any sort, though he had previously stated in the presence of the press that when he saw the film he felt about to vomit, his exact words being, as quoted in print: 'I must rush home at once, I think it's mal der mer.' In his various references to me in his printed works during three decades following my abuse of his 'original,' his stomach seemed never to have quieted down."[34] On the basis of his work on *Underworld*, Hecht was signed to a one-year contract by Paramount.

Buck Mulligan was based on gangster Dean (sometimes referred to as Dion) O'Banion, who was murdered in a flower shop. Ricardo Cortez was originally cast as the male lead. According to Tom Dardis, author of *Some Time in the Sun*, director Howard Hawks was an uncredited writer on the script.

The film's title was *Les Nuits de Chicago* in France, and *Paying the Penalty* in England. Filming took four weeks.

According to Kevin Brownlow, "Although it was adapted from a Ben Hecht treatment about the Cicero and South Side mob of Chicago—and although Hecht was a Chicago journalist who had witnessed the rise of the racketeers—the film was essentially the product of von Sternberg's imagination. The incidents, cleverly elaborated in Charles Furthman's story and Robert N. Lee's scenario, would have made an outstanding social film; as it was, von Sternberg turned them into a brilliant and almost poetic melodrama about the ethics of loyalty."[35] Brownlow concluded that the film, though "it had very little to do with reality," was "a magnificent piece of filmcraft."[36]

The studio did not have high hopes upon its release. Von Sternberg described how the film, "because of a dearth of product, [was] sneaked into the largest theatre in New York, unadvertised and with no advance notice of any kind."[37] It didn't matter. Word quickly spread. "Without benefit of the tush and gush or normal publicity which heralds each film as the greatest ever produced, my film opened at ten in the morning to avoid a review by the press, no critic being awake that early. Three hours later, no one knows how or why, Times Square was blocked by a huge crowd seeking to gain admission to the theatre, a crowd that stayed there and forced the theatre to stay open all night and remain open all night for the balance of the long run, thus inaugurating the era of gangster films and exhibitions of films around the clock."[38] According to von Sternberg, Jesse L. Lasky expressed his gratitude by giving him a medal as well as a $10,000 check.

On August 19, 1927, the Metropolitan Theater in Los Angeles held a tribute for the cast and crew. Although Brent was on the list of expected attendees, she had left for a New York vacation. Attendees included actors Bancroft, Kohler, and Brook.

Von Sternberg called the film "an experiment in photographic violence and montage."[39] He also claimed that the scene with the kitten was a blatant attempt to make the film more commercial. There are strong similarities between Bull and the character of Thunderbolt in the film of the same name (von Sternberg's first talkie). In fact, according to Thomas Leitch, *Thunderbolt* "was a virtual remake."[40] *Thunderbolt* (1929) starred George Bancroft, Fay Wray, and Richard Arlen.

Feathers' character is so named because of the prevalence of feathers in her costume. Von Sternberg had feathers sewed into Brent's underclothes. She wasn't kidding when she said, "I wear feathers all over." Marlene Dietrich's character was also named Feathers in *Shanghai Express*, and Angie Dickinson's character used the name in *Rio Bravo*. Writer Tom Dardis also found similarities between Feathers and the Marie Browning (Lauren Bacall) role in *To Have and Have Not*.

The *New York Times* named *Underworld* one the year's ten best. Long after her film career had ended, Brent understood that *Underworld* was an important film. "*Underworld* is a classic example of a gangster picture, because it's a picture of gangsterism. And he [von Sternberg] had people doing what they were supposed to do. I think it was wonderful. I really do. The last time I saw it, I still thought it was good."[41]

A newspaper ad proclaimed: "A thriller that will thrill you! A tale of modern gangster feuds—of No-mans Land in 20th century metropolis—that—and much more."

There was intriguing talk in 1937 about a sound remake that would star Akim Tamiroff, Lloyd Nolan, and Gail Patrick. However, it never happened.

Here's a little story that's guaranteed to make you see George Bancroft's performance in a different light. Brent described Bancroft as having "the reactions of a little boy. I don't mean he was retarded [which usually means that the speaker thinks the person is *semi*-retarded]." Brent explained that she and Bancroft had lunch with Priscilla Dean and her husband Leslie Arnold. They were discussing the film. "[H]e said, 'Do you realize why we were as good as we were in *Underworld*?' And I said, 'Because we had a damn good director.' And he said, 'No, it was because in the love scenes I always thought of my mother.' Does that make sense? Priscilla nearly fell out of her chair! That was George Bancroft!'"[42]

Bancroft, at least according to James Card, was the key to the film's success. "It was in 1927, with *Underworld*, that Sternberg hit his magnificent stride. It was a most fortunate bit of casting that he was able to use George Bancroft as his charismatic gangster. Not only was Bancroft the Charles Bronson of the pre-dialogue era, he was probably the very first of the screen villains who managed to have something really likable about him.... Bancroft had a visual laugh so hearty and robust that one felt sure it was being heard, though the film was silent. His craggy, rugged features would fragment into the merriest of laughter.... Then casting that smooth British performer Clive Brook as the gentleman drunk taken over by the gangster, he achieved an effective contrast to the beefy, extroverted American Attila."[43] There are lots of shots of Bancroft heartily laughing, and he comes across as a kind of maniacal brute.

Bancroft was born in Philadelphia in 1882. After attending the Naval Academy, Bancroft served in the Navy. He first worked as a theater manager but eventually became an actor, first on stage and then in movies. *Pony Express* was his first big role. Budd Schulberg described Bancroft in unflattering terms in his autobiography: "[T]o say that fame went to his head is understatement. Like fire down a cotton suit it spread to his chest, his pelvis, and down to his toes. As *Underworld* drew rave notices and lines around the block from New York to Rome, George Bancroft began to talk differently, walk differently, eat differently, think differently. I could see it in the way he drove through the main studio gate to his redecorated dressing room. When he waved at old Mac, the gateman who had been there forever, George's little flip of the hand was not so much patronizing as what one would expect of a British monarch acknowledging the salute of a loyal subject."[44] Brent's columnist friend Dorothy Herzog chastised Bancroft in 1929 when he acted as though he couldn't remember Brent's name. "Dear, dear George and Miss Brent only made three pictures together in succession and he can't remember the name. Still, I suppose one in pictures does meet so many people."[45]

Bancroft, who made $6,000 a week at the height of his career, died in 1956. As for his legendary laugh, Bancroft explained that he'd developed it to distinguish himself from Wallace Beery. "That laugh took a lot of effort ... and it's worth a lot of dough. I had to work out something individual. When the public sees a big guy on the screen it automatically supposes him to be Wallace Beery."[46]

Larry Semon was a former silent film comedian who'd made films for Vitagraph and Pathe. A huge star at one time, he later became a director for Mack Sennett and Paramount. He eventually lost his fortune, had a nervous breakdown, and contracted tuberculosis. He died in a sanitarium in October 1928 at the age of 37, though some question the circumstances surrounding his death. At the time he died, he was married to actress Dorothy Dwan. It's difficult to understand why he's in this film as he seems to exist only to make faces and act a bit creepy. Perhaps von Sternberg hired him as a favor.

Fred Kohler, born in Missouri in 1888, lost part of his right hand in a mining accident. He often played villains, especially in Westerns. Kohler died of a heart attack in 1938. Kohler is a great heavy and gives an intense performance in *Underworld*. He also appeared with Brent in *The Dragnet* (1928), *The Showdown* (1928), and *Daughter of Shanghai* (1937).

Helen Lynch, born in Montana in 1900, was a WAMPAS Baby Star of 1923. She began her film career in 1918. Married at one time to actor turned reporter Carroll Nye, Lynch died in 1965. She also appeared with Brent in *The Showdown* (1928) and *Why Bring That Up?* (1929).

Jerry Mandy was born Gerard Mandia in Utica, New York, in 1892. Sometimes billed as Ricardo Mandia, he appeared in more than a hundred films before his death in 1945. Though Mandy usually played waiters, barbers, cooks, and laborers, he does a hilarious turn as the "illustrious" Dr. Mandy in the Thelma Todd–ZaSu Pitts short *Let's Do Things*.

Josef von Sternberg (1894–1969) was born Jonas Sternberg in what is now Austria. He received Oscar nominations for *Morocco* (1930) and *Shanghai Express* (1932), both of which starred Marlene Dietrich. One of film history's greatest directors, he also directed Brent in *The Last Command* (1928) and *The Dragnet* (1928).

Writer Charles Furthman also worked on *The Last Command* and *Broadway*. Born in Chicago in 1884, he was the brother of writer Jules Furthman. He died in 1936.

*Reviews:* "[It] is a compelling subject, one that has a distinctly original vein.... Evelyn Brent is very attractive and she gives a capable performance as 'Feathers.' Sometimes Mr. von Sternberg shows that he is too fond of posing her looking away from the persons with whom she is supposed to be conversing, but that is his fault" (*New York Times*, August 22, 1927).

"...a whale of a film yarn.... *Underworld* runs 75 minutes and while it might stand a little chopping it grips right through" (*Variety*, August 24, 1927).

"If the baby has to go barefooted this winter, if the roof leaks like a sieve, and even if the lizzie needs gasoline, dig down into the jeans and go see *Underworld*.... The tale is told with an almost total absence of the usual movie hokum. Only at the end when the gangster admits that he has been in the wrong all the way is there a sop thrown in to the censors. Throughout, *Underworld* is played at a terrific pitch—suspense toward the end is almost nerve-wracking, and there is raw, vivid drama from beginning to end. It is very likely to create the furore [sic] on the screen that *Chicago* did on the stage." (*Los Angeles Times*, August 27, 1927).

"George Bancroft makes a powerful study of 'Bull' that you won't forget. It's the best role and performance of his screen career. Evelyn Brent is perfect as Feathers..." (*Syracuse Herald*, August 28, 1927).

"*Underworld* is just about the best underworld picture that has come along Melodrama it is, but melodrama that is human, that keeps its actors people, while unraveling a plot developed through the interplay of human temperaments, passions, feelings. Cinematically it is modern, in the stride of the art.... *Underworld* is a film of integrity on the part of director, scenario writer, actors and cameraman, done with back-bone..." (*National Board of Review Magazine*, August 1927).

"[S]cenes roll off the film with a lusty realism that makes it all the more regrettable that the producers should have seen fit to resort to the invariable Hollywood alchemy of turning even the gunman's heart to gold" (*Time*, September 5, 1927).

"A thrilling, and in spots, intensely gripping photoplay of the underworld.... [I]t is in the directorial and camera treatment that the picture is made to stand head and shoulders above any other cinema of like nature that can be called to mind" (*Atlanta Constitution*, September 13, 1927).

"Without a trace of doubt, it's the one great crook melodrama. There has never been anything like it" *Charleston Daily Mail* [West Virginia], October 17, 1927). This particular reviewer, who called himself (or herself) the Gallery God, really liked this picture. Another review in the same newspaper on December 17 stated: "*Underworld* is one of the two or three best pictures the Gallery God has seen since the [sic] 1927 was an infant in swaddling clothes.... When you see it, do your darndest to arrive for the start of the film. But see it anyway even if you see it backwards."

"Great story, great direction, great acting..." (*Photoplay*, October 1927).

"Often regarded as the first true gangster picture, *Underworld* is a vivid melodrama, elementary and sentimental, closer to *Othello* than to *Little Caesar* or *The Public Enemy* (Kevin Thomas, *Los Angeles Times*, July 21, 1987).

According to film historian Kevin Brownlow, "It was the film that began the gangster cycle, and it remains the masterpiece of the genre, containing all the elements which became clichés in later pictures."[47]

"...a dark, compelling crime picture with a strong, tense story and three fine performances from George Bancroft, Clive Brook (almost unrecognizable in the opening scenes as a shabby down-and-out) and a splendidly sultry Evelyn Brent" (Ivan Butler, *Silent Magic: Rediscovering the Silent Film Era*, p. 156).

"Long before Cagney or Robinson triggered a gat over

at Warner Bros., George Bancroft was the first gangster star in *Underworld*, beginning a genre that was to reach its peak of popularity in the early talking era. It was also a double first for Ben Hecht, who had not written for the screen before, and who carried off his first Academy Award for best original story.... The combined narrative and visual excitements had extraordinary impact.... [T]he public poured in" (John Douglas Eames, *The Paramount Story*, p. 46).

## Women's Wares

(Tiffany Productions) 5614 ft. 6 reels. 70 min. Released on October 1, 1927.

*Survival Status:* British Film Institute/National Film and Television Archive (London)

*Credits:* Director, Arthur Gregor; scenario, Frances Hyland; story, E. Morton Hough; photography, Chester Lyons; film editor, Desmond O'Brien; set decoration, Burgess Beall.

*Cast:* Evelyn Brent (Dolly Morton); Bert Lytell (Robert Crane); Larry Kent (Jimmie Hayes); Gertrude Short (Maisie Duncan); Myrtle Stedman (Mrs. James Crane); Richard Tucker (Frank Stanton); Cissy Fitzgerald (Mrs. Frank Stanton); Sylvia Ashton (Patron); Stanhope Wheatcroft (Floorwalker); Gino Corrado (Modiste); Robert Bolder (Boarder); James Mack (Patron).

The brief synopsis in the May 1928 *Photoplay* described the romantic drama: "Evelyn Brent as a beautiful model who is being constantly annoyed by naughty men." An Ogden, Utah, newspaper blurb stated, "The women will like this picture as the showing of wonderful gowns throughout the picture brings gasps of amazement."[48]

Bert Lytell, born in New York City in 1885, was a silent film star who made his film debut in 1917. Lytell was still acting on television into the 1950s until his death in 1954. Known for his early portrayals of the Lone Wolf and Boston Blackie, he was briefly married to Claire Windsor.

Myrtle Stedman was born in Chicago in 1885. Known as "The Girl with the Pearly Eyes," she appeared in films with then-husband Marshall Stedman. She died in 1938.

Cissy Fitzgerald, born in England in 1873, died in 1941. Known as "The Girl with the Wink," she first appeared on film in 1896 as, yes, a winking girl.

Gino Corrado was born in Florence, Italy, in 1893. He made his film debut in 1916 and worked steadily into the 1950s, specializing in waiters and cooks. Corrado died in 1982. He also appeared with Brent in *Daughter of Shanghai* (1938).

*Reviews:* "The plot of *Women's Wares* makes a story by A.A. Milne, written for his six-year-old son, sound like a dissertation on the universe by one of the early Germany philosophers—so simple is it.... Evelyn Brent, Dolly the model, is nice to look upon, even though you feel all along that her gold-digging tendencies will change for the moral uplift of everyone concerned" (*New York Times*, November 15, 1927).

"Direction apparently handicapped by script, but still not satisfactory" (*Variety*, November 23, 1927).

## Beau Sabreur

(Paramount Famous Lasky Corp.) 6704 ft. 7 reels. 67 min. Released on January 7, 1928.

*Survival Status:* Trailer released on video (*More Treasures from the American Film Archives, 1894–1931*)

*Credits:* Producers, Jesse L. Lasky, Adolph Zukor; director, John Waters; adaptation; Tom J. Geraghty; based on the novel *Beau Sabreur* by Percival Christopher Wren; titles, Julian Johnson; photography, C. Edgar Schoenbaum; film editor, Rose Lowenger.

*Cast:* Gary Cooper (Major Henri de Beaujolais); Evelyn Brent (Mary Vanbrugh); Noah Beery (Sheikh El Hammel); William Powell (Becque); Roscoe Karns (Buddy); Mitchell Lewis (Suleman the Strong); Arnold Kent (Raoul de Redon); Raoul Paoli (Dufour); Joan Standing (Maudie); Frank Reicher (General de Beaujolais); Oscar Smith (Djikki).

French Legionnaire Henri becomes known as Beau Sabreur after winning a duel against Becque. Henri's uncle implores him to give up women and serve France. He sends him to the desert where he meets American writer Mary Vanbrugh. Henri's vow to his uncle becomes difficult to keep when Mary gets involved in Becque's attempted vengeance. Henri kills Becque and professes his love for Mary.

Writer Percival Christopher Wren also wrote *Beau Geste*. Beau Sabreur translates to Beautiful Swordsman.

Following her success in *Underworld*, Paramount was eager to showcase Brent in another film. Husband Bernie Fineman announced Brent for the role in June 1927.

The biggest criticism against *Beau Geste* had been that it lacked any comedic elements. *Beau Sabreur* tried to address that complaint.

At least one writer has suggested that Paramount also had "a great deal of desert footage left from its brilliant 1926 production of *Beau Geste*."[49] In fact, the budget for *Beau Geste*'s sequel was almost cut in half, and Paramount used desert footage for *Beau Sabreur* that had not been used in the first production.

William Powell and Noah Beery were in *Beau Geste*, but since their characters were killed they were cast here in different roles. The original female lead was Esther Ralston, but Brent replaced her. The original director was James Cruze, who would direct Brent in *The Mating Call*, but he was replaced (momentarily) by William A. Wellman who pleaded that after his success on *Wings* he should be given a better picture. Little-known John Waters (no relation to the contemporary filmmaker) was hired.

*Beau Geste* had been filmed in Buttercup Valley near Yuma, Arizona, and the sequel used Red Rock Canyon in the Mojave Desert (about two hundred miles from Hollywood) and Guadalupe, California. *The Ten Commandments* also used the desert location at Guadalupe. Writer Frank Thompson provides us with some insight on how the budget was spent. "In advance of the actors' arrival, nine carpenters and assorted technicians were sent to Guadalupe to construct a prop tent, a hospital tent, a large tent with seats, a film room with loading dock, a water pipeline, water tank, and tank platform. A projection room was constructed and fitted out with projector and editing equipment. In all, one hundred fifty people were housed in the desert for fifteen days, which called for 1,590 lunches that cost Paramount $1.10 apiece."[50]

A literal city rose in the desert dunes during production. "Yesterday a barren spot on the great sand dunes of California; today it has a population of between 500 and 1000 men, women and children, and with a lighting plant, a hospital, a police force, a sewerage system, in fact, every adjunct of an up-to-date town [except] a newspaper [though the set apparently had a very able publicist!] and a chamber of commerce."[51] The contractor was W.L. Anderson, who had experience creating Hollywood cities through his work on *The Ten Commandments* and *The Winning of Barbara Worth*. "Comfort was the predominant note in the construction. Sabreur is 200 miles from Hollywood, fifty miles from a town of any importance whatsoever, and it was appreciated that the people who were going out there to live had to have much better accommodations than the nomadic tribesman they were to portray."[52]

The principal actors were given up-scale tents. "Each principal will have a private two-room tent, equipped with a bath and dressing-room, hot and cold running water, electric lights, a comfortable bed, not a camp cot. The rooms will be comfortable size, as the tents are 16 × 24. Tents for the atmosphere players are 16x16, arranged to accommodate five persons. For bathing there will be a twenty-unit shower bath building. An innovation in mess-hall accommodations will be tried out at Sabreur. The community dining hall, seating 1000 persons, and which will care for an average of 750 daily, will have comfortable chairs, such as found in a high-class restaurant, rather than hard wooden benches, and all tables will be kept covered with fresh linen daily."[53]

Filming began in July 1927 which necessitated the Guadalupe set. "Ordinarily the company would have been sent to the desert, but July being a hot month, Guadalupe must suffice. This was all very well, except that July is a month of fogs at Guadalupe and Waters was forced to wait until almost noon for the sun, then his difficulties were just begun. With the sun overhead, the nice long shadows of the desert were not to be obtained. Wait until later in the day? No, more fog."[54] Despite these obstacles, the film was finished in six weeks.

The desert fight scene required three days of filming and 35 cases of dynamite. According to an article in the *Los Angeles Times*, the film was the first to utilize radio communication. "The director, John Waters, sat near the first camera, with a radio telephone at his mouth. One mile away, where the warriors first appear, was another staff, the assistant director, Dick Johnston, and several aides linked up to Waters' direction by radio telephone. Waters gave the orders, which were transmitted over the air

waves, and Johnston and his helpers carried them out."[55] Fortunately, the careful planning meant there were no human or animal casualties.

The one thousand horses used in the film were rounded up in California, Montana, Wyoming, Texas, and Oregon. "One of the hardest jobs ever given Jack Moore, superintendent of the 1000-acre Paramount ranch in the foothills north of Hollywood, was that of rounding up 1000 steeds to aid in making *Beau Sabreur*.... It was for a fact such a strenuous task that Moore has been confined to a Southern California hospital ever since the animals were gotten together. He worked himself into a state of nervous collapse. 'I don't think that there are that many horses in all of California now,' Moore says.... 'When Director John Waters gave me the order, I sort of laughed. Thought it would be simple. I was wrong. It was just as simple as corralling 200 camels, which were also needed.... He had to circularize every menagerie and zoo in the United States to locate that many.'"[56]

In the book there were two American boys. However, in the film the American boys became Arab sheiks.

The film, most critics agree, did not come close to the grandeur of *Beau Geste*, but it was somewhat successful at the box office. Unfortunately, the film is now lost (though the trailer survives).

Admission to *Beau Geste* was more than the usual price. For example, in Utah the charge was thirty-five cents for adults (usually thirty cents), and a dime (usually a nickel) for children.

A third film was based on the last book of P.C. Wren's trilogy. *Beau Ideal* with Ralph Forbes and Loretta Young is considered the worst of the adaptations. Frank Thompson called it "a dreadful film, stilted and dull."[57]

Director John Waters began working in the film industry as a stagehand when he was 11. He worked as a camera operator, prop man, and electrician before being promoted to assistant director. He stayed in this position for eleven years until he was finally given the director's chair on *Desert Gold*. "Johnny Waters is known on the Paramount lot as 'that practical guy.' He just goes ahead and does the job without fuss or moody contemplation of the 'artistic values' to be derived from the script, taking what is set before him and making a picture of it as best he can."[58] Waters directed a handful of other films, but then became an assistant director again. He won an Oscar for Best Assistant Director in 1934 for *Viva Villa!* Born in New York City in 1893, he died in 1965.

Born Frank James Cooper in Helena, Montana, in 1901, Gary Cooper won Oscars for *Sergeant York* (1941) and *High Noon* (1952). He also received an Honorary Oscar in 1961 for lifetime achievement. In addition, Cooper received nominations for *Mr. Deeds Goes to Town* (1936), *The Pride of the Yankees* (1942), and *For Whom the Bell Tolls* (1943). Cooper died in 1961. He also appeared with Brent in *Para-*

*mount on Parade* (1930) and *Hollywood Boulevard* (1936).

Noah Beery, born in Kansas City, Missouri, in 1892, was the brother of Wallace Beery. Noah specialized in villain parts; his son was film and TV actor Noah Beery, Jr. He was married to actress Marguerite Lindsay from 1910 until his death in 1946.

Joan Standing, born in England in 1903, died in 1979. She made her film debut in 1919 and appeared in films until 1940.

Frank Reicher, who played a French officer, was once John Waters' boss when Reicher was a director. Born in Munich, Germany, in 1875, he died in 1965. Reicher also appeared with Brent in *King of Gamblers* (1937).

Arnold Kent, born Lido Manetti in Italy in 1899, died after being hit by a car in 1928. He also appeared with Brent in *The Showdown* (1928).

*Reviews*: "So magnificent are some of the desert scenes ... that yesterday afternoon an audience in the Paramount Theatre was stirred to applause.... Excellent direction, thoughtful casting and fine acting are contained in this offering.... Gary Cooper's work as Major Beaujolais is splendid.... Evelyn Brent and William Powell, who are both in *The Last Command*, also acquit themselves with distinction..." (Mordaunt Hall, *New York Times*, January 23, 1928).

"This tale is far under the horsepower of which [*Beau] Geste* could boast, and all in all is amongst the weakest features the Paramount has shown lately" (*Variety*, January 25, 1928).

"[I]t is above the average weekly-change attraction. It will suffer, however, because it so inevitably invites comparison with the other and better film, the similarity extending even to the title and the reappearance of at least two of the characters of *Beau Geste*. The fault most apparent ... is the absence of a great love theme, for it was this that dominated all else in the original production" (*Los Angeles Times*, January 30, 1928).

"Evelyn Brent ... does well indeed as the somewhat helpless heroine.... The sand of the desert ... is seen to fine effect, either snapping its angry yellow veil in the windy darkness, puffing smokily into the air after an explosion, or merely lying still under the sun like a quilt of shining yellow snow" (*Time*, February 6, 1928).

"The heart interest is put into the hands of Gary Cooper and Evelyn Brent and they managed to convey a lack of fervor that was either the result of histrionic limitations or inferior direction. In fact the entire story was put forth in half-hearted fashion..." (*Oakland Tribune*, February 13, 1928).

"Not another *Beau Geste*, but a thrilling and picturesque tale, nevertheless. You'll like Evelyn Brent, Gary Cooper, William Powell and Noah Beery" (*Photoplay*, May 1928).

"It would seem that the author of *Beau Geste* just couldn't let well enough alone.... *Beau Sabreur* is a tolerably interesting story.... Evelyn Brent is seen in the rather silly role of Mary Vanbrugh.... The picture has been beautifully produced, with all the care expected of an exceptional one. While it is far from dull, its pulse barely reaches normal" (*Picture Play*, May 1928).

"*Beau Sabreur* merely goes over familiar ground. It is well-enough staged, and is competently acted by Noah Beery. Gary Cooper is too grim as the hero, but Evelyn Brent reveals acting ability which shows that her talent flashed in *Underworld* is genuine" (*Motion Picture News*).

"Gary Cooper carries the hero part well. Evelyn Brent makes silly love interest worthwhile. William Powell a great heavy, as usual" (*Film Daily*).

## The Last Command

(Paramount Famous Lasky Corp.) 8154 ft. 9 reels. 90 min. Released on January 21, 1928.

*Survival Status*: Arhiva Nationala de Filme (Bucharest); Cinémathèque Royale (Brussels); Cineteca del Friuli (Gemona); Danish Film Institute (Copenhagen); George Eastman House (Rochester); Harvard Film Archive (Cambridge); Museum of Modern Art (New York City); UCLA Film and Television Archive (Los Angeles). Released on video. (Paramount, 88 min.)

*Credits*: Producers, Jesse L. Lasky, Adolph Zukor; supervising producer, J. G. Bachmann; associate producer, B. P. Schulberg; director, Josef von Sternberg; screenplay and adaptation, John F. Goodrich; story, Lajos Biro; titles, Herman J. Mankiewicz; photography, Bert Glennon; art direction, Nicholas Kobliansky; film editor, William Shea; set decoration, Hans Dreier; makeup, Fred C. Ryle.

*Cast*: Emil Jannings (General Dolgorucki [Grand Duke Sergius Alexander]); Evelyn Brent (Natalie Dabrova); William Powell (Leo Andreyev); Nicholas Soussanin (Adjutant); Michael Visaroff (Serge, the bodyguard); Jack Raymond (Assistant); Viacheslav Savitsky (Private); Fritz Feld (Revolutionist); Harry Semels (Soldier extra); Alexander Ikonnikov, Nicholas Kobliansky (Drillmasters).

The film starts with a title card telling us it's Hollywood in 1928. "The Magic Empire of the Twentieth Century! The Mecca of the World! To this Hollywood had come Leo Andreyev, a Russian director...."

Andreyev searches through a stack of photos for actors and is not happy with what he's seeing. As he pulls out a cigarette, all of his assistants immediately offer to light it for him, a wry comment on Hollywood sycophants. He finally stops looking through the piles when he sees the photo of Sergius Alexander. On the back of the photo he reads: "Claims to have been commanding general of Russian Army and cousin to czar. Little film experience—works for $7.50 a day." The director wants to cast him as a general. An assistant telephones the boarding house where he lives. The former general is frail and timid. He shuffles to the phone and is told to report at six A.M. the following morning.

The next title card reads "The Bread Line of Hollywood," and we see hundreds of desperate men behind the studio gates. Once the gate is opened, the men surge forward, crowding each other as they make their way inside the studio. Sergius receives his general's uniform, boots, cap, and rifle amidst a rude, shoving mob. A man mocks him for a physical tic—he persistently shakes his head as though saying "no." Sergius apologizes. "Excuse me, please—I can't help it—I—I had a great shock once!"

Sergius pins a medal on his uniform. When asked about it, he explains that the czar had given it to him. He is again mocked. These extras in the dressing room with him are truly a bunch of ill-mannered ruffians.

We are now treated to a flashback: "Imperial Russia—1917. Proud, majestic, haughty—seemingly eternal as the ages! On a dozen far-flung battle fronts, Russia was engaged in a death grapple with the enemy." We next see a particularly effective sequence beginning with a medium shot of a woman and her infant sitting on a snow bank. The camera tracks slowly back to reveal they are just a tiny part of the events on a busy city street where masses of desperate people, soldiers and citizens alike, are in the grip of war. All are in a mad rush, coming and going in all directions. As the camera continues to track back, the woman and child, a microcosm of the suffering of a whole nation, disappear from sight behind the wave of humanity. After the scenes showing bedlam in Russia, we meet the general. "Tireless in the defense of a crumbling empire was the Grand Duke Sergius Alexander, cousin to the Czar, and Commanding General of the Russian Armies." Proud, perhaps even arrogant, he is observed by revolutionists Natalie and Leo. "Let him strut a little longer!" Leo tells her. "His days are numbered." Natalie, who looks world-weary as well as drop-dead gorgeous, echoes his sentiment: "The days of *all* who are dragging Russia down are numbered!"

In a remarkable scene, Leo and Natalie are detained and taken to the general's office. When Leo gets smart with him, the general brutally strikes him with a whip and arrests him. After he is struck, Leo's glare at the general leaves no doubt that he will neither forget nor forgive. As for Natalie, the general sizes her up and likes what he sees. He asks her to accompany her to the new headquarters. She agrees.

The general dines with Natalie and she begins to understand that he is a principled man who is perturbed by the czar, especially requests that endanger his troops. The general tells her he would gladly die for Russia. She invites him to her room for coffee. Upon arriving, he begins making love to her but sees a gun hidden beneath a pillow. He offers her a cigarette, but she requests her own. The general walks to her dressing table, turning his back. Natalie pulls out the gun and stands. In a great mirror shot we see Natalie pointing the gun at the general's back. But she swoons and collapses. He helps her to her feet and asks her why she didn't shoot. "I suppose it was because I couldn't kill—anyone—who loves Russia as much as you do!" He takes her head in his hands. "From now on you are my prisoner of war—and my prisoner of love."

The general, his staff, and Natalie travel on a train that has been targeted by the revolutionaries. "His Imperial Highness will be here in five minutes! Let's give him the greatest reception he has ever had!" a revolutionary announces to the crowd. When it appears that the angry mob plans to kill the general, a passionate Natalie steps to the front of them. "This is the end, your Imperial Highness! It is our turn now! Let's hang him in Petrograd—for all the world to see!" The crowd overpowers and beats him. Natalie again steps forward. "Look at him! The greatest man in Russia—greater even than the Czar!" She spits upon him. "Make him sweat as *we* have sweated! Make him stoke our train to Petrograd!" The crowd, mocking him, put him back on the train. He is forced to shovel coal.

Meanwhile, two men fight over Natalie. One has stolen the general's coat. "That woman," he says, "belongs with me—she goes with the coat!" The other shoots him to death and takes the coat. The revolutionaries party on the train while Natalie suddenly disappears. She joins the general in the coal car. Now collapsed, he pushes her away. "Don't you understand?" she explains. "It was the only way I could save your life. I love you!" She gives him the pearls he'd given her. "These pearls will pay your way out of Russia!"

With her help, he escapes from the train, jumping into a snow bank. Natalie, however, remains on the train. He watches as a bridge collapses, and the train falls into the icy river. We now see that this is when he acquired the head shaking tic.

"And so the backwash of a tortured nation had carried still another extra to Hollywood." Leo, who escaped, is now a fancy pants directors. The extras report to the set. An assistant insists that the general wear a particular medal in a specific place. The general argues that it isn't accurate. "I've made twenty Russian pictures," the assistant claims. "You can't tell me anything about Russia!"

As we near the conclusion, Leo confronts the general. He puts the medal in the right place on the general's jacket. Leo asks for a whip. "I have waited ten years for this moment, Your Imperial Highness," Leo tells the general. "The same coat, the same uniform, the same man—only the times have changed!"

Leo gives the general his instructions. He tells him to whip a man. "We won't have to rehearse that scene—I know you can use a whip!" As they start the scene, Leo asks that the Russian National Anthem be played. The general is transported back. He seems to believe he is truly fighting the war again. "People of Russia, you are being led by traitors—we must win or Russia will perish!" he says in a line that echoes a previous one in the film. His enthusiastic acting frightens the crew. "Long Live Russia!" he proclaims and then collapses. Leo cradles him. "Have we won?" the general asks. Leo assures him he has, and the general dies in his arms. "Tough luck!" the assistant says. "That guy was a great actor." Leo looks at him. "He was more than a great actor—he was a great man." Leo lifts up the Russian flag and covers the general's body with it. The camera pulls back, and the scene fades out.

If you see only one Evelyn Brent film, make it *The Last Command*, a masterpiece of silent filmmaking. The picture is compelling and features some of Brent's finest acting. Brent reportedly studied German during the production, convinced it would help her screen performance. It certainly didn't hurt.

The working titles were *The Road to Glory* and *The General*. The film was titled *Crepuscule du Gloire* in

France. According to von Sternberg, the picture "was made in five weeks, though it seemed like five years."[59] Early drafts of the script used a strictly chronological order with no flashbacks. In addition, the train wreck and death of Natalie were added; in earlier versions, Natalie survived and became a Hollywood actress.

An argument could be made that there is a strong parallel between the general's life in Russia and then in Hollywood. The unruly extras are an American version of the mob of revolutionaries who humiliated and mocked the general at the train before it left for Petrograd. The medal, the uniform, his role as the general, and Andreyev's film direction (he was a Russian theatre director at the time of the revolution) are all part of the general's life playing out again, but this time with a different result. For all of his suffering (he's probably relived that day every day for the past ten years), the general is given a second chance. He dies accomplishing his greatest wish, leading Russia to victory.

Von Sternberg made his first film, *The Salvation Hunters*, in 1925. After being fired from MGM's *The Exquisite Sinner* in 1926, he landed at Paramount. It was here that von Sternberg's style was honed. According to film curator and historian James Card, "Along with his growing concern for composition, in his early Paramount films Sternberg discovered what would become his most powerful trademark, overshadowing even his long, long dissolves and his crowded, overwhelmingly detailed frames. It was his close-ups. The usual Hollywood close-up was a head-and-shoulders portrait. The Russian close-up was a dynamic, full-frame face, often cropping off the top of the head and the neck of the subject. But the Sternberg close-up was something of a mystical experience for the beholder, particularly if the subject was a woman. He usually had his actress smoking a cigarette. The translucent, drifting clouds of smoke wrapped the girl in a shimmer haze. Sternberg understood lighting better than any other director. He understood his camera lenses better than many a cinematographer. He was, in fact, the only Hollywood director who was a member of the American Society of Cinematographers. Any ordinary actress caught in Joe's idealizing compositions and his caressing lighting glowed like Garbo at her best." Card further pointed out that it was in *The Last Command* "that Sternberg, with his close-ups of Emil Jannings, William Powell and Evelyn Brent, began to toy with transcendentalism in his screen-filling faces, which we can actually see 'turning into poetry.'"[60] Von Sternberg used some of his own previous experiences as assistant to a director when directing the assistant in *The Last Command*, including lighting the director's cigarettes.

Brent's character is compelling and sexy. According to Kevin Brownlow, "Von Sternberg was a master of cinematic eroticism.... Few directors have displayed such intelligence with such scenes; a moment in the locomotive in the flashback of *The Last Com-*

*mand* when Evelyn Brent distracts a sentry from Jannings' escape by making love to him is an example of von Sternberg's mastery. As Jannings kills the engineer with a shovel, Evelyn Brent, embracing the sentry, clenches her teeth and gasps—a brilliant piece of visual double-entendre."[61]

The idea for the film came from a conversation von Sternberg shared with director Ernst Lubitsch. In fact, there was a real-life Hollywood extra (using the name Theodore Lodi) who'd worked as a Russian restaurant manager. His real name was General Lodijenski, and he was a former member of the Imperial Russian Army. "Thousands of people in [New York] will remember having eaten a few years ago at the most authentically atmospheric restaurant, probably, which ever represented a foreign colony in a distant land. It was on the midtown east side, a Russian restaurant kept by a distinguished aristocrat of the old regime, a formal loyal General of the Czar. When the Communist revolution flared up, the General was fortunate to escape from home with his life. His first job in the New World was as a stableman. After a time some friends financed him and he opened his café. Real princesses served at the tables. The food, the music, the tobacco, the decorations—all were Russian of the best kind. But the General's less fortunate compatriots elected him to be their meal ticket, and he hadn't the heart to turn them away. So when a movie actress at the Long Island studios invited him to play a type in one of her pictures he accepted gladly, and later he went to Hollywood. Now he is reported to be 'just another extra,' even as the hero of the film."[62]

Lubitsch felt the real life of a movie extra–former Russian general had little potential for reel life.[63] However, von Sternberg was able to develop the idea into a compelling full-length picture that deals not only with the Russian revolution but also reveals the dark side of Hollywood. Von Sternberg took credit for the story, though official credit went to Lajos Biro because "Mr. Biro had been carried on the payroll for years and that this somehow had to be justified."[64] At Hollywood's first Academy Awards, Biro was honored with a certificate of honorable mention in the Best Writing (Original Story) category.

Emil Jannings claimed that the idea for the film originated with him after a meeting at Paramount with an extra who had once been a Russian general; this claim is dubious. There is no denying that Jannings' acting is brilliant. He ended up winning the Best Actor Award for his work in this film and *The Way of All Flesh*. Sternberg was a big fan of the actor. "[H]is importance as a major personality of his time must be reconstructed. Not only was he the most prominent actor of his day, acknowledged as such by critic and public alike, but also the most famous representative of the powerful German stage that had become so effective under the guidance of Max Reinhardt. His name had become a household word, respected and honored."[65] Even so, von Sternberg discovered that Jannings was a high maintenance actor who demanded attention. "His shyness was coupled with an intense jealousy, and from the moment the film began he behaved as if we were married. The slightest attention I gave to other actors was an act of infidelity toward him, and he quivered like a deserted woman whenever I ignored him for a second to instruct others in the same scene."[66]

Jannings also created chaos on the set by giving instructions to actors and crew. Furthermore, he could be temperamental. "The film was complicated enough without him, and the part he had to play was not easy either. He had to be meek as the Hollywood extra, and arrogant when portraying the commanding general of the Russian army, but somehow he always managed to have his moods twisted. When he was on the stage as the beggarly extra he behaved like a mighty overlord, and when he donned the pompous uniform of the bemedaled Russian general, he stood before me like a schoolboy waiting to be reprimanded, and I would have to pump him up like a bicycle tire."[67] Jannings also sometimes behaved childishly. "To direct a child is one thing, but when the youngster weighs close to three hundred pounds it is not easy to laugh at all his pranks.... When the film was 'wrapped up,' I thanked Emil for his cooperation and told him that under no circumstances, were he the last remaining actor on earth, would I ever again court the doubtful pleasure of directing him."[68] Despite this statement, von Sternberg did indeed work with Jannings again in *The Blue Angel*, the 1930 classic with Marlene Dietrich.

Brent was impressed with Jannings' performance. "He is superb! In his most frenzied moments he is not rushed—because the German language, which he uses almost entirely, gives him time for thought."[69] According to Brent, Jannings had a lucrative contract. "I remember it was the talk of the studio. He had all the concessions.... He had a car at his disposal and all the things that nobody I knew had at that time. Anyway, Jannings came in with an interpreter, and they would say something, and the guy would interpret it into German, then wait for an answer, which he would interpret back into English. I thought that was funny because he spoke English, Jannings did. A few days later I said, 'What's the big idea?' and he said, 'When I don't speak English, I'm a smart boy.' He heard what they said, then he thought it out and gave his answer. It was very smart ... very cute."[70]

Von Sternberg hired many Russian extras, including former military leaders. For example, Viacheslav Savitsky was a general for the Kuban Cossacks. Alexander Ikonnikov had been a colonel with the Imperial Foot Guards. In addition, the son of a Russian princess, Nicholas Kobliansky, had served as a captain with the Guards. "All three were members of the Czar's regime, and went through the revolution without a scratch and made their way to America. But it was different in motion pictures.... [A]ction in the scenes of the revolution called for them to be seized by a mob, dragged from a train,

stripped of their uniforms, and made prisoners. When the 350 extras used in the scene had finished their realistic acting, the three Russians were nursing bruises and cuts which had never been their lot in the stormy days of the Czar's downfall."[71]

When the film was completed, the studio was reluctant to release it because it seemed too damning of Hollywood. Producer Otto Kahn stepped in and insisted the film be released. *New York Times* critic Mordaunt Hall named the film one of the ten best films of 1928.

The role of Czar Nicholas was played by Paramount assistant casting director Tom Ford. "Ford spent two days in a vain search for just the right type. At length one of the Russian ex-generals of the technical staff clapped Ford on the shoulder and said, 'You're the man, yourself. You have his eyes and features, his build and carriage.' Ford was rushed into whiskers and he played the part."[72]

Von Sternberg personally chose William Powell to play the film director. Powell, however, decided he never wanted to work with the director again, going so far as to include this stipulation in his contract. He did work with the director again, though, in *The Dragnet*.

Fashion historians will notice that Brent's gowns are more in the style of 1928 than World War I. This might be one of the film's few flaws.

Much of the shooting took place in 90° weather. Powell and Brent suffered on the hot set while wearing heavy furs and boots.

Jannings, born in Switzerland in 1884, moved to Germany when his American film career ended primarily due to his heavy accent. He was a supporter of the Nazi regime and appeared in an anti–British film titled *Ohm Kruger* in 1941. Jannings died in Austria in 1950.

Jack Raymond appeared in many films as an extra. He also appeared with Brent in *Night Club Scandal* (1937). Born in Minneapolis in 1901, he died in 1951.

Nicholas Soussanin was born in Yalta in 1889. He was married to actress Olga Baclanova from 1929 to 1939. His son was actor Nicholas Saunders, and his grandchildren include actress Lanna Saunders and jazz musician Theo Saunders. Soussanin died in 1975.

Michael Visaroff was born in Moscow in 1892. He graduated from the Principal Dramatic School in Russia. He also appeared with Brent in *The Mad Empress* (1939). Some sources also list him as a cast member in *Woman Trap* (1929). Visaroff died in 1951.

German-born Fritz Feld was married to character actress Virginia Christine, best known for portraying Mrs. Olson on Folger's Coffee TV commercials in the 1960s and 1970s. Feld, often cast as a waiter or maitre d', was known for making a popping noise with his hand and mouth. He was born in 1900 and died in 1993. He also appeared in *Broadway* (1929).

Shep Houghton, born in 1914, was a teenager when he went into the movie business. *The Last Command* was only his second film. Some sources indicate he also appeared in *Underworld*. His long career included many television appearances such as *Wagon Train, Perry Mason, The Lucy-Desi Comedy Hour, The Untouchables, The Twilight Zone, My Three Sons, The Andy Griffith Show, The Dick Van Dyke Show, The Loretta Young Show, Hogan's Heroes, Mannix,* and The *Mary Tyler Moore Show.* He retired in 1976.

Nicholas Kobliansky, born in Russia in 1888, served as a technical advisor on films dealing with Russian themes such as *Scarlet Dawn* (1932) and *British Agent* (1934). He died in 1976.

Character actor Harry Semels, born in New York in 1887, began his career in 1917. He amassed well over 300 film credits before his death in 1946.

A Stanford University graduate, cinematographer Bert Glennon was nominated for Oscars for his work on *Drums Along the Mohawk* (1939), *Stagecoach* (1939), and *Dive Bomber* (1941). He was the father of cinematographer James Glennon; his granddaughter is actress Meghan Glennon.

Art director Hans Dreier won Oscars for his work on *Frenchman's Creek* (1944) and *Samson and Delilah* (1949). He received 21 other nominations. Born in Germany in 1885, he died in 1965.

Herman Mankiewicz was the brother of writer-director Joseph Mankiewicz. A former theatre critic, Herman won an Oscar for writing 1941's *Citizen Kane* (it was shared with Orson Welles). He also received an Oscar nomination for co-writing (with Jo Swerling) *The Pride of the Yankees* (1942). He also worked with Brent on *His Tiger Lady* (1928), *The Dragnet* (1928), *A Night of Mystery* (1928), and *The Mating Call* (1928). Born in New York City in 1897, he died in 1953.

*Reviews:* Keven Brownlow noticed a flaw in the film's story, but still felt it was a powerful film. "Andreyev encountered the Grand Duke once, when he was arrested, when the Grand Duke struck him. He could not have known about the general's true personality since he never saw him or Natacha again. Aside from this lapse, *The Last Command* is a most unusual and effective production. At no stage does it try to present an accurate picture of the revolution—von Sternberg had no interest in realism—but as a rich character study it is unforgettable."[73]

"This production has its forced moments, its sluggish incidents, but the chronicle is equipped with a double strain of suspense. It strikes one as a good short story turned to excellent account in film form.... Evelyn Brent is pleasing as the girl who helps the general" (*New York Times*, January 23, 1928).

"It's exceptional for a regular program release, even for Paramount.... Jannings is an elegant and eloquent actor.... Evelyn Brent you will like immediately, and William Powell, giving a corking performance in a double sided role" (*Variety*, January 25, 1928).

*The Los Angeles Times* reviewer noted that Jannings received an extended ovation from theatergoers. In fact, his final scene was quite effective. "It is a radiant bit of action. And Jannings succeeds in imbuing it with an almost supernatural frenzy, the impression of which will prove unforgettable. A number of people were visibly affected by this scene during the showing last night." The reviewer concluded, "In spite of its flaws, *The Last Command* is a picture to be warmly commended. In general quality and in the novelty of its ideas, it is high above the average. It struck me, too, that the studio scenes, even if—perhaps slightly exaggerated, were exceptional in other respects. They are far ahead of any scenes heretofore presented that have essayed to depict movieland" (*Los Angeles Times*, January 28, 1928).

"*The Last Command* is indubitably a powerful film. Clumsy-faced, blacksmith-muscled, thick-fingered Emil Jannings, the thoroughly unhandsome hero, is the most finished, the most subtle cinemactor [sic] in the U.S. He does everything slowly; smiles break across his face like a gradual sunrise, his sorrows have accumulated intensity. In this picture, he is ably supported by lords, soldiers, peasants, and most notably by Evelyn Brent who is the heroine" (*Time*, January 30, 1928).

"Evelyn Brent acquits herself most creditably and displays enough beauty and brains to disturb an army.... Von Sternberg gives us in this picture the best inside portrayal of studio activity that has ever been put on the screen, also tremendously realistic background both in studio and behind the scenes on Russian front. A thrilling melodrama" (*Photoplay*, March 1928).

"In a word, Emil Jannings compromises with Hollywood. The result, while neither fish, flesh nor fowl, is nevertheless fairly satisfactory" (*Motion Picture*, May 1928).

"A powerful and tragic story.... Thanks to the magnificent acting of Emil Jannings, this film is the most popular crying-fest of the season" (*Photoplay*, May 1928).

"Superb, magnificent—all the most extravagant adjectives belong to Emil Jannings.... William Powell is striking, as always.... Evelyn Brent is the only woman in the cast.... It is one of her most effective performances" (*Picture Play*, May 1928).

"...an exceptional silent film ... with a controlled, striking style. Holding up extremely well, it can still be shown to almost any audience and produce a remarkable effect.... The performances in *The Last Command* are excellent. It is certainly by far Emil Jannings' finest American role.... Evelyn Brent, von Sternberg's pre–Dietrich *femme fatale* and lady of mystery, projected a complex, intelligent, and yet sensual woman" (Rudy Behlmer & Tony Thomas, *Hollywood's Hollywood*, pp. 169–170).

## The Showdown

(Paramount Famous–Lasky) 7616 ft. 8 reels. 77 min. Released on February 25, 1928.

*Survival Status:* Library of Congress (Washington).

*Credits*: Producers, Jesse L. Lasky, Adolph Zukor; director, Victor Schertzinger; adaptation and continuity, Ethel Doherty, Hope Loring; based on the play *Wildcat* by Houston Branch; titles, John Farrow; photography, Victor Milner; film editor, George Nichols Jr.

*Cast*: George Bancroft (Cardan); Evelyn Brent (Sibyl Shelton); Neil Hamilton (Wilson Shelton); Fred Kohler (Winter); Helen Lynch (Goldie); Arnold Kent (Hugh Pickerell); Leslie Fenton (Kilgore Shelton); George Kuwa (Willie).

Sibyl and Wilson Shelton arrive in Mexico to look for oil. Sibyl and Cardan fall in love, but Cardan resists the temptation. He engages Wilton in a card game and fixes it so Wilton wins the oil lease. The oil well blows, and the Sheltons become instantly wealthy. Cardan leaves the camp, alone.

George Bancroft reportedly chose this screenplay himself. Advertising played up the reteaming of Bancroft and Brent: "George Bancroft and Evelyn Brent, stars of the sensational photodrama, *Underworld*, provide new thrills in *The Showdown*, Paramount's powerful picture of strong men and willful women."

Director Victor Schertzinger was born in Pennsylvania in 1890. He received an Oscar nomination for *One Night of Love* (1934). Schertzinger was also a musician and composer whose songs included "Tangerine" and "I Remember You." He died in 1941. Schertzinger's name also appeared in the credits for *Paramount on Parade* (1930).

Writer John Farrow was married to Maureen O'-Sullivan, and their daughter was Mia Farrow. He won an Oscar for co-writing *Around the World in Eighty Days* (1956) and received an Oscar nomination for directing *Wake Island* (1942). Born in Australia in 1904, he died in 1963.

Writer Ethel Doherty (1889–1974) also worked on the script for *Home on the Range* (1935). Writer Hope Loring was born in England in 1894 and died in Spain in 1959. She also worked on the screenplay for *Interference* (1928).

*Reviews:* "This film ... is sadly lacking in an imaginative quality and also true human psychology. Most of the dramatic developments are wrought with little or no suspense and the characters are not given credit for much intelligence.... Mr. Hamilton's acting in this film only deserves mention because it is so poor, so utterly wanting in anything approaching natural actions in the circumstances. Evelyn Brent is comely, but either she or Mr. Schertzinger are to blame for her sudden recovery from a frightful struggle, and also for taking silks and laces to this godless spot" (*New York Times*, March 5, 1928).

"A picture of considerable dramatic vitality, cynical in some of its phases and a wide departure from the screen formula of romantic story.... The action of the whole cast is admirable, especially admirable in its simplicity. Even Evelyn Brent's heroine in distress isn't overdone" (*Variety*, March 7, 1928).

"A picture teeming with splendid acting, but a story which leaves a questionable taste in your mouth. Droning oil wells, merciless tropic heat, the menacing attitude of lonely, desperate male beings will depress you as they depress the young American woman who invades the Mexican oil well region" (*Photoplay*, May 1928).

"A battle between two brawny giants and a card game with the woman and the oil well as the stakes are the high points" (*Syracuse Herald*, June 3, 1928).

"A heavy-breather set in Mexican jungle country, *The Showdown* gave ticket buyers 84 minutes of impassioned melodrama.... Evelyn Brent ... invested the central role with a kind of suppressed frenzy, very effective." (John Douglas Eames, *The Paramount Story*, p. 55).

## A Night of Mystery

(Paramount Famous–Lasky) 5741 ft. 6 reels. 60 min. Released on April 7, 1928.
*Survival Status:* UCLA Film and Television Archive (Los Angeles).
*Credits*: Producers, Jesse L. Lasky, Adolph Zukor; director, Lothar Mendes; scenario and adaptation, Ernest Vajda; based on the novel *Ferréol* by Victorien Sardou; titles, Herman J. Mankiewicz; photography, Harry Fischbeck; film editor, Frances Marsh.
*Cast*: Adolphe Menjou (Captain Ferréol); Evelyn Brent

(Gilberte Boismartel); Nora Lane (Thérèse D'Egremont); William Collier, Jr. (Jérôme D'Egremont); Raoul Paoli (Marcasse); Claude King (Marquis Boismartel); Frank Leigh (Rochemore); William P. Bert (Rochemore's secretary).

Romance was combined with a murder mystery in this drama, which is also known as *The Code of Honour*.

Director Lothar Mendes was born in Berlin in 1894. He also directed Brent in *Interference* (1928). Mendes was married to actress Dorothy Mackaill from 1926 to 1928. He died in London in 1974.

Writer Ernest Vajda also supervised the production. He wrote such plays as *The Harem* and *Grounds for Divorce*. Vajda claimed that he wrote twelve hours a day—every day. "Too many playwrights fail in their motion-picture efforts because they are too lazy, too much engrossed in their own comfort.... Find out what the business is all about, then go to work. Put your shoulder to the wheel twelve hours a day. That's my advice."[74]

Adolphe Menjou was born in Pittsburgh, Pennsylvania, in 1890. He began his career in the silent era and received an Oscar nomination for the talkie *The Front Page* (1931). One of his last performances was in *Pollyanna* (1960) as Mr. Pendergast. A member of the John Birch Society, he testified as a friendly witness before the House Committee on Un-American Activities. Menjou, married for many years to actress Verree Teasdale, died in 1963. He also appeared with Brent in *His Tiger Lady* (1928).

Raoul Paoli, who also appeared with Brent in *Beau Sabreur* (1927), was a French Olympic athlete who participated in a multitude of sports, including rugby, boxing, rowing, the shot put and discus, and wrestling. During the filming of *A Night of Mystery*, he taught William Collier, Jr., how to throw the discus. "Collier started with a throw of only a few yards, and ended by coming within fifteen feet of the athlete's throws."[75] Paoli died in 1960.

William (Buster) Collier, Jr., was born Charles Gall, Jr., in New York City in 1902. He was a child actor in silent films beginning in 1915. When he stopped acting in 1935 he became a producer. In the 1950s he produced television's *Mr. and Mrs. North*. Collier died in 1987.

Nora Lane was born in Chester, Illinois, in 1905. She committed suicide on October 16, 1948, in Glendale, California.

Claude King also appeared with Brent in *It Couldn't Have Happened—But It Did* (1936) and *Jungle Jim* (1937). The founder of the Screen Actors Guild (SAG) was born in England in 1875 and died in 1941.

*Reviews:* "It is a complicated story, heavily handled. The different threads of the story are loosely woven. Situations lack clarity. In spite of its faults, however, the picture retains interest. There are some excellent court scenes" (*Los Angeles Times*, April 10, 1928).

"It is a chronicle that is not exactly plausible, and the mentalities of the characters are decidedly man-made....

All this chiefly due to Lothar Mendes's none too brilliant direction.... Evelyn Brent has rather a thankless role with which she does all that is possible" (*New York Times*, April 16, 1928).

"Indifferent Menjou film.... A straightaway murder plot without a chance of pace. Little action and no comedy.... Nobody stands out in the cast" (*Variety*, April 18, 1928).

"Your loss if you miss it" (*Photoplay*, May, 1928).

"Evelyn Brent—well, by this time you surely should have detected the high esteem in which this department holds the glittering Evelyn. Miss Brent does beautifully as always..." (G. Worthington Post, *Wellsboro Gazette* [Pennsylvania], August 2, 1928).

"Neither the cast ... nor the direction by Lothar Mendes did anything to lubricate the story's arthritic joints" (John Douglas Eames, *The Paramount Story*, p. 55).

## The Dragnet

(Paramount Famous Lasky Corp.) 7866 ft. 8 reels. Released on May 23, 1928.

*Survival Status:* Presumed lost.

*Credits:* Director, Josef von Sternberg; scenario, Charles Furthman, Jules Furthman; adaptation; Jules Furthman; story, Oliver H. P. Garrett; titles, Herman J. Mankiewicz; photography, Harold Rosson; film editor, Helen Lewis; set decoration, Hans Dreier.

*Cast:* George Bancroft (Two-Gun Nolan); Evelyn Brent (The Magpie); William Powell (Dapper Frank Trent); Fred Kohler ("Gabby" Steve); Francis McDonald (Sniper Dawson); Leslie Fenton (Shakespeare).

Police officer Nolan tries to rid his city of gangs. He mistakenly believes he is responsible for a death, quits his job, and goes on a toot. Finally, he is told the truth by the Magpie and wreaks vengeance upon those responsible.

This was directed by Josef von Sternberg. Many consider it one of his lesser films. Ivan Butler calls it a "minor work."[76] The working titles were *The Night Stick* and *Blackjack*.

Written by former tabloid reporter Oliver H.P. Garrett, this is another gangster film with George Bancroft and Evelyn Brent. Bancroft was not easy to work with at this point in his career. Von Sternberg gave him instructions for a particular scene: When the director shouted "Bang!" Bancroft was to grab the staircase and turn. When von Sternberg shouted "Bang! Bang!" Bancroft was to fall. Bancroft agreed, and the director began filming. He shouted "Bang!" several times, but each time Bancroft ignored him. A furious von Sternberg confronted the star. "Don't shout at me, Joe. Of course, I heard you. But just remember this: One shot can't stop Bancroft."[77] This story became a familiar punchline in Paramount producer Schulberg's home, and when young Budd went to see the film in a theater he burst into laughter when the scene appeared. "Father tried to shush me. I was destroying one of the most dramatic moments in the picture. People were looking at me. I held my hand over my mouth until the fit passed."[78]

This was not a pleasant set. According to Schulberg, "As George's fame kept mounting to tidal-wave pretentions, von Sternberg's defense was simply to ignore the antics of his star. Nobody could acquire instant deafness more quickly than Joe. They made a remarkable pair. Bancroft whose fame had transformed into an impregnable fortress, and von Sternberg whose artistic arrogance regarded all actors as empty-headed puppets to be jerked this way and that in the firm grip of the puppeteer."[79]

A special set was created on Paramount's lot featuring a city jail and police station. Advertising proclaimed "Vivid, powerful drama of the Law and Gangland! The most sensational picture of the year, made by von Sternberg, producer of *Underworld!*" and "BANCROFT has the town on edge again. Bancroft on both sides of the law—as a cop and a culprit. If you are one of those who thought *Underworld* just about the last word in crook melodramas, don't let this one catch you napping."

*Reviews:* "Josef von Sternberg ... has done a very efficient piece of work in this film. Some of the scenes may be theatrical and farfetched, and occasionally the action may drag rather boringly, but the production on the whole is good.... The acting is excellent" (*Los Angeles Times*, May 22, 1928).

***Tough gal Brent with George Bancroft in* The Dragnet *(1928).***

"Evelyn Brent, best 'tough girl' interpreter in the movies, carries thru her part admirably, tho [sic] she may be accused of overplaying her character" (*Davenport Democrat and Leader* [Iowa], May 27, 1928).

"Notwithstanding George Bancroft's derisive laugh, Evelyn Brent's striking plumed headgear, and Josef von Sternberg's generous display of slaughter ... the film ... is an emphatically mediocre effort.... It failed even to make an impression on a small boy in the audience yesterday afternoon. This youngster said to his mother: 'Isn't this an awful picture?' His mother agreed in a whisper" (*New York Times*, June 4, 1928).

"As an underworld with unusual rapidity and plenty of action it must compare most favorably with, if not above, that other *Underworld*.... Evelyn Brent is the girl, always doing well in playing but not always looking so well. In a few scenes, though, she looks peachy with those close fitting hats" (*Variety*, June 6, 1928).

"A worthy successor to *Underworld* and other gangland films.... [Brent] displays a startling penchant for black and white coats. She has a relatively unimportant part, but furnishes the necessary love element" (*Zanesville Signal* [Ohio], September 7, 1928).

"Vivid and swiftly moving underworld story with Grade-A acting by George Bancroft, William Powell and Evelyn Brent" (*Photoplay*).

"A von Sternberg picture always meant interesting visual and atmospheric touches..., and here he took a crime drama that in other hands might have been pedestrian and transformed it into something vivid and individualistic. While not first-rate von Sternberg, it is one of his more creditable efforts nevertheless" (Lawrence J. Quirk, *The Complete Films of William Powell*).

## His Tiger Lady

[Alternate titles; *Tiger Lady*; *The Tiger Lady*; *His Tiger Wife*; *Love Is Incurable*] (Paramount Famous Lasky Corp.) 4998 ft. 5 reels. 57 min. Released on May 27, 1928.

*Survival Status:* Presumed lost.

*Credits*: Producers, Jesse L. Lasky, Adolph Zukor; director, Hobart Henley; adaptation, Ernest Vajda; based on the novel *La Grande-duchesse et le garçon d'étage, comédie en trois actes* by Alfred Savoir; titles, Herman J. Mankiewicz; photography, Harry Fischbeck; film editor, Alyson Shaffer; costumes, Travis Banton; circus animals; Al G. Barnes.

*Cast*: Adolphe Menjou (Henri, the "super"); Evelyn Brent (The Tiger Lady); Rose Dione (Madame Duval); Emile Chautard (Stage manager); Mario Carillo (The Duke); Leonardo De Vesa (The Count); Jules Raucourt (The Marquis); Jewel (Herself, an elephant); Pocahontas (Herself, a tiger).

Brent plays a capricious lady of royalty in Paris who insists that commoner (and bit actor in the Folies Bergere) Henri show his love for her by spending a night in a tiger's cage. Fortunately for Henri, the tiger has passed on to tiger heaven, and he wins the hand of his beloved.

Brent replaced Ruth Chatterton. Menjou delayed his honeymoon (coincidentally, to Paris) to finish the picture. His new wife was actress Kathryn Carver. They divorced in 1934.

An elephant and three tigers were borrowed from the M.G. Barnes circus. The main tiger weighed 500 pounds and was named Pocahontas Barnes. Al-

though she was described as tame, her handlers "took no chances." Four sharpshooters were at the ready ... just in case. Menjou was reportedly so unhinged at the idea of stepping into a tiger's cage (who can blame him?) that it took three takes (and, finally, notes written on his sleeve) to get the scene the director wanted.[80]

Director Hobart Henley was also a silent film actor. He was married to Broadway and film actress Corinne Barker, who died in August 1928, a few months after the film was released. Henley died in 1964.

Rose Dione was born in Paris in 1875. She is perhaps best known as Madame Tetrallini in *Freaks* (1932). Dione died in 1936.

Emile Chautard was George Archainbaud's stepfather. Born in France in 1864, he was a silent film actor, director, writer, and producer. He died in 1934.

*Reviews:* "*His Tiger Lady* is rich in costly gowns and costumes, stage trappings and elaborate sets. Its scenes of the Paris variety are authentic and excellently presented. Life backstage in the sequences at the beginning of the picture is realistic and well portrayed. But little more may be said in favor of the production.... The plot is so trite, and Menjou's screen character so negative, that the picture is almost wholly unconvincing and lacking in appeal" (*Los Angeles Times*, May 13, 1928).

"...a clever, fantastic picture.... This yarn moves with celerity and Mr. Menjou gives a splendid portrayal of humility and arrogance. Evelyn Brent is imperious and charming as the Tiger Lady. Hobart Henley's direction is excellent, the scenes in the restaurant being alive with imagination" (*New York Times*, May 28, 1928).

"A typical Menjou cream puff. Unreal, unconvincing, unimportant, but moderately amusing.... Miss Brent looks great" (*Variety*, May 30, 1928).

"*His Tiger Lady* ... becomes rather thin toward the end and lacks the incisive brilliance of some of Adolphe Menjou's previous pictures. However, it has kept audiences highly amused and Mr. Menjou's subtlety, if you will pardon a hackneyed word, has never been more in evidence. As much cannot be said of the sequence where Evelyn Brent appears in a Shubert negligee, flings herself on a couch and squirms. But her conception of the part is excellent in its poise and she presents a distinguished and glamorous figure" (*Los Angeles Times*, June 3, 1928).

"Fair farce" (*Time*, June 11, 1928).

"Old-fashioned story, tricked out in fancy costumes and made palatable by the suave acting of Adolphe Menjou and Evelyn Brent" (*Photoplay*, August 1928).

"Miss Brent ... appears surprised and startled when the scenario gives her an opportunity to act. As a matter of fact, the whole film is dead from beginning to end. A couple more like it, and Adolphe Menjou will be completely done" (Bill Marks, *Warren Tribune* [Pennsylvania], August 3, 1928).

"A cinema fairy tale of no particular originality.... The picture achieves its excuse for being in the performances of Adolphe Menjou and Evelyn Brent.... Mr. Menjou acts with customary distinction, but is getting too old for such foolishness. As for Miss Brent, she has the finest figure of any Countess the writer has met. It is especially commendable in a garment designed to represent a spider's web. It is rumored that Theda Bara, when she saw it, gnashed her teeth" (*Dallas Morning News*, August 18, 1928).

"[A]n attempt at adult entertainment which often is not quite mature. Sophistication that doesn't quite come off is as woeful as an ostrich plume in the rain.... Evelyn Brent. ... lends her sulky beauty and slithering carriage to great effect, but ... she fails to strike the proper note" (G. Worthington Post, *Wellsboro Gazette* [Pennsylvania], September 6, 1928).

## The Mating Call

(Caddo Co.) 6352 ft. 7 reels. 72 min. Released on August 16, 1928.

*Survival Status:* University of Nevada, Las Vegas (UNLV). Released on video (Flicker Alley)

*Credits*: Producer, Howard Hughes; director, James Cruze; adaptation, Walter Woods; based on the novel *The Mating Call* by Rex Beach; titles, Herman J. Mankiewicz; photography, Ira Morgan; film editor, Walter Woods.

*Cast*: Thomas Meighan (Leslie Hatten); Evelyn Brent (Rose Henderson); Renee Adoree (Catharine); Alan Roscoe (Lon Henderson); Gardner James (Marvin Swallow); Helen Foster (Jessie); Luke Cosgrave (Judge Peebles); Cyril Chadwick (Anderson); Will R. Walling (Uncle Billy).

Leslie Hatten has gone off to war, leaving behind his lovely wife Rose. It's been three years since they've seen each other. Once he returns to his village, he learns a lot has changed. Rose's parents had the marriage annulled because she wasn't of age, and Rose has since married wealthy lawyer Lon Henderson.

Rose, however, is still interested in Les. We know she's a sophisticated woman because when Les returns from working in the fields of his farm she's waiting for him in a chair, smoking a cigarette. It's a nice shot—all you can see is the back of the chair, the top of her hat, one arm holding a cigarette—and then Les' expression when he sees her.

"You look like Hell," she says to him, though she's looking at him in a way that suggests she doesn't care. They shake hands. "I heard you were a hermit—never called on anyone—so I thought I'd break the ice," she says.

He asks why she didn't bring Lon with her. "Why should I—Three's a crowd. Besides, Lon annoys me. He's too loyal—to other women. So I'm going to do exactly as *I* please." Les asks her to leave, but she tries to seduce him. "I dare you to kiss me and then tell me to go!"

Les pushes her out the door and locks the door behind her. The little spitfire breaks out the door's window with a pick. He lifts her into his arms and deposits her in her sports car, while all the while fighting off her kisses. "Think it over, Les. You're going to be awfully lonesome out here," she teases before driving off to return to her mansion.

Rose discovers Jessie's handkerchief in Lon's car and realizes he's having an affair with the young girl. Rose mentions seeing Les, and Lon threatens to have him run out of town. He is a member of the Order (a secret organization with hood-wearing members ... think Ku Klux Klan), and, according to him, "It is the duty of our Organization to safeguard the honor of our womenfolk!"

Rose lets him know she knows about Jessie, and they tussle over the handkerchief as Jessie and her elderly relative, Judge Peebles, arrive for a visit. Jessie lies about seeing Lon and claims she had tea with Les.

Soon after, Rose drops off flowers for Les at his house. Lon reports Les to the Order, and Les gets a message on his door:

IT IS THE DUTY OF THIS ORGANIZATION TO PROTECT THE HONOR OF OUR HOMES— YOUR RELATIONS WITH A CERTAIN MARRIED WOMAN MUST CEASE.—THE ORDER

Les receives another visit from Rose. He complains about the flowers. "Don't get frightened—I just dropped in to say goodbye. I'm leaving Evergreen." Les and Rose are unaware they're being watched by the Order. "Lon and I are through!" Rose explains. "Too many women—too many quarrels—life's too short!"

She spills a basin of water on her clothing and insists she change her outfit. She sends Les out to her car to get her suitcase. She tells him he brought in the wrong bag and sends him back to the car again. Meanwhile, she starts undressing. Wearing a very suggestive gown, Rose tries to seduce Les. At first, he appears to be made of stone. Finally, he kisses her. They are interrupted by a knock on the door. Just when the Order is on the verge of teaching him a lesson, Lon drives up and says he'll take over. The Order leaves.

Rose confronts Lon. "How do you like it—when your wife borrows your own morals?" Lon pulls a

*A stylish profile from 1928.*

gun on Les, but Les quickly overpowers him. "Don't worry—either of you!" Les announces. "I'm already married!" He lies and says he was married in France and is awaiting his wife's arrival.

Rose takes it hard, and Lon threatens to kill him if Les sees Rose again. Les decides that the best course of action is to get a wife. "Not a baby-faced doll from around here—but a real woman who wants a home—and is willing to work for it! And I know where to find one." So he goes to K-Mart—no, we're kidding. But it's almost as good. He goes to *Ellis Island*. Yep, he's going to get one of those immigrant girls who'll be happy to clean his house and, um, meet his needs.

Upon his arrival at Ellis Island, Les is told about a family that will be deported unless he steps in. Pretty Catharine asks if he'll help. He touches her little chin and says, "I need a woman. I'll take you and your parents with me—if you'll marry me." How utterly romantic. Naturally, she's aghast at the idea, and so are her parents. However, the man in charge disagrees: "This gentleman has a farm and he needs a wife to help him work it. I think you're all lucky, if you ask me."

Her parents still refuse, but Catharine reluctantly agrees. Les slaps a ring on her finger and they are married. They all go back to the farm. (The parents are in a couple more scenes, but then pretty much disappear with no explanation.) Les takes her into his bedroom and announces: "This is *our* room." He starts to kiss her but then changes his mind and decides to sleep on the fold-out sofa.

The next morning, Catharine is in the kitchen cheerfully cooking breakfast. Les tries to reassure her that she should feel welcome. Later, when Catharine is scrubbing the floor, Rose arrives for a visit. She accidentally gets a bucket full of water thrown on her when enters the kitchen. While Catharine is polishing Rose's shoes, Les returns from the fields.

"This is just a friendly call," Rose insists. "I've met your servant, but where's the bride?" she asks. He pretends the wife hasn't arrived yet. Catharine has a fit. "So I'm good enough to be your *woman*—but not good enough to meet your friends!" Les, who obviously knows nothing about women, just rubs his head.

Another guy who knows nothing about women is Lon. He tells Jessie he won't marry her and wants his love letters returned. Soon, Marvin, a much more suitable love interest for Jessie, proposes to her. She asks for time to think it over and slips Lon's letters into Marvin's pocket.

Les finds Jessie's body submerged in water—she's drowned herself. Lon leads members of the Order to believe Les had something to do with her death since her body was found on his property.

The next scene offers a nighttime meeting of the Order. Yep, there are hoods, a bonfire, and a kind of trial. The first person is a young boy who is accused of being shiftless and not helping support his mother. He gets away with a warning. The next guy is a wife

beater. He's not nearly as apologetic. So they strap him to a wooden cross and whip the heck out of him.

Meanwhile, back at the farm (in the most adorable scene of the film), Catharine bathes a piglet in a basin of water. Even Les, who doesn't have much of a personality, thinks it's cute. Just after Catharine puts the baby pig to bed, Les is warned that the Order is coming for him.

He escapes but can't find Catharine. Les discovers Catharine swimming nude (a gratuitous and quite revealing scene) in the farm's pond. She's offended, believing he was spying on her. They go back to the farmhouse, but the Order is waiting for him. Catharine tries to protect him, but Les is taken to the meeting where he is charged with causing Jessie's suicide. Les pleads his case but to no avail.

In another part of town, Marvin is found near Lon's body. He claims he didn't kill him. While that is being sorted out, Les is, yep, strapped to a cross and beaten with a whip. Marvin is brought to the meeting and says again that he didn't kill Lon—but planned to. He shows the Order the letters Lon had written to Jessie. They stop punishing Les. Appalled by Lon's letters, the Order decides to save Marvin and make it look like Lon committed suicide. We see Judge Peebles cleaning his gun and realize he was the murderer.

Les returns home to Catharine. They've bonded, probably over the piglet and nude bathing, and embrace.

There are two reasons to watch this film. It's an interesting look at societal problems faced following World War I. During the war, women had gained more freedom. With the end of the war, however, there was great difficulty getting women to go back to the roles they'd previously accepted. The film reflects this. Rose is a shallow and virtueless woman who does not value the role of good wife. Brent is good in the role. However, the character is one-dimensional and unsympathetic.

The second reason to view this film is to see the charms of Renee Adoree. She does not arrive until the film is almost half over, but she steals the picture. Born Emilie Louise Victorine Reeves in France on September 30, 1898, Adoree lived only thirty-five years, dying of tuberculosis on October 5, 1933. She is probably best known for her appearance in *The Big Parade* (1925) with John Gilbert.

This was the third film produced by Caddo Company. The first two were *Two Arabian Knights* and *The Racket*. These three films are among Howard Hughes' first pictures. He also produced *Swell Hogan* (never released) and *Everybody's Acting* (1926). Brent was approached about appearing in *The Racket* but turned it down.

Some sources list Herman J. Mankiewicz and Delmer Daves as uncredited extras. The budget for *The Mating Call* was approximately $400,000. The film was based on a novel of the same name published in 1927. Novelist Rex Beach was a prolific writer who had many of his works adapted into film, including *The Spoilers*, *The Silver Horde*, and *The Mating Call*. Born in Atwood, Michigan, in 1877, he committed suicide in 1949.

A copy of the film was stored at the University of Nevada at Las Vegas in the Howard Hughes archive. It was recently restored by Flicker Alley and Advanced Digital Services, and subsequently shown on Turner Classic Movies. According to Jeff Masino, Flicker Alley's owner, the restoration was painstaking: "With an electronic filter and then moving frame-by-frame, the digital artisans physically removed splice marks, scratches and nitrate damage."[81]

Much was made in magazines and newspapers of Brent's sophisticated costumes throughout the film. Indeed, her fashions offer a great view of what fashionable late–1920s women might wear. However, since the film is supposed to take place right after the war, the fashions were not true to the period.

One small town Texas movie theater owner cheerfully reported to the *Exhibitors Herald-World* the following: "Picture follows original story unusually well and handles the Ku Klux angle wonderfully; both Kluck and Anti-Kluck can see this good picture."

Director James Cruze was born Jens Bosen in Utah in 1884. Previously married to actresses Betty Compson and Marguerite Snow, he was also an actor and producer. Cruze died in 1942. Cruze was a friend of actor Luke Cosgrave's. "Everyone asked the reason for Jim's great success," Cosgrave wrote, "and his ability to make so many great pictures in such rapid succession. The reason was because he was a charmer, and could read the thoughts of people. He had a subtle art of wheedling them to express clearly the thought of the scene; and then photographed it. Some say you can photograph disembodied spirits. Jim tried to photograph carefully the story, as told by the expressive souls of men and women while in their natural element, the human form divine."[82]

Born in Ireland, Cosgrave (1862–1949) had an autobiography published after his death, *Theater Tonight*. In the book Cosgrave described Brent's character as "that charmingly sweet little devil who leads the poor boy into danger."[83] Cosgrave posed for illustrator William King when *The Mating Call* was published in *Cosmopolitan*. This was before Cosgrave was cast in the movie, and he was King's model for a Russian character.

Alan Roscoe was born in Nashville, Tennessee, in 1886. Also known as Albert Roscoe, he began his film career in 1915. Roscoe often co-starred with Theda Bara. He died in 1933.

Born in New York, Gardner James was once married to screenwriter Marian Constance Blackton, daughter of producer J. Stuart Blackton. He died in 1953.

Helen Foster, born in Independence, Kansas, in 1906, was a WAMPAS Baby Star in 1929. She died Christmas Day, 1982.

*Reviews*: "*The Mating Call* ... is drama of sordid proportions, however brilliant the acting.... Evelyn Brent displays at times a lively representation of a woman tired of her husband. Essentially it is unsympathetic ... and while the part is hardly likable, Miss Brent has breathed such wholehearted vividness into it that from the standpoint of interest it ranks high in showmanship.... Renee Adoree is quite effectively pleasing" (*Los Angeles Times*, September 23, 1928).

"It is too much [plot] for one picture, for James Cruze, the director, has been compelled to hasten over his episodes in order to get everything in.... Miss Brent gives a stunning performance, except that when she expresses curiosity she is tempted to exaggerate it by frowning" (*New York Times*, October 8, 1928).

"Picture's best assets is a first rate sympathetic role for Renee Adoree. Another is the presence of some pretty high powered sex sequences and a third, although value of this may be doubtful, is topical interest of Klan activity" (*Variety*, October 10, 1928).

"Best shot: Renee Adoree in swimming at night in a coal black river. Good entertainment" (*Time*, October 22, 1928).

## *Interference*

(Paramount) 7487 ft. 10 reels. 90 min. Released on November 5, 1928

*Survival Status:* UCLA Film and Television Archive (Los Angeles).

*Credits*: Associate producer, J.G. Bachman; director of dialogue scenes, Roy J. Pomeroy; director of silent versions, Lothar Mendes; screenplay adaptation, Hope Loring; based on the play *Interference, a Play in Three Acts* by Roland Pertwee, Harold Dearden; continuity, Louise Long; dialogue, Ernest Pascal; titles, Julian Johnson; photography, J. Roy Hunt; film editor, George Nichols, Jr.; sound, Franklin Hansen; recording and photographic engineers, Farciot Edouart, Albert De Sart, Franklin Hansen.

*Cast*: William Powell (Philip Voaze); Evelyn Brent (Deborah Kane); Clive Brook (Sir John Marlay); Doris Kenyon (Faith Marlay); Tom Ricketts (Charles Smith); Brandon Hurst (Inspector Haynes); Louis Payne (Childers); Wilfred Noy (Dr. Gray); Donald Stuart (Freddie); Raymond Lawrence (Reporter); Doro Merande (Deborah's Maid); Clyde Cook (Driver).

Philip Voaze, assumed killed in World War I action, attends his own memorial service in London. One of the mourners is Deborah Kane, and, boy, is she surprised to see *him*. She follows him until she's able to confront him. Evelyn Brent's first words ever said on film are "Philip! It *is* you, Philip!"

He tells her he's changed his name to Julian Akroyd. "It suited my purpose to let Philip Voaze remain dead," he says. "You'll always be Philip Voaze to me," she says, explaining that she's missed him terribly.

Philip doesn't feel the same. "After all, our life together was not exactly harmonious," he reminds her. Turns out he'd left Deborah to marry Faith. Deborah quickly tells him that Faith has married another man. It's apparent Deborah is still bitter. "Still the same old vengeful Deborah," Philip says.

When Deborah realizes Philip is ill, she tells him she'll do anything for him. He asks her to get out of his life. She leaves in a huff.

Sir John Marlay is a medical doctor who has recently been honored for important research. While he and wife Faith are celebrating, Faith gets a surprise visit from Deborah who informs her that Philip is alive and in London. Deborah blackmails Faith, telling her she has incriminating letters that Faith wrote to Philip. (In this scene, Brent stumbles a bit on her line about the Royal Society. Apparently Pomeroy decided the flub wasn't noticeable enough for a retake.) "Now I have the upper hand," she says with satisfaction. Before she leaves, she gets a check from Faith—and Deborah promises that John will get a blank postcard every morning, just to remind her that she's still in the picture.

After John receives several blank postcards, Deborah calls Faith and asks for additional money. John is unable to give her the money, and Faith considers suicide.

Meanwhile, Julian (Philip) has arrived for an appointment with John, not realizing Faith is his wife. They have an awkward reconciliation. Faith tells him about Deborah's blackmail. Philip takes the medicine bottle (acid hydrocyanic) away from Faith, scolding her that suicide is not the answer. Philip agrees to go to Deborah's apartment and reason with her.

John examines Philip and tells him he has an aneurism of the aorta. "It's like carrying a large bomb in your breast," Sir John explains to Philip. He tells Philip he doesn't have long to live.

Philip tells John his true identity and informs him about the letters. Angrily, John tells Philip to stay out of his affairs. He gets Deborah's address (it appears that he has the tiniest address book in the world).

Faith visits Deborah's apartment to tell her she couldn't get the money. (Check out Brent's revealing

***Gypsy chic in the late 1920s.***

satin pajamas.) While there, John arrives. Faith hides. John asks for the letters. "I'm afraid they're rather expensive," Deborah cheerfully explains. He tells her he won't pay. "You're interfering with the happiness of my wife and myself. I intend to put a stop to that interference. Permanently." He asks for her hand. She gives it to him reluctantly. He pokes her with a gold pencil, letting her know he could easily silence her. He leaves, telling her he'll return later that night for her answer.

"Do, Sir John, I'll be delighted to see you," she says sarcastically.

Faith tells Deborah that Philip must have told John. Deborah becomes convinced that Philip and Faith are still lovers, and she is not happy about it. "You've got the man you call your husband. Home, love, all the luck. All the simple, easy things. But it isn't enough for you. You want Philip, too! You want a little excitement. Well, you shall have it!" Enraged with jealousy, Deborah throws Faith out of her apartment.

Deborah sends a note to John and then calls the newspaper office to ask that someone be sent to her apartment. She wants to give them a story about John.

Philip arrives at her apartment, drunk. He tells Deborah he will marry her if she gives him the letters. "I'll say you always loved me," she says as she composes the note to Faith that will accompany the letters. "And she can go to the devil." Deborah finishes the note but sees Philip reading Faith's letters with a moony look. It makes her jealous, and they argue.

"Filthy drunkard," she sneers at him. "Good for nothing. Good for no one."

"Good enough for you," he replies.

Philip pours the contents of the medicine bottle into Deborah's drink. "Deborah, let's put an end to *all* quarrelling." She dies almost immediately in a surprisingly subtle death scene. Philip is so stunned by Deborah's quick death that he stares at her dead body, glances at the shot glass that contained the poison, looks back to her body, and musters a "hmm."

Later that night, John returns to Deborah's apartment and finds her body. He discovers his wife's handkerchief and bag—and the medicine bottle that came from his office. He removes the label from the bottle and places the bottle in Deborah's hand. He then pretends he cannot get her to answer the door and is let into her apartment. The body is "discovered," and the police are called in.

The reporter shows up, and John is excused. The inspector, however, realizes that Deborah was left-handed, and she's holding the bottle in her right hand. He looks for the stopper but can't find it, though he does locate a receipt for Lady Marlay. Finally, the inspector realizes the poison was poured into a flower arrangement. The inspector concludes that Deborah was murdered.

Meanwhile, John tells Faith that he's made Deborah's death look like a suicide. He assumes Faith murdered her. He asks Faith about the letters, but she says she hasn't got them. Philip arrives and says he is leaving England in the morning. "I've managed to do what you asked me," he says to Faith as he hands her the letters. The inspector arrives and questions Faith and Philip. He wants to compare the bottle to the ones in Sir John's cabinet.

Philip holds up the stopper and confesses to Deborah's murder. "I can't bear interferences," Philip says wearily. He is arrested and taken away.

"I was mad. I shall never forgive myself," John says.

"Why, there's nothing to forgive," Faith replies.

Paramount's first talkie film was based on a successful play. Director Roy Pomeroy, a special effects trouble-shooter, was shrewd enough to know he had the opportunity of a lifetime. "Roy J. Pomeroy had been the man of the hour at Paramount after *Wings* began its road-show engagements with striking sound effects in January 1928. He was already justly famous for his photographic parting of the Red Sea in DeMille's *The Ten Commandments* in 1923. He was also supervising Paramount's radio experiments, chaired the technical committee of the Five-Cornered Committee, installed Western Electric gear at Astoria and thereby learned talking-picture recording techniques firsthand from the ERPI [Electrical Research Products, Inc.] technicians. When Pomeroy returned to Hollywood, he told Lasky that sound was so complicated that only he could direct the studio's talking films."[84] Pomeroy suffered from a huge ego, which eventually led to the end of his career. "Success seems to have transformed him into the archetypal tyrannical soundman."

David O. Selznick began working at Paramount in 1928 and immediately ran into conflicts with the dictatorial director who insisted on controlling every aspect of filmmaking. "[A]fter a period of a few months it became apparent that other studios were making sound pictures and maybe there were other gods that could be obtained. Schulberg contacted the Western Electric authorities. They sent out their technicians, who had no ambitions other than to do a good technical job; and the new king was toppled from his throne. Within a few weeks everyone in the studio knew all they needed to know about sound, and in an amazingly short space of time the transition was made and we were making sound pictures along the same assembly-line methods that were employed for the silent pictures."[85] Pomeroy had overplayed his hand.

Most critics found the film innovative. According to Alexander Walker, "There were some scenes ... that advanced the creative use of sound. Hearing Evelyn Brent's disconsolate weeping when William Powell breaks with her, but *seeing* only his face in medium close-up wondering what her next move will be, is one of the earliest examples of sound being separated from the image so as to increase the drama of the visible scene. Up to then, and indeed for quite a time afterwards, audiences were presumed to need the sight of Miss Brent in order to link her with the sound of sobbing. The reaction shot was now charged with a new emotion, impossible in the silent movie. (One contemporary critic actually inferred from this innovation that it would reduce the cost of constructing sets which had got to be seen for actors who had only got to be heard!)"[86]

*Lux Radio* adapted the film for a November 28, 1938, broadcast. Mary Astor played Brent's role, and Herbert Marshall and Leslie Howard co-starred.

Paramount produced a silent version, directed by Lothar Mendes, that was used as a template for the talkie. Critics favored the sound version, finding the silent version "overdone and intrusive."[87]

The film began with a prologue by Daniel Frohman which explained the importance of the sound film. *Interference* set a box office record of $103,000 at Broadway's Paramount Theatre in 1929.

On August 22, 1928, the *Los Angeles Times* reported that *Interference* would be the first Paramount film that would not use extras.[88] This report was not true; there are lots of extras in the film, especially in the early memorial scene.

*Interference* was one of the first films that used screen tests for gowns. "Each of the gowns worn by Evelyn Brent in *Interference* ... was worn by her before a testing camera before being finally accepted for use in the production. 'To perfectly meet the needs of the screen, clothes must appear as well to the camera lens as to the eye,' says Travis Banton, Paramount's costume designer. 'They must also show their wearer to that person's best advantage. A dress that might be very becoming to Miss Brent off the screen might not look so well on the silver-screen. The screen test for dresses is a simple and effective means of deciding all questions.'"[89]

In a sense, cinema regressed with the introduction of talkies. It's important to remember that the best dialogue films of 1928 and 1929 do not compare well to the best silent films of those same years. Filmmakers working with dialogue had not yet gotten it right. Silent films, on the other hand, had been around for decades and were reaching their artistic heights. The 1928 peak year for silents contrasted sharply with the most primitive year for talkies. No talkie from the early years of the sound era will knock your socks off except for *Applause* and perhaps a couple others. *Interference* is pretty good for a late 1928/early 1929 dialogue film, which isn't saying a whole lot. Compared to other films from other years, it is a snoozefest. It put the talk in talkie.

Poor Doris Kenyon fares the worst. She appears self-conscious when delivering her lines. It must have been a nightmare playing opposite her. She gives a horrible performance, complete with hand-wringing and chest-clutching. Even worse, she sounds like she's saying her words phonetically. Try not to wince when she speaks her lines. Brent, Powell, and Brook are much more natural. Brent received top billing.

Kenyon was born in Syracuse, New York, in 1897. A silent film star, she continued making films until the late 1930s and gave much better performances in later pictures. She made a film comeback in the 1950s and later appeared on television. Kenyon was married four times. Her first husband was Milton Sills who died in 1930. Her second marriage was to playwright Arthur Hopkins; that marriage was annulled. She had a brief marriage to Albert David Lasker and then married Bronislaw Mylnarski in 1947. The marriage lasted until Mylnarski's death in 1971. Kenyon died in Beverly Hills in 1979. Doris Day is said to be named after her.

Brandon Hurst also appeared with Brent in *Secret Orders* (1926). He was born in London in 1866 and enjoyed a long career in silent and dialogue films until his death in 1947.

Tom Ricketts was born in London in 1853. A Shakespearean actor, he was also an early Hollywood director and writer. He died in 1939.

Louis Payne was married to actress Mrs. Leslie Carter. Born in Pennsylvania in 1873, Payne died in 1953. He also appeared with Brent in *Alias Mary Flynn* (1925).

Wilfred Noy, born in London in 1883, was Leslie Howard's uncle. Noy was also a writer, producer, and director. He died in 1948.

Donald Stuart was born in London in 1898. A stage and radio actor, Stuart died in 1944 of a heart attack.

Clyde Cook was nicknamed the Kangaroo Boy. Born in Australia in 1891, he appeared in many films, including some of the Keystone Cops pictures. Cook died in 1984.

Doro Merande was born in Columbia, Kansas, in 1892. The familiar character actor, sometimes using the name Dora Matthews, was a scene stealer extraordinaire. Also a stage actress, she ended her career on such television shows as *The Twilight Zone* and *The Jackie Gleason Show*. She died in 1975.

Writer Louise Long (1886–1966) also worked on the script for *Woman Trap* (1929).

*Reviews:* "[T]he audible screen adaptation of the play *Interference* is in many respects so remarkable that it may change the opinion of countless skeptics concerning talking photoplays. The vocal reproductions are extraordinarily fine and the incidental sounds have been registered with consummate intelligence. As a play it would naturally be considered far from perfect, but as a specimen in the strides made by the talking picture it is something to create no little wonderment.... Evelyn Brent does fine work as Deborah Kane" (*New York Times*, November 17, 1928).

"*Interference* is the finest talking production as a production yet turned out in dialog. It possesses all the elegance of gowning, suavity and gorgeous setting that distinguished Paramount's swanky dramas during the silent era. Yet with all these favorable points *Interference* is indifferent screen entertainment.... Miss Brent. ... is remarkable considering her total lack of experience [sic] on the speaking stage. She should avoid pajama costumes; they do not become her" (*Variety*, November 21, 1928).

"[I]ts smoothness, credibility and tastefulness are freely acknowledged. Its appeal from every standpoint is adult. However, in spite of this it is dull and some of the issues are confused" (*Los Angeles Times*, November 25, 1928).

"Evelyn Brent and Clive Brook were excellent; William Powell the best. All managed their voices as though they were used to them and not, as many talking picture actors, as though they were hot mashed potatoes" (*Time*, November 26, 1928).

"[W]ell made.... The story is a dandy.... Evelyn Brent is as alluring as ever, but her lines are read not nearly as well as those of Doris Kenyon" (The Gallery God, *Charleston Daily Mail* [West Virginia], January 1, 1929).

"Historically, [Paramount's] most important event of 1928 was the making of *Interference*, its first all-dialogue feature. Commercially, it was money in the bank. Artistically, alas, it left something to be desired. Trapped in a tiny stage sound-proofed by inventive trouble-shooter Roy Pomeroy, the cast seemed to be immobilized by microphone paralysis" (John Douglas Eames, *The Paramount Story*, p. 58).

## *Broadway*

(Universal Pictures) 9661 ft. 12 reels. 105 min. Released on May 27, 1929.

*Survival Status:* Archives du Film du CNC (Bois d'Arcy); Cinémathèque Royale (Brussels); Cineteca Italiana (Milano); Library of Congress (Washington).

*Credits:* Producers, Carl Laemmle, Carl Laemmle, Jr.; director, Pál Fejös; scenario, Edward T. Lowe, Jr., Charles Furthman; based on the play *Broadway* by Jed Harris, Philip Dunning and George Abbott; dialogue, Edward T. Lowe, Jr.; titles, Tom Reed; photography, Hal Mohr; special effects; Frank H. Booth; art direction, Charles D. Hall; film editors, Robert Carlisle, Edward L. Cahn: supervising editor, Maurice Pivar; costume design, Johanna Mathieson; makeup and hair, Dotha Hippe; music, Howard Jackson; sound engineer, C. Roy Hunter; sound system monitor, Harold I. Smith; dance numbers, Maurice L. Kusell; songs, "Broadway, The Chicken or the Egg," "Hot Footin' It," "Hittin' the Ceiling" and "Sing a Little Love Song," music and lyrics by Con Conrad, Archie Gottler, Sidney Mitchell.

*Cast:* Glenn Tryon (Roy Lane); Evelyn Brent (Pearl); Merna Kennedy (Billie Moore); Thomas Jackson (Dan McCorn); Robert Ellis (Steve Crandall); Otis Harlan ("Porky" Thompson); Paul Porcasi (Nick Verdis); Marion Lord (Lil Rice); Fritz Feld (Mose Levett); Leslie Fenton ("Scar" Edwards); Arthur Housman (Dolph); George Davis (Joe); Betty Francisco (Mazie); Edythe Flynn (Ruby); Florence Dudley (Ann); Ruby McCoy (Grace); Gus Arnheim and His Cocoanut Grove Ambassadors.

The film begins with aerial exterior shots of New York at night. With special effects magic we see a skyscraper-tall figure walking amongst Broadway buildings. He pours a drink and then pours the liquid over the buildings. After the credits there is a lively montage of theatres with their marquees lit, dancing girls, performances, etc. The montage takes us right to the doors of the trendy Paradise Night Club.

Backstage, club manager Nick Verdis watches disapprovingly as Roy Lane, club headliner and second-rate hoofer, puts the chorus girls through their paces. The girls' rehearsal session is uninspired. Nick, in his thick Greek accent, says to one chorus girl, "Pearl, will you watch what you're doing?" Pearl subtly replies, "Ahh, go fry an egg."

Nick tells the group, "This show ain't bad ... it's lousy." He says that last night a customer had told him, "Outside your place it says The Paradise Club—

the *best* cabaret in New York. That's what is *says*. And then he walks out." The girls quickly point out that no-show Billie Moore should take the brunt of the blame for not even bothering to come to rehearsal.

Nick plans to let Billie go, but Roy, who partners with Billie in the act, doesn't want her fired. Roy is in love with Billie and defends her absence to Nick. "You're gonna make one big mistake if you let her out." For emphasis, Roy adds, "Where could ya get a guy ta do what *I'm doin'* for the coffee and cake money you're payin' me? Ya' see, it ain't only that I can dance ... I got *PER-SON-AL-ITY*." Despite continuous jabs from fellow performers regarding his talent, or lack thereof, Roy is a trouper and all about the act. He is decent and likable but naïve. He is also a dreamer whose ambition is bigger than his talent. He sees his name in lights and daydreams that his act with Billie will some day make the big time. Nicknames like "Small-time," "Ham and egger," and "Oil can" do not stop him from pursuing his life's ambition.

Billie, later described by a club chorus girl as a "professional virgin," finally shows up at the club. When questioned by Roy as to why she was late, she admits that she was out with Steve Crandall. Roy, jealous, gives her some advice: "Lay off those big sugar daddies.... They're only after one thing."

Crandall arrives at the club. Verdis acts like his manservant, taking Crandall's hat, coat, and walking stick. It's evident that Crandall runs the show. Roy asks roughneck Crandall to lay off good girl Billie. Crandall is unmoved by Roy's plea.

Crandall's rival, bootlegger "Scar" Edwards, unexpectedly shows up backstage at the club. Edwards,

*A flapper look from 1929.*

furious with Crandall for hijacking his liquor and cutting into his territory, arrives alone and unarmed for a showdown. That's right, alone *and* unarmed. "Scar" tells Crandall, "You guys stay down in your own territory and leave my trucks alone, see! Because I've got the dope on ya, see. *You* croaked O'Connell." Alone and unarmed was not the smartest way to arrive for a showdown with Crandall. Crandall proves it by gleefully shooting "Scar" in the back, see?

Edwards and henchman Dolph carry the lifeless body out the back of the club but are interrupted by Billie and Roy. "Hey, who's the drunk?" Roy asks. Crandall tells him, "It's just one of the boys." The body is tossed into the back of a truck. Pearl, believing she heard a shot, is told that the noise was part of a battle number being staged by the band.

Roy performs a song-and-dance number with the chorus ("Hittin' the Ceiling") when homicide detective Dan McCorn enters. Although McCorn sits at a table and calmly reads a newspaper, he is at the club for business, not pleasure. (By the way, every number in this picture sounds like it's being performed by the Munchkins.)

Backstage, Billie tells Roy that his big dream might instead just be a "pipe dream." Roy thinks the act is sure-fire and tells her his dream will come true and that pretty soon they'll be making $700 a week, "just as true as if I were standin' here handin' you the money right now." Roy, still trying to convince a skeptical Billie, deftly manages to bring up the prickly subject of her involvement with Crandall. Billie doesn't think she "ought to miss out on a chance to go out with a big man like Mr. Crandall." Roy asks Billie to go out later that night, but Billie plans to attend Crandall's party. Roy asks, "Are you *fallin'* for this Crandall guy?" Billie stammers, "Why the very idea! Why, Mr. Crandall just considers me like a friend, or, or just sort of a pal." Roy replies, "Oh, I suppose he's going to adopt you.... It's your career I'm thinkin' of, that's all. Billie we can't let nuthin' stand in our way. I see our name in lights right now: *ROY LANE* ... and Company.'"

Crandall asks Billie, whom he often calls by the pet name "cute fella," to forget about the drunk he and Dolph were helping out of the club earlier. He presents her with a bracelet before returning to his office. Billie gushes.

McCorn, cool and competent, enters Crandall's office and grills Crandall. He tells him that the body of "Scar" was discovered and asks Crandall if he has an alibi. Crandall replies that he was at the club all night. McCorn then leaves the office and checks out some of the girls. Although he recognizes Pearl, she denies having seen him before.

Roy, the very definition of a trouper, gives the dancers a pep talk before they go on stage for the next number. "Remember, every night a first night, and they all paid for their seats. Heavy cover. So we gotta be good. Make 'em like it. Smile at 'em." Roy notices Billie's bracelet and insists she return it. She refuses, and they argue. Verdis steps in and tells Roy to get it together. "Nobody can tell you that I don't give my customers a hundred percent," Roy claims. "Every performance. The night my old man died, I went on ... at the Regent Theater in Danbury. And I gave one of the best performances I ever gave in my life." Roy starts to break up. "And even if a Jane ... I've pinned all my hopes ... and faith on ... was goin' to *Hell*, I'd still go on and do my best. Line up, kids. Now remember, this is the cue. Cut 'em deep and let 'em bleed." They go on, and the club crowd goes wild (most likely from the effect of bootleg whiskey rather than the song and dance number).

Backstage after the routine, Billie has second thoughts about accepting the bracelet from Crandall. There has been talk among the girls, and she fears that accepting the expensive gift will lead to misconceptions. Crandall easily convinces the naive girl otherwise. Crandall then says, "I'm crazy about you. Honest. No foolin'. Don't listen to what they say, Kitty. I'll take care of you." He tries to kiss Billie, but Roy interrupts.

Roy confronts Crandall, and Crandall laughs him off. Roy then pleads his case to Billie. He tells her, "I'm no prude. I'm for light wines and beers. But if a girl wants to get ahead in this racket, she shouldn't *start* her career by partyin' around with a lotta roughnecks." He once again demands that Billie return the bracelet to Crandall. After more bickering, Roy earnestly but awkwardly asks for Billie's hand. "I guess you know pretty well ... that I'm strong for ya. Only I ain't said nuthin' about it on account of my old man just died in here recently. [It's assumed he meant the *man* died, not the act.] But since this big four-flusher, Steve Crandall, is talkin' about a weddin' ring, it's time I played my ace. Listen, honey, how 'bout gettin' hitched up?"

Billie, not quite ready for a marriage proposal, hesitates. "Roy, I don't know. Gee, I don't know what to say." Roy, getting desperate, says, "God knows I'm for ya ... and if you'll just say the words that you're for me.... Well, I won't let out no yells or nuthin' like that, but I'd sure feel like doin' just that little thing." But Billie doesn't think they ought to talk about marrying when "you're so poor." Roy calls her a gold digger. Billie is angered by the accusation and tells Roy she's going to Crandall's party, "just to show you."

Roy conspires with a friend to have a telegram sent later that night from Trenton. Pearl and McCorn run into each other backstage. McCorn knows Pearl is Edwards' girl and asks if she is working at the club to keep "tabs on this bunch for 'Scar,' I mean Jim." Pearl replies, "Yeah, the lot of dirty skunks. They wouldn't stop at nuthin'." Pearl tells McCorn that she and Edwards are going to be married. She also mentions that Edwards told her at breakfast that he was coming down to the club for a showdown with Crandall. McCorn replies, "Thanks, Mrs. Edwards."

Roy and Billie argue backstage again. Roy parts with, "First, the artist, that's me. Second, the human bein'. I done everything I could to appeal to your

better instincts. There's nuthin' up the sleeve as far as I'm concerned. So if ya wanna be sore, I guess that's how it'll hafta be. That's all." Billie turns and walks away in a huff.

McCorn confronts Crandall as Pearl and the chorus girls come down the dressing room steps. Pearl collapses when she overhears Crandall say to McCorn, 'Why get all steamed up 'cause a nuisance like 'Scar' Edwards gets bumped off?" Pearl angrily stares at Crandall because she knows he murdered Edwards.

Billie attends Crandall's party with the rest of the girls. The party is for the rough Chicago crowd, in town as muscle for Crandall while he takes over Edwards' territory. One of the Chicago cavemen tries to force himself on Billie, but Crandall comes to her rescue. Crandall, weak-kneed for Billie, can no longer contain himself. "It's all right, little fella. Don't worry. Everything's all right.... I won't let nobody bother you. I love you, little fella. I love you. I'd *do murder* for you."

The charmer tries to kiss Billie, but she pulls away. Billie receives Roy's fake telegram telling her that her mother is ill. Roy comforts her and offers to take her home to Trenton. Another telegram arrives. It's real, and it's from Billie's mom, telling her to stay at the party and have a good time. Billie is beside herself when she finds out that Roy was responsible for the ruse. She tells him, "Oh, it's as dirty a trick as you could ever do.... I won't listen to ya. I don't want anything to do with ya, you ... oh, ya, ya big *sap*." The words cut deeply into Roy. The girls leave, and Roy is surrounded by the Chicago boys and Crandall. Crandall punches Roy. Quickly on his feet, Roy goes after Crandall. Crandall pulls a gun, but it falls to the floor. Roy picks it up. It's the same gun Crandall used to shoot 'Scar.' Roy points it at Crandall. McCorn arrives just in time to disarm Roy. Even though Roy says it's not his gun, McCorn asks, "Have you got a permit to carry this?" Roy, never missing a chance to toot his own horn, replies, "Of course not. I'm the chief performer here, mister. *Roy Lane*." McCorn then asks, "Did you ever hear of the Sullivan Act?" Roy stops to think about it, and with his one-track mind replies, "Sullivan ... no, what time is it playin'?"

Crandall's crowd doesn't want McCorn to confiscate the gun for obvious reasons. McCorn explains that he's already protected Crandall from 'Scar''s gang. Roy pipes up and tells McCorn he saw Crandall with a man who had a scar earlier that night. McCorn asks Billie if she saw Crandall helping a drunken man out the door. Billie lies for Crandall and says it never happened. As Roy is taken away, he threatens to kill Crandall if he touches Billie. After seeing that Crandall is untouchable, Pearl's hatred for him grows stronger.

Morning. We again take an aerial trip through New York's skyline. Back inside the Paradise Club, the cleaning staff is hard at work.

By showtime, Roy has been released and returns to the club. He says he's quitting, but Verdis appeals to

Roy's ego by telling him that the crowds are asking for him. Hambone Roy falls for the ruse. Roy runs into Billie, who tries to break the ice by saying, "I'm terribly glad you didn't get hurt or anything." Roy says the act is over. "Last night, you lied to save him, and *against* me." Billie replies, "Yes, but I didn't know. And you have no right to talk to me that way. All the girls around here always saying I'm too good ... and you're saying I'm too *bad*. Oh, I *hate* this darn place!"

Roy, sensing he has the upper hand, says, "Say, there's another thing too. Last night you called me a big *sap* ... in the presence of *several* witnesses." Billie says angrily, "Oh, shut up. That's just what you are, and I'll tell you sumthin' else. Last night when I went home all alone, I asked my mother if a girl was terribly in love with a person, so much that it was just like love at first sight, was it all right to marry 'em, even if they was poor? Now ... how would you like to go to the *devil*?!" She turns her back on Roy and goes into her dressing room.

Crandall, riding in a taxi cab on his way to the club, is shot at from another cab that pulls up alongside. The bullet goes through the window of his cab, narrowly misses his head, traveling through his hat. Crandall, severely shaken, doesn't see the shooter clearly.

Crandall arrives at the club and is a nervous wreck. Believing "Scar"'s gang is after him, he steps up security. Pearl arrives at the club looking frazzled. She runs up to the dressing room, changes into her costume, comes downstairs, and overhears Crandall tell Verdis his plan to take Billie on a trip. She also hears Crandall admit to killing Edwards.

Verdis gives Roy and Billie a chance to premiere a duet at the club. Roy is confident, but Billie is nervous and gets stage fright. Roy talks her through it, but her nervousness is apparent on stage.

Backstage, Pearl, armed, confronts Crandall: "Turn around, rat. I don't want to give it to you the way you did him—in the back." Crandall begs for mercy. He gets none. Pearl goes on, "I'm giving you more chance than you gave him. I'm lookin' at you, and the last thing you'll see before you go ... Jim Edwards' woman, who swore she'd get you. Whine, you *rat*." She pulls the trigger and says, "I knew you would." Crandall stumbles into his office and dies.

Roy and Billie get their big chance but the act doesn't go over big, which doesn't surprise several veteran members of the troupe. McCorn discovers Crandall's body, and Verdis tries to blame Roy for the murder. Knowing full well that Pearl did it, McCorn has sympathy for her and declares that Crandall committed suicide.

Before going on for the next number, Roy gets a card from a booking agent: "I can offer you ... and partner, Chambersburg and Pottsville next week." It's not Broadway, but what the heck. Roy kisses Billie. Pearl glances at the office door, behind which Crandall's dead body lies. Roy, Billie, and Pearl all got what they wanted ... well, sort of. Roy says, "I see

our names in lights right now. Roy Lane ... and Company. Remember, we're all artists. Here we go."

The concluding number is "Hittin' the Ceiling" again (in early two-strip Technicolor). Pearl appears to be going through the motions.

In a word, wow. It's hard to believe that *Interference* and *Broadway* were produced around the same time. *Interference* is static, stagey, and has little camera movement. *Broadway*, on the other hand, glories in camera movement and tricks. Busby Berkeley must have seen this film and committed it to memory as it is very reminiscent of his swooping crane camera technique. In essence, this is truly a *moving* picture.

Film buffs should seek it out just to experience a film by Dr. Pál Fejös. The play had been on Broadway for two years and was familiar to many moviegoers. The dilemma for director Fejös and producer Carl Laemmle was clear: "They had to satisfy those who went to see *Broadway* and at the same time refrain from presenting something that had already been shown...."[90] In the play, all the action took place backstage at the Paradise Club. "The happenings in the night club itself were described, but not shown. Here, in the picturization of the play lay the greatest opportunity to enhance the cinematic value of the film. Mr. Laemmle, together with Dr. Paul Fejös, envisioned a night club which should be symbolic not only of one of Broadway's nocturnal resorts, not only of Broadway itself, but a compendium of New York."[91]

The soundstage would hold not only the Paradise Club but other important settings as well. The result was the largest soundstage yet built—340 feet by 150 feet, and 70 feet high. Furthermore, the sets and lighting were used to great effect. "An example of ultramodern decoration, as a whole, each of the six fifty-foot columns built to support the roof was a separate skyscraper, graduated in size toward the top and illuminated from within by lights representing windows. On the walls of the set were painted other skyscrapers, sloping in a futuristic fashion outward into space from huge bases to the skyline, where begin the inverted pyramids supporting the roof. Inside of these pyramids and shining through them, were more lights. A kaleidoscope of color crashed downward upon the black 'marble' floor and the hundreds of tables and chairs, of various shapes and color combinations and cubistic shapes, seating the gay crowd of revelers. Against the decorative curtains forming the entertainers' entrance to the café a lighted model of the 'L' railroad roared upon a trellised arc. It disappeared behind one of the tiers of twenty-odd boxes bracketed upon the walls half-way between the floor and roof; boxes constructed in a variety of forms, painted in all colors and lighted by table lamps in conformity with the general design. Gigantic figures in cubistic form were against the walls. In the main entrance hall, behind and at the side of the six black marble columns surmounted by opaque lanterns stood the Princess of Pleasure—a carved figure—greeting her subjects as they entered the café. There appeared an ocean liner, ablaze with lights, making her way seaward from the merry whirl. Everywhere were hints and suggestions of designs, all symbolic of some particular phase of New York. And into this, beneath the 4,000,000 watts of light banked above, whirled the revue of thirty girls. All this pageantry of color and of motion was photographed in both color and Technicolor. The result, as seen upon the screen, embodies all the 'atmosphere' of the Great White Way in a single setting."[92] Thomas E. Jackson and Paul Porcasi, who appeared in the stage production, joined the film cast along with Glenn Tryon and Merna Kennedy, who played the leads.

Cinematographer Hal Mohr was responsible for filming the extraordinary scenes. According to writer Donald Albrecht, new equipment was developed. "So huge were the film's sets ... that they could not be photographed with regular equipment, and a special set-up had to be built: the Broadway camera crane, which cost $50,000 [some estimate the cost at $75,000] and had an arm extending forty feet. From the opening shots, in which the viewer travels along the canyons of Times Square and glides into the Paradise Club, Mohr's mobile camera is the perfect guide to explore Hall's vertiginous, Art Deco space filled with merrymakers perched on balconies."[93] Mohr (who was married to actress Evelyn Venable) ultimately won Oscars for *A Midsummer Night's Dream* (1935) and *Phantom of the Opera* (1943). He received a nomination for *The Four Poster* (1952). Born in San Francisco in 1894, he died in 1974.

Director Fejös traveled to New York twice for research and filming. One of his best ideas never made it to film because of the cost. "At one time he was so enthused over a scene which would show a panoramic Broadway taken from an outside elevator way to the top of the New York Times Building that he had plans drawn and actually secured permission from *The Times* to take the shot. But the cost of the elevator and the insurance were so staggering that he had to abandon the idea."[94]

Meanwhile, art director Charles D. Hall and Fejös created a set whose "décor would have engulfed 'the Palace, the Winter Garden, and the Hippodrome all in one.'"[95] The Paradise Club set was said to be the largest set in the history of film. (A *Billboard* critic thought it resembled the Cathedral of St. John the Divine.) Throughout the film, the skyscraper—a favorite symbol of Art Deco photographers and artists—is shown. "While modern architects expressed skyscrapers functionally as flat-topped stacks of horizontal floors, movie skyscrapers took their cues from the innumerable Art Deco skyscrapers of the 1920s. Like the Chrysler Building, they resembled nothing so much as modern-day Gothic cathedrals, tall arrows aspiring to the sky. Vertical black and silver stripes, a standard Art Deco motif, emphasize the height of the miniature skyscrapers that decorate the Paradise Club of Broadway, while rendered in the club's backcloth replicate the optical illusion of converging verticals familiar from the skyscraper photographs of Berenice Abbott and Edward Steichen."[96]

The set design was so complex and elaborate that a "Photoplay Appreciation" class at the University of Southern California requested a variety of photographs to study it. "Great scientific and engineering interest is attached to the lighting of this set because of the difficulties which had to be overcome in order that the entire interior of the Paradise Club might be illuminated from above. This was necessary so that the entire scenes could be photographed as a whole, without floor lights being used."[97]

In addition, two streets in Universal City were recreated as Broadway. "Two blocks of roadway at Universal City, constructed and peopled to resemble the famous thoroughfare, so even a native New Yorker would feel at home there, has been named 'Broadway' by Carl Laemmle, Jr. The street was built for scenes in *Broadway*.... Literally everything from the white way had been transferred to the studio for the production. Players, costumes, sets, atmosphere and dialogue from the stage hit were found on this street at Universal City."[98]

Fejös, born in what is now Hungary in 1884, is one of film's most remarkable directors. He is also relatively unknown and largely forgotten. He left Hollywood in 1930 and made some films in Europe, including documentaries. A brilliant man, he also studied biology and chemistry, and eventually left filmmaking to become an archeologist. He died in Romania in 1960.

Tryon and Kennedy play such dim bulbs they do seem a good match (though no one wishes them to have children). Still, their performances, especially Kennedy's, are weak for leads. Brent and Jackson are the better performers. They have strong chemistry, and there is a hint of attraction between the gun moll and bull. Second-billed behind Tryon, Brent is sullen in almost every one of her scenes and scantily clad throughout the picture.

A sound and silent version were released. (A sound version, minus the two-strip Technicolor ending, was screened at the Museum of Modern Art several years ago.) Historian William K. Everson explained that releasing a film in sound and silent versions was "not a difficult process, since the extreme camera mobility retained the 'look' of a silent film and made cutting easy. The musical numbers were trimmed down to emphasize size and spectacle rather than the songs themselves, and dialogue exchanges were likewise shortened by the use of titles. Although there were problems with the new sound equipment, it *was* possible to design a film release in both versions, the silent one usually being one to two reels shorter than the sound."[99]

The play ran for two years on, yes, Broadway with Lee Tracy in the lead. Thomas Jackson created the role of the detective on stage. Laemmle purchased the screen rights for $225,000; when it was decided that the film would become a sound production, an additional $25,000 was paid for dialogue rights.[100] According to Richard Barrios, "*Broadway* was another result of Carl Laemmle's quest for class and coin. The smash 1927 melodrama ... seemed to condense all the dark brash myths about Prohibition into one parcel confined entirely to the backstage area of a seedy nightclub. The ambitious hoofer, sweet chorine, ruthless lech of a gangster, smart police detective, and vengeful moll all spout dialogue couched in the most colorful and evocative slang possible this side of decency."[101]

The budget was reportedly $1.5 million, but it wasn't unusual for studios to exaggerate these figures. *Broadway* was one of the first Hollywood productions that cost more than a million dollars. It was a favored project of Carl Laemmle, Jr., the son of Universal's president. Because of its success, many films imitated it, including *Broadway Nights*, *Broadway Babies*, and *Backstage*.

One of the highlights of the production is the chorus girls. According to the *Los Angeles Times*, "Each girl in the ensemble, which performs in a variety of presentations on the mirror-like black parquet floor of the Paradise Night Club ... was specially selected for beauty of form, feature, and terpsichorean talent, and the group as a whole underwent rigorous training at the hands of Maurice Kusell for many weeks."[102] New songs were written specifically for the film, including "Broadway," "Hittin' the Ceiling," "The Chicken and the Egg," and "Sing a Little Love Song."

The Los Angeles premiere at the Biltmore was a big deal with many celebrities on hand, including Douglas Fairbanks, Jr., and Joan Crawford, Laura La Plante and William A. Seiter, Sue Carol, Sid Grauman, and Mr. and Mrs. Cliff Edwards. Brent did not like her performance and did not attend the premiere, although many of her co-stars did.

Everson enjoyed the art deco influence on the film and its sets. "With an excellent set design by Charles D. Hall—and a traveling camera crane designed specifically for the occasion—the huge night-club set, in which the camera swooped and pounced from dizzy heights, represented a bizarre sign of Hollywood's recognition of this new pictorial art. Not only was it Art-Deco to an extreme degree, but it showed recognizable traces of German expressionism, too."[103] Everson compared it to *Dr. Mabuse* (1922) and *Metropolis* (1926). Richard Barrios declared it "a one-of-a-kind transitional piece, an uncommonly baroque hybrid.... Virtual virtuosity is on one end of *Broadway*, audible histrionics are on the other, and in between is a limbo dumping ground for the musical numbers."[104]

Bette Davis played the role of Pearl in a Massachusetts production early in her career. Vivian Vance also played the role on stage. *Broadway* was remade in 1942 with George Raft, Pat O'Brien, Janet Blair, and Broderick Crawford. Anne Gwynne played the role of Pearl, and William A. Seiter (who attended the 1929 *Broadway*'s Biltmore premiere) directed.

Advertising described Pearl as: "beautiful, cold, indifferent on the surface ... burning fires beneath ... the dancer whose curling lip and insolent eye masks an aching heart." The film was proclaimed "The Greatest Melodrama the Screen Has Ever Known." Ads billed the film as "Exactly as presented on B'Way" and also promised that it featured "All talk—songs and shooting!"

Art director Charles D. Hall was born in England in 1888. He received Oscar nominations for *Merrily We Live* (1938) and *Captain Fury* (1939). He died in 1970.

Glenn Tryon also wrote, produced, and directed films. He was born in Idaho in 1898 and died in 1970. Formerly a song-and-dance vaudeville performer, he was divorced from actresses Jane Frazee and Lillian Hall. Tryon later directed Brent in *The Law West of Tombstone* (1938).

Merna Kennedy, born Maude Kahler in 1908 in Kankakee, Illinois, was briefly married to Busby Berkely in the mid–1930s. She died of a heart attack in 1944. Her role was originally intended for Betty Bronson.

Thomas E. Jackson was often cast as a detective, most notably in *Little Caesar* (1930) and *The Woman in the Window* (1944). He was also a successful stage producer, responsible for *Gentlemen of the Press* and *Ten Per Cent*. Born on July 4, 1886, he died in 1967. Jackson also appeared with Brent in *Hollywood Boulevard* (1936).

Robert Ellis was married and divorced from writer Helen Logan and actress May Allison (Allison later married James Quirk, editor of *Photoplay*; and became the magazine's editor following her husband's death). Ellis later married actress Vera Reynolds in 1926, and they remained married until her death in 1962. Ellis died in 1974. Ellis, who also wrote and directed, appeared with Brent in *Silk Stocking Sal* (1924), *Lady Robinhood* (1925), and *Forbidden Cargo* (1925).

Otis Harlan (1865–1940) was the voice of Happy in *Snow White and the Seven Dwarfs* (193X). Paul Porcasi was born in Italy in 1879. The popular character actor often played restaurant owners, chefs, waiters, and bartenders. He died in 1946. For stage actress Marion Lord (1886–1942), this was her first film role.

Leslie Fenton was born in Liverpool in 1902. His brother was writer Francis Fenton. Married to Ann Dvorak from 1932 to 1945, Fenton gave up acting to become a director. He appeared in several films with Brent including *The Showdown* (1928), *The Dragnet* (1928), *Woman Trap* (1929), and *The Pagan Lady* (1931). He died in 1978.

Arthur Housman (1889–1942) specialized in playing drunks. Unfortunately, he had a real-life drinking problem which led to his death. Born Elizabeth Barton in Arkansas in 1900, Betty Francisco was a WAMPAS Baby Star in 1923. She died of a heart attack in 1950. Gus Arnheim was born in Philadelphia, Pennsylvania, in 1887. The bandleader and songwriter died in 1955.

Writers Jed Harris and Tom Reed were nominated for an Oscar for co-writing *Night People* (1954).

*Reviews:* "[U]nusually good production.... Excellent casting.... Evelyn Brent will probably be first choice for good acting.... The final scene of a carnival night in the cabaret was done in Technicolor, giving a corking finish to a corking picture" (*Variety*, May 29, 1929).

"[G]ood melodrama.... The acting is variable.... In the opinion of many the outstanding members of the cast are two recruits from the stage play, Thomas E. Jackson and Paul Porcasi, but to those of us who are still loyal to the screen much can be found to admire in Glenn Tryon's highly expert performance as the hoofer [and] in Evelyn Brent's sullen study of revenge..." (*Los Angeles Times*, June 2, 1929).

"Features of the cops-&-robbers subplot which once seemed original have been used so often in other films that they are stale stuff by now. Best shot: Evelyn Brent in evening clothes" (*Time*, June 10, 1929).

"[Brent] gave a remarkably good performance. And if you never have seen Evelyn in a dancing costume, you want to. She has a figure that would make the German war debt look sick by comparison" (Dan Thomas, *Port Arthur News*, June 30, 1929).

"[A]n expert drama, with concise dialogue, tense melodrama, and, for the most part, good acting.... Tryon is surprisingly good in a difficult part. But he has keen competition in Thomas E. Jackson, a member of the stage cast, and Evelyn Brent, as the vengeful chorus girl, who steal the show.... [Y]ou will not be disappointed" (*Photoplay*, August 1929).

## *Fast Company*

(Paramount Famous–Lasky) 8 reels. 80 min. Released on August 30, 1929.

*Survival Status:* UCLA Film and Television Archive (Los Angeles).

*Credits:* Director, A. Edward Sutherland; screenplay, Walton Butterfield, Patrick Kearney, Florence Ryerson; adaptation, Walton Butterfield, Patrick Kearney; based on the play *Elmer the Great* by Ring Lardner, George M. Cohan; dialogue, Joseph L. Mankiewicz; photography, Edward Cronjager; film editor, Jane Loring; sound, Eugene Merritt; songs, "You Want Lovin', I Want Love," words and music by Sam Coslow.

*Cast:* Evelyn Brent (Evelyn Corey); Jack Oakie (Elmer Kane); Richard "Skeets" Gallagher (Bert Wade); Sam Hardy (Dave Walker); Arthur Housman (Barney Barlow); Gwen Lee (Rosie La Clerq); Chester Conklin (C. of C. President); E. H. Calvert (Platt); Eugenie Besserer (Mrs. Kane); Bert Rome (Hank Gordon); Irish Meusel, Arnold "Jigger" Statz, Truck Hannah, Gus Sanberg, Ivan Olson, Wally Rehg, Jack Adams, George Boehler, Howard Burkett, Red Rollings, Frank Greene, Lez Smith (themselves, baseball players).

Jack Oakie is Elmer Kane, a baseball star whom scout Bert Wade is desperate to sign. Wade enlists the aid of Evelyn Corey to seduce Elmer into signing. Elmer not only signs but also falls in love with Evelyn. The romance, however, does not progress well, and his hitting is affected.

Some newspapers proclaimed this the first all-talking baseball film. The film was based on *Elmer the Great*, a stage play by Ring Lardner which ran in several cities in 1928, and starred Walter Huston and Kay Francis before they began their film careers. This was the first of three Hollywood films based on the play. The second was *Elmer the Great* (1933), directed by Mervyn LeRoy, which featured Joe E. Brown, Patricia Ellis, and Frank McHugh, with Claire Dodd playing Evelyn. *Cowboy Quarterback* (1939), directed by Noel M. Smith, featured Bert Wheeler, Marie Wilson, and William Demarest, with Gloria Dickson as Evelyn.

Partly as a result of his writing for this film, Joseph Mankiewicz was named by *The Los Angeles Record* as one of the ten best dialogue writers and received a salary increase.

The filmmakers struggled with the problems associated with the then-new talkies. "In those days we used to start shooting at Paramount after five in the afternoon, and we'd shoot until five in the morning, because we were using the old silent stages, with enormous carpets, and tapestries hung down the walls for soundproofing. The reason we'd start at five was because that's when the traffic got quieter, so that the mikes wouldn't pick up the traffic noise."[105]

This was Chester Conklin's first movie without his trademark whiskers. Advertising proclaimed it was "Vibrant with Action!"

The film follows what Mankiewicz referred to as "the Oakie formula": "He was the sap who spoke in malapropisms, the ingenuous country bumpkin al-

*Sam Hardy, Gwen Lee, and Brent bicker in* Fast Company *(1929).*

ways taken for a ride by the society girl. He found out just in time that she was wrong for him and wound up with the more plain and virtuous girl—Mary Brian or the equivalent."[106] Oakie was a former broker's assistant who enjoyed a vaudeville career before breaking into films. Born Lewis Delaney Offield in Sedalia, Missouri, in 1903, he made his film debut in 1923. Early in his career he was often teamed with Richard "Skeets" Gallagher. Oakie died in 1978.

"Skeets" Gallagher was born in Terre Haute, Indiana, in 1891 and died in 1955. Sam Hardy made his film debut in 1915. Born in New Haven, Connecticut (he attended Yale), in 1883, he died in 1935. Eugenie Besserer made her film debut in 1910 as Auntie Em in *The Wonderful Wizard of Oz*. Born in Watertown, New York, in 1868, she died in 1934.

*Reviews:* "A thoroughly entertaining screen adaptation.... Mr. Oakie is splendid in his characterization and commendable work is done by Richard Gallagher as Wade, Evelyn Brent in the role of the actress and Gwen Lee, a friend of Evelyn's 'who was fired from a job at the Five-and-Ten because she couldn't remember the prices'" (*New York Times*, October 5, 1929).

"It is not belly laugh entertainment, but it is uncommonly agreeable light comedy buttressed by humanity and an idea" (*Variety*, October 9, 1929).

"Oakie, Brent, Gallagher] do their stuff in a very handy manner.... The direction thruout [sic] is very good and several shots of the 1928 [World Series] have been employed to advantage" (*Billboard*, October 12, 1929).

Critic Whitney Williams thought Brent's character was unsympathetic, but loved the movie. "[Y]ou can't afford to miss *Fast Company* ... that is, if you want a laugh a minute.... Jack Oakie is ideally cast.... The story is highly amusing.... So much so, in fact, that the audience is quite content to forget that the plot is somewhat trite.... Particular attention must be paid to the dialogue. It is bright and sparkling throughout" (*Los Angeles Times*, October 23, 1929).

"The honors belong to Jack Oakie as the conceited small town baseball star" (*Photoplay*, November 1929).

## Woman Trap

(Paramount Famous–Lasky) 80 min. Released on August 30, 1929.
*Survival Status:* UCLA Film and Television Archive (Los Angeles).
*Credits:* Director, William A. Wellman; screenplay and dialogue, Bartlett Cormack; scenario; Louise Long; based on the play *Brothers* by Edwin Burke; photography, Henry Gerrard; film editor, Alyson Shaffer; sound, Earl Hayman.
*Cast:* Hal Skelly (Dan Malone); Chester Morris (Ray Malone); Evelyn Brent (Kitty Evans); William B. Davidson (Watts); Effie Ellsler (Mrs. Malone); Guy Oliver (Mr. Evans); Leslie Fenton (Eddie Evans); Charles Giblyn (Smith); Joseph Mankiewicz (Reporter); Wilson Hummell (Detective captain); Sailor Billy Vincent (Himself, a boxer); Virginia Bruce (Nurse).

It's 1927. Police officer Dan Malone's kid brother Ray is often on the other side of the law. Ray likes to run around with Eddie Evans, who hangs out with mobsters.

Eddie's sister Kitty wants Dan to intervene. She and Dan have been dating off and on for years. She arrives at the Malones' one morning with fire in her eyes. One look at her and Dan says, "Uh-oh. The war is on." Kitty complains that Dan is not doing enough to keep "the kids" in line. "What do you think Eddie and Ray are trucking? Dry goods?"

Ma Malone also suggests that Dan do something about Ray. "Ray goes as the wind blows.... Like his father before him," Mrs. Malone complains to Dan. She's convinced he's hanging with the wrong crowd and probably involved in trucking alcohol. Ma also wants Dan to marry Kitty, "though you couldn't support a canary."

Dan has a talk with Ray, and Ray assures him that he's not doing anything too illegal. Eddie's father arrives to tell Ray to stay away from Eddie. The argument escalates, and Mr. Evans hits Ray in the back of the head with a cane. Dan picks up a silver cleaning bottle and throws it. Unfortunately, the liquid hits Ma, blinding her.

Kitty tells Dan it's his fault "for letting one thing lead to another till ... till this happened." They end up arguing, and Kitty stalks off.

One night Ray drives a car to the warehouse as a favor for Eddie, but the cops are waiting. They give chase. There's a terrific fight scene in an elevator. Finally, a gun goes off. The cop has been shot. Ray escapes, but leaves behind a cuff link.

"Your duty is to find the guy that shot that federal dick," Dan is told. He sees the cuff link and realizes his brother was involved.

It's now June 1929. "The law lies in the end of a policeman's night-stick," says a sign on the captain's desk. The desk now belongs to Dan Malone. He's developed a reputation for being tough. Perhaps too tough.

Dan gets a letter from Ray telling him he shot the federal officer—and figures he'll get caught eventually—but right now he's serving five years for a bank robbery. Ray asks Dan to tell Ma he's dead.

Dan tells Ma that Ray was killed in a logging accident after saving a little girl. While Dan and his mother are in church praying for Ray's soul, the City Civic League is bombed. (The camera must have been mounted on or near a horse-drawn carriage because hoofbeats are clearly heard in the exterior establishing shot. The explosion itself is a great, perhaps lucky, shot. The building explodes, and the City Civic League sign propels end over end directly towards the camera.)

A man is killed in the bombing, and Eddie is captured. A newspaper headline reads: "EDDIE EVANS GUILTY OF MURDER." The next one reads: "GOVERNOR REFUSES EVANS APPEAL." The final one reads: "EVANS TO HANG AT NINE A.M."

After Eddie is killed, a bitter Kitty confronts Dan. "You used *him* as your answer to the underworld.... They'd have let him go if you hadn't been such a ... such a god of justice!" She warns him, "But I'm hard too now and cold inside myself like you. Only harder and colder. So I'm going to get you. That's what I wanted to tell you. I'm going to get you some way where it'll hurt. Break you into little pieces and step on 'em till you cry like I've been crying." (There are some nice visual touches in this scene. As Kitty is talking about the hanging of her brother to "the god of justice," notice the shadow behind her. It appears to be coming from a shade pull, and obviously represents a hangman's noose swinging. Behind Dan's head is the shadow of a guillotine. Also, note that in the two-shot the shadows from the prison bars are visible behind the pair. The prison bars behind Dan are visible in other scenes as well.)

Ray escapes from prison and hides in his home watching his mother say "goodnight to the boy." In a particularly maudlin scene his mother, who doesn't know Ray is in the room, pats his bed and says, "Goodnight, Sonny." (Notice how Ray appears to be behind prison bars—in this case, it's the bars of the bed headboard. This is a recurring visual theme, perhaps telling us that Ray is doomed.)

Ray finds Kitty. (In this scene we experience an interesting use of early sound. The sound of giggling, almost hysterical girls comes from another room, creating a sharp contrast with the mood between Kitty and Ray. Notice, also, the wallpaper behind Ray has vertical bars on it.) Kitty lies to Ray, telling him Eddie's undercover. "But I can get to him." She'll bring Eddie to him and wants his address. "It's 36 River Street. The name's Wilson. See?" She promises to be there at 6.

Kitty calls Dan's office and informs his assistant Watts (who is not a big fan of Dan's). Watts convinces Dan to go to 36 River Street. Meanwhile, Ray is spotted by the officer he shot a couple years ago, and there is a struggle. The officer is accidentally killed.

Kitty arrives to meet Ray. He tells her about the officer and says he has to leave. Kitty has second thoughts about turning in Ray. Dan arrives and is surprised to see Kitty. She pleads with him to go away. He sees Ray. "You double-crossed me, huh?" Dan asks Kitty.

Dan tries to help Ray escape, but a bitter Watts stops him. 'You call the wagon. I can't take him," Dan laments.

Ray hides a gun in his pocket, says he needs to get his toothbrush, steps into the bathroom and shoots himself. A grieving Kitty tries to comfort Dan. "You said you'd make me cry," Dan says. "Well, I'm doing it."

"Dan, forgive me."

"I can't think very well. Maybe you ought to forgive me, too. And the Lord forgive the both of us."

"Dan."

"Kitty."

*Woman Trap* is a 1929 all-talking film, so allowances must be made. Morris is good. Skelly is a hambone. His Dan Malone is a stupid man, and not very likable. Skelly is unable to bring even the slightest bit of intelligence to the characterization. There's a bit much of Mother love, which was a hugely popular theme in films and popular music of the late twenties and early thirties. But overall, it is a well-directed film with a lot of nice visual touches.

Brent was second-billed and does a very good job. She shows range as she changes from a good-hearted but concerned young woman to one made bitter and cold by her losses.

The film is an adaptation of Edwin Burke's one-act play *Brothers*, which was purchased in May 1929. A better title for the film might have been *Jackass Brothers*. These boys will get on your nerves something terrible with their obnoxious horseplay. Both of them need to grow up.

Walter Huston was originally cast in the Hal Skelly role. Director Wellman kept pressing Skelly to make one specific entrance with more force. A frustrated Skelly finally opened the door, interrupting a tense scene between Brent and Morris. He broke everyone up by riding in on a bicycle he'd borrowed from a prop man.[107]

Skelly could never be considered a handsome man. The dancer, born in Wisconsin in 1892, joined the circus when he was young and later became a stage star. Skelly's film career came to an abrupt end when he was killed in an automobile accident in Connecticut in 1934. Though Skelly received good reviews during his lifetime, he doesn't hold up well.

In contrast, charismatic Chester Morris is still watchable today. He was born in New York in 1901. Nominated for an Oscar for his work in *Alibi* (1929), Morris enjoyed a long career in films and television. Diagnosed with cancer, he committed suicide in 1970 while appearing in a stage production at the Bucks County Playhouse in Pennsylvania. Morris' performances are usually energetic and strong. There's a James Dean and early Brando quality to him. It's surprising he's not better known.

According to a July 8, 1929 report in the *Los Angeles Times*, Donald Davis, the son of playwright Owen Davis, was hired to help with dialogue.

William B. Davidson, born in New York in 1888, appeared in literally hundreds of films beginning around 1914. Previously he'd been a college football star for Columbia University, and his early roles were as a leading man. He died in 1947. Davidson also appeared with Brent in *The Silver Horde* (1930).

Effie Ellsler was born in Cleveland in 1855. A long-time stage actor, she made her film debut in 1926. When Ellsler was appearing on stage in *The Bat* in January 1922, her husband Frank Weston visited her after the second act. He collapsed and died. "Miss Ellsler hastily summoned help, then stepped out on the stage and played her part to the final curtain."[108] Described as "one of the sweetest old ladies in Hollywood," Ellsler died in 1942.

Guy Oliver, born in Chicago in 1878, began his film career in 1911. He died in 1932. Charles Giblyn had once been a silent movie director before turning to acting, often in bits. He died in 1934. Wilson Hummel was often billed as Clarence Wilson. Born in Ohio in 1876, he died in 1941. Sailor Vincent, born in Massachusetts in 1901, was also a stuntman in many films. Vincent appeared on television shows in the 1960s including *Gunsmoke* and *Twilight Zone*. He died in 1966.

Lovely Virginia Bruce began her film career in 1929 at the age of 19. After testing for this film, she got the part as well as a long-term contract. Born in Minnesota in 1910, she married John Gilbert in 1932; they divorced two years later. She enjoyed a long career, eventually appearing on television in the 1950s. She died in 1982.

Director William Wellman, known as "Wild Bill," won an Oscar for co-writing *A Star is Born* (1937). Born in 1896 in Massachusetts, Wellman received a Lifetime Achievement Award from the Directors Guild in 1973. He died in 1975.

Bartlett Cormack (1898–1942) was best known for writing the stage hit *The Racket*. Edwin Burke (1889–1944) won an Oscar for his adaptation of *Bad Girl* (1931).

*Reviews:* "A talking film with extravagant and unconvincing action, verbose dialogue and patches of sentimentality.... Hal Skelly, who is featured in *The Dance of Life*, ... adds a second excellent performance to his credit. There are also others who do good work in this offering, particularly Evelyn Brent and Chester Morris" (*New York Times*, August 31, 1929).

"Flaws can be picked, but the ... ensemble passes muster as reasonably intense melodrama" (*Variety*, September 11, 1929).

"For two years the crime wave has flooded the film market, yet this production rises above the hackneyed and commands attention" (*Photoplay*, October 1929).

## Why Bring That Up?

(Paramount Famous–Lasky) 80 min. Released on October 4, 1929.

*Survival Status:* UCLA Film and Television Archive (Los Angeles).

*Credits:* Director, George Abbott; adaptation, George Abbott, Hector Turnbull; dialogue, Hector Turnbull; story, Octavus Roy Cohen; titles, George Marion Jr.; photography, J. Roy Hunt; film editor, William Shea; sound, Harry D. Mills; songs, "Do I Know What I Am Doing While I'm in Love" by Leo Robin and Richard A. Whiting; "Shoo Shoo Boogie Boo," by Leo Robin, Sam Coslow, Richard A. Whiting.

*Cast:* Charles Mack (Charlie); George Moran (George); Evelyn Brent (Betty); Harry Green (Irving); Bert Swor (Bert); Freeman Wood (Powell); Lawrence Leslie (Casey); Helen Lynch (Marie); Selmer Jackson (Eddie); Jack Luden (Treasurer); Monte Collins, Jr. (Skeets); George Thompson (Doorman); Eddie Kane (Manager); Charles Hall (Tough).

Betty breaks up George's vaudeville act when she breaks his partner's heart. George teams up with Charlie, but Betty returns in an attempt to swindle George in a stock market deal.

For some viewers today, the success of Moran and Mack is inexplicable. Richard Barrios was not a fan. "Their routines, obviously an offshoot of the minstrel tradition, contained enough lazy drawling to sink a battleship, and this type of humor was still viable for many white Americans. (*Variety* once observed that the team's popularity extended to some black audiences as well.) After many decades, the reasons for their success may seem mysterious. In other

practitioners of racially insensitive humor there can often be divined reasons for success, comprehension if not acceptance or appreciation. Not so with Moran and Mack; seen and heard today, they are not broad enough to be outrageous, just two men with minstrel makeup telling stories. The stereotypes, as obvious and unseemly as could be, just lie there—blackface for its own sake, without reference to vitality or humor, much less humanity."[109]

Still, the film was very successful, though the act broke up. Bert Swor became Moran for the next feature, *Anybody's War*. Some believe the success of Moran and Mack declined when the similar *The Amos 'n' Andy Show* became a huge radio success.

Advertisers billed the picture in this way: "Here they are! The funniest men in the world in a romantic musical! A show that had all New York laughing! A $7.70 musical comedy unequalled on any stage!," "The Two Black Crows—MORAN and MACK—in their first ALL TALKING Production," and "NOW—HEAR THEM ON THE SCREEN—Funnier than ever!"

The film was originally titled *Backstage Blues*, and was supposed to include actual events that had occurred in their stage careers. Charles Mack was born Charles Sellers in White Cloud, Kansas, in 1887. He died January 11, 1934, in a car accident in Mesa, Arizona. George Moran was born George Searcy in Elwood, Kansas, in 1881. He died in 1949.

Harry Green, born Henry Blitzer in New York City in 1892, was a lawyer before he made his screen debut in 1929. He died in 1958. Bert Swor, born in Paris, Tennessee, in 1878, died in 1943. Lawrence Leslie, born in 1908, appeared in only three films before his death on July 15, 1930, in New York City. Eddie Kane also appeared with Brent in *Framed* (1930). The busy character actor was born in St. Louis in 1889. He died in 1969. Selmer Jackson, sometimes billed as Selmar Jackson, also appeared with Brent in *Madonna of the Streets* (1930), *Jungle Jim* (1937) and *Stage Struck* (1948). Born in Iowa in 1888, he died in 1971 after a long career that began in the silent era.

*Reviews:* "[A]n inconsequential but enjoyable trifle with an atmosphere of the theater so authentic that we begin to grow fidgety about our own exit-cue long before it was given.... Evelyn Brent walks easily through the part" (*Los Angeles Times*, October 5, 1929).

"This audible film is ably produced by George Abbott, playwright and stage director.... Up to the last quarter it is extremely funny, particularly in those passages where Moran and Mack do some of their well-known skits" (*New York Times*, October 5, 1929).

"The nationally known vaude routine of the blackface comedians, Moran and Mack, stretched out on a fragile story frame.... [I]t amounts to an acceptable program picture that never gets very near to bigness.... Miss Brent is, as usual, the looker and trouper" (*Variety*, October 9, 1929).

"The Two Black Crows are funny as ever.... Evelyn Brent makes an attractive gold digger as only she can" (*Billboard*, October 12, 1929).

"The two idols of the phonograph records are at their best in burnt cork. Without the shellac it is evident that they aren't such a much [sic] at heavy emoting" (*Photoplay*, October 1929).

"A fair comedy, with some rather neat work by this city's Evelyn Brent as a she-villain" (*Syracuse Herald*, December 26, 1929).

## Darkened Rooms

(Paramount Famous–Lasky) 70 min. Released on November 15, 1929.

*Survival Status:* Library of Congress (Washington); UCLA Film and Television Archive (Los Angeles).

*Credits:* Director, Louis Gasnier; adaptation, Melville Baker, Patrick J. Kearney; based on the short story *Darkened Rooms* by Philip Hamilton Gibbs; dialogue, Melville Baker, Patrick Kearney; titles, Richard H. Digges, Jr.; photography, Archie J. Stout; film editor, Frances Marsh.

*Cast:* Evelyn Brent (Ellen); Neil Hamilton (Emory Jago); Doris Hill (Joyce Clayton); David Newell (Billy); Gale Henry (Madame Silvara); Wallace MacDonald (Bert Nelson); Blanche Craig (Mrs. Fogarty); E. H. Calvert (Mr. Clayton); Sammy Bricker (Sailor); Oscar Smith (Oscar).

The film opens at a nighttime carnival on the boardwalk. We are next inside the office of fake psychic Madame Silvara, who is giving a $2 reading. Hoping to do better, she enlists the help of photographer Emory to produce fake spiritual photographs. Emory decides he wants to get into the psychic racket because he sees big money in it. "All I need is some good customers," he says.

Emory returns to his shop and finds Ellen waiting for him. She's a dancer who needs publicity pictures. He quotes her a price for a package. She's shocked. "Six dollars? You are an optimist, aren't you?" She can't afford them. "I've already hocked everything but my underwear," she wearily says. He offers to let Ellen pay him after she gets a job. "With my luck, you'll have a full beard by then," she says.

Ellen collapses while he's preparing to take her photograph. (It's a clever shot. Ellen is seen upside down through the cameras lens, and appears to fall 'upward' when she faints.) Emory asks her when she last ate. "I'm not old enough to remember that far back," she says. "Tough racket being a girl and broke," she explains when he gets her coffee and a hot dog.

He "hypnotizes" her and tells her to return to the shop that night at 8 PM. "Not a chance in the world," she says with a laugh. However, sure enough, she returns that night, though she claims she did it because she was hungry. "No," he says, "I made you come back." Instead of finding Emory creepy, she's taken with him.

Emory hires her to be his assistant. Ellen's first job is to pose with Madame Silvara and pretend to be a dead woman. She later overhears Emory talking to Madame Silvera about a job where he plans to scam a rich woman, Joyce Clayton, who lost Dick, her husband-to-be, in an airplane accident. Emory tells Ellen he's got a big part for her. Ellen's interested. "I'll play a bloodhound in *Uncle Tom's Cabin* if you want me to."

Ellen has second thoughts once they arrive at the Clayton house. "It's crooked and dangerous," she says, but goes along with the scam.

During the séance, Ellen (identified as Emory's sister) goes into a trance, pretends to be the dead aviator, and wants to speak to Joyce. This upsets Joyce and her new beau, Billy. Having heard enough, Billy turns on the lights, ending the séance.

Joyce visits the photography studio, followed by Billy, who warns Emory not to upset her again. Another séance is conducted, and Joyce again "hears" from her dead boyfriend. Billy stops the séance and warns Emory and Ellen that he'll have them arrested if they see Joyce again. "Oh, Emory, I was afraid this would happen," Ellen says. "I've always known it was wrong and dangerous."

Emory wants to continue the scam, but Ellen pleads with him to stop. She tells him she'll stop working with him. "All right, then" he says. "I'll work alone."

Joyce makes plans to travel overseas but wants to see Emory before she leaves. Emory tells her he has a message from Dick.

Ellen comes up with an ingenious plan: She hires actor friend Bert to impersonate Dick's ghost. The séance begins. Emory tells Joyce he'll be using a slate this time. He puts the slate under the table after having her examine it. In a moment, Emory retrieves the slate. It now has a message on it: "Joyce Dear—There are many troubles threatening you. Trust Emory Jago—He will tell you what to do." It is signed "Dick."

Joyce exclaims that it's Dick's handwriting. Suddenly they hear the sound of an airplane. Joyce hears "Dick," telling her he's come to warn her—and to save her from Emory. There's a spectral image of a man dressed like an aviator. "He has only the power to deceive you," the spirit continues. He tells Joyce to marry Billy and forget him, and then orders her to leave Emory's.

We now see Ellen is making the sound of the airplane with a vacuum cleaner. Bert comes in dressed like an aviator.

"Did he fall for it?" Ellen asks.

"He'll never get over it," Bert says.

A shaken Emory asks Ellen not to leave him. "I've had a terrible shock," he says. "I'm through monkeying with that stuff forever," he says in despair. "Why be just a fake spiritualist when you're a good photographer?" Ellen asks.

Emory and Ellen attend to a frequent customer (a homely sailor who keeps bringing in girls—and can't seem to keep his hands off them) and stand arm in arm.

Brent received top billing in this cynical melodrama. The photography and sets create a moody, slightly depressing atmosphere. Brent is charming and quite believable as the world-weary but decent young woman. Neil Hamilton, however, delivers his lines ponderously. A former Arrow shirt model, Hamilton is pleasing to the eye, but as an actor he is often stiffer than his Arrow shirt collars. He lacks the warmth needed to be a likable lead and might have been better suited as a caddish villain rather than a romantic lead.

For some reason they made poor Oscar Dixon pretend to have a stutter. A terrible stutter. Hilarity does *not* ensue.

William Powell was originally announced in January 1929 as the male lead. Jean Arthur was originally cast as Joyce. Wallace MacDonald was specifically chosen by director Gasnier "because he possesses the ability to talk like a chunk of ectoplasm."[110] This was director Gasnier's first talkie, and he believed directing dialogue films was much easier than silents. He credited two things: his stage training and the fact that many of the technical problems associated with sound were not his responsibility, but those of the technicians.[111] Gasnier also directed Brent's *Slightly Scarlet* (1930). Born in Paris in 1875, he was an actor, director, and producer of silent films in France for many years and directed the *Perils of Pauline* series. However—perhaps unfairly—he is best known as the director of the cult favorite *Reefer Madness* (1936). He died in Hollywood in 1963.

Archie Stout began working as an assistant for Mack Sennett in 1916. The much-experienced cameraman was asked to work on Brent's first starring role for Paramount. Stout explained that he got his inspiration from Rembrandt. "In *Darkened Rooms*, Stout throws lights on Miss Brent from above and below her face, from the right and to the left, but never allows a straight flat light to flood her features. When the action of the story causes her to travel cross the room, the lights follow her always, maintaining the same effects on her face. In contrast to the lighting arranged for the star is that employed for Doris Hill, who supports her in the picture. Her rounded features are at their best when lit by a brilliant straight white spot."[112] Stout deserves much of the credit for Brent's attractiveness in this film. Born in Iowa in 1886, Stout often worked with director John Ford. He won an Oscar for *The Quiet Man* (1952). Stout died in 1973.

Newspaper advertisements referred to Brent as "The Queen of Melodrama in her first starring role." The ad proclaimed: "Thrills! Mystery! Breathtaking Romance! Sir Philip Gibbs' sensational expose of society's wolves. It will hold you spell-bound with its hair-raising excitement. Don't miss it." Another focused on Brent: "She held you spellbound in *Interference*. Her voice thrilled you in *Woman Trap*. You saw her love in *Fast Company*. Evelyn Brent is more stirring, more thrilling than ever in her first starring picture. See and hear her." Another said: "She Cheats for the Man She Loves." One ad targeted the plot: "Thrill to this Love Exposé of this Spiritualist Medium 'Racket'—See and Hear the Secrets of the 'Great Beyond.'"

Neil Hamilton was a favorite male lead in silents and in the early 1930s. Born in Lynn, Massachusetts, in 1899, he also modeled for true-story magazines. Hamilton was an amateur, though very serious, magician, and a member of the American Magicians'

Society. He married Elsa Whitmer in 1922, and they remained married until his death in 1984. Hamilton's later work was on television. Perhaps his best known role was Police Commissioner Gordon on TV's *Batman* in the 1960s. He also appeared with Brent in *The Showdown* (1928), *The World Gone Mad* (1933), and *Dangerous Lady* (1941).

Born in Missouri in 1905, David Newell appeared on stage before he started his film career in 1929. He became a makeup artist in the late 1940s. Newell died in 1980.

Writer-director-producer-actor Wallace MacDonald was born in Canada in 1891. MacDonald appeared in several Charles Chaplin films in the silent era. The popular character actor began producing films in 1937. He died in 1978. He also appeared with Brent in *The Pagan Lady* (1931).

Blanche Craig's (1866–1940) first film appearance was in *Traffic in Souls* (1913). E.H. Calvert was also a silent film director. Born in Virginia in 1863, he began his acting career in 1912. Calvert, also known as Captain E.H. Calvert, died in 1941. He also appeared with Brent in *Fast Company* (1929). Doris Hill was born in Roswell, New Mexico, in 1905. Hill appeared in her first film in 1926. She made several Westerns in the 1930s, and her final appearance was in 1934. Hill died in Arizona in 1976.

Writer Melville Baker was the son of playwright Robert M. Baker. Born in Massachusetts in 1901, Baker died in France in 1958. Playwright Patrick J. Kearney, born in Delaware in 1893, also wrote the adaptation for *Fast Company* (1929). Kearney, who wrote the stage version of *An American Tragedy*, committed suicide in 1933.

*Reviews:* "A number of photographic effects, especially in the spirit scenes and medium trances, are extremely spooky. Evelyn Brent, as the fake medium, almost convinces the audience, as well as the wealthy prospect, that she is holding a genuine converse [sic] with the invisible world beyond the veil. In all, it is a powerful as well as an enjoyable production, furnishing enough chills to delight mystery seekers, enough psychology to satisfy the astute, and just enough romance to please everybody" (*Atlanta Constitution*, November 15, 1929).

"O. Henry might have written *Darkened Rooms*, but he didn't. It isn't such a much [sic] despite light handling and a unique twist. This little comedy-drammer is about a photographer who thinks he's a spiritualist, and a gal who proves that he isn't. Evelyn Brent is the star, but Neil Hamilton wins the bacon as the photographer" (*Photoplay*, December 1929).

"Incongruous story with the incidental action holding spotty interest.... Seances ... are the most entertaining" (*Variety*, December 18, 1929).

"[A] low-budget, taut little drama which gave Neil Hamilton his best part since *Beau Geste*..." (John Douglas Eames, *The Paramount Story*, p. 67).

## *Slightly Scarlet*

(Paramount Famous–Lasky) 72 min. Released on February 16, 1930.

*Survival Status:* UCLA Film and Television Archive (Los Angeles).

*Credits*: Directors, Louis Gasnier, Edwin H. Knopf; screenplay; Howard Estabrook, Joseph L. Mankiewicz; story, Percy Heath; titles, Gerald Geraghty; photography, Allen Siegler; film editor, Eda Warren.

*Cast*: Evelyn Brent (Lucy Stavrin); Clive Brook (Hon. Courtenay Parkes); Paul Lukas (Malatroff); Eugene Pallette (Sylvester Corbett); Helen Ware (Mrs. Corbett); Virginia Bruce (Enid Corbett); Henry Wadsworth (Sandy Weyman); Claud Allister (Albert Hawkins); Christiane Yves (Marie); Morgan Farley (Malatroff's victim); Georges Renavent (Inspector); Charles Sullivan (Chauffeur).

Paris. Courtenay and Lucy live across from each other's hotel. Courtenay sends Lucy a note with flowers: "Permit to express neighborly greetings—and may I await a friendly nod? Hopefully Courtenay Parkes."

While Courtenay awaits her answer, he sees a newspaper blurb: "Sylvester Corbett, Youngstown millionaire, has purchased for his wife, the famous pearl necklace formerly owned by the Maharajah of Khamboul. Mr. and Mrs. Corbett, with their daughter, Enid, are enjoying the Riviera season at Nice, where they have rented a villa." Apparently rebuffed by Lucy who responds to the note by closing the curtains, Courtenay plans a visit to Nice.

Meanwhile, Lucy is called to Malatroff's office. She's reluctant to work for him again, but he shows her a replica of the necklace. He asks her to pretend to be the American widow of an Austrian count. "I want to be free," she says. "Not always cut off from everybody. Guarding every word I say." He tells her she will always be "part of my machine.... To me you are number 14. And number 14 leaves for Nice tonight."

Lucy refuses. Malatroff brings in another agent who pleads for his life. Malatroff callously—and ominously—plays the organ when the man is taken out of the office, struggling and begging. Lucy reconsiders.

"If I do this, will it be the last thing you'll ever ask of me?" she asks.

He agrees. "If you are successful."

Lucy arrives at the Corbett family's Nice villa. Mr. Corbett is unhappy because they have been in Nice and have yet to make inroads into Nice society. In this amusing scene, Mr. Corbett gets increasingly angry while Enid sings musical scales. Her singing gets more and more annoying, building to a sort of crescendo, until he finally explodes (the expression on Enid's face when he blows up at her is priceless). Needless to say, they are glad to see that Countess Stavrin has come to see them. Actually, she explains, her car is stuck in a ditch and needs help getting out. While waiting, Lucy discusses jewelry with Mrs. Corbett. She learns that Mr. Corbett paid $500,000 for the necklace.

Lucy is alarmed to hear that the police have arrived. However, they are there because the Corbetts have enlisted their help in finding their dog. Courtenay and his butler, who are renting the villa next to the Corbetts', find the dog. Courtenay returns the dog to a very relieved Mrs. Corbett, who then introduces Courtenay to Lucy. There is a flicker of recognition.

Courtenay and Lucy are invited to dine with the Corbetts the following night. Mrs. Corbett wears the necklace. Lucy asks to try on the necklace, and while her chauffeur creates a disturbance she tries to exchange it with the replica. However, Courtenay foils her plan.

Courtenay and Lucy have an intimate talk after dinner. Lucy explains that she thought Courtenay was flirting with her maid, and he mistook her closing the curtains as a rebuff. Courtenay takes her to her hotel. She invites him to lunch the next day with the Corbetts.

Malatroff has been waiting for Lucy's return. She tells him she hasn't gotten the necklace yet. He tells her Courtenay is a detective. "We will attend to him," he assures her. Malatroff tells Lucy he must have the necklace by the following night.

At lunch the next day, Malatroff is seated at a table not far from Lucy's party. While discussing the availability of a villa, Lucy receives a note from him: "Impossible to get villa M." She tells her tablemates that she will now have to go away from Nice because she has not found a suitable villa. The Corbetts invite her to stay with them.

After lunch, Lucy returns with the Corbetts. Before retiring for the night, she asks Mr. Corbett to keep her jewels in the safe. She watches as he opens the safe. (After the two leave the room, notice the large spider web shadow visible on the wall. The same shadow is there when Lucy returns to the safe later that evening.)

Enid's callow boyfriend Sandy confronts Courtenay, wanting to know his intentions. Courtenay assures him that he is not going to ask Enid to marry

***Evelyn with Clive Brook in*** Slightly Scarlet ***(1930).***

him—and that he's in love with the countess. Sandy sees Lucy at the bottom of the stairs. He tells her he knows what she's up to—and that Courtenay is outside. "Lucy, can't you see that with just a little encouragement I shall probably tell you I love you?" Courtenay asks her.

"Yes."

"And you're not going to give me that encouragement?"

"I can't. I can't."

He implores her. Just as they're about to embrace, an accordion player begins playing. She is reminded of Malatroff. She abruptly turns away. Hurt, Courtenay tells her, "To think I nearly changed my plans ... for you. Good night."

In one of the film's best scenes, Lucy opens the safe and exchanges the necklaces. A flashlight spot follows her about the room. She sees a man at the safe. It's Courtenay. Lucy drops something. The flashlight begins searching for her again. Finally, she's illuminated. "Congratulations," she says cynically.

"I'm sorry," he says.

"Never mind the regrets. It's all right with me. You know what this reminds me of? Back home once I was pinched by a traffic cop for speeding. He was dressed in plain clothes. He was on a motorcycle with a sidecar that had groceries painted on it. Good idea, wasn't it? Well, you used charm like that cop used a sidecar. You wouldn't fight in the open. You're afraid." She asks him what he's going to do with her. He tells him he's beaten her to it and shows her the necklace. He's a robber, too.

She tells him this was going to be her last job, and then she was going straight. Courtenay tells her that what he meant earlier was that because of her, he was on the verge of quitting, too.

"Well, why don't we quit?" she asks.

"That would be more thrilling than any adventure I've ever known," he says. He starts to put the necklace back in the safe.

"Just a minute, dear," she says. "Don't you think we might as well let them have the real one?"

Courtenay carefully examines the necklaces and then looks at his beloved. "My compliments," he says sincerely.

"A gift to the Corbett family from the future Mrs. Courtenay Parkes and fiancé."

They embrace and kiss, but we see the shadow of a man. It's Malatroff. He asks for the necklace. Courtenay overpowers him. In the struggle, Malatroff is killed. The police charge in, guns drawn. Lucy and Courtenay are arrested.

The inspector questions them. Their stories don't match, and the inspector wants to get to the bottom of it. "The situation is simply this," Lucy explains. "I'm very much in love with Mr. Parkes and—"

The inspector agrees the excuse sounds plausible. He is given a message and then comes back to inform Courtenay that they owe him a debt of gratitude. "You have rid us of the worst criminal in Europe. That man was Malatroff."

Similar in plot to Ernst Lubitsch's 1932 *Trouble in Paradise*, this one also features elegant, sophisticated thieves. One of the picture's flaws is typical of the time period: limitations caused by sound. "The static camera work of *Slightly Scarlet* is indicative of the restrictions imposed on the early talkies by the need to muffle the noise of the camera by enclosing it in a soundproofed booth. The stagey tableaus and theatrical delivery of dialogue are attributable to the collaboration of a theater director (Edwin Knopf) with a silent film director (Louis Gasnier). These odd collaborations were devised by the front office to help the actors accommodate themselves to spoken dialogue and at the same time to school theater directors in film technique."[113]

Brent no longer had Archie Stout photographing her—and what a difference it made. Though top-billed, she is not always filmed in a flattering way. Brent doesn't get a close-up in the whole picture. Actually, no one did. The director's stage influence perhaps had a hand in this. This was Virginia Bruce's biggest role to date. Clive Brook was at his most charming as the debonair jewel thief who courts Brent.

Henry Wadsworth was a successful stage actor, appearing in *Applause* and other shows, before being signed to appear in *Slightly Scarlet*. Born in Kentucky in 1897, Wadsworth died in 1974.

Paul Lukas was born in Hungary in 1891. Lukas, who also performed on stage, won an Academy Award for *Watch on the Rhine* (1943). He died in 1971.

Eugene Pallette was one of Hollywood's most familiar character actors. Born in Winfield, Kansas, in 1889, he made his first film in 1913. A scene stealer who became a right wing zealot after World War II, he died in 1954. He also appeared with Brent in *The Cyclone Rider* (1924).

Helen Ware, born Helen Remer in San Francisco in 1877, was a stage actress. Married to Frederick Burt, she died in 1939.

Claud Allister played many butlers during his career. Born in London in 1888, Allister was a stage actor when he began his film career in 1929. He was the voice of Rat in Disney's *The Wind in the Willows* (1949). Allister died in 1970.

Morgan Farley was born in New York State in 1898. He enjoyed a long career and made many television appearances on such shows as *The Big Valley*, *Star Trek*, and *The Wild Wild West*. Georges Renavent, born in Paris in 1894, was married to character actor Selena Royle. He died in Mexico in 1969. Charles Sullivan, born in Louisiana in 1899, amassed more than four hundred film credits, usually as an extra. He was also a stunt man. He died in 1972. Oscar Smith was born in Kansas in 1885. As an African-American actor in the 1920s, '30s, and '40s, he played many janitors, porters, and servants. He died in 1956. He also appeared with Brent in *Beau Sabreur* (1928).

This film was remade in 1930 as *L'Enigmatique Monsieur Parkes* with Adolphe Menjou and Claudette Colbert.

*Evelyn Brent appeared on several magazine covers between 1928 and 1931.*

Reviews: "*Slightly Scarlet* is pure hokum of the ancient motion picture fashion, but it is dressed up in a new atmosphere and made interesting entertainment by treatment of story, the actors and the direction.... Evelyn Brent does exceptionally well as the mysterious feminine thief....

*Slightly Scarlet* is a most enjoyable production" (*Los Angeles Record*, February 22, 1930).

"[A] talking picture that actually keeps one guessing.... [I]n ringing its praises, it should not be forgotten that Clive Brook, that smooth and reliable actor, gives another thoroughly sound performance. His partner is Evelyn Brent, who handles her role competently" (*New York Times*, March 1, 1930).

"This is a production that ought to win favor with picture-goers who go in for intelligent things in the films. All the earmarks of matureness of mind are there, and from first to last it reveals itself as a neat piece of work, possessed of great smoothness and consistency of action. There is class in every foot of it..." (*Film Daily*, March 2, 1930).

"More than slightly foolish, this decorative melodrama of jewel thieves at work and play on the Riviera belongs to a comparatively new but increasingly comprehensive category of sound-cinemas. Its story is insipid and a lot of its talk ridiculous, but it is so well-made, its sets are so pretty, and its people so competent that within the scope of its intention it is hard to find fault with it.... Best shot: what Miss Brent found on her way to the safe" (*Time*, March 10, 1930).

"Nothing new, but engaging and interesting. Fair program fare.... Fans will accept it in a spirit of passive enjoyment and promptly forget" (*Variety*, April 2, 1930).

"It brings to screen audiences again that interesting co-starring team of Evelyn Brent and Clive Brook, last seen in *Interference*. *Slightly Scarlet* scarcely allows for characterization that Miss Brent and Brook had in *Interference*, but nevertheless they make the most of their roles" (*Illustrated Daily News*, April 18, 1930).

"A pleasing mixture of drama, suspense, mystery and comedy.... Especially good is Evelyn Brent and Clive Brook" (*Los Angeles Examiner*, April 18, 1930).

"Miss Brent is excellent" (*Los Angeles Review*, April 18, 1930).

"The picture tends to meander along in the opening sequences, turning to incidental side-tracks for support. Yet, the struggle in the closing scenes between Clive Brook and Paul Lukas may be called one of the best and most vivid to reach the talking screen. The sound element is used to advantage, with only outlines of the participants seen. Conflict is conveyed more to the ear than the eye" (*Los Angeles Times*, April 19, 1930).

"Evelyn Brent as society thief on the Riviera. Her best since *Interference*." (*Photoplay*, July 1930)

## *Framed*

(RKO Productions) 68 min. Released on March 16, 1930.

*Survival Status:* Library of Congress (Washington, D.C.). Released on video (RKO).

*Credits*: Producer, William LeBaron; associate producer, Henry Hobart; director, George Archainbaud; screenplay, Paul Schofield; dialogue, Wallace Smith; photography, Leo Tover; art director, Max Ree; film editor, Jack Kitchin; recording engineer, Clem Portman.

*Cast*: Evelyn Brent (Rose Manning); Regis Toomey (Jimmy McArthur [Carter]); Ralf Harolde (Chuck Gaines); Maurice Black (Bing Murdock); William Holden (Inspector McArthur); Robert Emmet O'Connor (Sergeant Schultze); Eddie Kane (Headwaiter); Mary Gordon (Mrs. Potter—Cleaning Woman).

*Framed* starts off with a great scene: Rose is surrounded by belligerent cops who grill her with questions. She keeps telling them she knows nothing. Finally, Inspector McArthur talks to her alone. One of his officers has been killed, and the inspector suspects Rose's father had something to do with it. She's asked to identify a man. "I never saw him before in my life," Rose says.

McArthur finally tells her the bad news. "Your father is dead, Rose."

"You and your coppers, you murdered him! You've taken away the only thing I had in the world." Grief-stricken, she vows revenge. "I'll get back at you, Mr. Butch McArthur! I'll get back at you!"

The title card (yep, they were still using them) reads: "Five years brought a new fashion in crime—and a new kind of 'holdup.'" Rose is now working as a hostess at the Little Casino, a speakeasy. Chuck, who is obsessed with his fingernails, runs the joint. He's the guy she refused to identify the night her father was killed. Chuck orders Bing to kill Johnny the Goat. "It's the guys who knew you *when* that know too much," Chuck explains to dim-witted Bing.

Chuck wants to marry Rose, but she claims she must first get revenge against McArthur. "That's all I've been waiting for ever since that night. It's the only reason I stick in this racket." She gets her chance. Police officers come to the Little Casino to ask questions about Johnny's murder. A sergeant tells Rose that the man he saw her sitting with—a young man she knows as Jimmy Carter—is actually Butch McArthur's son.

This is Rose's golden opportunity to get back at McArthur. She insists that Jimmy tell his father about their relationship. Jimmy's dad is not happy about the news. "There are two times when nobody can give a man advice," Butch says. "One is when he's drinking himself to death. The other is when he's in love. Or thinks he is." Still, Butch tries. "Rose Manning is framing you to get me," he insists. A rift develops between father and son. An enraged Butch goes to see Chuck. "You're trying to dirty up my boy, you rat, to get even with me."

Rose overhears the conversation and comes in to gloat. Butch tells her she'll never marry Jimmy. "Well, there is one thing in the way," she says smugly. "I don't like his family connections."

After McArthur leaves, Rose says, "I've waited five years for this, and it's sweet." Chuck fears that Rose has fallen for Jimmy, so he orders Bing to kill Jimmy. Rose pleads with Chuck, but he tells her Jimmy will be killed at midnight. Chuck can't wait to get his hands on Rose. "Tonight's the night. For me and for you," he tells her. When Rose threatens to tell McArthur, Chuck locks her in a room, promising to let her out at midnight.

Chuck tells Jimmy he's planning a surprise engagement party for Rose. He asks Jimmy to be in front of Webber's drug store at midnight. Jimmy says he'll pick up some flowers first. Chuck suggests he pick up a wreath.

Butch has received a tip that Jimmy is at the Little Casino. He orders a raid. Meanwhile, Rose escapes and picks up Jimmy in front of Webber's before Bing can get there. They go back to her apartment. Rose tries to make Jimmy leave by telling him she never loved him.

Chuck arrives, and Jimmy hides. Chuck tells Rose that he sent Bing to kill McArthur. He hears a noise in Rose's bedroom and realizes Jimmy is in there. "This is perfect," he says. "Bing's looking for the old man, and I take the boy."

Chuck goes in the bedroom, and Rose hears two shots. Jimmy walks out, holding a gun. He and Rose embrace. "I did it, Rose. With his own gun. And I'm glad of it." Rose sends Jimmy away to help his father.

Bing comes to Rose's apartment. He tells her he shot at Butch but didn't hit him. He did, however, kill another police officer. He wants Rose to be his alibi. He also wants something else from Rose. When McArthur arrives, Rose provides Bing's alibi.

The sergeant finds a gun in Bing's coat. Rose tries to keep the sergeant out of her bedroom. "Getting particular, aren't you?" Butch cracks.

Rose frames Bing for Chuck's murder. Bing is bemused. "Ain't that the limit? I've done many the errand for that guy, and I'm never grabbed. Here's one I don't do. And you nail me."

In the final scene, Rose is again seated with a bunch of cops shouting questions at her. This time she's calm, amused. "You boys will pardon me if I don't seem interested in these parlor games of yours."

"Wait till McArthur gets ahold of you," one warns.

McArthur enters the room and orders the others out. "You win, Butch McArthur," Rose says. "I go up, and I don't marry your boy." Butch tells her Jimmy has told him everything. "That boy's too darn square to get along in this world," Rose says.

Butch tells her she can go. Before she leaves, Butch asks her to identify a prisoner. "I don't know him," Rose immediately says.

"Even before you see him?"

It's Jimmy. Before leaving them alone, McArthur says, "Rose, my girl, try and forget your objections to his family." Rose and Jimmy embrace. McArthur closes the door behind him.

Brent and Toomey were signed for the roles in December 1929. The RKO lot was the same one Brent had worked on when she was employed at F.B.O. According to a blurb written by Brent's friend Dorothy Herzog, Brent received a pretty severe kick on the ankle during one of the film's scenes. "Betty's wounded ankle did a Zeppelin pronto."[114]

Top-billed again, Brent carries this excellent film. She's improving as an actress with every talkie role, and this picture shows that she could excel when given a meaty part. This is a much better role than what she was given at Paramount. She's got star quality and is in almost every scene. Her role and performance is reminiscent of Barbara Stanwyck. It's important to remember that Stanwyck was not yet a star when Brent made this picture.

Although likable, Toomey can't hold his own with Brent, and the two lack chemistry. In fact, Brent seems to have lots more chemistry with veteran character actor William Holden. The William Holden who appears in this film is not the guy you're thinking of. *This* William Holden was born in Rochester, New York, in 1862 and was a character actor. He died in 1932.

Toomey was born in Pittsburgh, Pennsylvania, in 1898. He enjoyed a long film career, beginning with *Alibi* in 1929. His many television appearances included *December Bride*, *Four Star Playhouse*, and *Petticoat Junction*. He died in 1991. Toomey also appeared with Brent in *Again ... Pioneers* (1950).

Ralf Harolde was born in Pittsburgh, Pennsylvania in 1899. He appeared as an extra in Brent's *The Last Train from Madrid* (1937). He died in 1974. Maurice Black was born in Queens, New York, in 1891. He began his career in 1928 and appeared in more than one hundred films before his death in 1938.

Robert Emmet O'Connor was born in Milwaukee, Wisconsin, in 1885. Often playing a police officer, he appeared in more than two hundred silent and sound films. He also appeared on the *Annie Oakley* TV series in the 1950s. He died in 1962. Mary Gordon is best known for playing Mrs. Hudson, Sherlock Holmes' landlady in films and on radio. Born in Scotland in 1882, she died in 1963.

Cinematographer Leo Tover did excellent work on this film. Born in New Haven, Connecticut, in 1902, he received Oscar nominations for *Hold Back the Dawn* (1941) and *The Heiress* (1949). Tover died in 1964. He also worked with Brent on *Love's Greatest Mistake* (1927), *The Silver Horde* (1930), *Traveling Husbands* (1931), and *Night Club Scandal* (1937).

Art director Max Ree was also a costume designer. Born in Denmark in 1889, he designed Brent's costumes in *The Silver Horde* (1930) and *Traveling Husbands* (1931). Ree won an Oscar for art direction for *Cimarron* (1931). He died in 1953.

*Reviews:* "Miss Brent, as usual, gives a satisfactory performance in the character of the avenging girl, but the picture is so shot through with hackneyed situations, melodramatic acting of a type reserved for the less pretentious films, and reminds one so strongly of *Broadway*, *The Racket*, and dozens of similar efforts..." (*New York Times*, March 29, 1930).

"[*Framed*] holds the attention admirably. Sustaining of the suspense, without disturbing the smoothness of the continuity, is another outstanding trait.... Regis Toomey is opposite Miss Brent. His is an outstanding performance, matching nicely that of the heroine's" (*Variety*, April 2, 1930).

"[A]n excellent program picture ... admirably directed ... and acted with distinction by Evelyn Brent, the triteness of the story being a regrettable handicap" (*Los Angeles Times*, April 6, 1930).

"The picture carries a new theme for underworld drama and the superb direction of George Archainbaud and particularly clever dialogue of Wallace Smith should place it among the best of the season" (*Los Angeles Examiner*, May 2, 1930).

"[T]he picture is crammed with action and boasts some excellent performances.... Miss Brent, she of the sullen beauty, contributes her usual fine performance. But the picture belongs to Ralf Harolde, who is so villainous that you'll want to beat him on the head the next time you see him on the street for making so much trouble for our hero and heroine" (*Illustrated Daily News* [Los Angeles], May 2, 1930).

"Evelyn Brent in an underworld story that gets across. Good trick climax. See it" (*Photoplay*, July 1930).

## Paramount on Parade

(Paramount Famous–Lasky) 101 min. Other sources list 102 and 112 min. Released on April 19, 1930.

*Survival Status:* UCLA Film and Television Archive (Los Angeles).

*Credits:* Producers, Albert S. Kaufman, Jesse L. Lasky, Adolph Zukor; supervisor, Elsie Janis; directors, Dorothy Arzner, Otto Brower, Edmund Goulding, Victor Heerman, Edwin H. Knopf, Rowland V. Lee, Ernst Lubitsch, Lothar Mendes, Victor Schertzinger, A. Edward Sutherland, Frank Tuttle; writer, Joseph L. Mankiewicz; directors of photography, Harry Fischbeck, Victor Milner; set decoration, John Wenger; dance ensembles director, David Bennett; editor, Merrill G. White; songs, Elsie Janis and Jack King; Ballard MacDonald and Dave Dreyer; Leo Robin and Ernesto De Curtis; L. Wolfe Gilbert and Abel Baer; Richard A. Whiting and Raymond B. Eagan; Whiting and Robin; David Franklin; Sam Coslow; Samuel Pokrass; incidental music, Howard Jackson.

*Cast:* Iris Adrian, Richard Arlen, Jean Arthur, Mischa Auer, William Austin, George Bancroft, Clara Bow, Evelyn Brent, Mary Brian, Clive Brook, Virginia Bruce, Nancy Carroll, Ruth Chatterton, Maurice Chevalier, Gary Cooper, Cecil Cunningham, Leon Errol, Stuart Erwin, Henry Fink, Kay Francis, Richard "Skeets" Gallagher, Edmund Goulding, Harry Green, Mitzi Green, Robert Greig, James Hall, Phillips Holmes, Helen Kane, Dennis King, Jack Luden, Abe Lyman & His Band, Fredric March, Nino Martini, Mitzi Mayfair, Marion Morgan Dancers, David Newell, Jack Oakie, Warner Oland, Zelma O'Neal, Eugene Pallette, Joan Peers, Jack Pennick, Russ Powell, William Powell, Charles "Buddy" Rogers, Lillian Roth, Rolfe Sedan, Stanley Smith, Fay Wray, Jane Keithley, Rosina Lawrence, Jeanette MacDonald, Al Norman, Ernst Rolf, Jackie Searl.

Paramount's most prestigious 1930 film began shooting on August 19, 1929, and wrapped on February 19, 1930. It was an important film for Paramount as well as the actors who were appearing in this early talkie. "Every contract player in the studio had been spending weeks and weeks preparing for his or her sequences for the picture. They were all carefully fitted for wardrobes that would suit the elegance they were to represent."[115] Paramount, like other studios of the time, used this type of revue to display their singing, dancing, talking stars. Other films of this ilk included *The William Fox Movietone Follies of 1929* (Fox), *Movietone Follies of 1930* (Fox), *Show of Shows* (Warner Bros.), and *Hollywood Revue of 1929* (MGM). Fay Wray, one of Paramount's stars, explained the film's genesis: "There was a roster of stars at Paramount and there was a roster of management. The roster of management made decisions for and about the roster of stars. It was difficult for them to make choices once the added factor of sound was involved. In a film called *Paramount on Parade*, they lumped every star, major and minor, into one musical under the guidance of eleven directors. The cast numbered almost fifty. The decision may have advanced sound and proved that Paramount could make a lot of it, but it did little for any individual."[116]

Unfortunately, a complete print does not exist because Paramount destroyed the original negative with the Technicolor sequences; in fact, until 1996, available prints excluded all Technicolor sequences, except the finale with Maurice Chevalier singing "Up on Top of a Rainbow," which existed only in black-and-white. The UCLA Archive has completed a partial restoration, including Technicolor sequences.

During the title credits, Kay Francis and George Bancroft stand behind the letter M as the title—*Paramount on Parade*—is shown. In the restored sequence, the title is displayed one letter at a time in black-and-white stills while the song "Paramount on Parade" is played in the background and the words displayed on the screen.

After the credits, the opening number is "Showgirls on Parade." In the restored version, stills of the chorus girls are shown. The next sequence includes Jack Oakie, "Skeets" Gallagher, and Leon Errol singing "We're the Masters of Ceremony." This is followed by "Love Time" with Charles (Buddy) Rogers and Lillian Roth on a cuckoo-clock set singing "Any Time's the Time to Fall in Love." The next scene is "Murder Will Out," a parody of detective mysteries with William Powell as Philo Vance, Clive Brook as Sherlock Holmes, Eugene Pallette as Sergeant Heath, Warner Oland as Dr. Fu Manchu, and Jack Oakie as the victim.

The best sketch, "Origin of the Apache," a slapstick vignette with Chevalier and Brent, appears about nineteen minutes into the revue and is introduced by Chevalier, who purports to show "the real origin of the Apache Dance." Directed by Ernst Lubitsch, who had masterfully directed Chevalier in *The Love Parade*, it crackles with sexual tension. Lubitsch's biographer Scott Eyman concluded that "Lubitsch had conquered sound the same way he had conquered silence, with clarity and a symmetrical grace ... and by making it look very easy."[117]

The scene has great back-and-forth dialogue and action. After Chevalier's introduction, Brent stalks into the elegant bedroom, obviously upset. Chevalier makes the mistake of asking her why she's troubled. "I say you flirted with the girl upon your right," she says to music. And it's on.

"Oh, that's silly. Let's not start a fight."

"You know you *did* flirt."

"No, dear."

"Yes, dear."

"*No,* dear."

The tone between the sophisticated couple gets more heated until they are shouting in each other's faces. Brent takes out a handkerchief and begins weeping as she tells him again that she saw him flirting. The next time she tells him, she's rubbing against him, flirting. She whispers in his ear. He whispers in hers. They kiss. She plays with his lips. He plays with hers. She playfully slaps him. He slaps her. She slaps him harder. He returns the favor. She shoves him. He shoves her. This continues until she slaps him again. They undress, slapping each other repeatedly. The last of their clothing comes off out of camera view. We just see the shoes, cuffs, lingerie, etc. being thrown. We next see the happy couple fully dressed and blissfully smiling, going off into the night. After holding the door open for Brent, Chevalier looks back at the audience and shrugs.

Brent's gown was carefully chosen. "The loops of a fishing net were the inspiration for the striking motif of brilliants on a gown of black satin.... The gown, which was designed by Paramount stylists, boasts a high waist line from which point of vantage the loops of crystals start their chic descent to the knees."[118]

Brent admitted in an interview that she wasn't the type of actress to offer suggestions, especially to someone like Lubitsch. "Although many actors did. Lubitsch had the best answer for actors' suggestions.... An actor would go up to him and Lubitsch would listen very carefully and say, 'You think so?' and the actor would say, 'Yes,' and he would say, 'I *don't* think so.' ... Oh, I learned a lot from Lubitsch. He's a great director."[119]

Next in *Paramount on Parade* is "Song of the Gondolier" with Italian tenor Nino Martini in a Technicolor sketch singing "Torna a Sorrento." This is followed by "In a Hospital," a comedy sketch with Leon Errol, David Newell, and Jean Arthur. Then Jack Oakie and Zelma O'Neal appear in "In a Girl's Gym," singing "I'm in Training for You."

Kay Francis appears in the next scene, "The Toreador," a restored Technicolor musical number. This number is notable because it is the only time in her career Francis appeared in Technicolor. It's followed by Ruth Chatterton in "The Montmartre Girl." Complete with French accent, she sings "My Marine" to Stuart Erwin, Stanley Smith, and Fredric March in a Paris cafe. Chevalier appears in the next sketch, "Park in Paris," as a police officer patrolling the park and singing "All I Want Is Just One Girl." Little Mitzi Green then does an impersonation of Chevalier singing the same song, just after she's impersonated Charlie Mack of Moran and Mack warbling, yep, "All I Want Is Just One Girl."

"The Schoolroom" features Helen Kane as a teacher, singing "What Did Cleopatra Say?" while the students answer, "Boop Boopa Doop." "Skeets" Gallagher and Dennis King then appear in "The Gallows Song," a Technicolor musical number featuring the song "Nichavo!" The sound is missing for most of this sequence, which was filmed on the set of the Technicolor operetta *The Vagabond King,* though the song by Dennis King has been restored. Next, Nancy Carroll and chorus appear in "Dance Mad," singing and dancing to "Dancing to Save Your Sole," accompanied by Abe Lyman's Band. "Dream Girl," a Technicolor sketch with Jean Arthur, Richard Arlen, Mary Brian, Gary Cooper, James Hall, Fay Wray, and others features the song "Let Us Drink to the Girl of My Dreams." The sound is missing, so the song's words are shown on the screen. The next number is "The Redhead," featuring Clara Bow, with Jack Oakie, "Skeets" Gallagher, and 42 sailors singing along to "I'm True to the Navy Now."

Kay Francis and George Bancroft appear with Cecil Cunningham in an amusing sketch titled "Impulses." The Technicolor finale, which, again, exists only in black and white, is "The Rainbow Revels," with Chevalier and an all-female chorus.

Advertisers were quite imaginative in how they billed this picture: "We'll be there and we'll do our stuff for you! ... The intimate big party of the stars! ... Comedy! Drama! Singing! Dancing! ... as exciting as New Year's Eve ... as enticing as a June Night!"

Maurice Chevalier was born in Paris in 1888. He received Oscar nominations for *The Love Parade* (1929) and *The Big Pond* (1930). In 1959 the Academy gave Chevalier an Honorary Award for lifetime achievement. He also won a Tony Award in 1968 for his one-man show. Chevalier, whose theme song was "Louise," died in 1972 in Paris.

Director Ernst Lubitsch, born in Berlin, Germany, in 1892, was one of Hollywood's greatest directors. He received Oscar nominations for *The Patriot* (1928), *The Love Parade* (1929), and *Heaven Can Wait* (1943). He also received an Honorary Oscar for lifetime achievement in 1947. Lubitsch directed such classic films as *Trouble in Paradise* (1932), *Ninotchka* (1939), and *The Shop Around the Corner* (1940). He died of a heart attack in 1947.

*Reviews:* "With its smashing lineup of popular personalities, plus a load of comedy and specially enjoyable performances by Maurice Chevalier, little Mitzi Green, and Nino Martini, an unusually promising singer from abroad, this revue should get over everywhere with a bang" (*Film Daily,* April 20, 1930).

"[I]n a class by itself. Real entertainment.... *Paramount on Parade* witnesses the first production of this kind linking together with an almost incredible smoothness achievements from the smallest technical detail to the greatest artistic endeavor ... Rialto audiences applauded each of the skits, sketches and musical numbers" (*Variety,* April 23, 1930).

"Offering no startling departures but consistently amusing and pleasing to the eye, *Paramount on Parade* contains much that will appeal to the followers of screen revues. Its two brightest lights are Maurice Chevalier and little Mitzi Green" (*Los Angeles Evening Herald,* April 25, 1930).

"Its primary purpose is to offer entertainment, and this it does in varied and constantly changing moods. Frankly, the revue isn't up to the standard fans have been led to expect from Paramount. It doesn't originate or create anything particularly novel. The color sequences are poor, possibly because of the wide screen.... However, these flaws may be overlooked in view of the amount and class of talent presented" (*Los Angeles Examiner,* April 25, 1930).

"Of all the revues, this is the only one that has captured everything expected of a first-class Broadway show.... In short, the picture is wholly a delight" (*Los Angeles Times,* April 27, 1930).

"[A] genuinely enjoyable piece of work, one that is much more enjoyable than any of the film revues that have appeared on Broadway.... One of the conspicuously clever features is 'Origin of the Apache' Dance..." (*New York Times,* April 27, 1930).

"This is one of those elaborate miscellanies with which the big production companies utilize the spare time of the stars on contract to them. It is an unusually good one—rapid, handsome, brightened with flashes of wit probably put in by Elsie Janis, who supervised it.... Best sketch: Maurice Chevalier and Evelyn Brent in 'The Origin of the Apache'" (*Time*, May 5, 1930).

"Pretty dull entertainment. Kept alive by M. Chevalier who, with Evelyn Brent, furnishes one of the best bits in 'The Origin of the Apache'" (*The New Movie Magazine*, September 1930).

"[I]t was more good-humoured, relaxed, rhythmical, sophisticated, confident of itself and far more risqué as well than *Hollywood Revue*."[120]

"Seen today, the total effect is wearisome after a while" (Lawrence J. Quirk, *The Films of Fredric March*, p. 58).

## The Silver Horde

(RKO Radio Pictures Inc.) 75 min. Released on October 25, 1930.

*Survival Status:* UCLA Film and Television Archive (Los Angeles).

*Credits:* Producer, William LeBaron; associate producer, William Sistrom; director, George Archainbaud; assistant director, Thomas Atkins; adaptation and dialogue, Wallace Smith; based on the novel *The Silver Horde* by Rex Beach; photography, John W. Boyle, Leo Tover; scenery and costumes, Max Rée; film editor, Otto Ludwig; recording engineer, Clem Portman.

*Cast:* Evelyn Brent (Cherry Malotte); Louis Wolheim (George Balt); Joel McCrea (Boyd Emerson); Raymond Hatton (Fraser); Jean Arthur (Mildred Wayland); Gavin Gordon (Fred Marsh); Blanche Sweet (Queenie); Purnell Pratt (Wayne Wayland); William Davidson (Thomas Hilliard); Ivan Linow (Svenson).

"Alaska—and two weary men struggle to the end of a long, long trail." Boyd and Fraser arrive in town on a dogsled. But they're not exactly welcomed until they're rescued by Cherry. "I'm boss around here," she informs them. She also tells them they've walked into a dangerous situation. "It's about as peaceful as smoking a cigarette on a keg of dynamite. You've walked into a neat little knock-down and drag-out, mister." Cherry is feuding with the salmon syndicate, and they're trying to force her out of town.

Boyd tells Cherry that he's had a lot of bad breaks as a gold miner. She waxes philosophic. "There's something bigger than finding a gold mine. And that's ... finding yourself." Boyd explains that he's broke and would do anything to get money. She sends him to Seattle to get money from friend Tom Hilliard to finance a fishing operation.

Meanwhile, spoiled and selfish Mildred plans to marry Boyd. Her dad, Wayne Wayland wants her to marry Fred, Cherry's nemesis. Boyd confronts Fred and tells him he plans to run a fishery in the town. Fred isn't impressed. "What an infant," he tells Wayne.

Tom's financing dries up. Cherry is called to Seattle to investigate. At the Café Marcino, Cherry has dinner with Tom, and Boyd arrives with Mildred. Tom tells Cherry that the deal is being held up by Fred and Wayne, and he realizes that Cherry has fallen in love with Boyd.

Cherry sees Boyd dancing with Mildred, and Tom tells her she is the daughter of Wayland. According

to Tom, Wayland is blocking the deal so Mildred won't marry Boyd. Cherry asks if Tom is going to let him get away with it. "It's up to you, Cherry." She goes back to Tom's apartment. Later, Tom phones Boyd to tell him the loan has been approved. We see Tom light Cherry's cigarette.

Boyd mistakenly thinks Mildred fixed it for him. Before leaving, Cherry concludes her deal with Tom. "Emerson gets the $200,000, and you get my ... copper mine."

Everyone returns to Alaska. Fred threatens Boyd and hints that Cherry played a part in his getting the money. For no good reason, Boyd and Swenson have a bare-chested wrestling-boxing match which Boyd wins.

"From the depths of the sea moves the vast, heroic tribe of salmon—the Silver Horde." We are now treated to the sight of the salmon harvest, from gathering them out of the traps to the final canned product. (Vegetarians and animal rights activists might want to cover their eyes during this scene.)

"Emerson's success forces Marsh to show his hand." Fred warns Cherry that if the traps continue to run, he'll have his men wreck them. A violent confrontation results, and Boyd's men win. Boyd confronts Mildred, and she tells him she is upset with him about his involvement with Cherry. She calls her a "hanger-on in men's camps." Boyd defends Cherry. Mildred breaks their engagement.

Boyd asks Fraser about Cherry, and he confirms that the rumors are true. "That kind of a woman..." Boyd says. Fraser also tells him that's how he got Tom Hilliard's money.

Cherry brings friend Queenie back from Nome. Meanwhile, Mildred pays Cherry a visit. Queenie eyes Mildred and calls her a "high-toned wench." Mildred and Cherry admit they're in love with the same man. "When I love a man, I don't need any rules," Cherry tells Mildred. Mildred insults her, but Cherry isn't offended. "You don't have to put me in my place. I know about me." Cherry insists Mildred listen to her. "I love Boyd. I'm not ashamed of it." Mildred tells her she no longer wants Boyd. "You'll take him," Cherry tells her. "Because you've been taking things all your life."

Cherry stops just before she strikes Mildred. "Oh, don't be scared. I won't dirty my hands on you. I'm Cherry Malotte! They know about me from San Francisco to Sitka. My reputation's got marks on it I couldn't rub off if I wanted to! I am what I am! I don't know how they finally settle things in this world or the next, but when the day comes I'll stand there with my chin up and take what's coming to me. And I wouldn't trade places with you, you white-livered, sweet-smelling hypocrite, if they gave me a one-way ticket to Hell! Now get out of here!"

Eventually an angry, inebriated Boyd confronts Cherry. He's upset because of the talk about her. "Tell me it's not true," he pleads.

"It's true all right," she concedes. "Everybody knows about Cherry Malotte." She tells him to go back to Mildred; she knows Mildred will take him back.

"*You* know. What can a woman of your kind know about her?" Boyd starts calling her names. They're so bad we only see Queenie's horrified reaction in another room.

"Well," a hurt Cherry says, "you've certainly named a few names all right."

"Yes, I could have loved you," Boyd says. "That's the kind of a fool I've been, thinking you were a pal. Helping me find myself. I found myself all right. And I found out about you!" Boyd is enraged and almost chokes her.

Queenie comforts Cherry after Boyd leaves. "He ain't worth crying about, honey. No guy is." Queenie also insists that Boyd is in love with her. Cherry and Queenie go to see Mildred, Fred, and Wayne on their yacht. Turns out Fred is already married to Queenie. "I thought she was dead," Fred lamely replies.

"You mean you wished I was dead," Queenie cheerfully says. "But I ain't." Cherry tells Mildred she'll send Boyd to her. "Don't let him go again," she gently warns.

Sobered up, Boyd feels awful about what he said to Cherry. He's told Cherry is on the yacht, so he rushes to her. Mildred assumes he's there to see her. She begs him to embrace her, but he hurries off and goes to Cherry's.

"Oh, forgive me, Cherry. There's no past. No yesterday. Only tomorrow. And tomorrow. Oh, Cherry, I love you so." While he's talking, the camera continues to slowly pull back. They embrace.

Top-billed, Brent is marvelous in this film, especially in the scene with Jean Arthur. She brings complexity to the role of a woman with a past.

The movie was based on Rex Beach's novel of the same name, published in 1909. This novel was adapted several times. In the first version (1914), Kathlyn Williams played Cherry Malotte. Betty Compson portrayed her in *The Spoilers* (1930), and Marlene Dietrich did the honors in the 1942 version of *The Spoilers*. The film was remade yet again in 1955 with Anne Baxter playing Cherry.

In April 1930, Louella O. Parsons reported that Edwin Carewe had wanted Brent for *The Spoilers*, "but Betty was tied up and couldn't accept his offer.... Betty is not a girl who acts hastily so she read *The Silver Horde* carefully before she agreed to play the part."[121] Parsons also reported that Ben Lyon was considered for the part that eventually went to McCrea.

This is a great film to watch on a hot summer day. If you watch it in the winter, the early shots of snow and ice are just about guaranteed to make you shiver. Locations included Ketchikan and Loring, Alaska. The production was filmed on location in July 1930. The cast returned at the end of July and filmed interior scenes in August.

Blanche Sweet did not join the cast until they'd returned from Alaska. According to Parsons, Brent recommended Sweet for the role. "That's what I call being a good sport," Parsons wrote.[122]

One newspaper writer suggested the film could be titled *The Private Life of a Salmon* because of the intense obsession of director George Archainbaud to get some unusual footage. "Every phase of salmon activity is being photographed.... One innovation being introduced is a waterproof case for standard cameras which will be lowered into the rivers for photographing the salmon during their 'run.'"[123]

Some genius decided the lead dog on a dog sled should be black instead of white so the dog was dyed. However, his fellow dogs no longer recognized him, and the result was a dog fight. The dye was removed until the dogs were leashed to the sled—and then reapplied.

Advertisements billed it in this way: "A one man woman in a world of men!" Other advertising used this tagline: "One Woman—in a Land of Men." And this one was also used: "Rex Beach's Sledge-Fisted Romance of the Great Alaskan Salmon Run."

Handsome Joel McCrea was born in South Pasadena, California, in 1905. Best known for his appearances in Westerns, he also proved adept in dramas and comedies. He retired to become a rancher and died in 1990. McCrea was married for more than fifty years to Frances Dee. He's a bit stiff in some early scenes, but there is no denying the chemistry between Brent and McCrea. Indeed, they were reported to have an affair during production. At the time, Brent was married to Harry Edwards. McCrea married Dee in October 1933.

Born in Red Oak, Iowa, Raymond Hatton appeared in more than five hundred films, beginning in 1909. He was married to Frances Hatton in 1909 until her death on October 16, 1971. Raymond died five days later of a heart attack. Hatton also appeared with Brent in *Jungle Jim* (1937) and *Raiders of the South* (1947).

Jean Arthur, born Gladys Greene in Plattsburgh, New York, in 1900, was one of Hollywood's leading ladies in the 1930s and 1940s. She received an Oscar nomination for her performance in *The More the Merrier* (1943). Following her retirement from films, she taught drama at Vassar. She died in 1991. Unfortunately, this is a thankless role for Arthur, and she does not bring depth to the shallow, selfish rich girl. She can bring considerable charm to a role, but not in this picture.

Gavin Gordon was born in Mississippi in 1901. His long career began in 1929. In the 1950s and 1960s he appeared frequently on television shows including *Alfred Hitchcock Presents, How to Marry a Millionaire,* and *Petticoat Junction.* He died in 1983.

Blanche Sweet, born in Chicago in 1896, was a silent film star when she was still a child. *The Silver Horde* was her last film appearance, though she made television appearances in the 1950s. Married at one time to Marshall Neilan, she later married actor Raymond Hackett. Sweet died in 1986.

Purnell Pratt, born in Bethel, Illinois, in 1885,

made his film debut in the silent era. He died in 1941. He also appeared with Brent in *Traveling Husbands* (1931) and *Hollywood Boulevard* (1936).

Ivan Linow was born in Latvia in 1888. He made his film debut in silent motion pictures in 1921. He died in London in 1940. He also appeared with Brent in *Madonna of the Streets* (1930).

*Reviews:* "Beautiful photography, intelligence in direction or wit in dialogue might have lifted the story out of its rut, but as it is this production is dull and trivial.... [T]he most interesting feature of the film is that showing the process of canning fish. The dramatic climax, when Mildred confronts Cherry in the back room of a dive and denounces her for dragging Boyd down to her own level, elicited laughter from yesterday's audience..." (*New York Times*, October 25, 1930).

"Popular novel rates fair screen entertainment with fine cast and some stirring action.... Louis Wolheim and Evelyn Brent give sterling performances, and the cast throughout is well picked.... The love interest gets rather wobbly toward the close, with the audience wondering who the hero really is in love with. But the fine trouping of Evelyn Brent makes it sound more convincing than it really is" (*Film Daily*, October 26, 1930).

"*The Silver Horde* ... is vigorous and effective ... because it is well-directed, interestingly photographed and yields excellent performances, even though the dialogue sometimes is pitched in terms too florid to create much realism" (*Los Angeles Times*, November 2, 1930).

"Evelyn Brent ... plays one of the best roles of her screen career.... Her performance and that of Raymond Hatton helps to relieve the slowness of the direction.... Jean Arthur is decorative, if somewhat ineffective" (*Syracuse Herald*, November 9, 1930).

"The comedy of Raymond Hatton and Louis Wolheim; the splendid acting of Evelyn Brent; the brief but very fine appearance of Blanche Sweet, and the catching and canning of salmon, are the most interesting scenes in the picture.... Evelyn Brent as Cherry Malotte, known from Nome to everywhere, plays the part as only Evelyn Brent can" (*Los Angeles Record*, November 21, 1930).

"*The Silver Horde* ... can be dismissed easily by the true picture lover.... It is a plotty, confused, childish fafair [sic] with one thing in its favor—the beautiful shots of the great hordes of fish whirling down the foaming river and some of the river salmon pouring into the fishing boats from the burdened nets.... Evelyn Brent as Cherry was good. She did everything she could with the theatrical part to make it believable, and, as usual, in her big emotional scene placed [sic] it with reserve and conviction" (*Dallas Morning News*, November 22, 1930).

"The incoherent filming [is] disappointing.... As it stands, the best remembered moments are offered by the travelogue shots through the canning factory and Evelyn Brent's magnificent dramatic climax as she defends her love for the boy" (*Motion Picture*, December 1930).

"Rex Beach's red-corpuscled yarn becomes tingling photoplay, and gives Evelyn Brent opportunity for a blisteringly hot portrayal" (*Photoplay*, December, 1930).

## *Madonna of the Streets*

(Columbia Pictures) 77 min. Released on November 21, 1930.

*Survival Status:* Library of Congress (Washington, D.C.).

*Credits:* Producer Harry Cohn; director; John S. Robertson; assistant director, C. C. Coleman; adaptation, continuity and dialogue, Jo Swerling; based on the novel *The Ragged Messenger* by William Babington Maxwell; photography, Sol Polito; art direction, Edward Jewell; technical director, Edward Shulter; film editor, Gene Havlick; sound engineer, Ben Harper.

*Cast:* Evelyn Brent (May); Robert Ames (Morton); Ivan Linow (Slumguillion); Josephine Dunn (Marion); Edwards Davis (Clark); Zack Williams (Blink); Ed Brady (Ramsey); Richard Tucker (Kingsley); Selmer Jackson (Kingley's Partner).

The film was set on San Francisco's Barbary Coast. Jack Holt was considered for a role. *The Ragged Messenger* had first been adapted into a 1917 film that starred Violet Hopson, Gerald Ames, Basil Gill, and George Foley. In 1924 *Madonna of the Streets* was released with Alla Nazimova, Milton Sills, and Wallace Beery.

John S. Robertson had a varied career. At one time he was leading man to Maude Adams on stage and he later starred in films at Vitagraph studios in Brooklyn. As a director, he was concerned with setting the atmosphere in a film. "Visual impressions tend to fix an idea with greater success than a verbal explanation in the minds of an audience, and for this reason, thinks John Robertson, more attention is being paid by motion-picture executives in making backgrounds authentic and properly atmospheric."[124] The opening of *Madonna of the Streets* is indicative of his approach. "The opening scene shows a foggy night. Wretched forms passing along the damp streets are vaguely outlined in the mists. Street lights are reflected on the wet sidewalk. A starved cur sneaks by in the eerie light."[125]

Writer Jo Swerling, who also wrote the screenplay for *Attorney for the Defense* (1932), was born in Russia in 1893. He received an Oscar nomination (along with Herman J. Mankiewicz) for *The Pride of the Yankees* (1942) and won a Tony Award (with Abe Burrows) in 1951 for *Guys and Dolls*. Swerling, who also wrote the screenplays for *Lifeboat* (1944) and *Leave Her to Heaven* (1945), contributed to the scripts for *Gone with the Wind* (1939) and *It's a Wonderful Life* (1946). He died in 1964.

Robert Ames, born in Hartford, Connecticut, in 1889, appeared in only about 25 films. One of his ex-wives was writer Frances Goodrich. Ames died in New York at the young age of 42 under mysterious circumstances.

Zack Williams, born in Louisiana in 1884, often played slaves, Africans, and other similar roles. He died in 1958.

*Reviews:* "Miss Brent and Mr. Ames deliver their usual competent performances, and John Robertson's direction is good" (*New York Times*, November 29, 1930).

"Ancient hoke related simply amid the drab surroundings of the Frisco waterfront.... It's a fair program[m]er.... If Madonna means something lovely looking sad, it wasn't Evelyn Brent in this film. Gayer colors suit her..." (*Variety*, December 3, 1930).

"*Madonna of the Streets* possibly will appeal to simple-hearted fans. It's nice enough" (*Illustrated Daily News* [Los Angeles], December 26, 1930).

"Mr. Robertson has taken a story of the usual melodramatic quality, and has added to it the genius of stage technique which makes the picture ring true. Where lesser directors would allow their stars to go into emotional debauch over the circumstances of the film, Robertson has caused them to register their suffering in silence" (*Los Angeles Evening Express*, December 26, 1930).

"The theme of the picture, dealing with a girl's attempt to victimize a charity worker who had inherited money she claimed, held few chances for either a display of smartness or action.... [T]he sequences were drawn-out, the speeches filled to overflowing with words and the production slowed up almost to the point of irritation on the part of the person who twisted uneasily in his theater chair" (*Los Angeles Times*, December 26, 1930).

"Evelyn Brent triumphs over the old yarn about the regeneration of a lady crook" (*Photoplay*, April 1931).

## Traveling Husbands

(RKO Radio Pictures) Released on August 7, 1931.

*Survival Status:* The Museum of Modern Art (New York City); UCLA Film and Television Archive (Los Angeles).

*Credits:* Producer, William LeBaron; associate producer, Myles Connolly; director, Paul Sloane; assistant director, Charles Kerr; writing, adaptation and dialogue, Humphrey Pearson; photography, Leo Tover ; second unit photography, Lloyd Knetchel; film editor, Archie F. Marshek; scenery and costumes, Max Ree; musical director, Max Steiner; sound recording, Clem Portman; song, "There's a Sob in My Heart," music and lyrics by Max Steiner.

*Cast:* Evelyn Brent (Ruby Smith); Frank Albertson (Barry Greene); Constance Cummings (Ellen Wilson); Hugh Herbert (Hymie Schwartz); Dorothy Peterson (Martha Hall); Gwen Lee (Mabel); Frank McHugh (Pinkie); Carl Miller (Ben Hall); Stanley Fields (Dan Murphy); Rita La Roy (Daisy); Lucille Williams (Vera); Purnell Pratt (J. C. Wilson); Spencer Charters (Joe); Tom Francis (Walter).

The credits are superimposed on a shot of a train speeding by at night. (The film's theme song, "There's a Sob in My Heart" is played during the opening credits.) Inside the train we see men smoking and chatting loudly. A group of traveling salesmen play cards and discuss how tough it is to be on the road.

Barry gets some good news about the J.C. Wilson account and ends up in Detroit. While waiting to see Wilson, he meets Wilson's daughter, Ellen. Unfortunately, he thinks she's a fellow salesperson and gives her advice and encouragement. One of his gems is "They all look alike in a Turkish bath." He also tells her, "Remember, you're just as important as he is." He gives her his pitch for the Bulldog safety pin but is interrupted by Wilson's assistant. "Your father will see you now, Miss Wilson."

Dad's upset with Ellen for ordering an airplane, and she's not happy that he's rarely home. They argue and exchange some ugly comments. "I'm not an employee," Ellen reminds him. "You can't fire me." She storms out.

Barry never gets his opportunity to see Wilson. Ellen later drives up in a convertible. They commiserate. "I'm going to knock this town right off its pin," Ellen boasts. "How'd you like to go along?" Well, who wouldn't? She drops him off at the Hotel Savron, and they agree to meet later in the hotel lobby. "Remember," she says, "I'm out to break the bad reputation record."

Barry receives a terse telegram from his company (by the way, his company's motto is "Mother's Friend for Half a Century"): "Get the J.C. Wilson business or consider yourself fired. Cordially, Bulldog Company." Barry sends a note to Ellen who's waiting in the lobby: "Dear Miss Wilson—Sorry, but stuck with important appointment. Big business deal pending. Hurriedly, Barry Green" Disappointed, Ellen tears up the note but remains at the hotel.

Meanwhile, the hotel has received many complaints about too much noise coming from room 520. Traveling salesmen, including Pinkie and Hymie, have made that room their home and invited young women in. Mabel phones Ruby (is that a marijuana cigarette Mabel is smoking?) and suggests she come by. When she arrives at the hotel, she is recognized and unwelcome. She asks Barry to help her get up to the room. On the way, they're both shocked to see Ben Hall with Ellen Wilson. Neither is happy about it. Barry says Ben is a chaser. "I'm no lily myself," Barry says, "but I never do any chasing."

"Don't start," Ruby advises. "You'd get terribly discouraged."

Before Barry gets on the elevator with Ruby, he's warned by hotel security man Dan. But Barry tells Dan he knows what she's about. The party starts (be sure to check out Hugh Herbert's funky dancing).

Meanwhile, we see a nice montage of Ellen and Ben out on the town. Finally, Ben brings Ellen back to his hotel room which adjoins 520. Ruby listens at the door and sighs. The party continues until there's a sharp knocking followed by cries of "Barry! Barry!" Ellen hurries into the room.

Ben gives Barry a look. "Working my territory, eh?" The two struggle in Ben's room while Ruby looks sad and hides on the balcony. Dan comes to investigate, and we hear a gunshot. When the door opens, Ben is on the floor, wounded. Barry stands over him with a gun. Barry says they were struggling over the gun, and he assumes it went off. No one is allowed to leave until the crime is investigated.

In a simple but poignant scene that follows, note the use of church bells in the background. The morning after the tragedy, upon hearing the bells, Vera says, "People are goin' to church ... down there."

Ruby talks to Ellen. "I'll bet your mother's proud of you," she scolds Ellen.

"I haven't any mother."

"Oh," Ruby says knowingly, "another one of those dames without a mother. So that's your alibi. You'll be telling me next you never had a chance." Ruby grills her about her relationship with Ben. "Just trying to get a line on excuses you refined chippies dig up for your funny business.... Well, you never can tell when you'll pick up a few good pointers. Maybe we aren't working the same trade...."

Ellen tells her she'd only just met Ben. Ellen leaves and sends Barry in. "As I get it," Ruby tells Barry, "she never had a mother, and you might do." Pinkie asks Ruby what Ellen is like. "Something like me if she was better-looking." Ruby is told that Ben's wife has been sent for. This information sends Ruby off on a rant. "Don't you wish we got the breaks their wives get?" she asks the other ladies in the room. "All you give us is carfare home when the party's over."

We see an index card the hotel has on Ben: "BEN HALL—CHICAGO—REGULAR GUEST BUSINESS, MACHINERY—CREDIT A. NOTE: HEAVY SPENDER. DRINKS TOO MUCH. WEAKNESS FOR WOMEN. BAD SCANDAL, HOTEL HARRISON, DETROIT, 1930, WITH RUBY SMITH—PROFESSIONAL."

A nurse brings the bullet that was removed from Ben; it matches Barry's gun. Barry is arrested, but before he is taken away, Ruby confesses. Ben's wife asks her why. "Why does a lady usually shoot a gentleman? Not for target practice." Ruby gets in her face. "I shot Ben Hall because I hate him. And because he changed my evening stroll from an exercise to—to an occupation." Ruby tells her she caught him with a "bleary blond" on his last visit to Detroit. Ruby adds, "Nobody was ever crazy about each other like Ben and me. Sometimes ... it was kind of spiritual." Ruby says she wanted Mrs. Hall's life. The wife explains that it's not all it's cracked up to be. Still, she says she and Ben love each other. "You want me to lose one of my tears over you?" Ruby asks.

When Mrs. Hall is told Ben will recover, she asks that the police not be involved. "Let's keep our chins up," she cheerfully tells Ruby. "Goodbye. Good luck." She sincerely squeezes Ruby's arm and leaves.

Barry and Ellen leave, on their way to have dinner with Mr. Wilson. Ruby is alone, crying against a door. "What a flat tire I turned out to be," she says to Dan. She gives Dan money and asks him to buy flowers for Ben. "Tell him they're from his little...." She reconsiders and decides it best not to tell him anything. Dan tells her to move along. The salesmen have to get some rest because if they don't sell their goods they won't eat. "Yep, me too," Ruby says. She takes a long look at the room and then salutes the men. "So long, suckers."

Hymie is so overcome, he writes a telegram to his wife: "Mama buy fur coat you wanted home next week." Another salesman calls to order flowers for his wife. "I wish I had someone to send something to," Pinkie regretfully says. "And had something to send."

This is an excellent pre–Code gem. Bitter and cynical, this picture offers great art deco sets and is fast-moving and well-acted, except for Frank Albertson who shouts every line of dialogue as though he were a 12-year-old boy. Dorothy Peterson starts off a little slow, but has a wonderful toe-to-toe scene with Brent. Hugh Herbert and Constance Cummings are excellent, and Frank McHugh, as usual, does a fine supporting job. Carl Miller, however, does not have

the necessary charm to convince viewers that so many women are crazy about him.

Brent was announced as the female lead in January 1931. She again received top billing. Claudia Dell, Mae Clarke, and James Gleason were at one time or another announced as cast members. Kitty Kelly and Joan Marsh were also up for roles in the picture but eventually replaced.

Costumer Max Ree commented, "Miss Brent has excellent taste in the selection of her off-stage wardrobe. This is mirrored in her screen costuming for, I feel, she is one of the best-dressed women on the screen." According to a publicity article, "[Ree] studied her with great care and in the dressy scenes of the picture chose materials for her that would accentuate her vivid beauty, the brilliance of her eyes, the cameo-clarity of her features. Her clothes give her a sophisticated, worldly ease on the screen and endow her with a confidence that is vital in the type of role *Traveling Husbands* demanded of her."[126]

Composer Max Steiner wrote the song "A Sob in My Heart" especially for this picture. Born in 1888 in what is now Austria, Steiner was one of Hollywood's most successful composers. He received numerous Academy Award nominations and won Oscars for *The Informer* (1935), *Now, Voyager* (1942), and *Since You Went Away* (1944). He died in 1971.

Director Paul Sloane, born in New York in 1893, began his career in 1916. It's not known why Sloane isn't better known—or why he didn't get more Hollywood jobs. He displays a deft, intelligent touch in several scenes in this picture. In 1950 he wrote, directed, and produced the low-budget *The Sun Sets at Dawn*. His last credit was a 1952 Japanese film titled *Feng ye qing*, which he produced and directed. He died in 1963.

Writer Humphrey Pearson was born in 1894. He died in Palm Springs, California, in 1937 after a mysterious shooting. Ironically, his last credit was for writing the screenplay for *Palm Springs* (1936). Pearson's screenplay for *Traveling Husbands* is a cut above, and he remains an intriguing but obscure Hollywood figure.

Frank Albertson was born in Minnesota in 1909 and died in 1964. A veteran character actor, he played the obnoxious Sam Wainwright in *It's a Wonderful Life* (1946) as well as the braggart Tom Cassidy in *Psycho* (1960). Albertson also appeared in many television shows near the end of his career. Albertson later appeared with Brent in *Silent Witness* (1943).

Constance Cummings was born Constance Halverstadt in Seattle in 1910. Married to British writer Benn W. Levy, she moved to England in 1934. One of her best performances was in *Blithe Spirit* (1945). She died in England in 2005. Cummings also appears with Brent in *Attorney for the Defense* (1932).

Scene-stealer Hugh Herbert was born in 1897 in Binghamton, New York. A playwright and stage actor in addition to his work in film, his long career ended with his death in 1952. His mannerisms and expressions are said to be the inspiration for Daffy Duck.

Dorothy Peterson, born in Hector, Minnesota, on December 25, 1897, began acting in 1930. She turned to television in the 1950s. Peterson died in New York in 1979. Peterson also appeared with Brent in *Attorney for the Defense* (1932).

Gwen Lee was a WAMPAS Baby Star in 1928. Born Gwendolyn La Pinski in Hastings, Nebraska, in 1904, she also appeared with Brent in *Fast Company* (1929) and *The Pagan Lady* (1931). She died in 1961 in Reno, Nevada.

Frank McHugh was born in Homestead, Pennsylvania, in 1898. His long acting career began in childhood as his parents owned a stock company. He ended his career with many television appearances in the 1950s and 1960s. He died in 1981. McHugh was married for almost fifty years to film editor Dorothy Spencer, who received Oscar nominations for *Stagecoach* (1939), *Decision Before Dawn* (1951), *Cleopatra* (1963), and *Earthquake* (1974).

Stanley Fields was born in Pennsylvania in 1883. A former boxer and vaudevillian, he died in 1941. Rita La Roy was born Ina Stuart in France in 1907. She is sometimes credited as Rita LeRoy, along with other variations. She received an Emmy nomination for Most Outstanding Television Personality in 1949. LaRoy sold yachts after retiring from show business. She died in 1993. Spencer Charters, born in Duncannon, Pennsylvania, in 1875, was a popular character actor who appeared in more than two hundred films. He committed suicide in 1943. Tom Francis, also credited as Tom Herbert, was Hugh Herbert's brother. Born in New York in 1888, he made his screen debut in this film (1931). He died in 1946.

*Reviews:* "Good acting and ease in direction.... Evelyn Brent does one of her dependable villaining portraits" (*Los Angeles Times*, May 10, 1931).

"[A] very well-knitted story.... Paul Sloane ... has handled these kind of tales before and knows where the punches lie" (*Variety*, August 11, 1931).

"It is admirably made, the various elements are deftly joined, the state of affairs remains clear and intelligible. Behind it are several sharp and plausible characterizations of moments of pungent realism ... Miss Brent as usual gives a luminous performance" (*Dallas Morning News*, August 21, 1931).

"Excellent photography and direction, good acting" (*Syracuse Herald*, August 22, 1931).

"Caustic wise-cracks and rowdy fun enliven the doings of *Traveling Husbands*.... Evelyn Brent is ... fine as the discarded woman" (*Los Angeles Evening Herald*, August 29, 1931).

"The conversation between the wife and the other woman is beautifully acted by Dorothy Peterson and Miss Brent" (*Los Angeles Examiner*, August 29, 1931).

"Risqué but not objectionably so. Top-notch acting, with Evelyn Brent in the lead" (*Photoplay*, September, 1931).

"Snappy fare for the more or less sophisticated, but leave the children at home.... Evelyn Brent is excellent as an embattled 'party girl' whose repartee and reputation are equally colorful" (*Screenland*, November 1931).

## The Pagan Lady

(Columbia Pictures Corp.) 77 min. Released on September 8, 1931

*Survival Status:* Library of Congress (Washington, D.C.).

*Credits:* Producer, H. D. Edwards; director, John Francis Dillon; assistant director, Arthur Black; screenplay, Benjamin Glazer; based on the play *The Pagan Lady* by William DuBois; photography, Norbert Brodine, Gus Peterson; film editor, Viola Lawrence; sound engineer, Edward Bernds; technical director, Charles A. Cadwallader.

*Cast:* Evelyn Brent (Dot Hunter); Conrad Nagel (Ernest Todd); Charles Bickford (Dingo Mike Hunter); Roland Young ("Doc" Heath); William Farnum (Malcolm Todd); Lucille Gleason (Nellie); Leslie Fenton (Jerry Willis); Gwen Lee (Gwen Willis); Wallace MacDonald (Francisco); Almeda Fowler (Belle); Adrian Morris (Snooper); Madame Sul-Te-Wan (Carla).

The film begins in Havana where Dot works in a seedy bar. "This place is full of fresh guys tonight," Dot complains to her friend. That is quite an understatement.

Dingo Mike asks Dot to make him a "New Life Cocktail." She asks him how to make it. Turns out it's got just about everything in it, including absinthe and egg shells. "Sounds more like Sudden Death to me," Dot quips. She charges him $8. He tells her the regular price is $2. "Two if you drink it," she challenges.

Minutes later, she warns Dingo that he's being set up: Two guys are waiting for him outside the bar. Francisco hears that Dot has been flirting with Dingo, and he wants her to account for her time.

"Listen here, spic," she says, "I just work here. If I want to go out and count the waves, I'll do it. See?"

***Evelyn in* The Pagan Lady *(1931).***

Dingo reappears and tells Francisco he's taken care of the two guys. "Come on, beautiful, get your things," he tells Dot. "We're pulling out of here." He picks up Dot like she's a toy and sets her up high in the bar. "Say, what's the idea?" she asks.

"I don't want to see you get mussed up, baby." A fight ensues. Dingo emerges victorious and takes Dot to Miami where he's a bootlegger. "I knew you were my medicine, and good or bad, I'd have to take you," Dot tells him on the way. She also tells him, "While it lasts, let's make it beautiful. Let's act nice with each other. That's all I mean." Dingo takes her to Nellie's boardinghouse. He soon leaves on a trip, though not without leaving strict instructions for Dot: "Now get this through your dome. You're mine, and mine you're gonna stay."

After Dingo leaves, she admits to Doc Heath that she's jumpy and nervous. He suggests she needs "variety." She gets it when reformers Malcolm and Ernest Todd show up at the boardinghouse. "The devil is still far too active," Malcolm tells his friend Heath. "We are determined to crush out vice in every form." Malcolm and his nephew certainly have their work cut out for them at the boarding house. Dot turns on her sultry charm when she first lays eyes on timid Ernest. "We could sit and watch the waves pounding on the sand bar. How does that sound?" she asks, though it's clear she's not talking about waves. Or a sand bar.

Ernest tells Heath that he and his uncle have decided he will not marry. "My talents don't run in that direction," he explains. Later he confesses to his uncle that he's unhappy and wants to give up his career. Malcolm admits that he, too, suffered from temptation. He solved it in a unique way. "I found the strength to drive her [a temptress he knew in Africa] back to darkness. That night I smeared my naked body with wild honey. Lashed myself to the wall for the insects to mortify till dawn. My first victory and my last." Ernest fervently prays for God's help.

A few days later, Ernest comes to Dot's assistance when fellow boarder Jerry hits on her. Jerry laughs when Ernest calls her Mrs. Hunter. "Mrs. Hunter, my foot! That's Dingo's moll. A dame he picked up in Havana."

"It's true what he said," Dot admits. "I'm not Mrs. Hunter." She runs out to the beach. Ernest follows. "I'm not your kind," Dot tells him. "Well, you were the first fella who ever stood up when I came into a room. Or ran to open a door for me or even talked to me without going on the make. A girl appreciates things like that. Especially a girl like me."

Ernest admits to Heath that he's fallen in love with Dot. Later Ernest and Dot discuss their views on religion. "My God is different," Dot tells Ernest. "He's in the first smell of morning and that last big red laugh they call the sunset. He's in those waves out there. He's right here now, feeling sorry at the way we're straining to put Him into words. Ain't any words for my God, Ernie. He's just there. Like the stars are there. He's always been, and He always will

be." She also admits, "I'm a bad egg. But He knows I haven't always wanted to be." Ernest asks her to marry him. "One thing no man has ever asked me," Dot says. "And it had to be you." She tells him she loves Dingo.

A rainstorm disrupts their conversation, and they spend the night on the island. Gwen can't wait to tell Malcolm that his nephew and Dot spent the night together. Dingo arrives and demands to know where Dot is.

Heath rows out to the island with Malcolm and tells Dot that Dingo is back. She tells him she's decided to marry Ernest. "I love what he is," she says. "I love what he stands for. I'm going to be what he wants me to be if it'll make him happy." In reality, she's doing it so Dingo won't kill Ernest.

Uncle Malcolm obviously doesn't like the idea. "Surely you must understand that you and Ernest stand as far apart as the poles."

"Well," Dot says, "just the same, we're beatin' it on the first train."

Ernest tells his uncle that he loves her. "Then this creature means more to you than your hope of Heaven?" Uncle Malcolm asks.

"I never felt nearer Heaven than today," Ernest tells him.

They head back with Dot saying, "The worst is yet to come." (Heath notices that Dot has written DINGO in the sand.)

Dingo confronts Dot. She tells him that she and Ernest love each other and are going to be married. "You're going to treat this kid right," a resigned Dingo cautions Ernest. "Or I'll get you wherever you are. And I'll make you wish you never was born."

"I won't forget you, Dingo," Dot tells him. "You've sure been white to me."

"What a tough guy I've turned out to be," Dingo complains when he lets them leave. Before they catch their train, Ernest and Dot listen to a sermon. Dot sees how it affects Ernest and advises him to go back to his uncle. She promises him she won't go back to her old life.

A drunken Heath tells Dingo that Dot decided to marry Ernest because she feared Dingo would kill him. Dingo, realizing Dot is not in love with Ernest, rushes off to find her. We hear a train whistle. Dot quickly boards the train as it's pulling away, but Dingo yanks her off. He tells her he'll marry her. "I don't want nobody else but you," he says. He also says he'll give up bootlegging and get a job on the police force. They kiss.

The story was supposedly based on the real-life adventures of rum-runner "Dago" Mike and his Havana girlfriend.[127] This picture was produced by Evelyn's husband Harry Edwards. Of course, Brent received top billing ahead of Nagel and Bickford, and she was photographed beautifully. The steamy, interesting film is quite good, as is the cast. It's difficult to understand, in fact, why the film failed at the box office. The script is good, and Bickford and Brent have strong chemistry. The picture's early scenes were filmed outside Havana, Cuba, in the Cantina del Diablo.

Roland Young produced a large number of sketches of cast members and sets while working on the project. It'll be just a matter of time before they begin to appear on eBay, if they haven't already.

Elizabeth Yeaman did a news blurb on the previous careers of *The Pagan Lady*'s cast members. "Every principal started in life in some other profession and eventually gravitated to the screen. Evelyn Brent, for instance, studied to be a school teacher. Conrad Nagel was a key clerk and telephone operator in a little mid-west town. Charles Bickford was a coal passer on the Roosevelt. Roland Young was turning into an architect when he determined to follow his yearnings instead of the line of least resistance. William Farnum and his brother Dustin were creating a 'kid circus' up in New England. Benjamin Glazer, who wrote the screenplay, was in the manufacturing business and Lucile Gleason thought she was destined for a domestic science teacher. And there you are."[128]

Born in Iowa in 1897, Conrad Nagel was a silent film star who made his film debut in 1918 as Laurie in *Little Women*. He was one of the founders of the Academy of Motion Picture Arts and Sciences and served as its president from 1932 to 1933. In the latter part of his career, he made many television appearances. Nagel died in 1970.

Charles Bickford was born in Cambridge, Massachusetts, on New Year's Day, 1891. A remarkable performer and person, he wrote about his adventures in his autobiography *Bulls, Balls, Bicycles & Actors*. Bickford received Oscar nominations for *The Song of Bernadette* (1943), *The Farmer's Daughter* (1947), and *Johnny Belinda* (1948). His final performances were in such television shows as *Playhouse 90, The Dick Powell Show*, and *The Virginian*. He died in 1967.

Roland Young was born in London in 1887. A successful stage performer, he appeared in silent films but became much more successful in the 1930s and 1940s as a character actor. Nominated for an Oscar for his work in *Topper* (1937), he died in 1953.

William Farnum, born in Boston in 1876, made his film debut in 1914 and eventually became a successful silent film star. He also was a noted stage actor. Farnum, whose brothers were Dustin and Marshall, died in 1953. His eulogy was read by Pat O'Brien.

Lucille (sometimes spelled Lucile) Gleason was born in Pasadena, California, in 1888. She died in 1947. A celebrated stage actress, she made her film debut in 1929. Gleason was one of the founding members of the Screen Actors Guild. She was married to James Gleason from 1905 until her death in 1947. Adrian Morris was Chester Morris' brother. Born in Mount Vernon, New York, in 1903, he appeared in small roles in the 1930s and 1940s. Morris died in 1941. Born Nellie Conley in Louisville, Kentucky, in 1873, Madame Sul-Te-Wan was the child of freed slaves. She was reported to be the first African-American to sign a film contract. Sul-Te-Wan appeared in such films as *The Birth of a Nation* (1915), *Intolerance* (1916), *Maid of Salem* (1937), and *Carmen Jones* (1954). She died in 1959.

Director John Francis Dillon was born in New York in 1884. An actor as well as a director (he also dabbled in producing and writing), he began his career at Keystone in 1913. Dillon died of a heart attack in 1934.

Writer (and producer) Benjamin Glazer was born in Ireland in 1887. He was one of the founders of the Academy of Motion Picture Arts and Sciences. Glazer won Oscars for *Seventh Heaven* (1929) and *Arise, My Love* (1940). He died in 1956.

Cinematographer Norbert Brodine was born in St. Joseph, Missouri, in 1896. He began his film career in 1919 and went on to receive Oscar nominations for *Merrily We Live* (1938), *Lady of the Tropics* (1939), and *The Frogmen* (1951). He also won an Emmy for an episode of *Letter to Loretta* in 1957. He died in 1970. Editor Viola Lawrence (1894–1973) received Oscar nominations for *Pal Joey* (1957) and *Pepe* (1960).

*Reviews:* "[I]t begins well but is another of those films that is not a little disappointing after it reaches the halfway mark. It has good performances by Roland Young, Charles Bickford, Evelyn Brent and Conrad Nagel..." (*New York Times*, September 21, 1931).

"[T]he story keeps on faltering ... right up to its foolish finish.... Only sacrilegious thoughts would stop any audience laughing outright at the antique ideas and dialog between William Farnum as the reformer and Nagel as his sappy student" (*Variety*, September 22, 1931).

"William Farnum as the vice reformer brings a forceful portrayal to the screen, as does Charles Bickford" (*Los Angeles Evening Herald*, October 30, 1931).

"[It] provides much amusement, presents a splendid cast and shows some fine photography. Evelyn Brent ... does her part in a manner that wins for her the sympathy of the audience" (*Los Angeles Record*, October 30, 1931).

"*Pagan Lady* is pretty strong melodrama enlivened with meaty—at times, torrid—dialogue and many comedy situations. *Pagan Lady* has a generally excellent cast.... Norman Brodine is responsible for some occasionally really beautiful photography" (*Los Angeles Times*, October 31, 1931).

"The Sadie Thompson theme in a new dress, with Evelyn Brent wearing it becomingly" (*Photoplay*, December 1931).

## *The Mad Parade*

(Liberty Productions Co.) 63 min. Released on September 18, 1931.

*Survival Status:* [1940 Re-issue] Library of Congress (Washington, D.C.).

*Credits:* Producer, Herman M. Gumbin; supervisor, M. H. Hoffman; director, William Beaudine; screenplay, Frank R. Conklin, Henry McCarthy; writing, Doris Malloy, Gertrude Orr; photography, Charles Van Enger; second camera, Glenn Kershner, Ernest Miller; assistant camera, Dean Dailey, Harold Graham, James Higgins, Oliver Sigurdson; film editor, Richard Cahoon, sound engineer, William R. Fox.

*Cast*: Evelyn Brent (Monica Dale [also known as "Duchess"]); Irene Rich (Mrs. [Betty] Schuyler); Louise Fazenda (Fanny Smithers); Lilyan Tashman (Lil Wheeler); Marceline Day (Dorothy Quinlan); Fritzi Ridgeway (Prudence Graham [also known as "Snoop"]); June Clyde (Janice Lee [also known as "Speed"]); Elizabeth Keating (Bluebell Jones); Helen Keating (Rosemary Jones).

The film begins with thrilling World War I stock footage, including airplanes, zeppelins, and so on. We next see a sign that says in part: "THIS MAY NOT BE A REGULAR UNIT OF THIS MANS [sic] ARMY—BUT, IF YOU THINK WE DON'T MAKE AS GOOD DOUGHNUTS AS THEY DO, COME IN AND TRY 'EM."

One of the first things you realize is that for some reason, everyone hates Snoop. "Listen, I may have to live with you," Lil complains, "but I'll be damned if I'll drink with you."

The medical aid station appears to have been fashioned from an abandoned-requisitioned French chateau-castle, complete with wine cellar. The grim, depressing surroundings for the aid workers often results in bickering, especially about romantic entanglements. Snoop hints to Janice that Monica is seeing her boyfriend Tony. That, in fact, she stayed out all night with him.

When a relaxed Monica returns from leave (wearing an evening dress), she senses something is up. "Boy, this silence is deafening. You must have been talking about me." Her good mood quickly disappears when Snoop says something about her being with Tony. Monica grabs Snoop and twists her arm, shoves a cigarette between her own lips, and slaps Snoop's face. It's pretty darn impressive.

Just after escaping an air raid, the women rally around Dorothy, who has received the sad news that boyfriend Jim has been killed. "Snap out of it, Dot.... You're not the only one that's lost a man in the war," Monica tells her.

After sending Dorothy to help in the canteen, Snoop says the absolute wrong thing—and with a smirk. "Anyway, now she knows where he is."

"Get out of here, you worm!" Monica shrieks. There is definitely some bad blood between these two.

Betty tells Monica that a complaint has been made about her conduct during her last leave. If it happens again, she'll be returned to the United States. "I couldn't stand it," Monica says. "What would I do in the States?" Monica complains that there's a double standard. Men can act however they want when they're on leave because of the war. "We're not women any more," she tells Betty. "I'm not. You don't suppose I can go through it, living in mud, smelling the dead and still come out of it like I was. Betty, I kissed a man once. He was dying. He got in the way of a shell. I'll never forget the sight. Just a *thing* with two blind eyes. He was off his nut and thought I was his wife. I kissed him and heard the rattle. I went on my first bender after that. I got cock-eyed for the first time." We get a sense of how damaged Monica has become as a result of the war. "Blood, rats, shells! They didn't know about things like that at home."

Just as Janice starts to quiz Monica about her relationship with Tony, the women get orders to relocate the aid station. They move the ambulance trucks at night and get caught in the middle of hostilities. One of the trucks is hit, and Dorothy is hurt. After holing up in a foxhole, Lil discovers Snoop hiding in a dugout. They get Dorothy inside, but she is terribly injured. Monica decides they should stay with her.

While the others are resting, Lil asks Monica about Tony. She admits she's fallen for him—and he feels the same way about her. Lil suggests she not see him any more. "You know, there ought to be a law against marriage," Lil says. "It's ruined so many grand passions." Monica tells Lil about the night she met Tony and tells her she won't leave him. "He's all I've got. The war and Tony. My whole world."

**Lilyan Tashman, Louise Fazenda, Irene Rich, and Brent in the all-female war film** The Mad Parade *(1931).*

Janice overhears the conversation and confronts Monica. Monica gives her the "It just happened" excuse, but Janice isn't buying it. She cries and tells Monica she's rotten. "All right, I'm rotten. So is this," Monica says. "The whole mad parade." Janice tells her she loves Tony. "Mine's the only kind there is," Monica tells Janice. "The other doesn't count up here. It's now or never. That's love. It means life for a moment." Janice tells Monica that Tony will leave her when the war is over. "You're warped, hopeless," she tells Monica.

Snoop butts in and mocks Monica, telling her she plans to tell Betty and have Monica sent back to the States "with your hair in a braid." Snoop keeps jabbing at Monica. "Your hard-boiled days are over, sweetheart. You're going back home in disgrace."

Monica eyes a hand grenade sitting on a table. Snoop turns her back, laughing. Monica doesn't hesitate. She picks up the grenade and throws it at Snoop. There's a terrible explosion. Lil and Fannie look. It's horrifying. Fannie runs out of the dugout.

Monica doesn't miss a beat. She tells Janice she's still not going to let Tony go. "It's right to kill if it's war. But if a dirty, little sneak comes along and tries to knife you in the back, it's wrong to defend yourself. To step on her like the rat she was. You wouldn't do what I did. You haven't got the guts to hit back! And if you think I'll give up the man I love, you're crazy!"

Dorothy's moans silence them. Janice goes to her, but Dorothy tells her she wants Monica. Dorothy finally dies.

The other truck shows up, and Lil and Fannie lead the others to the dugout. Betty looks at Snoop's body and asks Monica what happened. "Of course it was an accident," Betty says, obviously unsure.

"Ask Janice," Monica says.

Janice covers for her. The women are now trapped behind the lines. They draw to see who goes for help. Janice draws the marked paper. Monica wants to shake her hand, but Janice refuses. "All right. Have it your way. I don't blame you. I think you're the bravest one of us all," Monica tells her.

Monica then confesses to Betty about murdering Snoop. "After all, this is war, and it was Snoop or me." She turns to Janice. "I don't want anything that doesn't belong to me." She lies and tells Janice that Tony really loves her.

Monica fearlessly runs out of the dugout. Amid exploding shells and machine gunfire, she's hit but continues forward. Finally she arrives at a dugout. A man makes a call and asks for a ceasefire. The women back in the dugout clutch each other. Suddenly, there is quiet. "Oh, she must have made it!" Lil cries out.

Monica lies in the dugout. She's told that the ambulance will soon arrive. "Don't worry about your outfit," a man says. "The shelling stopped, and they're okay." Monica smiles and dies. The soldiers cover Monica with a blanket. "Boy, that dame had plenty of guts." Another soldier responds, "I'll say she did."

For Lilyan Tashman fans, this is a must-see. Whether she's dabbing alcohol behind her ears like it's perfume or delivering the best lines, she's a tie-wearing delight. After finding out that one of the twins had emptied her hot water bottle to get rid of the "terrible smell," Tashman replies, "And I had to break one of the commandments to get this terrible smell!"

All the major studios turned this one down. Herman M. Gumbin, who had never produced a film before, took a chance and bought the rights. This was his only film credit.

Writers Gertrude Orr and Doris Malloy based their story, "Women Like Men," on their own experiences as ambulance drivers. *Women Like Men* was considered as a title for the film. The film was re-released in 1936 with the title *Forgotten Women*, and again in 1940, this time titled *War Angels*.

*The Mad Parade* is an interesting film that might actually play better today than it did during its time period. All cast members are female, though you occasionally hear or see part of a man. Though it does suffer from being too tied to its stage origins, the picture provides fascinating performances from its strong cast. The best performances are by Brent, Ridgeway, Tashman, and Fazenda.

Brent helped June Clyde get her role, but behind-the-scenes chatter suggests that Brent was ambitious, and, if not ruthless, then certainly concerned about her career. Watch for the scene where Janice (Clyde) goes to Monica (Brent) and asks her to leave their mutual lover. The scene was originally written that Monica would remain stoic and cold. However, Brent apparently realized it'd become a scene-stealer for Clyde. According to a *Photoplay* article, Brent rethought her portrayal. "Betty [Brent] unbent and allowed herself to weep a little. Stole a little of June's stuff, to put it in bald-faced language. The director ordered a retake. When [Brent] found she wasn't allowed to cry, she managed to make some error. She forgot her lines; she moved in the wrong way; she made other technical mistakes. Now, it is difficult to do an emotional scene over and over. Each time you do it, you lose some of the spontaneity of the action. Your makeup becomes spotty; your temper unruly. But if Betty could make her little pal June less effective, the audience would give her less attention. Finally the director snapped at her, 'We'll use this take no matter what you do, Betty!' And Betty unbent, became a trifle sorry she was taking this girl's man from her!"[129] Clyde remained diplomatic, insisting that she wasn't angry. "I don't blame Betty. It was hard, of course. But it was Betty's picture. She was the *star*. It was her business to protect her interests but it was my business to protect mine. I grit my teeth and tried to do it better each time no matter what happened."[130]

Cast members were given special instructions from director Beaudine concerning their costumes. "Beaudine told us to get them dirty, to let the dog sleep on them, to mop the floor with them."[131]

When publicizing the movie, Beaudine stressed how difficult the set was for the actresses. "It was remarkable that no serious injury occurred among this assemblage of feminine players because of the hardships the actresses were forced to endure during production.... Every player at some time or other was hurt by flying dirt, missiles and debris, caused by bursting shells and exploding ground charges. Lilyan Tashman was knocked into a trench when a nervous powder expert set off a charge too soon; Marceline Day and the Keating twins were temporarily blinded by a wave of flying dirt, caused by a dynamite charge; Irene Rich strained her back while digging a truck out of a mud hole, and Evelyn Brent was shocked and bruised when thrown out of the seat of the truck."[132]

Cast and crew truly could not tell the difference between identical twins Helen and Elizabeth Keating. They appeared in only one other film, *Up the River* (1930).

At one time, ZaSu Pitts and Marion Nixon were considered for roles. Dale Fuller and Mae Busch tried out for the role Fritzi Ridgeway won. Some scenes were reshot in an attempt to make Brent's character more likable.

Director William Beaudine later complained that the film was edited to the point of nonsense. Born in New York in 1892, he was also an actor, writer and occasional producer. Called "One Shot" for obvious reasons, he became known as a master of low-budget films. Later in his career he directed many television shows. Beaudine also directed Brent in *Emergency Landing* (1941), *Bowery Champs* (1944), *The Golden Eye* (1948), and the television show *Elfego Baca*. He died in 1970.

Silent screen star Irene Rich was born Irene Luther in Buffalo, New York, in 1891. Rich later became successful on radio and the stage. She died in 1988.

Born in Indiana in 1895, Louise Fazenda was a popular silent comedienne who went on to do quite well in sound films. She was married to producer Hal B. Wallis (nicknamed "The Prisoner of Fazenda") and became known for her philanthropic activities. She died in 1962.

Lilyan Tashman was born in Brooklyn in 1899 and died of cancer in 1934. Notorious for her lesbian activities despite marrying actor Edmund Lowe in 1925, she was an interesting silent and sound film star who started her career in the Ziegfeld Follies.

Marceline Day was born in Colorado in 1908. She began her career in silent films and retired in 1933. After her retirement she refused all interviews and would not discuss her career. Her sister was Alice Day. Marceline died in 2000.

Fritzi Ridgeway was born in Butte, Montana, in 1898 and began her film career in 1916. Married to Russian musical director and conductor Constantin Bakaleinikoff, she died in 1961.

June Clyde was born June Tetrazini in St. Joseph, Missouri, in 1909. By the age of seven she was appearing on stage as Baby Tetrazini. Her film career began in 1929. Married to director Thornton Freeland, she died in 1987.

Henry McCarty, also known as Henry McCarthy, was a silent film director as well as a writer. Born in San Francisco in 1882, he died in Hollywood in 1954. Frank Roland Conklin was a prolific screenwriter with more than one hundred credits. Born in 1903 in New Jersey, he began his career in 1919. He died in 1963. Writer Gertrude Orr was born in Covington, Kentucky, in 1891. She attended Vassar College and then became a reporter for the *Denver Post*. Orr wrote several silent film scenarios before working on *The Mad Parade*. She also wrote the screenplay for *Without Children* (1935). Orr died in Washington, D.C. in 1971. Doris Malloy was born in New York in 1901. Her first film credit was for writing the silent Western *The Wild Horse Stampede* (1926), which starred Fay Wray. She died in Los Angeles in 1955.

*Reviews:* "It is a forced story of an unusual group of girls which lacks the quality of naturalness. ... Monica is acted by Evelyn Brent, who does quite well by her role" (*New York Times*, September 19, 1931).

"[T]his is product that has its strong moments. It also has its toddering [sic] side.... The scene in which one of the girls, a trouble maker, threatens another with exposure for serious violation of conduct rules, ending in murder by a grenade, is the strongest" (*Variety*, September 22, 1931).

"*The Mad Parade* is a picture that is not pleasant.... Evelyn Brent and Lilyan Tashman ... fought for supremacy as the pseudo-mannish characterizations they portrayed, with Miss Brent getting a slight edge" (*Illustrated Daily News* [Los Angeles], September 25, 1931).

"After the fairly accurate realism of *All Quiet on the Western Front*, it comes as a shock to find the screen still turning out such war hokum as *The Mad Parade*.... The pain is all the more localized in the neck by the wasting of some good acting on it. ... [Brent] manages to struggle through the absurdities of the picture with a suggestion of the fury and desperation of women in war" (*Los Angeles Evening Herald*, September 25, 1931).

"While it is unevenly interesting, it is distinctly novel and the cast includes favorite players. Fault is found with the roughness of some of the speeches, especially those allotted to Lilyan Tashman, but it is a fact that almost every word that Miss Tashman utters is good for a laugh" (*Los Angeles Times*, September 27, 1931).

"*The Mad Parade* is neither an unusual nor a particularly interesting picture" (*Time*, September 28, 1931).

"The women's side of the war done brilliantly by an all-feminine cast" (*Photoplay*, November 1931).

"[I]t is worth seeing for its originality. Hardly a superior film, nevertheless it has its points. Miss Brent. ... makes you believe her speeches about what war has done to her character" (*Picture Play*, December 1931).

When the film was re-released in 1936 with the title *Forgotten Women*, *Film Daily* provided this review: "Weak war drama with all-woman cast too talky in cross-fire conversation" (May 13, 1936).

## High Pressure

(Warner Bros. Pictures, Inc.) 74 min. Released on January 30, 1932.

*Survival Status:* UCLA Film and Television Archive (Los Angeles).

*Credits*: Director, Mervyn LeRoy; screenplay, Joseph Jackson; based on the play *Hot Money* by Aben Kandel; photography, Robert Kurrle; second camera, Al Greene; assistant camera, John Sepek; still photographer, Charles Scott Welbourne; art direction, Anton Grot; film editor, Ralph Dawson; costumes, Earl Luick; sound, Al Riggs; Vitaphone orchestra conducted by Leo F. Forbstein.

*Cast*: William Powell (Gar Evans); Evelyn Brent (Francine Dale); George Sidney (Ginsberg); John Wray (Jimmy Moore); Evalyn Knapp (Helen); Guy Kibbee (Clifford Gray); Frank McHugh (Mike Donahey); Oscar Apfel (B.B.B.M.); Ben Alexander (Geoffrey); Harold Waldridge (Vanderbilt); Charles Middleton (Mr. Banks); Polly Walters (Millie); Luis Alberni (Colombo); Harry Beresford (Dr. Rudolph); Lucien Littlefield (Oscar Brown); Charles Judels (Salvatore); Alison Skipworth (Mrs. Miller); Maurice Black (Poppolus); Bobby Watson (The Baron); Andre Luguet (Mr. Rodriguez).

Mike and Ginsberg are looking for promoter Gar Evans, but no one has seen him in days, including girlfriend Francine who has absolutely had it with him this time. Finally, Mike takes Ginsberg to the Koko Kola Club, a speakeasy, and finds Gar. Unfortunately, he is passed out. Mike and Ginsberg start to drag him out of the club but are told they need to settle his bill first—$108. "Hey, we don't want to buy him. We just want to rent him," Ginsberg complains but reluctantly pays.

After Gar's sauna, shower, and rubdown, Mike pitches an idea to her. Ginsberg knows an inventor who has a process that will make rubber out of sewage. "Tons and tons of it, Gar," Mike enthusiastically says. "Get yourself into that picture. Tons and tons of sewage. Begins everywhere and ends nowhere."

"Gentlemen, there's no romance in sewage," Gar disdainfully replies. However, he quickly warms up to the idea and decides to call the company the Golden Gate Artificial Rubber Company. Gar has big plans and asks Ginsberg to put up $25,000 to get the company started. It suddenly occurs to Gar, however, that he's forgotten all about Francine. Gar wants Mike to run interference for him with her. "Tell her this is the last time," he suggests.

"That's what I told her the last time," Mike says. They set up the company in a pricey building on Park Avenue. Mike tells Gar he had no luck getting Francine to come back. "Without her this deal is jinxed," Gar complains. He sends Mike off to try again.

Francine tells Mike she's been on a merry-go-round with Gar for five years, "and right now is where I get off." She tells Mike she plans to marry Mr. Rodriguez.

Gar introduces company president Clifford Gray to Ginsberg. Gray shows up in a tattered suit and is clearly a down-and-outer. Still, Gar has made him president of several companies because he *looks* like one. "Nobody in the world can sit in a chair the way he does," he crows.

While Ginsberg scurries off to find the inventor, Gar interviews Helen to be his private secretary. She agrees, and Gar quickly enlists Geoffrey, her fiancé, to write publicity for the company.

Just before Gar's big sales speech, Francine arrives. She's not in a good mood. She asks him if he got his Bromo Seltzer. "That's what you said you were going for. Five days ago." She gives him back jewelry he bought her. He apparently ran out on her when they were on the verge of getting married. "What do you think I am?" she angrily asks. "A luck charm for you?" She tells him life with him is like "living in a revolving door" and adds that she's met a Bolivian who has asked her to move with him to South America and marry him. "I'd like the feeling once of being called Mrs." Gar begs. No way, Francine declares. "You've played football with me long enough, and I'm tired of being kicked around. You're just a drunken, no-good, irresponsible scoundrel!"

Just as Francine is about to leave, she gets a good look at Helen. Now jealous, she changes her mind and decides to stay.

"Are you a red-blooded he-man?" Gar begins his speech. The rousing address fires up the crowd and convinces them the product will make them a fortune. (Gar's speech incorporates risk-taking pioneers and visionaries such as Daniel Boone, Robert Fulton, the Wright Brothers, Charles Lindbergh—and the Warner Brothers who "pioneered Vitaphone talking pictures").

Soon the company is thriving in large part because salesmen are pumping up the stock. "You'll double

**William Powell and Brent in** High Pressure **(1932).**

your money in less than six months" and "I wouldn't steer you wrong" are some of the pitches we hear from the boiler room. The company has everything but a product because Ginsberg still hasn't found the inventor.

Mr. Banks represents rubber manufacturers and wants to inspect the product. He also tells Gar they are prepared to pay $50,000 for the patent. Gar laughs at him, and Banks leaves in a huff, telling him that he will need to prove the process if they want to continue selling stock.

To make matters worse, Francine catches Gar in yet another lie. When he promises to tell her the truth, she says, "That'll be a novelty." To prove he's on the level, Gar signs over 51 percent of the company to her. "Now when the payoff comes, you'll be the big boss. What do you think of that?" Francine kisses him.

Helen tells Gar she has a "friend" who wants to invest $300 in company shares. Gar is at first reluctant but finally agrees. Helen kisses him just as Geoffrey walks in and gets the wrong idea. He tells Francine, and she and Geoffrey demand an explanation. "Go on," Francine tells Gar, "I like bedtime stories." Just then the attorney general's men come in. They seize the company's cash and books and will no longer allow any additional shares to be sold.

Stupid Helen pipes up and admits she gave Gar her life savings to buy stock. "Well, Gar, this is the rummiest thing you've done yet," Francine says, hands on hips. "Selling stock to that kid. Now you have promoted yourself right out of my life.... You couldn't sell me another share of Gar Evens Common. *Awful* common."

Finally, the inventor shows up. Turns out he's a fraud. He bought his chemistry degree for $17.50 from a degree mill Gar once ran. Still, the inventor convinces Gar and Ginsberg he has studied chemistry for years, and they put him in the lab to, yes, convert sewage into rubber. Gar invites scientists to visit the lab. The newspaper headline reads: ARTIFICIAL RUBBER CO. DEFIES INJUNCTION: INVITES SCIENTISTS TO TEST PROCESS. Turns out the inventor is a major kook. He tells Gar and Ginsberg his next big idea is to raise hens that will lay Easter eggs—already colored. Then he begins dancing around the lab, laughing hysterically.

Gar is advised to leave Ginsberg and Gray holding the bag, but Gar refuses. Banks comes to Gar with a deal: He'll clear up the stockholders' losses with interest and reimburse Gar's expenses, plus a bonus of $100,000 (they also want Mr. Gray, the president of the company, because he's impressed them). In return, Banks wants the company's controlling interest. Gar, of course, agrees.

Gar sends Mike to find Francine because they need the stock certificate, but she has accepted the marriage offer from the Bolivian and is at the steamship office. Gar, Mike, and Ginsberg hurry to find her. Gar promises her the world. He continues his pleas while they search through her trunk for the stock certificate. Once it's located, Gar sends Ginsberg to deliver it to Banks.

Francine finally relents, even though she knows she shouldn't. Just then Mike shows up with a new deal, an Alaskan gold mining deal. Gar tells Mike he's through. He escorts Francine away from the ship. Mike tells him the deal includes marble, too. Still not interested, Gar says. But then Mike tells him about the spruce tree forest that produces lightweight wood. Gar is hooked, going on and on about the potential. Francine gives him "here we go again" look. (The ship's whistle is used as a raspberry in this scene.) In the final scene we see Gar giving a highly energetic speech to salesmen. They love it.

The best lines are Francine's, and Brent delivers them like a pro. The worst lines are Ginsberg's, and George Sidney, unfortunately, gives an annoying performance. Polly Walters, in a bit as the ditzy blonde receptionist, has a particularly naughty line near the end of the picture. When Mr. Gray comes to her with a floral arrangement wrapped around him, he asks, "Where do I think I should put this?"

"Oh, Mr. Grant," she coos (decades before *The Mary Tyler Moore Show*).

As some critics have pointed out, there is something grim-faced and sullen about Evelyn in this film. Perhaps she made the decision to play the character that way, or maybe she was indeed feeling anxious about the direction her career was taking. The movie is not very good. Although it has the always-charming and energetic William Powell (giving a terrific performance) and the reliable Frank McHugh, the humor is lame, the script weak, and the direction feeble. Mervyn LeRoy would become a much better director; this is not one of his best efforts.

It's difficult to make a comedy about Depression-era scammers who steal life savings from suckers who fall for too-good-to-believe stock pitches. Gar expresses some regret, but he is unethical, unscrupulous, and unlikable. In addition, the idea of using sewage is distasteful—what were they thinking?

There are some nice camera shots, including one of the building lit up in neon lights with the name of the company emblazoned on the side. Anton Grot does a great job with the sets, including some gorgeous art deco furniture (notice, particularly, Gar and Francine's desks).

Shooting began on October 27, 1931. Powell received first billing. He had recently received a large contract from his new employer Warner Bros. "Evelyn Brent, looking rather tired and her luster of the Paramount days somewhat depleted, is on hand as Powell's love interest (reportedly at his request, so as to revive her flagging fortunes circa 1932)."[133]

In the following year, 1932, Warner Bros. made a French version of the film. Everything was the same—production studio, sets, and script—except for the performers. Powell was replaced by Andre Luguet (who played Brent's Bolivian love interest in *High Pressure*), and Brent by Lucienne Radisse. The French version was titled *Le bluffeur* (*The Bluffer*).

Within a few years, voice dubbing and subtitles came into widespread use, and this type of parallel production ceased. The film was remade in 1936 by Warner Brothers as *Hot Money*. Directed by William C. McGann, it starred Ross Alexander and Beverly Roberts.

Mervyn LeRoy was born in San Francisco in 1900. A cousin of Jesse Lasky, he worked in various areas of film before becoming a director in 1927. LeRoy received an Oscar nomination for *Random Harvest* (1942). He died in 1987.

George Sidney was born Sammy Greenfield in Hungary in 1876. Sidney appeared as Cohen in several Cohens and Kellys films in the 1920s and 1930s. He died in 1945.

Charles Middleton came from a wealthy family; his grandfather was one of the signers of the Declaration of Independence. He is best known for playing Ming the Merciless in the Flash Gordon serials. Born in Elizabethtown, Kentucky, in 1874, he died in 1949.

John Wray was born in Philadelphia in 1887. Also a writer, he began his film career in 1929. Wray died in 1940. He also appeared with Brent in *The President's Mystery* (1936).

Evelyn Knapp was the sister of band leader Orville Knapp (he died at the age of 32 in a 1936 airplane crash). Born Pauline Evelyn Knapp in Kansas City, Missouri, in 1908, she at one time had a dance act with her brother. This was Knapp's first film since a back injury the previous spring. She died in 1981.

Guy Kibbee was born in El Paso, Texas, in 1882. Kibbee was a stage actor until signed by Warner Brothers in 1931. A popular character actor for more than two decades, he died in 1956.

In addition to acting, Oscar Apfel was a director, actor, and producer. Apfel was born in Cleveland, Ohio, in 1878 and began his career as a silent film director in 1911, later becoming a character actor. Apfel died in 1938. Lucien Littlefield was born in San Antonio, Texas, in 1895. He enjoyed a long film and television career that began in 1914. Littlefield died in 1960. He also appeared with Brent in *Silent Witness* (1943). Former child actor Ben Alexander later costarred with Jack Webb on the radio and TV versions of *Dragnet*. A one-time radio announcer, he was born in Nevada in 1911 and died in 1969. Harold Waldridge was born in New Orleans in 1905. Often cast as in Jewish roles, he died in 1957. Harry Beresford was born in London in 1863. Married to actress Kitty Gordon, he appeared in many films in the 1930s. Beresford died in 1944. Alison Skipworth was born in London in 1863. Nicknamed "Skippy," she enjoyed much success on Broadway and was a familiar face in many 1930s movies. She appeared in several films as W.C. Fields' foil. She died in 1952. Andre Luguet, born in France in 1882, began his film career in 1910. He co-directed and starred in the French version of *High Pressure*, *Le bluffeur*, in 1932. Luguet died in 1979. Polly Walters was born Maud Walters in Columbus, Ohio, in 1913. She made a career out of playing dumb blonde switchboard operators. Walters died in 1994.

*Reviews:* "By all means see this film. It is one of the good ones" (*Los Angeles Evening Herald Express*, January 15, 1932).

"[A] fine piece of fast-moving colorful entertainment.... It is an amusingly told, crisply presented production, and should further along the prestige of Mervyn, who with every vehicle displays his smooth, keen technique, clever judgment, and knowledge of just what entertainment is in motion pictures.... Evelyn Brent has another of her matter-of-fact female characterizations, and is her usual frowning self" (*Illustrated Daily News* [Los Angeles], January 15, 1932).

"The plot developments are fairly ingenious, if not unexpected, and although middle section slows up to a noticeable degree, the star always puts on a good show of energy. Between him and the others, *High Pressure* is good for several smiles and even, I should add, a leer or two.... Miss Brent and Evelyn Knapp make charming alternate vis-a-vis" (*Los Angeles Times*, January 16, 1932).

"William Powell is in his element.... It is a brightly written and constantly amusing film.... Evelyn Brent is attractive and competent..." (*New York Times*, February 1, 1932).

"There is still a better story in the stock racket, and maybe somebody will write it..." (*Variety*, February 2, 1932).

"[R]apid, trivial, dextrous and absurd. Good shot: Powell, rewarded with $100,000 for his synthetic rubber company, planning to capitalize a concern for making wooden airplanes" (*Time*, February 8, 1932).

"Both Powell and Evelyn Brent are splendid" (*Photoplay*, April 1932).

## *Attorney for the Defense*

(Columbia Pictures Corp.) 70 min. Released on May 21, 1932.

*Survival Status:* Library of Congress (Washington, D.C.).

*Credits:* Producer, Harry Cohn; director, Irving Cummings; assistant director, David Selman; story; J. K. McGuinness; adaptation and dialogue, Jo Swerling; photography, Ted Tetzlaff; film editor, Gene Havlick; sound engineer; Russell Malmgren.

*Cast:* Edmund Lowe (William J. Burton); Evelyn Brent (Val Lorraine); Constance Cummings (Ruth Barry); Donald Dillaway (Paul Wallace); Douglas Haig (Paul Wallace, as a boy); Dorothy Peterson (Mrs. Wallace); Bradley Page (Nick Quinn); Nat Pendleton (Mugg); Dwight Frye (James Wallace); Wallis Clark (District Attorney Crowell); Clarence Muse (Jeff).

James Wallace, sentenced to death, is enraged with district attorney Burton. "I'm just another headline for you," he accuses. "The eighteenth guy you've railroaded to the electric chair. Because you want the governor's chair." As Wallace is dragged from the courtroom he continues yelling: "I'm no murderer! You *are*! You are!" His wife and son (child actor Douglas Haig is very annoying in this picture) weep.

In a must-see scene, Burton goes to the Beverly Apartments to see girlfriend Val. "Cigarette me, Nicky," Val requests from her other boyfriend, just before Burton walks into her lavish apartment. Val pretends to be happy to see Burton. She asks him what she should order from room service. "Why don't you go on a cheese diet?" Burton suggests. "It's good for rats."

"What's eating you? Did you get up on the wrong side of the bed this morning?" she asks angrily.

"No," he calmly replies. "You did." Burton tells Nick he won't have to sneak into Val's any more. "A two-time gal for a small-time crook," Burton says, suggesting Nick move in. He also warns Nick to stay out of his courtroom.

Headline: "ELECTROCUTE INNOCENT MAN! Wallace Convicted Last July, Cleared By Confession." The newspaper editor is all over the story: "Does the city need an executioner for a district attorney? A persecutor for a prosecutor?"

Burton writes a letter to the governor resigning his position and stating that he's going to become a defense attorney. He visits the Wallace family and hears sobbing come from within their apartment. (In this scene, notice the nice transition from the happy family in the neighboring apartment enjoying supper together, and closing the door on Burton, to the unhappy scene inside the Wallace apartment. The pleasant music coming from within the neighbor's apartment briefly overlaps with the sobbing coming from within the Wallace apartment.) Burton tells the Wallaces that he's left his estate to them. "Now in the meantime, all I've got is yours whenever you want it." He leaves his wallet.

In *The American Weekly*, we see an article with the headline: "HOW BILL BURTON ATONED FOR THE 'LEGAL MURDER' OF JAMES WALLACE: FORMER PROSECUTOR, NOW LEADING CRIMINAL LAWYER, WILLS ENTIRE ESTATE TO WIDOW AND UNDERTAKES EDUCATION OF THE WALLACE BOY." In a diary entry, the following is written: "Paul graduates today from Black Rock Academy. Mr. Burton wants him to go to Jefferson Law College."

Paul Wallace has become a college football star and is now close to graduation. Burton plans to hire him to work in his office. Val comes to Burton's office. She wants him to help Nick get out of a bust. "Billy, I used to mean something to you. For old time's sake, won't you—won't you do this for me?" He refuses, and she threatens him.

Nick comes up with a great idea: He tells Val to go after Paul. "I've always wanted to tackle a football hero," she says. For his part, Nick decides to go after Burton's chauffeur Mugg. Burton has some incriminating papers about him in his safe, so Nick offers Mugg $5,000 to crack the safe. Mugg turns it down because he was the one who cracked *Nick's* safe to get the papers in the *first* place. "An artist like me couldn't think of pulling the same job twice."

Mrs. Wallace tells Burton that Paul has been seeing a lot of a woman named Val. Burton tells Val to lay off Paul. Val tells Paul that Burton ordered her not to see him any more. "He's been after me ever since I met him," she explains. "If you only knew how rotten he is."

Paul confronts Burton. "Val Lorraine has just one interest in men," Burton explains to him. "And that is to take them for everything they've got. Including the gold in their teeth. She's no good." Paul angrily tells Burton he plans to marry Val.

Paul breaks into Burton's safe, steals the papers concerning Nick, and gives them to Val. "Oh, you don't know how happy you've made me, Paulie boy," she coos.

Val calls Burton and tells him to come by and pick up Paul—and to bring his checkbook. She offers to give the papers back for a fee. If he's not interested, she plans to offer them to Nick. "You know me, the highest bidder," she says. Paul overhears the conversation and gets a crazy look on his face. When Butler arrives, Val is dead and Paul is drunk.

Paul can't remember what happened. Burton sends him home. As Burton attempts to clean up the scene and find the papers, elevator operator-liquor supplier Jeff sees him. "It's all right, boy [the stereotyping of African-American characters in this one is hard to take]," Burton tells him. "Call the police. The number's Spring 7-3100."

Burton is jailed. His long-suffering assistant Ruth wants to hire lawyer Steiner, even though he's charging $50,000—$25,000 in advance—but she can't get anyone to help out on the fee. She tells Burton to represent himself. She also makes a confession: "The real reason I never got married was because you didn't ask me."

The trial is a big deal and is broadcast over the radio. The prosecutor makes a compelling case. Burton doesn't seem to be helping his cause at all. (There are a couple of great lines when Nick is on the stand. The district attorney asks if Burton was a regular visitor of Val's. "Visitor?" Nick asks incredulously. "Boarder," Nick clarifies. Ruth objects, and the district attorney turns to her. "You *should* object, Miss Barry," he says.)

Finally, when it seems certain Burton will be found guilty, he establishes that Nick is the murderer. "There's the man," Burton says, pointing at Nick, "who killed Valeska Lorraine!"

In the final scene, Burton proposes to Ruth. "I'm about to propose marriage to the grandest girl in the world, name of Barry. What about it, honey? Will you take dictation forever? Yours very truly, William J. Burton."

Edmund Lowe received top billing and deserves it. He's wonderful, very watchable. Often cast as a cad, he was assigned the Warren William pre–Code type roles by Fox and Columbia. Brent was second-billed and is glamorous as the evil Val.

The picture is loaded with great lines and solid performances. This rarely seen film was shown in 2000 at the Cinecon. Advertising used this slogan: "Men Were Cold Cases ... Women Were Warm Mysteries."

Edmund Lowe was born in San Jose, California, in 1890. Married to Lilyan Tashman from 1925 until her death in 1934, he began his career in the silent film era. In the 1950s he played David Chase in TV's *Front Page Detective*. Lowe died in 1971.

Character actor Donald Dillaway was born in New York in 1903. He began his career in 1930 and ended it with a variety of television appearances on such shows as *Perry Mason*, *The Munsters*, and *The Big Valley*. He died in 1982.

Bradley Page, born in Seattle, Washington, in 1901, began his screen career in 1931. He died in 1985. Page also appears with Brent in *The Law West of Tombstone* (1938) and *Silent Witness* (1943).

Nat Pendleton was born in Davenport, Iowa, in 1895. A college, Olympic, and professional wrestler, he died in 1967.

Dwight Frye was born in Salina, Kansas, in 1899. The stage actor became best known for his appearances in horror films, especially *Dracula* (1931) and *Frankenstein* (1931). The rock group Alice Cooper included the song "The Ballad of Dwight Fry" (Fry is the actual spelling of his last name) on the album *Love It to Death*. Frye died in 1943.

Wallis Clark was born in Essex, England, in 1882. He made his film debut in 1931 and amassed more than 100 film and television credits before his death in 1961. Clark also appeared with Brent in *The World Gone Mad* (1933). Clarence Muse, born in Baltimore, Maryland, in 1899, was inducted into the Black Filmmakers Hall of Fame in 1973. He died in 1979. Douglas Haig was born in New Orleans in 1920. He made his first film in 1928 and his last in 1937.

Director Irving Cummings was born in New York in 1888 and died in 1959. A former Broadway and silent film actor, he received an Oscar nomination for directing *Old Arizona* (1928). Cummings is best known for directing 20th Century–Fox films in the 1930s and 1940s, some of which featured Shirley Temple and Betty Grable.

Writer J. K. McGuinness was born in New York in 1893. He provided the story for *A Night at the Opera* (1935) and wrote the screenplay for *Rio Grande* (1950). McGuinness, who produced some films in the 1920s and 1930s, died in 1950.

Cinematographer (and director) Ted Tetzlaff was born in Los Angeles in 1903. Son of a race car driver and stuntman, he received an Oscar nomination for *The Talk of the Town* (1942). He died in 1995.

*Reviews:* "Although it is often melodramatic and scarcely convincing, and Mr. Lowe does not always succeed in lending to his portrayal the necessary sincerity—which, it is true, would not be an easy matter in the circumstances—its last scene was greeted with applause from an audience yesterday afternoon.... Evelyn Brent is capable as the sinister Val..." (*New York Times*, May 28, 1932).

"Essentially the narrative is trite, hashed-over.... It's all pretty far-fetched and improbable, but sustained by good direction and able performances" (*Variety*, May 31, 1932).

"All the actors are industrious but the material is banal, the direction clodhopper, the dialog dimwitted" (*Time*, June 6, 1932).

"[Y]ou may rest assured that this picture is good entertainment.... Evelyn Brent is colorful as the scarlet woman..." (*Hollywood Citizen News*, July 4, 1932).

"It's a corking thriller and it will keep anyone in his seat to the finish" (*Los Angeles Examiner*, July 4, 1932).

"Eddie Lowe ... turn[s] in one of the best performances of his career.... Betty Brent, perfectly cast, does a grand job of acting. The picture is splendidly produced, moves fast, thrills you with the unexpected.... It's good heart-thumping movie stuff" (*Movie Mirror*, July 1932).

"If you think you are fed up with courtroom pictures, don't make up your mind to pass them by until you have seen this. And don't miss the performance of Edmund Lowe, who carries off the honors. Evelyn Brent is seductive and does excellent work..." (*Photoplay*, July 1932).

## *The Crusader*

(Majestic Pictures Corp.) 72 min. Released on October 1, 1932.

*Survival Status:* [Re-release *Near Zero Hour*] Library of Congress (Washington, D.C.). Released on video (Sinister Cinema)

*Credits:* Director, Frank Strayer; story, Wilson Collison; adaptation; Edward T. Lowe; photography, Ira Morgan; art direction, Daniel Hall; film editor, Otis Garrett; sound, Earl Crain.

*Cast:* Evelyn Brent (Tess Brandon); H. B. Warner (Phillip Brandon); Lew Cody (Jimmy Dale); Ned Sparks (Eddie Crane); Walter Byron (Joe Carson); Marceline Day (Marcia Brandon); John St. Polis (Robert Henley); Arthur Hoyt (Oscar Shane); Ara Haswell (Madge); Joseph Girard (Corrigan); Syd Saylor (Harry Smaltz); Lloyd Ingraham (Alton).

Newspaperman Eddie Crane is out to get district attorney Phil Brandon. He's just too much of a crusader and goody-goody. Crane also blames him for the execution of a woman who some believed was simply protecting her honor.

Crane gets hold of a story that's guaranteed to hurt Brandon. It involves a scandal concerning Brandon's wife Tess. As colleague Shane says, "It's a pip of a story, all right." (Get used to that phrase because you're going to hear him say it about a hundred times.) Newspaper editor Henley doesn't want to print the story until it checks out.

Meanwhile, there's tension at the Brandon house between Marcia, Brandon's sister, and Tess. Tess warns Marcia that boyfriend Carson is a gangster. Marcia unpleasantly tells her it's none of her business. Tess puts in a call to former lover Jimmy Dale. They agree to meet.

"District Attorney's Wife Former Hostess in a Night Club" is the headline Crane pitches to his editor. The editor still isn't happy about it. Crane is fit to be tied. "Listen, you yellow belly. Tess Marlin was hostess in Jimmy Dale's Silver Bowl in [sic] 50th Street, New York, three years ago. She was a hot Mama and his girl. Get that? *His* girl."

Meanwhile, Tess meets with Jimmy at the Peacock Inn. He promises to talk to Marcia's beau and convince him to "drop the kid and get out of town." Jimmy, still crazy about Tess, wants her to protect herself and not let anyone know her true identity. Tess tells him that Marcia seems to have been on to her from the beginning. "She knows I don't belong."

Brandon continues to be a ruthless district attorney. He indicts the police chief on a bribery charge. Even members of the Citizens League have had it with him. They meet with him and remind him that they elected him to close speakeasies and road houses. Why, they ask, hasn't he closed the Peacock Inn? As they hastily leave, one of the hypocrites accidentally drops his "medicine" bottle.

Back at the Peacock Inn, Jimmy has a confrontation with prostitute Madge whom he asks not to frequent his establishment. "Have you ever seen one of the new hundred dollar bills?" he asks.

"Haven't seen one of the old ones yet," she sniffs. He gives her one—if she gets out and stays out. He advises her to go home to Mother. "You're the first man that ever talked decent to me, Mr. Dale," she says.

She recognizes that dirty dog Crane (a frequent patron of her services) on her way out. He wants to question Jimmy about the Silver Bowl. He specifically asks about Brandon's wife, but Jimmy denies knowing her. Unfortunately, Tess has just driven up. Tess tells Jimmy she's decided to tell Brandon who she is. Jimmy advises against it, and, again, assures her that he'll take care of it. He tells her to deny knowing him, no matter what happens. She agrees.

Later that night, Carson shows up at the Peacock Inn with Marcia. Jimmy asks him to drop the district attorney's sister, but Carson refuses. Carson tells Jimmy he knows about him and Tess, and then points a gun, concealed in his pocket, at Jimmy. "You spill. I spill. See?" Carson says.

A drunken Crane calls his editor and tells him he'll have a front page story for him soon. (This newspaper guy is unbelievable. In an earlier scene, after Jimmy comped his caviar dinner, Crane arrogantly signed the check. Then, while the waiter stood by, he flipped a coin and slapped it down hard on the table. He lifted his hand. The waiter moved to take the meager tip, but Crane snatched up the coin, telling the waiter, nope, he lost. Sheesh. He's definitely a stereotype of a newspaperman from the early talkie era. An aggressive, uncouth, hard-drinking, usually drunk, womanizing, frequently broke, do-anything-and-hurt-anyone-for-a-story type. He helps himself to freebies at every opportunity, often cigars, a handful of cigarettes, and, always, food.)

Still at the club, Carson starts to molest Marcia. "Don't be a child," he cajoles when she tries to get away. They struggle, his gun falls out, and Marcia shoots him.

She faints when Jimmy breaks into the room. Jimmy instructs that she be taken home and that Tess be told. Crane comes in and assumes it was Tess who fired the shot. "I shot him," Jimmy says.

"Yeah? Congratulations."

Jimmy tells him it was self defense. Crane doesn't buy it. He tells Jimmy he saw Tess in his office earlier and wants to know if she was the one who shot Carson. The cops are called. Jimmy continues to insist to Crane that he did it.

Marcia arrives home, and she's a heck of a lot more pleasant to Tess now (of course, now she's in big trouble, and Tess was right about Carson). Crane arrives at the Brandon house and tells the Asian-

American servant (in a racially insensitive scene) that he's a cop. Crane confronts Tess about seeing her in Jimmy's office—and says he saw her carried out after Carson was shot. He also tells her that Jimmy claims to be the shooter. Tess tells him she was the shooter.

After he leaves (the dolt puts a lit cigarette in an antique vase on his way out), Marcia tells Tess she'll confess to the murder. "You were not in that room tonight. Do you understand?" Tess asks.

Marcia is understandably curious why Tess is protecting her. "I'm not shielding you. I'm thinking of Phil," Tess says. Marcia says she'll tell Phil herself. "Have you ever had one thought that didn't concern yourself?" Tess asks, and we don't think it's a rhetorical question. "You've hated me from the moment your brother married me," she says a few minutes later. She tells Marcia that tomorrow's newspapers will tell the truth. "I was Jimmy Dale's sweetheart. And lived with him for a year." Believe it or not, Tess ends up comforting Marcia.

Police grill Jimmy, but he won't break. Meanwhile, Henley has second thoughts about running Crane's story. He wants to instead use this lead: "MYSTERY WOMAN INVOLVED IN MURDER! MAN SHOT IN PRIVATE DINING ROOM AT PEACOCK INN: Unknown Woman Spirited Away in Killing."

Crane and Henley go to Brandon's office. Jimmy soon joins them. "This is going to be good," Crane crows. Jimmy continues to say he is guilty and that no woman was involved. "Mr. Dale is lying. There was a woman in the room," Brandon announces. He asks who it was. Crane can't wait to tell Brandon. "You asked for it, and I'm going to give it to you right in the face. The woman in that room was your wife."

Brandon asks Henley if it's true. "I killed the name, Phil. I wouldn't run it."

Brandon asks for Tess to come up. Brandon tells Henley he knows about his wife's past. "Crane is the type of reporter who is a disgrace to any American newspaper," he says in a huge understatement. He goes on to say, "If my wife was anyone's sweetheart before she met me, I'm proud that it was a man who had the courage and principal to go to the electric chair in defense of a woman's good name." He adds that he still loves his wife. Henley says the story will not be printed. Brandon then drops the bombshell, telling everyone the woman in the private dining room was his sister. "Corrigan, go to my home. Arrest my sister for the murder of Jerry Lynn [Carson's real name]."

In the next scene, Crane has hired a lip reader to snoop using a telescope. He's spying on the jury room in Marcia's trial. Crane takes over (notice the lip reader flipping off Crane with gusto) and gives a play by play, ending with, "And the verdict is ... not guilty."

The headline reads: "JURY ACQUITS BRANDON GIRL!" Brandon comes out of the courtroom smiling, arm in arm with Marcia and Tess. In the final scene, Crane has a chat with Jimmy. Jimmy tells him he's leaving for Paris. Crane whispers something in

Jimmy's ear, but Jimmy shakes his head. "They don't allow 'em to come through the mail."

"Okay! Bring 'em back with ya."

The film starts off slow and talky, but the melodrama eventually packs a punch. Brent is still gorgeous, but this low-budget picture is a sign of things to come. There's also a hauntingly sad look about her. Brent was dealing with some difficult personal and professional issues when this was made.

The film was also released with the title *Should a Woman Tell?* The biggest flaw in the picture is Brandon's character. He's a sanctimonious, finger-pointing hypocrite who deserves his comeuppance. Also, the film's ending suggests that the rich and powerful deserve to get treated differently by the justice system.

Marceline Day also appeared with Brent in *The Mad Parade.* Her performance this time is much better, though the character is unsympathetic.

This was said to be H.B. Warner's one-thousandth role. [134] He was second-billed, behind Brent. Born Harry Byron Warner in London in 1875, Warner came from an acting family and performed on Broadway before making his film debut in 1914. He received an Oscar nomination for *Lost Horizon* (1937), but is probably best known for playing Mr. Gower, the elderly druggist in *It's a Wonderful Life* (1946). Warner died in 1958.

Lew Cody began his film career in 1914 and became a silent film star. Born Lewis Joseph Cote in New Hampshire in 1884, he was married to Mabel Normand from 1926 until her death in 1930. Cody died in 1934.

Ned Sparks had a gift for playing cynical. Born Edward Arthur Sparkman in Canada in 1883, he began his film career in 1915 but became famous with sound pictures. Lloyds of London once issued an insurance policy preventing damage to his career should anyone obtain a photograph of him smiling. He died in 1957.

Character actor Walter Byron, born in England in 1899, made his film debut in 1928 and died in 1972. John St. Polis was born in New Orleans, Louisiana, in 1873. He appeared in more than a hundred films following his screen debut in 1914, including playing alongside Mary Pickford in *Coquette* (1929), her first talkie. He also appeared with Brent in *Held to Answer* (1923), *The World Gone Mad* (1933) and *Mr. Wong, Detective* (1938). St. Polis died in 1946. Born in Colorado in 1874, Arthur Hoyt was a familiar face to moviegoers. He began his career in 1914 and is credited with almost three hundred motion picture appearances. Hoyt died in 1953. This was Ara Haswell's second appearance; her screen debut was in *I Take This Woman* in 1931. Joseph W. Girard was born in Williamsport, Pennsylvania, in 1871. He also appears with Brent in *The World Gone Mad* (1933). Girard died in 1949. Syd Saylor was born in Chicago in 1895. His long film and television career began in 1926 and included many appearances in Westerns. In the 1950s he was on the *Bozo, the Clown* television

show in Hollywood. Saylor died in 1962. He also appeared with Brent in *The World Gone Mad* (1933). Lloyd Ingraham was born in Rochelle, Illinois, in 1874. His film career began in 1913 and included credits for acting, directing, and writing. Ingraham died in 1956. He directed Brent in *Midnight Molly* (1925), and also appeared with her in *The World Gone Mad* (1933) and *The Seventh Victim* (1943).

Director Frank Strayer was born in Altoona, Pennsylvania in 1891. He directed many of the Blondie films in the 1930s and 1940s. He died in 1964. Writer Edward T. Lowe was born in Nashville, Tennessee, in 1890. Also a producer, he worked on Bulldog Drummond and Charlie Chan films, along with many other "B" pictures. Lowe's name appeared in the credits for *Broadway* (1928), *The World Gone Mad* (1933), *Daughter of Shanghai* (1938), and *Tip-Off Girls* (1938). Lowe died in 1973.

*Reviews:* "Thoroughly fine entertainment. Good story, excellent direction and strong, well-balanced cast.... Evelyn Brent ... and Lew Cody ... are both convincing" (*Film Daily,* October 5, 1932).

"*The Crusader* manages to combine most of the archaic elements of gangster-newspaper-administration film stories in an awkwardly arranged production.... Ned Sparks gives a good performance.... The rest of the cast ... never seems able to rise above the commonplaces of the lines and situations" (*New York Times,* October 8, 1932).

"Artificial characters throughout make *The Crusader* just another indie.... Producers can thank the director and the adapter for what might have been a good all around feature, being just what it is. There's no excuse, even in the indie field these days, for timid city editors, reporters who bulldoze managing editors and police chiefs, and for district attorneys who take up several minutes of film running time to preach to newspapermen" (*Variety,* October 11, 1932).

"This picture has action, suspense, and comedy.... Direction, acting, and settings are of high standard" (*Harrison's Reports,* October 29, 1932).

## *The World Gone Mad*

(Majestic Pictures Corp.) 80 min. Released on April 14, 1933.

*Survival Status:* Library of Congress (Washington, D.C.).

*Credits:* Producer, Phil Goldstein; director, Christy Cabanne; screen story, Edward T. Lowe; photography, Ira Morgan; art direction, Daniel Hall; film editor, Otis Garrett; sound engineer, Dean C. Daily.

*Cast:* Pat O'Brien (Andy Terrell); Evelyn Brent (Carlotta Lamont); Neil Hamilton (Lionel Houston); Mary Brian (Diane Cromwell); Louis Calhern (Christopher Bruno); J. Carrol Naish (Ramon Salvadore); Buster Phelps (Ralph Henderson); Richard Tucker (Graham Gaines); John St. Polis (Grover Cromwell); Geneva Mitchell (Evelyn Henderson); Wallis Clark (Avery Henderson); Huntley Gordon (Osborne); Max Davidson (Cohen); Joe Girard (Nichols); Lloyd Ingraham (Baird); Inez Courtney (Susan Bibens—telephone operator); Chester Gan (Andy's servant); Syd Saylor (Collins—janitor).

The opening shots feature a montage of skyscrapers. The camera zooms in on a sign: CROMWELL INVESTMENT CORPORATION. We're taken to

Mr. Cromwell's private office where he is advising an elderly company on an investment. The couple tell him, "Your word is good enough for us." Unfortunately, Cromwell's business associates are not so honest. Accountant Kemp warns Graham Gaines that he's been asked to meet with the district attorney. Gaines tells him to let him do the worrying.

The camera zooms into a directory inside one of the buildings: CONTINENTAL IMPORTING AND EXPORTING COMPANY. Christopher Bruno is listed as the president, and the office is 910. Bruno makes a deal with Gaines for $20,000 to knock off the district attorney. It goes down the chain of command until the last criminal says, "For one thousand dollar [sic] he is done, my friend." Oily hitman Ramon calmly returns to reading his book, *The Life and Loves of Casanova.*

Newspaperman Andy begs district attorney Avery Henderson for a story. Henderson says he can't yet tell him the details, but he's working on a case involving an investment scam. That night Henderson receives a phone call from "Nina," who pleads with him not to prosecute boyfriend Harley (an employee at Suburban Utilities). "I have evidence which proves there are others involved besides Harley. I'll give it to you if you'll just give him a chance." Henderson agrees to meet her at her apartment. She hangs up the phone and smiles at Ramon. He's polishing a gun.

Henderson goes to the apartment and is killed by Ramon. Andy arrives at the newspaper office (notice the signs designed to inspire the reporters, including one that says "Tell it ... in the FIRST PARAGRAPH"). He receives the shocking news about Henderson's murder. Even worse, Henderson was set up so it looks like he was keeping a love nest. He's not only dead, but his reputation as a family man is destroyed. Andy doesn't buy it, so he investigates. Meanwhile, Lionel Houston is made the new district attorney. The complication is that he's dating Diane Cromwell, daughter of the president of the corporation that was being investigated by Henderson.

Andy's investigation leads him to Ramon. He advises him to get out of town before he's arrested. Henderson's widow tells Andy and Lionel that her husband was in contact with a Harley Kemp at Suburban Utilities. She gives Lionel notes her husband had taken that seem to show Kemp was spending far more than he was earning. Lionel re-opens the investigation into Suburban Utilities. Gaines orders a hit on Lionel; this time the price is $30,000.

Andy, who apparently knows everybody in town, meets Bruno at a nightclub. A big-time womanizer with a black book filled with women's names and numbers, Andy eyes the performer. "She's *mine,*" Bruno harshly tells him. Bruno introduces him to Carlotta, his girlfriend (the woman who pretended to be Nina). Andy dances with Carlotta and tells her he has a message for her from Ramon. He follows her to her dressing room, and they hit it off. Bruno is not happy to find Andy playing footsie with her.

"DISTRICT ATTORNEY VICTIM OF HIT AND RUN DRIVER!: Lionel Houston Cheats Death in Auto Crash." Although Lionel is unhurt, he soon gets word that Harley Kemp "just blew his brains out."

Andy makes a date with Carlotta via the telephone. This is a cute scene where she pretends he's her dressmaker because Bruno is in the same room with her. The conversation is loaded with double entendres.

Lionel receives a note from dead man Harley Kemp: "Houston: I've falsified Suburban Utilities statements for over a year. The Cromwell Investment Corporation is rotten from top to bottom. It's more than I can face—so I'm taking the only way out. Harley Kemp." Lionel confronts Cromwell. It doesn't go well. Cromwell is indignant, and Diane takes her dad's side. Diane falls apart when Lionel leaves in a huff. "Never mind, sweetheart," Cromwell consoles. "If he's that big a fool, you don't want him." Cromwell leaves a message for Gaines to come to his house on an urgent matter.

In the next scene, Andy and Carlotta are drunk in bed together. Much of the scene is shot in shadows. At one point Carlotta says she wants to find her earring. She asks that the light be turned on. "Hey," she suddenly says, "what are you doing?" "I'm finding your earring," Andy says. "Well," she complains, "you look somewheres else."

Suddenly a light is turned on. Ramon is there with a gun. Carlotta tenderly kisses Ramon. "Well, if I'm not seven different kinds of a sap," Andy complains.

"You're not mad at me, are you, sucker?" Carlotta playfully asks.

Bruno shows up, and the bad guys force Andy to call Lionel. Andy tells Lionel he's sick and asks that he come to his apartment.

Gaines arrives at Cromwell's and is shown Kemp's note. He tells Cromwell it's true. "It was easy to start," Gaines confesses. "Impossible to stop." Cromwell tells Gaines he has a plan. They leave together with Cromwell driving. Diane finds a note from her father: "Diane—I find that Gaines has wrecked the company. I did not know—but by trusting him I am equally responsible. The insurance which Gaines and I carry for the corporation will help make good the losses of those who had faith in me. Don't blame Houston—Forgive me, dear—Dad." Cromwell intentionally causes an automobile accident, killing himself and Gaines.

Meanwhile, Lionel arrives at Andy's apartment. Ramon pulls a gun on him. After untying Andy, they come out of Andy's bedroom only to be confronted by a good guy with a gun. Ramon is shot, and Carlotta hurries to him (Bruno finally realizes Carlotta has been two-timing him). Andy phones widow Henderson and reads her the headline in the next edition: "AVERY HENDERSON EXONERATED: District Attorney Victim of Frame-Up."

Months pass. Andy arrives late at the marriage ceremony between Lionel and Diane without pants (don't ask). Everyone laughs.

Brent is a great femme fatale. She's sexy and evil

and could have had a wonderful career playing this kind of modern vamp.

The flick has a great cast, and O'Brien is particularly good in this fun cheapie. He is a master of fast talking, and you get to see him at his best here. Hamilton is only a little bit less stiff than in *Darkened Rooms*.

On February 12, 1933, the *New York Times* reported that Brent and O'Brien had been cast in *The Public Be Damned*. The British release title was *The Public Be Hanged*. Brent received second billing after O'Brien. This was her second film with low-budget Majestic Pictures.

O'Brien was born in Milwaukee, Wisconsin, in 1899. Originally a stage performer, he began his long film and television career in 1930. His last television performance was as Uncle Joe on *Happy Days*. O'Brien died in 1983.

Mary Brian, born Louise Byrdie Dantzler in Corsicana, Texas, in 1906, was nicknamed "The Sweetest Girl in Pictures." She made her screen debut as Wendy in *Peter Pan* (1924). Brian died in 2002.

Louis Calhern was born Carl Vogt in Brooklyn in 1895. His four wives (all marriages ended in divorce) were Ilka Chase, Julia Hoyt, Natalie Schafer, and Marianne Stewart. Nominated for an Oscar for *The Magnificent Yankee* (1950), he died in 1956.

J. Carrol Naish was born in New York in 1896. He received Oscar nominations for *Sahara* (1943) and *A Medal for Benny* (1945). He also appeared with Brent in *Night Club Scandal* (1937), *Daughter of Shanghai* (1937), *Tip-Off Girls* (1938), and *Forced Landing* (1941). Naish, who often played ethnic characters, died in 1973.

Buster Phelps, born Silas Vernon Phelps, Jr., in Los Angeles in 1926, made his film debut in 1930. His last film credit was in 1949, and he died in 1983. Richard Tucker was born in Brooklyn in 1884. He began acting in films in 1911. Credited with being the first member of the Screen Actors Guild, he died in 1942. He appeared with Brent in *Women's Wares* (1927), *Madonna of the Streets* (1930), *The World Gone Mad* (1933), and *Symphony of Living* (1935). Geneva Mitchell was born in Medarsyville, Indiana, in 1908. A former Ziegfeld chorus girl, she suffered from poor health, eventually dying in 1949. She was once a fiancée of Lowell Sherman. Huntley Gordon was born in Canada in 1887. He made his film debut in 1916. Sometimes credited as Huntly Gordon, he died in 1956. He also appeared with Brent in *The Glorious Lady* (1919). Max Davidson began his film career in 1912. Born in Berlin, Germany, in 1875, he died in 1950. Chester Gan, born in San Francisco in 1908, began his career in 1932. Often typecast in stereotypical Asian roles, he appeared in a hundred or so films before his death in 1959.

Producer Phil Goldstone was born in Poland in 1893. Also a director, he was the founder of the Motion Picture Relief Fund. Goldstone, sometimes credited as Phil Stone, died in 1963.

Director Christy Cabanne was born in St. Louis, Missouri, in 1888. Cabanne was also an actor, writer, and producer. He began his career in 1911 and was D.W. Griffith's assistant on such films as *The Birth of a Nation* (1915) and *Intolerance* (1916). He died in 1950.

*Reviews:* "Excellent cast registers strong in first-rate drama.... A lot of suspenseful entertainment and clever comedy.... [T]he cast carry on intelligently and convincingly" (*Film Daily*, April 15, 1933).

"It is a picture which is constantly implausible, but through the audacity of its incidents it does succeed in inveigling one's attention.... It matters not whether what [the characters] do is logical as long as it does not hinder the flow of the narrative" (*New York Times*, April 15, 1933).

"Newspaper-reporter vs. crook story developed with many persuasive angles, a neat turn of humor, but weakened by inexpert literary handling.... Cast of standard names delivers excellent service in the telling, though the names may not mean a great deal on the marquee" (*Variety*, April 18, 1933).

"A fairly exciting melodrama; it arouses human interest and suspense, and although at times the story is implausible it holds one's attention to the very end" (*Harrison's Reports*, April 22, 1933).

"[I]t has fallen short of satisfying audiences to the degree promised by excellent performances and a lively story.... There are too many characters and too many issues" (*Los Angeles Times*, April 23, 1933).

"Good enough for any theatre. Some might consider a little strange. Pleased our patrons" (*Motion Picture Herald*, September 23, 1933).

## Home on the Range

[Alternate Title: *Zane Grey's Home on the Range*] (Paramount) 55 min. Released on December 21, 1934.

*Survival Status:* Library of Congress (Washington, D.C.)

*Credits:* Producers, Adolph Zukor, Harold Hurley; executive producer, Emanuel Cohen; director, Arthur Jacobson; screenplay, Ethel Doherty, Grant Garrett; adaptation, Charles Logue; based on the novel *Code of the West* by Zane Grey; photography, William C. Mellor; art direction, Hans Dreier, Earl Hedrick; film editor, Jack Dennis.

*Cast:* Jackie Coogan (Jack Hatfield); Randolph Scott (Tom Hatfield); Evelyn Brent (Georgie Haley); Dean Jagger (Boyd Thurman); Addison Richards (Beady Pierce); Fuzzy Knight ("Cracker" Williams); Ann Sheridan (Elsie Brownly); Allen Wood ("Flash" Roberts); Richard Carle (James Butts); Howard Wilson (Bill Morris); Philip Morris (Benson); Albert Hart (Undertaker); Ralph Remley (Brown); C. L. Sherwood (Shorty); Francis Sayles (Hotel clerk); Jack Clark (Sheriff); Alfred Delcambre (Lem); Joe Morrison.

The working title was *Code of the West*. However, the title was changed when the producers received permission to use the song title. Since it was after the film was shot, retakes were shot which incorporated the song.

Some filming took place at Malibu Lake. One of the co-stars was Ghost, a horse who was apparently treated better than the stars. "The night was pretty cold and Evelyn Brent and Randolph Scott weren't feeling too well because of slight cases of the grip. On location at Malibu Lake they were told to stand by for a plunge into the cold waters.... They were to make the plunge astride Ghost, a trained horse. Everything was set when the owner of Ghost rushed in and said: 'I can't let Ghost do that. Get him a double. He might get pneumonia.' 'Some nag,' mumbled Brent and Scott as a substitute was brought up for the animal."[135]

In 1922, Famous Players–Lasky released a silent version bearing the novel's title. Evelyn's part was played by Constance Bennett, and Scott's by Owen Moore.

Publicity materials declared: "All the thrills of the pioneer days in a fighting story of Western justice shot from the end of a six-gun!"

Jackie Coogan, born in Los Angeles in 1914, was a child star who made a fortune. Unfortunately, his mother looted his bank account. As a result, the California legislature passed the Coogan Act (also known as the Child Actors Bill) which protected the earnings of young actors. Coogan was married to Betty Grable from 1937 to 1939. Known as Uncle Fester to baby boomers when he appeared on *The Addams Family* in the 1960s, Coogan died in 1984.

Randolph Scott was born in Virginia in 1898 and became one of Hollywood's most popular Western actors. He died in 1987.

Dean Jagger, born in Ohio in 1903, won an Oscar for *Twelve O'clock High* (1949) and received Emmy nominations for *Mr. Novak* in the 1960s. He died in 1991.

Ann Sheridan, then billed as Clara Lou Sheridan, played dance hall girl Elsie. Born in Denton, Texas, in 1915, Sheridan became a popular leading lady in the 1930s and 1940s. She died in 1967 while working on the television show *Pistols 'n' Petticoats.*

*Reviews:* "It is good entertainment for those who like horse 'operys'" (*Illustrated Daily News* [Los Angeles], December 26, 1934).

"This film is chiefly remarkable for the comeback of Evelyn Brent, who shows up nicely despite her long absence from the screen; the reappearance of a grown-up Jackie Coogan as the hero's kid brother; and the work of Ann Sheridan in her first part of any length" (*Dallas Morning News*, January 6, 1935).

"Good Western with plenty [of] action and bringing back Jackie Coogan in [a] grownup role" (*Film Daily*, February 8, 1935).

"It's a picture which ... follows tried and well-beaten paths, developing its menace in the same old way.... Picture is short on running time, 54 minutes, and pans out as fair entertainment" (*Variety*, February 12, 1935).

"The narrative progresses by fits and starts, with depressing interims during which you have the suspicion that the scenarists are just behind the camera working up something for the next scene" (*New York Times*, February 13, 1935).

"This is an up-to-date Western.... Evelyn Brent is the girl card-sharp who goes straight.... A few more like this should make Westerns more popular" (*Photoplay*, February 1935).

## Symphony of Living

(Invincible Pictures Corp.) 73 min. Released on January 20, 1935.

*Survival Status:* British Film Institute/National Film and Television Archive (London); Library of Congress (Washington, D.C.); The Museum of Modern Art (New York City). Released on video (Alpha).

*Credits*: Producer, Maury M. Cohen; supervisor, Lon Young; director, Frank R. Strayer; assistant director, Melville Shyer; story and adaptation, Charles Spencer Belden; photography, M. A. Andersen; art director, Edward C. Jewell; film editor, Roland Reed; music director, Lee Zahler; recording engineer, L. E. Clark.

*Cast:* Evelyn Brent (Paula Grieg); Al Shean (Adolph Grieg); Charles Judels (Rozzini); John Darrow (Richard Grieg); Albert Conti (Mancini); Lester Lee (Carl Rupert); Richard Tucker (Michael Rupert); Gigi Parrish (Carmen Rozzini); John Harron (Herb Livingstone); Ferike Boros (Mary Schultz); Ferdinand Schuman-Heink (The doctor); Carl Stockdale (Judge); William Worthington (Symphony Chairman); Dimitrios Alexis (Music lover); Les Goodwins (Oboe player); Gregory Golubeff (Musician); John Winters (Midget).

The film opens at a concert hall. Adolph is a capable symphony violinist whose home life is not so sweet. He's raised a couple of kids, Richard and Paula, who are lazy, insolent brats. "You and Richard," Adolph complains to Paula, "you only care for a good time."

Just before Adolph gets the opportunity to play his dream solo in Offenbach's *Orpheus in Hades* he suffers a hand injury. "Well, it's your own fault," Richard says. Adolph suggests Richard and Paula get a job to help out. "Paula ain't the type, and I can't find anything that suits me!" Richard says.

Paula sends a telegram from Atlantic City to her brother: "MARRIED MICHAEL HERE TONIGHT TOLD YOU I WAS MEANT FOR ORCHIDS INSTEAD OF ONIONS." Richard pawns his dad's cello and leaves town. He leaves a note for his dad: "I'll mail you the pawn ticket on your cello—I'm tired of this place, too. R." His kids are creeps, and Adolph's heart is broken.

Two years later, Adolph reads a blurb about Paula in the newspaper: "Mr. and Mrs. Michael Rupert have returned to their home at Meadowbrook after a two-year tour of the world. Long Island social circles will be made gayer by the arrival of Mrs. Rupert...."

Although Adolph's career and finances have taken a downward turn, it appears Paula is doing fine. We see her in her mansion with young son Carl. She's still a huge bitch. The child starts banging on the piano, and brittle, tightly wound Paula has a fit, telling the nanny, "Marie, haven't I told you to keep him away from the piano? That noise would drive anyone mad." She also says, "Keep him away from anything musical. I know what I'm talking about."

Her much older husband lays into her. "Paula, you're about as selfish and shallow as anyone could be." Neither partner feels he or she got a good deal from the marriage. "I see no reason for showing a charm and happiness I don't feel," Paula sullenly says.

**Symphony of Living *pressbook cover (1935).***

Richard shows up at Adolph's, borrows money, and uses his address for mail fraud. Finally, the cops come and arrest Richard. Paula's husband reads about it in the newspaper. He tells Paula he wants a separation. At first, she's resistant, but he offers her a financial settlement. "Hmm. A change might do me good at that," she concludes. Michael suggests he keep Carl, and, in return, he'll give her $50,000. "Make it a hundred thousand," Paula counters. They settle at $75,000 with the condition that Paula stays away from both of them. "You've been an uncongenial wife and a disinterested mother for years," Michael tells her. "Save your compliments," Paula says. She agrees to the settlement. "You get the cash," Michael concludes. "I keep Carl." (Poor Carl has overheard the conversation: *Hello, Dr. Freud!*)

Michael goes on a long trip and leaves Carl in the care of his former nurse, Mary. This being a Hollywood movie, Mary hires Adolph to teach Carl the violin. Neither knows they're related. After two years of training, Carl auditions in front of Mancini. They plan a recital. However, evil Paula enters the picture again. Unknowingly, she runs into them at the concert hall and comes up with a different plan for Carl's future. "You're coming home with Mother." She wants to take him to Europe for additional training.

Headline: "SENSATIONAL COURT BATTLE OVER BOY PRODIGY." The custody battle between Michael and Paula is decided when the judge lets Carl choose who he wants as custodian. "Why," he says, "I choose my grandfather, Adolph Grieg." That night, Carl is soloist at the concert. He's a sensation.

Brent received top billing over Shean. Her role is the meanest, most despicable character she probably ever played. There is not an ounce of warmth in Paula. Director Strayer discovered that Brent was often better in rehearsals than when the film was running. According to the film's pressbook, "He did not mention it to her, but he arranged a secret signal with his staff to start the camera and sound recorder without her knowing it. One of the most dramatic scenes in the production was photographed while she thought she was rehearsing, and Director Strayer says it is one of the most gripping scenes in the en-

They go to the Cosmopolitan Concert Hall that night for a concert, and Paula is shocked to see her father hanging around outside. He hurries up to her, but she turns away. Her husband, not knowing who he is, drops a donation in Adolph's hat. Adolph weeps.

Later that night, a couple of Adolph's friends discover him asleep outside the concert hall. Mancini and Rossini feed the poor man and help him start the Adolph Grieg Studio of Music. Of course, most of his students are unmotivated and untalented.

Meanwhile, Paula tells Richard about the Grieg studio and suggests he hit him up for money. She also fires her son's violin teacher. "Your father allows you to have these teachers, but he doesn't have to stay here and listen to them." She sighs and shakes her head. "You're your grandfather all over again." Paula has never told Carl about Adolph. When he eagerly asks about him, she says, "It's impolite to ask questions." She also tells Carl to forget about music. Carl is heartbroken.

tire picture."[136] Strayer did not, however, identify the scene.

According to the pressbook, assistant director Melville Shyer, not terribly surprisingly, had a tough time finding a midget who could play the bass violin. Finally, Shyer found a non-actor, Los Angeles department store executive John Winters.

*Symphony of Living* is a poignant film that works mainly due to the efforts of former vaudeville star Shean. He's a sympathetic figure, almost pathetic, who retains his goodness despite terrible setbacks and disappointments—and rotten kids. It's one of those films, like Yasujiro Ozu's *Tokyo Story* (1953), that makes you want to call your parents and apologize for every bad thing you've ever done.

Born Alfred Schoenberg in Germany in 1868, Shean was raised in the United States where he teamed with partner Gallagher for a popular vaudeville team. Their theme song was "Absolutely, Mr. Gallagher—Positively, Mr. Shean." An uncle to the Marx Brothers, Shean enjoyed a successful career as a character actor in the 1930s and 1940s. He died in 1949.

Charles Judels, born in the Netherlands in 1882, began his long film career in 1915. He was the voice of Stromboli in *Jiminy Cricket's Christmas*. Judels also appeared with Brent in *High Pressure* (1932). Adept at various accents, he died in 1969.

Lester Lee was thirteen when he appeared in *Symphony of Living*. The child prodigy had been a soloist with the Los Angeles Philharmonic Orchestra.

Born Harry Simpson in New Jersey in 1907, John Darrow was an actor in the 1920s and 1930s before turning his attention to talent agenting in the mid–1930s. He died in 1980.

Albert Conti was born in 1887 in what is now Trieste, Italy. A discovery of Erich von Stroheim, he made his film debut in 1923 and eventually quit acting to work in MGM's wardrobe department. He died in 1967. Conti also appeared with Brent in *Hollywood Boulevard* (1936).

Gigi Parrish was a 1934 WAMPAS Baby Star. Born Katherine Gertrude McElray in Cambridge, Massachusetts, in 1912, she married writer and artist Dillwynn Parrish (cousin of Maxfield Parrish) when she was 15. They divorced in 1936, and the following year she married John Weld. Parrish and Weld owned a Laguna Beach, California, newspaper from 1949 to 1965. She died in 2006.

John Harron was born in New York in 1903. His brother was silent movie star Robert Harron (who died under mysterious conditions in 1920). Married to actress Betty Westmore, Harron died in 1939 of spinal meningitis. Ferdinand Schuman-Heink was born in Germany in 1893. The son of opera singer Madame Ernestine Schuman-Heink, he died in 1958. Ferike Boros, born in Hungary in 1880, was a familiar face to moviegoers in the 1930s and 1940s. She died in 1951. Carl Stockdale, born in Worthington, Minnesota, in 1874, began his long career in 1913. By the time he died in 1953, he had appeared in more

than two hundred films. He also appeared with Brent in *Dangerous Lady* (1941). William Worthington was born in Troy, New York, in 1872. He made his film debut in 1913 and was also a silent film director. Worthington died in 1941. Les Goodwins, born in London in 1899, was primarily a writer and director—not an actor. He directed several Mexican Spitfire films and eventually turned his attention to directing television, including such shows as *Highway Patrol*, *My Favorite Martian*, and *F Troop*. Goodwins died in 1969.

Writer Charles Spencer Belden was born in Montclair, New Jersey, in 1904. He wrote the play that *Mystery of the Wax Museum* (1933) was based on, along with several Charlie Chan screenplays. Belden died in 1954.

*Reviews:* "Way above average for a programmer.... [T]here's so much good heart and home appeal it wins through over and above the fluff" (*Variety*, July 3, 1935).

"Certain emotional power and good music relieve the tedium and pathos of this story of a thwarted genius who finds triumph in the glories of his prodigy" (*Photoplay*, August 1935).

## *Without Children*

(Liberty Pictures Corp.) 85 min. Released on April 15, 1935.

*Survival Status:* Library of Congress (Washington, D.C.).

*Credits:* Producer, M. H. Hoffman; associate producer, M. H. Hoffman Jr.; director, William Nigh; suggested by the short story "Eyes of Youth" by Mrs. Woodrow Wilson; story, continuity and dialogue, Gertrude Orr; photography, Harry Neumann; film editor, Mildred Johnston; music supervisor, A. F. Meyer; sound, R. E. Tyler; production manager, Rudolph Flothow.

*Cast:* Marguerite Churchill (Sue Cole); Bruce Cabot (David F. Cole); Evelyn Brent (Shirley Ross Cole); Reginald Denny (Phil Graham); Dorothy Lee (Carol Cole); William Janney (David "Sonny" Cole, Jr.); Dickie Moore (David "Sonny" Cole, Jr., as a child); Cora Sue Collins (Carol Cole, as a child); Lillian Harmer (Frieda); Joan Woodbury (Secretary).

In this low-budget drama, an architect's affair leads to divorce. He leaves for Europe with his new wife while the first wife struggles to raise their two children. Finally, he realizes his family needs him and returns to them.

Production took place in August 1934. It was re-released in 1936 with a new title, *Penthouse Party*.

Nancy Mann Waddel Wilson, also known as Mrs. Wilson Woodrow and Mrs. Woodrow Wilson, was born Nancy Mann in 1875. She died in 1935. And, no, the writer was *not* the wife of the president. She was the estranged wife of Wilson's cousin James Wilson Woodrow—and a woman with a pretty savvy marketing strategy.

Marguerite Churchill was born in Kansas City, Missouri, in 1910. She made her film debut in 1929 but appeared in less than thirty films. Churchill was married to actor George O'Brien from 1933 to 1948. Her children included novelist Darcy O'Brien and classical bassist Orin O'Brien. Churchill died in Oklahoma in 2000. She had a memorable role in *Dracula's Daughter* (1936).

Bruce Cabot, born Etienne Pelissier Jacques de Bujac in Carlsbad, New Mexico, in 1904, made his film debut in 1931 and was still making occasional film and television appearances up until his death in 1972. His best-known film might have been *King Kong* (1933). One of his ex-wives was actress Adrienne Ames.

Dorothy Lee, born Marjorie Millsap in Los Angeles in 1911, was a former vaudevillian and big band singer. She married at least six times, including one oh-so-brief marriage in 1931 to gossip columnist Jimmy Fidler. Lee, who often appeared in Wheeler and Woolsey films, died in San Diego in 1999.

Child actor Dickie Moore was born John Richard Moore, Jr., in Los Angeles in 1925. He made his first film appearances in the late 1920s and became quite popular in the 1930s. Moore eventually left motion pictures and became a public relations executive. In 1988 he married actress Jane Powell.

Cora Sue Collins, born in Beckley, West Virginia, in 1927, made her film debut in 1927. She made her last film in 1945. William Janney was born in New York City in 1908. He made his film debut in 1929 and appeared in films until 1937. He died in 1992. Janney also appeared with Brent in *Hopalong Cassidy Returns* (1936). Born Joanne Woodbury in Los Angeles in 1915, Joan Woodbury was trained as a dancer. She specialized in exotic roles as well as Westerns. She is probably best remember for playing the title character in *Brenda Starr, Reporter*, a 1945 Columbia serial. Divorced from Henry Wilcoxon, she later became a stage producer and director and cofounded the Valley Player's Guild in Palm Springs with second husband Ray Mitchell. Woodbury, a great-niece of the Woodbury Soap's founder, died in 1989.

## The Nitwits

(RKO Radio Pictures) 81 min. Released on June 7, 1935.
*Survival Status:* British Film Institute/National Film and Television Archive (London); UCLA Film and Television Archive (Los Angeles).
*Credits:* Associate producer, Lee Marcus; director, George Stevens; screenplay, Al Boasberg, Fred Guiol; story, Stuart Palmer; contributor to dialogue, Grant Garrett; contributor to comedy construction, Leslie Goodwins; photography, Edward Cronjager; art direction, Van Nest Polglase; art direction associate, Perry Ferguson; film editor, John Lockert; musical director, Roy Webb; sound, P. J. Faulkner, Jr.; music and lyrics, "Music in my Heart" by Dorothy Fields and Jimmy McHugh; "You Opened My Eyes" by L. Wolfe Gilbert and Felix Bernard.
*Cast:* Bert Wheeler (Johnny); Robert Woolsey (Newton); Fred Keating (William Darrell); Betty Grable (Mary Roberts); Evelyn Brent (Alice Lake); Erik Rhodes (George Clark); Hale Hamilton (Winfield Lake); Charles Wilson (Captain Jennings); Arthur Aylesworth (Lurch); Willie Best (Sleepy); Lew Kelly (J. Gabriel Hazel); Dorothy Granger (Phyllis); Edgar Dearing (Officer Barney Riley); Donald Haines (Hal); Arthur Treacher.

The movie begins with a rendition of "You Opened My Eyes" by several different performers on the fifth floor of the Lake Publishing Company. The company's motto is "LAKE SONGS MAKE THE WORLD SING."

In the same building, Johnny works with Newton at a cigar stand. Inventor Newton has come up with a machine that makes people tell the truth. "It's the greatest idea I've ever had," Newton says. "And, boy, you know I've had a lot of them."

"Yeah, but none of them ever worked," Johnny replies.

"A mere coincidence," Newton tells him.

Johnny's girlfriend Mary works for lecherous Mr. Lake at the music publishing company. Mr. Lake's wife visits him in his office to show him a fourth letter promising the notorious criminal "Black Widow" will strike unless money is paid.

The Lakes interview private detective Darrell. We are next treated to a song-and-dance (mostly song) routine with Mary and Johnny singing "Music in my Heart." (This version appears on the Betty Grable CD compilation *The Pin-Up Girl* [Jasmine Records].) In an entertaining scene Newton pitches a song to Mr. Lake. The song, "The Black Widow Is Gonna Get You If You Don't Watch Out," only succeeds in scaring the fire out of Mr. Lake. (The movie may be spoofing the novelty song "Lon Chaney's Gonna Get You If You Don't Watch Out," which was performed by Gus Edwards in *The Hollywood Revue of 1929.*)

Johnny makes Mary quit her job when he catches Mr. Lake pawing her. Although the Lakes have decided to hire Darrell, the detective fails to save Mr. Lake's life. A toy spider is lowered from the ceiling onto Mr. Lake's desk. When he looks up at the ceiling, he is shot and killed. Mary is found hiding on the balcony with a gun and is arrested.

Mrs. Lake receives another note from the Black Widow. Frightened, she decides to pay. Darrell and the police lay a trap for the Black Widow. Hilarity ensues as a series of events that night results in the identification and capture of the Black Widow. The climax takes place in a stage costume and property warehouse. The Black Widow turns out to be Darrell.

This is an enjoyable, fun film that runs a bit too long (and has entirely too many scenes of all manner of heavy items—bottles, crockery, and even a bathtub—crashing onto skulls) but still has a few giggles. In one of the best scenes, Wheeler and Woolsey borrow a pair of stilts to visit Mary in jail. These aren't just any stilts—they're the tallest stilts you're likely to ever see. After Wheeler mistakenly sings to several hardened criminals, he finally finds Mary (still in her smart and snazzy plaid outfit instead of jail-issue garb), and they begin a rendition of "You Opened My Eyes."

The picture is loaded with great lines. At one point, the captain asks Newton if he shot Lake in self-defense. Newton replies, "No, I shot him through the heart."

Songwriter Lew Kelly asks Newton, "I'm trying to

find a rhyme—what goes with oranges?" "Gin," replies Newton, without missing a beat.

Wheeler and Woolsey might be one of the most underrated comedy duos in pictures. At the time they were a popular comedy team who often spoofed Hollywood films; they're largely forgotten now. Previous pictures had poked fun at costume dramas, gangster and prison pictures, war films, and Westerns. This one spoofs murder mysteries. For those not familiar with Wheeler and Woolsey, their act has a real vaudeville feel, which makes sense since they were popular vaudeville performers. Woolsey, 49 when he died of a kidney ailment only three years after this film was released, is similar to an older George Burns, complete with ever-present cigar and black, round eyeglasses. He even physically favors Burns. (A comparison could also be made with Walter Catlett who used glasses and cigars as props.) Born in Oakland, California, in 1888, Woolsey had a hard luck childhood. He was a jockey and then a bellboy before he became a vaudeville entertainer. Woolsey died on Halloween 1938 in Malibu.

Bert Wheeler was born in New Jersey in 1895. With first wife Margaret (Betty) Grae, he formed a vaudeville team that performed until their divorce in 1926. The following year he was teamed with Woolsey in Ziegfeld's stage version of Rio Rita. They made the film version in 1929. Wheeler continued his acting career after Woolsey's death, but not with the same amount of success. His last work was on television, including playing Smokey Joe on TV's Brave Eagle in 1956. He died in 1968.

Brent was fifth-billed and has a thankless role as the cold, mean-spirited, jealous wife of murder victim Mr. Lake. She does fine, but the role is one-dimensional and asks little of her. She has no memorable lines. Costumers Bernard Newman and Edith Clark chose furs and glamorous black designs for Brent in this film. She is a red herring, dressed like a black widow and playing a not-so-grieving wife.

Working titles included Nitwits and Murder Song. The budget was $239,000. Much of the money was probably spent on the stunning art deco sets supervised by Van Nest Polglase (born in Brooklyn, New York in 1898), who was also responsible for the set design on Citizen Kane (1941), and received Oscar nominations for his work on The Gay Divorcee (1934), Top Hat (1935), Carefree (1938), Love Affair (1939), and My Favorite Wife (1940). Polglase, who'd studied architecture and interior design, died in a house fire in 1968.

Someone may have been pulling someone's leg, but Elizabeth Yeaman reported in February 1935 that the film would not be a typical Wheeler and Woolsey comedy. "It is not a gag comedy in any sense of the word. It is a dramatic story, I am told, and Wheeler and Woolsey will merely [be] featured as comedy relief in the film."[137]

Director George Stevens went on to direct such wonderful films as Gunga Din (1939), The Talk of the Town (1942), I Remember Mama (1948), and Shane (1953). He won Oscars for A Place in the Sun (1951) and Giant (1956). Born in Oakland, California, in 1904, he died in 1975.

Writer Fred Guiol was also a director, producer, and all-around general film crewperson. Born in San Francisco in 1898, he began his career with D.W. Griffith. Guiol often worked with director George Stevens. He received an Oscar nomination (with Ivan Moffat) for writing Giant (1956). Guiol died in 1964.

Mystery and detective novelist Stuart Palmer (1905–1968) provided the story. He was the creator of Hildegarde Withers, who became a character in several RKO programmers starring Edna May Oliver.

It would take several more years and pictures before Betty Grable became a star, but you can clearly see her charm and sweet personality in this early effort. She also sings and dances, which is exactly what you want from Grable. Born Elizabeth Ruth Grable in St. Louis, Missouri, in 1916, she was one of Hollywood's top stars in the 1940s. Her film career began in 1929, but it wasn't until years later that she became a sensation, particularly as a pin-up model and musical film star. Married and divorced from Jackie Coogan and Harry James, she died in 1973.

Fred Keating was born in New York in 1897. He made his screen debut in 1934 and then appeared in only a handful of film appearances. He died in 1961. Erik Rhodes was born in what is now Oklahoma in 1906. He began his film career in 1934 and died in 1990. Hale Hamilton was born in Fort Madison, Iowa, in 1883. He began his long career in 1915, appearing in many films, particularly in the 1930s. He died in 1942. Charles Wilson began his film career in the late 1920s. Born in New York in 1894, he appeared in hundreds of films until his death in 1948. Arthur

**Despite her smile, Brent was struggling by the mid–1930s.**

Aylesworth was born in Rhode Island in 1883. He also appears with Brent in *The President's Mystery* (1936). He died in 1946. Arthur Treacher, born in England in 1894, played the British gentleman who keeps falling down the stairs with tennis net, rackets, and balls. He was often cast as a butler in Hollywood pictures. Those who grew up in the 1960s will remember him as Merv Griffin's talk show co-host. He was also the spokesperson for the fast food company Arthur Treacher's Fish and Chips. Treacher died in 1975.

Typical of movies of its time period, *The Nitwits* features numerous examples of racial insensitivity. Blacks are shown playing dice and gambling; getting frightened and wide-eyed; and appearing a tad lazy. According to the Internet Movie Database, Willie Best, who played Sleepy, told an interviewer in 1934: "I often think about these roles I have to play. Most of them are pretty broad. Sometimes I tell the director and he cuts out the real bad parts.... But what's an actor going to do? Either you do it or get out." Best, who was also billed as Sleep 'n' Eat, was born in Sunflower, Mississippi, in 1913. In addition to his film acting, he was a regular on television shows such as *Waterfront*, *The Stu Erwin Show*, and *My Little Margie*. He died in 1962.

Born in St. Louis, Missouri, in 1879, Lew Kelly appeared in more than two hundred films before his death in 1944. Dorothy Granger was born in New London, Ohio, in 1912. A beauty contest winner, she made more than two hundred film and television appearances (mostly comedies and Westerns) and retired in the 1960s. She died in 1995. Donald Haines, born in 1918, made his screen debut in 1930. He played Skinny in several Bowery Boys films. Haines was killed in action in World War II in 1941. Edgar Dearing (1893–1974) was born in Ceres, California. He later appeared with Brent in *Hollywood Boulevard* (1936) and *Ellery Queen and the Murder Ring* (1941), again playing policemen in both films. Dearing, who often played cops, began his career in 1924 in the Harold Lloyd film *Hot Water* playing a motorcycle cop. Dearing made more than three hundred film and television appearances.

Reviews: "It moves swiftly, it has some very funny gags and it attains a lightness and sureness which makes it most entertaining..." (*Los Angeles Examiner*, June 14, 1935).

"If you are looking for a picture which combines pathos, slapstick comedy, murder, and very funny gags, you won't have to look farther than Warners' Downtown this week where *The Nitwits* is current. The title doesn't do justice to the picture. I doubt if any title could be made to fit the film" (*Los Angeles Evening Herald Express*, June 14, 1935).

"Not a bad job, but [it] runs too long for best results in spite of some undeniably funny business and a finish that moves with the speed of the oldtime pantomime slapstick" (*Variety*, June 26, 1935).

"Wheeler and Woolsey mixed up in a murder case are at their funniest. The gags and giggles and roars are so fast you have to hang on or roll in the aisle.... It is rowdy, hilarious, and not a dull moment" (*Photoplay*, August 1935).

# Speed Limited

(Regent Pictures, Inc.) 56 min. Released November 26, 1935.

*Survival Status:* UCLA Film and Television Archive (Los Angeles).

*Credits:* Producer, George P. Regan, Jr.; director, Al Herman; story and screenplay, Ralph Graves; photography, William Hyer; film editor, Dan Milner; settings, Fred Preble; assistant director, Gordon Griffith; sound, Dave Stoner.

*Cast:* Ralph Graves (Jerry Paley); Evelyn Brent (Natalie); Claudia Dell (Marjorie); Andy Rice, Jr. (Smitty); Walter Worden (G-man); Vance Carroll (Tommy); Snowflake (Porter); Gordon Griffith (G-man); Ellen Corby (Secretary); Bobby Burns (Farmer); Ray Turner (Porter with telegram).

Jerry Paley is kidnapped from a train and taken to District 14, Department of Justice. It turns out to be a gag pulled by his FBI buddies who were instructed to "kidnap" him from the California Limited on his way to a Hollywood vacation.

"Well, that's ... uh ... rather disconcerting," a disappointed Paley says.

The ransom money from a kidnapping gang has been traced to Las Vegas. Paley is sent there and meets Marjorie, who develops a major crush on him. Natalie, one of the gangsters, tries to change a hundred in a drugstore, but the attendant calls the police. She is followed by the cops, crashes her car, but manages to escape. When Marjorie shows up at the crime scene, Paley tells her to go home to her husband. "I don't love my husband," she explains.

Marjorie returns to her car, and finds Natalie hiding inside, pointing a gun at her. "One peep out of you, and I'll plug you. Come on, sister, get going." Marjorie is friendly to Natalie as she drives. "What's your racket?" Natalie finally asks cheerful Marjorie. "Well, right now it's the divorce racket," Marjorie replies. Natalie warns Marjorie that she's in trouble—and Marjorie might end up in hot water herself. "A little hot water would feel pretty good right now," Marjorie replies.

Paley has followed the car to Marjorie's house. Natalie escapes again by shooting out the gas tank in Marjorie's car and taking off in Paley's vehicle.

Paley tells Marjorie he's taking her to jail. He drives her in her car, which, of course, runs out of gas (Paley doesn't seem too bright). After a series of events that are neither amusing nor integral to the plot, Marjorie is arrested but quickly bailed out by her attorney. She leaves a note for Paley: "Jerry dear: I need a 'g' man in my family. Would you be interested in a special assignment? Marjorie."

Turns out Marjorie is an heiress whose divorce has just gone through. She gets on her private railway car and is soon joined by Natalie, who wants to return Marjorie's coat. "My life wouldn't be worth a nickel if anyone knew I was here," Natalie tells her. Marjorie asks her to stay, but Natalie says she can't.

Paley, who has been invited to the car by Marjorie, arrives and sees a newspaper headline: "MARJORIE SUTTON DIVORCES PROMINENT BANKER."

After Natalie gets off the train, Paley follows her to a drugstore and calls for reinforcements. Meanwhile, Natalie asks her gang to clear out, but they refuse. There's a shootout. Natalie is wounded but manages to escape. The headline reads: "G-MAN SMITH KILLED IN FIGHT WITH GANGSTERS: Ring Leaders of Band Escape During Gun Battle."

Paley lights into Marjorie, blaming her for Smitty's death. Paley travels back east with Smitty's body, though Marjorie begs him to stay. When he refuses, she has her private car attached to the train so she can travel with him.

The bad guys commandeer Marjorie's rail car. Marjorie finds a seriously wounded Natalie. When Marjorie tries to find a doctor, the gangsters pull a gun on her.

Paley finds out that Marjorie's rail car is attached to his train and goes back to talk to her. The bad guys pull a gun on him ("Stick 'em up, copper!"). Paley quickly overpowers them. Next thing you know, Paley and a bad guy are on top of the train, struggling.

Meanwhile, Marjorie comforts a dying Natalie. "I'm not so ... terribly bad," Natalie says. "Really, I'm not."

Back to the men struggling on top of the train. Would you be terribly surprised if we told you that Paley wins the struggle? Back inside the train, Marjorie is shot. Another gun battle, and another bad guy dies and Paley is wounded.

In the final scene, Marjorie asks in the hospital if Paley is all right. "I'm afraid so," the doctor says. Paley ends the film by pushing Marjorie's wheelchair, advising the nurse, "I think I can look after this young lady."

The character of Marjorie was based on Barbara Hutton. Notice how they cleverly changed the name to Sutton from Hutton.

This one is *really, really* bad. The editing is a mess. The direction and writing are mediocre. And the acting isn't so hot, either. Certainly no one expected anyone to carefully review this film more than seventy years later and examine it closely. Still, no one could have thought at the time that the film was good or even fair. Everyone had to know this was a stinkeroo. A November 24, 1935, article in the *Zanesville Signal* blamed the whole thing on star Ralph Graves: "*Speed Limited* is his own brain child, an original story which he wrote and adapted for the screen." Graves was not only a terrible writer but a pretty poor actor too. He himself once said, "I was no actor."[138] He got that right. Brent's not terrible—and neither is Claudia Dell—but both had to be desperate to take these roles. As an actor, Graves is unexpressive and lacks charisma. Also, and, most annoyingly, his head is too big for his body.

Graves was a former silent screen star who began his career in 1918. He was also a director. Anthony Slide included a controversial interview with him in his book *Silent Players: A Biographical and Autobiographical Study of 100 Silent Film Actors and Actresses.*

Among the secrets Graves revealed was a two-year affair with director Mack Sennett. Born Ralph Horsburgh in Cleveland, Ohio, in 1900, Graves died in 1977.

Born Claudia Dell Smith in San Antonio in 1909, Dell is said to be the model for the first Columbia Pictures logo. A former Ziegfeld chorus girl, Dell died in 1977. She also appears with Brent in *The Mad Empress* (1939).

*Speed Unlimited* was Andy Rice's only film credit as an actor, though he did receive a handful of credits for screenwriting and lyric writing. He died in 1963.

Gordon Griffith (1907–1958) was born in Chicago. A child actor who made his debut in 1913, Griffith's early credits included Charles Chaplin films. He eventually became production manager at Columbia Pictures. Fred "Snowflake" Toones, born in North Carolina in 1906, amassed more than two hundred film credits, usually typecast as porter, butler, waiter, etc. He died in 1962. Born Ellen Hansen in Racine, Wisconsin, in 1911, Ellen Corby is best known for her Emmy-winning performance in the television show *The Waltons*. She also received an Oscar nomination for *I Remember Mama* (1949). Corby died in 1999. Bobby Burns was an actor and director during the silent film era. Born in Philadelphia in 1878, he made his film debut in 1908 and ended his career on the television show *Adventures of the Sea Hawk*. He died in 1966. Ray Turner was born in New Mexico in 1895. He made his screen debut in 1924 and, like Snow Flake, often played stereotypical African-American characters. He died in 1981.

Al Herman, sometimes credited as Albert Herman, was a writer, actor, producer, and director. He directed dozens of Mickey Rooney (in the role of Mickey McGuire) comedy shorts in the 1920s and 1930s. Born Adam Herman Foelker in Troy, New York, in 1887, he died in 1958.

It's difficult to find reviews of the film, leading us to believe it had limited distribution.

*Review:* "A dreary picture about a brave FBI agent hot on the trail of some kidnapers while romancing a dim-witted, flaky, divorced socialite. The story is bad enough, but the film shows no sign of having been made by anyone with an iota of technical knowledge" (http://www.tvguide.com/movies/speed-limited/118658).

## Song of the Trail

(Ambassador Pictures) 68 min. Released on February 24, 1936.

*Survival Status:* UCLA Film and Television Archive (Los Angeles). Released on video (VCI, 61 min.).

*Credits:* Producer, Maurice H. Conn; supervisor, Charles Hutchison; director, Russell Hopton; based on the short story "Playing with Fire" by James Oliver Curwood; screen adaptation, George Sayre, Barry Barringer; photography, Arthur Reed; film editor, Richard G. Wray; set design, Harry Williams; costumes, Harry Kusnick; musical director, Stetson Humphrey; sound engineer, Corson Jowett; songs and lyrics, Didheart Conn; songs, "Song of the Trail," "My Heart's on the Plains,"

"Let Me Whisper My Love" and "Nell Was the Belle of the Prairie."

*Cast*: Kermit Maynard (Jim Carter); Evelyn Brent (Myra); Fuzzy Knight (Pudge); Antoinette Lees (Betty Hobson); George Hayes (Ben Hobson); Lynette London (Marie); Wheeler Oakman (Bob Arnold); Lee Shumway (Stone); Roger Williams (Miller); Charles McMurphy (Curtis); Rocky (Himself); Horace Murphy (Sheriff); Ray Gallagher (Blore).

Jim Carter comes into town and learns about a rodeo competition. One of his competitors will be pretty Betty Hobson. "There's a girl that could make a clay pigeon out of me any time she wanted to," Jim says.

Betty's dad Ben Hobson has a gambling problem, and Bob Arnold takes advantage by stealing the deed to Ben's mine in a fixed poker game (he's using five aces). An enraged Ben threatens to kill the cheaters: "I'll get even with ya if it takes the rest of my life."

Using the distraction of the rodeo, Ben steals the deed back from Bob. When two of Bob's cohorts, Stone and Curtis, are murdered during the shooting contest, Ben is accused and rides off to hide. The bad guys find him, but Carter intervenes despite their protests that they've been deputized. "You lay a hand on Mr. Hobson, and you won't be deputized. You'll be paralyzed. With lead poisoning," Carter remarks. These lines are typical of the script.

Bob realizes Ben has stolen the deed, and there are several more chases and fights until Carter and Bob have a final face-off. Carter delivers the knockout blow: "Here's that fifth ace in your deck," he says. In the last scene, Carter and Betty stand arm in arm and wave goodbye to Carter's friends. They embrace and kiss.

Brent received second billing after Kermit Maynard, playing yet another tough-talking character, this time a saloon girl. There's one scene that's particularly reminiscent of Brent in her heyday: She's sitting with another saloon girl and is advised not to trust Bob. "Well, you're not me, and nobody's asking you to trust *Bob* Arnold. So use that mouth of yours to chew steak with, and you'll stay out of trouble." She also has an early scene where she tries to seduce Carter but quickly gives up. "Say, I owe you an apology, mister. I thought you were a sap. But all I can get out of you is giggles, and they don't pay dividends. I'll be seeing you."

You've got to look hard to find good acting in this one. There is some nice scenery, and lots of trick riding and rope tricks, in addition to some good fight scenes with the amazingly agile Maynard. The tagline for the film was "A symphony of the range, played with instruments of death!"

Kermit Maynard was Ken Maynard's younger brother. Born in Indiana in 1897, Kermit was also billed as Tex Maynard. Though he never achieved the fame of his brother, Kermit made close to three hundred film and television appearances. He died in 1971. His horse Rocky appeared in several films with him.

Popular sidekick Fuzzy Knight was born in West Virginia in 1901. He got his start as a musician in vaudeville before he entered films in 1929. Knight died in 1976. He also appeared with Brent in *Home on the Range* (1934).

Antoinette Lees was sometimes billed as Andrea Leeds. She became a much better actress with experience and was nominated for an Oscar for *Stage Door* (1937). She was considered for the role of Melanie in *Gone with the Wind* (1939). Lees retired from films in 1940 to raise a family. Born in 1914 in Butte, Montana, she died in 1984.

George Hayes, also known as Gabby Hayes, was born in Wellsville, New York, in 1885. He and wife Olive Ireland had a popular vaudeville act before he entered movies and became a favorite character actor and Western sidekick. The erudite, well-dressed gentleman was in real life the opposite of his on-screen persona. He died in 1969. He also appeared with Brent in *Hopalong Cassidy Returns* (1936).

Wheeler Oakman was born Vivian Eichelberger in Washington, D.C., in 1890. Oakman, who made his film debut in 1912, almost always played villains. He also appeared with Brent in *Bowery Champs* (1944). Oakman died in 1949.

Lee Shumway was born in Salt Lake City, Utah, in 1884. He began his career in the silent film era and appeared in more than four hundred films, many of them Westerns. He also appeared with Brent in *Night Club Scandal* (1937) and *Daughter of Shanghai* (1937). Shumway died in 1959.

Director Russell Hopton was born in New York in 1900. Primarily an actor who appeared in more than a hundred movies, Hopton directed only this film and *Black Gold* (1936). He committed suicide in 1945.

Writer James Oliver Curwood was born in 1878 and died in 1927 of blood poisoning after being bitten by a spider. Many of his novels focused on nature and the outdoors and were adapted into films. His Michigan home has been turned into a museum.

This was Lynette London's only film appearance. Composer Didheart Conn was producer Maurice Conn's sister.

*Reviews*: "Never for a moment diverges from the standard track.... Title won't help any and is just another example of non-inventiveness of labelers. Kids will revel in the yarn's opening shots of preparation and practice for a rodeo and the rodeo proper which, once again, serves as Maynard's excuse to exhibit his cowhand past" (*Variety*, December 23, 1936).

"Fast outdoor picture rates tops in Western class, with an abundance of comedy and acrobatics" (*Film Daily*, March 27, 1937).

## *It Couldn't Have Happened— But It Did*

(Invincible Pictures) 70 min. Released on August 1, 1936.
*Survival Status*: [Incomplete] British Film Institute/National Film and Television Archive (London) Released on video (Alpha, 70 min., Sinister Cinema).

*Credits*: Producer, Maury M. Cohen; supervisor, Herbert S. Cohen; director, Phil Rosen; assistant director, Melville Shyer; original story and screenplay, Arthur T. Horman; photography, M. A. Andersen; art director, Edward C. Jewell; film editor, Roland D. Reed; recording engineer, Richard Tyler.

*Cast*: Reginald Denny (Greg Stone); Evelyn Brent (Beverly Blake); Jack La Rue (Smiley Clark); Inez Courtney (Linda Sands); John [Hugh] Marlowe (Edward Forrest); Claude King (Ellis Holden); Bryant Washburn (Norman Carter); Robert Homans (Lt. O'Neill); Crauford Kent (Bob Bennett); Robert Frazer (Lloyd Schaefer); Miki Morita (Hashi); Emily La Rue (Ingenue); Henry Herbert (Sherwood); Lynton Brent (Landsdale); Broderick O'Farrell (Johnson); Dian Manners (Louise).

Stage star Beverly Blake is on the warpath at rehearsals for a new play. She is upset with actor Bob Bennett and wants her husband (and producer) Ellis Holden to fire him. "I'm not going to be upstaged and mis-cued by a ham like Bennett," says the tart-tongued diva.

"The oftener I see that woman, the better I like rattlesnakes," quips Linda, assistant to playwright Greg Stone. Edward Forrest doesn't feel the same. He's having an affair with Beverly. She's a busy woman because she's also having an affair with Norman Carter.

When Carter and Holden are murdered pushy Linda insists that the reluctant Stone solve the crime. After going through a multitude of suspects and clues, Stone writes a script that re-enacts the murders. The suspects sit in the audience, and the curtain opens to show a set that includes the offices of Carter and Holden as well as the outer office where Stone and Linda were working when the murders happened. As a nervous Beverly looks on, Stone establishes that Bob killed the two men—at Beverly's request.

The working titles of this film included *Divided by Two* and *It Couldn't Have Happened*. Brent received second billing after Denny. She is charmingly devious in her few scenes.

It's a fun comedy mystery if you don't expect too much from it. Denny and Courtney are the stars, and they make a cute couple. Denny is debonair and not terribly curious, while Courtney is spunky and sharp as a tack. The script has some good lines, and the performances are solid. Unfortunately, the film has the distinction of having one of the worst titles ever. One of the settings used was the Mayan Theater at 1038 Hill Street in downtown Los Angeles.

The movie had an unusual wrap party in July 1936. "The time was midnight, and the place a waffle parlor, but the occasion for the party was the fact that the last scene for ... *Divided by Two* had just been shot. Waiters appeared on the sound stage as from nowhere, bearing trays of cooling drinks and delectable food. Inez Courtney, the engaging young comedienne who has the leading role ... and her husband, Marquis Luigi Filiasi, were the hosts. And the producers, the cast, and entire staff were the guests of the very unexpected party."[139]

Reginald Denny also appeared with Brent in *Without Children* (1935). Born in England in 1891, Denny made his film debut in 1915. He was a pilot in World War I (and a pretty fair boxer in his regiment). He later became a manufacturer of model plane kits and also founded Radioplane, a manufacturer of military drones (Marilyn Monroe was once an employee in his factory). Denny's film career was a long one, encompassing many silent films, several Bulldog Drummond movies (he played Algy Longworth), and an appearance on TV's *Batman* as King Boris. Denny died in 1967.

Jack La Rue was born Gaspere Biondolillo in New York in 1902. He was in several Broadway productions before he made his film debut in 1925. Often cast as a gangster, he made more than one hundred film and television appearances. La Rue was also a narrator for TV's *Lights Out*. He died in 1984. He also appeared with Brent in *The Pay Off* (1942) and *Robin Hood of Monterey* (1947).

Inez Courtney was born in New York in 1908. The talented Courtney was a successful Broadway musical comedy performer (*Good News*, among others) before going into films. She gave energetic performances which often showcased her singing and dancing. After a promising start, her career slowed down. Late in her career, she had a subdued, un–Courtney-like role in Lubitsch's *The Shop Around the Corner* (1940). She retired in 1940 and died in 1975. Courtney is a delightful performer and deserves to be better known.

John Marlowe, also billed as Hugh Marlowe, was born Hugh Hipple in Philadelphia in 1911. The film and stage actor made his film debut in 1936. He made dozens of films but is probably best remembered for his television work, including a long stint on the soap opera *Another World*. Marlowe died in 1982.

Bryant Washburn (1889–1964) was born Franklyn Bryant Washburn III in Chicago. He began his film career in 1911 and made hundreds of film appearances. He also appeared with Brent in *My Husband's Wives* (1924), *Hollywood Boulevard* (1936), and *Jungle Jim* (1937).

Robert Homans, born in Malden, Massachusetts, in 1877, made his film debut in the silent era. He eventually appeared in hundreds of films, often playing police officers. Homans died in 1947. Crauford Kent was born in London in 1881 and made his first film appearance in 1915. He died in 1953. Robert Frazer also appeared with Brent in *Secret Orders* (1926), *Daughter of the Tong* (1939), and *The Mad Empress* (1939). Born in Worcester, Massachusetts, in 1891, he made his film debut in 1912 and appeared in more than two hundred films until his death in 1944. Miki Morita (also known as Mike Morita) almost always played Asian servants in the dozens of films in which he appeared. Born in 1897 in Chicago, Lynton Brent made his film debut in 1930. He appeared in more than two hundred films and died in 1981. He also appeared with Brent in *Mr. Wong, Detective* (1938).

Director Phil Rosen was born in what is now Poland in 1888. He began his career as a cinematographer (and was a founding member of the American Society of Cinematographers) for Edison in 1912. He died in 1951. Rosen was assistant director on *Fool's Gold* (1919) and also directed *The President's Mystery* (1935).

*Reviews:* "Miss Courtney shines despite phoney lines, phoney situations and stupid story development.... Whole production bears marks of quickie effort.... Phil Rosen's direction is far below the standard of his more recent independent efforts" (*Variety*, September 16, 1936).

## *Hollywood Boulevard*

(Paramount Pictures) 75 min. August 21, 1936.
*Survival Status:* UCLA Film and Television Archive (Los Angeles).
*Credits:* Producers, Adolph Zukor, A. M. Botsford; executive producer, William LeBaron; associate producer, Edward F. Cline; director, Robert Florey; assistant dirctor, Joe Lefert; screenplay, Marguerite Roberts; story, Max Marcin, Faith Thomas; photography, Karl Struss, George Clemens; art director, Hans Dreier, Earl Hedrick; editors, Harvey Johnston, William Shea; interior decorations, A. E. Freudeman: musical director and composer, Boris Morros; sound recording, Walter Oberst, Louis Mesenkop.
*Cast:* John Halliday (John Blakeford); Marsha Hunt (Patricia Blakeford); Robert Cummings (Jay Wallace); C. Henry Gordon (Jordan Winslow); Esther Ralston (Flora Moore, an actress); Esther Dale (Martha); Frieda Inescort (Alice Winslow); Albert Conti (Mr. Sanford); Thomas Jackson (Detective); Oscar Apfel (Dr. Inslo); Purnell Pratt (Mr. Steinman); Hyman Fink (Snapshot "Hymie"); Irving Bacon (Gus, bartender); Richard Powell (Pete Moran); Rita La Roy (Nella); Francis X. Bushman (Director of desert scene); Maurice Costello (Director); Betty Compson (Betty); Mae Marsh (Carlotta Blakeford); Charles Ray (Charlie Smith, the assistant director); Herbert Rawlinson (Manager of Grauman's Chinese Theater); Jane Novak (Mrs. Steinman); Bryant Washburn (Robert Martin); Jack Mulhall, Creighton Hale, Gary Cooper (Men at bar); Roy D'Arcy (The sheik); Ruth Clifford (Nurse); Jack Mower (Frank Stucky); Frank Mayo, Harry Myers, Eleanore Whitney (Themselves); Mabel Forrest (Mother); Tom Kennedy (Bouncer); Pat O'Malley (Dancer); Bert Roach (Scenarist); Lois Kent (Little girl); Gregory Gaye (Russian writer); Ed Cecil (Butler); Lowell Drew (Doorman at Trocadero); Phil Tead (Master of ceremonies); Robert E. Homans (Gray); Eddie Dunn (Grip); Monte Vandergrift (Electrician); Kitty McHugh (Secretary); Matty Roubert (Newsboy); Frances Morris (Moran's secretary); Ed Dearing (Motor policeman); Charles Williams (Reporter); Otto Yamaoka (Thomas); Gertrude Simpson (Gossip); Johnny Fletcher (Vendor); Joanne Dudley (Girl in Pullman); Hal Prince (Police radio announcer); Charles Morton (Guest); Margaret Harrison (Guest); John Sylvester (Guest); William Desmond (Guest); Edmund Burns (Guest); James Ford (Guest); Franklin Parker, William Wayne (Workmen—Brown Derby); Eddie Room, Margaret Hourian, G. H. Gordon, William Farnum.

Fading star John Blakeford is talked into writing his memoirs by Winslow, the sleazy tabloid publisher of *Modern Truth*. The actor is desperate for the prom-

ised $25,000 and allows the editors to embellish. This leads to complications with his estranged daughter Patricia, ex-wife Carlotta, and former mistress Alice, who is now the wife of the tabloid publisher. Blakeford pleads with the publisher (unaware of his wife's previous relationship) to stop running the memoir, but he refuses.

Alice shoots Blakeford, afraid he'll write about their affair. Blakeford's daughter is mistakenly accused. Patricia's boyfriend finds a Dictaphone recording that implicates Alice. He confronts the Winslows, and Alice and her husband hurry to the hospital to assure Blakeford that no additional memoirs will be published. The police officer asks Blakeford who shot him.

"Who shot me? Why, it was an accident. I'll tell you more about it when I'm stronger." Everyone leaves the hospital room, but Blakeford calls back his daughter. "Your old man's still a pretty good actor. Huh?"

Although references indicate that Brent's scenes were deleted, we believe her silhouette is used in an early scene right after the credits run. Look for her profile—and her telltale jawline—after the stoplight changes. She is facing the Brown Derby sign.

Gary Cooper's appearance was unbilled. At this point in his career, he was a huge star and likely did the bit as a favor to friend John Halliday.

This is a great idea for a film, and the scenes present a kind of 1930s Hollywood travelogue with shots of the Brown Derby, the Trocadero, Grauman's Chinese Theater, the Ambassador Hotel, and more. We also get to see silent stars such as Francis X. Bushman, Maurice Costello, Charles Ray, Mae Marsh, and Esther Ralston, though some performances are tentative and awkward as though they're not quite sure they should be participating in this endeavor—or exactly what the director wanted.

Director Florey was a huge fan of Hollywood and often used the setting for his pictures, including *The Life and Death of 9413—A Hollywood Extra* and *The Preview Murder Mystery*. According to Brian Taves, "The warm reception accorded *The Preview Murder Mystery* caused producer A.M. Botsford to call on Florey for another story of filmland to be constructed around the title *Hollywood Boulevard*. After a few days he came up with a vague plot which was speedily approved. Florey's concept was to fashion an entire picture around the appearance of a host of old favorites seen in supporting cameo roles. *Hollywood Boulevard* would be a virtual Grand Hotel of stars of the silent days, twenty-three in all, more than any other film of its time."[140]

Florey's idea was for each new sequence to start with an establishing shot of a well-known Hollywood place. Filming was completed in June 1936, and Florey left for Nevada to work on *Outcast*. Unfortunately, the editing was brutal. "[T]he production's supervisor, Eddie Cline (a Keystone relic), ordered the editor to remove all shots not absolutely essential to the plotline.... Upon returning to the studio

[Florey] was sickened by what had been done to *Hollywood Boulevard*. 'More than eighteen extremely interesting exteriors vanished, and it became all plot and no more Hollywood,' he said. Mae Marsh and Gary Cooper had their roles reduced, and Harold Lloyd's cameo was completely eliminated."[141]

In the Editor's Foreword to Taves' book on Florey, Anthony Slide wrote, "I think my favorite Robert Florey is *Hollywood Boulevard*; here the director is presenting a very personal view of Hollywood, a community and a way of life he knows and has come to love. Here also, Robert Florey has brought together all the 'great' names of the past, many reduced by this time to extra work, and once more allowed them to be an integral part of the filmmaking process."[142]

Absolutely. If you love Hollywood, you're going to love this film. Florey also captures the indignities faced when a Hollywood actor loses fame and fortune. It's cynical but not mean-spirited. The film's theme had to be particularly poignant for Brent. In an early scene, a newsboy sells a paper to Blakeford, telling him his picture's in it. It is indeed, along with the embarrassing headline: "JOHN BLAKEFORD SUED BY TAILOR." This was around the time that Brent also had her name in the newspaper for various lawsuits.

Florey, born in Paris in 1900, became a film devotee after watching George Melies make his magical silent films. Florey was also at one time an assistant to French director Louis Feuillade as well as a journalist who often wrote about films and filmmaking. His film credits include *The Cocoanuts* (1929), *Murders in the Rue Morgue* (1932), *The Desert Song* (1943), *God Is My Co-Pilot* (1945), and *The Beast With Five Fingers* (1946). At one point he was picked to direct *Frankenstein* (1931), but the job eventually went to James Whale. After his film career ended, he went into television directing, eventually winning the first Directors Guild award for Television Direction in 1953 for his work on the *Four Star Playhouse* production "The Last Voyage," which starred Charles Boyer and Regis Toomey. Florey died in 1979.

Marguerite Roberts co-wrote *Hollywood Boulevard* with an uncredited Florey. Of the collaboration, she said, "I found him to be a charming and talented man and very tolerant of a tyro screenwriter.... I considered it a prize assignment."[143] Born in 1905 in Greeley, Colorado, Roberts and husband John Sandford were blacklisted when they refused to cooperate with the House Un-American Activities Committee in the 1950s. Roberts made a comeback in the 1960s and wrote the screenplay *True Grit* (1969). She died in 1989.

In some ways, John Halliday fit the character of John Blakeford. Born in 1880 in Brooklyn, New York, Halliday began his film career in 1911 and was indeed a leading man for some time. However, when *Hollywood Boulevard* was made, Halliday's heyday was over. He made only a handful of films after this one and died in 1947.

Born in Chicago in 1917, Marsha Hunt began her long film and television career in 1935. *Hollywood Boulevard* was only her fifth film. Married to writer Robert Presnell, Jr., from 1946 until his death in 1986, Hunt suffered career problems due to her political activities. Nevertheless, she stayed active in theatre and television and appeared in a film as recently as 2008.

Robert Cummings' performances often straddle an uncomfortable line between charming and demented. This one, unfortunately, leans more towards the demented side. He plays a screenwriter who comes dangerously close to needing a restraining order. Cummings was born in Joplin, Missouri, in 1908. He made his film debut in 1933 and did well in several films but received most of his success on television. Cummings was nominated multiple times for Emmys for *The Bob Cummings Show*. A pilot and health food enthusiast, he died in 1990. He also appeared with Brent in *The Last Train from Madrid* (1937).

C. Henry Gordon (1883–1940), born in New York, made his first film appearance in 1930. He often played ethnic characters. Esther Ralston was born into a family of entertainers in Bar Harbor, Maine, in 1902. First known as Baby Esther, Ralston became a successful silent film star nicknamed "The American Venus." Like Brent, Ralston ended up losing her fortune. She died in 1994. Esther Dale was born in Beaufort, South Carolina, in 1885. A former lieder singer, she made her film debut in 1934. Dale appeared in more than one hundred films and television episodes before her death in 1961. She also appeared with Brent in *Wrecking Crew* (1942). Frieda Inescort, always a compelling screen presence, was born in Scotland in 1901. She developed multiple sclerosis in 1932. Inescort, who was also a stage actress, made her film debut in 1935 and died in 1976. Irving Bacon was born in St. Joseph, Missouri, in 1893. A familiar face, this character actor ended up with more than five hundred credits. His brother was director Lloyd Bacon. Irving Bacon also appeared with Brent in *Hopalong Cassidy Returns* (1936) and *Tip-Off Girls* (1938). He died in 1965.

Francis X. Bushman, born in Baltimore, Maryland, in 1883, was a silent film star who made his first film in 1911. Nicknamed "King of the Movies," Bushman's grave has these words inscribed on it. He died in 1966. Maurice Costello was the father of Dolores and Helene. In 1939, Costello was so broke he sued his daughters for support. Born in Pittsburgh, Pennsylvania, in 1877, Costello was a highly successful silent film actor and director nicknamed "The Dimpled Darling." The great-grandfather of Drew Barrymore, he died in 1950. Betty Compson was born in Beaver, Utah, in 1897. Nominated for an Oscar for *The Barker* (1928), she'd made her debut in 1915. Compson, a successful silent film star, was married to director James Cruze from 1925 to 1930. Upon retirement, she owned a company called Ashtrays Unlimited. Compson died in 1974.

Mae Marsh was born in 1894 in what was then called New Mexico Territory. She entered films in 1910 and became a silent film star, earning $2,500 a week. She lost her fortune and returned to films after Wall Street's 1929 crash. Marsh appeared in close to two hundred films until her death in 1968.

Charles Ray was born in Jacksonville, Illinois, in 1891. A producer, director and sometimes writer, he was also a successful silent film star. However, when he self-produced *The Courtship of Miles Standish* (1923) he lost his fortune. He struggled the remainder of his career. Ray, a onetime millionaire, reportedly earned $7.50 a day on *Hollywood Boulevard*. Ray died in 1943 of an infected tooth.

Jane Novak was born in St. Louis, Missouri, in 1896. She made her film debut in 1913 and became a popular silent film star. Novak made a fortune with investments in film production and real estate but lost it in the 1929 stock market crash. She continued to act sporadically and published a cookbook in the 1970s. She died in 1990.

Herbert Rawlinson was born in England in 1885. He made his film debut in 1911. Once a leading man, he became a character actor in his later years. He died in 1953 after working on an Ed Wood, Jr., film, *Jail Bait* (1954). Rawlinson also appeared with Brent in *Silent Witness* (1943).

*Reviews:* "It has unexpected virtues, having one of the best scripts ever possessed by a behind-the-scenes-in-Hollywood picture" (*Variety*, September 23, 1936).

## The President's Mystery

(Republic Pictures) 52 min. Released on October 8, 1936.

*Survival Status:* UCLA Film and Television Archive (Los Angeles). Released on video (Classic Collectors Series, 52 min.).

*Credits*: Producer, Nat Levine; executive producer, Albert E. Levoy; associate producer, Burt Kelly; director, Phil Rosen; assistant director, Ray Culley; based on the novel *The President's Mystery Story*, story conceived by Franklin D. Roosevelt and written as a serial for *Liberty Magazine* by Rupert Hughes, Samuel Hopkins Adams, Anthony Abbot [Fulton Oursler], Rita Weiman, S. S. Van Dine and John Erskine; screenplay, Lester Cole, Nathanael West; photography, Ernest Miller; film editor, Robert Simpson; editorial supervisor, Murray Seldeen; costumes, Eloise; music settings, Dr. Hugo Riesenfeld; music supervisor, Harry Grey; sound engineer, Harry Jones.

*Cast:* Henry Wilcoxon (James Blake, later known as Carter); Betty Furness (Charlotte Brown); Sidney Blackmer (George Sartos); Evelyn Brent (Ilka Blake); Barnett Parker (Roger, Blake's butler); Mel Ruick (Andrew, Sartos' chauffeur); Wade Boteler (Sheriff); John Wray (Shane); Guy Usher (Police lieutenant); Robert E. Homans (Sergeant); Si Jenks (Earl); Arthur Aylesworth (Joe Reed); June Johnson.

FOREWORD: President Franklin D. Roosevelt, talking with a magazine editor on one of his favorite subjects—mystery stories—advanced the question: "How can a man disappear with five million dollars of his own money in negotiable form and not be traced?" Challenged by this, the editor enlisted the aid of six famous authors. The result was a thrilling story. The same problem intrigued the producers of this photoplay, and in another form it is now brought to the screen. The proceeds of the sale of the plot, both for publication and motion picture rights, have been given voluntarily by the publisher to the Georgia Warm Springs Foundation."

Wealthy attorney Blake sees firsthand how his lobbying efforts for big business in Washington, D.C., hurt local communities and workers. He begins to question his values. At his mansion, he sees the magazine story suggested by President Roosevelt. Blake has a serious discussion with bitchy wife Ilka, suggesting they lead empty, shallow lives, and perhaps they should go away and start anew. She's not receptive to the idea. "I *detest* fishing!" she tells him.

Black liquidates his financial holdings. Meanwhile, two-timing Ilka is accidentally killed by her lover's chauffeur. Believe it or not, at about the exact same time Blake fakes his own death. When his "body" is found, the case is "solved," and it's assumed Blake killed his wife and then committed suicide.

Blake, now using the name Carter, joins forces with cannery owner Charlotte Brown. George Sartos, a representative of National Cannery (and Ilka's former lover), meets with "Carter." Sartos recognizes Blake and lets him know he's on to him. Blake is arrested. Sartos and his associates get the townspeople riled up. They riot and break into the warehouse. Blake "escapes" from jail (with the help of the sheriff) and shows up to give a rousing speech. The co-op ("Springvale Co-Operative Eat More for Less") is saved.

Meanwhile, Blake's fey butler gets Sartos' chauffeur's confession that he accidentally killed Ilka, and bad guy Sartos is arrested for inciting a riot. In the final scene, Blake tells Charlotte they're going to be married before they head to Washington, D.C. A fleet of trucks roll out of town with boxes of the co-op's products.

Brent was fourth-billed and had only a minimal part. The film is not terribly interesting. It's one of those films where much of the plot is told in newspaper and magazine headlines, montages, and long speeches. It's a message film that is, frankly, boring.

The idea for this movie indeed came from President Franklin Delano Roosevelt. "One day last year [1935] Franklin D. Roosevelt remarked to Editor Fulton Oursler of *Liberty* that he had a good idea for a mystery story. Smart Editor Oursler pounced on the idea, [and] got the President's permission to have it written up for *Liberty* in six installments.... Last November the first installment appeared, accompanied by the President's picture on the cover, an article inside explaining the story's origin. A loud editorial coup, *The President's Mystery Story* was snapped up by Hollywood, which has made from it an adaptation which reeks of New Deal propaganda and good melodrama."[144] The story ran in the magazine from November 16 to December 21, 1935. The story was eventually published in book form by Farrar in 1935.

The tagline was "The thriller that speaks right out!" In the United Kingdom the film was released with the title *One for All*.

The seven writers who contributed to the novel each wrote one chapter. Samuel Hopkins Adams (1871–1958) was also known as Warner Fabian. He also wrote the novel *Flaming Youth* (1923) which was made into a Colleen Moore movie. John Erskine (1879–1951) also wrote the novel *The Private Life of Helen of Troy* (1927). Rupert Hughes (1872–1956), Howard Hughes' uncle, directed several silent films. Fulton Oursler (1893–1952) was a playwright and novelist who used the pen name Anthony Abbot. S. S. Van Dine (1887–1939) was the author of the Philo Vance detective stories. Rita Weiman (1885–1954) was a playwright and novelist. Her novel *One Man's Secret* was adapted into the screenplay *Possessed* (1947).

Nathanael West was born Nathan Weinstein in 1903 in New York and died with wife Eileen McKinney (her sister Ruth wrote about her in *My Sister Eileen*) in an automobile accident in 1940. West's novels included *Miss Lonelyhearts* and *The Day of the Locust*.

Lester Cole was born in New York in 1904. One of the Hollywood Ten, he served a year in prison for refusing to testify about his political beliefs. He died in 1985.

Henry Wilcoxon, a Liam Neeson lookalike, was born in the British West Indies in 1905. He began his film career in 1931 and was best known for his appearances in Cecil B. DeMille's films, including *Cleopatra* (1934) and *Samson and Delilah* (1949). Wilcoxon died in 1984.

Betty Furness, born in New York in 1916, was borrowed from MGM for this film. She made her film debut in 1932. A teenage model, she later became a TV spokesperson for Westinghouse. Furness, who was Betty Grable's maid of honor when she married Harry James, also served as Director of Consumer Affairs for New York City. Furness died in 1994.

Character actor Sidney Blackmer was born in Salisbury, North Carolina, in 1895. His long acting career included performances on radio, film, television, and the stage. He was awarded a Tony for *Come Back, Little Sheba* in 1950. He was also very good in *Rosemary's Baby* (1968). Married to actress Lenore Ulric from 1929 to 1938, Blackmer died in 1973.

Barnett Parker, born in Yorkshire, England, in 1886, made his film debut in 1915 and was sometimes billed as Burnett Parker. A "confirmed bachelor," he died in 1941.

Mel Ruick, born in Boise, Idaho, in 1898, made his film debut in 1935 and he became a familiar face to television viewers in the 1950s and 1960s. He died on Christmas Eve 1972. Wade Boteler was born in California in 1888. He made hundreds of film appearances, often playing police officers. Boteler died in 1943. He also appeared with Brent in *Tip-Off Girls*

(1938). This was June Johnson's first role She was the daughter of Chic Johnson, part of the vaudeville team of Olsen and Johnson. Born in St. Louis, Missouri, in 1918, she died in 1987.

*Reviews:* "Phil Rosen's direction is fluid. Dr. Hugo Riesenfeld's score [is] admirable and the cast uniformly competent.... In its melodramatic way, *The President's Mystery* is a well-constructed essay on one means of achieving a more abundant life, and it is an interesting picture as well" (*New York Times*, October 19, 1936).

"Chief mystery ... is why the producers attempted to improve on the *Liberty Magazine* version.... If the original ... had been transferred to the screen as a mystery yarn and nothing else, Republic might have had something.... Considering the way the original has been manhandled, director Phil Rosen has done a creditable job. He maneuvered his mob scenes effectively to mount to a climax that was the highlight of the film" (*Variety*, October 21, 1936).

"A splendid job of acting is done by Wilcoxon, who is a star whether called that or not, while Barnett Parker carves a big niche for himself as a comedian in a butler role. Betty Furness proves her excellent acing ability again, as do Sidney Blackmer, Evelyn Brent, et al." (*Los Angeles Times*, October 29, 1936).

## Hopalong Cassidy Returns

(Harry Sherman Productions) 75 min. Released on October 16, 1936.

*Survival Status*: UCLA Film and Television Archive (Los Angeles). Released on video (USTO/ Sagebrush Entertainment).

*Credits*: Producer; George A. Hirliman; associate producer, Eugene Strong; director, Nate Watt; assistant director, U. O. Smith, D. M. Abrahams; story, Clarence E. Mulford; screenplay and dialogue, Harrison Jacobs; photography, Archie Stout; art direction, Lewis Rachmil; film editor, Robert Warwick, Jr.; wardrobe, Al Kennedy; sound engineer, Earl Sitar; special effects, Mel Wolf.

*Cast*: William Boyd (Hopalong Cassidy); George Hayes (Windy Halliday); Gail Sheridan (Mary Saunders); Evelyn Brent (Lilli Marsh); Stephen Morris [Morris Ankrum] (Blackie); William Janney (Buddy Cassidy); Irving Bacon (Peg Leg Holden); Grant Richards (Bob Claiborne); John Beck (Robert Saunders); Al St. John (Luke); Ernie Adams (Benson); Joe Rickson (Buck); Ray Whitley (Davis); Claude Smith (Dugan).

Peg Leg finds gold. Not the brightest guy in the world, he announces it to the whole town of Mesa Grande. And then proceeds to get drunk. Feigning concern, the cunning and seductive Lilli Marsh, owner of the Crystal Slipper, quickly sets upon Peg Leg to find out the location of the mine. "Here's to your mine, Peg Leg," she toasts.

"Here's to yours," he says in return. Truer words were never spoken. Before Peg Leg can make his claim at the county seat, he's murdered and the location map is missing.

Newspaper editor Robert Saunders writes a damning editorial about Lilli and her cohorts. Lilli proposes that the wheelchair-bound man be made marshal of the lawless town. Bob recruits old friend Hopalong Cassidy to help him.

Hopalong first meets Lilli when her horse is frightened by a snake. He rescues her. "I'll try to even things up some way if I can, Mr. Cassidy," she promises.

Before Cassidy and younger brother Buddy get into town, Bob is brutally attacked in front of his daughter Mary. Bob's dying words to Cassidy are a plea to make the town a fit place to live in. Suspicion turns to Lilli concerning the murders of Peg Leg and Bob. Hopalong, now the new marshal, finds his way to Lilli's saloon. "You're not going to let that piece of tin keep us from being friends, are you?" Lilli coquettishly asks as she fingers Hopalong's badge.

Hopalong shows how tough he is and then says goodnight. A saloon girl remarks, "Say, look at Lilli. She don't know whether to kiss the new marshal or kill him."

Hopalong and Lilli spar for control of the town. There's conflict between the two as well as unmistakable flirting and sexual tension. "Good luck, Mr. Cassidy," Lilli says at one point. "May the best man win." She later says, "Lilli Marsh never runs away from anything. Or anybody. Besides, if I were to leave, who'd look after you?"

After cleaning up the town, all that's left of the bad guys is Lilli and Blackie. Lilli prevents Blackie from assassinating Hopalong. However, Blackie shoots her, and Lilli crumples to the floor. Cassidy kills Blackie and cradles a dying Lilli. "I've been wanting to even the score with you, Mr. Cassidy. I guess I have, haven't I?"

"You've more than evened it," he replies.

Lilli strokes his face and says, "Somehow ... you ... you make me wish I'd met you ten years sooner. Just knowing you made me want to do so many things I'd forgotten how to do."

"I knew you had a decent streak in you somewhere. That's why I wanted to give you a chance."

Lilli asks that the mine deed be given to Mary Saunders (her father shared it with Peg Leg). "Would it be asking too much if ... if I asked you to kiss me?" Hopalong does, right on the lips, and Lilli peacefully dies. Hopalong and sidekick Windy leave town, though Buddy stays behind with Mary. "Some womenfolk have a way of changing a man's mind without him even knowing it," Hopalong muses. "Funny...."

Brent, fourth-billed, is glamorous in a meaty role reminiscent of her underworld molls. "And remember this, I'm still boss!" she snarls at one point. For the most part, she's very glamorous, though she does have to wear an unfortunate dress that had to be someone's idea of a joke. Not even Kay Francis would have looked good in it.

The film is entertaining. William Boyd is always a charming actor. It's an opportunity, too, to hear Gabby Hayes' unique utterances. Yur durn tootin'!

It was announced in August 1936 that Brent had replaced Helen Flint as Lilli. While filming *Hopalong Cassidy Returns* that month, Evelyn and her colleagues turned into real-life heroes when a fire broke out in Kernville, the town where they were working. According to an Associated Press article in the *Dallas Morning News* on August 21, 1936, "A company of

seventy-five motion picture actors, including William Boyd and Evelyn Brent, turned fire fighters here Thursday and saved the town from destruction. A cowboy actor was awakened by the smell of smoke at 3:30 am. He grabbed his six shooter, and emptied it into the air, awakening the remainder of the company. All members of the troupe joined and subdued the blaze which destroyed a barroom and service station with an estimated loss of $5,000."[145]

Taglines included: "Hopalong Cassidy meets the Queen of Mesa Grande and matches his wits and heart against her brains and beauty" and "She was more ruthless than any man ... and more dangerous!"

The originator of the Hopalong Cassidy character, writer Clarence E. Mulford, was born in Streator, Illinois, in 1883. He was reportedly unhappy with the changes William Boyd made to his character, thinking Hopalong had become too genteel. Mulford died in 1956.

Boyd was a hugely popular cowboy actor. Born in Hendrysburg, Ohio, in 1895, he was a silent film star before starring in his first Hopalong Cassidy movie in 1935. The character made Boyd a very rich man. He also licensed the character and earned millions in merchandizing. Boyd died in 1972.

Gail Sheridan was born Shirley Mingins in Seattle, Washington, in 1916. She appeared in only nine films before quitting in 1937. Her last film, *Hills of Wyoming*, was another Hopalong Cassidy picture. She died in 1982.

Stephen Morris, also known as Morris Ankrum, was born Stephen Morris Nussbaum in Danville, Illinois, in 1896. Before becoming a character actor he was a college professor and attorney. Ankrum appeared in many Westerns and science fiction films until his death in 1964. He also appeared with Brent in *Wide Open Town* (1941) playing the role of the kindly newspaper editor.

Grant Richards was born in New York City in 1911. He appeared on many radio and television shows until his death in a car accident in 1963.

Writer Harrison Jacobs was born in Pennsylvania in 1892. He wrote many Western screenplays including other Hopalong Cassidy pictures. He died in 1968.

*Reviews:* "Stacks up as best of the Hop-Along Cassidy pictures with good plot and plenty of action" (*Film Daily*, October 12, 1936).

"Supposed to be No. 7 in the Hopalong Cassidy series of Westerns, this new one not only fails to measure up to all its possibilities but also shows how miserably the producers have fallen down in developing original promise of the series. It is difficult to pin full responsibility on any one individual, for it looks as though the film scripter, director, dialog writers and casters all erred or were hurried in their tasks" (*Variety*, January 6, 1937).

"By far one of the best of the Cassidy series, with plenty of true Western atmosphere, punch, pep and bravado.... Boyd does his best work to date. Evelyn Brent plays a villainess with finesse and charm" (*Movie Mirror*, January 1937).

"The best Western we've played for a long while. Full

of action and interesting all the way through.... A nice picture and a nice business" (*Motion Picture Herald*, February 20, 1937).

## Jungle Jim

(Universal Pictures) 12 chapters, 232 min. Released on January 8, 1937.

*Survival Status:* UCLA Film and Television Archive (Los Angeles). Released on video (VCI).

*Credits:* Associate producers, Ben Koenig, Henry MacRae; directors, Ford Beebe, Cliff Smith; screenplay, Wyndham Gittens, Norman S. Hall, Ray Trampe; based on the newspaper feature *Jungle Jim* owned and copyrighted by King Features Syndicate; photography, Jerry Ash; film editors, Louis Sackin, Alvin Todd, Edward Todd; art director, Ralph DeLacy; supervising editor, Saul A. Goodkind; words and music ("I'm Takin' the Jungle Trail"), Kay Kellogg.

*Cast:* Grant Withers (Jim "Jungle Jim" Bradley); Betty Jane Rhodes (Joan Redmond/Mrs. Tom Redmond); Raymond Hatton (Malay Mike); Evelyn Brent (Shanghai Lil); Henry Brandon (The Cobra); Bryant Washburn (Bruce Redmond); Claude King (Territorial Consul Gilbert); Selmer Jackson (Attorney Tyler); Al Bridge (Slade); Paul Sutton (LaBat); Al Duvall (Kolu); Frank Mayo (Tom Redmond); J.P. McGowan (Ship Captain J.S. Robinson); Frank McGlynn, Jr. (Red Hallihan).

Shipwreck survivor Joan grows up in the jungle and is called the Lion Goddess by the natives. Fifteen years later her uncle comes to Africa because she's inherited a fortune—and he wants to get her out of the way so he can nab it. Jungle Jim and sidekick Malay Mike battle the uncle as well as Shanghai Lil and the Cobra, murderers who have escaped from London. In the end, Jim and Joan emerge victorious and sail away together.

If you've never seen a movie serial before, they can be fun. Keep in mind, however, that serials were meant to be seen in chapters, one per week. Each chapter ended with a cliffhanger where it seemed the hero could not possibly make it out alive. But he or she did. Every time. Frankly, most serials lose their impact when chapters are viewed back to back.

This was a 12-episode serial. The chapters were "Into the Lion's Den," "The Cobra Strikes," "The Menacing Herd," "The Killer's Trail," "The Bridge of Terror," "Drums of Doom," "The Earth Trembles," "The Killer Lion," "The Devil Bird," "Descending Doom," "In the Cobra's Coils," and "The Last Safari."

*Jungle Jim* is loaded with thrills, though it's strictly escapist fare. It's filled with wild animals, African natives, and tons of plot. Everything but fine acting. Grant Withers may have been miscast as Jungle Jim. He just doesn't seem to have whatever it takes to be a larger-than-life hero. Brent plays Shanghai Lil, and is not the least bit subtle. The poor thing seemed totally uncomfortable with her lines and out of place in the jungle setting. Here's a sample line: "Now we are in for it. How are we going to control the natives when they find out their Lion Goddess is dead?"

Sheesh. Still, she photographs beautifully and took the job because she needed the money and perhaps thought the role might lead to something else. Brent was announced for the role in October 1936. According to the *Los Angeles Examiner*, "The acquisition of this well known player ... points to the growing importance of serials."[146]

Since this was a Universal production, you can find leftover sets. One to look for is a stairway that was also used in *Frankenstein* (1931).

Taglines included "12 ROARING CHAPTERS AMONG WILD MEN and BEASTS OF PREY!," "Based Upon The Sensational King Feature Newspaper Strip by ALEX RAYMOND," "GANGWAY, JUNGLE! HERE COMES JIM! ... With a knife, a rifle and a murderous fist he saves the girl he loves from the perils of the African veldt! Don't miss a single one of these 12 thrilling chapters!," "YOU'LL TINGLE TO A MILLION THRILLS When you see Alex Raymond's mighty jungle serial come roaring on the screen! 12 pulse-pounding chapters! Don't miss one!," "It's SOCK-A-SECOND DRAMA! Alex Raymond's (creator of *Flash Gordon*) mighty jungle serial now comes roaring to the screen! 12 thrill-thronged chapters!"

Betty Jane Rhodes was born in Rockford, Illinois, in 1921. She was a radio performer while still a child and later went on to have a singing career. She was only sixteen years old when she made *Jungle Jim*.

Grant Withers, born in Pueblo, Colorado, in 1904, began his career in 1925. When he was 26 he eloped with 17-year-old Loretta Young (the marriage was later annulled). Withers appeared in many films and television episodes until his suicide in 1959. He also appeared with Brent in *Mr. Wong, Detective* (1938) and *Daughter of the Tong* (1939).

Henry Brandon was born Heinrich von Kleinbach in Berlin, Germany, in 1912. The tall (6'5") actor was often cast as a villain such as in *Drums of Fu Manchu* (1940). Brandon was Mark Herron's partner (Judy Garland's ex-husband) for many years and died in 1990.

Born in New Rochelle, New York, in 1909, Alex Raymond died in a car accident in 1956.

Screenwriter Wyndham Gittens, born in the West Indies in 1885, also wrote for *Holt of the Secret Service* (1941). He died in 1967.

*Reviews:* "The first three chapters are loaded with ... all sorts of thrills and suspense" (*Film Daily*, December 23, 1936).

"For the serial crew, *Jim* will be found a satisfier" (*Variety*, February 24, 1937).

"In execution, *Jungle Jim* is a clumsy serial. It uses large doses of library footage of jungle animals and the footage never matches the footage of the actors. Frequently, the actors must battle lions (Joan commands an entire pride), but the lions are always clearly stuffed and only move thanks to the furious rolls and thrusts of their attackers. Still, regardless of the risible elements, which are many, *Jungle Jim* is still good fun" (Gary Johnson, *Images Journal*).

## King of Gamblers

(Paramount Pictures) 78 min. Released on April 23, 1937.
*Survival Status*: UCLA Film and Television Archive (Los Angeles).

*Credits*: Producers, Adolph Zukor, Paul Jones; executive producer, William LeBaron; director, Robert Florey; assistant director, John Burch; screenplay, Doris Anderson; story, Tiffany Thayer; contributors to treatment, Ben Hecht, Charles MacArthur; photography, Harry Fischbeck; art direction, Hans Dreier, Robert Odell; film editor, Harvey Johnston; interior decoration, A. E. Freudeman; music director, Boris Morros; sound recording, Harry Mills, Louis Mesenkop; songs, "Hate to Talk About Myself," music and lyrics by Ralph Rainger, Leo Robin and Richard A. Whiting, "I'm Feelin' High," music and lyrics by Burton Lane and Ralph Freed.

*Cast*: Claire Trevor (Dixie Moore); Lloyd Nolan (Jim Adams); Akim Tamiroff (Steve Kalkas); Larry Crabbe (Eddie); Helen Burgess (Jackie Nolan); Porter Hall (George Kramer); Harvey Stephens (J.G. Temple); Barlowe Borland (Mr. Parker); Purnell Pratt (Strohm); Colin Tapley (Joe); Paul Fix (Charlie); Cecil Cunningham (Big Edna); Robert Gleckler (Ed Murkil); Nick Lukats (Taxi driver); Fay Holden (Nurse); John Patterson (Freddie); Evelyn Brent (Cora); Estelle Ettere (Laura); Priscilla Lawson (Grace); Harry Strang (Simeley); Richard Terry (Solly); Connie Tom (Tika); Harry Worth (Chris); Alphonse Martell (Headwaiter); Aileen Ransom (Hat check girl); George Magrill (Tough waiter); Wally Maher (Mechanic); Garry Owen (Fred—Attendant); Mildred Gover (Black maid); Frank Reicher (Temple's valet); Priscilla Moran (Secretary); Gertrude Messinger (Telephone operator); Frank Puglia (Barber); Ralph M. Remley (Customer); Henry Roquemore (Man at table); Stanley Blystone (Man at table); Russell Hicks (Man at Temple's table); Natalie Moorhead, Lelah Tyler, Rita La Roy, Helen Davis (Women at table).

The film gets off to a rousing start: We see colorful street scenes including children playing. Then we hear a barber complaining about the politics involving the slot machine in his shop. Suddenly there's an explosion, and we see a newspaper headline stating that children have been killed in the explosion. Gangster Steve Kalkas, the czar of the slot machines, kills the man who killed the kids, but the murders set off a chain of events that doom him.

On a drunken binge after getting jilted, newspaper reporter Jim Adams shows up at Kalkas' Palm Parade nightclub and buys a kiss from singer Dixie. He ends up at Dixie's apartment where he spends the night. Badly hung-over the next day, he says, "I *was* feeling open-hearted wasn't I? I suppose I didn't hold back on anything." Dixie responds with a laugh, "Don't worry ... you did."

They obviously hit it off, but Jim is sent on an assignment to London. Dixie has a fight with roommate Jackie, who is going to Havana with crook Temple. (Dixie and Jackie have an intense relationship and behave more like lovers than friends.) Kalkas, who has been after Dixie, makes his move. He sets her up in a luxurious apartment.

Temple returns from Havana and tells Kalkas he wants out. Kalkas kills Temple (it's a chilling scene as he sends Temple to his death down an elevator shaft).

Jackie is kidnapped and sent to Big Edna's so she'll remain quiet.

Dixie later finds Jackie in a hospital (she'd been drugged and thrown in a river). Dixie contacts Jim and asks for his help. He arrives at the hospital, but Jackie dies before she can tell anyone what happened. Jim finds a note in Jackie's purse: "Gave Cora my fur coat to get her to phone Dixie."

Jim begins investigating. He finds an address for Big Edna and goes to the slums. Cora and Chris also live in the broken-down boardinghouse. (Note the camera angles, shots, and set design that appear to be a Florey homage to German Expressionism. The whole boardinghouse scene, from a visual standpoint, is pretty near brilliant.) No one living there could be considered a pleasant person. Everyone squabbles, especially Cora and Chris (Brent once again shows her talent for slapping). Jim finds Jackie's clothes at the boardinghouse and gets part of the phone number for the ring leader.

Unfortunately, Dixie tells Kalkas what they know. Jim comes to Dixie's apartment and tells Kalkas even more, including the part of the phone number. Dixie says it sounds familiar. Kalkas pretends to call the police commissioner and set up a meeting. After Kalkas leaves, Dixie is sure that Jim has some questions about why she's living in Kalkas' fancy apartment.

"Listen, Dixie," Jim says. "I'm still on Jackie's assignment. When I clean that up. ... give you the beating of your life and then marry you quick just like that [snaps fingers].... Now, you have your hairbrush ready, and be sure it's a good hard one."

After Jim leaves for the meeting, Dixie remembers the rest of the phone number and dials it. Kalkas answers. Dixie alerts the police and Kramer, Jim's editor. In the climax, Kalkas and Jim fight. Meanwhile, Dixie arrives at the building and calls Kalkas' private elevator. Kalkas, thinking the elevator is waiting, steps into the elevator shaft and falls to his death.

"You suicidal dimwit!" Kramer greets Jim.

Jim hurries to embrace Dixie. "Jim," Kramer reminds him, "you've got to put the paper to bed. And I mean the *paper*." Jim and Dixie walk off arm in arm. Kramer smiles.

Evelyn Brent was not listed in the beginning screen credits, though she is the final name on the ending credits. We can thank old friend Robert Florey for including her at all. She has one scene, and it's a remarkable one because it's with Cecil Cunningham and Harry Worth. They're slovenly, low-class miscreants who hate the world and each other.

The movie, a little-known gem, is quite entertaining and loaded with great actors, including the wonderful Claire Trevor, Akim Tamiroff, and Lloyd Nolan. It also has interesting camera shots, angles, and edits. Pretty good dialogue, too. The working title was *The Kid from Paradise*. The film was also released with the title *Czar of the Slot-Machines*.

Lloyd Nolan described what it was like to work with Robert Florey: "I soon found out he knew the script backwards; he also knew the cuts and additions to be made—and just about how many days he expected to come in under schedule. He knew what sets could be converted, in a matter of minutes, by adding a ship's lifeboat, an arbor, park benches, a reversible doorway, etc., to the background with, of course, an artist's change of lighting." Lloyd also described the working conditions on these low-budget pictures: "Most of the time [Florey] would try to finish a 'B' in three six-day weeks, with only a half-hour for lunch. Studio policy was to work you on Saturday until midnight, then give you a twelve o'-clock call Monday. By the time you got home and got to sleep you probably slept all day Sunday, too, and then started again Monday. They were long, hard-working hours."[147]

This was the second film Evelyn made with Louise Brooks. The first was *Love 'Em and Leave 'Em*. Brooks was supposed to play Jim's former lover Joyce Beaton in an early scene. However, her scenes were cut from the final edit.

Brian Taves found *King of Gamblers* to be "an unexpectedly virtuoso item that turned out as well as a programmer could." It set the stage for Florey's low-budget gangster picture career. "*King of Gamblers* ... inaugurated a long series of middle- to low-budget gangster thrillers that came increasingly to dominate the assignments Paramount gave Florey in the next few years. It was certainly an auspicious beginning. Shot in March 1937, *King of Gamblers* was planned as only routine product but turned out to be near showcase quality. The film was singled out from among the run of untrumpeted movies by critics for the high quality of its script, direction, and acting."[148]

According to Taves, the success of the picture can partly be attributed to the script. "The screenplay, one of the best Florey was ever given, was based on a story by crime novelist Tiffany Thayer. The rather complex tale moves at breakneck speed.... To the intriguing script, fully-rounded characters and quality acting, Florey added superb timing, which came together to make a film of terrific excitement. His imaginative touches enlightened the photography and atmosphere of *King of Gamblers*, traits that developed into typical hallmarks of his later thrillers at Paramount. A number of interesting angles are used, particularly in Evelyn Brent's waterfront dive, shot with heavily oblique compositions and using Nolan's movement into an overhead shot and concealment behind shadowy curtains to reveal the danger he is in.... By the end of the year, Florey would direct a virtual remake, *Dangerous to Know*, with the emphasis on character rather than mystery, accenting the tragic elements of the story."[149]

Writer Tiffany Thayer was born in Freeport, Illinois, in 1902. She also wrote the novels *Thirteen Women* and *Call Her Savage* which were made into movies. Thayer died in 1959.

Claire Trevor was born Claire Wemlinger in New York City in 1910. She made her film debut in 1933 and became one of Hollywood's most dependably interesting actresses. Trevor won an Oscar for *Key Largo* (1948) and received nominations for *Dead End* (1937) and *The High and the Mighty* (1954). She also won an Emmy for her performance in "Dodsworth," an episode of *Producer's Showcase*. In 1954 she received an Emmy nomination for "Ladies in Retirement," an episode of *Lux Video Theatre*. Nicknamed the Queen of Film Noir, she died in 2000.

Born in San Francisco in 1902, Lloyd Nolan appeared on stage before making his film debut in 1935 and appeared in more than a hundred films and television episodes before his death in 1985. He won an Emmy in 1955 for playing Capt. Queeg in "The Caine Mutiny Court-Martial," an episode of *Ford Star Jubilee*. He also received an Emmy nomination for *Julia*. Nolan married Robert Florey's widow Virginia Dabney in January 1983. He also appeared with Brent in *Tip-Off Girls* (1938).

Akim Tamiroff was born in 1899 in what is now Tbilisi, Russia. He received Oscar nominations for *The General Died at Dawn* (1936) and *For Whom the Bell Tolls* (1943). He died in 1972.

Larry Crabbe, also known as Buster Crabbe, was born Clarence Linden Crabbe in Oakland, California, in 1907. An Olympic swimmer, he made his film debut in 1930. Crabbe has the distinction of being the only man to play Tarzan, Buck Rogers and Flash Gordon. He died in 1983. Crabbe also appeared with Brent in *Daughter of Shanghai* (1938) and *Tip-Off Girls* (1938).

Porter Hall was born in Ohio in 1888. He was a stage actor before making his film debut in 1931. Hall worked steadily in films and on television until his death in 1953.

Harvey Stephens was born in Los Angeles in 1901. The character actor made his film debut in 1931 and appeared in more than one hundred films and television shows. He died in 1986. Stephens also appeared with Brent in *Night Club Scandal* (1937), *Tip-Off Girls* (1938), and *Ellery Queen and the Murder Ring* (1941).

Barlowe Borland was born in Scotland in 1887 and died in 1948. Borland also appeared with Brent in *Night Club Scandal* (1937) and *Tip-Off Girls* (1938). Helen Burgess, born in Portland, Oregon, in 1916, died on April 7, 1937, shortly after *King of Gamblers* was made. She was working on the set of *Night of Mystery* when she developed pneumonia. She died a few weeks before she turned 21 and appeared in only four films. She was briefly married to Herbert Rutherford in 1937; the marriage was annulled the same year. Cecil Cunningham was a veteran character actor, often seen with a short, mannish haircut. Born in St. Louis, Missouri, in 1888, the tall (5'8") actress made her film debut in 1929. She was briefly married (1915–1917) to songwriter Jean C. Havez and died in 1959. Cunningham also appeared with Brent in *Paramount on Parade* (1930), *Night Club Scandal* (1937), and *Daughter of Shanghai* (1937). Harry Worth was born in England in 1903. He began his career in 1919 in British films. When he came to the

United States, he first acted on stage before making his American film debut in 1935. He died in 1975. He also appeared with Brent in *The Last Train from Madrid* (1937) and *Forced Landing* (1941). Natalie Moorhead was born in Pittsburgh, Pennsylvania, in 1898. She began her film career in 1929 and was a distinctive actress in many films. She retired from films in 1940 and died in 1992.

*Reviews:* "It is knock-down, drag-out melodrama all the way, but so well conceived and edited that it rates as one of Hollywood's better gangster pieces. ... sure-fire stuff.... [I]t's Tamiroff's picture all the way" (*Syracuse Herald*, June 5, 1937).

"This meller is of the old gangster school of pix, but well enough done to rate okay in the smaller spots solo.... Picture moves pretty fast, despite a poor cutting job. Dialog is generally good, and so's Robert Florey's direction" (*Variety*, July 7, 1937).

"Freshness and originality are lacking from the story.... But Robert Florey has directed with keenness and authority, enlivening his work with surprising touches and generated tension and suspense of such a high order that the picture becomes absorbing, thrilling and very much worthwhile. Last, but far from least, the acting is as fine as can be found in any current picture" (*Los Angeles Times*, July 11, 1937).

"In the late thirties Paramount was notable for the best low-budget, fast-paced program pictures in the business. *King of Gamblers*, for instance, showed some of its more expensive brethren how to hold audience attention every minute, even if motivations were sometimes foggy and loose narrative ends left dangling" (John Douglas Eames, *The Paramount Story*, p. 126).

## The Last Train from Madrid

(Paramount Pictures) 83 min. Released on June 18, 1937.
*Survival Status:* UCLA Film and Television Archive (Los Angeles).
*Credits:* Producers, Adolph Zukor, George M. Arthur; executive producer, William LeBaron; director, James Hogan; associate director, Hugh Bennett; assistant director, Roland Asher; screenplay, Louis Stevens, Robert Wyler; story, Paul Hervey Fox, Elsie Fox; contributor to screenplay construction and dialogue, True Boardman; photography, Harry Fischbeck; art direction, Hans Dreier, Earl Hedrick; film editor, Everett Douglas; interior decorations, A. E. Freudeman; musical director, Boris Morros; sound recording, Gene Merritt, Louis Mesenkop.
*Cast:* Dorothy Lamour (Carmelita Castillo); Lew Ayres (Bill Dexter); Gilbert Roland (Eduardo de Soto); Karen Morley (Helene Rafitto); Lionel Atwill (Colonel Vigo); Helen Mack (Lola); Robert Cummings (Juan Ramos); Olympe Bradna (Maria Ronda); Anthony Quinn (Captain Ricardo Alvarez); Lee Bowman (Michael Balk); Jack Perrin (Guard); Harry Semels (Guard); Frank Leyva (Chauffeur); Roland Rego (Officer); Frank Lyman (Officer); Merrill McCormick (Officer); Robert Strange (Officer); George Lloyd (Intelligence officer); Louise Carter (Rosa Delgado); Henry Hale (Dias); Karl Hackett (Herrera); Hooper Atchley (Martin); Otto Hoffman (Fernando); John Oliver (Orderly); John Picorri (First hotel clerk); Peter De Rey (Second hotel clerk); Allan Garcia (Third hotel clerk); Dan Colette (Fourth hotel clerk); Guy D'Ennery (Dignified man); Ralf Harolde (Spanish man); Joseph de Stefani (Factory owner); Nigel de Brulier (Philosopher); John Marshall (Clerk); Stanley Price

(Clerk); Sam Appel (Warden); Stanley Fields (Avila); Francis McDonald (Mora); George Magrill, Carl Harbaugh, Jack Gardner, Sid D'Albrook, Robert Middlemass, Bert LeBaron (Militiamen); George MacQuarrie (Driver); Rollo Lloyd (Hernandez); Henry Brandon (Radio announcer); Louis Natheaux (Headwaiter); Maurice Cass (Waiter); Alonzo Price (Leader); Harry Worth (Gomez); Donald Reed (Husband); Leonard Sues (Young man); Harry Woods (Government man); Ben Hendricks (Perez); George Lollier (Secret Service man); Bob O'Connor, Stanley Andrews (Secret Service men); Hallene Hill (Mother); Francis Ford (Pedro); Reynolds Denniston (Stationmaster); Adele St. Maur (Mother); Yvonne Pelletier (Daughter); Bess Flowers (Saleswoman); Carlos de Valdez (Carlos Ronda); Charles Middleton (Warden); Gordon De Main (Gonzales); Bonita Weber (Woman soldier); Tiny Rowland (Turnkey); Sid Nene (Man in railroad station); Evelyn Brent (Soldier); Charles Stevens, Sharon Lewis, Ricca Allen, Libby Taylor.

The film begins with the sights and sounds of a fast-moving train. "Out of War have come the world's greatest dramas—dramas all the more challenging to the imagination because their basis is real. This is such a story—an account of fictional characters caught in beleaguered Madrid, fired with one common desire—Escape. We neither uphold nor condemn either faction of the Spanish conflict. This is a story of people—not of causes."

Only one more train will leave Madrid. In order to be on that train, one must have a special pass. Citizens are desperate to leave.

Captain Ricardo Alvarez is an old friend of Eduardo, a political prisoner who is brought to Madrid. Out of loyalty, Ricardo allows Eduardo to go free. Eduardo returns to girlfriend Carmelita, who plans to leave on the train, only to find out that she is now Ricardo's girlfriend.

Meanwhile, soldiers march off to war. "What's the matter, my dove, aren't you enjoying our war?" a woman soldier (Evelyn Brent) asks Maria. Maria complains that she doesn't like the war and wants to get to Madrid. "I understand," the woman replies. "It's no fun shooting strange men before you've had a chance to find out you don't like them." The marchers are bombed and seek cover. "Here's your chance, kid! Run for it!" This is Brent's only scene; she is not listed in the credits. Maria catches a ride with American reporter Bill Dexter (at gunpoint) and explains that she must get to Madrid because her father is being executed.

These are just two of the stories told in this long film. All the stories are melodramatic and reach their climax when the time nears for the train to leave. Although most of the cast is good, the script does not seem genuine or cohesive. Though it had great potential, the plot feels contrived and soap operaish, relying too much on clichés rather than on originality. Still, the final fifteen minutes pack a wallop.

The best scenes are the ones with Karen Morley. She brings a sophisticated *film noir* feel to her role. "You cheap, little-minded fool," she says to Michael, who is indeed that—and more—and then shoots him with a cold look on her beautiful face.

Original director Al Santell was replaced by James Hogan. Hogan, born in Lowell, Massachusetts, in 1890, began his career in the silent film era. He directed several Bulldog Drummond and Ellery Queen films in the 1930s and 1940s and died in 1943.

Writer Louis Stevens at first insisted on full writing credit. However, producer George M. Arthur convinced Stevens to share credit with Robert Wyler. Wyler was later nominated (with Philip Yordan) for an Oscar for *Detective Story* (1951).

The original story was pursued by other studios, but Paramount won the bidding war. Paul Hervey Fox received $10,000 for the story. Novelist Fox and his Cuban wife Elsie were the parents of the excellent writer Paula Fox (Courtney Love's grandmother) who wrote about them in her memoir *Borrowed Finery*. "[Paul Hervey Fox] told me he'd written the entire movie in a week while Elsie, my mother, handed him Benzedrine tablets from the bed upon which she lay, doing crossword puzzles and lighting cigarette after cigarette."[150] Neither Fox was a good parent, and they eventually divorced.

It was announced in April 1937 that Brent was joining the cast of *The Last Train from Madrid*. Told in *Grand Hotel* style, this film was one of Hollywood's first movies about the Spanish Civil War. Gilbert Roland, who apparently thought it important at the time, ordered all cast members to shave off moustaches so theirs wouldn't compete with his. Alan Ladd and Cecil B. DeMille had bit parts. Some scenes were filmed in Palencia, Spain. Others, probably the ones with Dorothy Lamour, were filmed at DeMille's bungalow on the Paramount lot. The tagline was "Thousands Flee As Bombs Rain On Madrid."

Dorothy Lamour, born Mary Leta Dorothy Slaton in New Orleans in 1914, is best known for the *Road* pictures she made with Bing Crosby and Bob Hope. She's also known as "The Sarong Girl." Lamour, who started her career as a big band singer, died in 1996.

Lew Ayres, who is very similar to Jack Lemmon in looks and acting style, was born in Minnesota in 1908. He received an Oscar nomination for *Johnny Belinda* (1948) and an Emmy nomination for an episode of *Kung Fu*. During World War II he was a conscientious objector who worked as a medic and chaplain's aid. Ayres, who married and divorced Lola Lane and Ginger Rogers, died in 1996.

Gilbert Roland was born Luis Antonio Dámaso de Alonso in Mexico in 1905. He began his career as an extra in silent films in the 1920s and was still making film and television appearances into the 1980s. Roland, who was briefly married to Constance Bennett, died in 1994. It was reported in the pressbook that Roland's father, Don Francisco de Alonso, had a bit part in the film. Roland also appeared with Brent in *Robin Hood of Monterey* (1947).

Karen Morley, born Mildred Linton in Ottumwa, Iowa, in 1909, saw her career suffer because of her political activities. She and husband Lloyd Gough were blacklisted in the 1950s. A longtime supporter of liberal causes, she ran an unsuccessful campaign for New York lieutenant governor in 1954. Morley, a sensation in *Scarface* (1932), died in 2003.

Lionel Atwill was born in London in 1885. Atwill's career was damaged by a scandal involving a 1940 sex party at his home. He was eventually put on probation after being convicted of perjury during the grand jury probe. Atwill died in 1946. He also appeared with Brent in *The Mad Empress* (1939).

Helen Mack, born in Rock Island, Illinois, in 1913, was a child star who performed on vaudeville and in movies. She made her last film with Monogram in 1945. Mack later became a radio producer and scriptwriter. Mack died in 1986.

Robert Middlemass was born in Connecticut in 1883 and died in 1949. He also appeared with Brent in *The Pay Off* (1942). Born in Paris in 1920, Olympe Bradna was a dancer at the Folies-Bergere. Her first film was in 1933 and her last in 1941. Anthony Quinn was born Antonio Rudolfo Oaxaca Quinn in Mexico in 1913. He won Oscars for *Viva Zapata!* (1952) and *Lust for Life* (1956) and received nominations for *Wild Is the Wind* (1957) and *Zorbas the Greek* (1964). His first wife was Katherine DeMille, daughter of Cecil B. DeMille. Quinn, who died in 2001, also appeared with Brent in *Daughter of Shanghai* (1937) and *Tip-Off Girls* (1938). Lee Bowman, born in Cincinnati in 1914, made his film debut in 1937. He appeared in many television shows in the 1950s and 1960s, including *The Adventures of Ellery Queen* in 1951, and died in 1979. Francis Ford, born in Portland, Maine, in 1881, was the brother of director John Ford. He was a writer, director and actor. He also appeared with Brent in *Bowery Champs* (1944). Ford died in 1953.

*Reviews:* "Bolstered by an intriguing title, picture is weak on cast names and has a befuddled tale to tell. Main difficulty is the half dozen intrigues within narrow confines" (*Variety*, June 23, 1937).

"An action-packed drama of modern Spain with timely subject material and a good story, but the dialogue is an insult to intelligence" (*Photoplay*, September 1937).

"Strongly cast [but] production was otherwise deplorable. James Hogan's direction ... had a slapdash air, and for realism of time and place it might as well have been *The Last Subway from the Bronx*. Although slammed by critics, it brought pretty good attendance, doubtless drawn by so many well-known players" (John Douglas Eames, *The Paramount Story*, p. 128).

## *Night Club Scandal*

(Paramount Pictures) 72 min. Released on November 19, 1937.

*Survival Status:* UCLA Film and Television Archive (Los Angeles).

*Credits:* Producers, Adolph Zukor, Harold Hurley, William Lackey; executive producer, William LeBaron; director, Ralph Murphy; assistant director, Mel Epstein; based on the play *Riddle Me This* by Daniel N. Rubin; screenplay, Lillie Hayward; photography, Leo Tover; art direction, Hans Dreier, Earl Hedrick; film editor, Archie

Marshek; interior decorations, A. E. Freudeman; music director; Boris Morros; sound recording; Philip Wisdom, Richard Olson; songs, "No More Tears," words and music by Ralph Freed and Burton Lane.

*Cast*: John Barrymore (Dr. Ernest Tindal); Lynne Overman (Russell Kirk); Charles Bickford (Capt. McKinley); Louise Campbell (Vera Marlan); Elizabeth Patterson (Mrs. Elvira Ward); Harvey Stephens (Frank Marlan); Cecil Cunningham (Mrs. Alvin); Evelyn Brent (Julia Reed); J. Carrol Naish (Jack Reed); Barlowe Borland (Dr. Sully); John Sheehan (Duffy); George Guhl (Brown); Frank O'Connor (Alcott); Leonard Willey (Dr. Goodman); George Offerman, Jr. (Messenger boy); Lee Shumway (Policeman); Dorothy Howe (Marlan maid); Herbert Ashley (Doorman); Jack Raymond (Cab driver); Mack Gray (Reed's assistant); Robert Brister (District attorney); Dick Cramer (Prison guard); John Hamilton (Governor); Fred Warren (Waiter); Spec O'Donnell (Copy boy); Dudley Clements (Mullins); Franklin Parker (Reporter); Reginald Simpson (Secretary).

We see Ernest S. Tindal's medical bag. He walks out of his bedroom with a stethoscope around his neck. Ominous music plays. It ought to, because he's just killed his wife.

Tindal goes to the Columbine Club. Jack Reed owns the club, and Captain McKinley is keeping a close eye on the joint because Jack's a gangster.

Vera is having dinner at the club with brother Frank, who is in a rush to leave for a date with Mrs. Tindal. As the waiter brings the check, Vera says to Frank, "It must be love." "No, ma'am," the waiter deadpans, "eight dollars and fifteen cents." (The actors—Harvey Stephens and Louise Campbell—appear uncomfortable having to chuckle at that godawful line. There are plenty of good lines to make up for it.)

Frank discovers Mrs. Tindal's body. He pleads with Vera to give him an alibi. When the police investigate they find annoying reporter Russell Kirk, a burr in McKinley's pants, already there. He gives the report to his newspaper: "She was killed while her husband was at a banquet delivering a lecture on how to live to be a ripe old age. She got her throat caught in her sweetheart's fingers. Yeah. Certainly there was a sweetheart. She was 25, and her husband was 50. Write your own story."

Tindal arrives home and pretends to be grief-stricken, enraged, etc. His alibi is provided by Mrs. Ward. She heard Mrs. Tindal playing the piano after Tindal left for his banquet. The cook, Mrs. Alvin, arrives and tells everyone that Mrs. Tindal was having an affair. She's a venomous old thing. "She had it comin' to her too," she adds.

McKinley takes Frank in for questioning. A watch charm found in Mrs. Tindal's clutched hand matches Frank's. Mrs. Alvin identifies Frank's voice as the one she heard arguing with Mrs. Tindal. Vera provides the fake alibi for Frank, but Kirk tells McKinley that Vera went home alone. With the evidence mounting, Frank finally admits he found the body but didn't kill Mrs. Tindal.

Kirk tries to persuade McKinley to wait to sign a complaint against Frank. "Listen, nitwit, a man could walk into a house, kill the owner, be photographed in a mirror standing over the body with a weapon in his hand, and if nobody saw him commit the murder, it's still circumstantial evidence," McKinley gruffly tells him. "But you're the only jackass in the world that would believe he didn't do it."

Frank is tried and found guilty. Meanwhile, Kirk has fallen for Vera and wants to prove Frank's innocence before he's executed. "He always was a sucker for a good-looking dame," McKinley says.

Kirk demonstrates to McKinley that Frank couldn't have committed the murder and turns the attention to Jack Reed. Tindal gives Jack and Julia a heads-up that McKinley is on his way. Jack tries to escape but is shot by McKinley. Meanwhile, Kirk is unable to get a stay of execution for Frank.

Kirk finds a business card that he picked up at the murder scene. It's for the Famous Music Co. One of the items they sell is player pianos. Yep. Tindal had bought a player piano. Meanwhile, Julia, Jack's wife, has called Tindal to minister to her husband's wounds. Tindal kills Jack, telling Julia the bullet was too near his heart and nothing could be done.

Julia arrives at McKinley's office. The grief-stricken widow is armed. "But you had the law on your side so you could shoot. Well, I'm giving that lead right back—!" She fires at McKinley but is overpowered. Kirk arrives with the news that McKinley's bullet didn't kill Jack—the doctor who operated on him did. Julia finally tells them it was Tindal.

In the climax, they all head to the apartment. Kirk explains that Tindal committed the murder. He demonstrates how the player piano was set up to play after the doctor left the apartment. Tindal is arrested.

McKinley puts in a good word for Kirk with Vera. However, she tells him she's engaged. "You ... You're very sweet," she finally says to Kirk before leaving.

"You certainly are *very* sweet," McKinley chimes in.

"Ah, shut up!"

"Well, that's that," McKinley says.

Filming began in August 1937. The working title was *City Hall Scandal*. Neither title is very good.

Evelyn's part isn't large, but she does have a few nice scenes and gets to sing "No More Tears" at a beautiful night club. Her voice is deep and pleasant; too bad she didn't get to sing in other pictures.

This picture was a loose remake of *Guilty as Hell* (1932). In that version, Noel Francis played Julia Reed, and Ralph Ince, Brent's former director, was Julia's ill-fated husband. Elizabeth Patterson played the same role in both productions. Other actors in the 1932 production included Edmund Lowe, Victor McLaglen, Richard Arlen, Adrienne Ames, and Henry Stephenson.

*Night Club Scandal* is a good hard-boiled comedy based on the play *Riddle Me This*. It doesn't try to be anything more than it is. An aging and fading John Barrymore—he'd be dead in five years—phones in his performance. He was at the point in his career where his difficulty remembering lines necessitated that his lines be written on an off-set blackboard.

Notice in this film how he's often looking off, seemingly at nothing and no one. This was the second time Evelyn had worked with Barrymore, though twenty years had passed since they were together in *Raffles, the Amateur Cracksman*. Barrymore had aged considerably, Brent less so. Barrymore received top billing, and Brent was billed eighth.

Charles Bickford does a great job as a gruff, nononsense detective. Bickford's career had almost ended two years before while filming *East of Java* when he was nearly killed by a lion. Bickford and Lynne Overman make a great team. Overman plays the Frank McHugh–type role a bit obnoxiously at first, but his final scene when he realizes he won't get the girl is poignant and believable. Overman, born in Maryville, Missouri, in 1887, died in 1943 of a heart attack.

This was one of Louise Campbell's first films, and she's quite good as the loyal sister. She sounds a bit like a cross between June Allyson and Jean Arthur. Campbell was born Louise Weisbecker in Chicago in 1911. Married to actor Horace MacMahon from 1937 until his death in 1971, she died in 1997.

Elizabeth Patterson, born in Savannah, Tennessee, in 1875, was the daughter of a Confederate soldier. She was a stage star but did not make a film until she was in her 50s. She is probably best known for playing Lucy's babysitter Mrs. Trumbull on *I Love Lucy*. She's very good in this film, playing a ZaSu Pitts–type character. Patterson died in 1966.

Two years after this film, Dorothy Howe won the "Gateway to Hollywood" talent search sponsored by Jesse Lasky, and her name was changed to Virginia Vale. Born in Dallas, Texas, in 1920, she died in 2006. John Hamilton, who played the governor, is best known for playing Perry White on TV's *Adventures of Superman*. Born in Pennsylvania in 1887, he died in 1958.

Director Ralph Murphy, briefly married to actress Gloria Dickson, turned his attention to directing television shows in the 1950s. His small-screen credits included *Mr. & Mrs. North*, *Lassie*, *Broken Arrow*, and *The Many Loves of Dobie Gillis*. Born in Connecticut in 1895, he died in 1967.

Screenwriter Lillie Hayward (born in St. Paul, Minnesota in 1891), sister of actress Seena Owen, was a prolific screenwriter who eventually wrote for Disney including such films as *The Shaggy Dog*. Hayward was a silent film actress from 1911 to 1918. Married to writer Jerry Sackheim, she died in 1977.

*Reviews*: "Murder story with breezy comedy via Overman is pleasing entertainment" (*Film Daily*, October 21, 1937).

"Though not especially 'ambitious' in a productional sense, the film itself—largely in consequence—may be counted among the more tolerable of recent corpse operas" (*New York Times*, November 12, 1937).

"The old formula about dumb cops and smart newspaper guys following themselves around through a simple murder case. And in the customary, lazy film fashion, the only way to solve the first death is by compelling the culprit to commit another.... The camera work is okay, and

the nite club set is only a background of apparent sumptuousness, not fitting into the scheme of the plot" (*Variety*, December 22, 1937).

"The memory had gone, along with much of the famous good looks. But—*Night Club Scandal* made clear—[John Barrymore's] inimitable style was still intact. It brought a touch of class and a fizz of excitement to a grade B whodunit..." (John Douglas Eames, *The Paramount Story*, p. 123).

## Sudden Bill Dorn

(Universal Pictures) 60 min. Released on December 1, 1937.

*Survival Status*: Autry National Center (Los Angeles); British Film Institute/National Film and Television Archive (London); UCLA Film and Television Archive (Los Angeles).

*Credits*: Director, Ray Taylor; assistant director, W. B. Eason; screenplay, Frances Guihan; story, Jackson Gregory; photography, Allen Thompson, John Hickson; art direction, Ralph Berger; film editor, Bernard Loftus; sound supervisor; L. John Myers.

*Cast*: Buck Jones (Bill Dorn); Noel Francis (Lorna Kent); Evelyn Brent (Diana Villegas); Frank McGlynn Sr. (Cap Jenks [Captain Asbury Jinks]); Lee Phelps (Ken Fairchild); Harold Hodge (Mike Bundy); Ted Adams (Fontana); Mabel Colcord (Maggie); Wm. Lawrence (Hank Smith); Tom Chatterton (Stock Morgan); Ezra Paulette (Curly O'Connor); Carlos J. de Valdez (Don Francis); Chas. Le Moyne (Sheriff); Red Hightower (Bud Williams); Adolph Milar (Tony).

Prospector Bundy discovers gold at the Kent ranch but keeps it secret. He tries to take the ranch away from Bill's niece Lorna. An explosion ultimately reveals Bundy's secret.

A tagline was "A RIDIN'-BLAST of HE-MAN FURY!"

Noel Francis, a former Ziegfeld girl, was born in Texas in 1906. Her best known role might have been in *I Am a Fugitive from a Chain Gang* (1932). She never married and died in 1959.

Frank McGlynn, Sr., was the father of actor Frank McGlynn, Jr., who appeared in the *Jungle Jim* serial with Brent. The elder McGlynn often portrayed Abraham Lincoln in films. Born in San Francisco in 1866, he died in 1951.

Director Ray Taylor began his silent film career in 1926. He directed well over a hundred films and television episodes, specializing in Westerns and science fiction. Born in Minnesota in 1888, he died in 1952.

*Reviews*: "Despite [the] uneven tempo, *Sudden Bill Dorn* easily is Buck Jones' best in months.... Evelyn Brent strives ardently to make something of that sketchy Senorita character" (*Variety*, January 12, 1938).

## Daughter of Shanghai

(Paramount Pictures) 67 min. Released on December 16, 1937.

*Survival status*: Library of Congress (Washington, D.C.); Archive: UCLA Film and Television Archive (Los Angeles).

*Credits*: Producers, Adolph Zukor, Edward T. Lowe;

executive producer, William LeBaron; director, Robert Florey; assistant director, Stanley Goldsmith; screenplay, Gladys Unger, Garnett Weston; based on the story "Honor Bright" by Garnett Weston; photography, Charles Schoenbaum; art direction; Hans Dreier, Robert Odell; film editor, Ellsworth Hoagland; interior decorations, A. E. Freudeman; music director, Boris Morros; sound recording, Charles Hisserich, Richard Olson.

*Cast*: Anna May Wong (Lan Ying Lin); Charles Bickford (Otto Hartman); Larry Crabbe (Andrew Sleete); Cecil Cunningham (Mrs. Mary Hunt); J. Carrol Naish (Frank Barden); Anthony Quinn (Harry Morgan); John Patterson (James Lang); Evelyn Brent (Olga Derey); Philip Ahn (Kim Lee); Fred Kohler (Captain Gulner); Guy Bates Post (Lloyd Burkett); Virginia Dabney (Rita, a dancer); Ching Wah Lee (Quan Lin); Frank Sully (Jake Kelly); Ernest Whitman (Sam Blike); Maurice Liu (Ah Fong); Mrs. Wong Wing (Amah); Paul Fix (Miles); Gwen Kenyon (Phone girl); Charles Wilson (Schwartz); John Hart (Sailor); Layne Tom, Jr. (Chinese candy vendor); Michael Wu (Yung Woo); Mae Busch (Lil); Bill Powell (Carib waiter); Carmen Bailey (Dancer); Paulita Arvizu (Dancer); Carmen La Roux (Dancer); Tina Menard (Dancer); Gino Corrado (Interpreter); Alex Woloshin (Gypsy); Agostino Borgato (Gypsy); Bruce Wong (Chinese); Andre P. Marsaudon (South American); Billy Jones, Jimmie Dundee, Chick Collins (Seamen who fight); Harry Strang (Sailor); Lee Shumway (Ship's officer); Pierre Watkin (Mr. Yorkland); Rebecca Wassem, Marie Burton, Paula de Cardo, Alma Ross, Blanca Vischer, Norah Gale, Harriette Haddon, Joyce Mathews, Helaine Moler.

"FOREIGN HORDE FLOODS U.S." screams a headline in a San Francisco newspaper. The next headline is "HUMAN CARGO PAYOFF TOTALS MILLIONS!" Next: "UNCOVER COAST SMUGGLING RING." Finally, we see "AIRPLANES USED TO LAND ALIENS."

In a particularly chilling scene we see an airplane loaded with, yes, human cargo being tailed by a government plane. Unable to lose it, Harry Morgan (no, not *that* Harry Morgan—this one is played by Anthony Quinn) opens a trap door and sends the unfortunates hurtling into the ocean. That, my friend, is cold. Even colder is Morgan's comment: "There goes $6,000."

Government agent Kim Lee is assigned to work on the case. Meanwhile, the smugglers try to involve Chinese importer Quan Lin, but he refuses. Lin and daughter Lan Ying are kidnapped. Lin is shot and killed. Their car is dumped into the water, but Lan Ying escapes.

She and her father were supposed to meet with antique collector Mrs. Hunt and Lee so she goes to the house and tells her what happened. Unfortunately, Lan Ying does not realize that Mrs. Hunt is the ringleader.

Lan Ying goes off in search of a man named Hartman and finds him on the island of Port O' Juan. Pretending she wants to be a dancer in his club, Lan Ying tries to meet with Hartman. First, though, she has to go through harsh Olga. "He don't need anyone. He told me so," she barks. Despite Olga's efforts, Lan Ying finally meets grumpy Hartman. He likes what he sees and decides to hire her.

Meanwhile, Lee has also made his way to the island. Billed as "Daughter of Shanghai," Lan Ying dances and is recognized by Lee. They agree to travel back to San Francisco together. Before they leave, Lee steals Hartman's transaction book. Captain Gulner quickly realizes the two are conspiring and takes them prisoner.

As the smugglers wait for the ship to arrive, they remain curious about the two who were captured. "Sharks won't be particular," Andrew (played by Larry Crabbe, who at times in this film looks remarkably like Burt Reynolds) says with a smile.

Lee and Lan Ying escape. Unfortunately, they escape to one of Mrs. Hunt's houses. Still unaware that she's a bad guy, Lan Ying tries to tell her everything that's happened. Suddenly, however, she sees a notation in Hartman's book. "So that's it," she says. "You're the boss."

"My dear," Mrs. Hunt corrects, "I'm a businesswoman."

Although tied up, Lee manages to make a phone call (he's a very limber man). In addition, Mrs. Hunt's chauffeur Kelly helps Lee and Lan Ying. The police arrive.

"How would you like to live in Washington?" Lee asks Lan Ying.

"Perhaps a change of climate is just what I need."

The two lovebirds speak some words of Chinese between them.

Mrs. Hunt wants to know how long she'll be in prison. "When you get out of jail, my grandchildren will be enjoying my Social Security checks," Kelly tells her. (The first Social Security payments were issued in January 1937.)

*Daughter of Shanghai* was filmed in the fall of 1937; the working title was *Across the River*. It was made in three weeks. At one point Paramount wanted to use the title *Daughter of the Tong* but changed their minds. It was released as *Daughter of the Orient* in the United Kingdom. *Daughter of Shanghai* was added to the National Film Registry in 2006. It's a very good "B" movie that is a cut above, mainly due to the efforts of Robert Florey and a strong cast. Florey collected Chinese furniture and used some of his own pieces on the set.

This is one of Anthony Quinn's first efforts, and, typically, he's cast as a menacing goon. Quinn was once married to Katherine DeMille, daughter of director Cecil B. DeMille.

Evelyn Brent was announced as an addition to the cast in September 1937. She was billed eighth and played a jealous, tightly wound woman who packed quite a glare.

Florey and fellow director Nick Grinde enjoyed a strange competition. Each tried to include, whenever possible, a character who holds an electric fan. In *Daughter of Shanghai*, you'll see Charles Bickford doing the honors.

The film was an attempt to revitalize the career of Anna May Wong. This was a sympathetic part for Wong, and her first feature film in two years. Her refusal to accept a subordinate role in *The Good Earth* (1937), and then leaving for China after Luise Rainer got the lead, made her unpopular in Hollywood. Her last important American film had been *Daughter of the Dragon* (1931). Florey had previously worked with Wong on *A Study in Scarlet* (1932). Many of the gowns Wong wore in the film were ones she'd purchased in Peking. Biographer Graham Russell Gao Hodges described one unique costume: "[It] ... was made of blue Chinese crepe with a brocaded plum blossom pattern. Piping of three shades of blue satin accented the costume. The trousers were blue silk, with an oriental knot pattern applied over the net."[151] Notice that Wong, true to Chinese custom, does not wear clothing that shows her legs. According to Philip Leibfried and Chei Mi Lane, "As entertaining as it is, *Daughter of Shanghai* marked the beginning of the long road downward for Anna May Wong's career. She would no longer star in 'A' pictures. In fact she would appear in only one, and that was to be her last film."[152]

Publicity suggested that Wong and Ahn would marry in real life too. However, bisexual Wong refused to play along, insisting that she felt no romantic feelings for the reportedly gay Ahn, though they were great friends. Wong was still considered star material at the time and received a little more than $4,000 for her work on the film. Ahn, on the other hand, received $1,000.

Wong was born in Wong Liu Tsong in Los Angeles in 1905. Her cousin was cinematographer James Wong Howe. Her career began in silent films, and she also enjoyed a vaudeville and nightclub career. A fascinating actress and woman, she died in 1961.

Ahn was actually Korean, not Chinese. Born in Los Angeles in 1905, he made his film debut in 1935. Ahn is best known for his many television appearances including playing Master Kan in *Kung Fu*. He died in 1978.

Florey married Atlanta-born actress Virginia Dabney on October 25, 1939. In addition to *Daughter of Shanghai*, she was often cast in his films but retired shortly after their marriage. Dabney was born in Atlanta, Georgia, in 1907. After Florey's death, she married Lloyd Nolan in 1983. Dabney died in 1991.

"The ever-popular" Mae Busch, born in Australia in 1891, began her film career in 1912. Convent-educated, she was known as "The Versatile Vamp." She's perhaps best known for playing Oliver Hardy's wife in several films. Busch died in 1946.

This was John Hart's first film. Born in Los Angeles in 1917, he became a popular television performer. He was Hawkeye Cutler on TV's *Hawkeye and the Last of the Mohicans* and the Lone Ranger in the 1950s television version. He also appeared with Brent in *Tip-Off Girls* (1938).

Pierre Watkin, born in Sioux City, Iowa, in 1889, made his film debut in 1932. He racked up close to four hundred film and television appearances until his death in 1960. He also appeared with Brent in *Tip-Off Girls* (1938) and *Ellery Queen and the Murder Ring* (1941).

*Reviews:* "A tense, melodramatic atmosphere ... is successfully maintained.... An unusually competent cast saves the film from the worst consequences of certain inevitable banalities" (*New York Times*, December 24, 1937).

"Good example of Hollywood's efficiency in turning out palatable trifles.... Robert Florey's direction is capable enough and several scenic shots are colorful, photography and sound are capably handled. For a frankly secondrate offering, *Daughter of Shanghai* isn't half bad" (*Variety*, December 29, 1937).

"It is well made, holding enough punch for action houses ... well paced, with the necessary melodramatic angles" (*Motion Picture Exhibitor*, January 1, 1938).

"[A] thrilling tale" (*Los Angeles Evening Herald Express*, January 6, 1938).

According to Brian Taves, "*Daughter of Shanghai* was a quickly-paced topical exploitation thriller dealing with the always timely subject of illegal immigration.... The direction, set design, and photography are well above the 'B' level and the perils-of-Anna type plot. The movie was made with a knowing sense of humor that glosses over the unlikelihood of many of the twists in plot, the players imbuing some of their more unfortunate lines with a subtly amusing tongue-in-cheek quality. The photography is extremely dark, as if taking place entirely at night, with only a few interiors well illuminated. This produces a sense of menace and uncertainty in every scene" (Brian Taves, *Robert Florey*, pp. 206–07).

"As a Paramount B-movie, *Daughter of Shanghai* is quite well executed. While the editing and acting (from minor actors) are somewhat underwhelming, the production values are very good. The film is overall an improvement in its less exoticized portrayal of Asian characters. *Daughter of Shanghai* was touted as a positive depiction of Chinese people. If "positive" refers to screentime and speaking parts (and close-ups for that matter), then Florey's film delivers with respect to shot composition and plot. On the other hand, being in the foreground is only part of a broader issue" (Stina Chyn, Turner Classic Movies website).

## *Tip-Off Girls*

(Paramount Pictures) 61 min. Released on March 25, 1938.

*Survival status:* UCLA Film and Television Archive (Los Angeles).

*Credits:* Producer, Adolph Zukor; executive producer, William LeBaron; associate producer, Edward T. Lowe; director, Louis King; based on the article "Hunting the Highway Pirates" by William E. Frazer; original screenplay, Maxwell Shane, Robert Yost, Stuart Anthony; photography, Theodor Sparkuhl; art direction, Hans Dreier, Robert Odell; film editor, Ellsworth Hoagland; interior decorations, A. E. Freudeman; musical director, Boris Morros; sound recording, Charles Hisserich, Walter Oberst.

*Cast:* Mary Carlisle (Marjorie Rogers); Lloyd Nolan (Bob Anders); Roscoe Karns (Tom Benson); Larry Crabbe (Red Deegan); J. Carrol Naish (Joseph Valkus); Evelyn Brent (Rena Terry); Anthony Quinn (Marty); Benny Baker (Scotty); Harvey Stephens (Jason Baardue); Irving Bacon (Sam); Gertrude Short ("Boots" Milburn); Archie Twitchell (Hensler); Barlowe Borland (Blacky); Pierre Watkin (George Murkil); John Hart, Harry Templeton, Vic Demoruelle, Jr., Jack Pennick, Ethan Laidlaw, Stanley King (Truck drivers); Stanley Price (Louis); Phillip Warren (Steve); Wade Boteler (Pete, weighing cop); John Patterson (Jim); Frank Austin (Gus); Richard Allen (Police lieutenant); Stanley Andrews (Police sergeant); Oscar G. Hendrian (Hijacker); Barbara Jackon (Nurse); Wally Dean (First businessman); Field Norton (Second businessman); Frank Mayo (Third businessman); Pat West (Proprietor); Al Herman (Proprietor); Wally Maher (Garage attendant); Harry Fleischmann (Cop); Willard Kent (Cop); Joyce Mathews (Tessie); Ruth Rogers, Laurie Lane, Margaret Randall, Cheryl Walker (Waitresses); Lola Jensen, Paula de Cardo, Marion Weldon, Gloria Williams.

The film begins with a couple of truckers coming across a woman lying in the road. They stop to help. It turns out to be a stick-up. The woman lying in the road, Rena, is praised by thug Marty. "That's my job, Marty," Rena cheerfully replies, "pleasing Deegan."

Headlines proclaim: "TRUCK COMPANIES FACE RUIN FROM ROAD ROBBERS!," "MILLIONS LOST TO HIGHWAY PIRATES!," and "TRUCKMEN DEMAND FEDERAL AID!"

At Deegan's warehouse, pirated shipments keep coming in with goods varying from furs to cigarettes to silk. "Rena, you're the greatest little tip-off gal in the game," Deegan compliments his girlfriend (he should—Brent looks great in this one) and then hands her one of the furs.

Stenographer Marjorie Rogers gets involved in this business because she works for ruthless truck company owner Joseph Valkus, who helps fence the goods. (Maybe it's us, but it seems this film is loaded with double entendres and sexual innuendo. For one thing, they can't seem to say dictation enough. Also, during one dictation episode, the letter begins, "My Dear Johnson." Perhaps the writers were having a bit of fun.)

Things start going badly for Deegan and his boys when his hijackers are hijacked by Bob Anders and Tom Benson. When Anders and Benson are caught by Deegan, they ask to be cut in. Deegan invites them to join his outfit.

Rena expresses doubts about Anders. "I don't know. Just a funny little feeling," she says. Turns out, she's absolutely right. While he's pretending to help the Deegan gang by roughing up a policeman, he's actually telling him where he'll leave his report. Anders is one of the good guys in the police and FBI investigation.

Someone has been tipping off "hijackers" about Valkus' trucks. He starts putting the heat on Deegan. Meanwhile, Anders is getting closer to Valkus' secretary Marjorie.

Marty and Rena catch Tom giving the FBI a tip. Anders is meeting with Valkus when Tom is brought in. "There's your stool pigeon," Rena announces. Valkus hands Anders a gun to kill Tom. "Well, that makes you smarter than me, Valkus," Anders says with defeat in his voice. Still, Anders manages to turn on the dictograph, and Marjorie overhears the conversation. Unfortunately, she is caught.

Boots and Scotty are Marjorie's two dim-witted friends (not a brain between them). Marjorie leaves Boots a shorthand message to decipher.

In the climax, Tom and Marjorie take a truck to meet the "hijackers," actually FBI and police officers. Meanwhile, Boots tries to decipher her "shorthand lesson." Thrilled with herself, Boots has "figured" it out: "I know what Marge is doing. She's writing a detective story about hijacking, and she's making Mr. Valkus the villain." Scotty, who is apparently slightly more intelligent than Boots, suggests there might be something more to Marjorie's message. They call the police and tell them to go to Deegan's warehouse. They arrive in the nick of time because Anders is getting roughed up. Anders races to the meeting place. Deegan's men are captured.

In the final scene Anders and Marjorie are on their honeymoon. "From now on, Mrs. Anders," he says, "you take all your dictation from me." (There they go again.)

Brent was sixth-billed. It's a good "B" film but lacks the distinctive touch that someone like Robert Florey could have brought to it. Still, the actors, especially Brent, Carlisle, Nolan, and Naish, are quite good.

The film's working title was *Highway Racketeers*. Filmed in January 1938, it was based on an article, "Hunting the Highway Pirates," written by William E. Frazer which appeared in *American Magazine* in January 1937. Ads proclaimed it "Paramount's thrilling exposé of America's $10-million highway hijacking racket!"

Born in Boston in 1912, Mary Carlisle was a WAMPAS Baby Star in 1932. She made her movie debut in 1930 and was a popular leading actress in the 1930s. Carlisle married actor and future movie executive James Blakeley and made her last film in 1943.

Roscoe Karns was born in San Bernardino, California, in 1891. The character actor began his long career in 1915. He later played Rocky King on the 1950s television series *Inside Detective*. Karns died in 1970. He also appeared with Brent in *Beau Sabreur* (1928).

Benny Baker, born in St. Louis in 1907, made his film debut in 1930. He made many television appearances from the 1950s to the 1980s and was a semi-regular on *Surfside 6* and *F Troop*. He died in 1994.

Gertrude Short was born in Cincinnati in 1902. Cousin of Blanche Sweet and the daughter of actor Lew Short, she began her career in vaudeville. Short often played telephone operators throughout her career and starred in many comedy shorts. Her husband was actor-director-writer Scott Pembroke. She died in 1968. Short also appeared with Brent in *Women's Wares* (1927).

Joyce Mathews was born in New York in 1919. A showgirl when she was a teenager, Mathews was married seven times to four different husbands, including Milton Berle (twice), Billy Rose (twice), and Don Beddoe. She died in 1999.

Born in Virginia in 1898, Louis King began directing films in 1921 and ended his career directing television shows including *Gunsmoke* and *Adventures of*

*Wild Bill Hickok.* The brother of director Henry King, he died in 1962.

Writer Maxwell Shane was also a producer and director. Born in Paterson, New Jersey, in 1905, he also worked with Brent on *Forced Landing* (1941) and *Wrecking Crew* (1942). Shane later produced the television shows *M Squad* and *Thriller.* He died in 1983.

*Reviews:* "Though melodrama of a familiar brand, it is so well done that it has a freshness of appeal.... Evelyn Brent, ideal for the part, figures prominently in the action and does very well" (*Variety,* March 23, 1938).

"Told swiftly, in a clean, straight line, and convincingly performed ... *Tip-Off Girls* is a good, B-plus action picture" (*New York Times,* March 25, 1938).

"As the gangster–G-men type of pictures go, this one has as many thrills and as much suspense as any of them" (*The Film Daily,* March 26, 1938).

"[A] smoothly knit shocker.... J. Carrol Naish is capital.... Lloyd Nolan ... couldn't fumble a role if he tried" (*Los Angeles Times,* May 13, 1938).

## *Mr. Wong, Detective*

(Monogram Pictures) 70 min. Released October 5, 1938.
*Survival Status:* Library of Congress (Washington, D.C.). Released on video (Alpha).
*Credits:* Producer, Scott R. Dunlap; associate producer, William Lackey; director, William Nigh; assistant director, W. B. Eason; based on characters created by Hugh Wiley in the "James Lee Wong" short stories in *Collier's*; screenplay, Houston Branch; photography, Harry Neumann; film editor, Russell Schoengarth; music director, Abe Meyer; recording engineer, Karl Zint; technical director, E. R. Hickson; production manager, C. J. Bigelow; makeup, Gordon Bau.
*Cast:* Boris Karloff (James Lee Wong); Grant Withers (Captain Sam Street); Maxine Jennings (Myra Ross); Evelyn Brent (Olga, also known as Countess Dubois); George Lloyd (Devlin); Lucien Prival (Anton Mohl, also known as the Baron); John St. Polis (Carl Roemer); William Gould (Theodore Meisle); Hooper Atchley (Christian Wilk); John Hamilton (Simon Dayton); Wilbur Mack (Russell); Lee Tong Foo (Tchin); Frank Bruno (Lascari); Lynton Brent (Detective Tommy), Grace Wood (Mrs. Roemer).

Simon Dayton enlists the aid of detective James Lee Wong because he fears that someone is trying to harm him and his company, Dayton Chemical. He *should* be worried. By the time Wong shows up the next morning to meet with him, Dayton has been murdered.

Disgruntled scientist Carl Roemer is suspected because he pointed a gun at Dayton earlier. The police think Dayton died of heart failure, but Wong discovers a small shard of glass and begins to investigate. Turns out Dayton died from poison gas. Wong determines that a glass grenade was somehow used.

Dayton's business partner Mr. Wilk is visiting with Countess Dubois and Wong when he receives a note sent from a jailed Roemer. "Mr. Wilk: You're in great danger. Stay in your study and call the police immediately for protection." Without telling anyone of the note, Wilk does as he's told and waits in his study. The police arrive, and Wilk is found dead. Wong finds another glass shard.

The police grill Roemer, and he tells the police that the last remaining business partner Mr. Meisle is the murderer. When the police go to Meisle's house to arrest him, they find him dead. Yep, Wong finds a glass shard. (Wong is quite clever to be able to tell the difference between this one and all the glass shards from the windows the cops broke to gain entry.)

Wong asks that Roemer be brought to his house. Meanwhile, Anton, the countess, and Lascari are waiting for the Chinese detective. They want Roemer's formula for poison gas, and Anton insists Wong turn it over. "This glass ball," Wong slowly explains, looking at the globe, "contains a concentration of the poison gas you're looking for.... The formula is of no use to you unless you understand its operation." An impatient Lascara jostles Wong's arm, and the glass ball breaks. "You've destroyed us all!" Wong exclaims. "The slightest exertion will kill you instantly. This room is filled with poison gas. Invisible. Colorless. Swift. It's in your lungs. Seeping into your bloodstream. There's no escape. Soon you'll feel a sensation of choking, a tingling in your fingers, a paralysis of your limbs. No pain." He continues to describe the symptoms, and as you might imagine, this bluff is pretty effective stuff. The bad guys try to make a run for it, but Wong holds them with a gun until the police and Roemer arrive.

Wong sits down with Roemer and shows him yet another glass ball. This one, Wong says, is filled with the gas. As he's talking we hear the sound of a police siren. "Your carriage approaches," Wong says to the criminals. Meanwhile, Roemer tries to escape. As he is detained, Wong points to the ball and shouts, "Watch that!" Sure enough, the ball explodes. Wong assures everyone the ball was actually empty.

Roemer had fixed the globes so that a police siren would trigger their explosion. In every case, the victim phoned the police himself. "Clever," Wong says, nodding. "Very clever, Roemer."

Filming began in August 1938. Brent was fourth-billed and is quite effective as a glamorous villain. The success of the picture, however, rests with the considerable charm of Boris Karloff in the role of Wong. There is an attempt to make a cute couple out of the police detective Street and secretary-girlfriend Myra, but their dialogue is not quite witty enough.

The Mr. Wong film series was produced in the hopes of successfully competing against other Asian detectives including Charlie Chan and Mr. Moto. It was based on Hugh Wiley's James Lee Wong short stories in *Collier's.*

Harold Huber also tested for the Mr. Wong role, though Karloff eventually won the part. There were five Mr. Wong films in the series. The others were *The Mystery of Mr. Wong* (1939), *Mr. Wong in Chinatown* (1939), *The Fatal Hour* (1940), and *Doomed to Die* (1940). *Phantom of Chinatown* (1940) again featured Grant Withers as Captain Street, but the lead character this time was Jimmy Wong (Keye Luke), and Karloff was not in the picture. William Nigh directed all five Karloff films, and Withers starred in all as well. Marjorie Reynolds replaced Maxine Jennings as the detective's girlfriend in three of the films.

*Mr. Wong, Detective* was remade in 1948 as *Docks of New Orleans*, a Charlie Chan vehicle which starred Roland Winters in the title role. It was directed by Derwin Abrahams; the setting was changed from San Francisco to New Orleans.

According to Karloff biographer Peter Underwood, "The role of the suave and meticulous Mr. Wong ... gave Karloff an opportunity to establish a character whose personal charm and quiet, scientific methods of detection provide a welcome change from the usual run of such films.... The whole series was effectively produced and the suspense invariably well sustained."[153]

Taglines for the film included "The most ingenious crime even conceived ... but the killer hadn't counted on the crafty Mr. Wong as his adversary!" and "Thousands asked to see *Collier's Magazine* famous detective on the screen ... here he is!"

William Nigh was born Emil Kreuske in Berlin, Wisconsin, in 1881. He began his career in the silent era and wrote, produced, acted, and directed. He died in 1955. Nigh also directed Brent in *Without Children* (1935).

Englishman Karloff was often cast as Asians. He played the evil title character in *The Mask of Fu Manchu* (1932) and also played Asian characters in *The Miracle Man* (1932) and *West of Shanghai* (1937). Karloff had previously appeared with Brent in *Forbidden Cargo* (1925) and *Lady Robinhood* (1925). Born William Henry Pratt in 1887, Karloff will always be remembered for his legendary role in *Frankenstein* (1931). He also provided the expert narration for the 1966 television special *How the Grinch Stole Christmas*. Karloff died in 1969.

Maxine Jennings, born in Portland, Oregon, in 1909, made most of her films between 1935 and 1938. She died in 1991.

*Reviews:* "[Karloff is] in splendid fashion. He completely immerses himself in the role with little makeup. Evelyn Brent, Grant Withers and others are good" (*Los Angeles Times*, October 13, 1938).

"It is true that Karloff, with his lantern face, looks about as Chinese as his parrot does, but at least he is distinctive and to that end suitable for an exotic role. Karloff should have no difficulty in soon establishing himself as a popular figure in his new role" (*The Cinema*, November 10, 1938).

"Next to having the detective himself turn out to be the murderer, we like the solution in *Mr. Wong, Detective*" (*New York Times*, November 21, 1938).

"First picture suffers from directorial and writing troubles, plus a combination of careless acting and haphazard casting.... Evelyn Brent ... familiar from silent screen days, makes acceptable the scheming Olga, one of the spy trio" (*Variety*, November 23, 1938).

## *The Law West of Tombstone*

(RKO Radio Pictures) 73 min. Released on November 17, 1938.

*Survival Status:* Library of Congress (Washington, D.C.).

*Credits:* Producer, Cliff Reid; production executive, Lee Marcus; director, Glenn Tryon; assistant director, Samuel Ruman; screenplay, John Twist, Clarence Upson Young; story, Clarence Upson Young; photography, J. Roy Hunt; art direction, Van Nest Polglase; art director associate, Albert D'Agostino; film editor, George Crone; musical director, Roy Webb; sound recording, Earl A. Wolcott.

*Cast:* Harry Carey (William "Bonanza Bill" Barker); Tim Holt (Ted, also known as "The Tonto Kid"); Evelyn Brent (Clara Martinez); Jean Rouverol (Nita Moseby); Clarence Kolb (Samuel Kent); Allan Lane (Danny Sanders); Esther Muir (Madame Mustache); Bradley Page (Doc Howard); Paul Guilfoyle (Bud McQuinn); Robert Moya (Chuy); Ward Bond (Mulligan P. Martinez); George Irving (Morton Dixon); Monte Montague (Clayt McQuinn).

New York, 1881. In front of the Hotel Grand Central, newspapermen await the arrival of Bill Barker, who claims he's hit it big with a mine.

Clara Martinez, known as the Barcelona Rose, is appearing in *The Fatal Fandango* with "50 SNAPPY SENORITAS." Bill tells the reporters that he's familiar with Clara. A headline reports: "Knew Clara Martinez 'way back when'—claims Bonanza Bill."

"Lies, lies, lies!" Clara complains to businessman and boyfriend Samuel Kent. She's pretending to be by way of Europe—not El Paso. She's even got a fake accent and a pet monkey.

Meanwhile, Kent receives a telegram reporting that Bill is a liar, horse thief, etc. At dinner with Kent and Clara that night at the Delmonico, turkey-eating Bill backs up Clara's story that they don't know each other. Turns out, in fact, the two have a daughter, Nita, who thinks both parents are dead.

Bill is arrested when he can't pay the dinner bill—$1,374.25. Kent pays the bill, but Bill is forced to leave town. Clara gives him her pet monkey with a note attached: "Just to remind you what you made of yourself during your visit to New York."

Bill returns to El Paso, declares himself the law west of Tombstone, and sets off to find the Tonto Kid. Prim and proper Nita (we know she's a good girl because her worst language is of the "fiddlesticks" variety) ends up with the Kid after he robs the train she's riding on. Bill comes to the rescue, and the Kid is allowed to escape. (When the Kid called him an "old jackass," truer words were never spoken.)

Nita and Bill end up in Martinez, a new town on the railroad. They're soon joined by the Kid and Danny, Nita's fiancé. Nita does not know that Danny is the Kid's partner in crime. The two robbers argue, and the Kid kills Danny in self-defense.

The Kid explains to Bill that Danny was no prize. In appreciation for saving his daughter from a lifetime of misery, Bill, now mayor of Martinez, defends him in a trial. Together, Bill and the Kid help Nita with her ranch.

On the day it looks like Bill is going to lose his election, Clara and Kent stop by on their way to California. This gives Bill some badly needed credibility because the townspeople were convinced he'd lied about knowing them. Bill also has an Indian "problem" so he solves this by getting the "smelly" Indians on the train with Clara and Kent. When a plump Indian baby is put in Clara's arms, she faints. This is supposed to be payback for the little monkey Clara gave to Bill. According to Bill, "I'll never forget a little present you made me when I left New York. Now, one good turn deserves another." After the train leaves, there's a successful shootout with the villainous McQuinn brothers.

In the final scenes, Bill is again telling his tall tales with an eager audience, including his paramour Madame Mustache, and the Kid and Nita rap on the door of the Justice of the Peace.

Brent was third-billed though she had few scenes. She played yet another sexy, glamorous role which she seemed to be specializing in at this stage in her career. This film needed much more of Brent. She stood out in all her scenes, and the film got a boost every time she was on screen.

The picture is an entertaining Western with a good cast, though the depiction of Native Americans is appalling. The studio was reportedly concerned about rights issues. Clearly, however, the Bill Barker character is similar to that of real-life Judge Roy Bean, who named a town after Lily Langtry and referred to himself as the Law West of the Pecos. Doc Howard is modeled on Doc Holliday, and the Tonto Kid is based on Billy the Kid. The villainous McQuinn brothers are based on the McLaury brothers—or perhaps the Clanton brothers. (Or a composite of the McLaurys and the Clantons.) Mrs. Mustache is reminiscent of Calamity Jane, though much more feminine.

The shooting took place in September and October of 1938 at the RKO Encino Ranch. Director Glenn Tryon is the same Glenn Tryon who co-starred with Brent in *Broadway* (1929). This is one of ten films Tryon directed in his career.

Harry Carey will never be called a subtle, nuanced performer. He always seems to be playing to the person sitting in the last row of the upper balcony. Born in New York in 1878, Carey received an Oscar nomination for *Mr. Smith Goes to Washington* (1939). He was a director, writer, producer, and actor during the silent film era and was best known for playing cowboys. Carey died in 1947.

Cutie pie Tim Holt was primarily known for playing cowboys, though he also appeared as the indulged, rich young man in Orson Welles' *The Magnificent Ambersons* (1942). Born Charles John Holt, Jr., in Beverly Hills in 1918 to actor Jack Holt and wife Margaret Woods, Tim was also a decorated (and wounded) World War II veteran. He died in 1973.

Jean Rouverol was born in St. Louis, Missouri, in 1916. She appeared as an actor in less than a dozen films. She and husband Hugo Black were blacklisted in the 1950s and moved to Mexico. She later moved back to the United States and turned her attention to writing. Rouverol received Emmy nominations for *The Guiding Light*.

Clarence Kolb, born in Cleveland, Ohio in 1874, had a successful vaudeville act with partner Max Dill. He's probably best known for playing Mr. Honeywell on the television series *My Little Margie*. Kolb died in 1964.

Allan Lane was the voice of TV's talking horse *Mr. Ed*. Born Harry Leonard Albershart in Indiana in 1909, Lane enjoyed a long career in film and on television (often playing cowboys). He died in 1973.

Esther Muir is a pleasure in just about every movie she appears. Born in Andes, New York, in 1903, she appeared on stage with the Marx Brothers in *A Day at the Races* and then also co-starred in the 1937 movie. Divorced from director Busby Berkeley and songwriter Sam Coslow, she died in 1995.

Ward Bond (1903–1960) is probably one of Hollywood's most recognizable character actors. Born in Nebraska, he began his career in 1929. Friends with John Wayne and John Ford, he appeared in many Westerns. Bond held strong rightwing views and was president of the Motion Picture Alliance for the Preservation of American Ideals, an organization that supported blacklisting. He also appeared with Brent in her episode of *Wagon Train*.

*Reviews:* "Neat outdoor production combines comedy and drama in most enjoyable manner" (*Film Daily*, November 15, 1938).

After detailing the plot, the *New York Times* asked, "Does this sound slightly wild and vague? So is the picture. For, in spite of some fancy script-writing and occasional touches of brightness, *The Law West of Tombstone* is mostly a series of shooting and drinking bouts, held together by a thread of coincidences. And as such it is just a cut above the ordinary 'Western'" (November 25, 1938).

"Carey has an old fave, Evelyn Brent, to back him up but she's confined to comparatively few shots.... Direction helps to smooth out spots that might otherwise drop the film into a burlesque of Westerns" (*Variety*, November 30, 1938).

## *Panama Lady*

(RKO Radio Pictures) 64 min. Released on May 12, 1939.

*Survival Status:* Library of Congress (Washington, D.C.).

*Credits:* Producer, Cliff Reid; production executive, Lee Marcus; director, Jack Hively; assistant director, J. Dewey Starkey; screenplay, Michael Kanin; story, Garrett Fort; photography, J. Roy Hunt; art director, Van Nest Polglase; art director associate, Albert D'Agostino; film editor, Theron Warth; wardrobe, Edward Stevenson; musical director, Roy Webb: sound recording, Hugh McDowell, Jr.; special effects, Vernon L. Walker.

*Cast:* Lucille Ball (Lucy); Allan Lane (Dennis McTeague); Steffi Duna (Cheema); Evelyn Brent (Lenore); Donald Briggs (Roy Harmon); Bernadene Hayes (Pearl); Abner Biberman (Elisha); William Pawley (Bartender); Earle Hodgins (Foreman).

The film begins with a montage of New York City scenes including skyscrapers and street scenes. Suddenly we hear the sound of someone calling out, "Lucy! Lucy!" (Yep, Lucille Ball's character's name is Lucy in this one. Even weirder, the voice belongs to Allan Lane, the voice of TV's *Mr. Ed*.) She's not happy to see Dennis McTeague because he brings up bad memories. (We wonder if someone wasn't a fan of Chicago novelist Frank Norris whose novel *McTeague* was about a dentist. The novel was the basis for the classic 1924 silent film *Greed*.) She has a flashback to their life in Panama.

Lenore is a weary bar owner. The place isn't doing any business so she has to fire the dancers including Lucy. One woman reminds her they have contracts. "Yeah? Use 'em for wrapping paper," Lenore cynically suggests.

Lucy asks boyfriend Roy to marry her but he refuses, accusing her of rushing him into marriage. It's easy to see that Roy is a no-good, but he's even worse than we thought. Lucy stows away on his plane and discovers he's smuggling guns. "You keep your pretty trap shut ... if you want to stay alive," he says without any charm at all. You're going to love another one of his lines: He matter-of-factly tells his smuggling buddies that Lucy's "just a bimbo I picked up in Panama. Thinks I'm gonna marry her."

Lucy is blindfolded and taken back to Panama. She goes to Lenore, pleading for a job. "Listen, kid," Lenora tells her. "You might be able to sell me that sob stuff if I didn't have a stomach full of my own."

McTeague, an old friend of Lenore's arrives, and this time he's loaded with money. Lenore and Pearl talk Lucy into getting McTeague drunk so they can roll him. McTeague passes out and comes to in a room in Lenore's bar. When he wakes up and realizes his money is gone, he has Lenore arrested. Lucy agrees to get McTeague's money back. However, when she takes him to Pearl's room to retrieve it, they discover Pearl is gone and so is the money.

Lucy travels with McTeague to South America where she'll work as housekeeper on his houseboat in order to pay off the money. Lucy, who still for whatever reason has it bad for Roy, writes him a note: "Roy, darling—Please come for me as soon as possible. I can explain everything. Lucy." She also leaves him a map.

Once she gets to the houseboat, McTeague introduces her to jealous Cheema, a young native woman who already lives with him. McTeague leaves for oil camp, and, upon his return, he and Lucy become closer. Meanwhile, Roy is indeed looking for Lucy: He's convinced that she spilled the beans about gun running and plans to kill her.

McTeague strikes oil. Roy arrives at the houseboat and finds out about the oil strike. He steals McTeague's paperwork so he can register the claim. Lucy pulls a gun on him. He throws a chair at her but is shot and killed. McTeague sends Lucy back to the States.

"It's like a nightmare. I can't forget it," Lucy says as we return to the present time, a year later. McTeague tells Lucy that Cheema shot Roy. He also tells her that he loves her and wants to marry her. Lucy isn't interested. She points at a limousine and

tells him it's waiting for her. She asks the limousine driver to play along and drive her around the block. He refuses.

Lucy trudges along the city street until a masher approaches. McTeague rescues her. The limousine pulls up—it's McTeague's. "Yours?" Lucy asks.

"Ours," McTeague says.

Brent was billed fourth, and she's good in a limited role. The movie starts off well but descends into some unlikely plot developments. Also, McTeague has a real dark side. His treatment of Cheema is inappropriate at best, and he's not always gentlemanly with Lucy either. The ending hardly seems like a happy ending because Lucy, desperate and unhappy, appears deeply disturbed by all that has happened.

Production began in February 1939. The working title was *The Second Shot*. It was a remake of RKO's *Panama Flo* (1932) which was directed by Ralph Murphy and starred Helen Twelvetrees.

This was director Jack Hively's (1910–1995) second effort at directing. He was also a film editor. Writer Garrett Fort, born in New York in 1900, is best known for his work on such horror films as *Dracula* (1931) and *Frankenstein* (1931). He committed suicide in 1945. Michael Kanin was the brother of writer Garson Kanin. Born in Rochester, New York, in 1910, he won an Oscar (shared with Ring Lardner, Jr.) for *Woman of the Year* (1942). He also received an Oscar nomination (shared with wife Fay Kanin) for *Teacher's Pet* (1958). Kanin died in 1993.

The legendary Lucille Ball was born in Jamestown, New York in 1911. Forever immortal through her work on the television show *I Love Lucy*, Ball began her film career in 1933. By the time she made *Panama Lady* she was already a seasoned veteran on the RKO lot. In this film she photographs beautifully and plays a glamour role. She died in 1989.

Steffi Duna, born Stephanie Berindey in Budapest, Hungary, in 1910, made her film debut in 1932. Married to Dennis O'Keefe from 1940 until his death in 1968, she died in 1992.

Donald Briggs was born in Chicago in 1911. He made his film debut in 1936 and ultimately made many television appearances. Briggs was a semi-regular as Eddie Collins on *The Lucy Show* in the 1960s. He died in 1986. Briggs did a fine job in this film as the blunt, scheming, cold-hearted boyfriend.

Bernadene Hayes was born in Chicago in 1903, and it was there that she became known as the Queen of Radio before she entered films in 1932. She died in 1987.

Abner Biberman, born in Milwaukee, Wisconsin, in 1909, was also a director and occasional writer. A onetime member of the Group Theatre Company, he became a television director working on such shows as *Ben Casey* and *The Fugitive*. Sometimes credited as Joel Judge, he died in 1977.

Reviews: "[A] run-of-the-mill feature..." (*Los Angeles Times*, May 5, 1939).

"*Panama Lady* is a dull, poor story that has few redeeming features.... [Donald Briggs] does well enough, along with Miss Brent, who's in a bit, and Lane, while Miss Ball has bitten off more than she can chew" (*Variety*, June 7, 1939).

## Daughter of the Tong

(Metropolitan Pictures) 56 min. Released July 11, 1939.
*Survival Status:* Released on video (Alpha, 53 min.).
*Credits:* Producers, Henry S. Webb, Lester F. Scott, Jr.; director, Raymond K. Johnson; assistant director, Ray Nazarro; story, George H. Plympton; continuity, Alan Merritt; photography, Elmer Dyer; film editor, Charles Diltz; musical director, Lee Zahler; sound technician, Clifford Ruberg.
*Cast:* Evelyn Brent (The Illustrious One, also known as Carney and The Daughter of the Tong); Grant Withers (Ralph Dickson); Dorothy Short (Marion Morgan); Dave O'Brien (Jerry Morgan); Richard Loo (Wong); Dirk Thane (Ward); Harry Harvey (Mugsy); Budd Buster (Lefty); Robert Frazer (Williams); Hal Taliaferro (Lawson); James Coleman (Hardy).

"Every American, regardless of class, position, or the community in which he lives, pays monetary tribute to the racketeers who direct the activities of the underworld. Local law enforcement agencies cope adequately with the small racketeer, but the big racketeer rules his kingdom from a position beyond the reach of local governments, challenging society with their ever increasing demands. Uncle Sam accepted this challenge and his answer was The Federal Bureau of Investigation, known as the F.B.I. and feared by every criminal in the United States. This organization is founded upon courage and faith; and in many cases has exacted the lives of those federal agents whose ideals strongly embody liberty and the rights of their fellow men. From the brilliantly lighted drawing rooms of society to the mysterious shadows of Chinatown these investigators work secretly. It is with those who dwell in these mysterious shadows that our story deals." Whew! That long-winded written introduction sets the stage for this programmer that doesn't have much substance.

After the killing of government agent Wilson, a newspaper headline reads: "CARNEY SUSPECTED IN LATEST OUTRAGE!" Notorious criminal Carney meets with her men about the headlines. "Don't worry," she says confidently. "I'm not afraid of words or the men who write them. They've fought me in their stupid papers for five years. And for five years I've taken what I've wanted in this town, and I'll keep on taking!"

Carney recruits Gallagher, who just escaped from the Atlanta penitentiary. Meanwhile, the FBI assigns Dickson to impersonate Gallagher—who has already been arrested.

Marion brings money to Jerry Morgan in room 406 of Carney's Oriental Hotel. Later, Dickson learns from Marion that Jerry is her brother and was Carney's partner in the importing business. The money was supposed to buy Jerry out of Carney's clutches.

Dickson returns to the hotel's fifth floor to find Carney. He overhears Carney and her men tell Jerry they're going to kill him. Dickson is captured. He

tells them he's Gallagher and demands to see Carney. "Sure about that?" she asks. "I'm Carney," she says when he says he's sure.

Lefty, who's actually a government agent, identifies Gallagher as his old partner from the Atlanta pen. Carney gives Dickson his assignment: "Mr. Morgan is resigning from our organization. Permanently. Are you ready to go to work?" She hands him a gun (unloaded), and he immediately turns it on her gang. "All right," Dickson says. "I'm taking Jerry, and the money goes with it."

Carney orders her men to take him. Lefty cuts off the lights, and a fight ensues. Jerry and Dickson escape. "Fool! Idiots! Imbeciles!" Carney shouts.

They give chase, and a long—*really long*—automobile chase follows. Dickson and Jerry are finally recaptured when bullets puncture the gas tank. They're brought back to the hotel. Carney orders Wong to give Dickson the "Oriental manicure" to make him talk. However, the authorities arrive before too much pain is inflicted. "You win, Gallagher," Carney says. "Whose mob is this?"

"Uncle Sam's," Dickson replies. He and Marion walk off, arm in arm.

Brent was top-billed here for the first time in a long time. She's sleek and glamorous as the Asian mastermind criminal and proved again that she could adeptly play a villain. She's much better than the material and certainly deserved better.

The movie is fair but lacks distinctiveness. Grant Withers is good as a tough guy F.B.I. agent who makes most of his decisions by flipping a coin. He also punches out more people than Mike Hammer. Harry Harvey is notable as a dim-witted gangster. However, it seems that many times the director is simply padding the movie with stock footage, chases, fights, and newspaper headlines.

Director Raymond K. Johnson was also known as Bernard B. Ray. He was born Benjamin T. Shamroy in Moscow in 1895 and was also a producer and writer. Under the name of Ray, he directed Brent in *Dangerous Lady* (1941). He died in 1964.

Writer George H. Plympton, born in Brooklyn in 1889, began his film career in 1912. He amassed more than two hundred credits, including serials such as *The Masked Marvel* (1943) and *Brenda Starr, Reporter* (1945). He died in 1972.

Dorothy Short was born in Philadelphia in 1915. She was married to fellow actor Dave O'Brien from 1936 until their divorce in 1954. Short appeared in the *Captain Midnight* serial as well as Pete Smith short films. She died in 1963.

Dave O'Brien was born David Poole Fronabarger in Big Spring, Texas, in 1912. He also wrote and directed using the name David Barclay. O'Brien often appeared in low-budget Westerns early in his career. He won an Emmy (and received a second nomination) for his work on *The Red Skelton Show*. He is best known for his appearances in the MGM Pete Smith shorts in which he played a doofus. O'Brien died in 1969.

Richard Loo was born in Hawaii in 1903. Married to agent (and occasional actress) Bessie Loo, he made his film debut in 1931 and ended up making hundreds of film and television appearances. He was Master Sun in *Kung Fu* and appeared in Toyota commercials until his death in 1983.

Harry Harvey (1901–1985), born in what is now Oklahoma, made his first film appearance in 1932. The popular character actor made close to four hundred film and television appearances. Harvey was Sheriff Blodgett on *The Roy Rogers Show*.

Budd Buster was born in Colorado in 1891. He began his career in 1933 and made more than three hundred film and television appearances, often in Westerns, until his death in 1965. Buster also appeared with Brent in *Westward Ho* (1942).

Hal Taliaferro was also known as Wally Wales. Born Floyd Talafierro Alderson in Wyoming in 1895, he began his film career in the silent era. Taliaferro often appeared in Westerns. He died in 1980.

*Review:* "Irredeemably bad in almost all aspects, *Daughter of the Tong* is made somewhat palatable by silent star Evelyn Brent.... Unfortunately, photography, direction, story line, and supporting cast ... are below par even for this kind of thing, making the viewing of *Daughter of the Tong* something of a chore at times" (Hans Wollenstein, *All Movie Guide*).

## The Mad Empress

(Hispano Continental Films) 72 min. Released on December 16, 1939.
*Survival Status:* UCLA Film and Television Archive (Los Angeles).
*Credits:* Producer-director, Miguel Contreras Torres; screenplay and dialogue, Jean Bart, Jerome Chodorov, Miguel Contreras Torres; photography, Alex Phillips, Arthur Martinelli; film editor, Carl Pierson; set designer, F. Paul Sylos; music directors, James Bradford, A. Esparza Oteo, Mario Talavera; sound recording, Farrell Redd; production managers, Bartlett Carré, P. Castelain, J. Centeno; production advisor, Lionel Atwill.
*Cast:* Medea de Novara (Empress Carlotta of Mexico); Lionel Atwill (General Bazaine); Conrad Nagel (Maximilian); Guy Bates Post (Louis Napoleon III); Evelyn Brent (Empress Eugenie); Claudia Dell (Agnes Salm); Frank McGlynn, Sr. (President Lincoln); Jason Robards (President Benito Juarez); Gustav von Seyffertitz (Metternick); Nigel de Brulier (Father Fisher); Michael Visaroff (Dr. Samuel Basch); Earl Gunn (Porfirio Diaz); George Regas (Escobedo); Rudolph Amendt ([Rudolph Anders] Hersfeld); Duncan Renaldo (Colonel Miguel Lopez); Graciela Romero (Madame Bazaine); Juan Rivero (Tomas Mejia); Rolfe Sedan (Tudos), Franklin Murrell (Grill).

Through the courtesy of the Mexican Government some of the important scenes in this picture—the Cathedral, the National Palace, the Empress' bedroom, the Castle and grounds of Chapultepec, and Queretaro—were taken in authentic places where the drama of Maximilian and Carlotta actually evolved.

Emperor Napoleon III of France and Empress Eugenie, [sic] dreamed of a Mexican Empire against the will of the Mexican people, who, under President Benito P. Juarez were desperately fighting for freedom and democracy. The crown of Mexico was offered by Napoleon to Maximilian of Hapsburg and to his consort, Princess Carlotta of Belgium, who accepted this perilous venture.

This sets up the military conflict between Juarez and Maximilian and Carlotta. The strain of the conflict drives Carlotta mad, and Maximilian is eventually defeated and executed by a firing squad. In the final scene, crazy Carlotta, who has returned to Europe, hears Maximilian call to her. She "sees" him, and then he disappears.

The real-life Carlotta died January 19, 1927, sixty years after Maximilian's execution. She continued to believe that Maximilian was alive and supposedly kept a little doll in bed with her whom she named Max. *Creepy!*

Brent received fifth-billing in this terrible movie. It offers great sets and costumes—and a god-awful script. Talk, talk, talk plus hammy performances equals boredom. Medea de Novara is a beautiful woman (with a profile remarkably similar to Brent's), but she was severely hampered by a clichéd, earnestly pretentious script. This is the kind of film that the fast-forward button was designed for. Enjoy the travelogue aspects of this one, but it wouldn't hurt to keep the sound off. Based on the evidence of this film, Torres might be one of the worst directors ever. Perhaps he suffered from a language problem, but nobody gives a good performance. Is it so bad it's good? It comes close. Torres was born in Mexico in 1899. A prolific filmmaker in his native country, he had credits as an actor, director, producer, writer, cinematographer, and editor. He died in 1981.

Medea de Novara was born Herminne Kindle Futcher in Lichtenstein in 1905. She appeared in only eleven films, including *Jesucristo y María Magdalena* (1946) which was also written and directed by husband Torres. De Novara also played Carlotta in *La Poloma* (1937) and *Caballeria del imperio* (1942). She died in 2001.

Jason Robards was the father of Oscar-winning actor Jason Robards, Jr. Born in Hillsdale, Michigan, in 1892, the elder Robards was a noted stage actor. He died in 1963.

Duncan Renaldo, born Renault Renaldo Duncan in Spain in 1904, was best known for his role in *The Cisco Kid*. He died in 1980. Graciela Romero was the sister of Cesar Romero. This was her only film credit.

Writer Jerome Chodorov survived this movie. Born in New York in 1911, he won two Tony awards for his collaboration on Broadway's *Wonderful Town* in 1953. He died in 2004.

Working titles included *Maximilian and Carlotta*, *Carlotta the Mad Empress*, *Juarez and Maximilian*, and *Maximilian*. In 1935, director Torres filmed a Spanish-language version titled *Juarez y Maximiliano*. It was filmed in Mexico City with wife Medea de Novara; Torres had the cooperation of the government who loaned cavalry troops to serve as extras. In addition, telephone poles were pulled down. Torres recycled scenes from this earlier picture and used them in *The Mad Empress*.

Production began in January 1938. In February, Torres, reportedly $18,000 in debt, stopped filming and did not begin again until a year later when Warner Brothers provided additional funding. Torres resumed filming at Talisman Studios in California after a deal was struck with the studio agreeing to distribute the picture. Eventually, Warner Bros. edited the film from 95 to 72 minutes (thank God). In June 1939 Warner Bros. released *Juarez*, a version of the same story. This one was directed by William Dieterle and starred Paul Muni, Bette Davis (as Carlotta), and Brian Aherne.

*Reviews*: "This picture will require much judicious cutting to become effective entertainment. Authentic Mexican backgrounds are used, but the lighting and camerawork on the exteriors could have been improved" (*Film Daily*, May 4, 1939).

"[I]t is necessary to state that the Mexican and prior-made product is not in the same league with *Juarez*—except in the matter of scenic backgrounds, which in *The Mad Empress* are generally superior.... For all its magnificent—and strictly authentic—background, *The Mad Empress* is little better than an academic leafing through the familiar pages of history, without life or emotional impact" (*New York Times*, February 15, 1940).

"Principal drawback to what might have been exciting is that everything is tediously unfolded, in episodic fashion" (*Variety*, February 21, 1940).

"Conrad Nagel and the beautiful [de Novara] made little impact as the protagonists, leaving the acting honors to Lionel Atwill as Bazaine" (Clive Hirschhorn, *The Warner Bros. Story*, p. 206).

## Emergency Landing

[Alternate title: *Robot Pilot*] (Producers Releasing) 67 min. Released on May 9, 1941.

*Survival Status*: British Film Institute/National Film and Television Archive (London). Released on video (Alpha).

*Credits*: Executive producer, George R. Batcheller; producer, Jed Buell; director, William Beaudine; assistant director, Edward Montfort; original story and screenplay, Martin Mooney; photography, Jack Greenhalgh; film editor, Robert Crandall; sound, Buddy Meyers; production manager, Peter Jones.

*Cast*: Forrest Tucker (Jerry Barton); Carol Hughes (Betty Lambert); Evelyn Brent (Maude Marshall); Emmett Vogan (Doc Williams); William Halligan (George B. Lambert); George Sherwood (Jones); Joaquin Edwards (Pedro); I. Stanford Jolley (Karl); Stanley Price (Otto); Joe Hartman (Capt. North); Paul Scott (Colonel); Billy Curtis (Judge).

Industrialist George Lambert gets a big defense contract. Meanwhile, test pilot Jerry Barton is working with inventor Doc Williams to develop a remote control plane. Lambert is too busy to see them so Jerry and Doc demonstrate a model while Lambert is golfing with daughter Betty. Lambert is impressed and schedules an appointment with Doc and Jerry. Betty is peeved, however, when the plane lands in a puddle and splashes her.

For the test, Jerry flies a real airplane, and Doc remotely takes over control at 3,000 feet. In order to convince everyone that he is not flying the plane, Jerry parachutes out. The plane crashes. Betty mocks Jerry when she sees him lying on the ground. "You know, you'd be much safer playing with my little nephew's scooter."

Jerry returns with Doc to the desert so they can work on the project. Meanwhile, Betty wants to go to Hollywood. Her father is vehemently against the idea. Once again, however, the spoiled brat gets her way. Aunt Maude goes with her. "Now, what in the world am I going to do in Hollywood?" Maude asks as they're driving. (The line was ironic considering Brent's problems with Hollywood.) "Oh," Betty says, "Barrymore's single again."

They meet up with Jerry again when he "arrests" them for stealing government gas. While Jerry and Betty continue to butt heads, Maude shows herself to be a good sport. Doc comments, "Now there's a woman with a sense of humor." Later, after Doc cooks for her, she quips, "You know, you'd make some fella a good wife."

Jerry wires Lambert: "THINK CAN TEACH YOUR DAUGHTER MUCH NEEDED LESSON." Lambert roars with laughter and sends his own telegram: "MY DEAR JERRY: GO TO IT. BETTY NEEDS DISCIPLINE DON'T SPARE MAUDE—SHE NEEDS LESSON, TOO. WILL DROP IN ON YOU IN A WEEK OR SO IF I CAN FIND THE PLACE.... THANKS.... BEST REGARDS—G.B. LAMBERT"

Jerry puts the two women to work on household chores (it's a rare sight to see Brent dusting and sweeping). Meanwhile we see a newspaper headline: "LAMBERT TESTS FIRST U.S. BOMBER: COMPLETED TWO WEEKS AHEAD OF SCHEDULE." During the test, foreign agents steal the plane.

Jerry and Doc learn that a plane has been stolen from Lambert. The plane crashes near Doc's cabin. One of the criminals is killed and the other shows up at the cabin and takes the robot plane. Unfortunately, Maude and Betty are hiding in it.

Jerry and Doc decide to run the test in order to bring the plane back. This time it works, and they capture the foreign agent. Lambert arrives and agrees to buy Doc's invention. Romance has blossomed between Jerry and Betty and between Doc and Maude.

In the final scene, the judge arrives. He's a cigar-smoking midget who quickly dispenses justice on the gas-stealing charge. "Twenty bucks or twenty days!" He's paid and leaves. Maude, looking stunned, turns toward the camera and asks with a puzzled expression, "Did you see what I saw?" (It's odd, but nice, to see her come out of character and talk to the audience.)

Brent's addition to the cast was announced on April 16, 1941. She was third-billed and played a smart, sophisticated role. For once, she was given a "normal" role and proved she was more than capable. It's nice to see Brent excel in a good, light comedy role; she had so few of them.

This is an entertaining little programmer that

mainly succeeds because of the strong cast. The worst thing about it is the stereotyping of the Mexican-American character. A lot of jokes are made at the expense of Pedro's fractured English. In addition, at one point Maude actually says, "All Mexicans' names are Pedro." Pedro corrects her. "Oh, no, no, senorita, I got a brother, his name was Pancho." Oh, brudder.

Taglines included "Daredevil Test Pilot vs. Society's Dizzest Deb!," "Trapped in the Plane of a Crazed Killer!," and "She'd lie to get her hands on his throat ... and he's trying to get his arms about her waist."

Forrest Tucker, born in Plainfield, Indiana, in 1919, is best known for playing Sergeant O'Rourke on TV's *F Troop*. He made his film debut in 1940 in *The Westerner*. This was his second film appearance. Tucker died in 1986.

Born in Chicago in 1910, Carol Hughes began her film career in 1935. Married to actor Frank Faylen from 1936 until his death in 1985, she's probably best known for playing Dale Arden in *Flash Gordon Conquers the Universe*. She died in 1995.

Emmett Vogan was born in Cleveland in 1893. The veteran character actor began his film career in 1934 and amassed close to five hundred credits before his death in 1969. He also appeared with Brent in *Dangerous Lady* (1941). William Halligan was born in Illinois in 1883 and died in 1957. Halligan also appeared with Brent in *The Seventh Victim* (1943). Joaquin Edwards was also known as Thornton Edwards. Born in Maine in 1894, he died in 1988. He also appeared with Brent in *Forced Landing* (1941) and *Robin Hood of Monterey* (1947). George Sherwood was born in what is now Poland in 1892. Married to Pauline Starke, he died in 1983. I. Stanford Jolley was born in New Jersey in 1900. He made his film debut in 1935 and appeared in more than three hundred films and television episodes. Daughter Sandra was married to Forrest Tucker from 1940 to 1950. Jolley died in 1978. Billy Curtis, born Luigi Curto in Springfield, Massachusetts, in 1909, made his film debut in *The Terror of Tiny Town* (1938). Sometimes billed as Little Billy, he also appeared in *The Wizard of Oz* (1939) and was McDonald's Mayor McCheese until his death in 1988.

Writer Martin Mooney also worked with Brent on *Silent Witness* (1943). Born in New York in 1896, he died in 1967.

*Reviews:* "Carol Hughes and Evelyn Brent overshadow the men in both name and performance, although neither sets any records" (*Variety*, June 18, 1941).

"This picture has a lot of entertainment value in its footage.... Tucker shows improvement as an actor and the other three are capable players, Miss Brent and Vogan being valuable additions to any cast" (*Film Daily*, July 10, 1941).

## Forced Landing

(Picture Corporation of America) 66 min. Released on July 1, 1941.

*Survival Status:* UCLA Film and Television Archive (Los Angeles).

*Credits:* Producers, William H. Pine, William C. Thomas; associate producer, John W. Rogers; director, Gordon Wiles; assistant director, Bart Carré; screenplay, Maxwell Shane, Edward Churchill; photography, John Alton; art direction, F. Paul Sylos; film editor, Robert Crandall; set decoration, Ben Berk; wardrobe, James Wade; music supervisor, Dimitri Tiomkin; songs, "Bandolero," music and lyrics by Frank Loesser and Victor Young; composer, Frank Loesser Victor Young; sound recording, Farrell Redd, W. M. Dalgleish; special effects, Fred Jackman; production manager, L. B. Merman; stunt pilots, Herb White, Garland Lincoln, Richard Probert, Joel Thorne.

*Cast:* Richard Arlen (Dan Kendall); Eva Gabor (Johanna Van Deuren); J. Carrol Naish (Andros Banshek); Nils Asther (Colonel Jan Golas); Evelyn Brent (Doctor's housekeeper); Mikhail Rasumny (Christmas); Victor Varconi (Hendrick Van Deuren); John Miljan (General Valdane); Frank Yaconelli (Zomar); Harold Goodwin (Petchnikoff); Thornton Edwards (Felig); Bobby Dillon (Nando); John Gallaudet (Major Xanders); Harry Worth (Doctor Vidalek).

In this war drama, hotshot American pilot Dan Kendall joins the air force of a South Pacific country. Kendall falls in love with a colonel's girlfriend which leads to several brushes with death. He eventually defeats the colonel and returns to America to live happily ever after with his girlfriend.

Mosaque was used as the name of a fictitious country to "avoid offending any nationality." Susan Hayward screen-tested for a role. Some scenes were filmed in Gopher Valley. A tagline for the film was "Fifth Column Raids Pacific Base!"

Gordon Wiles was influenced by F.W. Murnau and stage set design. He had won an Oscar in 1932 for *Transatlantic* and took his duties on this film quite seriously. "He started by rehearsing his actors three weeks on a bare stage, with all incidental business included. 'We rehearsed the script and walked it,' he says. Then he drafted his sets to fit the business and the walking. On the shooting-stage floor, circles were painted for camera setups and marked for lens (say, 24 mm.), height of camera (4ft. 6in.) and continuity (No.7—i.e., seventh shot of the day). To pre-indicate light sources, ordinary lamps were turned on and their shadows PAINTED on walls, floors, props. Then came the sets themselves—sections of sets, really built so closely to plan that 'if you moved two feet off the circle you wouldn't even find them.' These sections were on platforms with rollers underneath.... Painting the walls, etc.—'You can cover a dozen sets in one day with an air gun'—was to eliminate lighting delays. A single lighting platform supplied the illumination; the shadows were already taken care of."[154] After this film, Wiles directed only once more, *The Gangster* in 1947, though he continued to be hired as an art director and production designer. Wiles was born in St. Louis, Missouri, in 1902 and died in 1950.

Richard Arlen also appeared with Brent in *Paramount on Parade* (1930) and *Wrecking Crew* (1942). Arlen was born Cornelius Richard Van Mattimore in Charlottesville, Virginia, in 1900. He made his film debut in the silent film era and had his biggest hit with the World War I drama *Wings* (1927). He died in 1976.

Nils Asther was born in Denmark in 1897. He was raised in Sweden and made his film debut there in 1916 when he appeared in *Vingame* with director Mauritz Stiller. Asther came to Hollywood in the 1920s, but his career declined with the advent of sound, mainly because of his strong accent. He died in Sweden in 1981.

This was Eva Gabor's film debut. Born in Budapest in 1919 (or thereabouts), Gabor's sisters included Zsa Zsa and Magda. The Gabors were most famous for their multiple marriages. Eva played Lisa Douglas on TV's *Green Acres* in the 1960s. She died in 1995.

John Gallaudet, born in Philadelphia in 1903, played a judge on the TV series *Perry Mason*. Married to Wynne Gibson from 1927 to 1930, he died in 1983. Gallaudet also appeared with Brent in *Stage Struck* (1948).

Composer Dimitri Tiomkin was born in the Ukraine in 1894. Not only was he commemorated with a United States postal stamp, he won three Oscars (*High Noon* [1952], *The High and the Mighty* [1954], and *The Old Man and the Sea* [1958]), along with numerous nominations for other films. Tiomkin, married for many years to choreographer Albertina Rasch, died in 1979.

*Reviews:* "Naish goes far to steal the picture.... It will never gain higher than a 'B' rating, but it classifies very well in that province" (*Los Angeles Times*, July 1, 1941).

"You can't go wrong on this cast or finished product" (*Film Daily*, July 3, 1941).

"Gordon Wiles, former art director, pilots the picture at a fast pace, while editing displays several episodes of neat selection of background plates for process photography. The air shots and battle at the finish are expertly staged" (*Variety*, July 9, 1941).

"[A] good low-budget production" (*Los Angeles Times*, July 18, 1941).

## *Wide Open Town*

(Paramount Pictures) 78 min. Released on July 19, 1941.

*Survival Status:* The Museum of Modern Art (New York City). Released on video (U.S.T.O.).

*Credits*: Producer, Harry Sherman; associate producer, Lewis J. Rachmil; director, Lesley Selander; assistant director, Frederick Spencer; based on characters created by Clarence E. Mulford; screenplay, J. Benton Cheney, Harrison Jacobs; photography, Russell Harlan; art direction, Ralph Berger; supervising film editor, Sherman A. Rose; film editor, Carrol Lewis; set decoration, Emile Kuri; properties, Henry Donovan; wardrobe, Earl Moser; musical directors, Irvin Talbot, John Leipold; sound, Charles S. Althouse; sound recording, General Service Studios.

*Cast*: William Boyd (Hopalong Cassidy); Russell Hayden (Lucky Jenkins); Andy Clyde (California); Evelyn Brent (Belle Langtry); Victor Jory (Steve Fraser); Morris Ankrum (Jim Stuart); Bernice Kay (Joan Stuart); Kenneth Harlan (Tom Wilson); Roy Barcroft (Red); Glenn Strange (Ed Stark); Ed Cassidy (Brad Jackson); Jack Rockwell (Rancher); Bob Kortman, Frank Darien.

The first screen tells us, "Photographed at the base of Mount Whitney near Lone Pine, Calif." Belle Langtry owns the Paradise Saloon in Gunsight. The town has been going to hell in a handbasket since she bought the place. Editor Jim Stuart and daughter Joan resolve to do something about it. Prospector Pete gets drunk in Belle's saloon and spills the beans about his mine find to the flirtatious Belle. Soon he's dead and his location papers are missing.

Hopalong, who is looking for some cattle rustlers, meets Belle when she's on her way to the county seat to file papers for the claim. They meet cute. He thinks her horse is a runaway, and she thinks he's chasing her. After the miscommunication is cleared up, the flirtation begins. "Look me up in a couple of days," Belle coos to handsome Hopalong. "I might be able to show you around. Just ask for Belle Langtry at the Paradise."

Just as Hopalong and his crew get into town, the editor and his daughter are paid a visit by Steve and his cronies. They tear apart the newspaper office until Hopalong intervenes.

Hopalong becomes sheriff. When he tells the ruffians in the saloon that he means business, one of the saloon girls (again) says, "Belle looks like she doesn't know whether to kiss him or kill him." As Hopalong leaves the saloon, Belle prevents Steve from shooting him in the back. "Since when have you started doing things without being told?" she asks Steve. She promises him she'll take care of Hopalong, but Steve is jealous.

Later, Belle and her gang plan a major heist, but Hopalong outsmarts her. Steve tells Belle that it was a trap, and the two argue about what to do next.

Hopalong tells Belle she should leave town. She pulls a gun on him as he leaves (his back is turned), but can't shoot him. "Not being a woman, you wouldn't understand," she later tells Steve. "I'll take care of him in my own way." Meanwhile, Hopalong's sidekick California allows a prisoner to "escape," and the bad guy is followed to the hideout where Hopalong and his men find their rustled cattle.

Steve tells Belle she's no longer the boss. "You better change your brand of liquor, Steve," she advises. Steve tells her he thinks she's joined forces with Hopalong. "Shoot," he orders his men, "if she tries to make a break."

"You'll never get away with this, Steve," she warns.

Spunky Joan is captured and taken back to the place where Belle is being held. In the shootout climax, Steve threatens to shoot Joan unless Hoppy and his men leave town. Hopalong agrees.

Belle grabs a gun. "Throw down your guns or I'll start blasting," she orders. Belle and Joan escape, but Steve shoots through the door, wounding Belle.

Hopalong comforts Belle and Joan, and then goes up to Belle's room to find Steve. Hopalong is wounded in the shoulder, but Steve falls out the window as they struggle.

A tearful Belle boards a stagecoach on her way to prison. Hopalong tells her to let him know if she needs anything. "You might send me a nice, new hacksaw," she says. Hoppy gets a big laugh out of this.

This movie is remarkably similar to *Hopalong Cassidy Returns* (1936)—but without the kiss. In fact, the set looks the same, and even some of the same lines and scenes are repeated. It's kind of fun to watch them back to back. It's especially interesting to see what two old pros like Boyd and Brent do with identical lines about five years apart. Filming started around January 16, 1941. Working titles included *Men of Action* and *Law Comes to Gunsight*.

A reporter provided some insight on what it was like to work on a Hopalong Cassidy set: "Most of the films ... are made with a location company of at least sixty-five and they are made fast. Working hours are from sunup to sundown. The average shooting schedule takes two weeks and that means thirty to forty scenes a day. The shooting is more or less 'from the cuff.' The script is there, but everybody ad libs a little and Mr. Boyd usually paraphrases things to suit his own style. After all, by this time, he has begun to feel mighty like Hopalong himself."[155] In another interview, the formula for low-budget but profitable pictures was succinctly revealed: "Cost of an average picture is $100,000, while the shooting time runs about 90 hours. They make a lot of money."[156]

Russell Hayden was born Pate Lucid in Chico, California, in 1912. He played Lucky Jenkins in dozens of Hopalong Cassidy movies. Later he was a regular on the television series *Cowboy G-Men*. He died in 1981.

Andy Clyde was born in Scotland in 1892. A former vaudevillian and music hall performer, he was Hopalong's sidekick in many pictures. He later made many television appearances including George MacMichael on *The Real McCoys* and Cully Wilson on *Lassie*. Like Gabby Hayes, Clyde was nothing like the characters he played. The well-dressed, immaculately groomed gentleman died in 1967.

Victor Jory was born in Canada in 1902. His long movie and television career began in 1930. Jory also made many television appearances from the 1950s to the 1970s. He died in 1982.

Bernice Kay is better known as Cara Williams. Born Bernice Kamiat in Brooklyn in 1925, she received an Oscar nomination for *The Defiant Ones* (1958). She also received an Emmy nomination for her role on TV's *Pete and Gladys*. *Wide Open Town* was her film debut. She was married from 1952 to 1959 to John Drew Barrymore, who later became Drew's father. Before making the film, Kay and her mother were on welfare. She impressed a studio executive with an impression of Charlie McCarthy and was hired. During filming, Kay entertained Brent and Jory by imitating Bette Davis, ZaSu Pitts, Mae West, Luise Rainer, Fanny Brice, and Katharine Hepburn. She also reportedly did dead-on impressions of Brent and Jory.[157]

Roy Barcroft was born Howard Ravenscroft in Nebraska in 1902. He appeared in hundreds of Westerns in film and on television. He also appeared with Brent in one of her rare television appearances on *Elfego Baca*. Barcroft died in 1969.

Director Lesley Selander, born in Los Angeles in 1900, helmed many Western films in his career and then turned his attention to television. He received a Directors Guild Association nomination for Outstanding Directorial Achievement in Television for an episode of *Lassie*. Selander died in 1979. J. Benton Cheney was a film and television writer who specialized in Westerns. He also worked on the script for *Raiders of the South* (1947).

*Reviews:* "Good clean action entertainment with lots of comedy.... Mr. Sherman's record for making the best Westerns that can be made at any price doesn't suffer with this one" (*Film Daily*, July 30, 1941).

"Miss Brent turns in a fine performance as the brains of the gang, and advances considerably in her comeback attempt.... Script neatly mixes the various ingredients of gun and fist fights, wild rides, chases and general action expected from a Western" (*Variety*, July 30, 1941).

## *Dangerous Lady*

(Producers Releasing Corp.) 65 min. Released on September 12, 1941.

*Survival Status: Exists.* Released on video (*Classic Collectors Series*)

*Credits*; Executive producer, George R. Batcheller; producer-director, Bernard B. Ray; assistant director, Fred Santley; screenplay, Jack Natteford; additional dialogue, Sidney Sheldon; original story, Leslie T. White; photography, Jack Greenhalgh; art director, Fred Preble; film editor, Carl Himm; musical director, Clarence E. Wheeler; sound engineer, Ferol Redd; production manager, Robert Ray.

*Cast*: June Storey (Phyllis Martindel); Neil Hamilton (Duke Martindel); Douglas Fowley (Sergeant Brent); John Holland (Guy Kisling); Emmett Vogan (Dr. Grayson); Evelyn Brent (Hester Engel); Malcolm McTaggert (Joe Link); Greta Granstedt (Leila Bostwick); Carl Stockdale (Judge Harding); Jack Mulhall (Hotel Clerk); Kenneth Harlan (Det. Dunlap); John Ince (Capt. Newton); Terry Walker (Annie); Sheila Darcy (Reporter); James Aubrey (Janitor); William Dudley.

Detective Duke is married to attorney Phyllis. She doesn't want him working on any criminal cases. However, they quickly become involved in the Leila Bostwick case when they learn that Leila, accused of murdering a judge, might have been framed. After Leila escapes from jail, the Martindels try to solve the crime.

Duke and Phyllis tie the judge's murder to Guy Kinsling, a former business partner of Leila's. For a brief moment, the Martindels are in danger. However, after a struggle, the cops finally arrive and the bad guys are arrested. Leila is cleared of the murder charge.

In the final scene, Duke gets a telegram from a friend asking for help. "Papa's not going to take any more of those naughty criminal cases," Phyllis warns.

"Oh, no, my love," Duke says. He embraces and kisses Phyllis and then crosses his fingers behind her back. Meanwhile, she picks the telegram out of his pocket and puts it behind her back.

Brent was sixth-billed this time, and for the first time looks older and somewhat tired. She usually brings something distinctive to a role, but left it at home this time.

It tries to be *The Thin Man*, but it's not even *Mr. and Mrs. North*. The script for this mediocre comedy is bad, and the performances are even worse. The picture lacks charm, wit, and plausibility. It is also known as *Beware the Lady*.

June Storey, born in Canada in 1918, was best known for her many appearances in Westerns with Gene Autry. She died in 1991.

Douglas Fowley was born in the Bronx in 1911. The father of songwriter and producer Kim Fowley, he began his film career in 1933 and appeared in more than three hundred films and television episodes. Fowley died in 1998.

Greta Granstedt, born in Kansas in 1907, made her first film appearance in the late 1920s. The onetime roommate of adventurer Bessie Hyde (who disappeared in the Grand Canyon with her husband in 1928 under mysterious conditions) Greta's face was also familiar to television viewers in the 1950s and 1960s. She died in 1987.

Malcolm McTaggert, born in Nebraska in 1910, died in a swimming pool accident in 1949. He was also known as Bud McTaggert and Ward McTaggert. Jack Mulhall was born in Wappingers Falls, New York, in 1887. The character actor made his film debut in 1910 and ended up with more than four hundred film and television credits. Like Brent, he went from being a star to appearing in small roles. Mulhall died in 1979. He also appeared with Brent in *The Iron Will* (1916), *Hollywood Boulevard* (1936), *Silent Witness* (1943), and *Bowery Champs* (1944). John Holland (1908–1993), born in Nebraska, made his film debut in 1937 and ended his career with numerous television appearances. Sheila Darcy was married to actor Preston Foster from 1946 until his death in 1970. Born Rebecca Benedict Heffener in York, Pennsylvania, in 1914, she also appeared as the Dragon Lady in the serial *Terry and the Pirates*. Darcy died in 2004.

*Reviews:* "With its budgetary confines, this is a snappy comedy melodrama that is nicely handled all the way, although the yarn is on the weak side.... Evelyn Brent, Jack Mulhall, Kenneth Harlan ... turn in strong supporting bits" (*Film Daily*, October 13, 1941).

## Ellery Queen and the Murder Ring

(Columbia Pictures) 6256 ft. 70 min. Released on October 17, 1941.

*Survival Status:* Exists.

*Credits:* Producer, Larry Darmour; associate producer, Rudolph Flothow; director: James Hogan; assistant director, Carl Hiecke; screenplay, Eric Taylor, Gertrude Purcell; based on the novel *The Dutch Shoe Mystery* by Ellery Queen; photography, James S. Brown, Jr.; film editor, Dwight Caldwell; music, Lee Zahler; sound engineer, Tom Lambert.

*Cast:* Ralph Bellamy (Ellery Queen); Margaret Lindsay (Nikki Porter); Charley Grapewin (Inspector Queen); Mona Barrie (Miss Tracy); Paul Hurst (Bill Page); James Burke (Sgt. Velie); George Zucco (Dr. Janney); Blanche Yurka (Augusta Stack); Tom Dugan (Lew Thomas); Leon Ames (John Stack); Jean Fenwick (Alice Stack); Olin Howland (Dr. Williams); Dennis Moore (Dr. Dunn); Charlotte Wynters (Miss Fox); Pierre Watkin (Crothers); Evelyn Brent (Nurse in classroom); Barlowe Borland (Martin Butler); Don Brodie (Hospital Desk Supervisor); Dick Curtis (Policeman); Edgar Dearing (Motorcycle cop); Claire Du Brey (Nurse in corridor); Byron Foulger (Male nurse); Edward Gargan (Dumb henchman); Harrison Greene (Hospital elevator repairman); Harry Tyler (Henchman); Pat West (Ambulance attendant).

Ellery Queen feigns laryngitis to go undercover at a hospital to investigate alleged wrongdoing. Nikki Porter and hapless Police Sgt. Velie are on hand to throw monkey wrenches into the investigation. Although the film doesn't take itself too seriously and appears to be played largely for laughs, several unfortunate and unnecessary deaths take place before the culprit is finally brought to justice. An okay programmer featuring familiar faces and some not-too-subtle comedy relief.

Brent was unbilled in a thankless bit and had one short line of dialogue. She played a nurse locked in a closet after a surprise run-in with one of the villains.

Ralph Bellamy was born in 1904 in Chicago, Illinois. His prolific 60-year-plus film career began in 1931. A well respected actor of film, stage and television, received an honorary Oscar in 1987. Bellamy died in 1991. This was his fourth and final appearance as the master detective.

Margaret Lindsay was born Margaret Kies in 1910 in Dubuque, Iowa. She began her film career at Universal in 1932 and went on to brighten many Warner Bros. films in the 1930s. She enjoyed continued success throughout the 1940s moving between character roles in "A" films and leads in lower budgeted fare. Lindsay appeared on numerous television programs throughout the 1950s and 1960s. Lindsay, who lived for many years with actress Mary McCarty, died in 1981.

Charley Grapewin was born in 1869 in Xenia, Ohio. Although probably best known for his portrayal of Uncle Henry in *The Wizard of Oz* (1939), Grapewin appeared in many other classics such as *The Petrified Forest* (1936), *The Grapes of Wrath* (1940) and *They Died With Their Boots On* (1941). He made his last film appearance in 1951 and died in 1956.

Mona Barrie, born in 1909 in London, made her film debut in 1934. Though she never achieved stardom, Barrie had a respectable film career that spanned nearly twenty years. She appeared in W.C. Fields' last starring film *Never Give a Sucker an Even Break* (1941) and co-starred with Buck Jones in his last film *Dawn on the Great Divide* (1942). Barrie died in 1964.

Blanche Yurka was born in 1887 and raised in St. Paul, Minnesota. Opera singer, renowned stage actress, film character actress and author, the multitalented Yurka may be best remembered by film audiences for her compelling portrayal of Madame De

Farge in *A Tale of Two Cities* (1935). Yurka retired from acting in 1970 and died in 1974. She was divorced from Ian Keith.

Claire Du Brey was born in 1992 in Bonner's Ferry, Idaho. She made her film debut in 1916. A character actress and bit player with a career spanning more than 40 years and 200 films, Du Brey made her last film appearance in 1959. She was an intimate of Marie Dressler until their falling-out in 1932. Du Brey died in 1993 one month shy of her 101st birthday.

George Zucco, born in Manchester, England, in 1886, was a dependable character actor nicknamed "One Take Zucco." He often played doctors, and many of his appearances were in horror films. Zucco died in 1960. Jean Fenwick was the sister of Marian Marsh. Born in the West Indies in 1907, she died in 1998. Charlotte Wynters, born in Wheeling, West Virginia, in 1899, was married to Barton MacLane. She became a cattle rancher after her retirement and died in 1991.

*Reviews*: "The adventure, with its sideline comedy by-play, is generally acceptable diverting fare" (*Variety*, September 17, 1941).

"[T]here is nothing to recommend the picture except the fact that it finally comes to an end" (*New York Times*, October 21, 1941).

"*Ellery Queen and the Murder Ring* is a wearisome whodunit-as-if-anyone cared" (Walter Winchell, *The High Point Enterprise* [North Carolina], October 27, 1941).

## Holt of the Secret Service

(Columbia Pictures) 15 episodes, 278 min. Released November 21, 1941.

*Survival Status:* Library of Congress (Washington, D.C.). Released on Video (Alpha, Serial Squadron).

*Credits:* Director, James W. Horne; original screenplay, Basil Dickey, George H. Plympton, Wyndham Gittens; original music, Lee Zahler; cinematography, James S. Brown, Jr.; film editors, Dwight Caldwell, Earl Turner.

*Cast:* Jack Holt (Jack Holt / Nick Farrel); Evelyn Brent (Kay Drew, R49); Montague Shaw (Chief John W. Malloy); Tristram Coffin; (Ed Valden); John Ward ("Lucky" Arnold); Ted Adams (Quist); Joe McGuinn ("Crimp" Evans); Edward Hearn (Agent Jim Layton); Ray Parsons (John Severn, engraver); Jack Cheatham (Agent Frank).

Entrusted with two of America's most vital policing jobs—the safeguarding of our President and the protection of our currency against counterfeiters—the Men of the Secret Service are front line soldiers in the never ending war against crime. Standing not only between the Chief Executive and an assassin's bullet, but between the nation's currency and the vicious criminals who would despoil it, the Men of the Secret Service deserve our gratitude as well as our respect. Yet, too often, their reward is—Death!

In this 15-chapter serial, a Treasury Department engraver is kidnapped and the Secret Service assigns Jack Holt and Kay Drew to solve the case. Both are seasoned. According to Kay, "I've worked where gun molls' lives aren't worth a dime a dozen. Shoot the works. I'm ready." Holt pretends to be criminal Nick Farrel, and Kay will be his wife.

It takes a while, and there are many close calls, but Jack and Kay eventually defeat the criminals. In the conclusion, Jack and Kay are given a lengthy paid vacation. Kay says she's leaving the state. *The state?* "Yes, the state of matrimony." Jack chases after her, saying that he's going back on the job, and it's going to be a tough one. "Making Kay change her mind."

The supervisors chuckle, and one says that Kay is in for it "because Holt of the Secret Service always gets his ... uh, uh ... man."

This serial serves Brent much better than *Jungle Jim*. The serial itself is quite good—fast-paced and compelling. Brent is equally good as is Jack Holt. Brent gets to do some sneering and tough-talking ("Do you want me to weep in a bucket?" is just one of her great lines), and her role is very physical. *Holt of the Secret Service* provides another opportunity to see what Brent does best—play tough, gutsy women.

Taglines included: "MOST POPULAR ACTION STAR OF ALL TIME IN HIS FIRST SERIAL!," "The Hero Of 10,000 Adventures Tops 'Em All In His First Serial!," and "His First Serial Blasts a New Trail of Thrills!"

Born in New York, Holt (1888–1951) made his film debut in 1914 and became a silent film star, especially in Westerns. Holt will forever be referred to as "granite-jawed" for obvious reasons. He was the father of Tim Holt who worked with Brent in *The Law West of Tombstone* (1937).

Montague Shaw, sometimes billed as C. Montague Shaw, was born in Australia in 1882. He made his film debut in 1926 and appeared in many serials. Shaw died in 1968. Tristram Coffin was born in Mammoth, Utah, in 1909. He made his film debut in 1939 and was a regular on the TV show *26 Men*. He died in 1990.

Director James W. Horne, born in 1880 in San Francisco, was also a writer and occasional actor. Horne worked for Hal Roach and directed some of the Charley Chase and Laurel and Hardy pictures. He died in 1942. Writer Basil Dickey, born in Illinois in 1880, also wrote scripts for many other serials including *Beatrice Fairfax* (1916) and *Flash Gordon* (1936). He died in 1958.

*Reviews:* "Design of the piece is strictly for the kids, and it adds up to a disappointment in lots of ways.... One of the illusion-busters is the casting of Miss Brent, who, in no sense of the imagination could pass as the type one would want to protect, or would have to worry about taking care of herself.... Formula demands that the girl be demure, and Miss Brent hardly qualifies for that classification" (*Variety*, January 21, 1942).

## Westward Ho

(Republic Pictures) 56 min. Released on April 24, 1942.

*Survival Status*: UCLA Film and Television Archive (Los Angeles).

*Credits*: Associate producer, Louis Gray; director, John English; assistant director, George Webster; based on characters created by William Colt MacDonald; screenplay, Morton Grant, Doris Schroeder; original story, Morton Grant; photography, Reggie Lanning; art direction, Russell Kimball; film editor, William Thompson; music score, Cy Feuer.

*Cast*: Bob Steele ("Tucson" Smith); Tom Tyler ("Stony" Brooke); Rufe Davis ("Lullaby" Joslin); Evelyn Brent (Mrs. J.L. Healey); Donald Curtis (Rick West); Lois Collier (Anne Henderson); Emmett Lynn (Sheriff); John James (Jimmy Henderson); Tom Seidel (Wayne Henderson); Jack Kirk (Deputy); Budd Buster (Coffee); Kenne Duncan (Dallas); Bud Osborne (Red); Al Taylor (Hank); Monte Montague (Parker); Alfred Hall (Williams); Glen "Slim" Lucas (Driver); Jayne Hazard (Photographer's girl); Milt Kibbee (Photographer); Edmund Cobb (Mob member); Tony Roux (Waiter); James C. Morton (Superintendent); Joe De La Cruz (Bartender); Burr Caruth (Mantley).

When the Three Mesquiteers come into town, Lullaby is mistakenly assumed to be a bank robber. His buddies help him escape a hanging and then try to separate the good guys from the bad.

Brent played a villainous member of a corrupt banking association. She was announced as a cast member on March 3, 1942. This was part of a series of Westerns. The first film in the series was *The Three Mesquiteers* (1936), and the series continued until 1943.

Director John English, born in England in 1903, directed many Westerns, both film and television. He started as an editor in the silent film era. English died in 1969. Screenwriter Doris Schroeder began her career in 1913 writing silent scenarios. She eventually specialized in Westerns after talkies became popular. Schroeder died in 1981.

Cowboy star Bob Steele, born in Portland, Oregon, in 1907, was the son of director Robert N. Bradbury. He appeared in silent films as a child and then became known as a Western star. Steele played Trooper Duffy on *F Troop* and appeared on many television shows late in his career. He died in 1988.

Tom Tyler was born Vincent Markowsky in Port Henry, New York, in 1903. A champion weightlifter, he appeared in many Western serials but is probably best known for playing Captain Marvel in *Adventures of Captain Marvel* (1941). He died in 1954.

Rufe Davis, born in Vincent, Oklahoma, in 1908, ended his long film and television career by appearing on *Petticoat Junction* as Floyd Smoot (a character he also played on *Green Acres*). He died in 1974.

Lois Collier was born Madelyn Jones in Salley, South Carolina. She appeared in many low-budget films and serials in the 1940s. She also was a regular on TV's *Boston Blackie*. Collier died in 1999.

*Reviews:* "This is an above-average Western, with much action and a novel story.... Evelyn Brent, still looking attractive; Donald Curtis, John James and Emmett Lynn all are contributory factors to a punchy picture" (*Variety*, April 29, 1942).

"Western fans should find little complaint with the action and brand of villainy in this film.... There are good performances by Steele, Tyler, Davis, Miss Brent, Donald Curtis, Lois Collier, John James" (*Film Daily*, May 6, 1942).

# *Wrecking Crew*

(Paramount Pictures) 73 min. Released on November 7, 1942.

*Archive*: UCLA Film and Television Archive (Los Angeles). Released on video (Movies Unlimited)

*Credits*: Executive producers, William H. Pine, William C. Thomas; director, Frank McDonald; assistant director, Howard Pine; screenplay, Maxwell Shane, Richard Murphy; original story, Robert T. Shannon, Mauri Grashin; photography, Fred Jackman, Jr.; art direction, F. Paul Sylos; film editor, William Ziegler; music score, Freddy Rich; sound recording, Charles S. Althouse; special effects, Alex Widlicska.

*Cast:* Richard Arlen (Matt Carney); Chester Morris (Duke Mason); Jean Parker (Peggy Starr); Joe Sawyer (Freddy Bunce); Esther Dale (Mike O'Glendy); Alexander Granach (Joe Poska); Billy Nelson (Tom Kemp); Evelyn Brent (Martha Poska); William Hall (Red); Frank Melton (Pete); Fred Sherman (Emil); Alec Craig (Charley); Nigel de Brulier (Priest); Byron Foulger (Mission worker); Ralph Sanford (Worker); Grant Withers, Pat West.

The Great Western Hotel, built in 1902, is being torn down. "This is the story of the wreckers.... They tear down that others may build—Their lives are dedicated to the proposition that whatever goes up must come down, and the bigger they are ... the harder they fall." At the building site we see a sign: "THIS BUILDING BEING WRECKED BY O'-GLENDY WRECKING CO."

Duke Mason arrives to work on the project though he's considered a jinx. Old friend Matt Carney assigns him to take down the water tower. (Notice the not-so-subtle sign advertising a complete funeral for $125. Also, if you have a fear of heights you might want to skip this scene.) We're no experts on the construction business, but we have to think that OSHA would be all over these guys. There are lots of foolish hijinks on the tower, and the guys behave like jackasses. Anyway, if you like that male energy gone manic kind of thing, these guys are a scream.

The crew has a deadline to meet. Accidents start to happen, which adds to the superstition that Duke is a jinx.

Duke meets Peggy, a young woman who's down on her luck. He saves her when she jumps in the river. Matt meets her, and sparks fly. He and Duke persuade wrecking company owner Mike O'Glendy to hire her, and Carney and Duke vie for her attention.

Matt proposes to Peggy, but she asks for time. Mike tells her to marry Matt because marrying Duke would be "a ride on a roller coaster. You'd never be sure. You would have a lot of laughs, but a lot of tears, too. Mr. O'Glendy was like Duke. He was a lot of man, though."

Malcontent Kemp shows up drunk and asks for his job back. Duke refuses, and Kemp sabotages the site (in a New York minute he goes from malcontent to psychopath), releasing a wrecking ball (pretty thrilling scene, reminiscent of the first *Indiana Jones* movie), seriously injuring a worker. Matt blames Duke, and Duke quits. He asks Peggy to marry him, but she tells him she's marrying Matt.

Duke and Matt end up in a fistfight until Mike tells them a storm is bringing the building down. Duke insists he's quitting, and Peggy calls him a coward. "Help your brother in his hour of need" is the message Duke gets after leaving the worksite. He returns, just in time to rescue Matt who is trapped. "Well, I'm a rat if I don't and I'm a chump if I do. So I'm a chump."

He rescues Matt, but they're stuck on a crumbling wall. (They see, however, that the price of the funeral has been reduced to $75.) They are rescued by their fellow workers just before the wall falls.

In the final scene, Peggy has married Matt (thank God she didn't marry the maniac). They're on top of the Empire State Building. Duke and Mike are there too. Duke sits on the edge, picking at the building. "This wouldn't be so tough, Mike," he says. "Why, we could wreck this in less time than it takes to say—" Duke slips off the ledge. His friends help pull him back to safety. Everyone (except the audience) has a good laugh.

Brent did not even get an on-screen credit this time. She is miscast as the wife of an ill-fated, happy-go-lucky immigrant. She's fine but it's a role that just about anyone could have played.

The picture is only fair. It's apparently a guy movie showing the importance of camaraderie. Or maybe it's a dumb-guy movie showing the importance of choosing your friends wisely. Anyway, Chester Morris, who usually gives an energetic performance, is tuned even higher than usual. The special effects are the highlight of the film.

The film was based on a short story titled "Alley Cat." Joyce Mathews was considered for Jean Parker's role. Taglines included "Eyes High ... For Thrills!" and "THEY'LL WRECK ANYTHING ... A Skyscraper ... A Heartbreaker ... Or Each Other!" (A more accurate tagline would have been, "THEY WRECK EVERYTHING ... Friendships ... Relationships ... And everything else they're not supposed to!")

Frank McDonald, born in Baltimore, Maryland, in 1899, was a film and television director from 1934 to the 1960s. He worked on such television shows as *The Gene Autry Show* and *Get Smart*. Evelyn Keyes found him to be a nervous wreck on the set. "I've never seen anyone as terrified of directing as Frank McDonald,"[158] she said. He died in 1980.

Writer Mauri Grashin, born in Illinois in 1901, received an Oscar nomination for *Hide-Out* (1934). He died in 1991. Writer Richard Murphy was born in Boston in 1912. He received Oscar nominations for *Boomerang* (1947) and *The Desert Rats* (1953). Murphy created the 1960s television show *The Felony Squad*. He died in 1993.

Jean Parker, born Lois Mae Green in Deer Lodge, Montana, in 1915, made her film debut in 1931 and was a successful leading lady well into the 1940s. She was discovered when she won a poster painting contest. She died in 2005. Born in Canada in 1906, Joe Sawyer made his film debut in 1930 and appeared in more than two hundred films and television episodes. He died in 1982. Alexander Granach, born in the Ukraine in 1893, was a German film star who came to the United States after Hitler took power. He died in 1945.

*Reviews:* "Made to order for action fans.... Maxwell Shane and Richard Murphy have packed their screenplay solid with exciting and action-begetting incidents" (*Film Daily*, November 2, 1942).

"Script is crisply set up, focusing attention on the action throughout, while director Frank McDonald holds to a fast pace with scenes clipped to minimum" (*Variety*, November 4, 1942).

## The Pay Off

(Producers Releasing Corp.) 74 min. Released on November 24, 1942.

*Survival status:* Released on video (Alpha, 69 min.).

*Credits:* Executive producer, Leon Fromkess; producer, Jack Schwarz; associate producer, Harry D. Edwards; director, Arthur Dreifuss; assistant director, Edward M. Davis; dialogue director–screenplay, Edward Dein; screenplay–original story, Arthur Hoerl; photography, Ira Morgan; film editor, Charles Henkel, Jr.; music score composed and conducted by Charles Dant; sound engineer, Ben Winkler; production manager, Arthur Hammond.

*Cast:* Lee Tracy (Brad McKay); Tom Brown (Guy Norris); Tina Thayer (Phyllis Walker); Evelyn Brent (Alma Dorn); Jack La Rue (John Angus); Ian Keith (Inspector Thomas); Robert Middlemass (Lester Norris); John Maxwell (Vince Moroni); John Sheehan (Sergeant Brenen); Harry Bradley (Dr. Steele); Forrest Taylor (Hugh Walker); Pat Costello (Reporter).

The film begins by cleverly showing the credits with the use of newspaper headlines. (By the way, check out the other headlines: "WPB Shortens List of School Supplies," "Drummer Rich to Entertain with Solid Jive," etc.) In the opening scene, special prosecutor Lloyd Pearson is murdered. Newspaperman Brad McKay finds out that Pearson was dirty and had falsely implicated attorney Hugh Walker. Walker's daughter Phyllis gives McKay a key to a locker where she stored a package at her father's instruction. At some risk to his life, McKay retrieves the package and hides the $100,000 it contains (a payoff to Pearson) in his apartment.

McKay takes one of the marked bills to a gambling joint owned by Angus. He flirts with Alma, who works for Angus. Later, she sneaks into his apartment to find the package. McKay pretends she's shot him and milks it for everything he can, including getting a sweet kiss from her. Finally, he overpowers her. She tells him to turn her over to the police. "I wouldn't share you with anybody," he says. (This is a nice scene between the two old pros. Tracy *really* milks it. It looks like the two of them almost crack up at one point during the scene. There's also this nice piece of dialogue: She says, "Sorry, I didn't kill you," and he replies, "You do, baby.")

"You know, I should hate you," Alma says, "but women are such chumps."

The two join forces. McKay takes his evidence to his publisher Norris. Turns out Norris is the top man in the criminal enterprise. "The city remains a rotten, stinking cesspool," McKay says dejectedly upon learning the truth.

Angus' place is raided, and he's killed. McKay and Norris go to a warehouse. Norris thinks his son Guy has gone there and is walking into a shootout. Norris runs inside the warehouse shouting his son's name. He's shot and killed. When the newspaper reports the story, Norris is the hero. "It isn't true, I know," McKay says, "but it'll give the kid something to look up to. You know, something to fight for. Make this the best city in the world."

McKay gets Alma released from jail. She shows up at his apartment with a bottle of liquor (he'd mentioned to her that he proposes after drinking). Alma starts to walk away, and McKay asks her where she's going. "Where I belong," she says. McKay fires two shots. (Notice that the camera shot does not match—it must have been a retake. By the way, Tracy had gotten in trouble in March 1935 for firing five shots in his Hollywood apartment. Fortunately, no one was hurt. Tracy pleaded guilty to intoxication and was fined $100.) "Here's where you belong, baby!" They embrace and passionately kiss. The final shot is a newspaper with the headline "THE END." (Again, take a look at the fake headlines including "First-Aiders Take Part in Mock Raid.")

Brent, fourth-billed, looks glamorous and is more than competent in a small but important role.

Lee Tracy, who pokes fun at his own dissipated looks when he tells a photographer, "Don't forget to touch up the bags, under the bags, under my eyes," was trying to make a comeback. He gave an energetic performance in this snappy film with a nice jazzy score. Still a fast talker, he was quite good as a cynical reporter, and he and Brent, who had both been through the Hollywood wringer, had great chemistry. Tracy was born in Atlanta, Georgia, in 1898 and was, without a doubt, his own worst enemy. He was a hugely popular actor in the early 1930s, but his personal life, particularly his uncontrolled drinking, led to his decline. After a scandalous episode in Mexico City in 1934 while filming *Viva Villa!*, MGM took him off the picture and cancelled his contract. Tracy made a successful comeback, though he never reached the same level of success. He made only a few other film appearances after this picture, though he did appear on television in the 1950s and 1960s, most notably in *Martin Kane, Private Eye*. He received an Oscar nomination for 1964's *The Best Man* (he had received a Tony nomination for the play of the same name in 1960) and died in 1968.

There are numerous scenes of Tracy wisecracking on the telephone and using his famous telephone flip—he flips the phone receiver off the ringer into his hand. He used this flip to great effect in *The Strange Love of Molly Louvain* (1932). Tracy has great movement as an actor. He's never still. Nobody, except perhaps Cagney, moves around and through a set like Tracy. Director Dreifuss wisely keeps him moving throughout much of this film.

Taglines included "Tracy—the Great-Go-Getter.... Is Back in a Sensational Role!," "AN AIR-TIGHT ALIBI? He thought he had an air-tight alibi ... but a fast-talking newshawk punched holes in it!," and "HE'S BACK AGAIN.... The Fastest talking newshawk in his greatest role!"

Tom Brown was born in New York in 1913. He made his film debut in 1924 and was still acting on television throughout the 1970s. He was a regular on TV's *Mr. Lucky* and *Gunsmoke*. Brown died in 1990.

Tina Thayer appeared in only seven films. She made her debut in 1940, and her last film was in 1944.

Ian Keith was born in Boston in 1899. A Broadway star, he made his film debut in 1924. He died in 1960. Ex-wives included Ethel Clayton and Blanche Yurka. He also appeared with Brent in *Bowery Champs* (1944).

*Reviews:* "In his welcome return to the screen, Lee Tracy gives his usual snappy performance as a star newspaperman. The picture ... is easily one of the best to bear the PRC label" (*Film Daily*, November 24, 1942).

## Silent Witness

(Monogram Productions) 62 min. Released on January 10, 1943.

*Survival Status:* Library of Congress (Washington, D.C.).

*Credits:* Producer, Max M. King; director, Jean Yarbrough; assistant director, George Webster; second assistant, Gerd Oswald; story and screenplay, Martin Mooney; photography, Max Stengler; art director, David Milton; film editor, Carl Pierson; music score, Edward Kay; sound engineer, Glen Glenn.

*Cast:* Frank Albertson (Bruce Strong); Maris Wrixon (Betty Higgins); Bradley Page (Bob Holden); Milburn Stone (Joe Manson); Lucien Littlefield (Eastman); Evelyn Brent (Mrs. Roos); Jimmy Eagles (Carlos Jockey); Anthony Warde (Lou Manson); Jack Mulhall (Jed Kelly); John Ince (Mayor); Ace (Major); Joe Eggleston (Rancher); Sam McDaniel (Deacon); Paul Bryar (Blackie), Patsy Nash (Elsie), John Sheehan (Det. Dan Callahan), Jean Ames (Daisy); Virginia Carroll (Majorie Miller); Harry Harvey (Monk); Buzz Henry (Johnny Jergens); Olaf Hytten (Sidney); Margaret Armstrong (Mrs. Higgins); Herbert Rawlinson (Benjamin Yeager); Caroline Burke (Nurse); Henry Hall (Judge); Kenneth Harlan (Det. Jackson).

Gus is killed in his apartment by two assassins outside his building. District attorney Bob Holden and investigator Betty Higgins have an eyewitness, Mrs. Roos, who identifies the murderers as Joe and Lou Manson. Attorney Bruce Strong gets the case dismissed when he brings up a former shoplifting conviction for Mrs. Roos. It ruins her life.

Disgusted, Betty returns her engagement ring to Bruce. Meanwhile, the Manson brothers continue their crime spree. Their next caper is stealing silk from a warehouse. The brothers are arrested.

Bruce keeps trying to get Betty back, but she refuses unless he quits defending bad guys. Bruce finally tells Joe Manson he's finished with him. Manson says they're going after the district attorney. Bruce tries to warn Bob, but he is killed before he can get to him. Bob's dog Major is also wounded. Bruce is arrested for the murder.

Betty receives a note from Bruce that was mailed before he was arrested. He tells her that he's given up his criminal practice. Betty goes to see Bruce in jail, and she decides to help prove he's innocent. They need all the help they can get because the Mansons planted the murder weapon in Bruce's car. Bruce is convicted and sentenced to die.

Some kids find Major and tend to his wound. Their dad realizes the dog might be involved in the case and calls the authorities. When Betty shows up to identify Major, the dad gives them white cloth that was found in Major's mouth. It's a piece of overalls similar to ones worn by the Manson brothers. She brings the crooks in for a line-up. Unfortunately, a witness cannot make a positive identification, and the crooks are dismissed. However, the day is saved when Major attacks Lou. "I'll talk! I'll tell everything" the bad guy pleads. Joe is also arrested.

In the final scene Major receives an award from the mayor. Bruce returns the ring to Betty. The last line is delivered by one of the kids: "When he has puppies [Major—not Bruce], we'll give you one, Miss Higgins." It's supposed to be cute.

Production began on October 27, 1942. Martin Mooney and Max King were partners in a company and were supposed to co-produce the film. However, in November 1942 the partnership was dissolved. The film was released in the United Kingdom with the title *Attorney for the Defense*.

Brent slipped to eighth billing on this one. It's not a very good film. The script is awkward, and the performances are weak. This is not one of Brent's better performances. Taglines included "Even gangland's cleverest 'mouthpiece' meets his Waterloo with the D.A.'s blonde bombshell!"

Director Jean Yarbrough, born in Arkansas in 1900, started his career in the silent film era and ended it with many television assignments including *The Abbott and Costello Show, The Guns of Will Sonnett*, and *Death Valley Days*. He died in 1975.

Maris Wrixon was born in Pasco, Washington, in 1916 and made her film debut in 1939. She was married to editor Rudi Fehr from 1940 until his death in April 1999. She died in October of that same year.

Milburn Stone was best known for his role as Doc Adams on TV's *Gunsmoke* (he won an Emmy in 1968). Born in Kansas in 1904, he was part of a vaudeville team named Stone and Strain. He made his film debut in 1935 and died in 1980.

Anthony Warde was born in Pennsylvania in 1908 and died in 1975. He also appeared with Brent in *Stage Struck* (1948). Virginia Carroll was born Virginia Delight Carroll Broberg in Oklahoma in 1910. Married to *Dick Tracy* actor Ralph Byrd, she died in 1986. Carroll's name is incorrectly spelled "Carrol" in the opening credits. Sam McDaniel, actually nicknamed "Deacon," often appeared in stereotypical

African-American roles of porters, chauffeurs, etc. The brother of Hattie McDaniel, he was born in Wichita, Kansas, in 1886 and died in 1962. Ace the Wonder Dog appeared in sixteen films between 1938 and 1949.

*Reviews:* "[W]hile there are moments when you feel you have seen this picture before, due to the ingredients being familiar ... the sauce of suspense so nicely flavors it and there are so many little touches of human nature and comedy, as well as surprise moments, that the film is absorbing. Directing and acting, too, leave nothing to be desired" (*Los Angeles Times*, December 10, 1942).

## Spy Train

(Monogram Productions) 61 min. Released July 5, 1943.
*Survival Status:* Library of Congress (Washington, D.C.). Released on video (Movies Unlimited).
*Credits:* Producer, Max M. King; director, Harold Young; dialogue director, Harold Erickson; screenplay, Leslie Schwabacker, Bart Lytton; original story, Scott Littlefield; contributing writer, Wallace Sullivan; photography, Mack Stengler; set construction, David Milton; film editor, Martin G. Cohn; set dressings, Al Greenwood; sound engineer, Glen Glenn; makeup, Harry Ross; production manager, Dick L'Estrange.
*Cast:* Richard Travis (Bruce Grant); Catherine Craig (Jane Thornwald); Chick Chandler (Stew); Thelma White (Millie); Evelyn Brent (Frieda Molte); Warren Hymer (Herman Krantz); Paul McVey (Hugo Molte); Herbert Heyes (Max Thornwald); Steve Roberts (Chief Nazi); Bill Hunter (Detective); Napoleon Whiting (Porter); Gerald Brock (Italian spy); John Hamilton (Conductor); Forrest Taylor (Anderson); Dick Rush (Train conductor); Bill Kellogg (Detective); Snowflake Toones (Porter); Barbara Mace; Caroline Burke; Geo. Bronson.

At the Los Angeles train station, Jane Thornwald's maid Millie is unknowingly given a bag that holds a bomb timed to explode at 10:22 P.M.—or if it is opened. She and Jane board the train with it. Also aboard are writer Bruce Grant and his photographer friend Stew. Grant recognizes German agents Frieda and Hugo Molte; according to Stew, "They're crooked as corkscrews."

Grant meets Jane and learns she's reading one of his books. "Pretty good book," she says. "Who wrote it for you?"

"I'm glad you like it. Who read it to you?"

Grant wants to use Jane to get a meeting with her father, a publisher who has stopped printing his newspaper series on Nazi secrets. She is offended, and though there are plenty of sparks she doesn't trust him again until he's wrongly accused of stabbing Stew. Meanwhile, the bag that Millie brought on board gets tossed about, stolen, and re-stolen with none of the principals knowing it holds an explosive device.

Grant intercepts a wire sent to Frieda and learns that he has only a few moments before the bag explodes. He takes Frieda and Hugo off the train at gunpoint. The police stop Grant, and the Moltes run off with the bag despite Grant's plea to stop ("Molte, look out! That's loaded with a bomb!"). Molte doesn't believe him. "Just another stupid American trick," he says. Of course, the bag explodes, blowing him and his wife to bits.

Turns out the spy ring had put together photo composites that showed Jane posing with Hitler and Goering. They used the photos to get Jane's father to stop publishing Grant's articles. Thornwald agrees to resume publishing the articles immediately. Meanwhile, Jane tells Grant that she's finished his book and wants a dedication. Bruce writes "Dedicated to my wife Jane."

The direction is quite good, and the film is fast-paced and interesting. It starts off a little slowly, but the suspense ramps up big-time. Many train dramas, by their nature, are pretty thrilling and well-paced. The best feature intersecting diverse lives, small claustrophobic compartments, lots of cuts and edits—there's a lot going on. The director still has to do his job, though, for the film to be successful.

As the Moltes, Brent and McVey do the impossible—they almost make the murderous German spies sympathetic. At the same time, there's great chemistry between Travis and Craig. For their part, White and Chandler play charming sidekicks.

The working title was *Time Bomb*. Lewis D. Collins was assigned to direct this film, but was eventually replaced by the highly efficient Harold Young. Notice that in one of the scenes, as Hugo dictates a note to wife Frieda, she misspells the name of the composer Haydn (Heydn). Also, though they're on a steam train the whistle you'll hear is that of a diesel train.

Blandly handsome Richard Travis was born William Justice in New Mexico in 1913. He was a regular on *Cowboy G-Men* and *Code 3*. He died in 1989.

Born Thelma Wolpa in Lincoln, Nebraska, Thelma White (1910–2005) is unfortunately best known for her role in the cult film *Reefer Madness* (1936). White later became a talent agent representing such actors as Debbie Reynolds, Robert Blake, and Dolores Hart. A supposed autobiography was published after her death, and it is guaranteed to be one of the most unusual books you will ever read. She also appeared with Brent in *Bowery Champs* (1944).

Born Catherine Jewel Feltus in Bloomington, Indiana, in 1913, Catherine Craig made her film debut in 1940. She met fellow student Robert Preston when they attended the Pasadena Playhouse and married him on November 9, 1940. She died in 2004.

Chick Chandler was born in Kingston, New York, in 1905. He appeared in many films in the 1930s and 1940s and then became a popular character actor on television. He died in 1988.

Warren Hymer was born in New York in 1906. His parents were playwright John B. Hymer and actress Eleanor Kent. Hymer made his film debut in 1929, but heavy drinking eventually ruined his career and health. He died in1948.

Paul McVey was born in Boston in 1898. He appeared in well over a hundred movies until his death in 1973. Notice in the scene where Grant shows Jane

an excerpt from his book that McVey's last name is used: "One night, in a Munich beer hall, Bill McVey pointed out Frieda and Hugo Molte. He described them as a pair of despicable and dangerous criminals. Through one Herman Kranz they would contact rich would-be refugees and offer them a way of escape for a large fee. After the money had been paid, the victims would be turned over to the police and sent to concentration camps."

Director Harold Young was born in Portland, Oregon, in 1897. Also an editor and occasional actor, he died in 1972.

*Reviews:* "One can't deny that Monogram's *Spy Train* never stops moving; after all, it is set on a speeding train.... The Travis-Craig banter is incredibly sexist (he even gets away with gently slapping her face!), which in a way is oddly endearing" (Hal Erickson, *All Movie Guide*).

## *The Seventh Victim*

(RKO Radio Pictures) 71 min. Released August 21, 1943.

*Survival Status:* British Film Institute/National Film and Television Archive (London); UCLA Film and Television Archive (Los Angeles). Released on video (Warner Home Video).

*Credits:* Producer, Val Lewton; director, Mark Robson; assistant director, William Dorfman; writers, Charles O'Neal, DeWitt Bodeen; photography, Nicholas Musuraca; art directors, Albert S. D'Agostino, Walter E. Keller; editor, John Lockert; set decorators, Darrell Silvera, Harley Miller; gowns, Renie; musical director, C. Bakaleinikoff; music, Roy Webb; sound, John C. Grubb; dialogue supervisor, Jacqueline de Wit.

*Cast:* Tom Conway (Dr. Louis Judd); Jean Brooks (Jacqueline Gibson); Isabel Jewell (Frances); Kim Hunter (Mary Gibson); Evelyn Brent (Natalie Cortez); Erford Gage (Jason Hoag); Ben Bard (Mr. Brun); Hugh Beaumont (Gregory Ward); Chef Milani (Mr. Romari); Marguerita Sylva (Mrs. Romari); Mary Newton (Mrs. Redi); Wally Brown (Durk); Feodor Chaliapin (Lee); Jamesson Shade (Swenson); Eve March (Miss Gilchrist); Ottola Nesmith (Mrs. Lowood); Edythe Elliott (Mrs. Swift); Milton Kibbee (Joseph); Marianne Mosner (Miss Rowan); Elizabeth Russell (Mimi); Joan Barclay (Gladys); Barbara Hale (Young lover); William Halligan (Radeaux); Howard Mitchell, Bud Geary, Charles Phillips (Police officers); Lou Lubin (Irving August); Kernan Cripps (Police officer with Mary); Dewey Robinson (Conductor); Lloyd Ingraham (Watchman); Ann Summers (Miss Summers); Tiny Jones (News vendor); Adia Kuznetzoff (Ballet dancer); Patsy Nash (Nancy); Sarah Selby (Miss Gottschalk); Betty Roadman (Mrs. Wheeler); Eileen O'Malley (Mother); Lorna Dunn (Mother); Norma Nilsson (Girl); Wheaton Chambers, Ed Thomas (Men); Edith Conrad (Woman); Mary Halsey, Patti Brill (Bits); Richard Davies (Detective).

The film opens with the following lines from a cheery little sonnet by John Donne: "I runne to Death, and death meets me as fast, and all my pleasures are like yesterday." (The film attributes the quote to Holy Sonnet #7, but it's actually from Holy Sonnet #1.) Mary, who has been living at a girls' school, finds out that her sister Jacqueline is missing. She leaves for Greenwich Village to find her. Another pupil tells her not to come back: "One must have courage to really live in the world." How true.

Mary finds that Jacqueline has sold her company, the La Sagesse Cosmetics, to Mrs. Redi. This starts Mary on her search for her sister, but the mysteries pile up, and the search turns into a dark nightmare involving murders, lies, and terror. Turns out Jacqueline's friends are devil worshippers. In a particularly chilling scene reminiscent of Hitchcock's *Psycho* (1960), Mrs. Redi visits Mary while she's in the shower and strongly suggests she return to school. She adds that Jacqueline killed a man. "I warn you, Mary. Go back."

The Satanic cult has charged Jacqueline with betraying them because she told her psychiatrist about them, and now, they've decided, she must be killed. In the climax, the cultists have captured Jacqueline. They demand she drink poison. "It won't hurt," she's told. She refuses at first, but finally lifts the glass to her lips. Frances knocks the glass out of her hands, crying, "No! No, I can't let you, Jack. The only time I was ever happy was when I was with you." The Satanists allow her to leave but tell her they'll find her again. She returns to her room and hangs herself. Meanwhile, Mary and Gregory (Jacqueline's husband) admit they have fallen in love.

If you're into devil worship films, here's a dandy. This is one creepy movie. And Jacqueline Gibson is a freaky-deaky lady who is unforgettable in a haunting, troubling, disturbing way. "The girl ain't right" only hints at Jacqueline's unusualness. Often described as beautiful, which she is, this nut case plays peek-a-boo with her sister, keeps a noose hanging in her apartment, and has gotten involved with a cult that worships the dark side. She is also catnip to man, woman, and dog. Jacqueline has deserted her husband, had an affair with her psychiatrist, and shared an intense friendship with girlfriend Frances. (When she meets Mary, Frances spills the beans about her relationship with her sister. "Know her? My dear, we were *intimate*! The times we used to have together. I'll bet she never told you about that—you're too young.") Whew! After apparently too much fun in her short life, Jacqueline kills herself.

Richard Barrios further explored the lesbian plot point in his excellent book *Screening Out Gays*: "It might be argued that this movie equates gayness with devil worship or witchcraft, thus serving as a harbinger of the right-wing hysteria of forty and fifty years later. Yes, Pat Buchanan did issue the pronouncement, in 1990, that 'Promiscuous homosexuals appear literally hell-bent on Satanism and suicide.' But really, *The Seventh Victim* is not about any of that. Like many of Lewton's movies, it's about the destructive power of repression, the riskiness of conspiratorial secrecy, the high price paid by the world's misfits. Almost too overtly, it wears its subtlety and taste on its sleeve, and its secret world, be it devilish or gay or both, lingers far longer than more calculated movie frights."[159]

The only ending this film can have, of course, is Jacqueline's death. It's no surprise that she commits suicide.

In November 1942, DeWitt Bodeen was assigned to write the screenplay. The original story centered on a murder mystery among the Signal Hill oil wells. Charles O'Neal was hired in late February 1943 to revise the script, using input from Lewton. Jacques Tourneur was the original director, but ultimately Mark Robson, then an editor, was given his first shot at directing. Filming was started on May 5 and completed on May 29, 1943.

The film was made not long after Orson Welles was fired from RKO. When RKO decided to go with a different type of film, Lewton was brought in to produce low-budget horror films. However, there still remained a few vestiges of Welles' reign. For example, the girls' school scene was filmed on the same set as Orson Welles' *The Magnificent Ambersons* (1942).

*The Seventh Victim* has been described by Carlos Clarens in *An Illustrated History of Horror and Science-Fiction Films* as Lewton's masterpiece. "Rarely has a film succeeded so well in capturing the nocturnal menace of a large city, the terror underneath the everyday, the suggestion of hidden evil."[160] He also called it "hauntingly oppressive."[161]

Phil Hardy described it as a near masterpiece, pointing to its "evocative script," and opined that it matched *I Walked with a Zombie* (1943) "as a film haunted by death and despair, somehow contriving to live up to the doom-laden premise of its epigraph from a poem by John Donne."[162]

Doug McClelland found the film "somewhat overwritten, incomparably unnerving and original."[163] He also provided an interesting interpretation on why the movie seems so bizarre: "The film had a strange, dreamlike ambiguity. One explanation for it all could be that the schoolgirl [played by Kim Hunter], repressed and naïve, lost her grip on reality at her first contact with a complex adult world and fantasized the macabre events. Perhaps she was literally, as one character put it, 'half-crazy with anxiety.' This seemed particularly likely in light of Kim Hunter's almost somnambulant performance and her delivery of her lines in a hushed monotone. Everything she saw took on a seemingly bizarre quality, including her sister."[164] Maybe. The film's ambiguity also might have been due to the fact that this was Mark Robson's first directorial effort. Often there's a tendency among first-time directors to be a bit heavy-handed.

Many of Brent's scenes were cut, leading some fans to jump to conclusions about her absence from films. Screenwriter DeWitt Bodeen explained that "considerable material had been cut after filming to get the picture down to bottom-bill length. For instance, the minor character of the one-armed devil worshipper played by Evelyn Brent was originally more prominent as a concert pianist who had turned to the evil society in bitterness over the loss of her arm. This was not explained in the film, nor even suggested, causing some viewers to think veteran actress Brent, not as active then as she once was, actually had her arm amputated."[165] A newspaper reported that during production Brent sat so long on the set with her arm taped behind her that she required first aid.[166]

Taglines included "ROBBED OF THE WILL TO LOVE!" and "SLAVE to SATAN!"

Val Lewton was born Vladimir Leventon in what is now the Ukraine in 1904. He sometimes used the pseudonym Carlos Keith as a writer. Lewton, who wrote some scenes for *Gone with the Wind* (1939), died in 1951

Jean Brooks, who resembled Bettie Page divided by *The Addams Family*'s Carolyn Jones in this film, was born Ruby Kelly in Houston, Texas, in 1915. Sometimes billed as Jeanne Kelly, especially early in her career, Brooks was briefly married to writer-director Richard Brooks. A onetime big band singer, she worked three times with Val Lewton (*Youth Runs Wild*, *The Leopard Man*, and *The Seventh Victim*); her film career ended in the late 1940s. Brooks, usually blond in her roles, often played unstable characters. She died of alcoholism in 1963 in Richmond, California. Notice in the film how her fingernails are sometimes painted and then unpainted—sometimes in the same scene.

Tom Conway, brother of George Sanders, was born Thomas Charles Sanders in Russia in 1904. Probably best known for playing the Falcon in a series of films, he was also a radio star and a regular on *The Betty Hutton Show*. Conway also played Dr. Louis Judd in *Cat People* (1942). He died in 1967.

This was Kim Hunter's first film role. Born Janet Cole in Detroit in 1922, her long career was interrupted in the 1950s when she was blacklisted for being a Communist sympathizer. Hunter won an Oscar for *A Streetcar Named Desire* (1951) and became known to younger moviegoers for her performance as Zira in *Planet of the Apes* (1968). She died in 2002.

Isabel Jewell, born in Wyoming in 1907, made her film debut in 1932. Jewell, who played Emmy Slattery in *Gone with the Wind* (1939), died in 1972.

Elizabeth Russell, Rosalind Russell's sister-in-law, was a favorite of producer Val Lewton. The former fashion model also appeared in *Cat People* (1942), *The Curse of the Cat People* (1944), and *Bedlam* (1946). She was the model for Mary Meredith's portrait in *The Uninvited* (1944). Born in Philadelphia in 1916, she died in 2002.

Barbara Hale appeared in the subway scene. Born in DeKalb, Illinois, in 1922, she is best known for playing Della Street in scores of Perry Mason TV shows. She married actor Bill Williams, and her son is actor William Katt. Co-star Raymond Burr named an orchid after her—and also claimed she had one of Hollywood's best screams.

Born in 1912 in Massachusetts, Erford Gage enlisted in the Army in 1943 and was killed in the Philippines in March 1945. Hugh Beaumont was best known for playing Beaver's father in the TV show

*Leave It to Beaver*. Born in Lawrence, Kansas, in 1909, he made his film debut in 1940. An ordained minister and tree farmer, he died in 1982. Chef Milani, also credited as Joseph Milani, was born in Italy in 1892. *The Seventh Victim* was his first film; he was better known for his appearances on radio and television in his real-life career as a chef. He died in a car accident in 1965. Born Marguerite Alice Hélène Smith in Belgium in 1876, Marguerita Sylva appeared in only eight films. She died in a car accident in 1957.

Director Mark Robson was born in Canada in 1913. He received Oscar nominations for *Peyton Place* (1957) and *The Inn of the Sixth Happiness* (1958). Also an editor and producer, he died in 1978 during production on his final film, *Avalanche Express*.

Screenwriter Charles O'Neal was the father of Ryan O'Neal and grandfather of Tatum O'Neal. Nicknamed "Blackie," he was born in North Carolina in 1904 and died in 1996. Co-writer DeWitt Bodeen was born in California in 1908 and died in 1988. He also wrote screenplays for *The Curse of the Cat People* (1944), *I Remember Mama* (1948), and *Billy Budd* (1962). He wrote an article on Brent for *Films in Review* in 1976.

Reviews: "Although this melodrama leaves much to be desired, it should manage to get by with the type of audience for which it has been designed. Chiefly in the film's favor is its mood, which creates a feeling of doom.... Its chief fault is that it lacks clarity. The plot has been developed in a confusing manner. The end in particular will leave audiences in a bit of a quandary" (*Film Daily*, August 24, 1943).

"[W]e have no more notion of what *The Seventh Victim* ... is about than if we had watched the same picture run backward and upside down.... Apparently the people at the studio (RKO), where this picture was made, just had a collective nightmare, and this is the horrible result. Or maybe the projectionist is responsible. Maybe he did run it backward and upside down" (*New York Times*, September 18, 1943).

## Bowery Champs

(Monogram Pictures) 62 min. Released on November 14, 1944.

*Survival Status:* UCLA Film and Television Archive (Los Angeles).

*Credits:* Producers, Sam Katzman, Jack Dietz; associate producer, Barney Sarecky; director, William Beaudine; assistant directors, Arthur Hammond, Clark Paylow; original story and screenplay, Earl Snell; photography, Ira Morgan; art director, David Milton; film editor, John Link; musical director, Edward Kay; sound engineer, Tom Lambert; special effects, Ray Mercer; production manager, Ed Rote.

*Cast:* Leo Gorcey (Ethelbert Muggs McGinnis); Huntz Hall (Glimpy); Gabriel Dell (Jim Linzy); Billy Benedict (Skinny); Bobby Jordan (Bobby); Thelma White (Diane Gibson); Evelyn Brent (Gypsy Carmen); Ian Keith (Ken Duncan); Frank Jaquet (Lester Cartwright); Fred Kelsey (McGuire); Ann Sterling (Jane); Bill Ruhl (Lieutenant); Wheeler Oakman (Tom Wilson); Bud Gorman (Shorty); Jimmy Strand (Danny); Francis Ford (Scoop); Eddie Cherkose (Brother); Bernard Gorcey (Mr. Johnson); Betty Sinclair (Apartment Manager).

Gypsy Carmen, once the toast of Broadway, was cheated in her divorce with Wilson. As Muggs puts it so eloquently, "He kind of gypped the Gypsy." Gypsy confronts Wilson. She wants the amount of money she had before she married him. She pulls a gun on him, but he tells her that her securities are missing. Gypsy isn't buying it. He starts to call the police when he's shot. Puzzled, Gypsy looks at her gun and then gets the heck out of there.

Of course, Gypsy becomes the prime suspect. The East Side Kids investigate for their newspaper, *The Evening Express.* She tells them that she didn't fire the shot. The kids help her elude the police by using Skinny, dressed in Gypsy's clothing, as a decoy. They take Gypsy, now dressed in men's clothing, to their club. (They have to change their sign from "NO WOMEN ALLOWED" to "AIR RAID SHELTER.")

Skinny follows Diane to the Pussycat Café and leaves a message for the boys to join him. Carmen gets there before them and accuses Wilson's business manager Duncan of stealing her securities. Gypsy and Diane struggle (it's a pretty ferocious girl fight). The boys arrive, closely followed by the police. The headline in the newspaper reads: "POLICE ARREST WILSON KILLERS." The next headline is "KEN DUNCAN AND NIGHT CLUB SINGER CONFESS SHOOTING TOM WILSON." And the final newspaper headline says: "EAST SIDE KIDS HELP CLEAR GYPSY CARMEN." The boys celebrate in their clubhouse. The final shot is Muggs shoving a cream pie in Glimpy's face.

The working title of this film was *Mr. Muggs Meets a Deadline.* Considering it was shot in six days with a budget of $85,000, it's pretty good. If you're never seen an East Side Kids film, this is a good one to catch. The boys are charming and entertaining, and it's an hour full of chuckles. There are some funny lines, and the acting is above average.

It's always a treat to see Thelma White in anything. Here she plays a dumb floozy to perfection. The former vaudeville star also sings a number at the Pussycat Café. She was a friend of Brent's, and the two appear to be having a great time.

Not only does Brent cross-dress in this one, but one of the Kids does too when Skinny wears Gypsy's coat and hat. For those keeping track, this is the second incident of a Kid cross-dressing in a film. The first time it was Glimpy in *Clancy Street Boys* (1943). Also, according to Leonard Getz, it was the third time the bad guy was a restaurant owner. The same device had been used in *'Neath Brooklyn Bridge* (1942) and *Follow the Leader* (1944). Getz, who wrote a book about the entire series, summed up his entry in this way: "[T]here is no doubt that the original premise of these films—tough slum kids with soft hearts, victims of the environment, not given an even break—has been de-emphasized, opting for the charismatic appeal of Leo Gorcey and the silly comedy of Huntz Hall. *Bowery Champs* represents a turning point in the evolution of the kids' pictures."[167]

Bobby Jordan was not supposed to be in the movie. However, he was on leave from his military obligation and asked to appear. It was his first appearance in the series since *Ghosts on the Loose* (1943). It was also his last as an East Side Kid.

Taglines included "MASTER SLEUTH ON THE TRAIL!," "BAFFLING MYSTERY OF MURDER!," "SH-H-H ... IT'S MURDER," "A SPINE TINGLING MYSTERY!," and "THRILLS FOLLOW THRILLS ... and IT'S A FIGHT TO THE FINISH!"

Leo Gorcey was born in New York in 1917; his parents were vaudeville actors. Gorcey appeared in the play *Dead End* in 1937 and then starred in its film adaptation that same year. He died in 1969.

Huntz Hall was one of sixteen children. Born in New York in 1911, he later formed a nightclub act with fellow actor Gabriel Dell called Hall and Dell. Hall died in 1999.

Gabriel Dell, born in New York in 1919, received a Tony nomination for *Lamppost Reunion* in 1976. He died in 1988.

Billy Benedict was born in Haskell, Oklahoma, in 1917. He made his film debut in 1935 and went on to appear in many television shows from the 1950s throughout the 1980s. He died in 1999.

Bobby Jordan, born in Harrison, New York, in 1923, died of cirrhosis of the liver in 1965. He made his film debut in 1931 and enjoyed much success throughout the 1930s. However, after World War II his career floundered. He filed for bankruptcy in 1958.

Betty Sinclair was born in Liverpool, England, in 1907. She's best known for playing Mrs. Mandible in *Mr. Peepers* in 1952. She died in 1983. Eddie Cherkose, born in Detroit in 1912, was also a composer and songwriter. He died in 1999. Bernard Gorcey was the father of Leo. Born in Russia in 1886, he was part of a vaudeville team with wife Josephine. Gorcey died in a car accident in 1955. After his father's death, Leo did not appear in any new Bowery Boys movies.

Uncredited writer Morey Amsterdam is best known for playing Buddy Sorrell on *The Dick Van Dyke Show.* He received an Emmy nomination in 1966 for his work in the series. Born in Chicago in 1908, Amsterdam was a child performer in vaudeville. Nicknamed "The Human Joke Machine," he died in 1996.

## *Raiders of the South*

(Monogram Pictures) 57 min. Released on January 4, 1947.

*Survival Status:* Exists.

*Credits*: Producer, Scott R. Dunlap; director, Lambert Hillyer; assistant director, Eddie Davis; story and screenplay, J. Benton Cheney; photography, Harry Neumann; film editor, Roy Livingston; set decorator, Vin Taylor; music director, Edward Kay; recording engineer; Earl Sitar; recording; Paul Schmutz; production manager, Charles J. Bigelow; music, "Beautiful Dreamer" by Stephen Foster; songs, "Darling Nellie Gray," words and music by B. R. Hanby, "Sweet Betsy from Pike" and "Skip to My Lou," traditional; composer, Stephen Foster, B. R. Hanby.

*Cast*: Johnny Mack Brown (Capt. Brownell, also known as Johnny Langdon); Evelyn Brent (Belle Chambers); Raymond Hatton (Shorty Kendall); Reno Blair (Lynne Chambers); Marshall Reed (Larry Mason); John Hamilton (George Boone); John Merton (Preston Durant); Edwin Parker (Jeb Warren); Pierce Lyden (Marshal Jim Farley); Cactus Mack (Pete); Billy Dix (Preston); Dee Cooper (Wagon boss).

> 1865 brought to a close the Civil War, but the wounds of battle were still unhealed. Carpetbaggers and renegades roamed the land, leaving in their wake hatred and distrust. The situation became so critical that the Secret Service was called in to prevent martial law in many of the states.

Brent played a Yankee-hating (her husband was killed in the Civil War) outlaw. Reno Blair played her daughter. Johnny Mack Brown was a former Confederate soldier sent to investigate the raiders.

The working title of this film was *Draw When You're Ready*. Belle Chambers may have been based on outlaw Belle Starr. Taglines included: "Rugged story of the old brawling west ... when the Lone Star State was young!"

Director-writer Lambert Hillyer (1889–1969) was the son of actress Lydia Knott. Born in South Bend, Indiana, he was a vaudevillian and journalist before finding employment in motion pictures. He directed his first film in 1917 and specialized in Westerns. In the 1950s he directed episodes of *Highway Patrol* and *The Cisco Kid*.

Johnny Mack Brown, born in Alabama in 1904, was a football player at the University of Alabama before he became a Hollywood cowboy star. Known as the Dothan Antelope, he made his film debut in 1927 and eventually appeared in dozens of Westerns at Monogram in the 1940s and 1950s. Brown died in 1974.

Reno Browne, also known as Reno Blair, was born Josephine Ruth Clarke in Reno, Nevada, in 1921. She was a stuntwoman who appeared in several films with Brown. Married and divorced from cowboy star Lash La Rue, she died in 1991.

*Reviews*: "*Raiders of the South* is the biggest flop involving Dixie since Rankin, Talmadge and Bilbo" (*Kingsport News* [Tennessee], February 11, 1947).

## Robin Hood of Monterey

(Monogram Pictures) 56 min. Released on September 3, 1947.

*Survival Status*: British Film Institute/National Film and Television Archive (London). Released on video (VCI).

*Credits*: Producer, Jeffrey Bernerd; director, Christy Cabanne; assistant director; Eddie Davis; based on the character created by O. Henry; original story and screenplay, Bennett R. Cohen; additional dialogue, Gilbert Roland; photography, William Sickner; technical director, Ernest Hickson; film editor, Roy Livingston; set decorator, Vin Taylor; musical director, Edward J. Kay; recording engineer, Earl Sitar; recording, John Kean; special effects, Augie Lohman; makeup, Harry Ross; production supervisor, Glenn Cook.

*Cast*: Gilbert Roland (The Cisco Kid); Chris-Pin Martin (Pancho); Evelyn Brent (Maria Sanchez Belmonte); Jack La Rue (Don Ricardo Gonzales); Pedro de Cordoba (Don Carlos Belmonte); Donna DeMario [Donna Martell] (Lolita); Travis Kent (Eduardo Belmonte); Thornton Edwards (El Capitan); Nestor Paiva (Alcalde); Ernie Adams (Pablo); Julian Rivero (Dr. Martinez); Felipe Turich (Guard); Alex Montoya (Juan); Fred Cordova (Manuel); George Navarro (Player).

Eduardo asks the Cisco Kid to intervene in a conflict with his stepmother, Maria Sanchez Belmonte. She is having an affair with Don Ricardo and wants to get rid of Eduardo's father Don Carlos. Eduardo offers her money to leave, but she convinces Don Carlos that Eduardo is infatuated with her. An enraged Don Carlos pulls a gun on Eduardo. There's a struggle, and a gun goes off. Don Carlos is dead. "They quarreled. Eduardo killed him," Maria explains. Eduardo escapes and goes to Cisco.

The Cisco Kid and Pancho go to the ranch to investigate. Turns out Cisco and Maria knew each other back when, and each has something on the other. "Suppose we make a bargain. Silence for silence," Maria says. She immediately betrays Cisco and sends Don Ricardo to Pueblo de San Blas to get Cisco arrested. Meanwhile, Cisco discovers that the bullet that killed Don Carlos came from Maria's gun.

Cisco and Pancho get arrested. Maria and Don Ricardo come to town to attend Cisco's execution. "What a pity," Maria mockingly says when Cisco falls after being "shot." He escapes, however, because a friend has loaded the guns with blanks.

Eduardo returns to the ranch and is arrested. Cisco convinces the police chief that Eduardo is innocent. He promises to give himself up if Eduardo is released.

"You are the mistress of Belmonte," Maria says in front of her mirror, looking a lot like the evil Queen in *Snow White and the Seven Dwarfs*. "While you live no one shall take your place." Cisco confronts Maria. "I will not hesitate to kill again to keep my position," she tells him. "I will not lose what I have here." She offers him riches. The police chief hears her confession and arrests her and Don Ricardo. Eduardo and Lolita are reunited. Cisco keeps his word and turns himself in to the police chief. They share a toast, and the chief allows Cisco to leave.

The title on the title card is *The Cisco Kid in Robin Hood of Monterey*. The film is mediocre but does have some nice moments mainly due to the masculine charm of Gilbert Roland, who would make only one more Cisco Kid movie (*King of the Bandits*, 1947) after this one. Cisco and Pancho are remarkably affectionate throughout the film, often holding hands and leaning into each other.

According to Donna Martell, the film was produced at the Circle J Ranch in Newhall, California. The cast and crew stayed at the ranch for a week or so while filming in the warm summer.

Taglines included "HE'S TALL, DARK AND DANGEROUS! A Two-Gun Galahad Leaving a Trail of Kissing Women and Cussing Men!," "He Knows

His Own STRENGTH ... And A Woman's WEAK-NESS!," and "HE'S LAWLESS! ... and the Gals All Love It! That gay gunman of Old Mexico breaking laws and hearts in a new adventure!"

Jack La Rue, who had already appeared with Brent in several pictures, had just lost an election to the Los Angeles City Council. Chris-Pin Martin, born Ysabel Ponciana Chris-Pin Martin Piaz in Tucson, Arizona, in 1893, appeared as Pancho in several Cisco Kid pictures as well as Gordito in Zorro films. He died in 1953. Pedro de Cordoba was born in New York in 1881. Of Cuban-French heritage, he was a stage and radio actor who made his film debut in 1915. He died in 1950. Donna Martell was born Irene DeMario in Los Angeles in 1927. She made her film debut in *Apache Rose* (1947) with Roy Rogers. Married to award-winning sound editor Gene Corso, she appeared in many television shows in the 1950s and 1960s. In 2002 she was awarded a Golden Boot Award. Nestor Paiva was born in Fresno, California, in 1905 and made his film debut in 1937. Of Portuguese descent, he played Spanish, Greek, Russian, and African-American characters in film and on radio. Paiva died in 1966.

## Stage Struck

(Monogram Pictures) 71 min. Released on June 13, 1948.
*Survival Status:* Exists.
*Credits:* Producer, Jeffrey Bernerd; director, William Nigh; assistant director, Eddie Davis; screenplay, George Wallace Sayre, Agnes Christine Johnston; original story, George Wallace Sayre; photography, Harry Neumann; camera operator, William Margolies; stills, Scotty Welbourne; art director, Dave Milton; editorial supervisor, Otho Lovering; film editor, William Austin; set decorator, Ray Boltz, Jr.; musical director, Edward J. Kay; recording engineer, Earl Sitar; hair stylist, Loretta Francel; production manager; William Calihan, Jr.; script supervisor, Ilona Vas; grip, George Booker.
*Cast:* Kane Richmond (Nick Mantee); Audrey Long (Nancy Howard); Conrad Nagel (Lt. Williams); Ralph Byrd (Sgt. Tom Rainey); John Gallaudet (Benny Nordick); Anthony Warde (Barda); Pamela Blake (Janet Winters); Charles Trowbridge (Captain Webb); Nana Bryant (Mrs. Howard); Selmer Jackson (Ed Howard); Evelyn Brent (Miss Lloyd); Wanda McKay (Helen Howard); Jacqueline Thomas [Lyn Thomas] (Ruth Ames); Wilbur Mack (Professor Corella); Beverly Jons (Rose); Denise Kay, Gerry Pattison, Dorothy Douglas (Girls in nightclub); Valerie Ardis (Gloria, secretary); Helen Francell (Hat check girl); Andy Andrews (Police clerk); Gaylord Noblitt (Officer).

The movie begins ominously when we see Benny and a young woman struggle over a gun. She is killed, and Nick is the witness. The body, dumped in an alley, is later identified as Helen Howard.

Police Lt. Williams breaks the bad news to the Howard family. Miss Lloyd, Helen's elocution teacher, is interviewed. "She was an actress. A real actress." Miss Lloyd admits that Helen was her favorite student. "An old maid elocution teacher can get very lonely in a town like this," she says. "The two hours a week I spent here [at Helen's house] were

the bright spots in my life." Miss Lloyd also confesses that she lied to Helen about her career and blames herself for Helen becoming stage struck and going to New York.

Best friend Ruth is also interviewed, and the police learn that Helen worked at the Blue Jay Club. Helen's sister Nancy joins the investigation and gets a job at the Club.

In the climax, Nick and Benny realize who Nancy is. The sinister-looking Barda agrees to take Nancy with him to Central America. The police arrive. Barda, it turns out, is on the police force, and he's recorded confessions from Nick and Benny. "Nick, you know," Williams lectures, "when a man thinks he's smart, that's when he's dumb." (Ironically, the proverb was proved throughout the film by Williams himself.)

In the final scene we are back at the Bureau of Missing Persons. "Here's another one," Williams sadly says. "There's always another one.... I wish I could say to every girl, to these thousands of girls, 'Stay home with your mother and father. Stay home! *Stay home!*'"

Filmed in March 1948, this one is typical of the Monogram Pictures that tried to teach a lesson. In this case, young women were warned about going to New York (or Hollywood) to become stars.

Wow—not sure what happened to Conrad Nagel, but he certainly aged quickly. The script is not very good, and poor Nagel gets stuck with some of the worst lines in his career. At least he got to appear in dozens of scenes; Brent was limited to two.

Taglines included "Shocking! Direct from official police files come the startling true stories of thousands of missing girls!

Kane Richmond, born in Minneapolis in 1906, made his film debut in 1929. He appeared in many "B" films and serials. *Stage Struck* was his last film credit. He died in 1973.

Audrey Long was born in Orlando, Florida in 1922. She made more than thirty films between 1942 and 1952.

Pamela Blake, born Adele Pearce in Oakland in 1918, appeared in many low-budget films from 1934 to 1954. She was married at one time to Malcolm McTaggart. Wanda McKay, born Dorothy Quackenbush in Portland, Oregon, in 1915, was Miss American Aviation in 1938. She was married to Hoagy Carmichael from 1977 until his death in 1981. McKay died in 1996. She also appeared with Brent in *The Golden Eye* (1948). Jacqueline Thomas was better known as Lyn Thomas. Born in Indiana in 1929, she made her film debut in *Stage Struck*. Thomas appeared in many "B" movies and television shows throughout the 1950s. She died in 2004.

## The Golden Eye

(Monogram Pictures) 69 min. Released on August 29, 1948.
*Survival Status:* Library of Congress (Washington, D.C.).

*Credits*: Producer, James S. Burkett; director, William Beaudine; assistant director, Wesley Barry; based on characters created by Earl Derr Biggers; original screenplay, W. Scott Darling; photography, William Sickner; camera operator, John Martin; stills, Al St. Hilaire; art director, Dave Milton; supervising film editor, Otho Lovering; editor, Ace Herman; set decorator, Raymond Boltz, Jr.; musical director, Edward J. Kay; recording, Franklin Hansen; sound, John Kean; makeup, Webb Overlander; hair stylist, Lela Chambers; production supervisor, Allen K. Wood; script supervisor, Jules Levy; grip, Grant Tucker.

Cast: Roland Winters (Charlie Chan); Wanda McKay (Evelyn Manning); Mantan Moreland (Birmingham); Victor Sen Yung (Tommy Chan); Bruce Kellogg (Talbot Bartlett); Tim Ryan (Lt. Mike Ruark); Evelyn Brent (Sister Teresa); Ralph Dunn (Driscoll); Lois Austin (Mrs. Margaret Driscoll); Forrest Taylor (Manning); Lee "Lasses" White (Pete); Lee Tung Foo (Wong Fai); Michael Gaddis (Pursuer); Sam Flint (Dr. Groves); Geraldine Cobb (Girl in riding clothes); Mary Ann Hawkins, Aileen Babs Cox (Bathing girls); Edmund Cobb, John Merton (Miners); Jack Gargan (Voice from darkness).

Mr. Manning steps into Wong's Curio Shop in San Francisco's Chinatown because he's being followed. While there, a man shoots at him through the window. Fearing for his life, he and daughter Evelyn meet with detective Charlie Chan and invite him to their Lazy Y Ranch in Arizona to further investigate. They suspect the attack might have something to do with his Golden Eye goldmine.

By the time Chan arrives, Lt. Mike Ruark is already there because Manning keeps having "accidents." This time he's fallen into a mine shaft and is seriously injured. Ruark tells Chan that Manning's gold mine is suddenly profitable—for no good reason. Chan visits with Manning, who is heavily bandaged and unconscious.

It turns out the mine is being used to smuggle gold from Mexico. Sister Teresa, supposedly a nurse who has come to care for Manning, shows up at the mine after a shootout where Ruark is wounded. She's no nun, but a pretty tough cookie. (By the way, it's a scream to see Brent in a nun's habit.) "If that Chinese [sic] comes snooping around the mine, put a bullet into him and ask questions afterward," she orders.

The climax occurs at the ranch. Chan starts to cut away Manning's bandages when a woman begins screaming. It is not Manning under the bandages but Mrs. Driscoll, wife of the mining supervisor. Sister Teresa pulls a gun on Chan, but Evelyn wrestles with her until Ruark arrives.

Chan explains that Manning was killed and his body hidden in the mine. Driscoll arrives and pulls a gun, but Tommy gets him to drop it. Driscoll escapes but is shot by Bartlett, Evelyn's boyfriend. Chan identifies Bartlett as the ring leader. According to Chan, "Mr. Bartlett number one suspect from very first" because Bartlett was a little *too* helpful.

"Ain't that somethin'," Birmingham concludes. "*Ain't* that somethin'. Good gracious, oh me. That's Mr. Chan all over. When you think it is, it ain't, and when you think it ain't, that's just when it is." Birmingham laughs hysterically.

The working title was *The Mystery of the Golden Eye*. It's also known as *Charlie Chan and the Golden Eye* and *The Mystery of the Golden Eye*. Filming started on April 14 and was completed April 30, 1948.

There are many good films in the Charlie Chan series. This, we're sorry to say, isn't one of them. The real entertainment is provided by African-American chauffeur Birmingham and Charlie's son Tommy. They get to dress up like cowboys and generally act like fools. They bring much-needed humor to a movie that never takes off. Perhaps the best Chan quotation in this film is "People who listen at keyholes rarely hear good of themselves."

Writer Earl Derr Biggers was born in Warren, Ohio, in 1884. He created the Charlie Chan character after taking a break from writing Broadway plays. Biggers died in 1933.

Roland Winters, born in Boston in 1904, played Chan in six films from 1948 to 1949. A frequent television performer through the 1970s, he died in 1989.

Mantan Moreland, born in Monroe, Louisiana, in 1902, appeared in more than a dozen Charlie Chan pictures as well as many other Monogram films. He died in 1973.

Victor Sen Yung, born in San Francisco in 1915, played Hop Sing on *Bonanza*. Yung also portrayed Jimmy (sometimes Tommy) Chan in many Charlie Chan pictures. He also wrote a Chinese cookbook before his death in 1980.

Bruce Kellogg, sometimes billed as Bill Kellogg, was born in Wyoming in 1910 and died in 1967. He also appeared with Brent in *Spy Train* (1943).

Tim Ryan, also a writer, was born in New Jersey in 1899. Divorced from actress Irene Ryan, he died in 1956. Ryan appeared in five Charlie Chan films.

Reviews: "Winters' Charlie is consistently engaging and the teamwork with Moreland, Young and Ryan purrs along like a finely tuned motor. Lapses and weaknesses apart, it truly is the last successful film in the series" (Ken Hanke, *Charlie Chan at the Movies: History, Filmography, and Criticism*, pp. 244–45).

## *Again ... Pioneers*

(Protestant Film Commission) 72 min. Released November 2, 1950.

*Survival Status*: UCLA Film and Television Archive (Los Angeles).

*Credits*: Producer, Paul F. Heard; associate producer, Barney A. Sarecky; director, William Beaudine; assistant director, Doc Joos; original screenplay, Oviatt McConnell; additional sequences, Alan Shilin; photography, Marcel LePicard; art direction, Frank Sylos; film editor, Al Joseph; set dresser, Tommy Thompson; music score, Irving Gertz; sound engineer, Gary Harris; special effects, Ray Mercer; technical advisor, Frederick R. Thorne; business manager, Oren Evans; casting director, Maurice Golden.

*Cast*: Colleen Townsend (Sallie Keeler); Tom Powers (Ken Keeler); Sarah Padden (Ma Ashby); Regis Toomey (Dave Harley); Jimmy Hunt (Nathaniel Ashby); Evelyn Brent (Alice Keeler); Larry Olsen (Kenny Keeler); Larry Carr (Malcolm Keeler); Erville Alderson (Pa Ashby);

Peggy Wynne (Arla Ashby); Melinda Plowman (Rebecca Ashby); Gene Roth (Monty Barnes); Judith Allen (Mrs. Barnes); Harry Cheshire (Col. Garnet); Hart Wayne (Chief Marlin); Louis Mason (Farmer Reader); John Parlow (Matt Gans); Gertrude Astor (Mrs. Gans); Russell Hicks (Pete Galloway); Raymond Bond (Dr. Miles); William Neff (Minister); Connie Evans (Mrs. Brown); Francis Morris (Mrs. Lyon); Jerry Mickelsen (Trummy); Gary Pagett (Tom).

The film was a religious-oriented drama that received little distribution.

Colleen Townsend was born in Glendale, California, in 1928. She was an up-and-coming starlet in the late 1940s and then turned her attention to religion. She married Presbyterian minister Reverend Louis H. Evans, Jr., in 1950 and began a career of speaking and writing on religious themes.

Tom Powers, born in Kentucky in 1890, appeared in silent films and reached success on Broadway as a writer, director, and actor. He's probably best known for playing Barbara Stanwyck's doomed husband in *Double Indemnity* (1944). Powers died in 1955.

Sarah Padden was born in England in 1881. The popular character actress who appeared in many films and television shows made her film debut in 1926. She died in 1967.

Jimmy Hunt was born in Los Angeles in 1939. The onetime child actor made his film debut in 1947. He appeared in the 1953 science fiction film *Invaders from Mars* and had a cameo in the 1986 movie of the same name.

*Reviews:* "[M]ake it a point to see a picture entitled *Again Pioneers.* ... I saw it previewed the other afternoon and I haven't been able to get it out of my mind since. Its emotional shock is terrific. In my opinion, this modest little picture would be one of the most talked-about films of the year.... It is precisely the kind of picture that countless millions have been searching for in their theaters—and failed to find. It is also proof positive ... that the screen can be the greatest of all educational mediums" (Jimmy Fidler, *Joplin* [Missouri] *Globe,* November 11, 1950).

# Appendix A:
# Television Appearances

## Wagon Train

"The Lita Foladaire Story." 60 minutes. January 6, 1960. NBC.

*Credits:* Producer, Howard Christie; director, Jerry Hopper; teleplay, Jean Holloway; story, Helen Cooper; music score, Heinz Roemheld; photography, Benjamin H. Kline; art director, Howard E. Johnson; editorial supervisor, Richard G. Wray; film editor, William W. Moore; musical supervision, Stanley Wilson; set director, Ralph Sylos; assistant director, Carter De Haven III; sound, David H. Moriarty; costume supervisor, Vincent Dee; makeup, Jack Barron; hair stylist, Florence Bush.

*Cast:* Ward Bond (Major Seth Adams); Terry Wilson (Bill Hawks); Frank McGrath (Charlie); Diane Brewster (Lita Foladaire); Kent Smith (Jess Foladaire); Jay Novello (Carlotti); Richard Crane (Clay Foladaire); Paul Birch (Dan); Evelyn Brent (Mrs. Simmons); Tom Drake (Dr. John Cannon); Lurene Tuttle (Mrs. Willoughby).

Lita Foladaire is found severely beaten. When she dies of her injuries, Major Adams vows to seek justice since she was the wife of one of his former military buddies, Jess Foladaire. "She was the most beautiful woman who ever lived," comments Mrs. Foladaire's housekeeper, Mrs. Simmons, as Adams admires her portrait. This seems to be the general sentiment as Adams searches for her killer.

We learn that she married the much-older Jess Foladaire but eventually fell in love with his younger brother Clay. When Lita finally told Jess she was leaving him, he murdered her.

"I never met Lita Foladaire," Major Adams concluded, "but I know I'll remember her as long as I live."

The episode is an excellent one, compelling and well-acted. Flashbacks are effectively used. Brent, seen in several scenes, does not seem comfortable. Perhaps it was due to her time away from acting, but Brent is less subtle in this performance than in others. Lead actor Ward Bond died in November 1960.

Director Jerry Hopper, born in Oklahoma in 1907, was Glenda Farrell's cousin. Married to Marsha Hunt from 1938 to 1943, he was a popular television director who worked on shows including *The Fugitive* and *Voyage to the Bottom of the Sea*. Hopper died in 1988.

Born in Kansas City, Missouri, in 1931, Diane Brewster played the murdered wife of Richard Kim-

ble on the television show *The Fugitive*. She also played Beaver's schoolteacher on *Leave It to Beaver.* Brewster died in 1991.

Tom Drake was born in Brooklyn in 1918. He made his film debut in 1940 and went on to have a long acting career, particularly in television shows from the 1950s through the 1970s. He died in 1982.

Kent Smith was born in New York in 1907. He made his film debut in the 1930s and never quite rose to stardom despite several interesting performances including *Nora Prentiss* (1947) where his character is executed for his own murder. Smith, a regular on *Peyton Place* and *The Invaders*, died in 1985.

Lurene Tuttle was born in Indiana in 1907. She received an Emmy nomination for *Julia* in 1968. A notable radio performer as well, she died in 1986.

## Elfego Baco

"Friendly Enemies at Law." 60 minutes. March 18, 1960. ABC. The show was part of *Walt Disney Presents.*

*Credits:* Producer, James Pratt; director, William Beaudine; photographer, Lucien Ballard; art director, Stan Jolley; editor, Basil Wrangell; music, Franklyn Marks; teleplay, Barney Slater; sound, Robert O. Cook; set decorators, Emile Kuri, William L. Stevens; costumer, Chuck Keehne; makeup, Pat McNalley; hair stylist, Ruth Sandifer; unit manager, Roy Wade; assistant director, Ivan Volkman.

*Cast:* Robert Loggia (Elfego Baca); Roy Barcroft (Sheriff); Pat Crowley (Patricia Kettrick); John Kerr (Martin Dibler); Robert Lowery (Wade Cather); Barton MacLane (Rawls Kettrick); Ray Teal (Frank Oxford); Guinn Williams (Buffalo); Evelyn Brent (Mrs. Oxford).

Elfego Baca was a frontier lawyer practicing in New Mexico. Dedicated to the belief that no man is above the law, he defended the little guy against big cattle operations.

In this episode, Frank Oxford trades his horse Diablo to Baca in order to be defended. Rancher Kettrick has stolen 50 head of steer that belong to Oxford. Baca meets Kettrick's "fancy pants" lawyer Martin Dibler, and they ride to the Kettrick ranch where the rancher is informed of Oxford's claim. Kettrick refuses to allow Baca to examine the herd.

Baca meets with Oxford again and learns that other small ranchers have also had cattle stolen. While discussing the case, Oxford is wounded by a sniper. Mrs. Oxford is unsympathetic. "Frank brought this all on himself. I told him not to go hiring a lawyer." She tries to talk Baca into dropping the case. The other ranchers, fearing repercussions, agree.

Frustrated, Baca confronts Dibler. An indignant Dibler insists on fighting Baca—and gets a sound thrashing. Now thoroughly bonded, Dibler and Baca work together to get a warrant to search Kettrick's herd. Even with the warrant, Kettrick refuses.

Baca takes matters into his own hands and breaks into Kettrick's house. He finds evidence that Kettrick's foreman has been cheating him and the small ranchers. Kettrick agrees to settle the claims with the small ranchers.

Brent did not appear in the credits. She had only one scene as the weary wife of small-time rancher Frank Oxford. She'd clearly aged, but was certainly recognizable as Evelyn Brent. This television show is a cut above usual television fare, largely because of the creative talent.

Cinematographer Lucien Ballard was born in Oklahoma in 1908. He received an Oscar nomination for *The Caretakers* (1963). Ballard had previously worked with Brent's former director Josef von Sternberg. Married to Merle Oberon from 1945 to 1949, he died in 1988.

Writer Barney Slater, born in North Carolina in 1923, received an Oscar nomination (shared with Dudley Nichols and Joel Kane) for *The Tin Star* (1957). Mainly a television writer, he also supplied scripts for *Tombstone Territory* and *Lost in Space*. Slater was killed by a hit-and-run driver in 1978.

Barton MacLane, born in South Carolina in 1902, played General Peterson in the TV show *I Dream of Jeannie*. He died in 1969.

Patricia Crowley was born in Pennsylvania in 1929. The television actress made her debut in 1950. She played Joan Nash on TV's *Please Don't Eat the Daisies* in the 1960s.

Born in New York in 1930, Robert Loggia received an Oscar nomination for *Jagged Edge* (1985). He also received Emmy nominations for *Mancuso, FBI* and *Malcolm in the Middle*.

Born in New York in 1931, John Kerr was the son of actors Geoffrey Kerr and June Walker (his biological father was Franchot Tone). His credits included *Tea and Sympathy* (1956) and *South Pacific* (1958). A Harvard graduate, he also obtained a law degree from UCLA and became an attorney.

Guinn "Big Boy" Williams was born in Decatur, Texas, in 1899 and began his career in the silent film era. He appeared in dozens of Westerns in film and on television until his death in 1962.

Ray Teal was born in Grand Rapids, Michigan, in 1902. He played Sheriff Roy Coffee on *Bonanza* and played hundreds of other roles in film and on television until his death in 1976.

## Day in Court

30 minutes. July 12, 1963. ABC.

Brent also made an appearance on this daytime series.

# Appendix B: Chronology

| | | | | |
|---|---|---|---|---|
| 1895 [?] | Mary Elizabeth Riggs [Evelyn Brent] born, October 20. | | | *The Shadow of the East* |
| 1914 | *A Gentleman from Mississippi* | | | *The Arizona Express* |
| | *The Pit* | | | *The Plunderer* |
| 1915 | *The Heart of a Painted Woman* | | | *The Lone Chance* |
| | *The Shooting of Dan McGrew* | | | *The Desert Outlaw* |
| | *When Love Laughs* | | | *The Cyclone Rider* |
| 1916 | *The Lure of Heart's Desire* | | | *The Dangerous Flirt* |
| | *The Iron Will* | | | *My Husband's Wives* |
| | *The Soul Market* | | | *Silk Stocking Sal* |
| | *Playing With Fire* | | 1925 | *Midnight Molly* |
| | *The Spell of the Yukon* | | | *Forbidden Cargo* |
| | *The Weakness of Strength* | | | *Alias Mary Flynn* |
| | *The Iron Woman* | | | *Smooth as Satin* |
| 1917 | *The Millionaire's Double* | | | *Lady Robinhood* |
| | *To the Death* | | | *Three Wise Crooks* |
| | *Who's Your Neighbor?* | | | *Broadway Lady* |
| | *Raffles, the Amateur Cracksman* | | | *Twisted Tales: The Eternal Triangle?* |
| 1918 | *Daybreak* | | 1926 | *Queen o' Diamonds* |
| 1919 | *Help! Help! Police!* | | | *Secret Orders* |
| | *Fool's Gold* | | | *The Impostor* |
| | *The Other Man's Wife* | | | *The Jade Cup* |
| | *The Glorious Lady* | | | *Flame of the Argentine* |
| 1920 | *Border River* | | | *Love 'Em and Leave 'Em* |
| | *The Ruined Lady* (play) | | 1927 | *Love's Greatest Mistake* |
| | *The Shuttle of Life* | | | *Blind Alleys* |
| | *The Law Divine* | | | Brent and Fineman divorce. |
| 1921 | *Demos* | | | *Underworld* |
| | *The Door That Has No Key* | | | *Women's Wares* |
| | *Laughter and Tears* | | 1928 | *Beau Sabreur* |
| | *Sybil* | | | *The Last Command* |
| | *Sonia* | | | *The Showdown* |
| 1922 | *Circus Jim* | | | *A Night of Mystery* |
| | *The Spanish Jade* | | | *The Dragnet* |
| | *Trapped by the Mormons* | | | *His Tiger Lady* |
| | *The Experiment* | | | *The Mating Call* |
| | *Married to a Mormon* | | | *Interference* |
| | *Pages of Life* | | | Brent marries Henry Donald Edwards. |
| | Brent marries Bernhard Powell Fineman. | | 1929 | *Broadway* |
| 1923 | Brent is named one of the Wampas Baby Stars of 1923. | | | *Fast Company* |
| | | | | *Woman Trap* |
| | | | | *Why Bring That Up?* |
| | *Held to Answer* | | | *Darkened Rooms* |
| 1924 | *Loving Lies* | | 1930 | *Slightly Scarlet* |

|      |                                                                                      |      |                                                                           |
|------|--------------------------------------------------------------------------------------|------|---------------------------------------------------------------------------|
|      | *Framed*                                                                             |      | *The Law West of Tombstone*                                               |
|      | *Paramount on Parade*                                                                | 1939 | *Panama Lady*                                                             |
|      | *The Silver Horde*                                                                   |      | *Daughter of the Tong*                                                    |
|      | *Madonna of the Streets*                                                             |      | Brent tours in *Streets de Paree*                                         |
| 1931 | *Traveling Husbands*                                                                 |      | *The Mad Empress*                                                         |
|      | *Pagan Lady*                                                                         | 1941 | *Emergency Landing*                                                       |
|      | *The Mad Parade*                                                                     |      | *Forced Landing*                                                         |
| 1932 | *High Pressure*                                                                      |      | *Wide Open Town*                                                          |
|      | *Attorney for the Defense*                                                           |      | *Dangerous Lady*                                                         |
|      | *The Crusader*                                                                       |      | *Ellery Queen and the Murder Ring*                                       |
| 1933 | Vaudeville tour with Harry Fox in *Manhattan Merry-Go-Round*                         |      | *Holt of the Secret Service* (serial)                                    |
|      | *The World Gone Mad*                                                                 | 1942 | *Westward Ho*                                                            |
|      | Brent files for bankruptcy.                                                          |      | *Wrecking Crew*                                                          |
| 1934 | *Home on the Range*                                                                  |      | *The Pay Off*                                                            |
| 1935 | *Symphony of Living*                                                                 | 1943 | *Silent Witness*                                                         |
|      | *Without Children*                                                                   |      | *Spy Train*                                                             |
|      | *The Nitwits*                                                                        |      | *The Seventh Victim*                                                     |
|      | *Speed Limited*                                                                      | 1944 | *Bowery Champs*                                                          |
| 1936 | *Song of the Trail*                                                                  | 1947 | *Raiders of the South*                                                   |
|      | *It Couldn't Have Happened—But It Did*                                               |      | Brent and Edwards divorce.                                               |
|      | *Hollywood Boulevard*                                                                |      | *Robin Hood of Monterey*                                                 |
|      | *The President's Mystery*                                                            | 1948 | *Stage Struck*                                                          |
|      | *Hopalong Cassidy Returns*                                                           |      | Marriage announcement for Brent and Harry Fox                            |
| 1937 | *Jungle Jim* (serial)                                                                |      | *The Golden Eye*                                                        |
|      | *King of the Gamblers*                                                               | 1950 | *Again ... Pioneers*                                                    |
|      | *The Last Train from Madrid*                                                         | 1959 | Fox dies.                                                                |
|      | *Night Club Scandal*                                                                 | 1960 | *Wagon Train*: "The Lita Foladaire Story"                                |
|      | *Sudden Bill Dorn*                                                                   |      | *Elfego Baca, Attorney at Law*: "Friendly Enemies at Law"                |
|      | *Daughter of Shanghai*                                                               |      |                                                                           |
| 1938 | *Tip-Off Girls*                                                                      | 1963 | *Day in Court*                                                           |
|      | *Mr. Wong, Detective*                                                                | 1975 | Evelyn Brent dies, June 4.                                               |

# Chapter Notes

## Preface

1. "She Eats and Tells!," *Photoplay*, January 1931.

## Chapter 1

1. Ted Le Berthon, "Star, Once a Resident of Syracuse, Reveals Her Early Struggles," *Syracuse Herald*, August 17, 1930.

2. Gladys Hall, "Confessions of the Stars: Evelyn Brent Tells Her Untold Story," *Motion Picture Classic*, June 1929, p. 29.

3. On her passport applications for 1919 and 1921, Brent used October 20, 1895 as her birth date and wrote that she'd been born in Syracuse, New York. She used the name Elizabeth Riggs. Her address was 114 West 82nd Street, New York. Dorothy Reed (169 West 74th Street, New York) was her identifying witness and claimed she had known Riggs for 20 years. Along with the affidavit from Reed was a letter from the Lawrence Weber Photo Dramas film company: "The Bearer Elizabeth Riggs (Stage name Evelyn Brent) has been in our employ for sometime [sic] and is to continue in our employ for sometime to come. She wishes to go to England and France to perfect herself in certain studies necessary to her work with us." It was signed by Lawrence Weber, resident of the company, and dated December 10, 1919. On the 1921 passport application she wrote that her father's name was Arthur Riggs, that he was born in Florida and was now deceased.

4. Richard Lamparski, *Whatever Became Of...?* radio interview, WBAI-FM, January 7, 1969. A 1930 Dorothy Herzog column reported that Brent weighed seven and a half pounds when she was born. (Dorothy Herzog, *Tyrone Daily Herald* [Pennsylvania], January 24, 1930)

5. "Home in London, Career in Legit, Evelyn's Goals," *Syracuse Herald*, December 21, 1930. This article claimed she was born in 1899.

6. Gladys Hall, "Confessions of the Stars: Evelyn Brent Tells Her Untold Story," *Motion Picture Classic*, June 1929, pp. 28–29.

7. Ted Le Berthon, "Star, Once a Resident of Syracuse, Reveals Her Early Struggles," *Syracuse Herald*, August 17, 1930.

8. "Remembering That First Kiss," *Helena Independent*, July 21, 1929.

9. Gladys Hall, "Confessions of the Stars: Evelyn Brent Tells Her Untold Story," *Motion Picture Classic*, June 1929, pp. 29, 66.

10. Ruth Biery, "Suicide Never Pays," *Photoplay*, May 1928, p. 120.

11. According to DeWitt Bodeen's *Films in Review* article, this is the version Brent told in her later years.

12. In Ruth Biery's article "Suicide Never Pays," Brent claimed that she, her mother, and grandmother moved to Brooklyn from Florida when she was 14. In this version, her father died in Florida, and Brent skipped school to find studio work. Shortly after that, her grandmother died, and then her mother.

13. One newspaper listed her name as Mary Louise Riggs. See Hayden Hickok, *Syracuse Herald*, August 28, 1937.

14. "Evelyn Brent Will Play Pearl in *Broadway* Film," *Syracuse Herald*, December 19, 1928, p. 16.

15. "Evelyn Brent, Film Beauty, to Visit Here," *Syracuse Herald*, May 21, 1933.

16. Ted Le Berthon, "Star, Once a Resident of Syracuse, Reveals Her Early Struggles," *Syracuse Herald*, August 17, 1930.

17. Gladys Hall, "Confessions of the Stars: Evelyn Brent Tells Her Untold Story," *Motion Picture Classic*, June 1929, p. 66.

18. Alice L. Tildesley, "That Old Sweet O' Mine!," *Modesto News-Herald* [California], February 11, 1928. This is an interesting article that even has Franklin Pangborn recalling a childhood romance.

19. Chester B. Bahn, "Up and Down the Rialtos," *Syracuse Herald*, September 9, 1930. It was also reported by Mollie Merrick in a 1928 newspaper column that Brent was known in Syracuse as Minnie Riggs. "As Evelyn Brent's official birthplace is Tampa, Fla., and her official education was received in New York City,

imagine her embarrassment when a group of Syracuse ladies rise to announce that she is Minnie Riggs, with whom they once went to school in Syracuse." Mollie Merrick, "Hollywood in Person," *Atlanta Constitution*, August 28, 1926, p. 4F.

20. "It's 'No' When Evelyn Says So—But Cupid Yes," *Fitchburg Sentinel*, July 28, 1923.

21. "Home in London, Career in Legit, Evelyn's Goals," *Syracuse Herald*, December 21, 1930.

22. Helen Louise Walker, "No Complexes Here!," *Picture Play*, January 1928, p. 34. We found no evidence that Brent appeared in any films with Moore directing. They were both in the casts of *When Love Laughs* (1915) and *The Glorious Lady* (1919). It is possible that Moore directed *When Love Laughs*, but no reference has yet credited him.

23. Richard Lamparski, *Whatever Became Of...?* radio interview, WBAI-FM, January 7, 1969.

24. Ted Le Berthon, "Star, Once a Resident of Syracuse, Reveals Her Early Struggles," *Syracuse Herald*, August 17, 1930. When *The Shooting of Dan McGrew* was re-released in 1918, Brent's credit was changed from Betty Riggs to Evelyn Brent. Lou was played by Kathryn Adams. She also appeared with Brent in *Raffles* in 1917.

25. "Film Factory Burns with $300,000 Loss: Many Valuable Reels Destroyed in Éclair Company's Fort Lee Plant," *New York Times*, March 20, 1914, in Richard Koszarski, *Fort Lee: The Film Town*, p. 116.

26. Richard Koszarski, *Fort Lee: The Film Town*, p. 15.

27. Harry Waldman, *Maurice Tourneur*, p. 26.

28. Ibid., p. 37.

29. *Butter with My Bread*, Olga Petrova, in Richard Koszarski, *Fort Lee: The Film Town*, p. 237.

30. "They Learn Life Is Just Ups and Downs," *Los Angeles Times*, March 24, 1928, p. A9.

31. Gladys Hall, "Confessions of the Stars: Evelyn Brent Tells Her Untold Story," *Motion Picture Classic*, June 1929, p. 66.

32. Ted Le Berthon, "Star, Once a Resident of Syracuse, Reveals Her

Early Struggles," *Syracuse Herald*, August 17, 1930.

33. "The Woman Picture Maker: Madame Blaché, The Distinguished Producer, Tells Townsend Black of Her Wonder Work," in Richard Koszarski, *Fort Lee:The Film Town*, p. 132.

34. Olga Petrova, *Butter with My Bread*, p. 258.

35. Sharon Smith, *Women Who Make Movies*, p. 8.

36. Olga Petrova, *Butter with My Bread*, p. 258.

37. Ibid.

38. John Kobal, *People Will Talk*, p. 103.

39. Karen Ward Mahar, *Women Filmmakers in Early Hollywood*, p. 89.

40. Daisy Dean, "News Notes From Movieland, Girl Pilots Boat in Petrova Picture," *Racine Journal-News*, April 28, 1916.

41. "Notes of Plays and Players," *Waterloo Times-Tribune*, July 2, 1916.

42. "Evelyn Will Get Skate On," *Manitoba Free Press*, Winnipeg, November 4, 1916.

43. "Amusements," *Atlanta Constitution*, May 24, 1916, p. 18.

44. "Weekly Gossip of Legitimate and Film Activities," *Lima Daily News* [Ohio], January 21, 1917.

45. Gladys Hall, "Confessions of the Stars: Evelyn Brent Tells Her Untold Story," *Motion Picture Classic*, June 1929, p. 66.

46. Gladys Hall, "The Home-Loving Vamp," p. 54.

47. Gladys Hall, "Confessions of the Stars: Evelyn Brent Tells Her Untold Story," *Motion Picture Classic*, June 1929, p. 66.

48. Ibid. The film was unidentified, and we found no credit that listed her character as "Sin."

49. "Evelyn Brent Would Be a Soldier Bold, Says She'll Enlist as 'Man' if War is Declared," *Morning Olympian* [Washington], March 18, 1917. The United States joined the war effort in April 1917.

50. Ted Le Berthon, "Star, Once a Resident of Syracuse, Reveals Her Early Struggles," *Syracuse Herald*, August 17, 1930.

51. Ruth Biery, "Suicide Never Pays," *Photoplay*, May 1928, p. 120.

52. *The Millionaire's Double* [review], *Variety*, May 11, 1917.

53. DeWitt Bodeen, "Evelyn Brent," *Films in Review*, p. 339.

54. Alice L. Tildesley, "Personality Preferred to Prettiness," *Galveston Daily News*, April 21, 1929.

55. Richard Lamparski, *Whatever Became Of...?* radio interview, WBAI-FM, January 7, 1969. *Redemption*, based on a work by Tolstoy, opened on October 3, 1918, at the Plymouth Theatre. When it opened, Barrymore

was no longer in it, having been replaced by E.J. Ballantine. The play was successful, closing after 204 performances in March 1919.

56. Ruth Biery, "Suicide Never Pays," *Photoplay*, May 1928, p. 120. The Martha Mansfield film might have been *Broadway Bill*. Mansfield died on November 30, 1923, after suffering severe burns on the set of *The Warrens of Virginia*.

57. Ibid., p. 121.

58. "Photographed, Mitchell Lewis Is Star at the Strand," *Atlanta Constitution*, September 26, 1920, p. 6A.

59. *The Other Man's Wife* [review], *Variety*, June 20, 1919.

60. Gladys Hall, "Confessions of the Stars: Evelyn Brent Tells Her Untold Story," *Motion Picture Classic*, June 1929, p. 66.

61. Ted Le Berthon, "Star, Once a Resident of Syracuse, Reveals Her Early Struggles," *Syracuse Herald*, August 17, 1930.

62. Gladys Hall, "Confessions of the Stars: Evelyn Brent Tells Her Untold Story," *Motion Picture Classic*, June 1929, p. 66.

63. "Among the Movie Stars, "*Evening Courier and Reporter* [Waterloo, Iowa], November 20, 1920.

64. "Model Universal City Springs Up Jones Production, Inc. at Work Depicting Maine in Moving Pictures," *Daily Kennebec Journal* [Augusta, Maine], July 31, 1919.

65. "Silent Movies on Location in Augusta," Susan Caldon, *Kennebuc Journal* [Augusta, Maine], December 7, 1976.

66. Ibid.

67. Sometimes appendicitis has been used to provide an excuse for complications resulting from an abortion. In Brent's case, we found no evidence that she had an abortion.

68. A February 18, 1972, *Daily Kennebuc Journal* [Maine] article referred to the Brent film as *The Rider of the King Log* and incorrectly called it "Augusta's only movie." The article also mentioned Brent's appendicitis. Local resident Marjorie Lee Sewell informed the newspaper that she was asked to perform a stunt for Brent. "Mrs. Sewell ... figured in another scene where Evelyn Brent, a leading lady, was to gallop across a road and jump a fence. Evelyn Brent was recuperating from an appendectomy so the director substituted Mrs. Sewell for the scene, which Mrs. Sewell said, was never used." Mrs. Sewell received no pay for her services or for the use of her horse Dixie, though she was promised some photographs. "The director defaulted on this promise too but Mrs. Sewell concludes philosophically, 'It was all great fun, anyhow.'"

69. "Model Universal City Springs Up Jones Production, Inc. at Work Depicting Maine in Moving Pictures," *Daily Kennebec Journal* [Augusta, Maine], July 31, 1919.

70. "Evelyn Brent at Colonial Today," *Daily Kennebec Journal* [Augusta, Maine], December 3, 1919.

71. "Augusta Locals," *Daily Kennebec Journal* [Augusta, Maine], September 20, 1919.

72. "Actress Cites Detour Route to Film Fame," *Los Angeles Times*, August 7, 1927, p. C8.

73. Edna May Sperl became leading lady for the Jones Production Co. films after Brent left. According to a 1976 newspaper report, the company failed in 1922 after novelist Holman Day was hired. He and Jones could not get along, and Jones was eventually forced out.

74. Ted Le Berthon, "Star, Once a Resident of Syracuse, Reveals Her Early Struggles," *Syracuse Herald*, August 17, 1930.

75. Ruth Biery, "Suicide Never Pays," *Photoplay*, May 1928, p. 121. Brent applied for a passport and sailed for England in December 1919.

76. Gladys Hall, "Confessions of the Stars: Evelyn Brent Tells Her Untold Story," *Motion Picture Classic*, June 1929, pp. 66, 90.

## *Chapter 2*

1. Marquis Busby, "She Doesn't Want to Star," *Los Angeles Times*, June 3, 1928, p. D11.

2. Ruth Biery, "Suicide Never Pays," *Photoplay*, May 1928, p. 121.

3. Gladys Hall, "Confessions of the Stars: Evelyn Brent Tells Her Untold Story," *Motion Picture Classic*, June 1929, pp. 66, 90.

4. John Kobal, *People Will Talk*, p. 103.

5. Hayden Church, "British Actresses Lack Pep of American Cousins, Confess British Critics," *Atlanta Constitution*, October 3, 1920.

6. In her January 1969 interview with Richard Lamparski, Brent said that Bruce had been the stage manager.

7. Paul Bailey, *Three Queer Lives*, p. 128.

8. "America Likes Its Melodramas," *Los Angeles Times*, July 19, 1925, p. 17.

9. Gladys Hall, "Confessions of the Stars: Evelyn Brent Tells Her Untold Story," *Motion Picture Classic*, June 1929, pp. 66, 90.

10. Cited in DeWitt Bodeen, "Evelyn Brent," *Films in Review*, p. 343.

11. "The Film World," *London Times*, September 26, 1921, p. 8.

12. "The Screen," *The Decatur Review* [Illinois], January 18, 1922.

13. Ruth Biery, "Suicide Never Pays," *Photoplay*, May 1928, p. 121.

14. Gladys Hall, "Confessions of the Stars: Evelyn Brent Tells Her Untold Story," *Motion Picture Classic*, June 1929, pp. 66, 90.

15. Ruth Biery, "Suicide Never Pays," *Photoplay*, May 1928, pp. 121–22.

16. Marquis Busby, "She Doesn't Want to Star," *Los Angeles Times*, June 3, 1928, p. D11.

17. Ibid.

18. Gladys Hall, "Confessions of the Stars: Evelyn Brent Tells Her Untold Story," *Motion Picture Classic*, June 1929, pp. 66, 90.

19. Ruth Biery, "Suicide Never Pays," *Photoplay*, May 1928, p. 122.

20. Ibid.

21. Ted Le Berthon, "Star, Once a Resident of Syracuse, Reveals Her Early Struggles," *Syracuse Herald*, August 17, 1930. Brent did not identify the girlfriend.

22. Gladys Hall, "Confessions of the Stars: Evelyn Brent Tells Her Untold Story," *Motion Picture Classic*, June 1929, pp. 66, 90.

23. James W. Dean, "Critics Improved Movies, Not the Producers," *Modesto Evening News*, January 13, 1923.

## Chapter 3

1. "Film Stars Will Sue," *Los Angeles Times*, October 31, 1923, p. 11.

2. "Lubitsch to Direct Doug," *Los Angeles Times*, November 29, 1922, p. III.

3. Ibid.

4. Ibid.

5. Heather Paster. The apartment complex, damaged by earthquakes and neglect, has recently been renovated into luxury apartments by Jeffrey Rouze, who also restored the El Capitan Theater.

6. John Kobal, *Hollywood: The Years of Innocence*, p. 50.

7. "Succumbs to Cupid's Dart," *Los Angeles Times*, March 6, 1923.

8. "Muted Bells Find Tongue," *Los Angeles Times*, March 27, 1923.

9. Ibid.

10. Ibid.

11. Ibid.

12. Born September 14, 1897, Frances Fineman attended Barnard College and Radclyffe. She married writer John Gunther in 1927, and the couple traveled around the world, both working as writers. Gunther is best known for his book *Death Be Not Proud*, a memoir about their teenage son's death. Frances contributed the

book's final chapter. They also had a young daughter, Judith, who died at the age of four months. The Gunthers divorced in 1944. Frances Fineman reportedly had an affair with the future prime minister of India, Jawaharlal Nehru. Fineman, who had interests in Russian theatre, psychoanalysis, and Zionism, died in 1964 in Jerusalem. As far as meeting Frances during her school days, it's not conclusive. Fineman attended New York schools until she moved with her mother to Galveston, Texas, in 1911. She returned to New York in 1916 to attend Barnard College. She also studied at Houston's Rice Institute and Radcliffe before graduating from Barnard in 1921.

13. Gladys Hall, "Confessions of the Stars: Evelyn Brent Tells Her Untold Story," *Motion Picture Classic*, June 1929, pp. 28–29.

14. Ken Cuthbertson, *Inside: The Biography of John Gunther*, p. 68.

15. *Inside: The Biography of John Gunther* author Ken Cuthbertson states that Morris Brown sexually abused Frances and was emotionally, if not physically, abusive to his wife (p. 69).

16. Brent identified herself as Roman Catholic, especially later in life, and when she died, a rosary was held in her honor.

17. Roy Liebman, *The Wampas Baby Stars*, pp. 1–2.

18. Marquis Busby, "She Doesn't Want to Star," *Los Angeles Times*, June 3, 1928, p. D11.

19. "Out of Fairbanks Film," *Los Angeles Times*, May 19, 1923, p. 14.

20. John Kobal, *People Will Talk*, p. 107.

21. "Out of Fairbanks Film," *Los Angeles Times*, May 19, 1923, p. 14.

22. Ibid.

23. "Doug Picks Out Dancer," *The Ogden Standard Examiner* [Utah], June 17, 1923. Julanne Johnston's last film work was a small part in *Cleopatra* (1934). She died in Grosse Pointe, Michigan, in 1988.

24. "Film Star in Peril Making Sea Scene," *Thomson Review* [Illinois], April 7, 1927.

25. "Among the Movies," *Lincoln State Journal* [Nebraska], July 12, 1923.

26. "Cinema Unit Gives Fire Boat Thrill," *Los Angeles Times*, June 24, 1923, p. III28.

27. "Film Star in Peril Making Sea Scene," *Thomson Review* [Illinois], April 7, 1927.

28. "Miss Brent to Move to Metro Lot," *Los Angeles Times*, June 26, 1923, p. II19.

29. "Studio Goes to Sickabed Film Star," *Los Angeles Times*, August 1, 1923, p I110. As stated before, there

was confusion about Brent's nationality. In August 1924, the *London Times* referred to Brent as "the British actress."

30. "Here and Abroad," *The New York Times*, September 9, 1923.

31. Unidentified clipping.

32. *Held To Answer* [review], *Variety*, November 15, 1923.

33. "Hollywood in Pitiless Light," *Los Angeles Times*, August 19, 1923.

34. "It's 'No' When Evelyn Says So—But Cupid Yes," *Fitchburg Sentinel*, July 28, 1923.

35. Ibid.

36. "Evelyn Brent Will Make Career Here," *Los Angeles Times*, September 5, 1923, p. I111.

37. Ibid.

38. The lawsuit was reported in *The New York Times* on October 31, 1923. The law firm was O'Brien, Malevinsky, and Driscoll. On November 1, legal representatives for Pickford and Fairbanks said that Marguerite De La Motte might also be added to the suit because she was named in the story as well ("Attorneys Indicate that Miss De La Motte Might Be Fourth Plaintiff," *Los Angeles Times*, November 1, 1923, p. I11). It was also reported that Fairbanks had fired Brent because she had gained too much weight.

39. "Douglas and Mary Plan Libel Suit Against Publisher for Story of Quarrel Over Other Woman; She Promises to Assist in Action," *Nevada State Journal*, October 31, 1923.

40. "Film Stars Will Sue," *Los Angeles Times*, October 31, 1923, p. 11.

41. "Film Stars Will Sue," *Los Angeles Times*, October 31, 1923, p. 11. Marguerite De La Motte was also asked to become part of the lawsuit. As with Brent, it had been suggested that Pickford was unhappy with Fairbanks' attentions toward De La Motte and asked that she be fired. See "Star Asked to Aid Doug, Mary in Suit," *Modesto Evening News*, October 31, 1923.

42. "Mary and Doug Planning to Sue Paper for Libel," *Atlanta Constitution*, November 1, 1923, p. 15.

43. Ibid.

44. "Movie Fraternity Frowns on Doug and Mary's 'Stunt,'" *Decatur Review* [Illinois], November 1, 1923.

45. "Editor Replies to Charges of Mary and Doug," *Syracuse Herald*, December 25, 1923.

46. John Kobal, *People Will Talk*, p. 107. Brent also explained that she kept a photograph of friend George K. Arthur displayed. Reporters saw it and became convinced it was a photo of Fairbanks. This helped fuel the rumors.

47. Unidentified clipping.

48. "Feminine Heavy in Melo-

drama," *Los Angeles Times*, December 9, 1923, p. III33.

49. *Arizona Express* [review], *Variety*, April 23, 1924.

50. "Picture Players Scorn Danger in Reel Thriller," *Ada Evening News* [Oklahoma], April 11, 1924.

51. F.B.O. was located at 780 Gower Street in Hollywood

52. "America Likes Its Melodrama," *Los Angeles Times*, July 19, 1925, p. 17.

53. "British Director Amazed," *Los Angeles Times*, July 14, 1924, p. A5.

54. "At Last! Latest Style in 'Vamps,'" *Los Angeles Times*, July 27, 1924, p. B18.

55. *The Desert Outlaw* [review], *Variety*, November 12, 1924.

56. "The Orpheum," *Daily Courier* [Connellsville, Pennsylvania], February 20, 1925.

57. "Evelyn Brent Stars," *Los Angeles Times*, September 3, 1924, p. A11.

58. David J. Skal and Elias Savada, *Dark Carnival: The Secret World of Tod Browning*, p. 85.

59. Ibid.

60. *Dangerous Flirt* [review], *Variety*, December 17, 1924.

61. Ted Le Berthon, "Star, Once a Resident of Syracuse, Reveals Her Early Struggles," *Syracuse Herald*, August 17, 1930.

62. "Sick But Willing," *Los Angeles Times*, January 18, 1925, p. 27.

63. This is probably a reference to English poet John Masefield, who wrote "Sea-Fever."

64. Grace Kingsley, "Tea-Cup, Tete-a-Tete with Stella, the Star-Gazer," *Los Angeles Times*, February 11, 1925, p. C10.

65. "Directors Selected with Care," *Los Angeles Times*, February 15, 1925, p. 35. Fineman sounds a bit puffed up. You'd think he was making the greatest story ever told rather than a low-budget quickie.

66. Cynthia Lindsay, *Dear Boris*, p. 28.

67. DeWitt Bodeen, "Evelyn Brent," *Films in Review*, p. 345.

68. "Evelyn Brent Saved By Maid; Artery Severed," *Los Angeles Times*, March 15, 1925, p. 10.

69. "Actress Slashes Artery in Wrist," *Oakland Tribune*, March 14, 1925.

70. "Most Stars Confess to Having Jinx," *Los Angeles Times*, March 16, 1925, p. A9.

71. In the photo, Brent is wearing the same clothes and shoes as when she later rides an ostrich. She may have visited a petting zoo and been photographed with several different animals.

72. "Snapping, Hissing Reptiles the Crop on This Farm," *San Antonio Express*, March 22, 1925, p. B5.

73. "Cameragrams," *Helena Daily Independent* [Montana], March 11, 1925.

74. "The Days News in Pictures," *Hamilton Evening Journal* [Ohio], March 14, 1925.

75. "Fineman Sees Thrill Profit," *Los Angeles Times*, March 29, 1925, p. 39.

76. Ibid.

77. "Movies News Notes," *Olean Evening Herald* [New York], February 27, 1925.

78. "Evelyn Brent in New Role," *Los Angeles Times*, April 11, 1925.

79. "Studio and Stage," *Los Angeles Times*, April 18, 1925, p. A9.

80. "Film Beauty Will Play 'Plain' Role," *Los Angeles Times*, June 1, 1925, p. A7.

81. "America Likes Its Melodrama," *Los Angeles Times*, July 19, 1925, p. 17.

82. Ibid.

83. Ibid.

84. *Smooth as Satin* [review], *Variety*, June 24, 1925.

85. Unidentified clipping.

86. "Evelyn Brent Broadway Hit," *Davenport Democrat and Leader* [Iowa], June 21, 1925. In the August 20, 1926, *Syracuse Herald*, Chester Bahn suggested the opposite: "None of the pictures Miss Brent appeared in for F.B.O. has done any more than to just about clear."

87. *Kansas City Star* [Missouri], May 24, 1925.

88. "Stars Bar Corsets," *Los Angeles Times*, May 3, 1925, p. 29.

89. Ibid.

90. "Says Women Should Design Men's Wear," *Los Angeles Times*, May 13, 1925, p. A9.

91. "Evelyn Brent Bobs Her Hair," *Davenport Democrat and Leader* [Iowa], May 17, 1925.

92. "Bob Is Not So New," *Los Angeles Times*, May 25, 1925, p. 21.

93. "Studio and Stage," *Los Angeles Times*, June 2, 1925, p. A15.

94. "Finishes Picture," *Los Angeles Times*, July 5, 1925, p. D 10.

95. "Ince Says Miss Brent Looms As Great Star," *Los Angeles Times*, June 7, 1925, p. 23.

96. *Los Angeles Times*, June 29, 1925, p. A7.

97. "Lady Robber Forswears Horse," *Los Angeles Times*, July 12, 1925, p. H4.

98. "Film Star Assails 'Moron Publicity,'" *Port Arthur News*, August 2, 1925.

99. Russell J. Birdwell, *Ogden Standard-Examiner* [Utah], August 16, 1925.

100. "Request Cast of Actress's Ankle Which Won Prize," *Davenport Democrat and Leader* [Iowa], August 30, 1925.

101. "Evelyn Brent May Appear in Society Drama," *Los Angeles Times*, August 2, 1925, p. D12.

102. Ibid.

103. "Evelyn Brent Busy With New Crook Picture," *Los Angeles Times*, p. A7.

104. *Photoplay*, February 1926.

105. "Evelyn Leaves for East," *Los Angeles Times*, August 29, 1925, p. 7.

106. "Evelyn Brent Will Begin New Series," *Los Angeles Times*, September 13, 1925, p. 30.

107. "High Light of Comedy Helps Film," *Los Angeles Times*, September 13, 1925, p. 26.

108. "Miss Brent on Belated Honeymoon," *Syracuse Herald*, September 15, 1929.

109. "Fineman Not Leaving F.B.O.," *Los Angeles Times*, August 29, 1925, p. 7.

110. "Actress Departs on Eastern Trip," *Los Angeles Times*, August 29, 1925, p. 15.

111. Isabel Stuyvesant, "Society of Cinemaland," *Los Angeles Times*, September 6, 1925, p. 18. In a 1949 column, Jimmy Fidler recalled seeing 376 pairs of shoes in her closet. He did not tell us how long they took to count. (Fidler, "In Hollywood," *Tri-City Herald* [Pasco, Washington], January 7, 1949.)

112. "Evelyn Brent Steals March on Paris Shops," *Los Angeles Times*, October 7, 1925, p. A9.

113. "Evelyn Brent Mistaken for Society Crook," *Los Angeles Times*, October 11, 1925, p. 28.

114. To the great annoyance of film historians, Cecil B. DeMille used DeMille professionally and de Mille in private life.

115. Known as the Fox Figueroa Theatre, it was located at Santa Barbara Boulevard (the name has been changed to Martin Luther King, Jr. Blvd.) and Figueroa Street. The movie palace was demolished in the late 1960s.

116. Rosalind Shaffer, "Glimpses of Hollywood," *Atlanta Constitution*, November 29, 1925, p. D3.

117. "File Suit for $501,500," *Manitoba Free Press*, November 21, 1925. According to a report in the *Fresno Bee* (November 20, 1925), "The actress asked $100,000 exemplary damages on the attack charges, $150,000 actual damages for alleged fake imprisonment, $100,000 exemplary damages on this charge, $50,000 for 'loss of earning capacity.' $1,000 for counsel fees growing out of the false imprisonment charge and $500 for medical services."

118. "F.B.O., Studios, Manager, Sued On Actress' Charge," *Fresno Bee*, November 20, 1925.

119. "Sues for $501,500," *Port Arthur News*, December 8, 1925.

120. "Pretty Peggy Udell Pleads $500,000 Damages in Suit to Clear Name in Scandal," *Port Arthur News* [Texas], November 27, 1925.

121. Peggy's name was also sometimes spelled Unertal, Unertl, U'Nertle, Unertle, and N'ertle. In one newspaper she was said to be the daughter of Dr. and Mrs. John U N'ertle of Milwaukee, Wisconsin ("Drunk When Wed Man Declares," *Gettysburg Times*, June 6, 1922).

122. "Pretty Peggy Udell Gets Husband and Money," *News-Sentinel* [Fort Wayne, Indiana], July 30, 1922. Before the trial, Peggy went home to mother and gave a fascinating interview in the *Eau Claire Leader* (May 11, 1922). Briefly, her version was this: "It was love at first sight.... He loved me, I know he did, and I loved him. Just a case of too much mother-in-law." At the time, Udell was planning to sue Montgomery for $50,000 for slander. She said she still loved her husband: "But I'm young.... I'm going to forget and then I'm going to marry a man who will love me dearly and then a home and kiddies—that's my final aspiration." For a more cynical interview with Udell, see "Doughnuts and Divorce for Her Wedding Breakfast," *Charleston Daily Mail* [West Virginia], March 26, 1922. See also "Couple Is Married on Dare; He Rues It," *Nevada State Journal*, March 4, 1922.

123. "Peggy Udell Again Seeks Divorce," *Lincoln State Journal* [Nebraska], June 17, 1924. The newspaper also mentions she was seeking support for "her unborn child." The child was mentioned again in a *San Antonio Light* article ("Uneasy Peggy Udell, Sore and Sorry, Seeks a Convent," February 17, 1929) which referred to a daughter. Patricia Michon was (fortunately) raised by her grandparents and went on to have an acting career herself. For more information, see "Movie Actress from Milwaukee Comes to Town for an Afternoon, *Appleton Post-Crescent*, June 2, 1960.

124. "Actress Pays for Specs and All Is Forgiven Again," *San Antonio Light*, December 25, 1932. For more on the fight with Green as well as additional information about Udell, see the July 15, 1928, *San Antonio Light* article "Peggy Udell, Late of the 'Follies,' Tells Why She Socks 'Em."

125. "Uneasy Peggy Udell, Sore and Sorry, Seeks a Convent," *San Antonio Light*, February 17, 1929. See also "Noted Actress to Enter Convent," *Syracuse Herald*, February 3, 1929.

126. "Peggy Stars in Newark Nuptial Act," *Circleville Herald* [Ohio], March 18, 1930.

127. "Actress Pays for Specs and All Is Forgiven Again," *San Antonio Light*, December 25, 1932.

128. The other movies and advertised star were *Keep Smiling* (Monte Banks), *Fighting Heart* (Buck Jones), *Speed Wild* (Lefty Flynn), *Durand of the Bad Lands* (Buck Jones), *Percy* (Charles Ray), *The Desert Price* (All-Star Cast), *The Mysterious Stranger* (Richard Talmadge), *Satan in Sables* (All-Star Cast), and *The Freshman* (Harold Lloyd).

129. *Atlanta Constitution*, February 3, 1926, p. 16.

130. "Little Stories from Filmland," *Kansas City Star* [Missouri], February 7, 1926.

131. *Queen O' Diamonds* [review], *Variety*, April 28, 1926.

132. *Photoplay*, August 1926.

133. Unidentified clipping.

134. *Photoplay*, September 26, 1926.

135. Isabel Stuyvesant, "Society of Cinemaland," *Los Angeles Times*, May 16, 1926, p. C10.

136. "Up They Go—Or, the Art of Star Making," *Daily Messenger* [Canandaigua, New York], June 22, 1926.

137. "Actress Seeks Health Elixir," *Los Angeles Times*, July 14, 1926, p. A22.

138. Jack Woolridge, "Movieland," *Oakland Tribune*, July 25, 1926.

139. "Evelyn Brent Breaks Contract," *Los Angeles Times*, July 16, 1926, p. A8.

140. "Little Stories from Filmland," *Kansas City Star* [Missouri], July 25, 1926.

141. "Evelyn Brent 'Helen Wills' of Pictures," *Los Angeles Times*, August 15, 1926, p. C21.

## *Chapter 4*

1. Whitney Williams, "Under the Lights," *Los Angeles Times*, January 23, 1927, p. 13.

2. Frank Tuttle's memory might have been playing tricks on him. Brent did not appear with Bancroft until after *Love 'Em and Leave 'Em*.

3. Frank Tuttle, *They Started Talking*, p. 56.

4. Ibid., p. 57.

5. Ibid.

6. Barry Paris, *Louise Brooks*, p. 170.

7. Ibid.

8. Ibid.

9. Frank Tuttle, *They Started Talking*, p. 59.

10. "Evelyn Brent Joins Stellar Group in *Love 'Em and Leave 'Em*," *Los Angeles Times*, December 12, 1926, p. C27.

11. Ibid.

12. *Love's Greatest Mistake* [review], *Variety*, February 16, 1927.

13. "Roxy Theaters May Be Chain," *Los Angeles Times*, December 19, 1926, p. C21.

14. Mordaunt Hall, *New York Times*, March 1, 1927.

15. Whitney Williams, "Under the Lights," *Los Angeles Times*, February 7, 1926, p. 15.

16. "Columbia Signs Stars for Big Feature Movies," *Charleston Gazette* [West Virginia], February 24, 1927.

17. Martha Nye, "Society of Cinemaland," *Los Angeles Times*, February 20, 1927, p. C28.

18. Gladys Hall, "Confessions of the Stars: Evelyn Brent Tells Her Untold Story," *Motion Picture Classic*, June 1929, p. 90.

19. Ibid., p. 99.

20. Dorothy Herzog, "Backstage at Hollywood," *Waterloo Evening Courier* [Iowa], January 19, 1929.

21. "Bathing Girls Prepare for Annual Classic," *Los Angeles Times*, May 22, 1927, p. B8.

22. John Springer and Jack Hamilton, *They Had Faces Then*, p. 40.

23. "Studio Payrolls Not What They Used to Be," *Reno Evening Gazette*, January 22, 1927.

24. Kevin Brownlow, *The Parade's Gone By*, p. 195.

25. "Flashes from the Studios," *New York Times*, November 4, 1928.

26. James Card, quoted in Victoria A. Wilson, "Silent Knight," *Interview*, November 1, 1994.

27. "Favorites!," *Los Angeles Times*, May 15, 1927, p. 13.

28. John Kobal, *People Will Talk*, pp. 87–88. Brooksie, who was an equal opportunity insulter, also pointed out that Sternberg coaxed a great performance out of Betty Compson in *The Docks of New York*. She described Compson as "so soft, so frail, so delicate, so empty-headed that she was just meaningless on the screen." (Kobal, *People Will Talk*, p. 88)

29. Budd Schulberg, *Moving Pictures*, p. 242.

30. Blake Lucas, *Acting Style in Silent Films*, p. 41.

31. Josef von Sternberg, *Fun in a Chinese Laundry*, p. 216.

32. John Kobal, *People Will Talk*, p. 103.

33. Ruth Biery, "Suicide Never Pays," *Photoplay*, May 1928, p. 122.

34. Grace Kingsley, "Evelyn Brent's Fine Role," *Los Angeles Times*, December 31, 1926, p. A10.

35. "Environment Spurs Film Star's Work," *Los Angeles Times*, May 26, 1929, p. 17.

36. John Kobal, *People Will Talk*, p. 112.

37. Unidentified clipping.

38. John Kobal, *People Will Talk*, p. 113.

39. Richard Lamparski, *Whatever Became Of...?* radio interview, WBAI-FM, January 7, 1969.

40. Ibid.

41. Ibid.

42. John Kobal, *People Will Talk*, p. 109.

43. DeWitt Bodeen, "Evelyn Brent," *Films in Review*, p. 349.

44. *San Antonio Light* [Texas], June 24, 1928.

45. James Card, *Seductive Cinema*, p. 243.

46. William K. Everson, *American Silent Film*, p. 229.

47. Ibid., p. 230.

48. James Card, *Seductive Cinema*, p. 238.

49. "Dregs of Life Offer Vivid Tale," *Los Angeles Times*, August 27, 1927.

50. "Nine Big Pictures Scheduled," *Los Angeles Times*, August 10, 1927, p. A9.

51. "*Underworld* Makes Bit Hit in New York," *Los Angeles Times*, August 1927, p. D13.

52. Harry Hossent, *Gangster Movies*, p. 19.

53. Morris Gilbert, "Paris Cinema Chatter," *New York Times*, April 20, 1930, p. 104.

54. Richard Griffith, *The Movie Stars*, p. 335.

55. "Filmplayers Shy at Telephone Book," *Los Angeles Times*, August 27, 1928, p. A2.

56. *Women's Wares* [review], *Variety*, November 23, 1927.

57. Brent's attorneys were Milton M. Cohen and George D. Horne.

58. Ruth Biery, "Suicide Never Pays," *Photoplay*, May 1928, p. 122.

59. Alma Whitaker, "Evelyn Brent More Critical Than Ever of Own Work; Underworld Roles Seem Destiny," *Los Angeles Times*, June 16, 1929, p. C13.

60. Mollie Merrick, "Hollywood in Person," *Los Angeles Times*, March 9, 1930, p. B17.

61. Ted Le Berthon, "Star, Once a Resident of Syracuse, Reveals Her Early Struggles," *Syracuse Herald*, August 17, 1930.

62. Ruth Biery, "Suicide Never Pays," *Photoplay*, May 1928, p. 122.

63. "Mate Too Rude to Love, She Says," *Los Angeles Times*, August 17, 1927, p. A5.

64. "Evelyn Brent Gets Divorce," *New York Times*, August 18, 1927, p. 9. A couple years later, in September 1929, Mollie Merrick remarked on the friendship between Brent and Dean: "[They] have known each other since the days of silent struggles. Evelyn Brent is now a star. Priscilla Dean is a memory. But the friendship endures." Mollie Merrick, "Hollywood in Person," *Atlanta Constitution*, September 23, 1929, p. 4.

65. "Mate Too Rude to Love, She Says," *Los Angeles Times*, August 17, 1927, p. A5.

66. Bernie Fineman expressed this thought in an October 11, 1943, letter to his sister Frances. It was in response to a letter he received from her announcing her decision to divorce John Gunther. The letter was located in the Frances Fineman Gunther archive at the Schlesinger Library at the Radcliffe Institute for Advanced Study.

67. Myra Nye, "Society in Cinemaland," *Los Angeles Times*, March 4, 1928, p. C28.

68. At one point while at MGM, Fineman was instructed by Louis B. Mayer to have a talk with openly gay actor William Haines who was scheduled to appear in MGM's *Just a Gigolo* (1931). "In late February [1931], Billy was called into Fineman's office and told in no uncertain terms to leave the trademark William Haines wisecracks and mannerisms out of his performance. He was to play it straight—in all the meanings of the term. He was instructed to imitate Ronald Colman for the picture.... Then Fineman informed him he would be coached by Leslie Howard, the English actor newly arrived on the lot." From William J. Mann, *Wisecracker*, p. 180.

69. Anne Edwards, *The DeMilles*, p. 120.

70. Carol Easton, *No Intermissions*, p. 84.

71. Ibid., p. 84. Agnes and Margaret were themselves part–Jewish.

72. Margaret de Mille died in 1978.

73. Judith Fineman Donelan.

74. Agnes de Mille, *Speak to Me, Dance with Me*, p. 9. Agnes de Mille hinted that the marriage to Fineman was troubled partly due to high living. "Mag [Margaret] and her husband Bernie rented a palazzo on Belagio Road in Bel Air, absolutely opulent, with rolling lawns adjoining the greens of the Bel Air golf course.... Mag seemed to be living in fine style, but actually it was a false front. Bernie was undergoing the ghastly experience of waiting for a renewal of contract and each day they watched for invitations as sure clues. Several mornings after a big bash I found my sister weeping over the bills and over the lack of important calls." [p. 279] Eventually Fineman moved his family to London to seek work. "My sister, her husband and child, pursuing their waning fortunes, once more had moved and had now gone to London and were installed in Trevor Square with a wonderful nanny of quality, the sister-in-law of Sean O'Faolain. Bernie was trying to promote work in the British studios." [p. 300] The Finemans' marriage ended in England; Agnes de Mille described it as a "violent divorce." [p. 308]

75. Miriam Fineman was active in Israeli and Jewish causes. She died of a heart attack in her 336 Central Park West residence in October 1964.

76. Helen Louise Walker, "No Complexes Here!," *Picture Play*, January 1928, p. 34.

77. "Rock in Desert Background in Paramount Film," *Los Angeles Times*, August 27, 1927, p. C24.

78. Grace Kingsley, "Paramount Players Depart," *Los Angeles Times*, June 24, 1927, p. A8.

79. "Sleigh Riding in Sand," *Los Angeles Times*, July 13, 1927, p. A8.

80. Chester B. Bahn, "Up and Down the Rialtos," *Syracuse Herald*, July 16, 1927. Brent also reportedly injured her left hand on the set of *The Last Command*. Check out a very strange site: http://bonetrade.gregorywhitehead.com/sma/azindex.html. According to this site, "We are a small and dedicated organisation based in Baltimore, USA. Our aim is the 'resurrection' of actresses from the Golden era of silent cinema. To do this we are securing a large body of quality genetic material from a variety of sources which is subjected to rigorous testing to ensure its validity. Samples range from small tissue and blood samples to full bones and several preserved organs. We intend to work closely with science organisations to perfect safe and reliable human duplication techniques. We are already in discussion with several studios interested in becoming parents to these new stars of old." Among the actresses they claim to have specimens from are Mary Astor, Vilma Banky, Theda Bara, and Alice White. Brent's specimen is a blood-soaked cloth. We wonder who saved the cloth.

81. "Evelyn Brent Ill," *Los Angeles Times*, August 2, 1927, p. A18.

82. "Evelyn Brent Returns," *Los Angeles Times*, August 10, 1927, p. A8.

83. Dorothy Herzog, "Behind Hollywood Scenes," *Oxnard Daily Courier* [California], June 13, 1929.

84. "New *Beau* Film Stirs Spectators," *Los Angeles Times*, January 30, 1928, p. A7.

85. Frank B. Allen, "Trouping Is New to Evelyn Brent But She Likes It," *Waterloo Courier* [Iowa], January 26, 1940, p. 3.

86. *Beau Sabreur* [review], *Variety*, January 25, 1928.

87. Homer Dickens, *The Films of Gary Cooper*, p. 7.

88. John Engstead, *Star Shots*, p. 122.

89. Brent must have been confused about the dates. Valentino died on August 23, 1926, almost a year earlier than the supposed romance with Cooper.

90. John Kobal, *People Will Talk*, p. 106.

91. Richard Lamparski, *Whatever Became Of...?* radio interview, WBAI-FM, January 7, 1969.

92. Lawrence J. Quirk, *The Complete Films of William Powell*, p. 71.

93. "Actor Must Be Linguist," *Ogden Standard Examiner* [Utah], November 16, 1927.

94. Grace Kingsley, "Evelyn Exposes Genius," *Los Angeles Times*, January 15, 1928, p. C13.

95. Ibid.

96. Ibid.

97. Marquis Busby, "Hollywood's Scrappy Colony," *Motion Picture*, May 1931.

98. "Environment Spurs Film Star's Work," *Los Angeles Times*, May 26, 1929, p. 17.

99. "Russian Roles Most Difficult, She Declares," *Los Angeles Times*, November 13, 1927, p. C37.

100. "Russian Amazed at Star's Ability in His Language," *Los Angeles Times*, November 27, 1927, p. C30.

101. James Robert Parish and Don E. Stanke, *The Debonairs*, p. 423.

102. "Jannings Will Appear Tonight," *Los Angeles Times*, January 26, 1928, p. A11.

103. "*Last Command* Drama Potent," *Los Angeles Times*, January 28, 1926, p. A7.

104. DeWitt Bodeen, "Evelyn Brent," *Films in Review*, p. 347.

105. James Card, *Seductive Cinema*, pp. 237–38.

106. Ivan Butler, *Silent Magic: Rediscovering the Silent Film Era*, p. 165.

107. "Menjou's Next a Sardou Play," *Los Angeles Times*, January 6, 1928, p. A11.

108. Marquis Busby, *A Night of Mystery* [review], *Los Angeles Times*, April 10, 1928, p. A11.

109. *A Night of Mystery* [review], *Variety*, April 18, 1928.

110. "Evelyn Brent's Cabin Site," *Los Angeles Times*, January 18, 1928, p. A8.

111. Myra Nye, "Society in Cinemaland," *Los Angeles Times*, January 29, 1928, p. C24.

112. "Evelyn Brent to Travel," *Los Angeles Times*, February 1, 1928, p. 22. Also mentioned in Myra Nye's "Society of Cinemaland" in the *Los Angeles Times*, February 5, 1928, p. C18.

113. Helen Louise Walker, "No Complexes Here!," *Picture Play*, January 1928, p. 34.

114. Ibid., p. 35.

115. Ibid., p. 35.

116. Ibid., p. 106.

117. John Kobal, *People Will Talk*, p. 109.

118. Grace Kingsley, "Evelyn Brent's New Lead," *Los Angeles Times*, March 21, 1928, p. A8. Rena Vale went on to become a science fiction writer. She was also part of the Writers Project, and a former member of the Communist Party who became extremely anti–Red and testified against former and current members.

119. *His Tiger Lady* [review], *Los Angeles Times*, May 13, 1928, p. 14.

120. *His Tiger Lady* [review], *Variety*, May 30, 1928.

121. Grace Kingsley, "Paramount Lines Up Releases," *Los Angeles Times*, May 2, 1928, p. A8. The same article stated that Brook and Brent would also appear in *The Perfumed Trap*, which was apparently never made.

122. Ted Le Berthon, "Star, Once a Resident of Syracuse, Reveals Her Early Struggles," *Syracuse Herald*, August 17, 1930.

123. *The Showdown* [review], *Syracuse Herald*, June 3, 1928.

124. Mordaunt Hall, *New York Times*, June 10, 1928.

125. *Dragnet* [review], *Los Angeles Times*, May 1928, p. A11.

126. James Robert Parish and Don E. Stanke, *The Debonairs*, p. 423.

127. DeWitt Bodeen, "Evelyn Brent," *Films in Review*, p. 347.

128. Marquis Busby, "She Doesn't Want to Star," *Los Angeles Times*, June 3, 1928, p. D11.

129. Ibid.

130. *Mating Call* [review], *Los Angeles Times*, October 1, 1928, p. A7.

131. Dan Thomas, "Movie, Chat," *Olean Times* [New York], October 15, 1928.

132. Geoff Schumacher, *Howard Hughes: Power, Paranoia & Palace Intrigue*, p. 20.

133. Marquis Busby, "She Doesn't Want to Star," *Los Angeles Times*, June 3, 1928, p. D11.

134. Ruth Biery, "Suicide Never Pays," *Photoplay*, May 1928, p. 122.

135. Ibid.

## Chapter 5

1. Marquis Busby, "No More 'Shopping Tours,'" *Los Angeles Times*, November 4, 1928, p. C16.

2. May Mann, "Wetjen Gives Low-Down on Hollywood Characters," *Ogden Standard-Examiner* [Utah], October 6, 1940. Wetjen was a book author who occasionally wrote magazine articles.

3. John Kobal, *People Will Talk*, pp. 523–24.

4. Katherine Albert, "Temperamental? YES! What of It?," *Photoplay*, October 1929, p. 59.

5. Jesse Lasky, *The Sound and the Fury*, p. 105.

6. Ibid., p. 106.

7. Ibid., p. 106.

8. Ibid., pp. 106–07.

9. Ibid., p. 107.

10. Ibid., p. 107.

11. Ibid., p. 108.

12. "Talking Films Introduce Revolutionary Procedure," *Los Angeles Times*, October 14, 1928, p. B30.

13. Alexander Walker, *The Shattered Silents*, p. 106.

14. Clara Butt (1872–1936) was a tall (6'2") opera singer. According to her Wikipedia entry, Sir Thomas Beacham once said, "On a clear day, you could have heard her across the English Channel."

15. John Kobal, *People Will Talk*, p. 116.

16. Richard Lamparski, *Whatever Became Of...?* radio interview, WBAI-FM, January 7, 1969.

17. Frank B. Allen, "Trouping Is New to Evelyn Brent But She Likes It," *Waterloo Courier* [Iowa], January 26, 1940, p. 3.

18. Alexander Walker, *The Shattered Silents*, pp. 104–05.

19. "Paramount Voice Film at Carthay," *Los Angeles Times*, October 23, 1928, p. A11.

20. "All-Talkie, Eddie Cantor at T-D Today," *Oakland Tribune*, February 8, 1929.

21. Mordaunt Hall. "The Screen" [review of *Interference*], *New York Times*, November 17, 1928.

22. Ibid.

23. "Current Events in Cinemaland," *Los Angeles Times*, November 11, 1928, p. C21.

24. Dan Thomas, "Syracuse Girl Real Talkie Hit," *Syracuse Herald*, November 25, 1928.

25. Norbert Lusk, "East Approves Three Talkies," *Los Angeles Times*, November 25, 1928, p. C13.

26. Forney Wyly, "Broadway Banter," *Atlanta Constitution*, June 9, 1929, p. G19.

27. Marquis Busby, "No More 'Shopping Tours,'" *Los Angeles Times*, November 4, 1928, p. C16.

28. Ibid.

29. Ibid.

30. Ibid.

31. Grace Kingsley, "Evelyn Brent Heads Starward," *Los Angeles Times*, November 13, 1928, p. A10.

32. Anthony Slide, *Silent Topics*, p. 49.

33. Lillian Faderman & Stuart Timmons, *Gay L.A.: A History of Sex-*

ual *Outlaws, Power Politics, and Lipstick Lesbians*, p. 41.

34. John Kobal, *People Will Talk*, p. 101.

35. Telephone interview with David Chierichetti, August 17, 2008.

36. Cal York, "Gossip of All the Studios," *Photoplay*, February 1929, p. 48.

37. In Mollie Merrick's syndicated column on November 20, she wrote that Brent and Edwards went across the border to Mexico to marry because of California's law requiring a three-day announcement to wed before the ceremony could be held. *Lincoln State Journal*, November 20, 1928.

38. Forney Wyly, "Broadway Banter," *Atlanta Constitution*, December 30, 1928.

39. Cal York, "Gossip of All the Studios," *Photoplay*, February 1929, p. 46.

40. "Ring Misleading in This Instance," *Los Angeles Times*, September 18, 1928, p. A3.

41. He used his full name on his 1938 Social Security application.

42. Other sources list 1888 (World War I draft registration) and 1892 (1916 passport application) as birth years. Edwards' Social Security application uses the 1888 date. Much of the information about Edwards is from his 1916 and 1922 passport applications. Edwards could not locate his own birth certificate at the Bureau of Vital Records of New York City at the time of his 1916 passport application. No Manhattan birth record exists for any Harry Edwards born on April 11, 1887, or 1888.

43. 1922 passport application. In the 1916 application, his father was not listed as deceased. According to the 1922 passport application, his father was deceased.

44. Henry Edwards 1916 and 1922 passport applications.

45. Henry Edwards 1916 passport application

46. New York City attorney and American representative for the American Volunteer Motor Ambulance Corps. Eliot was brother of Richard Norton, overseas Ambulance Corps organizer, and "son of Charles Eliot Norton, Harvard's internationally celebrated professor of history, and his mother, Susan Segwick, had Boston Brahmin blood." From *Gentleman Volunteers: The Story of American Ambulance Drivers in the Great War, August 1914–September 1918* by Arlen J. Hansen.

47. 1917 draft card registration.

48. One of many writers who were members of the Ambulance Corps during the war, Conklin worked for Christie Studio until the early 1930s.

49. *Stardust and Shadows—Canadians in Early Hollywood* by Charles Foster, pp. 23–24.

50. Ibid., p. 28.

51. "Along with Al Christie and Frank Conklin," *Oakland Tribune*, May 14, 1922.

52. Ibid.

53. Gladys Hall, "Confessions of the Stars: Evelyn Brent Tells Her Untold Story," *Motion Picture Classic*, June 1929, p. 90.

54. "In Hollywood," *Lima Sunday News* [Ohio], December 2, 1928. See also *Syracuse Herald*, November 30, 1928. Interestingly, in her June 18, 1929, column, Dorothy Herzog included this short blurb: "[Gary] Cooper and [Andy] Lawler trudge into studio executives' offices and ask if they can go off for a weekend hunting together. 'Can Andy go bear huntin' with me?' Gary asks, a little boy to his stern fathers. They say no: just as they eventually may have put the squash on the friendship." (William J. Mann, *Behind the Screen*, p. 106.) Mann went on to explain, "Andy Lawler would remain embittered by his treatment by Paramount. Touted for a part in Nancy Carroll's *The Devil's Holiday*, he was inexplicably canned." Was Herzog retaliating? Or was she being used as a tool by Paramount?

55. William J. Mann, *Kate*, p. 236. See also p. 224.

56. "Evelyn Brent's Chauffeur Held After Argument," *Los Angeles Times*, February 13, 1929, p. A9.

## Chapter 6

1. "She Eats and Tells!," *Photoplay*, January 1931.

2. Edwards' FBI files were destroyed for unknown reasons.

3. "Censors Prefer Ice," *Amarillo Globe* [Texas], April 15, 1930.

4. Alyce Curtis, "Evelyn Brent Up-to-Date," pp. 65, 93.

5. "At the Theatres," *The Syracuse Herald*, June 20, 1933.

6. "Embassy Club Will Open Soon," *Los Angeles Times*, November 10, 1929, p. D3.

7. Myra Nye, "Society of Cinemaland," *Los Angeles Times*, February 16, 1930, p. A21.

8. Alma Whitaker, "Haute Monde Invades Colony," *Los Angeles Times*, October 6, 1929, p. B13.

9. Grace Kingsley, "Embassy to Open," *Los Angeles Times*, November 29, 1929, p. 14.

10. Louise Brooks, "Stardom and Evelyn Brent," January 13, 1975.

11. Margaret Chute, "The Brent's Due," *The Picturegoer*, February 1929, pp. 26–27.

12. Alma Whitaker, "Evelyn Brent More Critical Than Ever of Own Work; Underworld Roles Seem Destiny," *Los Angeles Times*, June 16, 1929, p. C13.

13. *Woman Trap* [review]. *Photoplay*, October 1929, p. 54.

14. Fleet Smith, "Six Young Stars Are Brought Out By Paramount Co.," *Zanesville Signal* [Ohio], June 23, 1929.

15. Cal York, "Gossip of All the Studios," *Photoplay*, September 1929, p. 50.

16. "She Eats and Tells!," *Photoplay*, January 1931.

17. Gladys Hall, "Confessions of the Stars: Evelyn Brent Tells Her Untold Story," *Motion Picture Classic*, June 1929, p. 90.

18. Ibid., p. 99. A 1932 blurb stated that though Brent collected perfume bottles, she did not use perfume. Relman Morin, "Cinematters," *Los Angeles Evening Herald Express*, August 1, 1932. In a different article, a bookseller described Brent as "one of the most voracious readers in the colony." He specifically mentioned Brent's purchases of first editions by Jeffers, Liam O'Flaherty, and Thomas Mann. (Robbin Coons, "Movie Stars Go Heavy on Good Reading," *Mason City Globe Gazette* [Iowa], May 5, 1931.)

19. On November 29, 1928, the *Modesto News-Herald* article "My Beauty Secret By Evelyn Brent As Told To Diana Dare" covered everything from diet to exercise to sleep. Among the nuggets of information: "A clear, glowing complexion was never acquired on a diet of fudge, sundaes and pastries.... I think it is a good beauty rule to have lots of friends. It keeps you busy smiling at them, and there is nothing better for the face than smiling.... My complexion is such that I don't need cosmetics, but the only rule I would lay down is the safe one of using too little of them rather than too much." An entire paragraph was devoted to massages. "I am a great believer in massage. There is nothing like a massage by an expert to stimulate the system and I feel like a new person after one. I would rather go without food than my weekly massage, I believe."

20. "She Eats and Tells!," *Photoplay*, January 1931.

21. Ibid.

22. Ibid.

23. Ibid.

24. Ibid.

25. Ibid.

26. Ibid.

27. Alyce Curtis, "Evelyn Brent Up-to-Date," pp. 64–65.

28. Ibid., p. 65.

29. Gladys Hall, "The Home-Loving Vamp," p. 54.

30. Alyce Curtis, "Evelyn Brent Up-to-Date," p. 65.

31. "Evelyn Brent in Emotional Picture Role," *Los Angeles Times*, March 17, 1929, p. C25.

32. Alma Whitaker, "Evelyn Brent More Critical Than Ever of Own Work; Underworld Roles Seem Destiny," *Los Angeles Times*, June 16, 1929, p. C13.

33. Katherine Albert, "Temperamental? YES! What of It?," *Photoplay*, October 1929, p. 59.

34. Alma Whitaker, "Evelyn Brent More Critical Than Ever of Own Work; Underworld Roles Seem Destiny," *Los Angeles Times*, June 16, 1929, p. C13.

35. Louella O. Parsons, *San Antonio Light*, January 5, 1930.

36. "Evelyn Brent Wants to Do Talkies Only," *Los Angeles Times*, April 14, 1929, p. C10.

37. "Kibitzer Came Out of the Garden of Eden," *Los Angeles Times*, September 22, 1929, p. 21.

38. "'Temperament?' It's Only Fighting for Square Deal in Movies, Say Stars," *Syracuse Herald*, September 29, 1929.

39. Katherine Albert, "Temperament? YES! What of It?," *Photoplay*, October 1929, p. 59.

40. "Moran and Mack Film Continues Paramount Run," *Los Angeles Times*, October 11, 1929, p. A11.

41. *Why Bring That Up?* [review], *Syracuse Herald*, December 21, 1929.

42. John Kobal, *People Will Talk*, p. 527.

43. Ted Le Berthon, "Star, Once a Resident of Syracuse, Reveals Her Early Struggles," *Syracuse Herald*, August 17, 1930.

44. Forney Wyly, "Broadway Banter," *Atlanta Constitution*, September 29, 1929, p. 116.

45. Chester B. Bahn, "Speaking Very Candidly," *Syracuse Herald*, April 10, 1932. According to Peter Underwood in *Death in Hollywood*, Edgar Wallace hosted a February 1932 dinner party for Genevieve Tobin, Evelyn Brent, Jesse Lasky, and Ricardo Cortez. "[W]ithin three days [February 10] he [Wallace] was dead, for the sore throat had turned to double pneumonia." (*Death in Hollywood*, p. 293.)

46. John Kobal, *People Will Talk*, pp. 114–15.

47. "Picture Folk Look Forward to Playtime," *Los Angeles Times*, July 14 1929, p. 16.

48. "Jaunt to Studioland," *Los Angeles Times*, July 21, 1929, p. H4.

49. "Music Devices Now Found in Stars' Rooms," *Los Angeles Times*, October 6, 1929, p. 31.

50. "Piano Business Booming," *Los Angeles Times*, November 17, 1929, p. 26.

51. Forney Wyly, "Broadway Banter," *Atlanta Constitution*, November 3, 1929, p. E3.

52. John Kobal, *People Will Talk*, p. 106.

53. *Darkened Rooms* [review], *Variety*, December 18, 1929.

54. "At the Theatres," *Kingston Daily Freeman* [New York], February 8, 1930.

55. *Darkened Rooms* [review], *Photoplay*, December 1929.

56. *Fast Company* [review], *Variety*, October 9, 1929.

57. "Oakie Goes to Bat," *Los Angeles Times*, August 18, 1929, p. 13.

58. *Photoplay*, November 1929, p. 55.

59. "Oklahoma and Oakie Same Things," *Los Angeles Times*, August 25, 1929, p. B11.

60. "Naturalism Keynote to Good Work," *Los Angeles Times*, October 13, 1929, p. B12.

61. "Talkies Driving Film Stars to Studious Ways," *The Bee* [Danville, Virginia], August 10, 1929.

62. "Miss Brent on Belated Honeymoon," *Syracuse Herald*, September 15, 1929.

63. Louella O. Parsons, "Elsie Janis Borrowed to Aid in Music Talkie," *San Antonio Light*, December 4, 1929.

64. Grace Kingsley, "Star May Return to Lasky," *Los Angeles Times*, December 17, 1929, p. A8.

65. Publicity materials mistakenly claimed that Brent was in the film. An Ogden, Utah, newspaper actually published ads with Brent in the credits for *The Return of Sherlock Holmes*. See *Ogden Standard-Examiner*, October 26 and 27, 1929.

66. Hubbard Keavy, "Stardom Thrust on Evelyn Brent," *Charleston Gazette* [West Virginia], December 1, 1929.

67. Ibid.

68. "Evelyn Brent Gets Contract from Columbia," *Los Angeles Times*, January 5, 1930, p. B27.

69. Mollie Merrick, "Hollywood in Person," *Montana Standard* [Butte], December 13, 1929.

70. Richard Lamparski, *Whatever Became Of...?* radio interview, WBAI-FM, January 7, 1969.

71. Ibid.

72. "Film Stars Shine at Wedding," *Los Angeles Times*, March 16, 1930, p. A10. Another newspaper article identified Charles Bowers as the best man (see Grace Kingsley, "Oh, the Bride and Groom Were Gay," *Los Angeles Times*, April 13, 1930, p. H5.)

73. "As Screen Stars Met at Altar," *Kingsport Times* [Tennessee], March 26, 1930.

74. Grace Kingsley, "Oh, the Bride and Groom Were Gay," *Los Angeles Times*, April 13, 1930, p. H5.

75. Richard Lamparski, *Whatever Became Of...?* radio interview, WBAI-FM, January 7, 1969.

76. "Film Dialogue Held Different from Captions," *Los Angeles Times*, January 26, 1930, p. B26.

77. Jessie Henderson, "Movie Crooks Do Not Show Reality, Says Evelyn Brent," *Appleton Post-Crescent* [Wisconsin], March 15, 1930.

78. Ibid.

79. *Slightly Scarlet* [review], *Variety*, April 2, 1930.

80. *Slightly Scarlet* [review], *Los Angeles Times*, April 19, 1930, p. A7.

81. *Film Daily*, March 2, 1930.

82. Harry Mines, *Illustrated Daily News* [Los Angeles], April 18, 1930.

83. Jimmy Starr, *Los Angeles Record*, February 22, 1930.

84. Louella O. Parsons, "Santa Claus Won't Forget Movie Stars," *San Antonio Light*, December 22, 1929.

85. "Evelyn Brent in Keith's Framed," *Syracuse Herald*, May 18, 1930.

86. Muriel Babcock, "Exploits in Night Club Recounted," *Los Angeles Times*, May 3, 1930, p. A7.

87. Chester B. Bahn., *Framed* [review], *Syracuse Herald*, May 18, 1930.

88. Kenneth R. Porter, *Los Angeles Examiner*, May 2, 1930.

89. Lawrence J. Quirk, *The Films of Fredric March*, p. 58.

90. Homer Dickens, *The Films of Gary Cooper*, p. 74.

91. Richard Barrios, *A Song in the Dark*, p. 180.

92. *Paramount on Parade* [review], *London Times*, June 17, 1930, p. 12.

93. John Kobal, *People Will Talk*, p. 111.

94. Ibid.

95. Edwin M. Bradley, *The First Hollywood Musicals*, p. 269.

96. Dorothy Herzog, "Behind the Scenes in Hollywood," *Sheboygan Press* [Wisconsin], May 12, 1930.

97. Scottish-born Buchanan, who later became a business partner of Harry D. Edwards, was in Hollywood to make *Monte Carlo* with director Ernst Lubitsch and Jeanette MacDonald. According to his biographer, "On this occasion, he had brought his mother out from England and they rented a house in Beverly Hills. They also brought with them their cook from New York [Buchanan had appeared on Broadway], who together with the Japanese and Filipino servants they employed locally, provided Jack with a more settled home base." From Michael Marshall's *Top Hat & Tails: The Story of Jack Buchanan*, p. 99.

## Chapter 7

1. Buck Rainey, *Sweethearts of the Sage*, p. 108.
2. Grace Kingsley, "Joel McCrea Plays Lead," *Los Angeles Times*, May 21, 1930, p. A8.
3. "Archainbaud to Direct," *Los Angeles Times*, June 5, 1930, p. A8. See also Grace Kingsley, "RKO Players to Alaska," *Los Angeles Times*, July 3, 1930, p. A6.
4. Grace Kingsley, "Too Hot for Them," *Los Angeles Times*, July 29, 1930, p. A8.
5. John Kobal, *People Will Talk*, p. 305.
6. Muriel Babcock, "Evelyn Brent Gets Contract," *Los Angeles Times*, September 10, 1930, p. 8. *Quest* was apparently never made.
7. Norbert Lusk, *Silver Horde* [review], *Los Angeles Times*, November 2, 1930, p. B10.
8. Dan Thomas, "Beach Novel Makes Good Talkie Fare," *Syracuse Herald*, November 6, 1930.
9. "At Syracuse Theaters," *Syracuse Herald*, August 21, 1930.
10. "Screenland Soon to Welcome Home Its Grande Dame," Mollie Merrick, *Dallas Morning News*, July 9, 1931.
11. John Scott, "Redemption Story Told on Screen," *Los Angeles Times*, December 26, 1930, p. A7.
12. *Illustrated Daily News* [Los Angeles], December 26, 1930.
13. *Los Angeles Examiner*, December 26, 1930.
14. "At Syracuse Theaters," *Syracuse Herald*, November 25, 1930.
15. "At Syracuse Theaters," *Syracuse Herald*, December 8, 1930.
16. Louella O. Parsons, *Los Angeles Examiner*, December 27, 1930.
17. Gladys Hall, "What Women Want to Know…," *Motion Picture*, December 1930, pp. 48, 108.
18. Ibid., p. 108.
19. Ibid., p. 108.
20. "Requests of Stars," *Los Angeles Evening Express*, December 6, 1930.
21. "Penthouses to be Built for Dressing Rooms," *Los Angeles Times*, January 27, 1931, p. A9.
22. Gladys Hall, "The Home-Loving Vamp," p. 83.
23. "Evelyn Brent in New Picture," *Los Angeles Times*, January 6, 1931, p. A13.
24. "Only Women to Have Roles in War Film Cast," *Los Angeles Times*, January 11, 1931, p. 21.
25. Relman Morin, *Los Angeles Record*, September 26, 1931.
26. Muriel Babcock, "Experiments in Films Flourish," *Los Angeles Times*, January 18, 1931, p. B11.
27. Louella O. Parsons, *Los Angeles Examiner*, September 25, 1931.

28. Norbert Lusk, *The Mad Parade* [review], *Los Angeles Times*, September 27, 1931, p. B9.
29. Eleanor Barnes, *Illustrated Daily News* [Los Angeles], September 25, 1931.
30. W.E. Oliver, "Long Distance Films Irk Stars," *Los Angeles Evening Herald*, September 26, 1931.
31. Ibid. The Noël Coward musical starred Peggy Wood.
32. Llewellyn Miller, *Los Angeles Record*, September 30, 1931.
33. "Unusual Superstition," *Los Angeles Times*, June 1, 1931, p. A7.
34. Elizabeth Yeaman, *Hollywood Daily Citizen*, March 20, 1931.
35. Michael Marshall, *Top Hat & Tails: The Story of Jack Buchanan*, p. 100.
36. Louella O. Parsons, *Los Angeles Examiner*, April 11, 1931.
37. Ibid., May 2, 1931.
38. *Pagan Lady* [review], *Variety*, September 22, 1931.
39. Harry Mines, *Illustrated Daily News* [Los Angeles], October 30, 1931.
40. "Solitaire Favored," *Los Angeles Times*, August 17, 1931, p. A7.
41. "Hollywood's Pagan Lady Is Just That in Latest Film," *Kingsport Times* [Tennessee], January 3, 1932.
42. "At Syracuse Theaters," *Syracuse Herald*, March 5, 1931. RKO also ultimately dropped Betty Compson and Jack Mulhall around the same time.
43. "Movies Move on Malibu," *Los Angeles Times*, July 12, 1931, p. B11.
44. Sara Hamilton, "Mad, Merry Malibu," *Photoplay*, September 1932.
45. Ibid.
46. Ibid.
47. "Home in London, Career in Legit, Evelyn's Goals," *Syracuse Herald*, December 21, 1930.
48. "Up and Down the Rialtos," *Syracuse Herald*, December 19, 1930. One magazine article claimed she owned 147 perfume bottles. Another article claimed it was 500 bottles.
49. Brent bought the *Huckleberry Finn* first edition from Jean Hersholt at an auction for $118. Hersholt, an avid collector himself, had purchased the book for $1.50. (Hubbard Keavy, "Screen Life in Hollywood," *Galveston Daily News*, November 25, 1932.)
50. "Montgomery and Powell Seen on Regent's Screen," *Syracuse Herald*, March 13, 1932.
51. Dorothy Herzog, "Behind the Scenes in Hollywood," *Sheboygan Journal* [Wisconsin], April 30, 1930.
52. Louella O. Parsons, *Los Angeles Examiner*, March 10, 1931.
53. Mollie Merrick, "Hollywood in Person," *Los Angeles Times*, April 1, 1931, p. A11.
54. Myrtle Gebhart, "$15,000 a

Year for Clothes," *Los Angeles Times*, June 5, 1932, p. H1.
55. Louella O. Parsons, "Hollywood Itself Latest Theme for Movie Stars," *Fresno Bee*, April 27, 1931.
56. Grace Kingsley, "Stars to Take Lengthy Trips," *Los Angeles Times*, p. A7.
57. Ibid.
58. Grace Kingsley, "Benefit Tea Successful," *Los Angeles Times*, May 5, 1931, p. A11. Years later, Damon Runyon asked a retiring railroad porter to name the most generous tippers. He hesitated only slightly before naming Lupe Velez and Evelyn Brent. (Damon Runyon, "The Brighter Side," *Chester Times* [Pennsylvania], February 23, 1938.)
59. Myra Nye, "Cinema of Cinemaland," *Los Angeles Times*, May 10, 1931, p. 26.
60. Mollie Merrick, "Hollywood in Person," *Los Angeles Times*, July 15, 1931, p. 11.
61. Roger Bryant, *William Powell: The Life and Films*, p. 86.
62. Grace Kingsley, "Evelyn Brent's Contract," *Los Angeles Times*, June 27, 1931, p. A7. Damita's first name was sometimes spelled with a "y."
63. Margaret Nye, "Society of Cinemaland," *Los Angeles Times*, July 19, 1931, p. 24. One article attributed Brent's constant tan to her habit of sunbathing on her home's roof. See "Bits of Gossip About Hollywood and Its Famous," *Reno Evening Gazette*, April 6, 1929.
64. "News of the Cafes," *Los Angeles Times*, July 29, 1931, p. A7.
65. Grace Kingsley, "Stars Narrowly Escape Drowning," *Los Angeles Times*, July 30, 1931, p. 11.
66. Louella O. Parsons, "Movie-Go-Round," *Los Angeles Examiner*, August 2, 1931.
67. Dan Thomas, "Evelyn Brent Bides Time on Beach Awaiting Work," *Piqua Daily Call* [Ohio], July 29, 1931.
68. Ibid.
69. Ibid.
70. Ibid.
71. Ibid.
72. Grace Kingsley, "Heard in Hollywood," *Los Angeles Times*, September 17, 1931, p. A9.
73. "Actress Moves," *Los Angeles Times*, October 15, 1931, p. A9.
74. Samuel Richard Mook, "Do Writers Dare Tell the Truth," *Picture Play*, December 1931.
75. *Los Angeles Evening Herald Express*, December 25, 1931.
76. "Taylor Suit Driver Says," *Los Angeles Times*, April 22, 1933, p. A1. In April 1933 court testimony, the chauffeur claimed he was not intoxicated, having had only one drink — a

glass of wine—hours before the accident. He denied Taylor's claim that Brent's maid had given him a bottle of gin.

77. Alma Whitaker, "Old-Time Headliners Lost in Shuffle," *Los Angeles Times*, December 6, 1931, p. B11.

78. "At Syracuse Theaters," *Syracuse Herald*, January 28, 1932.

79. Hans J. Wollstein, *Vixens, Floozies and Molls*, p. 126.

80. Louella O. Parsons, *Los Angeles Examiner*, October 15, 1931.

81. *Evening Tribune* [Albert Lea, Minnesota], February 23, 1932.

82. Norbert Lusk, *High Pressure* [review], *Los Angeles Times*, February 7, 1932, p. B11.

83. "Evelyn Dresses Up," *Los Angeles Times*, November 1, 1931, p. B17.

84. James Robert Parish and Don E. Stanke, The *Debonairs*, p. 430.

85. "Evelyn Brent May Sign Pact with Columbia," *Syracuse Herald*, March 20, 1932.

86. "Actress Sued for Gown Bills," *Los Angeles Times*, March 31, 1931, p. A10. Chanel, located at 3285 Wilshire Blvd., was represented by the law firm of Goldstone and Garbus.

87. Harrison Carroll, "Screenographs," *Los Angeles Evening Herald*, March 31, 1931.

88. Louella O. Parsons, *Los Angeles Examiner*, March 30, 1931.

89. Dan Thomas, "Shop Owners Cheat Stars," *El Paso Herald-Post*, August 8, 1931.

90. *Traveling Husbands* [review], *Variety*, August 11, 1931.

91. Philip K. Scheuer, "Drummers' Pastimes Depicted," *Los Angeles Times*, August 31, 1931, p. A7.

92. *Film Daily*, June 21, 1931.

93. Marquis Busby, *Los Angeles Examiner*, August 29, 1931.

94. "Actress Sued," *San Mateo Times and Daily News* [California], January 8, 1932.

95. "Clothiers Sue Screen Couple," *Los Angeles Times*, April 25, 1932, p. A3. The attorney who filed the complaint for the collection agency was L.W. Jaycox; the judge was Municipal Judge Carrell.

96. "Actress Ordered to Pay Book Bill," *Los Angeles Times*, April 28, 1932, p. A16. The order was made by Judge Kincaid of the Municipal Court. Brent was also sued under the name of Mrs. Harry Edwards.

97. "Furrier Sues Evelyn Brent," *Los Angeles Times*, April 30, 1932, p. A9. The suit was filed in Judge Crawford's court, and the complaining attorney was Milton D. Klein.

98. "Actress Sued By Dog Doctor," *Los Angeles Times*, August 6, 1932, p. A5.

99. Myrtle Gebhart, "Dog-Gone Hollywood," *Los Angeles Times*, May 15, 1932, p. J3.

100. Alyce Curtis, "Evelyn Brent Up-to-Date," p. 65.

101. "Film Actress Sued on $1200 Bill for Shoes," *Los Angeles Times*, September 27, 1932, p. A1. The case was filed in Judge Crawford's courtroom. In a January 29, 1929, column, Brent's shoe purchases were detailed: "[She] has just received a dozen pairs or more for spring and summer wear. She purchases shoes of linen and crepe de chine and kid in pastel shades. Also braided sandals, the stripe as delicate as tiny cords." ("'Back-Stage' Cycle Enters Field of Movie Production," *Edwardsville Intelligencer* [Iowa].)

102. "Evelyn Brent Faces Bill Suit," *Los Angeles Times*, November 25, 1932, p. A8.

103. "Hollywood Gossip, Poor Evelyn Can't Sleep," *Indiana Evening Gazette* [Pennsylvania], March 2, 1932.

104. "Film Spotlight Shuns Pioneers for Newcomers," *Syracuse Herald*, May 22, 1932.

105. Harrison Carroll, *Los Angeles Evening Herald Express*, July 18, 1932.

106. *Attorney for the Defense* [review], *Los Angeles Times*, May 31, 1932.

107. Louella O. Parsons, *Los Angeles Examiner*, July 4, 1932.

108. Louella O. Parsons, *San Antonio Light*, July 12, 1932.

109. Eleanor Barnes, *Illustrated Daily News* [Los Angeles], July 4, 1932.

110. Dan Thomas, "Hollywood Gossip," *The Frederick Post* [Maryland], October 15, 1932.

111. Edwin Martin, *Hollywood Citizen News*, January 9, 1933.

112. "Evelyn Brent Sued Over Lesson Books," *Los Angeles Times*, April 24, 1933.

113. Dan Thomas, "Where Money Takes Wings," *Helena* Independent [Montana], January 29, 1933.

114. Louella O. Parsons, *Los Angeles Examiner*, January 27, 1933.

115. Louella O. Parsons, "Movie Go Round," *San Antonio Light*, March 19, 1933.

116. *World Gone Mad* [review], *Los Angeles Times*, April 18, 1933.

117. Norbert Lusk, *The World Gone Mad* [review], *Los Angeles Times*, April 23, 1933, p. A3.

118. "Evelyn Brent Tires of Bad Woman Roles," *Zanesville Signal* [Ohio], July 9, 1933.

119. "Evelyn Brent Faces Tax Lien," *Los Angeles Times*, May 6, 1933, p. A12.

120. John Kobal, *People Will Talk*, p. 115.

# Chapter 8

1. "Evelyn Brent Back Again in Syracuse, Plans Visit to Scene of Her Childhood," *Syracuse Herald*, May 26, 1933.

2. Harry Fox used many different birth years when filling out official forms. His California death record and several newspaper obituaries used 1882. His World War I draft card and Social Security application used 1885. The 1920 census, 1924 passport application, and a *New York Times* article claimed 1887. On the 1930 census he wrote 1889. According to early official sources, his father's first name was Arthur.

3. According to George L. Fox biographer Laurence Senelick, "Harry Fox was lying" (personal e-mail correspondence, July 23, 2008). Best known for his Humpty Dumpty pantomime, the Boston-born Fox (1825–1877) was placed in an insane asylum in Somerville, Massachusetts, and shortly thereafter died at his sister's Cambridge home. See "Brilliant Revival of the Clown in the Drama," *Atlanta Constitution*, October 30, 1904. By the way, on his 1937 Social Security application, Harry claimed that George L. Fox was his *father* and that Mary McLean was his mother. According to the application, Fox was living at 1414 North Fuller in Hollywood.

4. Julie Malnig, *Dancing Till Dawn*, p. 26.

5. Richard M. Stephenson & Joseph Iaccarino, *The Complete Book of Ballroom Dancing*, p. 34.

6. Ibid., p. 32.

7. Gary Chapman, *The Delectable Dollies*, p. 36.

8. Ibid., p. 41.

9. Ibid., p. 47.

10. Diamond Jim Brady remembered Harry Fox in his will, bequeathing him a ring set containing 14 diamonds.

11. Gary Chapman, *The Delectable Dollies*, p. 47–48.

12. Ibid., p. 48.

13. *Stop! Look! Listen!* [review]. *New York Clipper*, January 1, 1915.

14. "Harry Fox Reveals Secret of Making All of 'Em Laugh," *Duluth News Tribune*, February 13, 1916.

15. "Dolly Sister Sues,"*Baltimore American*, June 12, 1917. Specifically named was actress Fay Atkins. For the reconciliation, see "Call Off a Divorce Suit," *Kansas City Star* [Missouri], June 28, 1917.

16. "Actress Regrets Divorce Action," *Philadelphia Enquirer*, July 15, 1917.

17. Gary Chapman, *The Delectable Dollies*, pp. 78–79.

18. Ibid., p. 79.

19. Ibid., pp. 79–80.

20. Harry apparently had no negative feelings. In 1936 he helped Jenny prove her American citizenship by writing affidavits on her behalf. Jenny committed suicide on June 1941 after several marriages and a disfiguring automobile accident. In 1945, the Betty Grable-June Haver musical *The Dolly Sisters* was released and in 1946 Fox unsuccessfully sued, claiming that his depiction in the film was belittling. Harry's third wife Beatrice Fox White also unsuccessfully sued.

21. "Their Hearts Keep Time with Their Feet," *Philadelphia Enquirer*, December 11, 1921.

22. This information came from Beatrice Curtis Fox's 1924 passport application. According to the application, Fox and Curtis married on February 5, 1921, which would have meant that Fox was still married to Dolly. It is more likely Fox and Curtis married on February 5, 1922, but it still leaves a mystery about why they lied on the passport.

23. "Harry Fox and Pretty Partner at Orpheum Tell Secrets," *Salt Lake Telegram*, November 26, 1920.

24. Richard M. Stephenson & Joseph Iaccarino, *The Complete Book of Ballroom Dancing*, p. 35.

25. From the February 9, 1922, *Oregonia*: "The marriage of Beatrice Curtis and Harry Fox took place in Akron, Ohio, last week. Miss Fox has been appearing with Mr. Fox in vaudeville.... The engagement of Miss Curtis to Mr. Fox has been known among their friends for quite some time. The new Mrs. Fox is a petite blonde. She appeared here last season at the Orpheum with Harry Fox."

26. *The Fox and the Bee* is also known as *Harry Fox and Beatrice Curtis in The Fox and the Bee*. Curtis sometimes used the nickname Bee.

27. Curtis occasionally appeared in films up until 1940. She died in 1963.

28. "Evelyn Brent Back Again in Syracuse, Plans Visit to Scene of Her Childhood," *Syracuse Herald*, May 26, 1933.

29. Ibid.

30. Ibid.

31. Ibid.

32. Ibid.

33. Ibid.

34. Chester B. Bahn, "Evelyn Brent Graces Stage at Paramount," *Syracuse Herald*, May 27, 1933.

35. Ibid.

36. "Tri-C Hostess," *Syracuse Herald*, May 25, 1933.

37. "More Tax Liens Files," *Los Angeles Times*, September 11, 1933, p. A3. Other stars who were named, and the amounts they owed: Priscilla Dean, $7100 (covering the years

1924–1926); Tallulah Bankhead, $104 (1931); Reginald Denny, $336 (1932); Fifi D'Orsay, $910 (1932); Monta Bell, $673 (1928); Natalie Moorhead, $143 (1932).

38. Chester B. Bahn, "Evelyn Brent Tells Frankly What's the Matter with Hollywood." *Syracuse Herald*, October 1, 1933.

39. Ibid.

40. Ibid.

41. Ibid.

42. Richard Griffith, *The Movie Stars*, p. 378. Wherever Brent appeared, it seemed the local mayor wanted to provide her with the key to the city. In Lawrence, Massachusetts, she ended up with a kiss instead when Mayor Billy White claimed he had run out of keys. ("Mayor White Had No Key But Made Good with Kiss," *Portsmouth Herald* [New Hampshire], October 26, 1933.)

43. Richard Griffith, *The Movie Stars*, p. 378.

44. Ted Le Berthon, "Star, Once a Resident of Syracuse, Reveals Her Early Struggles," *Syracuse Herald*, August 17, 1930.

45. "Film Siren Files Bankruptcy Plea," *Los Angeles Times*, September 1, 1933, p. 3.

46. "Business Records, Bankruptcy Proceedings, Southern District," *New York Times*, September 2, 1933, p. 16.

47. Other sources referred to the address as 344.

48. Philip Scheuer, "A Town Called Hollywood," *Los Angeles Times*, April 1, 1934, p. A1.

49. Jimmy Starr, *Los Angeles Evening Herald Express*, April 23, 1934.

50. "Theater News by Bildad," *Wisconsin State Journal* [Madison], May 3, 1934.

51. Louella O. Parsons, "Stage, Screen to Produce Play for Broadway Films," *San Antonio Light*, March 31, 1934, p. 3A.

52. Jerry Hoffman, *Los Angeles Examiner*, May 31, 1934. See also "Evelyn Brent and Husband Separate After Disagreement," *Syracuse Herald*, May 31, 1934.

53. Fred Curran, "Success Is Luck, Says Miss Brent, Tired of 'Trash,'" *Wisconsin State Journal*, May 3, 1934. In a September 30, 1928, *Davenport Democrat and Leader* article, she called Janet Gaynor "the finest motion picture actress in America."

54. Gladys Hall, "When a Star Falls," *Movie Mirror*, 1935, p. 83.

55. Ibid.

56. Carroll Nye, "Dial Gets New Political Feature," *Los Angeles Times*, July 23, 1934, p. 16.

57. Louella O. Parsons, *Los Angeles Examiner*, August 20, 1934.

58. Dan Thomas, "Evelyn Brent

May Get That Delayed Break," *Lima News* [Ohio], July 30, 1934.

59. "Miss Brent Testing," *Los Angeles Times*, September 12, 1934, p. 18.

60. Muriel Babcock, *Los Angeles Examiner*, December 26, 1934.

61. Dan Thomas, "Hollywood News and Gossip," *Lima News* [Ohio], September 6, 1934.

62. Dorothy Herzog, "The Strange Case of Miss Brent," unknown publication.

63. Ibid.

64. Louella O. Parsons, *Los Angeles Examiner*, November 1, 1934.

65. "Miss Brent Fights Suit," *Los Angeles Times*, April 6, 1935, p. A3. Sunshine Duncan was represented by Samuel S. Gelberg.

66. "Court Quashes Action Against Evelyn Brent," *Los Angeles Times*, May 8, 1935, p. A3.

67. Harrison Carroll, *Los Angeles Evening Herald Express*, May 20, 1935.

## Chapter 9

1. Gladys Hall, "When a Star Falls," *Movie Mirror*, 1935, p. 83.

2. Sidney Skolsky, *Hollywood Citizen News*, January 23, 1935.

3. Read Kendall, "Around and About Hollywood," *Los Angeles Times*, March 8, 1935, p. 13.

4. "Screen Folk Sued on Tax," *Los Angeles Times*, March 21, 1935, p. A1.

5. Gladys Hall, "When a Star Falls," *Movie Mirror*, 1935, p. 62.

6. Ibid., p. 83.

7. Ibid., p. 83.

8. Ibid., p. 83.

9. Ibid., p. 62.

10. Bill Daniels. "Talkie Topics." *Ogdensburg Advance* [Utah], October 19, 1935, p. 4.

11. *The Nitwits* [review], *Variety*, June 26, 1935.

12. Dan Thomas, "Hollywood Gossip," *Wisconsin Rapids Daily Tribune*, April 11, 1935.

13. The August 7, 1927, *San Antonio Express* reported that Brent enjoyed menthol cigarettes. Another columnist mentioned seeing Brent at the RKO dining area smoking "a carved ivory cigarette holder about a yard long" ("Up and Down the Boulevard," *Wisconsin State Journal* [Madison], August 24, 1930). Grace Siwek reported that Brent was not a smoker in the 1960s when she met her.

14. Dan Thomas, "Hollywood Gossip," *Wisconsin Rapids Daily Tribune*, April 11, 1935.

15. *Symphony of Living* [review], *Variety*, July 3, 1935.

16. *Symphony of Living* pressbook,

"Evelyn Brent Back After Stage Tour," 1935.

17. Robin Coons, "Evelyn Brent Content to Live Easy Going Life Free from Worry," *Amarillo Globe*, July 19, 1935.

18. "Evelyn Brent Must Pay 'Back Wages,'" *Oakland Tribune*, November 12, 1935. The trial was held in Municipal Judge Tyrrell's courtroom. The plaintiff's case was brought by Joseph J. Creem, chief of the division of labor statistics and law enforcement of the State Department of Labor.

19. "Actress Loses Employees' Suit," *Los Angeles Times*, November 12, 1935, p. A16.

20. "Evelyn Brent Wishes She Had Taken Pay Cut," *Los Angeles Examiner*, January 5, 1936.

21. *It Couldn't Have Happened—But It Did* [review], *Variety*, September 16, 1936.

22. *The President's Mystery* [review], *Variety*, October 21, 1936.

23. Norbert Lusk, "Film Information," *Los Angeles Times*, October 25, 1936, p. C3.

24. Tom Dardis, *Some Time in the Sun*, p. 151.

25. Ibid., pp. 151–52.

26. *Song of the Trail* [review], *Variety*, December 23, 1936.

27. "Kermit Maynard Rescuer," *Mansfield News Journal* [Ohio], July 24, 1936.

28. John Kobal, *People Will Talk*, p. 305.

29. The character's name, Merle, may have been a variation of Brent's birth initials M.E.R. In 1937, Dorothy Herzog was living in New York City. In her Social Security application, filled out in October of that year, she stated that she lived at 344 West 72nd Street. This is the address for the Chatsworth Apartments designed by John E. Scharsmith and built around the turn of the century. According to *The Guide to New York City Landmarks* by Andrew Dolkart and Matthew A. Postal, the building was designated as historic in 1984. "Prominently sited at the southern end of Riverside Park and Drive, the Beaux-Arts Chatsworth and its annex were built to house the affluent families moving into Upper West Side apartment houses in the early 20th century. The Chatsworth originally offered such amenities as a conservatory, a sun parlor, a café, a billiards room, a barber shop, a beauty salon, and electric bus service along West 72nd Street to and from Central Park" (p. 141). The building is still a desirable address. It's not unusual for an apartment to rent for more than $4,000 a month.

30. "Stars Move Frequently to New Homes," *Los Angeles Times*, December 19, 1937, p. C1. Although we suspect a connection to Al, we could find no information on Virginia Wertheimer.

31. Barry Paris, *Louise Brooks*, p. 378.

32. Lloyd Pantages, "I Cover Hollywood," *Los Angeles Examiner*, March 17, 1937.

33. Barry Paris, *Louise Brooks*, p. 378.

34. "Two Ex-Stars in Films Again," *Los Angeles Times*, April 2, 1937, p. 10.

35. Barry Paris, *Louise Brooks*, p. 378.

36. *King of Gamblers* [review], *Variety*, July 7, 1937.

37. "Best Performances in Current Pictures," *Los Angeles Times*, May 30, 1937, p. C1.

38. Norbert Lusk, "Unheralded Film Lauded by Broadway," *Los Angeles Times*, July 11, 1937, p. C3.

39. Louella O. Parsons, *San Antonio Light*, April 15, 1937.

40. *Film Daily*, October 12, 1936.

41. *Hopalong Cassidy Returns* [review], *Los Angeles Times*, January 6, 1937.

42. Obera H. Rawles, "Intimate Facts About Screen Stars of Yesterday," *Chester Times* [Pennsylvania], January 20, 1937.

43. *Jungle Jim* [review], *Variety*, February 24, 1937.

44. Paula Fox, *Borrowed Finery*, p. 103.

45. Read Kendall, "Around and About in Hollywood," *Los Angeles Times*, July 27, 1937.

46. "Jimmy Fidler in Hollywood," *Chronicle-Telegram* [Elyria, Ohio], August 23, 1937.

47. Harriet Parsons, *Fresno Bee*, July 26, 1937.

48. Louella O. Parsons, "News of Stage and Screen," *Fresno Bee*, August 28, 1938.

49. Richard Lamparski, *Whatever Became Of...?* radio interview, WBAI-FM, January 7, 1969.

50. Harrison Carroll, "Behind the Scenes in Hollywood," *Ogdensburg Advance* [Utah], September 11, 1937, p. 5.

51. *Apt Pupil*, *Brownsville Herald* [Texas], October 18, 1937.

52. Philip Leibfried and Chei Mi Lane, *Anna May Wong: A Complete Guide to Her Film, Stage, Radio and Television Work*.

53. Brian Taves, *Robert Florey*, p. 206.

54. Graham Russell Gao Hodges, *Anna May Wong: From Laundryman's Daughter to Hollywood Legend*, p. 184.

55. Dale Armstrong, "Mike Waits for Armstrong," *Los Angeles Times*, November 23, 1937, p. 14.

56. "Actress in Comeback," *Reno Evening Gazette* [Nevada], November 30, 1938.

57. Harrison Carroll, "Behind the Scenes in Hollywood," *Ogdensburg Advance* [Utah], September 30, 1938, p. 2.

58. Jimmy Fidler, "Anne Shirley, Suspended on Refusal to Take Role, Aids Unknown to Fame," *Charleston Daily Mail* [West Virginia], September 30, 1938.

59. *Hollywood Citizen News*, September 20, 1938.

60. "Western Film Melodrama Given Preview," *Los Angeles Times*, November 12, 1938, p. A7.

61. Philip K. Scheuer, *Tip-Off Girls* [review], *Los Angeles Times*, May 13, 1938, p. 15.

62. Richard Lamparski, *Whatever Became Of...?* radio interview, WBAI-FM, January 7, 1969.

63. Frederick C. Othman, "Stayed Away Too Long," *Corpus Christi Times*, January 21, 1938.

64. *Hollywood Citizen News*, January 4, 1939.

65. "Sentimental Directors Go for Old-Time Favorites," *Los Angeles Times*, March 26, 1939, p. C4.

66. Hedda Hopper, "Hedda Hopper's Hollywood," *Los Angeles Times*, May 19, 1939, p. A17.

67. Robbin Coons, "Today in Hollywood," *Lowell Sun* [Massachusetts], March 23, 1939.

68. Evelyn Brent, "Glamorous Screen Star in Person with *Streets de Paree*." *Burlington Daily Times-News* [North Carolina], November 6, 1939.

69. *Zanesville Signal* [Ohio], September 13, 1939.

70. Frank B. Allen, "Trouping Is New to Evelyn Brent But She Likes It," *Waterloo Courier [Iowa]*, January 26, 1940, p. 3.

71. Ibid.

72. "Identify Evelyn Brent!" [ad], *The Times Recorder* [Zanesville, Ohio], September 16, 1939.

73. "Evelyn Brent Noted Hollywood Star to Appear at State," *Morning Herald* [Uniontown, Pennsylvania], September 16, 1939.

74. Jean Gray Scott, "Evelyn Brent Receives Staff Member of *Times-News* in Her Dressing Room at the Theatre," *Burlington Daily Times-News* [North Carolina], November 8, 1939.

75. Ibid.

76. Ibid.

77. Frank B. Allen, "Trouping Is New to Evelyn Brent But She Likes It," *Waterloo Courier [Iowa]*, January 26, 1940, p. 3.

78. Ibid.

79. Ibid.

80. Ibid.

81. Ibid.

82. Jimmy Fidler, "Movieland," *Appleton Post-Crescent* [Wisconsin], October 7, 1940.

83. Paul Harrison, "Harrison in Hollywood," *Fitchburg Sentinel* [Massachusetts], September 24, 1940.

84. Paul Harrison, "Harrison in Hollywood," *Brownsville Herald* [Texas], September 6, 1941.

85. Philip K. Scheuer, "Town Called Hollywood," *Los Angeles Times*, June 1, 1941, p. C3.

86. *Forced Landing* [review], *Los Angeles Times*, July 1, 1941, p. 16.

87. *Film Daily*, July 30, 1941.

88. Louella O. Parsons, *Fresno Bee*, January 13, 1941.

89. Lee Shippey, "Lee Side o' L.A.," *Los Angeles Times*, October 13, 1941, p. A4.

90. Philip K. Scheuer, "Town Called Hollywood," *Los Angeles Times*, November 16, 1941, p. C3.

91. Robin Coons, "In Hollywood," *Gastonia Daily Gazette* [North Carolina], October 30, 1941.

92. *Film Daily*, May 6, 1942.

93. Louella O. Parsons, "Movie-Go-Round," *San Antonio Light*, April 5, 1942.

94. Untitled, unsigned article, *Daily News* [Huntington, Pennsylvania], April 24, 1942.

95. Sheilah Graham, "Hollywood in Person," *Dallas Morning News*, May 16, 1943.

96. DeWitt Bodeen, "Evelyn Brent," *Films in Review*, p. 349.

97. Doug McClelland, *The Golden Age of "B" Movies*, p. 176.

98. David Hayes and Brent Walker, *The Films of the Bowery Boys*, p. 80.

99. Edwin Schallert, "Evelyn Brent Returning in Outdoor Opus," *Los Angeles Times*, August 16, 1946, p. A7.

100. *New York Times*, August 19, 1946, p. 28.

101. Louella Parsons, *Syracuse Herald-Journal*, September 10, 1946.

102. An interesting character, Al Wertheimer was reportedly a member of the Detroit mobster organization "The Purple Gang." Author Paul R. Kavieff described the Gang as "one of the most ruthless organized crime groups in U.S. history. From the chaotic streets of Detroit's lower east side, this group of predominantly Jewish gangsters would muscle their way into the underworld by 1927, where they would remain through a five-year reign of terror. It left an estimated five hundred unsolved murders in its wake." According to David Wallace in *Hollywoodland*, some think that Lucky Luciano ordered the 1935 death of Thelma Todd, and the hit was carried out by the Purple Gang. Wertheimer was seriously in-jured in the mysterious November 20, 1937, automobile accident that claimed the life of Eddie Mannix's wife, 37-year-old Beatrice (sometimes referred to as Bernice). The accident happened at around 2:30 in the morning after the couple finished playing "bridge" at Wertheimer's night club, The Dunes, and were on their way in Wertheimer's convertible to a party at producer Joseph Schenck's Palm Springs house. "Wertheimer was traveling at a moderate rate of speed and struck the soft shoulder of the road when he turned out to avoid striking another automobile. His convertible roadster overturned.... Her body [Mannix] was crushed into the desert sand." See "Social Leader in Hollywood Dies in Auto Accident," *Waterloo Daily Courier* [Iowa], November 21, 1937. One has to wonder why Schenck would have had anything to do with Wertheimer. In 1937, during Schenck's income tax evasion trial, Wertheimer testified that he once turned Schenck's 7269 Hollywood Boulevard mansion into a casino while Schenck was in Europe. See "Hollywood Man Tells of Changing Magnate's Mansion Into Gambling House at Income Tax Trial," *Galveston Daily News*, March 14, 1941. By the way, Emil Jannings lived at that address in the 1920s.

103. Westbrook Pegler, "Fair Enough," *El Paso Herald-Post*, April 1, 1936.

104. "Cross-Suit Filed by Evelyn Brent," *Los Angeles Times*, April 29, 1947, p. 6.

105. "Income of Star Whittled," *San Antonio Light*, April 22, 1947.

106. "Ex-Screen Figures Trade Charges," *Wisconsin State Journal* [Madison], May 3, 1947. See also the *Los Angeles Evening Herald Express*, May 2, 1947.

107. "Ex-Producer with New Divorce Will Wed Today," *Los Angeles Times*, June 11, 1947, p. A1. This article repeatedly misspells Wertheimer "Wortheimer."

108. John Kobal, *People Will Talk*, p. 110.

109. Letter to Editor, Harry D. Edwards, *Time*, November 28, 1949. Edwards listed his residence as Hollywood, California.

110. Paul Parla, "Donna Martell: From Indian Princess to Astronaut," *Classic Images*, September 1997.

111. James King, telephone interview with Donna Martell, July 28, 2007.

112. Louella O. Parsons, "Betty Hutton Is to Star in the Broadway Story Picture," *Modesto Bee*, August 31, 1948.

113. Louella O. Parsons, "Holly-wood," *Galveston News*, March 3, 1950. According to Parsons, Brent "retired after a serious operation in 1942."

114. DeWitt Bodeen, "Evelyn Brent," *Films in Review*, p. 350.

## Chapter 10

1. DeWitt Bodeen, "Evelyn Brent," *Films in Review*, p. 350.

2. Erskine Johnson, "In Hollywood," *Portsmouth Herald* [New Hampshire], September 14, 1953.

3. "Chatterbox," *Dallas Morning News*, October 2, 1957.

4. *Lima News* [Ohio], July 25, 1959.

5. John Kobal, *People Will Talk*, p. 110.

6. Telephone interview, August 18, 2008.

7. "Double Celebration," *Winnipeg Free Press* [Manitoba], December 17, 1960.

8. John Kobal, *People Will Talk*, p. 108.

9. Mike Connolly, "Studs Lonigan Sole U.S. Entry," *Star-News* [Pasadena], October 27, 1960.

10. Louella O. Parsons, "Doris Day with Como Newest Plan," *San Antonio Light*, March 16, 1961.

11. Fred H. Russell, "Golden Era Stars Will be Seen on Series," *Bridgeport Post* [Connecticut], July 2, 1963.

12. Mike Connolly, "Notes from Hollywood," *Independent* (Pasadena), January 26, 1965. Mary Pickford is credited with founding the Motion Picture Country Home; Jean Hersholt also played a part in its success. We have found no other evidence that Evelyn Brent was a co-founder.

13. John Barbour, "Where Hollywood Grows Old," *Pacific Stars and Stripes* [Tokyo, Japan], August 18, 1978.

14. Louella O. Parsons, "Hollywood ... Beatty's Top Billing Demand Over Wife-to-Be Is Denied," *Anderson Daily Bulletin* [Indiana], February 18, 1965.

15. Richard Lamparski, *Whatever Became Of...?* radio interview, WBAI-FM, January 7, 1969.

16. According to one 1930 article, Brent's chauffeur "matched" her black car and white fur interior. "Her Negro chauffeur carries on the black-and-white color scheme, not only with his ebony face and ivory teeth, but in his uniform of smartest black, piped with white." Margaret Chute, "The Brent's Due," p. 26.

17. Richard Lamparski, *Whatever Became Of...?* radio interview, WBAI-FM, January 7, 1969.

18. Ibid.

19. Ibid.

20. Richard Lamparski, *Whatever Became Of...?* (Third Series), p. 207.

21. Dorothy Herzog died at the age of 89 on January 29, 1989, in New York.

22. Information and quotes were obtained in three telephone interviews with Grace Siwek (April 20, April 24, and May 8, 2008).

23. All quotes from Dick Balduzzi are from an August 18, 2008, telephone interview.

24. Ted LeBerthon, "School Teacher Career Halted for Screen Life," *Los Angeles Record*, June 24, 1930. While doing publicity for *Attorney for the Defense* in 1932, Brent told an interviewer that she still had—and used—two prayer books she received as gifts for her first communion 20 years before. "They are the only two mementoes of her childhood.... She cherishes them far more highly than a mother cherishes the first pair of baby shoes her child wears.... Since that time those prayer books have stayed wrapped except for one occasion each year, the anniversary of that first religious moment. Then in the sanctuary of a Catholic church in Hollywood that will stay nameless by Miss Brent's request, she secrets herself and spend [sic] an hour alone with her prayer books." (Strand, *Key West Citizen*, August 27, 1932.)

25. Dick Balduzzi said that Brent was by no means a heavy drinker. He also said that Brent was still smoking when Konrad met her but eventually stopped due to health problems.

26. John Kobal, *People Will Talk*, p. 99.

27. Grace Siwek remembered Dorothy and Evelyn owning a dog and a cat. She specifically recalled them sending her a photograph of the cat lounging in their fruit bowl. Dick Balduzzi also remembered the pets. According to Balduzzi, the dog died, but they had the cat for many years. "It was their baby. They pampered that cat like you wouldn't believe. Evelyn was very good about feeding it all the time, taking care of it."

28. John Kobal, *People Will Talk*, p. 102.

29. All quotes from Wesley Musick were obtained in a June 17, 2008, telephone interview.

30. Brent's star is located at 6548 Hollywood Boulevard.

31. Personal letter, Mona Malden, June 28, 2008.

32. Anthony Dexter played Rudolph Valentino in *Valentino* (1951).

33. Clive Hirschhorn, email correspondence, April 3, 2007.

34. All David Chierichetti quotes are from an August 17, 2008, telephone interview.

35. Most sources give Brent's height as 5'2".

36. Lou Valentino, email correspondence, April 2, 2007.

37. Anthony Slide, personal letter, February 12, 2007.

38. DeWitt Bodeen, "Evelyn Brent," *Films in Review*, p. 349.

39. Cynthia Lindsay, *Dear Boris*, p. 28.

40. "Evelyn Brent Rosary Tonight," *Pasadena Star-News*, June 6, 1975, p. A3. Brent's last address was 1904 Manning Avenue.

41. The location is Lot B-698, Grave 12.

42. Fox is buried in Lot B-697, Grave 12, and Brent is in Lot B-698, Grave 12. Dorothy Konrad, 91, died on December 29, 2003.

43. James Card, quoted in Victoria A. Wilson, "Silent Knight," *Interview*, November 1, 1994.

44. Anthony Slide, personal letter, February 12, 2007.

45. Buck Rainey, *Sweethearts of the Sage*, p. 110.

46. James Card, quote in Victoria A. Wilson, "Silent Knight," *Interview*, November 1, 1994.

47. Roy Liebman, *From Silents to Sound*, pp. 44–45.

48. DeWitt Bodeen, "Evelyn Brent," *Films in Review*, p. 339.

49. John Kobal, *People Will Talk*, p. 117.

# Filmography Notes

1. Harry Waldman, *Maurice Tourneur*, p. 26.

2. Alice Guy Blaché, *The Memoirs of Alice Guy Blaché*, p. 80.

3. "The Film Girl, Seen on the Screen," *Syracuse Herald*, September 2, 1916.

4. "Stellar Cast Seen in *The Iron Woman*," *The Iowa Recorder* [Greene], March 28, 1917.

5. *Who's Your Neighbor?* [advertisement], *Los Angeles Times*, December 4, 1917, p. II3.

6. Tom Benjey, *Keep A-Goin'*, p. 173.

7. Ibid., p. 185.

8. Jody Lawrence-Turner, "Fire Destroys Building with a Past: Flames from stolen car ruin park equipment," *Spokesman Review* [Spokane, Washington], November 8, 2006.

9. Tom Benjey, *Keep A-Goin'*, p. 175.

10. "Movie Mysteries Bared Interesting 'Inside Dope' Gleaned at Local Studio," *Daily Kennebuc Journal* [Augusta, Maine], December 22, 1919.

11. "Attractions at Merrimack Square," *Lowell Sun* [Massachusetts], April 12, 1924.

12. "Best Pictures," *Manitoba Free Press*, September 12, 1924.

13. David Butler, *David Butler*, p. 29.

14. "Society Crowd Is Caught by Camera," *Logansport Pharos-Times* [Indiana], June 25, 1924.

15. Rialto, *Hamilton Daily News* [Ohio], December 18, 1924.

16. John Kobal, *People Will Talk*, p. 111.

17. Grace Kingsley, "Flashes," *Los Angeles Times*, July 19, 1924, p. 7.

18. John Kobal, *People Will Talk*, p. 111.

19. "Theatres Today," *Albuquerque Morning Journal*, July 28, 1925.

20. "Stage People," *Kansas City Star* [Missouri], June 21, 1925.

21. "Screen Detective Has Unusual Record," *Los Angeles Times*, May13, 1913, p. 11.

22. "Buelah's Hollywood Letter," *Syracuse Herald*, July 12, 1925.

23. Ron Haydock, *Deerstalker! Holmes and Watson on Screen*, p. 65.

24. Rachel Low, *History of British Film: Volume IV, The History of the British Film 1918–1929*, p. 139.

25. Ibid., p. 140.

26. Frank Tuttle, *They Started Talking*, pp. 57–58.

27. "At the Movies," *Park Record*, January 1, 1927.

28. "New Football Hero Bucking Line in Films," *Los Angeles Times*, December 12, 1926, p. C31.

29. James Card, *Seductive Cinema*, p. 243.

30. Ibid., p. 303.

31. "Von Sternberg to Make It," *Los Angeles Times*, March 5, 1927, p. A6.

32. Josef von Sternberg, *Fun in a Chinese Laundry*, p. 215.

33. "Uptown Has *Underworld*," *Los Angeles Times*, September 2, 1927, p. A9.

34. Josef von Sternberg, *Fun in a Chinese Laundry*, p. 217.

35. Kevin Brownlow, *Behind the Mask of Innocence*, p. 204.

36. Ibid., p. 206.

37. Josef von Sternberg, *Fun in a Chinese Laundry*, p. 216.

38. Ibid., p. 216.

39. Ibid., p. 216.

40. Thomas Leitch, *Crime Movies*, p. 28.

41. John Kobal, *People Will Talk*, p. 112.

42. Ibid., p. 114. Apparently others thought Bancroft a bit of a dummy. Budd Schulberg quoted his father, producer B.P., as saying that Bancroft "had the courage and the simple faith of profound ignorance." Budd Schulberg, *Moving Pictures*, p. 247.

43. James Card, *Seductive Cinema*, pp. 243–44.

44. Budd Schulberg, *Moving Pictures*, p. 242.

45. Dorothy Herzog, "Backstage at Hollywood," *Waterloo Evening Courier* [Iowa], January 19, 1929.

46. "A Visit to a Studio Underworld Reveals Shooting Movie Stars," *Kansas City Star* [Missouri], May 27, 1928.

47. Kevin Brownlow, *The Parade's Gone By*, p. 195.

48. "Theatres," *Ogden Standard-Examiner* [Utah], February 15, 1928.

49. Homer Dickens, *The Films of Gary Cooper*, p. 46.

50. Frank Thompson, *Lost Films*, p. 208.

51. "City Springs Up Amid California Sand Dunes," *Los Angeles Times*, July 10, 1927, p. 19.

52. Ibid.

53. Ibid.

54. "Practicality Is Director's Guiding Star," *Los Angeles Times*, January 29, 1928, p. C10.

55. "Desert Battle Sequences Require Three Full Days," *Los Angeles Times*, July 24, 1927, p. 19.

56. "Official Tells Difficulty in Finding Steeds," *Los Angeles Times*, September 18, 1927, p. 32.

57. Frank Thompson, *Lost Films*, p. 209.

58. "Practicality Is Director's Guiding Star," *Los Angeles Times*, January 29, 1928, p. C10.

59. Josef von Sternberg, *Fun in a Chinese Laundry*, p. 131.

60. James Card, *Seductive Cinema*, p. 237.

61. Kevin Brownlow, *The Parade's Gone By*, p. 198.

62. "Emil Jannings in New Role of Ex-Despot," *New York Times*, January 22, 1928.

63. Ernst Lubitsch also made a Russian-themed film, *The Patriot* (1928) with Emil Jannings, now a lost film. Brent was at one time a cast member but was replaced by Florence Vidor. *The Patriot* received several Oscar nominations, and Hanns Kraly won for Best Writing.

64. Josef von Sternberg, *Fun in a Chinese Laundry*, p. 127.

65. Ibid., pp. 127–28.

66. Ibid., p. 129.

67. Ibid., p. 130.

68. Ibid., pp. 132–33.

69. "Foreign Words Believed Aid to Film Stars," *Los Angeles Times*, October 30, 1927, p. 34.

70. John Kobal, *People Will Talk*, pp. 115–16.

71. "Revolution in Film City Held More Dangerous," *Los Angeles Times*, February 27, 1928, p. A7.

72. "Emil Jannings in New Role of Ex-Despot," *New York Times*, January 22, 1928.

73. Kevin Brownlow, *The Parade's Gone By*, p. 197.

74. "Inspiration, Perspiration Tale Retold," *Los Angeles Times*, April 9, 1928, p. A7.

75. "Actors Throw Discs in Between 'Shots,'" *Los Angeles Times*, April 12, 1928, p. A11.

76. Ivan Butler, *Silent Magic: Rediscovering the Silent Film Era*, p. 167.

77. Budd Schulberg, *Moving Pictures*, p. 243.

78. Ibid., p. 244.

79. Ibid., p. 244.

80. "At the Theaters," *Port Arthur News* [Texas], August 9, 1928

81. Adam Bernstein, "Silent Films Speak Loudly for Hughes," p. Y06.

82. Luke Cosgrave, *Theater Tonight*, p. 228.

83. Ibid.

84. Donald Crafton, *The Talkies*, p. 285.

85. Ibid., p. 286.

86. Alexander Walker, *The Shattered Silents*, p. 105.

87. Ibid., p. 106.

88. "Supernumeraries Taboo," *Los Angeles Times*, August 22, 1928, p. A9.

89. "Screen Tests Given Gowns Worn in Movies," *Vidette-Messenger* [Valparaiso, Indiana], April 19, 1929.

90. "Broadway on Screen," *New York Times*, May 9, 1929, p. x4.

91. Ibid.

92. Ibid.

93. Donald Albrecht, *Designing Dreams*, p. 133.

94. "Broadway on Screen," *New York Times*, May 9, 1929, p. x4.

95. Donald Albrecht, *Designing Dreams*, p. 133.

96. Ibid., pp. 150–51.

97. "At the Movies," *Roosevelt* [Utah] *Standard*, November 28, 1929.

98. "Lonesome for the White Way? See Universal City," *Los Angeles Times*, January 20, 1929, p. C27.

99. William K. Everson, *American Silent Film*, p. 338.

100. Another article claimed the amount paid for the rights was $275,000. This same article reported that the production cost was $1.5 million. See "Record Price Paid," *Monitor Index-and Democrat* [Moberley, Missouri], October 12, 1929.

101. Richard Barrios, *A Song in the Dark*, p. 95.

102. "Chorus Numbers Called Feature of Broadway," *Los Angeles Times*, June 28, 1929, p. A11.

103. William K. Everson, *American Silent Film*, p. 314.

104. Richard Barrios, *A Song in the Dark*, p. 98.

105. Kenneth L. Geist, *Pictures Will Talk*, p. 29.

106. Ibid.

107. "Best Scenes of Films Cutups Never Pictured," *Syracuse Herald*, June 15, 1930.

108. "Chester B. Bahn's Stage and Film Chat," *Syracuse Herald*, June 10, 1929.

109. Richard Barrios, *A Song in the Dark*, p. 267.

110. Helen and Olive Parish, "Darkened Rooms, Thriller, Deals with 'Mediums,'" *Atlanta Constitution*, November 15, 1929, p. 11.

111. "Gasnier Finds Talkies Easier," *Syracuse Herald*, October 13, 1929.

112. "Cameraman's Work Due to Skill of Painter," *Los Angeles Times*, September 15, 1929, p. 25. See also Frederick A. Chase's "Ancient Artist Invented Light for Hollywood," *Olean Times* [New York], October 11, 1929.

113. Kenneth L. Geist, *Pictures Will Talk*, p. 33.

114. "Scouting the Sinema," January 6, 1930, *Los Angeles Evening Herald*.

115. *Jack Oakie's Double Takes*, p. 51.

116. Fay Wray, *On the Other Hand*, p. 104.

117. Scott Eyman, *Ernst Lubitsch: Laughter in Paradise*, p. 160.

118. "Fish Net Motifs of Brilliants in Gown," *Ogden Standard-Examiner* [Utah], February 25, 1930.

119. John Kobal, *People Will Talk*, p. 111.

120. Alexander Walker, *The Shattered Silents*, p. 186.

121. Louella O. Parsons, *Los Angeles Examiner*, April 22, 1930.

122. Louella O. Parsons, "Ban on Big House in Ohio Is Surprise," *San Antonio Light*, July 31, 1930.

123. "Beach Film to Depict Salmon Run in Alaska," *Los Angeles Times*, August 8, 1930, p. 11.

124. "Olden Days in Bay City Now Shown," *Los Angeles Times*, December 21, 1930, p. B23.

125. Ibid.

126. "Evelyn Brent Stars in Quimby Show," *Times Recorder* [Zanesville, Ohio], September 22, 1931.

127. "Evelyn Brent Plays Lead in Pagan Lady," *Los Angeles Times*, October 28, 1931, p. A9.

128. Elizabeth Yeaman, *Hollywood Daily Citizen*, June 3, 1931.

129. Frances Denton, "Must They Be Selfish to Win Screen Fame," *Photoplay*, November 1931, p. 37.

130. Ibid., pp. 37, 123.

131. Alma Whitaker, "Director's Whip Rules Feminine Rough-House," *Los Angeles Times*, January 25, 1931, p. B13.

132. "War Film Booked at Paramount," *Los Angeles Times*, September 22, 1931, p. A9.

133. Lawrence J. Quirk, *The Complete Films of William Powell*, p. 131.

134. "New Policy for Los Angeles Set," *Los Angeles Times*, December 25, 1932, p. B6.

135. Read Kendall, "Around and About in Hollywood," October 5, 1934, p. 15.

136. *Symphony of Living* pressbook, "Fans to See Rehearsals in Symphony of Living," 1935.

137. Elizabeth Yeaman, *Hollywood Citizen News*, February 27, 1935.

138. Anthony Slide, *Silent Players*, p. 159.

139. Reine Davies, "Hollywood Parade," *Los Angeles Examiner*, July 24, 1936.

140. Brian Taves, *Robert Florey*, p. 195.

141. Ibid., p. 195.

142. Ibid., pp. v–vi.

143. Ibid., p. 51.

144. "The New Pictures," *Time*, October 12, 1936.

145. "Film Actors Save Town from Fire," *Dallas Morning News*, August 29, 1936. *The Los Angeles Times* also reported the story, giving the location as Kernville. See "Film Group Helps Put Out Blaze," *Los Angeles Times*, August 21, 1936, p. 2.

146. "Evelyn Brent Cast," *Los Angeles Examiner*, October 1, 1936.

147. Brian Taves, *Robert Florey*, pp. xi–xii.

148. Ibid., p. 203.

149. Ibid., pp. 203–04.

150. Paula Fox, *Borrowed Finery*, p. 103.

151. Graham Russell Gao Hodges, *Anna May Wong: From Laundryman's Daughter to Hollywood Legend*, p. 186.

152. Philip Leibfried and Chei Mi Lane, *Anna May Wong: A Complete Guide to Her Film, Stage, Radio and Television Work*, p. 115.

153. Peter Underwood, *Horror Man*, p. 108.

154. Philip K. Scheuer, "Town Called Hollywood," *Los Angeles Times*, June 1, 1941, p. C3.

155. Theodore Strauss, "Cowboy and the Lady," *New York Times*, March 16, 1941, p. X5.

156. Louis Berg, "He Went Thataway," *Los Angeles Times*, January 11, 1948, p. E15.

157. "Jimmy Fidler in Hollywood," *Olean Times-Herald* [New York], February 11, 1941.

158. Frank McDonald, imdb.com, retrieved May 26, 2008.

159. Richard Barrios, *Screening Out Gays*, pp. 189–90.

160. Carlos Clarens, *An Illustrated History of Horror and Science-Fiction Films: The Classic Era 1895–1967*, p. 69.

161. Ibid., p. 70.

162. Phil Hardy, *The Encyclopedia of Horror Films*, p. 83.

163. Doug McClelland, *The Golden Age of "B" Movies*, p. 174.

164. Ibid., pp. 174–75.

165. Ibid., p. 176.

166. "Theater Topics," *Nebraska State Journal* [Lincoln], June 20, 1943.

167. Leonard Getz, *From Broadway to the Bowery*, p. 164.

# Bibliography

"Actor Must Be Linguist." *The Ogden* [Utah] *Standard Examiner,* November 16, 1927.

Albert, Katherine. "Temperamental? YES! What of It?" *Photoplay,* 1929.

Albrecht, Donald. *Designing Dreams: Modern Architecture in the Movies.* San Diego: Hennessey & Ingalls, 2000.

Bahn, Chester B. "Evelyn Brent Tells Frankly What's the Matter with Hollywood." *The Syracuse Herald,* October 1, 1933.

Bailey, Paul. *Three Queer Lives: An Alternative Biography of Fred Barnes, Naomi Jacob and Arthur Marshall.* London: Hamish Hamilton, 2001.

Barrios, Richard. *Screened Out: Playing Gay in Hollywood From Edison to Stonewall.* New York: Routledge, 2003.

_____. *A Song in the Dark: The Birth of the Musical Film.* New York: Oxford Press, 1995.

Behlmer, Rudy, and Tony Thomas. *Hollywood's Hollywood: The Movies About the Movies.* Secaucus, N.J.: Citadel, 1979.

Benjey, Tom. *Keep A-Goin': The Life of Lone Star Dietz.* Carlisle, Pa.: Tuxedo Press, 2006.

Berlin, Howard M. *The Charlie Chan Encyclopedia.* Jefferson, N.C.: McFarland, 2000.

Bernstein, Adam. "Silent Films Speak Loudly for Hughes." *Washington Post,* December 12, 2004.

Bickford, Charles. *Bulls Balls Bicycles & Actors.* New York: Paul S. Eriksson, 1965.

Biery, Ruth. "Suicide Never Pays." *Photoplay,* May 1928.

Blaché, Alice Guy. *The Memoirs of Alice Guy Blaché.* Translated by Roberta and Simone Blaché, edited by Anthony Slide. Metuchen, N.J.: Scarecrow, 1986.

Bodeen, DeWitt. "Evelyn Brent: 1899–1975." *Films in Review,* June 1976.

Bojarski, Richard, and Kenneth Beale. *The Films of Boris Karloff.* Secaucus, N.J.: Citadel, 1974.

Bradley, Edwin M. *The First Hollywood Musicals.* Jefferson, N.C.: McFarland, 1996.

Brooks, Louise. "Stardom and Evelyn Brent." Toronto Film Society, January 13, 1975.

Brownlow, Kevin. *Behind the Mask of Innocence.* Berkeley: University of California Press, 1990.

_____. *The Parade's Gone By.* New York: Alfred A. Knopf, 1969.

Bryant, Roger. *William Powell: The Life and Films.* Jefferson, N.C.: McFarland, 2006.

Buehrer, Beverley Bare. *Boris Karloff: A Bio-Bibliography.* Westport, Conn.: Greenwood, 1993.

Butler, David. *David Butler: Interviewed by Irene Kahn Atkins.* Metuchen, N.J.: Scarecrow, 1993.

Butler, Ivan. *Silent Magic: Rediscovering the Silent Film Era.* London: Columbus Books Limited, 1987.

Card, James. *Seductive Cinema: The Art of Silent Film.* Minneapolis: University of Minnesota Press, 1994.

Castelluccio, Frank, and Alvin Walker. *The Other Side of Ethel Mertz: The Life Story of Vivian Vance.* Manchester, Conn.: Knowledge, Ideas & Trends, 1998.

Chan, Anthony B. *Perpetually Cool: The Many Lives of Anna May Wong (1905–1961).* Lanham, Md.: Scarecrow, 2003.

Chapman, Gary. *The Delectable Dollies: The Dolly Sisters, Icons of the Jazz Age.* England: Sutton Publishing, 2006.

Chute, Margaret. "The Brent's Due." *The Picturegoer,* September 1929.

Clarens, Carlos. *Crime Movies: An Illustrated History.* New York: W.W. Norton, 1980.

_____. *An Illustrated History of Horror and Science-Fiction Films: The Classic Era 1895–1967.* New York: Da Capo, 1997.

Cosgrave, Luke. *Theater Tonight.* Hollywood: House-Warven, 1952.

Crafton, Donald. *The Talkies: American Cinema's Transition to Sound 1926–1931.* Berkeley: University of California Press, 1997.

Cuthbertson, Ken. *Inside: The Biography of John Gunther.* Chicago: Bonus Books, 1992.

Dardis, Tom. *Some Time in the Sun: The Hollywood Years of Fitzgerald, Faulkner, Nathanael West, Aldous Huxley, and James Agee.* New York: Scribner's, 1976.

de Mille, Agnes. *Speak to Me, Dance with Me.* Boston: Little, Brown, 1973.

Dickens, Homer. *The Films of Gary Cooper.* New York: Citadel Press, 1970.

Donaldson, Geoffrey. *Of Joy and Sorrow: A Filmography of Dutch Silent Fiction.* Netherlands: Stichting Nederlands Filmmuseum, 1997.

Dooley, Roger. *From Scarface to Scarlett: American Films in the 1930s.* New York: Harcourt Brace Jovanovich, 1979.

Eames, John Douglas. *The Paramount Story: The Complete History of the Studio and its 2,805 Films.* New York: Crown Publishers, 1985.

Easton, Carol. *No Intermissions: The Life of Agnes de Mille.* New York: Da Capo, 2000.

Edwards, Anne. *The DeMilles: An American Family.* New York: Harry N. Abrams, 1988.

Engstead, John. *Star Shots: Fifty Years of Pictures and Stories By One of Hollywood's Greatest Photographers*. New York: E.P. Dutton, 1978.

"Evelyn Brent, Actress, Asks for Divorce." *New York Times*, June 22, 1927.

"Evelyn Brent Gets Divorce." *New York Times*, August 18, 1927.

"Evelyn Brent, 75, Film Star of the 1920's." *New York Times*, June 8, 1975.

"Evelyn Brent Will Play Pearl in *Broadway* Film: Former Syracuse School Girl Picked for Universal's Costly Movie." *Syracuse Herald*, December 19, 1928.

Everson, William K. *American Silent Film*. New York: Da Capo, 1998.

Eyman, Scott. *Ernst Lubitsch: Laughter in Paradise*. New York: Simon & Schuster, 1993.

Faderman, Lillian, and Stuart Timmons. *Gay L.A.: A History of Sexual Outlaws, Power Politics, and Lipstick Lesbians*. New York: Basic Books, 2006.

"Fairbanks and Wife Order Suit for Libel." *New York Times*, October 31, 1923.

Finch, Christopher, and Linda Rosenkrantz. *Gone Hollywood*. Garden City, N.Y.: Doubleday, 1979.

Finler, Joel W. *The Movie Directors Story*. New York: Crescent, 1985.

Fox, Paula. *Borrowed Finery*. New York: Henry Holt, 2001.

Geist, Kenneth L. *Pictures Will Talk: The Life & Films of Joseph L. Mankiewicz*. New York: Da Capo, 1978.

Getz, Leonard. *From Broadway to the Bowery: A History and Filmography of the Dead End Kids, Little Tough Guys, East Side Kids and Bowery Boys Films, with Cast Biographies*. Jefferson, N.C.: McFarland, 2006.

Gifford, Denis. *Karloff: The Man, the Monster, the Movies*. New York: Curtis Books, 1973.

Griffith, Richard. *The Movie Stars*. Garden City, N.Y.: Doubleday, 1970.

_____, ed. *The Talkies: Articles and Illustrations from a Great Fan Magazine 1928–1940*. New York: Dover, 1971.

Hall, Gladys. "Confessions of the Stars: Evelyn Brent Tells Her Untold Story." *Motion Picture Classic*, June 1929.

_____. "What Women Want to Know: They Ask ... Evelyn Brent How to Escape Tragedy." *Motion Picture*, December 1930.

Hanke, Ken. *Charlie Chan at the Movies: History, Filmography, and Criticism*. Jefferson, N.C.: McFarland, 1989.

Hanson, Patricia King, and Gevinson, Alan. *The American Film Institute Catalog of Motion Pictures Produced in the United States: Feature Films, 1931–1940*. Berkeley: University of California Press, 1993.

Hardy, Phil. *The Encyclopedia of Horror Movies*. New York: Harper & Row, 1986.

"Harry Fox Is Dead at 76." *New York Times*, July 21, 1959.

Haydock, Ron. *Deerstalker! Holmes and Watson on Screen*. Metuchen, N.J.: Scarecrow, 1978.

Hayes, David, and Brent Walker. *The Films of The Bowery Boys*. Secaucus, N.J.: Citadel, 1984.

Herzog, Dorothy. *Intimate Strangers*. New York: Macaulay, 1933.

_____. *Some Like It Hot*. New York: Macaulay, 1930.

_____. *Undercover Woman*. New York: The Macaulay Company, 1937.

Hirschhorn, Clive. *The Warner Bros. Story*. New York: Crown Publishers, 1979.

Hodges, Graham Russell Gao. *Anna May Wong: From Laundryman's Daughter to Hollywood Legend*. New York: Palgrave Macmillan, 2004.

Hossent, Harry. *Gangster Movies: Gangsters, Hoodlums and Tough Guys of the Screen*. London: Octopus Books, 1974.

Hulse, Ed. *The Films of Betty Grable*. Burbank, Calif.: Riverwood, 1996.

Jensen, Paul M. *Boris Karloff and His Films*. Cranbury, N.J.: A.S. Barnes, 1974.

Kavieff, Paul R. *The Purple Gang: Organized Crime in Detroit 1910–1945*. Fort Lee, N.J.: Barricade Books, 2000.

Kear, Lynn, and John Rossman. *The Complete Kay Francis Career Record: All Film, Stage, Radio and Television Appearances*. Jefferson, N.C.: McFarland, 2008.

_____ and _____. *Kay Francis: A Passionate Life and Career*. Jefferson, N.C.: McFarland, 2006.

Kobal, John. *Hollywood: The Years of Innocence*. New York: Abbeville, 1985.

_____. *People Will Talk*. New York: Alfred A. Knopf, 1985.

Koszarski, Richard. *Fort Lee: The Film Town*. Rome, Italy: John Libbey Publishing, 2004.

Lacassin, Francis. "Out of Oblivion: Alice Guy Blaché." In *Sexual Stratagems: The World of Women in Film*, edited by Patricia Erens. New York: Horizon, 1979.

Lamparski, Richard. *Whatever Became Of...?* (Third Series). New York: Crown, 1970.

_____. *Whatever Became Of...?* (Fifth Series). New York: Crown, 1974.

Lasky, Jesse L. "The Sound and the Fury." In *The Grove Book of Hollywood*, edited by Christopher Silvester. New York: Grove, 1998.

Leibfried, Philip, and Chei Mi Lane. *Anna May Wong: A Complete Guide to Her Film, Stage, Radio, and Television Work*. Jefferson, N.C.: McFarland, 2004.

Leitch, Thomas. *Crime Films*. Cambridge University Press ebook, 2004.

Liebman, Roy. *From Silents to Sound: A Biographical Encyclopedia of Performers Who Made the Transition to Talking Pictures*. Jefferson, N.C.: McFarland, 1998.

_____. *The Wampas Baby Stars: A Biographical Dictionary, 1922–1934*. Jefferson, N.C.: McFarland, 2000.

Lindsay, Cynthia. *Dear Boris: The Life of William Henry Pratt a.k.a. Boris Karloff*. New York: Alfred A. Knopf, 1975.

Low, Rachel. *History of British Film: Volume IV, The History of the British Film 1918–1929*. New York: Routledge, 1996.

Lucas, Blake. "Acting Style in Silent Films." In *The Stars Appear*. Metuchen, N.J.: The Scarecrow, 1992.

MacCann, Richard Dyer. *The Stars Appear.* Metuchen, N.J.: Scarecrow, 1992.

Mahar, Karen Ward. *Women Filmmakers in Early Hollywood.* Baltimore: Johns Hopkins University Press, 2006.

Malnig, Julie. *Dancing Till Dawn: A Century of Exhibition Ballroom Dance.* New York: Greenwood, 1992.

Maltin, Leonard. *The Disney Films.* New York: Crown, 1984.

Mann, William J. *Behind the Screen: How Gays and Lesbians Shaped Hollywood, 1910–1969.* New York: Viking, 2001.

_____. *Kate: The Woman Who Was Hepburn.* New York: Henry Holt, 2006.

_____. *Wisecracker: The Life and Times of William Haines, Hollywood's First Openly Gay Star.* New York: Penguin Books, 1998.

Marill, Alvin H. *The Films of Anthony Quinn.* Secaucus, N.J.: Citadel, 1975.

Marshall, Michael. *Top Hat & Tails: The Story of Jack Buchanan.* London: Elm Tree Books, 1978.

McClelland, Doug. *The Golden Age of "B" Movies.* New York: Bonanza, 1978.

McMahan, Alison. *Alice Guy Blaché: Lost Visionary of the Cinema.* New York: Continuum International, 2002.

Mordden, Ethan. *The Hollywood Studios: House Style in the Golden Age of the Movies.* New York: Alfred A. Knopf, 1988.

"Movie Producer Bankrupt." *New York Times,* October 22, 1925.

Nollen, Scott Allen. *Boris Karloff: A Critical Account of His Screen, Stage, Radio, Television, and Recording Work.* Jefferson, N.C.: McFarland, 1991.

Oakie, Jack. *Jack Oakie's Double Takes.* San Francisco: Strawberry Hill Press, 1980.

Paris, Barry. *Louise Brooks: A Biography.* Minneapolis: University of Minnesota Press, 2000.

Parish, James Robert, ed. *The Great Movie Series.* Cranbury, N.J.: A.S. Barnes, 1971.

_____ and Don E. Stanke. *The Debonairs.* New Rochelle, N.Y.: Arlington, 1975.

Parla, Paul. "Donna Martell: From Indian Princess to Astronaut." *Classic Images,* http://www.classicimages.com/1997/september97/martell.html.

Paster, Heather. "Historic Hillview Apartments Restored." http://www.socal.com/articles/320-0.html

Petrova, Olga. *Butter with My Bread.* New York: The Bobbs-Merrill Company, 1942.

Pratt, George C. *Spellbound in Darkness: A History of the Silent Film.* Greenwich, Conn.: New York Graphic Society, 1973.

Quirk, Lawrence J. *The Complete Films of William Powell.* Secaucus, N.J.: Citadel, 1986.

_____. *The Films of Fredric March.* New York: Citadel, 1971.

Rainey, Buck. *Sweethearts of the Sage: Biographies and Filmographies of 258 Actresses Appearing in Western Movies.* Jefferson, N.C.: McFarland, 1992.

Ringgold, Gene, and DeWitt Bodeen. *Chevalier: The Films and Career of Maurice Chevalier.* Secaucus, N.J.: Citadel, 1973.

Schulberg, Budd. *Moving Pictures: Memories of a Hollywood Prince.* New York: Stein and Day, 1981.

Schultz, Margie. *Ann Sheridan: A Bio-Bibliography.* Westport, Conn.: Greenwood, 1997.

Schumacher, Geoff. *Howard Hughes: Power, Paranoia & Palace Intrigue.* Las Vegas: Stephens Press, 2008.

Silvester, Christopher. *The Grove Book of Hollywood.* New York: Grove, 1998.

Skal, David J., and Elias Savada. *Dark Carnival: The Secret World of Tod Browning.* New York: Anchor, 1995.

Slide, Anthony. *The Encyclopedia of Vaudeville.* Westport, Conn.: Greenwood, 1994.

_____. *Silent Players: A Biographical and Autobiographical Study of 100 Silent Film Actors and Actresses.* Lexington: University Press of Kentucky, 2002.

_____. *Silent Topics: Essays on Undocumented Areas of Silent Film.* Metuchen, N.J.: Scarecrow, 2004.

Smith, Sharon. *Women Who Make Movies.* New York: Hopkinson and Blake, 1975.

Springer, John, and Jack Hamilton. *They Had Faces Then.* Secaucus, N.J.: Citadel, 1974.

Stephenson, Richard M., and Joseph Iaccarino. *The Complete Book of Ballroom Dancing.* New York: Doubleday, 1980.

Taves, Brian. *Robert Florey: The French Expressionist.* Metuchen, N.J.: Scarecrow, 1987.

Thompson, Frank. *Lost Films: Important Movies That Disappeared.* New York: Carol, 1996.

Turk, Edward Baron. *Hollywood Diva.* Berkeley: University of California Press, 2000.

Tuttle, Frank. *They Started Talking.* Boalsburg, Pa.: BearManor, 2005.

Underwood, Peter. *Death in Hollywood.* Great Britain: Cleo Press, 1992.

_____. *Horror Man: The Life of Boris Karloff.* London: Leslie Frewin, 1972.

Von Sternberg, Josef. *Fun in a Chinese Laundry.* New York: Macmillan, 1965.

Waldman, Harry. *Maurice Tourneur: The Life and Films.* Jefferson, N.C.: McFarland, 2001.

Walker, Alexander. *The Shattered Silents: How the Talkies Came to Stay.* New York: William Morrow, 1979.

Wallace, David. *Hollywoodland.* New York: LA Weekly Books, 2002.

Watz, Edward. *Wheeler & Woolsey: The Vaudeville Comic Duo and Their Films, 1929–1937.* Jefferson, N.C.: McFarland, 1994.

Webb, Arthur. *The Clean Sweep: The Story of the Irish Hospitals Sweepstake.* Chicago: Henry Regnery, 1968.

White, Thelma, with Harry Preston. *Thelma Who? Almost 100 Years of Showbiz.* Lanham, Md.: Scarecrow, 2002.

Wilson, Victoria A. "Silent Knight" (interview with James Card). *Interview,* November 1, 1994.

Wollstein, Hans J. *Vixens, Floozies and Molls: 28 Actresses of Late 1920s and 1930s Hollywood.* Jefferson, N.C.: McFarland, 1999.

Wray, Fay. *On the Other Hand: A Life Story.* New York: St. Martin's, 1989.

# Index